Expanded Narration.
Das neue Erzählen.

Biennale des
bewegten Bildes 2013

Acknowledgments

B3 Moving Image Biennial 2013
Expanded Narration. Das neue Erzählen.
30.10.–03.11.2013
Frankfurt Rhein Main
b3biennale.com

Created by

in cooperation with

Funding Partners

Supported by   Hessian Ministry for Economy, Transport and State Development   European Union

B3 Parcours supported by   kulturfonds frankfurtrheinmain

Parcourspartners/venues   ALTANA Kulturstiftung
Astor Film Lounge   Atelierfrankfurt   Basis e.V.
Deutsches Filmmuseum   E-Kinos   Exzellenzcluster
Normative Orders   Frankfurter Kunstverein
Galerie Anita Beckers   Galerie Heike Strelow
Gibson Club   Haus am Dom   Hochschule für Musik und
Darstellende Kunst   Kai Middendorff Galerie   Kinothek
Asta Nielsen e.V.   MMK Museum für Moderne Kunst
Museum Angewandte Kunst   Museum für Kommunikation
Frankfurt   Museum Wiesbaden   Nassauischer
Kunstverein Wiesbaden   Portikus   Robert Johnson
Römerhallen   Schirn Kunsthalle Frankfurt   Städelschule
Weißfrauen Diakoniekirche   Weltkulturen Museum

Partners   Aventis Foundation   Brohm & v. Moers
Dr. Hauschka Kosmetik   FunDeMental Studios
Leo Burnett   Satis&fy   Sky Deutschland
Von Kelterborn/OSMO Collection   Wirtschaftsförderung
Frankfurt GmbH   **Hotelpartners**   Lindenberg
Nizza Hotel   Westin Hotels & Resorts   **Media Partners**
BlickpunktFilm   De:Bug   Frankfurter Allgemeine
Zeitung   GamesMarkt   HORIZONT   Journal Frankfurt
Medien Bulletin   Ströer Media AG   taz.die tageszeitung
Insurance Partner   ARTIMA

Imprint

Bibliographic information published by the Deutsche Nationalbibliothek
The Deutsche Nationalbibliothek lists this publication in the Deutsche Nationalbibliografie; detailed bibliographic data are available in the Internet at http://dnb.d-nb.de

© 2013 transcript Verlag, Bielefeld
All rights reserved. No part of this book may be reprinted or reproduced or utilized in any form or by any electronic, mechanical, or other means, now known or hereafter invented, including photocopying and recording, or in any information storage or retrieval system, without permission in writing from the publisher.

Published by
Bernd Kracke, Marc Ries
Hochschule für Gestaltung Offenbach
Schlossstr. 31, 63065 Offenbach am Main

Designers
Karin Rekowski
Supervision: Klaus Hesse, Nikolas Brückmann,
Yuriy Matveev (B3 Designstudio)

Editorial staff
Marc Ries, Norman Hildebrandt

Editing
Christine Taxer, Isa Bickmann, Keonaona Peterson

Translations
Geraldine Bleck, Jim Gussen, Steven Lindberg,
Marcel René Marburger, Robert Nusbaum,
Übersetzungsbüro Oskana Peters, Alan Shapiro,
Alexander Schneider, Mark Schreiber, Anja Wiesinger

Paper
90g/m² Fly Design, weiß

Typeface
Akkurat, Stone Serif

Production
brandbook, Frankfurt am Main

ISBN: 978-3-8376-2652-0

Contents

9   **Bernd Kracke, Marc Ries**
    Foreword

13 **Bernd Kracke**
    Whither (with) the Camera? B3, Part 1

21 **Marcel Schwierin**
    The New Narratives

29 **Marc Ries**
    Online Narration

43 **Hans Ulrich Reck**
    Beyond Structuralism: Extended Narratives between Texts and Images

55 **Ferdinand Schmatz**
    The Surge of Speech

59 **Usha Reber**
    It Will Have Been Reality: Alban Nikolai Herbst's Expanded Site of Writing

77 **Holger Kube-Ventura**
    Objects in a Mirror Are Closer Than They Appear: On Self-Portrayal in Contemporary Video Art.

95 **Rotraut Pape**
    Liberated Images and Sounds: Diving into the 360° Full-Dome-Cosmos

109 **Christian Janecke**
    Narrativity's Marginal Utility: Format and Immersion in Panoramic Dome Films

123 **Erkki Huhtamo**
Illusion and Its Reverse: About Artistic Explorations of Stereoscopic 3D

135 **Bjørn Melhus, Yves Netzhammer**
Time-Seeking Connections: Two interviews

149 **Eva Paulitsch, Uta Weyrich**
Loop Narration and Hyperlayered Narratives

161 **Sabine Breitsameter**
Listening While Out Walking: A Brief History of Soundwalking

---

175 **Martin Seel**
Varieties of Cinematic Narrative

185 **Vinzenz Hediger**
No Hurry, No Time: On the Proper Length of a Film

199 **Juliane Rebentisch**
Narrating Life: The Biopic and Its Deconstruction in Todd Haynes's *I'm Not There*

219 **Sabine Nessel, Winfried Pauleit**
Constructions of the Digital Film: Aesthetics, Narrative, Discourse

235 **Martin Gessmann**
Transmedia Storytelling and New Product Language in Film. Or: What Happens When Objects Even Speak

251 **Jos Diegel**
Spoiler Alert! You're Always Making Things without Beginnings or Ends, Big Pictures Full of Who Knows What Rubbish

257	**Steffen Huck, Diana Iljine, Sir Peter Jonas** A Narrative Revolution
267	**Christine Lang** »Gonna Break Bad?«—On Implicit Dramaturgy in *Breaking Bad*
281	**Alain Bieber** One Thousand and One: #Neuland
287	**Markus Kuhn** Of Lonely Girls, Prom Queens, and Cool Guys: Web Series as a New Audiovisual Form on the Internet
307	**Michel Reilhac** Gearing Up: Where Do We Stand with the Current Emergence of Interactive Storytelling?
321	**Claudia Söller-Eckert** Transmedia Storytelling and Participation Experience
341	**Ramón Reichert** Social Media Storytelling
359	**Stephan Günzel** Image and Narrative in the Computer Game
369	**Alan N. Shapiro** Software Code as Expanded Narration
385	**Jonas Englert, Norman Hildebrandt** Mothers, Can't We Please Come Back Home? This Freedom Fills Us with Anxiety

»... about once every hundred years everybody became conscious of this thing that everybody had come to do different things that is to say had come to do the same things in a different way in a way so different that everyone could come to know this thing know that it was a really different way and so of course a different way that had come to stay.«
Gertrude Stein

Foreword

Bernd Kracke

Marc Ries

The idea for this publication flashed through our mind during the work of developing a program for the first *B3 Moving Image Biennial* in Frankfurt am Main, 30.10. to 3.11.2013, which took *Expanded Narration. Das neue Erzählen* as its theme and followed the inkling that it is »a really different way« of narration that medial technologies now facilitate. In a reversal of Benjamin's image of a past which »rushes by,« a collection of differently motivated texts was to contemplate the images of those future worlds of narration, which, in the present, are already rushing by in many places, which we experience and, most of all, cocreate, but whose fine structure and influence on the communal and individual tissue become only indiscernibly and indistinctly resonant and visible in their utilization.

There are two levels on which the expansion of new narrative formats, in connection to the moving image, can be observed today. On the one hand are the serial formats on TV (and online), in which a narrative space is exploded over a multitude of episodes and holds unusual narrative potential. Furthermore, the transgressions of the boundaries of work and medium which are provoked by transmedial narration and whose integration of the audience into their dramaturgy offers irritating hybrids of authorship and collective participation. And there are new modes of narration that can be observed in the arts, which introduce a different politics of aesthetics, especially in the context of the ready availability of video technologies. Yet on the other hand, its also the micronarratives on the Internet, evoked by (video) blogs and especially platforms like Facebook, Twitter, and YouTube, which inextricably link their users, and their way of life, to the visual and audible forms of these daily applied media and which, as social media storytelling, offer a remarkable, if also contradictory, publicity to the previously intimate act of self-narration.

This book is itself conceived as a narrative, a polychromatic narrative drawn from different genres of text which react to these new phenomena in a way that transcends object and disciplines. They are notes, observations, and emphatic discussions by those who are directly involved in the production or exhibition of these new narratives; they are essayistic speculations, precise analyses, and theoretical models, that, from philosophy, literary theory and art and media theory, inquire into those works and processes which are characteristic for these narratives and thus become the focal point of a multitude of cultural and social movements. Their perspectives change continually, whether it be one of authorship, of »dividuality« or of the object currently investigated and thus this compilation includes representations of new film narratives and modes of narration in video art, TV shows, computer games, transmedial productions, micronarratives in the social network and expressive codes. Furthermore three literary texts have been included, which speak, within each particular singular form of writing, about that form within the whole of this departure to the new worlds of narration.

     We are glad that 30 (groups) of authors have agreed to pick up Gertrude Stein's reference to cultural time renewing itself every hundred years in the context of the new narration and to make this publication possible in unison with the explorations of the *B3 Moving Image Biennial*. Great thanks is due to the authors of this first alliance as well as to sponsors, supporters and partners.

Whither (with) the Camera? B3, Part 1

Bernd Kracke

'Twas a silent Big Bang, one that ushered in a new era in Chicago, Paris, New York and Berlin. Customers at the cafes and *variétés* could scarcely believe their eyes, and some were simply in shock. There were reports of panicked audience members running out of the movie theater or seeking shelter under tables and behind chairs as they saw a locomotive coming toward them during a showing of the movie *Arrival of a train at La Ciotat*. And that is of course assuming *movie* is even the right word for this entity.

Southern France. A small train platform in the summer sun. A steam locomotive is rapidly approaching, and as it does so grows steadily larger—a black monster portending disaster. The train passes by the audience at a terrifyingly close distance and comes to a stop. Totally serene passengers board and exit the train. And that was it. Only one showing, only 47 seconds—and a groundbreaking event nevertheless. Our horizons have since expanded exponentially: the camera has become our third eye.

Expansion of a New World

Still today, the Lumière brothers' legendary train snippet with a happy ending casts a magic spell over us all. Other movies of the time were mere carnie or peepshow fare, though they nonetheless created a sensation. People roared with laughter, yelled, were wildly enthusiastic, applauded. Movies were worth their weight in gold.

And so it wasn't long before growing excitement morphed into a growing industry. A cycle comprising investment, profits and reinvestment took hold—and with it the unstoppable expansion of a new world.

Soon virtually every city and town across the land had its Nickelodeon, Gem or Bijou. Premiers were held and critics wrote about them, and actors became stars. Movies were an inexhaustible topic of conversation à la »Have you seen…?« The moving image and all that went with it became a topic with enormous social repercussions. A medium that had once been the stuff of carnies and peepshows evolved into a new and compelling art form that transcended myriad existing boundaries.

The moving image then broke free of the confines of movie theaters via TV in viewers' living rooms. And then it spread from living rooms, offices and museums, becoming omnipresent thanks to the Internet, mobile devices, and immersion in every single moment of existence. Plus it now covers all the »brow« bases, from low to medium to high and beyond. The moving image has become a pivotal interface between technology and culture; its influence continues to grow apace. The moving image has expanded the horizons of music, the visual arts, research, learning, and the media—in short communication in all its myriad forms. And it is the democratic medium par excellence, open as it is to all comers.

An Audience Power Player

Woody Allen once said, »Everyone has a story to tell—at least one.« And although this statement dates back pretty far, who would have thought at the time that instead of making jokes as is his wont, Mr. Allen would predict the future? Presumably it's pretty much the same for everyone else nowadays as it was for him at the age of 16. Writing jokes and screenplays—and then of course his enthusiasm for stand-up comedians. But the prospect of being an eternal onlooker? A tough row to hoe for such an alert mind; and in the final analysis the moving image does have its side effects—namely learning to observe and the desire to emulate.

In the meantime the public—a learning and motivated organism if ever there was one—has turned out to be the world's most important movie producers. Millions upon millions of moving images are broadcast on TV daily. And some of them are even entertaining. What underlies them, though, is not so much an explicit business model, but rather a new kind of social behavior. But maybe not so new after all. Perhaps it's just the same old need to communicate, only in a new form. For today's smartphones and apps enable us to gain astonishing insights into each other's lives in the blink of an eye. Our world appears to be more dreamlike than anyone had thought. But conversely, established directors are glomming on to streaming as the wave of the future and are making movies for smartphones.

Every Tom, Dick and Harry Can Pick Up a Camera. But What Happens Then?

Well, life becomes unendingly amazing and fascinating. Telling stories with a camera is a matter of mind-set. Some are true believers and leave everything to happenstance. Happenstance? Things that appear to be happenstance may be something entirely different. Instinct, for example. The surroundings. A feel for the situation, for the decisive moment, for the impending event, for the meaningful point of view. In short, talent—the kind artists have. But a guarantee of success? No way.

And then there's the other camp, which favors leaving nothing to chance, who wonder to themselves what a craftsman might wonder: Whither (with) the camera? From which standpoint should the plot, scenes and sequences be recounted? From which (or whose) point of view should the story be told? And most important of all: What makes for a good yarn, and what's the best way to tell it?

When it comes to telling stories in moving images, craftsmanship and philosophy are pretty much intertwined. The Big Picture or Big Statement is revealed by minutiae, and vice versa. Rocket science it's not. But it's still a wee bit harder than it looks—particularly when you're looking to create a satisfying experience for the public time after time.

Between Old and New Narratives: B3

Many of the questions that we raise among ourselves time and time again have already been answered—to some extent at least. The past century has left us an amazingly rich narrative tradition that embraces experimentation and is astonishingly variegated. We can adopt any attitude we want toward those who have come before us. But we can't completely ignore them. Hovering in the background of every single motion picture story is a previous story that spurs us on to innovate, improve, invent.

And here—at this boundary between old and new narratives—is where the 2013 Moving Image Biennial comes in. Here's where it sets up its camera. The B3 Festival, B3 Parcours, and B3 Campus in particular—but also this book—seek to ferret out new needs, new desires, new dreams and new themes by taking a long, hard critical look at the confluence of past and present. New from top to bottom? Well, it's the same as for old and new media, in that the old ones refuse to curl up and die. Movie theater screens with their mammoth images and big sound remain the biggest kid, the heaviest hitter on the moving-image block. And there are other reasons, too, to avoid the pitfall of viewing the old and new from an either-or perspective, and to instead see what's happening today as a process of renewal.

Narratives That Don't Tell a Story

So let's take a look at the language of moving images. For this is a language that still today has no grammar and no set vocabulary in the usual sense of these terms. And what use would they be anyway? The world is the moving image's oyster. Words have to be synchronized, but images don't. They're perceived intuitively and more effortlessly and quickly than the mind can think. Thus moving images don't tell stories in the classic sense of the term—and are anything but abstract. What they do instead is present concrete and appealing dramatizations that leap from shot to shot; and in so doing they take in everything, including the poetry of the unseeable: feelings, motivations, inner states. The stuff of moving images? Colors and sounds, in an endless interplay with light, dialogue and atmosphere that create moods through gestures, action and a storyline. And the audience? Well they want to see for themselves, test the temperature of the narrative waters. The audience's dictum: Show me, don't tell me. Audiences go to the movies in search of a mirror of themselves.

Thus the audience, passive though it may seem, is in fact anything but inactive; or empathizes, anticipates and cocreates the whole damned time. When we read fiction, we shape the story in our minds; but when we watch a movie we tell ourselves the story on the basis of the sequence of images and events that unfold before our eyes. When it comes to many things in life, so much depends on empathy, seeing for ourselves, communicating; and so it is with cinematic narratives—a situation that is likely to remain unchanged for the foreseeable future. Despite the fact that everything else in life keeps running up against its own limitations.

Will the Standards of Today Stand the Test of Time?

New narratives are the fruit of constant pressure to change that is in turn attributable to the simultaneous contradictions found in every single media outlet. By which I mean: quality and ratings compete mercilessly with each other. This multiplicity and overstimulation have resulted in an insane competition for attention, whose new buzzword is *transmedia*. But audiences can only devote their time and attention to one event at a time. But which to choose? Well, if there was an easy answer to this question, neither this book nor the B3 would ever have seen the light of day. We are living in an era of differentiation and individualization—an era in which trial and error continue to be the main driving force behind the desire to advance into new territory.

Established stakeholders may have their recipes for success, some of which are calculated down to the minute, and often in dogmatic formats. But the fact remains that successful formats are copied almost instantaneously, and so often that after a while there really is nothing new under the sun; and formulas that work are worked to death. And so people cast about for something new, and the wheels of creativity begin to turn once again.

Seen in this complex and dynamic light, the 2013 Moving Image Biennial is a first attempt to capture and present the myriad facets and expanded possibilities of new narratives from a host of different perspectives. Perhaps the event will succeed in shifting the camera's perspective and see through the audience's eyes in new ways. For that's one of the ingredients of new narratives: a new way of seeing, a new perspective and—why not?—a new paradigm.

Bernd Kracke
is a professor of electronic media since 1999 at the Hochschule für Gestaltung (HfG) Offenbach and is also its president since 2006. He led the department for visual communication from 2001 to 2006. In 2000 he founded CrossMediaLab as a research and experimental platform for connecting analog and digtial technologies, as well as their innovative deployment in the context of art and design. He has built on his experiences of his work at MIT Cambridge/ USA (1979–1985), the Kunsthochschule für Medien Köln (1990–1999), as well his practice as a freelance media designer and media artist. Since 2008 he is speaker for the Hessische Film und Medienakademie (hFMA) presidency, a network of the 13 Hessian universities.
He initiated the B3 Biennal Frankfurt RheinMain, and took over its general direction in 2012.

The New Narratives

Marcel Schwierin

We are witnessing a fundamental change in video art—one that was also a central consideration in selecting the theme of the B3 Moving Image Biennial.

Beginning in around 2000, video art mainly took its cue from documentary filmmaking. Many artists were using documentary genres and methods, and classic documentary filmmakers such as Harun Farocki were even turning up at video art exhibitions and biennales.

But if you look at recent festival entries, particularly those from younger artists, it would appear that the dominance of the observing onlooker is being supplanted by a renewed desire for narrative. Such narratives cast a wide net, ranging from subtle fictionalizations of true events to the most fictitious of all film genres, sci-fi, which was heretofore the province of Hollywood and video games.

And if this still very tentatively posited observation (which mainly pertains to the last two to three years) is correct—in other words, if video art is indeed increasingly turning to narrative genres—then the question arises as to why this is the case. In short, what is driving this new interest in fiction, yes, even in fantasy formats?

Documentary Video Art

As has so often been the case in media history, the predominance of documentary video art was driven by technology. Documentary films used to be very expensive ventures whose crew normally comprised a director, cameraman and sound recordist. Documentaries were also cost-intensive, with each minute of completed film requiring upward of 10 to 20 minutes of raw footage. Thus documentaries were mostly the province of professional production companies.

But all this changed with the advent of digital film technology, whose semiautomatic video cameras to all intents and purposes obviated the need for a crew; plus the fact that material costs were next to nothing and editing could be done on a desktop computer, rather than in a film studio. This also placed documentaries within the financial reach of artists.

As a result, documentary video art became the key mainstay of the biennial circuit.

The Real and Virtual Worlds

At the same time the Internet gave birth to the so-called virtual world. And even though in its early days this virtual world was essentially more a mixture of hype and marketing than a genuine phenomenon, there was no mistaking the fact that it was a completely new information and reality medium whose esthetic manifestations tended toward excessive artificiality.

Hence video art documentaries were also a reaction to this virtual reality and its illusory promises of release from earthly cares (one need only think of the hype associated with so-called cybersex). The more pretentious the Internet was, the more down-to-earth video art documentaries became. And thus they gave the Internet a wide berth not only from an aesthetic standpoint but also in terms of the medium per se—the idea being that everything but the products of a limited art market can be found online. But this also constituted the fundamental contradiction of video documentaries—namely that the limitations of the video art market ran counter to its aim of enlightenment. Social criticism became a business; a mass medium turned into limited editions.

Professionalization of the Collectivity

If the advent of art documentaries is attributable to the advent of digital video cameras, the cellphone was yet another technological advance that was intrinsic to the transition to documentaries of the collective.

Ever since cellphone picture quality became good enough for large movie screens and certainly more than sufficient for computer screens, any witness to an event is potentially a documentary filmmaker. Such cellphone videos can be edited and posted on Web sites such as Mosireen (itself based on Web sites such as YouTube and Vimeo), which even first posts the raw footage and then the finished film.

This practice lends documentary videos a direct quality that neither classic TV shows, traditional documentary film crews, nor individual artists can hope to achieve. Moreover, the dissemination of such videos is totally in sync with what viewers want, as there is no commercial filter—be it a broadcaster or an art gallery edition—between filmmaker and viewer. Owing to this evolution, art documentaries—whose particular quality likewise lies in the artistic freedom afforded by their not being accountable to producers, editorial staffs and sponsors—have lost a certain relevance.

Endless Stories

Concomitant with this radical change in documentary filmmaking, cinematic narration has undergone a fundamental change. This genre was for many years dominated by feature films that were aped by TV via tertiary exploitation (with DVDs interposed) in its capacity as a creator of second-class moving images. But all this changed with the advent of new series formats such as *The Wire*, *Mad Men* and *Breaking Bad*, which at least temporarily have displaced feature films as the dominant medium in moving-image discourse.

What makes such series so special is that they are able to respond to viewer reactions as they develop their story arcs and characters. And unlike feature films, they lack a space outside of real life where viewers can experience the fantasy dimensions that are missing from their daily lives. Instead, such shows literally enter viewers' lives via the TV in their living room and by virtue of their following the characters' stories over multiple seasons. TV series heroes are much less adventurers than they are friends or relatives whose lives viewers follow with curiosity and a sense of personal investment. And thus it's no surprise that TV series and their characters are the subject of intense social media debate; and like politicians, series writers need to publicly justify the story arc decisions they make concerning their characters.

The Millionfold Narrative of the Self

But these epic series that are marketed worldwide pale in comparison to the web of narratives found on today's social media. Take Facebook for example, which describes itself thusly: »Facebook is all about the individual and collective experiences of you and your friends. It's filled with hundreds of millions of stories.« And with the introduction of the timeline function in 2011, whose use has since become mandatory, user entries are automatically converted into a chronological narrative of their lives. And because users know full well that such entries are to a certain degree public, this format has nothing in common with traditional autobiographical genres such as journals or photo albums. Facebook users document not only their lives, but also create idealized images of themselves—a far subtler species of avatar than heavy-handed Second Life animations. These new narratives of the self combine documentary and fictional elements to form an undistinguishable other.

New Narrative Forms in Video Art

Artists adopt these interwoven modalities to tell their stories using myriad methods drawn from both feature films and documentaries. I would like to discuss three representative works of this type.

In *Blind Ambition* (Hassan Khan, documenta 13) 27 actors in various squares in Cairo talk about all kinds of things in various settings such as cafés, shopping malls, or on the street. Due to the ever-changing characters and settings, as we watch, we have the feeling that we're eavesdropping on passers-by. The fact that the video was shot using a smartphone lends the images, despite their careful composition, a random quality while at the same time enabling the artist to shoot video fragments of daily life amid the hubbub of Cairo in a manner that goes unnoticed by bystanders.

Ho Tzu Nyen's complex installation *The Cloud of Unknowing* (54th Venice Biennale) is based on a book by the French philosopher Hubert Damisch about the use of clouds in European and Chinese painting. The film recounts eight characters' interactions with cloud-like appearances in their homes. Here too the narrative is extremely fragmented and the tableau-like scenes are more reminiscent of the—likewise narrative—photographs of Jeff Wall than they are of standard movie plot devices. The soundtrack is a mix of 200 pop songs about clouds, in the manner of a remixed playlist from the global cloud.

Because Laura Horelli's father was a diplomat, her family moved around a lot while she was growing up. In various works, she goes in search of fragments from her childhood, sometimes through either the places where she lived or through films and photographs. In her voiceovers, she directly addresses the characters in her films. In *Haukka-Pala* (2009), Horelli attempts to make contact with her mother via recordings of a Finnish TV cooking show in which her mother, who died young, was the main performer. Two years later, in *The Terrace*, she filmed at her family's former home in Nairobi and tried to contact the families she knew back then, as well as her former nanny and neighbors. Her mother is only a minor presence in this video via a handful of photographs, whereas in her latest work, *A Letter to Mother* (2013), she is once again the main character. If Horelli's individual videos present fragmentary memories, seen as a whole these works take on epic proportions; and like a novel about a family or even a TV series, the status of the various characters vary from one video to another.

Something all of the works discussed here have in common is that they alternate between various artistic strategies. The documentary dimension doesn't disappear altogether, but instead becomes one of many moments in the narrative. Places, people and actions are reflected by their media context, without the medium taking on the central McLuhanesque importance it once had in video art. Such reflections in turn become the fragmentary elements of new narratives which, precisely because they are not explicitly recounted, can develop in any direction. And in this lies their narrative freedom; which is why we find them so intriguing.

Marcel Schwierin
is a curator, filmmaker. He is also the cofounder of the Werkleitz Biennial, the experimental film database *cinovid* and the Arab Shorts festival in Cairo. Among his films are: *Die Bilder* (experimental, 1994), *Ewige Schönheit* (documentary, 2003). He regularly curates for the Werkleitz Biennial, the Goethe Institute, and the International Short Film Festival Oberhausen among other events. Since 2010 he is a film and video curator for transmediale.

Online
Narration

Marc Ries

1

Many children's books, like most other literature, are written in the past tense. I am not referring to the fairy tale, which indeed needs to employ a marked leap of time, »a long time ago...,« to create its fictional intangibility, but to the numerous stories which conjure a parallel present by means of their subject, thus suggesting a complicity with the life of the children, and yet conduct their narration in the preterite. At the moment of reading the stories are indeed already concluded; they are in a book between two covers. When reading such stories I continue to be irritated by this setting in what has gone before. I start reconstructing sentences into the present tense, but after a while, as this correction demands additional attention and distracts from the actual flow of reading, I fall back into the preset past tense of the story. It is my impression and suspicion that this transferring of the narrative into an earlier time makes it more difficult for the child to immerse itself in the story, to become part of it. This narrated time refers to an omniscient third-person narrator, who forbids his readers and listeners to pick up the narrative thread and follow it on a quasi-equal footing to him. Of course I cannot verify the assumption that a child—or is it only me?—would love to share in the immediate presence of an event and to experience itself as a coplayer in the narrated plot, but I nonetheless perceive that in their own stories, their little everyday inventions, children seek to surround themselves in their present with fictional siblings and acting animals and dolls, who take part in their lives as beings, which are narrated in the present tense. There is also no problem, within the story, to let day and night pass in a very short space of time—which may be one substantial reason for differentiating a narrated time which has passed and a constituting narrative time in literature. But with the onset of medial education the children encounter two further time techniques in narratives. Films, on the one hand, which also prefer to differentiate their narrated time from the present: Emil of Lönneberga also lived »a long time ago« even though the character is portrayed as timeless. On the other hand, TV shows become the object of medial desire; at first these are primarily animated (or animation-like) shows, like *Teletubbies* or *The Simpsons,* whose narratives take place exactly when the children are watching. The forces of attraction between this young audience and their favorite characters develop essentially through a shared present and, here and there, occasions of immediacy and concurrency in the experience of reality.

At the same time each day a host of juveniles arrives in Springfield, in the house of Homer Simpson and his family. They all do the same thing the Simpsons do: they watch TV. They share in the everyday life of Homer, Marge, Bart, Lisa and Maggie, the Western life of an average family, which hardly lends itself to heroic or glamorous identification, with joys, problems and absurdities both great and small. They encounter numerous contemporary conflicts and cultural references which have been built into the show. Most likely many of them have a Simpsons poster in their room or Bart mugs and T-shirts, perhaps even a map of Springfield. Because this life, the Simpsons collective, has become a part of their own cartography, of their own life; medial relationships (not copies), which the adolescents form within their own present and which, in the space between the media, facilitate the creation of their own life story.[1]

With a further densification of the medial environment —PC (Games), mobiles, Internet—the narratives (of the self) are liberated from their enthrallment to system media and their role models. Through Facebook, YouTube, text messages, Twitter and the like a young person can individualize their media usage and take part in social networks where they encounter a myriad of other narrators and share all kinds of things with them in a common present. Furthermore, as a witness, cocreator and protagonist of history they become an informer and narrator of political movements, narratives, which, via the direct representation of crisis in news channels or their reflection through comment and analysis in blogs, actualize events. The question remains how the New Narration, which is published in this way, can be represented with a cultural understanding and a new concept within culture theory and in what manner narration takes place—what distinguishes it from the authorities of the old narrative entities, literati and journalists alike?

---

[1] Also see my text: »Homers Home. Einige Nachüberlegungen zum Verständnis von Heimat,« in *Kritische Theorie zur Zeit. Festschrift für Christoph Türcke*, ed. Oliver Decker and Tobias Grave (Springe, 2008), 309–15.

2

Narrative is what anybody has to say in any way about anything that can happen has happened will happen in any way.
Gertrude Stein

To begin I would like to establish that (self-) narration and life story are necessarily interrelated, »that narrative structures cannot be extricated from the way humans live their lives.«[2] In pretechnological media time there were authorities of narration, which, in part, created master narratives, but always perceived themselves as public entities and there were many individual, small stories, which moved only within the circles of life-worlds and were often linked only to a few generations. Media technologies like blogs, text messages, Twitter, activities on Facebook, YouTube and Flickr also cater to a desire to narrate; they create versatile narratives, establish narrative enunciations which speak of a different diegesis, conjure a narrated world that is not like the ones we know from narrative literature. Today system narratives, which are created by cultural industries—cinema, TV, games—compete with narratives created by individuals which flow unregulated in open social media systems. The Internet has negated the hegemony of traditional, centralized narratives and enables the stream of life stories and everyday narratives to be produced, heard and seen by many. But, by now, system narratives, like transmedia storytelling, have begun to access the interconnected users for their own purposes, to bind them in corporate structures which are intended to produce at least an inkling of coauthorship and self-will. In any case the astonishing development of individual narratives on the net can be taken as a confirmation of »the narrative a priori of making oneself at home in the world.«[3]

What is a social medium? Such a medium is a technological structure facilitating and creating an exchange and (self-) reflexive sharing, hence a relational, nonparticular space which can be used by many.

Many social media expect, even provoke, a permanent level of use. The technologies' continual promptings to write to

---

[2] Dieter Thomä, *Erzähle dich selbst. Lebensgeschichte als philosophisches Problem* (Frankfurt am Main, 2007), 23.

[3] Albrecht Koschorke, *Wahrheit und Erfindung. Grundzüge einer Allgemeinen Erzähltheorie* (Frankfurt am Main, 2012), 16.

others, to share images and sounds and to take note of those sent by others creates a singularization of the messages, of the forms of texts and images; it extends, it elevates them into a narrative material made up of accounts of what one is doing just now, comments on current topics, insights into intimate events from which emerges a narration of one's own life intended for others who do the same with their lives. One can assume that the surprise regarding the fact that this infinite number of communications contains so little information or so much redundant content is valid only as long as the tremendous fabrication of narrated worlds full of fragments and contingencies within these communications has not been recognized in its actual expressive and existential power.

In the storyverse of the Internet a shift of significance can be observed, from the story-forming diegesis to a discourse of narration and the narrative act itself. The narrative theory of Gérard Genette introduced this tripartite and named discourse itself as its object, the modalities of narration, the narrative enunciation; the narration in social media has, in a peculiar manner, seen the narrative act itself become the center of its activities. In Genette's work the narrative act retains a certain ambiguity; it refers to the real or fictional situation in which it takes place on the one hand and to the act of narration within the author's own life story on the other—which must remain unquestioned as, from outside, it can only offer trivial insights into the relationship of work and biography.[4] But now the narrative activity on the net engenders a revaluation of both entities and the audience. Within Web 2.0 everyone is part of an audience which endows him with authorship as it is itself made up only of authors. While narration in the well-reviewed new TV serials is focused on a subtle expansion of the modalities of narration with the characters and the conception of the work itself remaining essentially the same, the inner logic of narrative is being expanded profoundly by means of the narrative act in social media as well as through transmedial narratology.

Formulated as a thesis, narratives in the new media are less meaningful in relation to a coherent story or imaginative *fabula*—here they are mostly redundant, formed by schemata or

[4] Gérard Genette, *Die Erzählung* (Paderborn, 1998), 12.

lost in everyday chimeras—than regarding the self-empowerment of a narrator in and with an audience which has never before been available. An audience which can be used and represented through individual media anytime and anywhere. It is equally important that the publication of the micronarratives happens in the knowledge that the audience not only reads, observes and hears, but that it writes, films and shares music itself. Each narrator in the universe of social media storytelling produces his narrative for other narrators, expects their narrative fragments and in turn creates new ones himself. Thus the narration of stories by the few for the many is overturned, qualified to the advantage of an extremely productive, horizontal fabrication of narratives which constitute medial events without an exclusive focus on the real events to which they relate. Narration and the narrative as a medial event become more meaningful than the story and its motivating plot. Hence the question concerning the desire which daily drives all these countless narrative acts is important because the many authors have no names, they know that and they do not wish to have any, just as their narratives do not claim to be either art or analysis. Thus the autobiographisms on the net are less of a cultural value but rather defining for the self-perception of individuals in ambiguous life situations. But how can this desired self-empowerment be realized?

3

Narration is, to a great extent, an unspecific medium [...]; its cultural achievement is less in division than in connection.
Albrecht Koschorke

Especially the diverse modes of narration on the net confirm an essential peculiarity of all medial communication. To communicate anything, a division or segmentation of that which is to be said or narrated is necessary. The strongly referential, that is referential to immediate events, narration in social networks must allow for medial-technological processes, which are defined by compartmentalization, reduction and selection (this is also true for affects that are to be communicated, like the internal references of dating fora). A narrative, an event, which has a certain effect, will, according to its medium, have to be reduced into sensory segments (speech, image, sound) as well as into parts, signs which translate the event into the intended forms. Where language is concerned this means sequencing the event into sentences made up of predefined elements, for image production the choosing of frames and perspectives, for sound the selection of sound sources. If transferred to the online technologies this process can be applied to tweets and blog entries, where informations essentially need to be segmented into a grid structure and saved in a relational database. Only through comprehensive processes of *dividere*, of division and segmentation, can communication take place and a promise of *participere,* of taking part, become tangible. Yet sharing is also effective on the level regarding the exchange of information. *Sharing* becomes a vital, even existential task for all active social network users. From *liking* on Facebook to the sharing of visual and audio files and the embedding of URLs the net thrives on an active mode of sharing. This accomplishes an offer implicated by media technologies to elude capital (P2P), to relativize identity (nicknames, avatars), to paraphrase community (*Second Life*).

The question how one narrates using the new media today is not solely concerned with the mode of narration, the *sjuzet* and the narrative act but with medial conditions that form the framework for, facilitate, even evoke actions on the net, namely protocols, software and sharing interfaces. It can be observed that the characteristics and contents of online narrative media, their technologies of writing and referencing as well as their publishing services, increasingly deterritorialized by APIs (application programming interfaces), circulating between different platforms, taken up by imperial networks like Facebook and YouTube, equipped with a simple IFTTT code, *If This Is Then That,* facilitate the sharing of data and narratives according to the distributive intentions of the actors (producers as well as readers, watchers and listeners). This results in migrational movements of messages, texts, videos and sounds between web places, emphasizing that there is no single origin of narratives any more but that they emerge, are communicated and shared simultaneously at different places.

In addition online narration picks up and amplifies the »ontological indifference« of stories.[5] Narration overrides, ignores the boundary between that which is true, binding, real and that which is fictional, nonactual, a game, deceit, that indispensable reference for functional systems. »Narration can be recognized or discarded as a technique for the transmission of knowledge, be in league with deeper truths or marred by the blemish of fraud. Ambiguity with regards to the alternate possibilities of true/untrue, then, pertains not only to the content of each single narrative but to the cultural validity of symbolic transactions employing the technique of narration in general.«[6] The ontological indifference of medial narration is part of the pact between online narrators using the most diverse levels intended for this purpose. On the one hand it touches on the »ecstasies of the ordinary« within the many social spaces [7] online. The simple act of somebody placing a camera in their teenage room and narrating their life in short clips, commenting on their mostly inconspicuous, average existence as such causes a stepping out, a tilting out of it, that is, out of the stasis, without the existence itself becoming exceptional. It seems as if its being something only gains a *something-contour* by its publication. Even if this existence is exposed as staged, not much changes. *Lonelygirl 15,* one of the first web serials created by 16-year-old Bree, who, in 2006, posted reports about her initially normal life on YouTube, points to the actual drive behind the ecstasy: even after having been unmasked as fictitious the show continued and remained popular despite being »acted.« It was the gesture of extension, of ecstasy that counted, not truthfulness.[8] »As a sphere of production within society that is unburdened of function the arts [and the cultural industry – MR] have developed fictional modes of representation, which permit the liberal use of material of doubtful veracity because they render their ontological indifference, or so it seems, to be without social consequences and hence harmless.«[9] Besides questions of truth and deontology, indifference has a further dimension in the

---

[5] Concerning »ontological difference,« see Koschorke, *Wahrheit und Erfindung,* 16 (see note 3).

[6] ibid., page 17.

[7] Birgit Richard, Alexander Ruhl: Der »Tag« ist das Bild. »Ich«-Sharing im kollektiven Universum der visualisierten Schlagworte, in *dating. 21. Liebesorganisation und Verabredungskultur,* Marc Ries et al. (ed.) (Bielefeld 2007), S. 173–192.

[8] The extension receives its sociological translation in the phrase »The extent to wich users...«; see the »honeycomb of social media« in Jan H. Kietzmann, Kristopher Hermkens, Ian P. McCarthy and Bruno S. Silvestre, »Social Media? Get Serious! Understanding the Functional Building Blocks of Social Media« (PDF), in: *Business Horizons* 54, no. 3 (2011): 241–51.

[9] Koschorke, *Wahrheit und Erfindung,* 18 (see note 3).

territory of the internet. It concerns the arbitrariness or expansion of the motifs and topics that become *narratable*, here experiencability meets the narratability of a life which struggles less with major questions but is guided by minor search movements, a groping through the small but ever-present scrub of the immediate surroundings, in the everyday entanglements which are barely considered by the systems. Narration happens with many and about infinitely much, which, condensed into information, contributes to the enrichment and abundance of the micronarratives which can be observed in the social network. The indifference or sovereignty with which the medium grants access and distribution to all things irritates the old centers of the literary administration of meaning but the benefits can hardly be dismissed. Here m*edia richness theory* may be right, which is founded upon the supposition »that the goal of any communication is the resolution of ambiguity and the reduction of uncertainty,« a goal which is motivated especially through the excessive reproduction of narratives.[10]

10
See Andreas M. Kaplan and Michael Haenlein, »Users of the World, Unite! The Challenge and Opportunities of Social Media,« *Business Horizons* 53, no. 1 (2010):

4

Stories are told to keep something at bay. In the most harmless but not least important case: boredom. Then, and more gravely: fear, which contains ignorance but also, and more elemental, unfamiliarity. Hans Blumenberg

In his ethnological studies concerning language Bronisław Malinowski has set a fundamental assessment at the beginning of his thoughts concerning a »new type of linguistic use—phatic communion«:

»[…] to a natural man another man's silence is not a reassuring factor, but on the contrary, something alarming and dangerous. […] The breaking of silence, the communion of words is the first act to establish links of fellowship, which is consummated only by the breaking of bread and the communion of food. The modern English expression, 'Nice day to-day' or the Melanesian phrase 'Whence comest thou?' are needed to get over the strange unpleasant tension which men feel when facing each other in silence. After the first formula, there comes a flow of language, purposeless expressions of preference or aversion, accounts of irrelevant happenings, comments on what is perfectly obvious. [...] There can be no doubt that we have a new type of linguistic use—phatic communion. [...] Each utterance is an act serving the direct aim of binding hearer to speaker by a tie of some social sentiment or other. [...] ›Phatic communion‹ serves to establish bonds of personal union between people brought together by the mere need of companionship and does not serve any purpose of communicating ideas.«[11]

I would like to apply Malinowski's analysis and his concept of the phatic in the context of new narration and to assume that the essential uncertainty, which Malinowski points to as explaining the origin of his invention of this new term —»...the strange unpleasant tension which men feel when facing each other in silence«—can not only be conceived as the trigger of an anthropological relational figure but as a symptomatology of society which we perceive as omnipresent today. *The world is silent*, *Weltenstille* is perceived as a constitutive threat to the process of civilization and as the origin of language, music and noise. On the one hand the silence of the world means a fundamental intransigence of nature, the failure of hermeneutical efforts to attain a representability of the world, the limits of an hearing and explaining access to natural processes, it means an »absolutism of reality« turned in silence against which »the conditions of his existence are nearly out of man's hold.«[12] On the other hand, silence—as semantic emptiness—is an effect of self-created abstraction as denuding of meaning that which exists. Here silence must be set in analogy to an omnipresent white noise of which the far-off murmur of the images, texts and sounds, which are universally lamented as simultaneously exceeding and devoid of meaning, tells us. In the self-produced, ubiquitous noise of a highly economized world the existential experience of an overwhelmed, alarmed, dangerous incomprehensibility, helplessness, of a dis-semantic, a negatively charged silence emerges. The attempts to face this threat can all be associated with the fundamental admission: *narrare necesse est*.

[11]
Bronsław Malinowksi, »The Problem of Meaning in Primitive Languages,« in *The Meaning of Meaning,* ed. C. K. Ogden and I. A. Richards (1923). Supplement I: 296–336. http://faculty.washington.edu/cbehler/glossary/malinowsPM.html (accessed September 23, 2013).

[12]
Hans Blumenberg, *Arbeit am Mythos* (Frankfurt am Main, 1979), 9.

Malinowski tells of a »phatic communion« which answers the silence. It is important that it is not one directed communication which is introduced here, but a communion as the desire, fundamental to every gathering of people, to communicate one's own presence via partaking in the presence of one or many others—be it symbolically, merely visually or purely audibly—to sever a part of one's own identity to form a community.

And yet the sociocohesive power of language is simultaneously linked to a relation with the (arti-) factual world, and is thus not only a kind of collective medial Eucharist celebrated with others, but also an invocation of the *deixis*, indexical acts of reference that facilitate an existential location of those present—however far apart they may be—continually interlocking them with the world via the *I, you, there, here...*

Twitter is possibly the most poignant example of such self-referential writing. Apparently the medium facilitates the speedy sending of news as *tweets,* which are messages of 140 characters. But the mere number of tweets sent out daily by 300 million active users shows that the creators only partly intended conventional communication, rather a stenographic passing on of their immediate life and work situation, minimal speech acts which mirror the actions, as caused or experienced or endured (one thinks of the situations akin to civil war all over the world) in the individual everyday life, acts which enable them to assure themselves of a territorial connection as well as of their desire not to be alone, to make each individual presence of the others perceptible against the silence of systems, institutions.

Concerning the medial modes of narrative in web spaces, it can be generally stated that it is not craftsmanship and formal quality which drives these texts and images, but the individual's early policy of desire to verify/testify its ephemeral, singular, vanishing occurrence with records to keep the fear, to keep the silence at bay. If these movements were intended for private or journalistic use in the first phase of technological media, so are they now for the sprawling collective space of an all-encompassing and omnipresent web. And both necessitate each other. One medium drives the other in order for its own presence to persist within it. The net evokes and provokes unfettered textual and photographic production to become the raw material for scenarios of exchange. Online texts and digital photography do not recognize the paradigm of the good or well-made work, they simply want to communicate, to record that which the individual sees at that moment, which it experiences and then publishes as quickly as possible to see it distributed in the global network. In this way all, or nearly all, events, both the irrelevant and the notable, enter the world a second time by means of their online existence.

Further aspects of these technological salvation fantasies can be supplied by the thoughts of Michel Foucault concerning photogenic painting in the nineteenth century: with the advent of photography the other fine arts were also set the task to seek the image itself behind or beside their painting, their drawing; an image, which, independently from its medium, from language and syntax, continually circulates, floats, wanders. In the present it is the Internet which provides the drive »to circulate images, to override them, to disguise them, to distort them, to make them red-hot, to freeze them, to variously translate them.«[13] Like these images the body, translated into medial forms, the acting, self-representing, disguising, distorting, the playing body experiences a new attraction concerning its use as an image.

[13] Michel Foucault, »Die photogene Malerei (Präsentation),« in idem, *Dits et Ecrits*, vol. 2, 1970–1975 (Frankfurt am Main, 2002), 871–82, here 872.

5

»... thankfully entertaining« Marcel Reich-Ranicki

One important question remains: How can one accommodate oneself with oneself if one is spread out into three entities with an obligation to each as an alter ego? These three entities are the *narrator* of the story (whether writing, filming...), the *protagonist*, i.e., the person who is being narrated about, and the *person,* that entity with whom »the narrative exceeds its own boundaries.« Even if »these three instances, which collude in this application of the narrative, ultimately refer to *one* person the identity which is being referred to is precarious.«[14] These models, developed by Dieter Thomä, show two variations which can be similarly applied to the mode of existence on the net and which I would like to comment on briefly.

There's the process of self-narration motivated by finding oneself and the invention of self manifested through blogs and Facebook. Thus the narrator perceives himself as an object because »the objectified self seems to be the prerequisite for making narration about it possible; on the other hand, that which one has attributed and is attributing to oneself remains trapped in the textual structure and becomes alienated from the acting entity. Via the detour of such objectification someone can arrive at an emphatic claim of who ›he himself‹ is; yet it is exactly in this claim that he remains separated from that which is happening to him or that which he happens to do right now.«[15]

On the other hand the way a person leads their life can converge with »the way he narrates something«. »This convergence happens especially when he does something. That which a person endures, perceives, experiences, feels—all that does not lend itself as easily to self-attribution as that which a person does (after they have done something and before they will do something). Here is a pragmatic neatness, a predefined context of meaning which can be rendered into narrative pretty much without loss. [...] Thus the narrator becomes the counterpart of the person that acts without being distracted by diffuse emotions or being swept away by overwhelming experiences.«[16] In this way the act seems to influence the often spontaneous, restless and indiscriminate writing and filming, for example on mobiles; the phatic nonparticularity which is characteristic for these fragments of experienced life, thus is in more or less radical contrast with the old, identity-centered narration.

Perhaps for many a kind of existential tension has emerged with their participation in the New Narrative modes on the net. None of them have »mislaid« the »primitively epic« quality of private life, as Robert Musil has his character Ulrich report.[17] But they link the foreshortening of the intellect, by

[14] Thomä, Erzähle dich selbst, 27 (see note 2).

[15] Ibid., page 171.

[16] Ibid., page 274.

[17] Robert Musil, *Der Mann ohne Eigenschaften*, Reinbek bei Hamburg, 1978, 648f.

means of which the narrative thread once directed the thread of life in a nice continuum, to a polyperspective entanglement within the infinite woven plane of the medial public. And, most important, their conversations are, while providing existential sustenance, often pretty entertaining.

Marc Ries
earned a doctoral degree in philosophy in 1995 at the Universität Wien. Cultural-theoretical and aesthetical issues give rise to studies on mass media, society and art. Visiting professor at the Friedrich-Schiller-Universität Jena and Hochschule für Graphik und Buchkunst Leipzig. Since 2010 Professor for sociology and media theory at the Hochschule für Gestaltung in Offenbach. 2009 concept and cocurator of the exhibition *talk.talk Das Interview als ästhetische Praxis* Leipzig/Graz/Salzburg. Selected publications: *Medienkulturen* (2002); copublisher: *DATING.21 Liebesorganisation und Verabredungskulturen* (2007).

Beyond Structuralism: Extended Narratives between Texts and Images

Hans Ulrich Reck

1. As Seen by Abraham A. Moles

›The evolutions we are seeing in images are based on the structural concept of the quantification of images in terms of selected points that can be teased from an original reality (icons). The most obvious procedure would be to simply record all existing points of reality and reproduce them in their entirety. But statistics, which are predicated on the constancy of the physical universe, teach us that reality could just as well be reproduced based on a random sample, whereby fewer elements would be incorporated than are reproduced. In the definitive image, truth is reconstructed using a limited amount of data, in which case the missing elements can be interpolated based on what is already known. This is the concept of random sample reconstruction of a curve or surface, which is reconstructed in its entirety using a number of known elements. This concept, which is the culmination of structural thinking, will be the driving force behind the evolution of images in the twenty-first century. ›The language of light‹ of classic photography will be supplanted by systematic deconstruction of the world and reconstruction of a point-for-point constant simulacrum that is nothing more than a random sample of the underlying reality. [...] Clear thinking will be driven by the schematization of the real, which will in turn reduce the superfluous richness of the ›thematic realm‹ to the limited capacities of information processing. This schematization will make the world easier to understand. [...] The core concept *image* has two aspects. First, visible images are the stuff of scientific theory that aims to explain the manifestations that appear under a microscope or that are captured by a camera. [...] Secondly, images result from a process that seeks to make the world more readily understandable. This in turn suggests that a new definition of *visible* may be required, namely the following: ›The visible comprises everything about the world that is visible and concealed, but which can be encompassed by a suitable technology.‹ In this sense, visible means objectifiable or discoverable. The technologies of discovery are those of evolution or development; and as with photography the latent image is there. The mechanisms of our intellects and technologies render invisible elements visible by discovering latent forms that our limited senses are unable to perceive.«[1]

That which the above passage formulated by aesthetics and information theorist Abraham A. Moles so succinctly expresses can serve here as a foil to generally applicable (from a poetic standpoint) narrative theory that exceeds the bounds of disparity between still images, moving images, poetry and texts. This has nothing to do with structural data compression but on the contrary involves the poetic decompression of data, i.e., its expansion. New narratives involve increased complexity and poetic interconnection, and need to break out and expand. This applies to both texts and images, and particularly to moving images. If data and sounds can be compressed using a sampling process, this can also be done with narrative texts and images without noticeable loss—which, if any, will only affect insignificant realms. Hence it is poetic form—not structural depictions (often represented in diagrams of technical processes)—that is the determining factor for narrative poetology. What counts here is not the world's understandability, but rather its mysteriousness; for otherwise the term *narrative* would be meaningless. For scientific narratives also include those involving the doings of the hermetic in a nontransparent domain; and clear statements in the sense of information only provide knowledge that can be compiled into sets of protocols. Narration is intrinsically a principle that exceeds the bounds of compression and protocol, the watchword here being *digression* rather than *compression*. For this, the following passage from Jorge Luis Borges provides a masterful representation and example.

2. As Seen by Jorge Luis Borges

»Five hundred years ago, the chief of an upper hexagon came upon a book as confusing as the others, but which had nearly two pages of homogeneous lines. He showed his find to a wandering decoder who told him the lines were written in Portuguese; others said they were Yiddish. Within a century, the language was established: a Samoyedic Lithuanian dialect of Guarani, with classical Arabian inflections. The content was also

[1] Abraham A. Moles, »Die thematische Visualisierung der Welt,« in *Tumult. Zeitschrift für Verkehrswissenschaft* no. 14, »Das Sichtbare« (1990): 111ff.

deciphered: some notions of combinative analysis, illustrated with examples of variations with unlimited repetition. These examples made it possible for a librarian of genius to discover the fundamental law of the Library. This scholar observed that all books, no matter how diverse, are composed of the same elements: the space, the period, the comma, the twenty-two letters of the alphabet. He also alleged a fact which travelers have confirmed: In the vast Library no two books are identical. From these two incontrovertible premises he deduced that the Library is total and that its shelves register all the possible combinations of the twenty-odd orthographical symbols (a number which, though extremely vast, is not infinite): Everything: the minutely detailed history of the future, the archangels' autobiographies, the faithful catalogues of the Library, thousands and thousands of false catalogues, the demonstration of the fallacy of those catalogues, the demonstration of the fallacy of the true catalogue, the Gnostic gospel of Basilides, the commentary on that gospel, the commentary on the commentary on that gospel, the true story of your death, the translation of every book in all languages, the interpolations of every book in all books. [...] The certitude that some shelf in some hexagon held valuable books and that these valuable books were inaccessible, seemed almost intolerable. A blasphemous sect suggested that the searches should cease and that all men should juggle letters and symbols until they constructed, by an improbable gift of chance, these canonical books. [...] [T]he Library is so enormous that any reduction of human origin is infinitesimal. The other: every copy is unique, irreplaceable, but (since the Library is total) there are always several hundred thousand imperfect facsimiles: works which differ only in a letter or a comma. [...] In truth, the Library includes all verbal structures, all variations permitted by the twenty-five orthographical symbols, but not a single example of absolute nonsense. [...] I cannot combine a number of characters which the divine Library has not already foreseen

        d h c m r l c h t d j

and which in one of its secret tongues harbors a terrible meaning. No one can articulate a syllable which is not filled with tenderness and fear, which is not, in one of these languages, the powerful name of a god. To speak is to fall into tautology. This wordy and useless epistle already exists in one of the thirty volumes of the five shelves of one of the innumerable hexagons—as well as its refutation. [...] The certitude that everything has been written negates us or turns us into phantoms. I know of districts in which the young men prostrate themselves before books and kiss their pages in a barbarous manner, but they do not know how to decipher a single letter. [...] The Library is unlimited and cyclical. If an eternal traveler were to traverse it in any direction, after centuries he would see that the same volumes were repeated in the same disorder (which, thus repeated, would be an order: the Order). My solitude is gladdened by this elegant hope.«[2]

The special alphabet that determines divine order in this text differs radically from media-sphere mechanization in the narrative of aggregations of time-theory dimensions: the aleatoric; that which is reproducible; variation; replication; generation. On the other hand, such time-spaces are extirpated by the mechanization of media arrangements and the hard-wiring of meaning and cognition to machines.

3. As Seen by Kazimir Malevich

Modern art culminates in or is intent on representing the nonrepresentable, rendering the nonvisible visible. The work of art becomes a momentary event in the process of experiencing art, which conveys the »imagelessness of absolutes.«[3] Hence the work of art can no longer be regarded as an object to be viewed or a medium of representation. It becomes the expression of problematic experiences that play out in the back and forth between the viewer and the work and which do not co-occur with its material equivalent, the work of art as text or image. And so in this dynamic, statements or elements that are recognizable as such only come into existence by removing meaning (signifiers) from symbols (that which is significant). The collapse of the representation of absolutes is attributable not only to the initiating movement of the viewer in respect to the work, but rather to the imminent dynamic, whereby the work seeks out a

[2] Jorge Luis Borges, »The Library of Babel« (1941), in *Labyrinths*, trans. James E. Irby (New York, 1962), 51–58.

[3] Georg Picht, *Kunst und Mythos*, 2nd ed. (Stuttgart, 1987), 74.

viewer who completes the work's message.⁴ This creation of the work's message from the standpoint of the viewer is the organizing principle of modern narratives, to which textual structure and image syntax are handmaidens.

In short, we can say this about stories in images, texts, or both: all the rhythmical quality that is ascribed to the language of images, i.e., musicality as a new guiding principle for the steadily expanding world of narratives now encompassing technology, species, genres, industries, and media, is becoming the archetypal experience of modern art, where time has displaced space as the field of experimentation. Nearly a century ago, around the time of the conceptual emergence of the urge toward expressionist form, Ernst Bloch, who had vehemently promoted this segregation, wrote: »the purely painterly, which many Impressionists are vaguely proud of having rediscovered, retreats before the drive toward expresion.«⁵ Henceforth, meanings arise from the process of abandoning oneself to the content of the artwork, rather than to the mere topography of themes, iconographies, and symbols. The tonality is internal; the sound of the image is the counterpart to the thrill experienced by a soul yearning to break free. Contemplation is regarded as no longer suitable for artworks. As living entities, narratives must be real-life experiences that always seek to clear the way for extension and expansion. Elsewhere in the same text, Bloch stated as follows in his remarkably emphatic and expressionistic language: »If however what the *sound* says comes from us, insofar as we place ourselves into it, and speak with this great macanthropic larynx, then that is no dream, but a solid ring of the soul, to which nothing corresponds only because nothing outside can, and because music as the inwardly utopian art lies completely beyond anything empirically demonstrable. [...] The servant's entrance of mere reflection has been forced open, and a different symbol appears than the allegorical kind that was alien to us, at least half extrahuman, that would have crushed us, burnt us up if it had become fully visible, like the uncovered Zeus, and whose still unresolved, transcendent ungraspability within the visible word, what is inclined toward us, had constituted its character as symbol.«⁶

[4] Umberto Eco, *The Open Work*, trans. Anna Cancogni (Cambridge, MA, 1989).

[5] Ernst Bloch, *Utopia,* trans. Anthony A. Nassar (Stanford, CA, 2000), 21.

[6] Ibid., p. 206.

4. As Seen by Witold Gombrowicz

Witold Gombrowicz, who tended to use the language of conflict, wrote a sharp scenario that revolved around the principle of narrative iteration (i.e., the continuation of its necessary expansion) in these terms: »You! People! You have no feel for painting! No clue! No understanding! You just don't get it. Me: Look at these three matches that I'm laying on the sand. Imagine that a group of people gets into a bitter argument about how these three matches can be arranged so that they will constitute the greatest possible revelation from an artistic standpoint. [...] [I]magine, if you will, that myriad experienced ›match artists‹ labor mightily at this task; some are more inventive, some less; hierarchies emerge; schools and styles emerge from all this; knowledge is developed. Why should this be absurd, I ask? Because, when all's said and done, people are able to express something about themselves and the world with these three matches. And ultimately, if we focused all our attention on these matches, we could discover the mystery of the cosmos. [...] All this is predicated on our looking inwardly to a sufficient degree. But the question is: is it worth it? is it worth it? is it worth it? [...] And I won't deny it: If you contemplate a Cézanne with this intensity, then Cézanne will become a revelation. But the question is: is it worth it? is it worth it? is it worth it? Why not look elsewhere for such revelations?«[7] Which leads us to this question: Why even seek revelations in art? Why not just follow the lead of narratives and perpetuate them?

[7] Witold Gombrowicz, »Sakrilegien,« in *Tagebüchern, 1953 bis 1967* (Frankfurt am Main, 2002), 140f.

5. A Few Words about Schleier, Fiction and Abstraction

In his 1905 book *Erkenntnis und Irrtum*, Ernst Mach provided a slew of examples from the »hard« sciences where happenstance plays a pivotal role.[8] In the book's foreword, Mach argues that scientific activities are deeply rooted in our instincts, but that we lose sight of science through poorly grasped assumptions and suppositions, lured on by the prospect of science's rational goals, which by no means provide us with a rational worldview.

[8] Ernst Mach, *Erkenntnis und Irrtum. Skizzen zur Psychologie der Forschung* (Darmstadt, 1991; facsimile of 5th edition publihed in Leipzig, 1926).

In the same spirit, though from a completely different point of view and with the same inspired tone, in 1954 Max Ernst wrote the following about his frottage series *Histoire Naturelle* (1926) in an essay entitled »Was ist Surrealismus« for an exhibition at Zürcher Kunsthaus: »The revolutionary meaning of this first and perhaps absurd description of nature will perhaps become clearer by virtue of the fact that similar results have emerged from modern microphysics. P. Jordan stated the following after measuring a weightless electron in movement and then measuring the location: ›But this distinction between the outer and inner realm essentially collapses in the face of experiments showing that things happen in the outside world which have an objective existence irrespective of any process of observation.‹ [...] Thus science substitutes itself for the knowledge of reactions that are caused by observational methodologies«[9] The refusal to accept the compartmentalization of documents, imagination and fiction: even entertaining the possibility that they exist was, shortly thereafter, the starting point for Michel Foucault's history of science in *Les Mots et les Choses* (1966).

The poetic inspiration of artists, as well as a paradigm shift in epistemological methods in the natural sciences (resulting from a revolution that was endured more than desired) are indicative of this disappearance of a factually consistent »objective reality,« independent of an observer and that clearly differentiates between the inner and outer realms.[10] »We've gotten to the point where the entire perceived world has become a sea of delusion, whereby curtain after curtain is pushed aside, until we believe that we are standing before a final curtain of reality upon whose surface only the shadows of electrons flit by mysteriously and almost imperceptibly. Rational understanding has the last word here: from the foreground of consciousness the world fades into the background of thought.«[11] This passage by Ernesto Grassi, where he so clearly explicates the keyword »nature« from Werner Heisenberg's *Das Naturbild der heutigen Physik*, dates from 1955. Back then, did knowledge of the world appear (like the world itself) to be forever beyond the reach of symbolic representation? Was this deeply felt, or was it merely a superficial assertion? Does this discourse harbor further, as yet

[9] Max Ernst, »Was ist Surrealismus,« in *Surrealismus in Paris, 1919–1939. Ein Lesebuch*, ed. Karlheinz Barck (Leipzig, 1990)

[10] Werner Heisenberg, *Das Naturbild der heutigen Physik* (Hamburg, 1955).

[11] Ernesto Grassi, *Die Macht der Phantasie. Zur Geschichte des abendländischen Denkens* (Königstein, 1979)

unperceived, interim stages in the human history of mistaking the facts—this time in terms of the impossibility of finding mathematical expression for a world that has become unimaginable, but that nonetheless remains calculable?

6. Metaphor, Polysemie and the Art of Fiction as a Perpetuation of Narrative

In *Museum without Walls* (1949) André Malraux predicted that in an age of mechanical reproduction fiction had irrevocably superceded style.[12] This, he wrote, inevitably resulted in playful training in the everyday representation of artifacts and mannerisms; which explains why the everyday world is being mediatized by growing expert knowledge of the recipient and, conversely, the hitherto untouchable worlds of the expert are, at the same time, characterized by an intense attention-seeking ritualization owing to the mediatization of asserted information.

The fiction of art gives way to the art of fiction, and the narratives never stop for producers and consumers alike. Everything is a priori grist for the mill of narrative perpetuation and expansion. Our era is notable not only for its telecommunication networks, consciousness industry, and disinformation masquerading as knowledge, but also for a general poetology of endless and steadily expanding narrative. And it is the same in the sciences, where rationalism no longer plays the preponderant role one would expect.

Reality is increasingly determined by fantasy and imagination, but at the same dependent upon it. There are no standards which could dictate the technical manipulations it might be wiser to qualitatively limit or prohibit. The actual guiding principle within the art of fiction—that characterize the randomness of any given imaginary museum or archive, whether in the arts or sciences—is the fragment. The fact that the whole world can thus become an image—whether as a substitute, reflection or ruination—is only one side of the process. It is only through the re-structuring of technical images into montages of images that

12
André Malraux, *Museum without Walls.*, in *The Voices of Silence*, trans. Stuart Gilbert (Princeton, 1978).

the naive reference to the object is overcome. Physical characteristics are displaced by comparative insights into the functional logic of artistic and scientific style—and today fictions. And they must be narrated before they actually exist.

Fiction is the ineluctable key to the creation of each model that renders reality comprehensible and thus ontologically real. The following passage by Andrei Markov is relevant here: If reducing complex data to a less complex program results in such program being able to reproduce the baseline volume of data, then this program *comprehends* this volume of data. A theory is a program that makes observations quantifiable. A program that tries to simulate a theory that is more complex than the theory that formed the basis of the program will provide better comprehension through self-development. Intelligence is more than just a metaphor for this. But it is not enough because, in point of fact, there is always a discrepancy. Speaking precisely is impossible. Every exact language is dependent on narrative elements, particularly metaphors, which meander, move, and are dynamic. They are »alive,« as Paul Ricœur has cogently shown.[13] And thus what emerges from expanded narrative and general poetology is a multiplicity of meaning, or as the French call it, *polysemie* (polysemy)—a term that means that an image or text can have various meanings depending on context. Things, images, symbols and words become »alien« or »foreign.« The identity of an image hinges on an internal dual coding: intrinsic sameness and heterogeneity, which allow for plurality and thus context openness. A system of symbols needs a specific attribute so that it can be open to context—although this attribute does not stem from the context per se. The characteristic ambivalence of contemporary artistic creations (texts, images, media) is attributable to the fact that only *polysemie* rather than a single-meaning identity allows knowledge to be conveyed. An image universe without *polysemie* would undermine the principle of signal economy, but would nonetheless expand vocabulary ad infinitum. Images exert an effect when they take the form of characteristic constructs and paradigmatic models; but in an apparent paradox, they can only do this if they exist in a single form. Media as art and art as medium comprise process-related and dynamic quantities, specific

13
Paul Ricœur, *Die lebendige Metapher* (Munich, 1986).

manifestations of creation, and relationships between particular contexts. And this in turn brings all types of media under one intellectual roof in terms of text, image, language and linguistics.

The dream of an exact, ideal, metaphor-free language is a twentieth-century dream that was brought to the highest level by Rudolf Carnap, but which has now disintegrated. For many years this dream appeared to be a viable option requiring tireless effort. However, to some extent this belief was attributable to the dogmatic view that any given rationale (e.g., as in early Wittgenstein) can always be expressed in perfectly accurate language. In line with this concept, all metaphors were regarded as metaphysics or as discourse leading to impurity and were thus spurned. But we moderns now have the opportunity to take model building as a starting point rather than representational theorems, the goal being not representation but rather self awareness of the processes of abstraction and narration. This involves expansion and new distinctions. Metaphors will be welcome to join the process at some point; will no longer be bothersome, and may even be able to make themselves useful. Abstractions, after being accentuated, are specifically structured processes involving the creation of a form and defining a hierarchy of the determining aspects of guiding choices and arrangements. They allow us to leave unimportant aspects by the wayside so that we may make wise choices among the important elements we decide to retain. This has indisputably become the literary, performance and characteristic core of fictional narration and of artistic representation in general. That new or expanded narratives come from a place beyond genres and types is a phenomenon that is only today coming into its own. It teaches us skepticism, agility and suppleness in all things and tests philosophy as discourse.

Hans Ulrich Reck
is a philosopher, an art theorist, a publisher and a curator. He is an art and media history professor at the Kunsthochschule für Medien in Cologne since 1995, past professor and director of the faculty for communication theory at the Hochschule für Angewandte Kunst in Vienna (1992–1995), and past lecturer at Basel and Zurich (1982–1995). His recent publications include: *Pier Paolo Pasolini – Poetisch Philosophisches Porträt* (2012); *Spiel Form Künste. Zu einer Kunstgeschichte des Improvisierens*, published by Bernd Ternes (2010); *Traum. Enzyklopädie* (2010); *Index Kreativität* (2007); *EIGENSINN DER BILDER. Bildtheorie oder Kunstphilosophie?* (2007); and *Das Bild zeigt das Bild selber als Abwesendes* (2007).

Ferdinand Schmatz
The Surge of Speech

1

Speech surges. It surges within us, urging us to put a name to what we perceive. Likewise allowing us to associate and classify, and thus be able to communicate our perceptions.

But not seldom is this order, this other-directed discourse, experienced as an external compulsion—generated by the systems which channel inner-linguistic insistence through the contexts surrounding such speech. And which are not merely limited to employing linguistic forms of expression to achieve their objectives.

These objectives are evident and, incidentally, have long lost their association with the given object or product. Opening our eyes to view the matter clearly, this means that actual realization means nothing other than setting boundaries within which the educated learn to cultivate those fields, so that their yields can be harvested by the systems.

This education occurs by means of penetrating, all-embracing media. It avails itself of words, but far more of imagery and other representative forms, by which it creates a reality that simulates a false transparency: everything is possible, whereby nothing is actually possible. And where abstract values become real and the real, even physical values, are reduced to abstracts, far removed from all individual experience.

It is thus less about language or speech than about the system of symbols, which are placed by the media machinery to impose order, in which I, you, we, become nothing more than the bearers of branded labels or stamped insignia. Order that does not produce its content from the individual needs of I, or the social group, but which suggests that its superficial values, in line with market demands, are profoundly our own.

That means the integration and requirement of speech and expressive forms as behavioral forms in individual as well as in social areas. Which represents nothing other than complying with standards, and alienation, relating not only to the object of abstract structures manufactured in remote-controlled machines, but to the entire attitude toward life.

2

Creativity or creative work surges. It surges into other works, which it visits, in order to toy and experiment with their medial resources, only to ultimately return to its original intention of a unified work of form and substance. As art, whereby form is not used as a means of communication, but rather is communication itself—which, within and without and far beyond itself, discusses, addresses, and portrays every politically and theoretically weighted-content of a standardized and limited reality and, by breaking down boundaries, seeks its transformation.

Interestingly, such work can also assume the form of other artistic media, which is likewise justified by the incursion of empirical realities. The actual, definitive intention of the work, to merely be this work, is not thereby restrained. On the contrary, opportunities for conveying its attendant message are enhanced.

3

This form is the intervention in a space or room, leaving the desk, the page, entering and taking a social space, that of the market itself—by means of definition, word and place.

The Word

—text from texts, a flood of symbols, a seeming chaos, that nonetheless has a pattern of order that inspires and influences. The school of the market! To elevate this influence into awareness, to thus transform it into a real and actual space in which action can be taken, yes, this applies to art:

In one specific place

—with media from other artistic areas—objects, photographs, video—an artistic expansion of the essential spoken medium that ultimately flows back into itself as text.

A work of works, a plural authorship that elects this specific space, to explore it and research within it, to analyze. That calls attention to specific conditions, in order to call attention, where possible, to the universally abstract, itself representative of the state of a socioeconomic, symbolic bond.

To that which represents standardization and automatism, effects and manipulation on the subconscious and the role played by the subject thus ensnared.

The artistic play is set against the gravitas of imprisonment, a type of revolt of the autonomous individual through the linguistically figurative, actionist forms of expression and behavior.

In this regard and ever more self-denigrating, language stands in the forefront as working material which is truncated by other forms of artistic expression, such as the physical act of transforming the introduced object(s) into an existing material and living world,

subject to capitalistic laws, yet freely suggested: as an attempt to act freely and allow others to participate.

The intervention in space is an interesting, yet long-lasting disruption of the status quo and its automatism by other means than that of speech or language alone, even when it involves poetry and literature!

Something like
SPEECH ROOM
Composed of
Sound Image Word—

A more actual than fragmentary space or room of text, textual images, text banners, text objects and diverse sketches in written, illustrated, and spoken form, as well as sung and musically performed.

The basis for this mobile space or room as a module for presentations, primarily in the areas of poetry and music, is a layout of 3 × 2 meters, extending from one wall, its perimeters marked with chalked lines.

These borders divide and define the room, inviting one to overstep its boundaries at the same time, actually referring to the essence of other forms of expression, as, too, to the symbolic crossing of borders within the area of literary language and poetry, all of which are interlinked with music, image, and the public space.

The room, our room, that of speech, that of the social group, the individual and the collective—
builds the basis for attracting the most diversified forms of artistic expression and giving them free reign, both within and outside one's own working area, of literature, of art, the university, the institute, the classroom.

Thus, it is to the edge of center that the venture stands, lies or drifts:

PURITY and SOUND, an artistic collaboration, an exciting interplay of poetry and music:

Word, phrase, tone and sound to be thematically and materially interwoven into a common basis, compositions of voice, instrument, borne by the spirit of enhancement, not only by poetry and music, but rather by dialogue forms which develop, produce and communicate their messages as purity and roughness, at one and the same time.

The SPEECH ROOM serves as a performance venue for the word-sound-compositions just as the layout from which the real and imaginary walls rise up—in the form of a public, open area where such textual and artistic works as objects of speech and other materials can be projected and introduced: and whose vertices can be substituted by a type of column, consisting of a word-image project—in the form of a newspaper, similar to, yet going beyond, the contextual display technique of Aby Warburg's *L'Atlas Mnémosyne* and its frieze.

Ferdinand Schmatz
writes poetry, prose and essays. He won several awards (Trakl, Artmann and Jandl). He teaches at the Universität für Angewandte Kunst in Vienna and runs the Institut für Sprachkunst. Schmatz lives in Vienna. Some of his publications are the following: *Maler als Stifter. Poetische Texte zur bildenden Kunst* (1997); *Farbenlehre* (with Heimo Zobernig, 1995); and his most recent works are: *Durchleuchtung. Ein wilder Roman aus Danja und Franz* (2007); *Quellen. Gedichte* (2010).

It Will Have Been Reality: Alban Nikolai Herbst's Expanded Site of Writing

Usha Reber

The *Expanded Narration* project offers a vague concept that speaks of innovating, networking, transcending boundaries but also of fuming and long-winded narratives. Thus a broad and ambiguous field is presented whose few pages I would like to illuminate with the help of the writing and narrating of Alban Nikolai Herbst, an author who lives in Berlin. Herbst coined the term *cyberrealism* for his work; he is also one of those authors who reflect in a highly precise way on their own writing, their methods of narrating and fabricating. Thus he certainly offers directions for ordering and interpreting his work. Such clues, which Herbst includes in his literary blog *Fiktionsraum* on twoday.net, will be examined below, and I will attempt to detect and analyze how the cyberrealistic method of narrative transcends boundaries.

In an earlier, comprehensive work I already devoted myself to Herbst's poetology in great detail concerning the aspect of metamorphic writing.[1] Several aspects are taken up here again and reexamined from a different perspective. The main question for this essay is: How can one narrate as literature and as art in new and expanded ways? Alban Nikolai Herbst asks himself this question again and again and responds to it with an aesthetic of possibility of »old forms in the present.« This establishes the focus of this analysis, which will investigate the relationship of time and narrative, of form and style, and thinking in/of possibilities.

Continuum/Compossibility

In his novel *Wolpertinger; oder, Das Blau*, published by Dielmann in 1993, Alban Nikolai Herbst placed his text beneath an epigraph from Jacques Lacan: »What is realized in my history is [...] the future anterior of what I will have been, given what I am in the process of becoming. *Lacan.*«[2] Indeed, the slightly paradoxical procedure of telling about a state in the past that is still occurring in the present is what forms a philosophical paradox of the predictability of what will have been can be applied to all of Herbst's writing and narrating. A paradox of (in)compossibility is presented that concerns both the temporal level(s) and the narrative coherence.

---

[1] Ursula Reber, *Formenverschleifung: Zu einer Theorie der Metamorphose* (Paderborn, 2009).

[2] Jacques Lacan, »The Function and Field of Speech and Language in Psychoanalysis,« in idem, *Écrits: The First Complete Edition in English*, trans. Bruce Fink with Héloïse Fink and Russell Grigg (New York, 2005), 197–268, esp. 248.

Alban Nikolai Herbst does not use this pair of terms in his reflections on poetology and cyberealism, but he is presumably very familiar with the principle of the »pyramid without a base.«³ It comes up under various names and in the context of several narrative techniques. It prominently controls the differentiation of events in his latest novel, *Argo. Anderswelt* (published in September 2013 by Elfenbein), as a »fog chamber« in which the »apparent infinity« becomes visible as »vapor trails; short, thin threads; and distended bodies like ghost caterpillars.«⁴ The principle is formulated more clearly in a note dated December 29, 2007:

»In the matrix of Cybernetic Realism, there are not only factual cognitions as components but also possibilities: that is the crucial aesthetic approach, that it is not an excluding poetic technique but rather an integrative one, which does *not* run aground on causal connections. For a novel, that means that the same narrative strands can split just like the narrated subjects and that these split narrative strands can each lead to different continuations of the plot, which are narrated in parallel, without placing an accent on any particular continuation.«⁵

The »pyramid without a base« cited above from Vogl, which is taken from Leibniz's *Theodicy* (sec. 416), provides the basic figure for Herbst's cyberrealism; moreover, the passage contains a formulation similar to the Lacan quotation cited above, if we note that to every possible world there corresponds a Roman prince Sextus Tarquinius, although not the same one to whom it is already implicit what he will become (sec. 414). But Herbst's poetic technique suspends the condition of compossibility, or rather he calls it into question or perhaps—we will see later—places it on a new foundation. In essence, all temporally and immanently separated compossibilities that in Leibniz are separated by the chambers in the pyramid are »possible together.« In that spirit, Herbst claims an »integrative« technique based on division. In contrast to the quotation above, which certainly complies with the rules of compossibility, of the unity of subject and predicat(ion), his stories do not proceed via integrative or integrating intersections.

3
See Joseph Vogl, »Was ist ein Ereignis,« lecture on October 26, 2003, at the ZKM symposium *Deleuze und die Künste: Wiederholung und Differenz*, http://on1.zkm.de/zkm/stories/storyReader $4048 (accessed July 31, 2013).

4
See Alban Nikolai Herbst, »Nebelkammer (1). Argo. Anderswelt. (64),« entry dated December 6, 2004, http://albannikolaiherbst.twoday.net/stories/428868 (accessed September 15, 2013).

5
See Alban Nikolai Herbst, »Desideria: Markus A. Hediger und Die Möglichkeitenpoetik,« in »Kyberrealism,« http://albannikolaiherbst.twoday.net/topics/KYBERREALISM/?start=40 (accessed July 31, 2013).

Unfolding/Splitting

Gilles Deleuze declared the fold, folds in all their variations, to be a principle for revealing the world in the Baroque, especially for Leibniz, for whom the world was folded into the soul, but the world was in turn the unfolding of the soul. In that sense, soul and world enfold or unfold each other, whereby the constant play of *développement* and *enveloppement*[6] is subject to constant reciprocal translation. The folds correspond to one another, but they can be reapplied again and again; folds are not static forms but open ones, which all but compel movement. It is not very surprising, really, that Alban Nikolai Herbst claims the fold for his poetology, when he observes in »Arbeitsnotat 11.11.2004: Zur praktischen Romantheorie. Argo. Anderswelt (46)«: »Interesting that ARGO functions like a self-generating text: folded in and out, folding worlds that comment on one another.«[7]

The autopoiesis of textual worlds in the form of an experimental setup, a play with possibilities of the medium, including disturbances from corrupt source code, seem like an analogy—and sometimes just like a mere assertion—in the novels. Whereas in *Wolpertinger* the fairy world is loaded by diskette onto the network of computers, full of the character of a game and the multiply refracted analogy to overlapping and overwriting cultures, and from there spills over into biological life in the pixelated, grainy style of early computer games and of comics, in *Thetis. Anderswelt*; *Buenos Aires. Anderswelt*; and *Argo. Anderswelt*, Herbst employs a cybernetic experimental setup of »world,« »otherworld,« and »Garraff« in such a way that programmed worlds develop on their own. The experimental setup blocks out a conformist real world because »world« should also be understood as a program. What was/is not planned in the experimental setup is the mutual interaction of incompossible worlds that originally existed separately. But it happens: first, various Deters characters exchange worlds, then the Broglier character transgresses the boundaries of the system, and the worlds begin the »commentary activity« via exchange and reaction.

»Is that why I disappeared from Garraff? I thought about that for a long time, and sometimes I still can't get it out of my

---

[6] Gilles Deleuze, *Difference and Repetition*, trans. Paul Patton (New York, 1994).

[7] Alban Nikolai Herbst, »Arbeitsnotat 11.11.2004: Zur praktischen Romantheorie. Argo. Anderswelt (46),« in »Panoramen der Anderswelt: Expeditionen ins Werk von Alban Nikolai Herbst,« selected and compiled by Ralf Schnell, copyediting: Johann P. Tammen, special issue, *die horen: Zeitschrift für Literatur, Kunst und Kritik* 53, no. 231 (2008): 134.

mind. Or can someone be doubled, so to speak, within the same reference system? That could explain the irregularities that apparently made any further separation of the otherworlds impossible. According to the first law of themodynamics [sic], when I came to Buenos Aires, I would have had to be extinguished from Beelitz and from the world as a whole. Unless Broglier and the other cyborgs who had left their world, and then I too (though *not* a cyborg), would have indeed—by means of our respective ›wandering,‹ let's call it—extended the closed systems by the other one in each case. That cannot be dismissed entirely. [...] According to my calculation, I have meanwhile been here almost exactly a year, so at best one could speak of ›fluctuation‹ if the temporal systems are not supposed to converge. So far I have found no indication of that. [...] Transsystematically wandering entities—to which I now belong as well—are, in a sense, stage and paralysis of data and physical worlds that are expanding into each other in complex ways. ([...] By transporting world, the transported is added to it. So it grows. Infinitely, I fear.)«[8]

The infinite growth is caused by the wanderers between worlds, who bring in things from the other world in the folds of their souls. Herbst demonstrates this impressively with a Deters character who brings a Dunckerstrasse from the world to Buenos Aires in the otherworld.[9] With the constant dovetailing of inner and outer concepts of the world, of corresponding compossibilities that are incompossible with each other, there seem to be only two possibilities in fact: either the implosion of the entire construct or the infinite expansion of incompossible elements into new compossibilities.[10]

The term *autopoiesis* has been applied to Herbst's novelistic worlds several times,[11] not least because Herbst himself never tires of suggesting it for his method or for the method of the texts themselves. It functions outstandingly well on the diegetic and semiotic levels, as a description of the narrative technique, and hence of the production of texts, but it should be used only within quotation marks and only with the awareness of the seduction by Herbst's subject and accompanying reflection. For even with the diversity of Herbst's worlds, and for all the narrated incompossibility, ultimately their compossibility holds, which is

[8] Alban Nikolai Herbst, »ARGO-ÜA (16). Gestrichenes. ›Transsystemisch,‹« http://albannikolaiherbst.twoday.net/stories/3140626/ (accessed August 3, 2013).

[9] Alban Nikolai Herbst, *Buenos Aires: Anderswelt; Kybernetischer Roman* (Berlin, 2001), 97.

[10] On this, see Ursula Reber, »Bauprinzipien des Ortswechsels,« in Reber, *Formenverschleifung* (see note 1), 376–87.

[11] See, for example, the contributions by Hans Richard Brittnacher, Christoph Jürgensen, and Renate Giacomuzzi, in *die horen* 53, no. 231 (2008).

meticulously produced very conservatively by the writer, the physical author. The harmony, the selecting intellect, that makes permits, in diverse and seemingly infinitely folded worlds, »expressive centers« to form, »in which, at each moment, the entire world is contained from a certain point of view,«[12] uses the nom de plume Alban Nikolai Herbst,[13] who has mastered his narrative »craft.« Herbst verbalizes that concern in several passages, particularly memorably in a note titled »Hängende und abgeschlossene Motive« (Hanging and completed motifs). On the one hand, he acknowledges there is »something parasitical« about the »hanging motif,« and that is confirmed by »narrative weaknesses,« when it loudly draws attention to itself as an incomplete motif that inserts »new narrative clusters.« On the other hand, Herbst emphasizes its functionality, insofar as it subliminally offers necessary elements to connect various narrative strands, but the author is dependent on highly precise design to preserve this subliminal quality.[14] Thus the »hanging motif« betrays the, as it were, system-internal function of the author as a *ratio sufficiens*, as the authority that ensures the compossibility of the narrated worlds.

Characters who are authors represent another important inventory of characters in his novels, if not the most important one of all. Especially in *Wolpertinger; oder, Das Blau*, the discourse of narrating, counternarrating, authorship versus autopoiesis overshadows the plot. A total of four author characters appear (who are of course further supplemented by other counterparts, especially female ones), one of whom remains nameless; two of whom share the same name, Hans Deters; and one who shares large parts of his biography with the two Deterses but has a different name, namely, Eckehard Cordes. The technique of transporting author characters into the narrated and narrating reality is twofold. Herbst uses both the principle of splitting, in which one author emerges from another, and so on, and that of folding, since every author unfolds a compossible world from himself, which—because the authors largely coincide with one another but at the same time pursue opposing, at times even hostile goals in their writing/creativity—have areas of intersection: »Although, however, if anyone, he was the one who lived

---

12
Deleuze, *Difference and Repetition* (see note 6), 48.

13
Alban Nikolai Herbst was baptized Alexander Michael von Ribbentrop; in 1981 he adopted the name Alban Nikolai Herbst, which he has used as a writer ever since.

14
Alban Nikolai Herbst, »Das hängende Motiv. Argo. Anderswelt. (204),« entry dated February 10, 2006,« http://albannikolaiherbst.twoday.net/stories/1540945/ (accessed August 2, 2013).

through this, he no longer had anything to do with it. It took me a long time to understand that. Unexpectedly, it has become my story and is becoming ever more so.«[15] And so during the enfolding of the respective worlds these overlappings of personnel result in the acute existence of incompossibilities that increasingly veer toward an implosion of all reality/ies.

The story of the author is ergo a different one than the one I am writing for him. But mine comes close to the facts. If, moreover, the author, under Alda's patronage, is writing the novel in the process of its creation, he needs an auxiliary structure that enables him to see himself. In this case, that's me. From that it is not difficult to see that we cannot be identical, and no more so than Hans Deters can still be similar to Ulf Laupeysser or Claus Falbin. It is, of course, problematic that Hans Deters does not exist—I assume—but the author and I do. On the other hand, those two are Deters's auxiliary structures and the author mine.[16]

Ulf Laupeysser and Claus Falbin are early identities/personalities of Deters I, from his previous novel, *Die Verwirrung des Gemüts* (1983), published by List in 1983. The splitting open and up, the production of doppelgängers, never ended and never ends; the existence of multiple identities and split personalities extends back before the beginning of every narrative or life history. Hence a third, new character comes aboard in the struggle over identity between Laupeysser and Falbin and then disembarks again Hans Deters in *Wolpertinger*.

In light of the fact that auxiliary structures for their part dream up and refine auxiliary structures, we are dealing with multiple identities, with »dividuals,« divisible people, rather than »in-dividuals,« indivisible people. On the level of the text and the sentence, the divided unity emerges as a constant change from the narrating »I« and »he,« as narrator-authors, each of whom takes the words out of the other's mouth:

»Cordes was reacting to something like that, I already saw the scene vividly in front of me; in such cases, you can only ever get out of there.«[17]

At times, two different subjects speak as »I« in one and the same sentence, and because one subject (noun) changes into

[15] Alban Nikolai Herbst, *Wolpertinger; oder, Das Blau* (Munich, 2000; orig. pub. 1993), 561.

[16] Ibid., 563.

[17] Alban Nikolai Herbst, »Argo. Anderswelt (2008), II, 7 auf 8,« *die horen* 53, no. 231 (2008): 27–28, esp. 28.

the other, the spaces also change immediately. So a sentence begins in Hamburg and ends in Frankfurt am Main, but naturally without any story of a journey.[18]

In this context, it is worth trying to follow Deleuze/Guattari by seeing Hans and Deters and Eckhard and Cordes and I and he as structures, that is, as a multiplicity subject to constant transformations or being »deterritorialized« and »reterritorialized.« If all the different narrators form a »population,« it is almost necessary by the laws of the structure that they are both an I and an I and he, that they are Hans Deters and not Hans Deters, and so on. Seen in this way, the territory of the narrators would be, in a sense, Hans Deters and I. As a result of deterritorializations, the latter is transformed into a he; in another, Hans Deters is transformed into the author, into Eckehard Cordes, into Herbst and is reterritorialized again, so that once again an I, a Hans, and a Deters are present. Thus the concept of »multiplicity« or of »population« permits the notion of a variable structure of narrators in which the narrative directions and intentions, the promises and desires, the subjectifications and objectifications change places. In such a narrative territory, which violates the usual pact between the reader, the narrator, the character, and the author concerning what should be understood as real and what as fiction, all of the people are both real and fictional; they are deterritorialized in stories that are told on top of one another, in which they are reterritorialized and become fiction.[19] This is not about an antithesis between the real and the fictional; rather, reality is the expression of the fictional as content and, conversely, of the fictional as the form for expressing reality as content in the aforementioned interplay of enfolding and unfolding.

Dividuality/Poetics of Possibilities

Dividuality is one principle of Herbst's cyberrealistic program. Christoph Jürgensen points out that Herbst formulated the subdivision of the subject into a population already at the beginning of his writing career, in 1985, in the context of his affirmation of technology, in the literary journal *Dschungelblätter*,[20] and from then on implemented it consistently in his literature. Not only does dividuality indeed guide the events in

18
Herbst, »Arbeitsnotat 11.11.2004« (see note 7), 134.

19
Anton Moosbach offers a clear and very convincing analysis of the character of Deters as a »conceptual persona for the concept of deterritorialization.« See Anton Moosbach, »Das Ribbentrop-Rhizom: Ein Experiment mit den Werken von Alban Nikolai Herbst und Gilles Deleuze/Félix Guattari,« thesis, Universität Zürich, 2005, available as a PDF at: http://www.die-dschungel.de/ANH/main.html, under »Sekundäres,« (accessed August 2, 2013.)

20
Christoph Jürgensen, »Unwirkliche Städte, unwirkliches Ich: Zum Verhältnis von Stadt und Individuum in Herbsts *Buenos Aires. Anderswelt*,« *die horen* 53, no. 231 (2008): 99–111, esp. 101.

the novels, but Alban Nikolai Herbst insists on it for his entire existence as a writer: He »confessed« in *Die Welt* on May 8, 1999, that not he but rather Hans Deters was the author of his works.[21] The text briefly demonstrates the overwriting, counterwriting, nonwriting familiar from the novels. With this deliberately designed confusion of authorship, narrator's voice, and (connection to) reality, he provides the »real« counterpart to the fact that he writes himself into his novels as the very real authorial character Herbst, since one day Hans Deters finds himself confronted in *Buenos Aires. Anderswelt* with a company sign on his front door reading: »Herbst & Deters. Fictioneers.« This very same sign results in further dovetailing with Herbst's blog account, where he also presents himself as a dividuality under the heading »Biography«: as the justiciar Gregor Lethen; the human speculator and esoteric Dietrich Daniello; the management consultant, traveling lecturer, and white slave trader Alexander von Ribbentrop; the disinformation scientist Hans Erich Deters; the ghostwriter Alban Nikolai Herbst; and the cybercharacter Titania Carthaga.

Herbst goes beyond dividualizing himself and incorporates his readers. The blog he has been writing since 2003 has a structure that permits readers to comment continuously, and at times they quite actively do so, so that discussions on specific themes ensue. One should, however, be cautious about the possibility of attributing specific comments to people, since Herbst employed not only the aforementioned »biographical« personae and avatars but also many others, with whose help he constantly comments on himself or at least moves discussions in the directions he wants. According to Renate Giacomuzzi, it has been verified that Paul Reichenbach is part of Herbst's dividuality.[22] Naturally, the inability to determine authorship places into Herbst's concept.

»While I was developing the procedure—or, better: while *it* developed—I have also accepted readers of my works into it to react to my work; in *Der Dschungel*, after all, that is very possible. For example, on November 29, 2005, a commentator who called himself *mimikry* wrote me as follows on the Literarisches Weblog [...]. So here is *mimikry's* comment.«*[23]

---

[21] Hans Erich Deters, »Eine Beichte: Wie ich zum Schreiben kam. (Gar nicht, ich kam zum Veröffentlichen),« *Die Welt*, May 8, 1999, http://www.die-dschungel.de/ANH/txt/pdf/schreiben.pdf (accessed August 3, 2013).

[22] Renate Giacomuzzi, »Die ›Dschungel.Anderswelt‹ und A. N. Herbsts ›Poetologie des literarischen Bloggens,‹« *die horen* 53, no. 231 (2008): 137–50, esp. 143.

[23] See Herbst, »Desideria« (see note 5).

But clicking on the link to the aforementioned comment leads, surprisingly, to an excerpt from the novel *Argo*, so that »mimikry,« with his programmatic name, can also be attributed to the Herbst dividuality. The footnote marked with the asterisk reads:

»[*: The very real Swiss author Markus A. Hediger wrote in reply three days later in *Der Dschungel*: ›The character in a novel Hediger (3). I see myself this way at least since I met the character in a novel Herbst in Berlin. And I'm extraordinarily confused for the reason, because now I can't get over the suspicion that Herbst really did invent me. Now I am a character in a novel who reads himself in variations.‹]«

In the continuation of comment and countercomment, the Herbst dividuality, as is to be expected, plays its game with authorship and the fictionality of the characters by seemingly revealing which contributors' names are characters he has invented and which are not. In the process, the characters speak out to correct him, in the familiar way, with regard, for example, to the date they were created. It is, however, certain that one character was created by an eBay auction in which one could bid on the role either of a secondary or a major character.[24]

Concerning mimikry commenting on or continuing the writing of the text of the novel, Herbst remarks he had »followed the trail left, that is, [he had] treated as fact [...] that which had been fantasized as the possible continuation of a novel's plot— that is, treated it as a matrix-like component with which [...] the poetic processes of calculation are worked through as a possibility [...] that—and this is important—certainly contradicted other possibilities.«[25] With that I have arrived again at the principle of (in)composibility and its order, which in Herbst's poetology is developed as one of the possibilities that necessarily strive to be realized. In the novel, a »beauty of availability and connection« is attributed to this poetics of possibilities.[26] In the selection and execution of the motifs, a form of isolation is suggested in the motivic that at the same time corresponds to the artful »impression of a possible arbitrariness.« This poetics of possibilities is expanded in the blog into an aesthetic of modalities of the cybernetic totality, which, by virtue of its lack of transparency to

---

[24] See Giacomuzzi, »Die ›Dschungel. Anderswelt‹« (see note 22), n. 22.

[25] See Herbst, »Desideria« (see note 5).

[26] Alban Nikolai Herbst, »Romantheorie. Argo. Anderswelt. (152). Kleine Theorie des Literarischen Bloggens (52),« entry dated September 30, 2005, http://albannikolaiherbst.twoday.net/stories/1018688/ (accessed August 4, 2013).

individuals, is called a »mythical« aesthetics.[27] Both the cybernetic totality and the mythical one should be understood as projects: On the one hand, their lack of transparency makes it possible to conclude the explanations of individual phenomena. Hence more and more (in)compossibles are added and connected (»linked«), but they always produce a new need for explanation. On the other hand, both systems question the individual, indivisibility itself, whose perspective is the only one from which the lack of coherence becomes evident.

Once again, we cannot take Herbst, the author, at his word but have to consider that this poetological program is also part of this same aesthetic. The claimed rebirth of myth from the computer corresponds to Herbst's style of implementing the aesthetic of modalities in literature. As noted above, however, this is a literary product, even though neither »the computer« nor a software program contributed to its development. The perception- and communication-related problem of modalities is better characterized in the section »ARGO-ÜA (23). Gestrichenes (ff.). Wirklichkeit & Gegenwart« in the reflection on the fictional permeation of the media and real present as a contemporary novel in a double sense:

»Because of the bitter cold, it could scarcely *be* the late October, early November, when this novel actually takes place; it takes more time to write it than the plot does [...]. So if it wants to remain a contemporary novel, the events have to push up, or at least drag along, the present, and specifically into a new present; this is in keeping with the idea of simultaneity (expressed in terms of the history of morals: with the presence of the past in the now, its metamorphosis). That just now occurred to Eckhard Cordes as an explanation, and he thought this hooking-into-one-another would have to lead to the individual narrative fragments becoming ever smaller; ultimately, they are, narrative points, entities, Whitehead would have said, which together, like thousands of pixels, create the planar image, the tableau, by means of the distance from them that someone adopts. If he stands too close, the image falls apart. Vilém Flusser observed that. He wrote, namely, that our reality is not constant *because* it is made up of points. It is

[27] Ibid.

perceived as closed and constant only because the brain interprets reality in this way [...].«

»Now, naturally, the reality points affect one another; that is what keeps reality together at all, like attractive and centrifugal forces do the little bodies of the molecule, and they in turn the cells and the body as a whole, which in turn interact in a very analogous way with other bodies and ultimately with the world and the cosmos; nevertheless, the nature of these forces is completely different; in poetry they are called inspiration.«[28]

The notion that the globalized present, in its multiply doubled, mirrored, and mediated simultaneous nonsimultaneities, has become untransparent has been reduced to a slogan at least since Jean Baudrillard. Herbst's modalities style functions as a productive mirror by realizing the »stream of narratives of simultaneities« in a poetological temporality that shifts the usual chronotope of the narrative into a level of consistency in which narrated time, the time of narration, and real-like time become a concept of time, become the aforementioned »narrative points,« which affect one another in the manner described in the passage from Lacan quoted at the beginning, which produces the completed future of the past as present.[29] Herbst works carefully and very consciously with »temporalization«; after all, his goal is to inscribe myth into his oeuvre, including his blog. The »cybernetician« uses the control circuit as his image:

»[B]etween the apparent restarting and the actual new beginning [of an estimated line—UR], a gap opens up. For what happens is precisely not an Eternal Recurrence of the Same, but rather the narrative portrays historical structures that are organized according to patterns that at the same time move forward irreversibly across continuous metalevels on the timeline. If one gets the impression a narrative cycle is returning to its beginning, not only have all of those involved but also the fundamental setting has changed. [...]«

»Using a thought game, that is, a model, it can be made clear that the spiral itself can be unfolded in the Fourth Dimension, namely, of time.«[30]

Once again, the fold accompanies Herbst's theoretical thinking, in this case the fold of a line turned—or folded—

---

[28] Alban Nikolai Herbst, »ARGO-ÜA (23). Gestrichenes (ff.). Wirklichkeit & Gegenwart,« http://albannikolai-herbst.twoday.net/topics/ARGO-ANDERSWELT/?start=40 (accessed August 4, 2013).

[29] I have explained various aspects of the structures of time-place and media in Reber, *Formenverschleifung* (see note 1), chaps. 5.4 and 5.6.

[30] Alban Nikolai Herbst, »Graphen der Erzählbewegung. Dritte Heidelberger Vorlesung (5). Aus der Erweiterung des Anfangs,« entry dated January 7, 2008, http://albannikolaiherbst.twoday.net/stories/4590233 (accessed August 4, 2013).

around and in itself to form a spiral, through which, Herbst goes on to say, the entire stream of stories flows as a whole.

The apparent constancy of this stream of stories—in Somadeva's *Kathasaritsagara*, written around the year 1000, it was still conceived as an ocean, that is, as the constancy of streams of stories—is composed of countless, ultimately infinitely many stories; adding them up results in this constant image (but this probably only means that the leaps assume vanishingly small dimensions). Nevertheless, if we take a single story from the stream, we can recognize the spiral and hence the leaps that perform the »beginnings« and »ends = restartings« of the spirals of rules as they relate to this one story. Now we see clearly that we are not dealing with redundancies.

This sudden switch is achieved by poetic inspiration. Ultimately, a novel is the shadow cast by a narrative body of four or more dimensions—that is, the reality based on it that results from its reasons—on the page of a book in the form of writing.

So, just as Deleuze calls the active folding of the soul its tendency, an expression of the present,[31] »if inclusion is extended to infinity in the past and the future, it is because it concerns first of all the living present that in each instance presides over their division,«[32] in a bunch of stories that constantly speak of the completed future, the stories of Herbst's figures and avatars take place in a constantly blurring, transitory now that, depending on the novel, never leaves the afternoon of a Thursday (or Wednesday), November 1, a noon, or the moment of sensation.

This transitory present, the constant presence, becomes visible in recurrent streams of perception and through the above-mentioned technique of taking just one story out of the stream in order to reveal the leaps, the gaps, within and also between them. One of the most important means to achieve this is with asyndetons, ellipses, that is, unconnected sentences without a subject. The characters to be narrated never come to act; sensory impressions are represented in the style of camera tracks and close-ups. Employing the cinematic image in literature makes it possible to present a pure space of perception and sensation: »Hence the observer and the observed fuse or interchange so rapidly that fusion is apparent. Instead of discourse—a

---

[31] Gilles Deleuze, »Incompossibility, Individuality, Liberty,« in idem, *The Fold: Leibniz and the Baroque*, trans. Tom Conley (Minneapolis, 1993), 67–85, esp. 80.

[32] Ibid., 80.

running between or running back and forth—there is intercourse, a running together.«[33]

By privileging perception and observation, the cinematic image objectivizes the classical (autonomous) subject, which is no longer alone with its view of the world and has interpretive authority over this view and what is perceived, but rather conditions the premise of the observer that he or she is also being constantly watched. This too amounts to adopting, by different means, a familiar structure: The narratability of myth, of mythic space, demands viewers. The gazes of the transformer, of the transforming power, and of the viewer intersect on the mutable surface of the body of the transformer. The body thus becomes the projection screen for the network of gazes. Herbst's postapocalyptic urban spaces, their squares, streets, and buildings in constant renovation and transformation, fulfill a dual function in this context: On the one hand, they also function as a projection screen for the viewers, without which it would not be possible to make the changes of name and shifts in the architecture visible. On the other hand, the interference is evident even on them, when the flickering of electronic images with a weak signal becomes visible on them or sceneries freeze as if due to bad WLAN reception. The space of sensations is determined more by the boundaries between the individual images, but the gaps between the shots.

The narrative time of novels—even when the past tense is used for long stretches, as is common in narrative literature—is the present, in keeping with the timelessness of mythical and semimythical characters such as Chill Borkenbord, Odysseus, Deidamia, and so on. The eyes of random viewers, who are not even observing but usually flooded with stimuli, adopt the role of the video camera: they perceive, record, and store, whereby the stream of what is perceived incessantly glides over them as crossing the surface of a screen.[34]

Pathos/Rhythm

Time's level of consistency interacts with another level of sensation, which produces the concept of pathos via language. Sensations, passions, and pathos are not narrated by Herbst but

[33] Mark Slade, *Language of Change: Moving Images of Man* (Toronto, 1970), 96.

[34] The fact that not only eyes but the bodies in general of the characters function as interfaces for the not exclusively visual images of the perception of their surroundings is obvious, at the very latest, in *Buenos Aires*, when they are literally used as screens, are scanned from ID cards, and chat messages run away.

actually produced by his style, his attitude. Herbst's writing employs all stylistic levels, from the earthy by way of verbalization of comics and computer games to the elegiac. On all these levels an imagistic and expressive language dominates, whose most characteristic feature is inversion, a word order that runs counter to normal word order. It is possible to regard moving the postpositional conjunctive adverb »namely« to the start of the sentence—a feature that makes Herbst's writing unambiguously recognizable, both in his novels and his blog—as more of a quirk. But the combination of stylistic levels and the almost obsessive use of odd and ancient rhetorical figures as style and stylization clearly places Alban N. Herbst in the ranks of Asian writers, for whom the ornament, the accessory, becomes the real message.[35]

In *Wolpertinger; oder, Das Blau*, passion and pathos, which belong to the mythical landscape and the mythical narrative as their motivation,[36] sometimes occur openly, sometimes in an ironic style. The drawing of the character of Lipom, an avatar of Oberon, and his elaborate, long-winded language, punctuated both by quotations from Gottfried Benn and by groans and moans, reveals Herbst's dilemma of how to tell a story with the aid of pathos that is at once ironic and not ironic.[37] In the unconditional cruelty, the pathos avoids the distance of irony in which »pathetician« and elf prince of rich and agile language works on eliminating the excluded middle; it celebrates passion and affect; it is in this respect and in every form cruel without any distance. As cruel as Lipom, who gradually sheds his mendacious, fictional confusion with the Deterses in favor of the spitefulness and magic that are characteristic of him and reveals himself to be a raving Dionysus of the underworld.[38]

Alban Nikolai Herbst elevates pathos to the level of an aesthetic program,[39] but this goes beyond mere rhetoric. Pathos as a literary strategy is opposed to the literary marketplace and entertainment, and in the form of a linguistic authenticity stylized in the medium of blog/logbook entries it transitions into lived experience, as is only logical for a dividual poetics of modalities, establishing, in this view, a holistic style. Renate Giacomuzzi has briefly sketched the unusualness and offensiveness of this style in several stages from the radical exposure of the

35
On this, see Hans Richard Brittnacher, »Der verspielte Untergang: Apokalypsen bei Alban Nikolai Herbst,« *die horen* 53, no. 231 (2008): 29–42, esp. 39–40.

36
On the complex of passions in myth, see Heinz-Peter Preusser, »Achilleus als Barde: Kybernetische Mythenkorrektur bei Alban Nikolai Herbst,« *die horen* 53, no. 231 (2008): 73–89.

37
See Alban Nikolai Herbst, »Das Innen ein Hotel (2). Korrespondenzen: An Albert Meier, Uni Kiel,« entry dated May 29, 2011, http://albannikolaiherbst.twoday.net/stories/zur-ironie-das-innen-ein-hotel-2-korrespondenzen-an-professor-albert-m (accessed September 17, 2013).

38
For a complete analysis of the Dionysian and the character of Lipom, see Reber, *Formenverschleifung* (see note 1), chap. 5.4.

39
On pathos as literary program, see Uwe Schütte, »Erzählen für morgen: Zur poetologischen Genealogie des Kybernetischen Realismus bei Alban Nikolai Herbst,« *die horen* 53, no. 231 (2008): 121–30, esp. 126–27.

private in the first web diary by way of the program of the martyr in the blog aesthetic to the involvement in the socially taboo practices of sadomasochistic passion.[40] In this form of a style in the sense of habit, it must absolutely be granted Giacomuzzi that the computer and the Internet have proven to be »ideal ›partners‹ for the author.«[41] In this Nietzschean experiment with giving form to one's own life, the possibilities of the blog and of the work diary have prepared the way for Herbst's fictioneers to unfold such a style of passions. But pathos and passions should not be understood (only) as themes: the experiment, even of the fictional style, between man and machine, author and Internet, private and public functions in a sense as the effect that causes the pathos to unfold.

Affect as physical state, as being affected by another body, and as interim space to the auction also reveals the true subject of the *Anderswelt* novels. As is clear from several of the poetological discussions on his blog, Alban Nikolai Herbst is fascinated by the neurosciences dealing with the material conditions of effect. In his artistic products that are published and distributed in book form on the book market, this basis for an affective poetology is made to disappear. The form in which affects are made to appear here and the readers are affected is representation in verbal images, in part evocation of emotion and passion, but far more effectively as the rhythmic shaping of linguistic form.

Herbst understands even language as such, in distinction from its grammatical form that constitutes the subject and consciousness, as a »system for communicating outside of emotion.«[42] Herbst works with »extralinguistic feeling« in order to cause affect to flow and to give the paths a level of expression, by introducing rhythm. Rhythmizing elements can be detected on all levels of his writing. Even simple reading reveals the sonata-like arrangement of the strands of (in)compossibility that in every book lead into a »Finale furioso« with variations. Motifs are assigned to the strands of (in)compossibility. Together with the transformations and intersections of worlds, such motifs are adjusted and converted to one another, syncopally at first, transgressing the boundaries of sentence, paragraph, and

[40] Giacomuzzi, »Die ›Dschungel.Anderswelt‹« (see note 22), 142–43.

[41] Ibid., 145.

[42] On this, see Alban Nikolai Herbst, comment on March 13, 2013, http://albannikolaiherbst.twoday.net/stories/326201419/.

chapter, so that the same feeling or sensation is attributed to different subjects.⁴³ Leitmotifs in the meter represent a kind of inner poetic memory; again and again, they resound separately from the actually narrating voices, like a warning: »Blood and brain are sprayed around the walls« in *Wolpertinger*, »Three things that enrich the poet: myths, poetic power and a store of ancient verse« and »the cattle of Thetra« in *Thetis*. In *Argo*, the structuring by leitmotifs recedes to the background in favor of a complete versification. Alban Nikolai Herbst discloses his reason and method; he makes himself concrete with a rewriting of Goethe's *Achilleis* in a transformation accurate in verse and meter.⁴⁴ Backed and mixed with quotations from other epic works such as *The Illiad*, these new verses run through the novel, offering a new rhythmic and motivic reasons for the exaltations of language and the effects of the bodies depicted.

»Schöne Literatur muss grausam sein!« (Belles-lettres must be cruel!) was the title of a poetological speech Alban Nikolai Herbst gave at the Deutsche Literaturkonferenz in Leipzig on March 23, 2002.⁴⁵ In it Herbst confessed to transgression, to the state of exception, in short: to a literary understanding of intensities. From it he derived the program of literature, granting space to pathos, above all as suffering, to the felt affect over morality, or to lend a voice without morality and in the process divide it among multiplicities, a voice that also breaks through the linguistic and hence (onto)logical structure of subject and object, simply sweeping over it. In other words, he called for an ecstatic, a cathartic literature.

It would not be going astray to recognize here models from ancient literary theory on the tragedy and epic, mediated by Nietzsche and Romanticism, then further developed in postmodernism.⁴⁶ What the aesthetic of modalities intends in a global world characterized by the simultaneity of nonsimultaneous stories »are *old forms in the present of the future* (›in the present as future‹)«⁴⁷ in accordance with an understanding of continuing folds of all sensations. Logically, Herbst exposes the bodies of his characters to excesses of violence,⁴⁸ places his own verbalized and »avatarized« body and his sensations on display in his blog to be commented on, understandably and openly subjects his textual

43
For examples of this, see Ursula Reber, »Avatarische Intensitäten: Affektive Landschaften in Alban Nikolai Herbsts Anderswelt-Romanen,« *die horen* 53, no. 231 (2008): 49–65, esp. 61.

44
See samples from the text in *die horen* 53, no. 231 (2008): 97–98.

45
Available at http://www.die-dschungel.de/ANH/txt/pdf/schoene_literatur.pdf (accessed August 5, 2013).

46
The poetological genealogy of Alban Nikolai Herbst's cyberrealism was compiled by Schütte, »Erzählen für morgen« (see note 39).

47
Alban Nikolai Herbst, »Weshalb Hexameter? The Archaic Revival, vampyroteuthisch. Zum Epilog. Argo. Anderswelt. (267),« http://albannikolaiherbst.twoday.net/stories/5145659/ (accessed August 5, 2013).

48
On this aspect, see Brittnacher, »Der verspielte Untergang/Apokalypsen« (see note 35), and Reber, *Formenverschleifung* (see note 1), chaps. 5.4 and 5.5.

body to endless deleting, correcting, over- and rewriting, and ultimately aims also at the bodies and memories of his readers in his desire to implant the overall impression of a disaster and to convert stability into instability.

Usha Reber
(1972) studied classic philology, German literature, and philosophy at the Philipps-Universität-Marburg; 2006 PhD at the University of Vienna, thesis: »Slurring Images: Toward a Theory of Metamorphosis« (2009). Since 2007 she is the director of the academic website *Kakanien revisited* (www.kakanien.ac.at) for SEE/CE studies, 2006/07 coordinator of the graduate program Cultures of Difference: Transformation in Central Europe. Her research interests and publications center around literary theory, intertextuality, postcolonial studies and fantasy literature.

Objects in a Mirror Are Closer Than They Appear: On Self-Portrayal in Contemporary Video Art.

Holger Kube Ventura

»Images, which learned how to move more than a century ago, have long since overtaken us. They have a dynamic life of their very own, are available everywhere round the clock, and can be subdivided into an infinite number of categories. The fact of the matter is that anyone can make a movie very quickly, for just about no money and with little technical expertise. Images stream through the Internet, gain millions of fans, and can be shared round the clock with a worldwide audience.«[1] This applies in particular to images of oneself, whereby the impact of this evolution is particularly noticeable in contemporary video art. In the fifty-year history of video art,[2] self-portraits and closed-circuit installations have always played a major role— as a way for the artist to position himself, for purposes of reflecting the viewer's vantage point, as a way of raising epistemological identity issues, or as narratives of the self. But ever since an era was ushered in where the daily production and distribution of self-referential moving images and of experimentally assumed roles in social networks has become the norm, new questions have arisen for many video artists. What meaning does the likeness of a person still have, and how does an image of a person differ from their reflection?

The erstwhile jarring representation of the technical frame of an image has now become the norm in video-clip culture. Even basic video-editing software for cellphones provides a full range of special effects, whereby closed circuits—once a thrilling experience allowing for a moving mirror image of oneself—are now the stuff of Skype conversations. Mediatization is ubiquitous.

In a world where mass-market audiovisual devices have long since been widely available—in other words in a world where every image and image of the self is permanently available, whereas their technical relativization and doubt are always ready to hand—what status does the image of a person have and to what extent can a viewer of such an image venture to identify with it?

This has become a burning issue in contemporary video art, a field where the work of many artists addresses the issue of the visual constitution of a subject: How do identities manifest

---

1
From an unpublished B3 Moving Image Biennial concept paper.

2
It is generally agreed that video art was »born« on the occasion of Nam June Paik's solo show *Exposition of Music—Electronic Vision* in March 1963 at Galerie Parnass in Wuppertal, Germany.

themselves in likenesses? What constitutes a speaking likeness and what constitutes a self-depiction? Where does my opposite number or counterpart come from and can I, as an artist, see myself in a reflection?

Most artists understandably take a pretty dim view of achieving identification via the likeness of a person and are instead interested in the conditions surrounding identification. Moreover, in their work they call role representation into question through devices such as reenactments and explore distinctive types of images, mirror images and counterimages. What's also central here are the various aesthetics that are found in deconstructions of images of the self in cases where the desire for such images is derailed or fanned out and the difference between form/frame/version and person emerges. Such strategies can be regarded as a response to the ubiquity of self-representations à la Facebook, and as an artistic corrective to this phenomenon.

On the occasion of the first edition of the B3 Moving Image Biennial in the fall of 2013, Frankfurter Kunstverein held a large group show titled *Per Speculum Me Video* (October 31, 2013– January 5, 2014). The exhibition's title says, in the »dead« language of Latin, that a self could or would see itself in a mirror. The title's wording has the effect of a long-forgotten spell that evokes the theory of French psychoanalyst Jacques Lacan on the relationship between self-awareness and the development of the self on the one hand, and recognizing oneself in a mirror on the other. The show was mainly composed of video installations, but there was also some photographic and acoustic work. In the following, I shall discuss, based on selected works, the significance of self-portraits and self-observation in contemporary video art, and in doing so I shall address the following issues: What has become of the former potential of closed-circuit concepts, and what form can role play in mirror images take on today?

The main difference between video and film technology is that video allows for simultaneous recording and playback. As early as 1936, live broadcasts of the Olympics were available in public TV lounges. But it was not until three decades later, when Sony came out with the first affordable portable video recording system, the Portapak, that it became possible for artists to create electronic mirror images of themselves. Soon thereafter, in the 1970s, oftentimes intimate self-reflections via closed circuits arising from observation and performance formed the basis for many video works. As a result, an interdisciplinary field came into existence that combined performance, theater, body experimentation and video. The preservable closed-circuit mirror images that could be generated using a video camera and monitor enabled artists such as Bruce Nauman and Peter Campus to explore their respective selves using moving images of themselves. Whereas in traditional theater a staged reality is performed, these new video performances explored self-staging in the truest sense of the term, whereby the lengths of the produced videos often corresponded to the length of the recorded event.[3]

Unlike film, an image being shot with a video camera that was plugged into a monitor could dispense with a tripod, whereby moving-image self-portraits and images of the self could be recorded, observed and corrected immediately and without outside assistance. Thus in the privacy of their studios, artists were able to transform experiments with their own likenesses into the form and content of works of art.

Friederike Pezold said this at the time: »Video enabled me to make the impossible possible in that I could stand in front of and behind the camera at the same time. Video enabled me to make the impossible possible in that I could be a painter and model at the same time! Subject and object at the same time! Image and likeness at the same time.«[4]

Video held out the promise of autonomy, reigning supreme over one's self and an increased public presence for artists. Valie Export, Ulrike Rosenbach, Rebecca Horn, Joan Jonas, Annegret Soltau and Barbara Hamman explored society's image of women and were able to develop and become established as artists mainly because video was not yet part of a male-dominated artistic canon.

Even in today's videos, gender roles still appear to be the domain of female artists, and it is perhaps no accident that the vast majority of the videos in the *Per Speculum Me Video* show were the work of female artists. Apart from Martin Brand (b. 1975, German, lives in Cologne) and Benny Nemerofsky Ramsay

---

3
The length and monotony of many 1970s video performances were often a veritable challenge for audiences. For example, Oliver Hirschbiegel, who at the time was a performance artist and is now a movie director, has said this: »Virtually all of this so-called video art was simply stupid and often far too long, one-dimensional and boring. («No Video-Kunst,« in Video in Kunst und Alltag. Vom kommerziellen zum kulturellen Videoclip, ed. Veruschka and Gábor Bódy [Cologne, 1986]). The art critic Alfred Nemeczek polemically titled his article on video art that appeared in the March 1983 issue of *Art*, »To Hell with Video Art!«

4
Friederike Pezold, »Die Geschichte der Videopionierin P. und ein Plädoyer für Video,« in *Schrägspur Videofestival*, ed. Hochschülerschaft an der TU Graz. Graz: 1985.

(b. 1973, Canadian, lives in Berlin), the following artists took part in the show: Pauline Boudry and Renate Lorenz (b. 1972/1963, Swiss/German, live in Berlin); Manuela Kasemir (b. 1981, German, lives in Leipzig); Sabine Marte (b. 1967, Austrian, lives in Vienna); Barbara Probst (b. 1964, German, lives in New York); Johanna Reich (b. 1977, German, lives in Cologne); Eva Weingärtner (1978, German, lives in Offenbach); and Gilda Weller (b. 1989, German, lives in Frankfurt).

Virtually all of Eva Weingärtner's videos center solely around the artist herself. Sometimes Weingärtner appears to be putting on a performance or a small chamber piece without an audience and for herself only, in a closed circuit comprising a camera, actor and control monitor. Other works seem like exercises or experiments depicting a specific sequence or state. In all of her videos, Weingärtner is succinct and tremendously exciting because despite her conceptual advance planning, she does unexpected albeit not shocking things.

The videos constantly come back to the issue of a person's perception of themselves versus that of others, the goal being to depict or conceal strengths and weaknesses. But in such works, who sees whom?

In most of Weingärtner's videos, the setting of the search for the self is readily apparent: production values are very basic, and sometimes her lighting, sound, props and camera angles are homemade in the truest sense of the term. Everything is authentic, in its as-is state, unpretentious and devoid of postproduction tampering of any kind. Her videos have such punch precisely because they are made in such a disarmingly simple manner, with minimal facial expressions and actions transforming themselves through calculated variations on an emotional roller-coaster ride. Nothing in these videos is accidental, meaningless or superficial; every moment of what's done and shown has its place in the cycle. A great deal occurs within a short space of time; concentration is maximally heightened for both the artist and viewer.

In the four-minute video *2me* (2010) we see a young woman who sees herself or engages with herself—or maybe she isn't aware of this at all. Be this as it may, she intently and motionlessly observes objects that are right near her mirror image.

Eva Weingärtner
2me, 2010
Video stills
© Eva Weingärtner

Eva Weingärtner
one me, 2013
Video still
© Eva Weingärtner

Her state of mind, as she does this, varies between critical, satisfied, horny and bored. She presses on the mirror, tastes it and kisses it, but never really approaches or moves away from it: she is genuinely chained to this mirror image and thus to her self. Each of her actions triggers further speculation about her state, which ranges from narcissism to autoeroticism to self-hatred. The simple and striking image of this autonomous physical interaction confronts the viewer with the whole gamut of possible relationships to oneself.

In *one me* (2013), Weingärtner's two-and-a-half-minute sequel to *2me* (2010), the young woman looks into the camera and thus at the viewer. This time her pursed lips appear to want to direct kissing, attraction and desire elsewhere—that is, if half her face weren't bathed in such harsh and intense shadows. Her face shows that in seeking the right distance from the camera, all that happens is that she once again encounters her own lips and her own likeness, which is a silhouette this time. And the viewer is in turn intrigued by the contrast between the transparency of her attempts and the tremendously precise way she addresses the viewer.

Weingärtner's videos are nothing if not daring. She puts herself out there, exposes herself. She experiences emotional highs and lows and doesn't shy away from first of all revealing them, second of all transcending them using artistic means, and third of all offering herself as a mirror image of the viewer, who recognizes herself in or through her. The video's protagonist becomes a vehicle for questions that go to the very heart of human existence. As with all outstanding performance artists, it remains unclear the extent to which the artist's intimate experiments and explorations are also explorations of the self and what exactly they have to do with Eva Weingärtner the person. She has stated the following in this regard: »My work is a large part of my identity. It's also a kind of confrontation with the self that I've been engaged in since I began making videos. In doing this, I hope to touch upon themes and states that mirror many people.«[5] And that is exactly what Weingärtner has succeeded in doing.

Many of Johanna Reich's videos are reminiscent of the pictorial space experiments of Peter Campus (b. 1937). Particularly in her series *The Presence of Absence*, Reich appears to be the

[5] Personal communication from the artist in an e-mail of November 8, 2012.

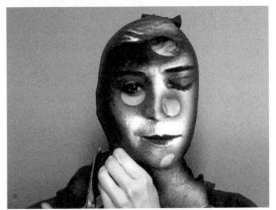

Johanna Reich
Kassandra, 2008
DV, PAL, 6 minutes
Video stills
© VG Bild-Kunst, Bonn 2013
Courtesy Galerie Anita Beckers, Frankfurt

successor to this American video pioneer. But also in videos such as the six-minute *Cassandra (Part 1 Transformations)* (2008), the artist explores the interactions between real surfaces and the expanse of a projection screen and the transformations that occur between cinematic space and real action in self-experiments.

In *Cassandra*, we first see a person with a pantyhose on their head, upon which a portrait of a woman is projected. The movements of this projected head are somewhat out of sync with the posture of the person, whose face doesn't seem to go with the body. The film portrait stares out into space while the protagonist (the artist herself) doesn't notice anything. But then she begins to cut out sections of the fabric with a large pair of scissors, an action that leaves gaping holes in the projection surface (and thus in the film portrait) and reveals the actress's face.

The two faces and their film likenesses are mixed together shot by shot. The farther the process advances, the better the protagonist/artist can see into the camera and thus look right into our eyes. At the same time, the remainder of the film portrait —particularly when its eyes move sideways—increasingly becomes a series of grimaces. Watching the situation unfold and the various portraits that are created is genuinely thrilling.

Other dimensions open up if you're familiar with Reich's sources and references in the video. The projected portrait is from Fritz Lang's two-part silent film *Dr. Mabuse the Gambler* (1920/21), which is meant to be a mysterious mirror image of the Weimar Republic. The self-portrait that emerges when the protagonist cuts a hole in the pantyhose (which evokes a gangster's mask) is a direct quote from and a reenactment of Sanja Iveković's video *Personal Cuts* (1982). In this work, which has likewise become virtually iconic, the artist leveled criticism at post-Tito nationalism by inserting the face of a young Yugoslavian between each shot of a propagandistic TV image. The title of Reich's video also gives the work greater meaning when you realize that the tragic figure of Cassandra from Greek mythology was a seer whose prophecies fell on deaf ears.

Some of Austrian artist Sabine Marte's videos also center around the incorporation and calling into question of real and cinematic space—an exploration that always serves to at

Sabine Marte
b-star, untötbar!, 2009
Video stills
Camera: Oliver Stotz
Location: Kleylehof im
Burgenland, Austria
© Sabine Marte

Sabine Marte
Finale, 2007
Video stills
Camera: Markus Marte
Location: Wrestling hall,
Götzis, Austria
© Sabine Marte

least implicitly explore situations where the subject observing herself relates to her immediate surroundings. Marte also films herself in her videos (in closed circuits) or focuses the camera on her immediate environs.

Marte's edgy, seven-minute-long video *b-star, untötbar!* (2009) unfolds in a powerfully unexpected fashion despite the fact that the setting remains virtually unchanged during the entire piece. We first see a shadowy close-up, bathed in excessively bright and monotone white light, of a faceless figure—the artist herself—sitting on a couch. Pretty much nothing happens in this irregularly flickering slow-motion footage, except that gradually we begin to hear loud noises—and then suddenly we hear a woman's voice. She talks in a fragmentary—and thus very poetic—manner about a woman (perhaps herself) who tried to find someone to talk to and in doing this »went through the whole film and forgot that it was fiction; she broke through the screen until it completely collapsed.« While she is saying this, the image stabilizes and we can clearly make out the woman on the couch, who stares into the camera and thus looks right at the viewer, although the woman is apparently forced to remain at this exact distance from the camera. Because now the background of the image has started to move chaotically. The couch and with it the fixed distance between the protagonist and her camera appear to be moving—as if a ghost were at work—through the roof of a house, and apparently must have flown right out of the roof. The entire room is in an uproar, but the woman on the couch takes no notice and continues to intensely stare into the camera.

But then the sounds generated by all the movement abruptly morph into music: we hear a beat and the voice becomes a Sprechgesang that is reminiscent of a Laurie Anderson piece, only to become minimalistic electronic pop music with a two-voice counterpoint refrain that goes, »I'm strong enough—to throw you up—into the sky—you learn to fly.—And you fall back—into my arms—I hold you tight—and then we dance.« The result: the whole situation is resolved by a happy end. The faceless and silent figure we saw at the outset—who then became a subject who was forced to withstand the chaos of her surroundings by concentrating on an Other (or by focusing on herself)—is ultimately transformed into a tender relationship with herself, where the inner and outer realms—which perhaps represent the past and present—have been overcome. The experimental video *b-star, untötbar!* is the story of a person coming to grips with themselves and their own existence—a story that can be becalming and motivating for others. At the *Per Speculum Me Video* show, *b-star, untötbar!* was projected onto a giant screen in a high-ceilinged 220-square-meter space that encouraged each audience member to adopt their own suitable and tolerable observational stance vis-à-vis that of Sabine Marte.

Marte does performance art in addition to her video work and also performs with the pop groups SV Damenkraft and Pendler. As in many of her videos, Pendler's music plays a pivotal role. We see an athlete—the artist herself—beating the hell out of a wrestling dummy. We don't really understand why this »dual combat« is so violent and aggressive—until it turns out that the video is being shown in reverse. In conjunction with Pendler's dark music, an extremely disturbing impression is created of this seemingly simple situation involving a woman training with a wrestling dummy. Was the video perhaps originally shot by Marte's trainer so that he could give her feedback about her wrestling technique? Be this as it may, the video being shown in reverse and the background music à la Lydia Lunch make this a very powerful work of art indeed.

»An awareness of yourself comes from a certain number of activities and you can't get it just thinking about yourself. It takes practice.«[6] This Bruce Nauman quote could—in homage to his work, which so radically called subjectivity into question—be seen as a gloss on Gilda Weller's video *Untitled* (2011), which was also shown at the *Per Speculum Me Video* show. *Untitled* is a precise and uncompromising cinematic composition, where three young women and their voices form a sensory complex concerning issues of identity, self-awareness, and male-female relationships. The three protagonists, who to all appearances are thinking aloud, are full of verve about the questions they're asking about happiness, security, and being a woman. But from the outset, it's unclear whether we're watching actresses studying a text or whether a serious questionnaire is meant. And if so, is

6
Bruce Nauman, cited in Kunst des 20. Jahrhunderts, ed. Ingo F. Walther. Cologne 2005, p. 598.

the questionnaire supposed to be providing a therapeutic mirror image via video with the goal of gauging the effect of actually speaking something aloud? Or perhaps the scene was originally intended to be part of an actual film. The sophisticated editing and the alternation of close-ups and extreme close-ups raises the intriguing question as to when and how a person, a real human being, appears to manifest themselves through their likeness. The video loop begins over again after six minutes and we barely notice the fact that it has ended or begun.

Ever since the advent of photography, photographs —which depict reality more accurately than handmade paintings or drawings—have been reworked, manipulated, and falsified. This also applies to moving images on video and film, particularly since digitalization made it possible to do what we please with every single pixel of every single image. For example, in his groundbreaking HDTV video *Steps* (1987), the experimental filmmaker Zbigniew Rybcynski interpolated images of camera-wielding tourists into the renowned Odessa steps sequence from Eisenstein's classic film *The Battleship Potemkin* (1925). And Steven Spielberg incorporated moving images of dinosaurs into *Jurassic Park* (1992)—images which, despite their undeniable photo-realist quality, were created without a camera. And while we've long since grown accustomed to manipulations of this kind and know that photographs don't necessarily show us reality, the fact remains that anyone who makes images using either a still or movie camera automatically joins the ranks of the creators of reality. What has perhaps been lost here, if anything, is merely the clear boundary that used to exist between fiction and never-never land.

Like the other artists whose work was shown at *Per Speculum Me Video,* the work of Manuela Kasemir also revolves around existentialistic profiles that can potentially result from self-observation. But Kasemir makes photographs, not videos, and her self-portraits are created not in closed circuits but instead partly after the fact using computer-aided image processing.

The *Urd* series—Urd being the Old German word for fate or the past—comprises seven small black-and-white pictures of a young person (the artist herself) doing household chores in an

Gilda Weller
o.T., 2011
Video still
Camera: Jonas Englert
© Gilda Weller

Manuela Kasemir
afraid of death, 2013
Photograph
75 cm × 60 cm
© Manuela Kasemir
Courtesy of the artist

old and apparently long-since-abandoned house. She hangs laundry in the attic, draws a bath, airs out a bedroom, brings in the mail.

These extremely poetic images accomplish two things. First, they tell of the abandoned interior of the previous occupants' former home and depict the traces of earlier periods in these peoples' lives. And secondly, the *Urd* photographs focus on this young person who has her whole life before her, but who nonetheless appears to have an invisible bond with this house and its past.

After you look at these images for a while, you feel that there is something inexplicable about these precisely composed pictures whose formal elements are handled to perfection. You begin to notice small details clearly indicating that the artist has processed each image using digital montage techniques. For example, you notice steam emerging from a teapot on a clearly nonfunctional stove; or family trees on the wallpaper; or hanging laundry turns out to be a series of figures; or it's unclear whether this person is a male or female.

The effect of these details is to ultimately cast doubt on the entire staging of the series, and thus on the relationship of the person shown in the pictures to the past and present. Kasemir, who took these pictures in the home where she spent the first twenty years of her life, says this about them: »I often dream about this place, this house. [...] A musty setting that I try to bring to life with my memories. Here, the past is merely the present. The past seeps through the crack at the bottom of every door and sticks to the wallpaper.«[7] And here too, Kasemir uses a self-portrait to call into question herself and her having come into being, as well as the circumstances and affiliations that have influenced this person and her social relationships. The artist appears to be conducting research into her own existence and in so doing refers in an exemplary manner to questions that go to the very heart of human existence and that just about any viewer would be likely to ask themselves as well.

Kasemir's photographs are contemporary takes on vanity photos. They show how art can ask the big questions about life— about becoming a person, being a person, and departing this life.

[7] From a talk given by the artist about her work on July 3, 2008, at Hochschule für Grafik und Buchkunst in Leipzig.

Manuela Kasemir
Urd, 2008
Change to: Series of 7 photographs, each 33 × 46 cm
© Manuela Kasemir | Courtesy of the artist

This aspect of Kasemir's work was particularly in evidence in her monumental 6.25-meter photo that was displayed on the Frankfurter Kunstverein facade during the *Per Speculum Me Video* show. The picture shows a person standing in front of a wall mirror, which, however, has no image reflected in it and remains black. The mirror appears to be making some lettering visible that is written by a thread that the person is apparently moving with her hands. In the mirror, we are able to decipher this: »I am afraid of death.« The mirror image allows the unspeakable to be spoken. The mirror allows me to see myself.

Holger Kube Ventura
is the director of the Frankfurter Kunstverein since 2009 and has curated, among other exhibitions: *Ohnmacht als Situation* (2013), *Malerei der ungewissen Gegenden* (2012), *Über die Metapher des Wachstums* (2011), *Das Wesen im Ding* (2010), *Bilder vom Künstler* (2009) and *Gemeinsam in die Zukunft* (2009). In 2001, he graduated with the thesis: *Study of Political-Artistic Concepts in the German-speaking regions in the 1990s*, publication 2008. He was curator at the board of the Kasseler Kunstverein from 1996–2000, the director of the Werkleitz Gesellschaft e.V. from 2001–03 and program coordinator with the Kulturstiftung des Bundes in Halle/Saale from 2004–09. Kuba Ventura is the author of over 100 art theoretical contributions.

Liberated Images and Sounds: Diving into the 360° Full-Dome-Cosmos

Rotraut Pape

Ralph Heinsohn,
Alien Action, 2004
45 minutes

As an artist, one learns and practices every day to make one's own virtual realities—what one has in mind, mental images, thoughts, feelings, ideas—*real*. In film and video, for example. However, free artistic thinking with technical visual media is always closely linked to the technological developments of each era. At the beginning of film history, the equipment was too heavy to move, so of course the motion picture did not move, and the eyes remained statically directed forward. The movie screen became a window through which one could collectively see, from the darkness of the exhibition hall, out to a distant world where workers left factories[1] or were shaved.[2] Photography plus motion, so to speak. Or the screen became a stage for scenes with life-size actors, made transportable in time and space, whom one could accompany on their magical trips to the moon.[3] Theater almost, but still silent. When the camera became more compact, lighter, equipped with sound and moveable, one was zoomed in closer to the action, one was among the players and could even hear them whisper. The canvas became a hole in the wall and the audience became voyeurs and accomplices—and with the development of television, all of that in real time. Video allowed simultaneous access to picture and sound, granted to artists without significant budgets access to the new mass medium of TV and, thanks to viewer ratings terror, gave to the shackled screen all-new content—as it had already been years before through the handy, user-friendly 16mm film and sound format, which enabled an independent film scene to arise, and technically compatible artworks could be shown in almost every movie theater. But no matter in which category or genre, or with which technology we have traveled in the last nearly 120 years, the film image format itself has changed little. Whether window, stage or keyhole, our media view of the world is still today forced into a rectangular cutout: this global dictate of the market-dominating companies could, up to now, only be counteracted by artists through an expanded cinema, or by means of arrangements of large-scale multichannel works with projections on multiple screens, or in always new installation constellations in response to the local requirements of a museum or alternative spaces. With the transition into the third millennium, all of our

[1]
La Sortie de l'usine Lumière à Lyon. (Filmed by Louis Lumière with the cinematograph on March 19, 1895. Workers leave his father's factory. He used the perforated film strip that is still in used today, not yet as celluloid, but made from a specially coated paper.)

[2]
The Barber Shop, Thomas Alva Edison, Black Marie Studio 1894. (The screening cost 10 cents—the same price as a shave.)

[3]
Le Voyage dans la Lune, Georges Méliès, 1902.

sense-extending media met up in a device that quickly comes to replace, or absorb into itself, all others: the computer. Everything runs together on this universal device: the classic analog audiovisual formats are finally compatible with each other and with the contemporary formats. Conceptual and aesthetic features permeate each other, and generate, together with the conscious and unconscious perception of the viewers, new creative potential. Formats and edge lengths are no longer rigid and inviolable. They can be digitally stretched and bent in all proportions and dimensions. The result is innovative cross-genre, genre-busting formats that are currently becoming possible in the audiovisual realm, and also retroactively in empowering older technologies.

The dome runs like a special place across our cultural history, as a shelter and place of worship (cave), an interface (church), as a manifestation of power (architecture) and spirituality (firmament). Is there anyone who has never been in the open air—ideally on a hill or a mountain with little light pollution—and looked at the stars and felt a connection to the afterlife or to infinity? This mother of all domes is now offered to us in the domesticated form of planetaria as a place for projections with new imaging techniques. The opto-mechanical device that previously filled these domes with light points can, after almost ninety years, no longer keep up with design requirements, especially since telescopes send us ever more detailed images from space, visualizing for us the moving cosmos. The offer[4] to develop short films specifically for the October 2006 inaugural all-dome laser projection in Europe at the Zeiss Planetarium in Jena provided an inspiring opportunity for the film/video students at the Art and Design University in Offenbach (Hochschule für Gestaltung, Offenbach—HfG) to liberate their images. However, it was difficult to imagine how to come to terms with the dimensions, technical conditions and requirements for filling this new screen. The dome measured 25 meters in diameter, the hemispherical 360° screen surrounded the audience and offered approximately 800 square meters of projection screen for one's creative thoughts. Each single image of the resulting film sequences had to be laid out as a square, with an edge length of up to a gigantic 4000 pixels. The laws of gravity and of the classic

4
From Micky Remann, lecturer in media events at the Bauhaus University Weimar, via Birgit Lehmann, lecturer for screenplays, HfG Offenbach Rotraut Pape, Professor, Department of Film | Video Art and Design 2006.

central perspective of design seem to be repealed: »up« is no longer at the top edge of a rectangular image, but in its round middle.

First, mental gymnastics—to be at all able to imagine all of that around oneself—then, in the absence of a media dome in the geographical area, to be unable to test—then, rendering madness, a new fashion disease, which occurs when man and machine are overwhelmed and reach their limits in the repeated attempt to create large single images one at a time mostly from multiple images, to fit them for the curvature of the dome using the appropriate plug-in[5] (from Portugal!), to calculate in a round way, and to render again from the computer with proper numbering and make them transportable. In cooperation with the Bauhaus University, Weimar,[6] the Muthesius Academy of Fine Arts and Design, Kiel,[7] the University of Applied Sciences, Kiel[8] and the Art and Design University of Offenbach,[9] the first FullDome festival in Germany took place at the Zeiss Planetarium in Jena[10] on March 16, 2007. All participants brought their mountains of data plus separate sound with them, the image sequences were sliced and stitched together on the spot by six impressive two-meter high computers, and then seamlessly written via six laser projectors into the dome. In the world's oldest operating planetarium,[11] we celebrated with all participants, supporters, mentors and a knowledgeable audience the different approaches of the artistic results in the new medium. What a breathtaking experience! What a great, luminous projection! What amazing sound! The HfG students had imagined their films during a whole semester, how they would work dramaturgically, how they would look, and how they would sound. The results exceeded all expectations: Ten art students had developed narrative short films that consider this whole very special spatial situation of immersive tangible film. *Expanded cinema = expanded consciousness.* Finally it is like how it is in real life: The audience is completely surrounded by images and needs to move to follow the stories. Each person sees a different film, from a different perspective. Released from the standpoint of the external observer, we no longer sit *in front of* the stage or the screen, but

---

[5] Navegar Foundation, Centro Multimeios Espinho, www.multimeios.pt

[6] Micky Remann/Wolfgang Kissel.

[7] Ralph Heinsohn/Tom Duscher.

[8] Eduard Thomas/Jürgen Rienow.

[9] Rotraut Pape/Birgit Lehmann.

[10] Jürgen Hellwig/Volkmar Schorcht.

[11] The Zeiss Planetarium in Jena opened on July 18, 1926. Starting from the end of July 1924, 80,000 people had already seen the first experimental demonstrations of the artificial night sky in a temporary dome on the roof of the Jena Zeiss works, hailed in the press as the »miracle of Jena.«

instead in the middle of it and move now as participating beholder in the center of the world.

Many worlds exist side by side. Owi Mahn[12] transforms the dome into an oversized vehicle in which all viewers find a seat on a fast-paced ride through the urban night. Each of the six windows, and all rear- and side-view mirrors, were filmed in the highest possible resolution and then these images were assembled together. We hear the driver who speaks loudly in a furor above free jazz and sit as helpless passengers as he swerves around the curves. Anna Pietocha[13] transforms the dome via animation into the insides of a rusted machine that rotates around itself, and which is on its last days. In a sentimental duet, the old machinist says good-bye to his iron companion and switches it off. Daniel Frerix[14] makes the dome into the inside of his head. The viewers—shrunk to the size of blood cells—see through the eyes. They see TV images from the World Cup soccer final in 1990, when Germany became the world champion. Depending on how the game is going, the nerve cells crackle, and spark-emitting brain currents give hints about the origin of feelings.

In the style of the Situationists, Jos Diegel[15] protests in scratched analog 16mm/35mm film against *Bigger Screens, Longer Necks*. Everything could consequently serve the virtual film, which plays in the head behind the eyelids, as a screen. Sentences gush from all six available sound sources. They overlap and penetrate both one another and the images that throw themselves flat under the dome and scrutinize all projects of immersion in a grand gesture. This controversial debate incited Christian Janecke[16] to hold annual lectures on immersion in art, especially for the student FullDome researchers: »To be fully immersed in an illusion is an old goal of art—but it is perhaps ultimately against art. Concentration on a highlighted point, area or object of study is not necessary. In place of the event compression of the image, the superimposable representation enters almost certainly within the space of the presentation [representation and presentation become nearly identical], in which the observer surrenders him- or herself, seeing, searching, and sometimes not being able to cope.«

12
Owi Mahn, *Autodrive*, 2007 (4:20 minutes).

13
Anna Pietocha, *Der Letzte Arbeitstag (The Last Workday)*, 2007 (5 minutes).

14
Daniel Frerix, *Gefühle im Gehirn (Feelings in the Brain)*, 2007 (1:46 minutes).

15
Jos Diegel, *Größere Leinwände, Längere Hälse (Bigger Screens, Longer Necks)*, 2008 (7 minutes).

16
Christian Janecke teaches art history in the basic, advanced, and doctoral degree programs at the HfG Offenbach.

As exciting as the first meetings of the immersive kind with one's own surround films were, so it was disillusioning to subsequently realize that one was perhaps essentially making a work that was going to be stuffed into some drawer—or, more precisely, onto some hard drive—because the places where you could present or study 360° dome movies were still sparse, and the media on which these volumes of data could be transported through time and space was bulky. Reluctantly, planetaria began worldwide to combine or replace their star projectors with new technologies from various manufacturers, but they still expected content for their venues—and continue to do so today—to come from astronomy or astrophysics. To show these new short films in our previously media dome–free region at all, we presented them sometimes in a mobile, inflatable dome,[17] or simply as round projections on the floor, around which one could move. Particularly impressive was a presentation in the Frankfurt Film Museum[18] which brought the films into close proximity to the historical phenakistoscopes of Stampfer (1833) and the zoetrope of Marey (1887), and brought to light media-archeological layers which reverberate to this day. Some students set about making their dome films retro-computationally suitable for projection on the conventional rectangular screen in order to be able to show them at all. The flat-screen version of *The Death of Love*[19] was shown at numerous festivals and was broadcast on TV. Both versions of *How to Disappear*[20] won international awards and recognition, including on the Internet. Somehow one is reminded of the last century, when the major US studios waged the concerted *Cinerama* attack against rapidly declining attendance in cinemas, triggered by the life-threatening spread of television in the early 1950s. The impressive curved semicircle of the 146° screen filled the field of vision almost entirely, and the film (three manually synchronized 35-mm projections) was almost physically tangible. The former blockbuster offered a roller-coaster ride[21] that brought the audiences to shriek—just like the arrival of a steam engine train at a railway station in France[22] filmed more than fifty years earlier by the Lumière brothers had—according to the well-nigh topical confusion of art and life—made people giddy from excitement. A worthy succes-

[17] Matthias Rode, www.fulldomedia.com.

[18] *Lost Media: Found.* Gallery exhibition of the HfG film class in the German Film Museum (Frankfurt am Main, 2009).

[19] Yehonatan Richter-Levin, *The Death of Love*, 2007 (2:30 minutes).

[20] Merlin Flügel, *Vom Verschwinden (How to Disappear)*, 2011 (4 minutes), VisuaLiszt-Award, FullDome Festival Jena 2011, Students-Nightlife-Award Platin, FH Kiel, Mediendom 2011, Best Narrative Award, Fulldome UK, Leicester 2012.

[21] Merian C. Cooper, *This Is Cinerama*, 1952.

[22] Auguste and Louis Lumière, *Arrivée d'un train à la Ciotat*, 1896.

sor to this group-dynamic approach that remains present in memory is Owi Mahn's dome film *Autodrive*. To win a moviegoing audience, it was upgraded to multichannel stereo sound and briefly brought the 3-D movie back from oblivion. But this was immediately overtaken by Cinemascope which was able to challenge 3-D at its weakest point—the new widescreen process worked without glasses. The market was—as one experiences again today in the dome movie universe—fragmented by numerous patents, and so flat-film versions were produced which could be shown anywhere. (*Miss Sadie Thompson*[23] came out in 2-D, 3-D standard, 2-D widescreen and 3-D widescreen. Alfred Hitchcock shot *Dial M for Murder*[24] in 3-D, but it was then distributed only in the classic format).

Since our first dome films preferentially thematized the dome as a closed ambient space, they were not edited. Then how do we perceive the environment? Hopefully uncut—otherwise we would probably be ill, asleep or on drugs! With us in the center, the environment moves faithfully around us, or with us when *we* move. Surround films in the mighty dome provide a telling example: »They enable the serving and, at the same time, the marking of that illusion in motion pictures to which, in the time *before* the invention of film, the great panoramas ultimately dedicated themselves only with fixed images without beginning and end.«[25] And could one not read the mechanically rotating viewing platforms on days of popular demand already as camera movement *avant la lettre*? Let us recall here also the wind-up *Moving Panorama* of Mont Blanc, which was presented at the beginning of the 1860s by Albert Smith at Windsor Castle before Queen Victoria, or the fact that the actual panorama rotunda was often underpinned with spaces to prepare for or to obtain the agreement of the audience through sequentially arranged stations of a narrative context in many individual images. But only with the help of cinematic moving images around and after 1900 (partly also in refined simulation of a visitors' site supposedly taking off from the ground), did it then become possible to suggest to the audience that it be moved. Correspondingly, the continuous camera movements of today's dome audience provide the full-dome-specific way of seemingly weightless

[23] *Miss Sadie Thompson*, film of the story by William Somerset Maugham with Rita Hayworth, 1953.

[24] Alfred Hitchcock, *Dial M for Murder*, 1954.

[25] From: »In The Thick of It—Immersion from an Art Historian's View.« Lecture by Christian Janecke, FullDome Festival Jena, 2012.

movement, and help the traditional or conventional planetaria films to go unedited from one place to go to another (flying and diving). In David Sarno's[26] film, the dome begins to dissolve. It looks glassy and presents the free view on all sides of an alien world in unhealthy colors. In the distance we see other glass domes that are being blown up by people in protective suits and breathing masks. We sense something ominous when the troop heads toward the glass dome under which *we* are sitting: »There are some still alive!« Gonzalo Arilla[27] converts the dome into the rectangular room of a boy who prefers to shoot green Martians to pixel nirvana rather than to do his homework. His favorite game is a cult classic game with high immersive potential for addiction. We are located spatially between him and his computer. We have to move quickly between different positions, like the umpire in a tennis match has to quickly move his head, and we have the unusual freedom to choose—either for cause or for effect. From different perspectives, as hunter or hunted, we experience close up how this modern sorcerer[28] plunges deeper into action, and the ghosts that he conjures can no longer be controlled by him when his whole room dissolves into the playing field. Based on text fragments from *A Streetcar Named Desire* by Tennessee Williams, Thorsten Greiner[29] lets the main character Blanche hallucinate a thousand changes in her own small cuboid world. It sensitively touches the audience's sense of balance when the dome filled with throbbing ashlar synchronized to music loses its form, breaks, grows or collapses. Anna Pietocha[30] makes precisely the right point about the situation of the actively involved audience and the new performative possibilities: the film begins in the dark, we hear approaching steps, a kind of lid opens noisily high above our heads, a hand reaches in and fishes a wriggling person from our midst. A real scream from the audience at the right moment completely removes the distance between audience and film and made the ninety-second film a very special experience. With support from the Hesse Film and Media Academy (hFMA),[31] other interested students from the Hessian university network were able to get to know, explore and apply the innovative potential of the new medium. Group excursions to the research dome at Carl Zeiss in Jena for the

[26] David Sarno, HfG, *Aufräumarbeiten (Cleanup)*, 2007 (3:50 minutes).

[27] Gonzalo Arilla, *Space Defender, Version 2.0*, 2007/08 (2:21 minutes), HfG.

[28] »Good! The sorcerer, my old master left me here alone today! Now his spirits, for a change, my own wishes shall obey!«, J. W. Goethe, 1797. (translated by Brigitte Dubiel)

[29] Thorsten Greiner, *50 Prozent Illusion (50 Percent Illusion)*, 2008 (5:05 minutes). Audience Award, 2. FullDome Festival Jena, Best Artistic Production Award, Domefest Chicago 2008.

[30] Anna Pietocha, *Mit Haut und Haaren (With Skin and Hair)*, 2008 (1:26 minutes).

[31] The Hessian Film and Media Academy is a network of thirteen Hessian universities. It was founded in 2007.

32 Micky Remann, Volkmar Schorcht, Jürgen Hellwig with Tobias Wiethoff, André Wünscher, Hannes Wagner and many others.

annual dome initiation workshop,[32] with subsequent midnight meetings in the large downtown planetarium, deepened exchanges with experienced practitioners from Weimar and beyond. Technical format requirements and criteria for the next season were developed and adopted. The formats and compression schemas with which the first films were made were too diverse. Eduard Thomas from the media dome of the University of Applied Sciences, Kiel, invited students to screenings and in-depth coaching and facilitated intensive shoptalk, e.g., with Ralph Heinsohn, visionary dome-film pioneer, who, in 2004 with his graduation film *Alien Action* at the Muthesius Academy of Fine Art and Design, Kiel, had virtually represented all of us by discussing virulent full-dome questions in his film. The experimental search for knowledge in the areas of technology, perspective, dramaturgy, content, narrative structure, interaction, etc. was driven by a growing, often changing, but always motivated group of student pioneers interested in the new, in ever more places, the refreshing results annually performed in spring at the FullDome Festival before a knowledgeable audience. Soon, professional full-dome shows were also presented at the festival, but they were almost exclusively expressions of worship of the starry cosmos and therefore strictly committed to the Planetarium—or in the opposite weightless direction penetrating to the depths of the seas. Mostly these science shows are realized as glossy computer animations, unidirectionally ideal for 30° tilted domes with screwed-down armchairs, and have a maximum duration of 50 minutes.

If it were up to us, one would have to immediately remove the chairs from all dome theaters, in order to move freely in these new walkable projections or, depending on the film, also easily set up! We are in favor of the multidirectional full-dome experience! We are opposed to digital wallpaper with all-around acoustic irradiation and the light-years of endless flight through the power of the stars! We await concepts, images and sounds that include new, inevitably polylinear viewpoints, enacted through the unpredictable multiperspective view of the moving observer, integrating decision-dependent narration and design forms, and bring in real-life film! This turned out, however, to be particularly difficult because flat-picture cameras until now yield only a fraction of the required edge length. We experimented with adapted content and DIY possibilities in order to produce high-resolution real-film dome masters. Students from Darmstadt[33] solved the problem with a story in which some young people armed with flashlights search a house. In their light cones, excerpts of the premises appear, flashing here and there with blurred borders in the dialogue-rich dark, each providing the best possible resolution. Matthias Winckelmann[34] managed a quantum leap in terms of image quality with an experimental stop-motion film whose real single images he, by means of an A3 scanner, generously »photographed« and, through further complex processing, was able to digitize. *Chaos, Ksmos, Mu!* won the Best Experimental prize at the prestigious DomeFest USA, and attracted further international attention to the lively full-dome avant-garde in Germany. Using two digital cameras side by side, Thorsten Greiner[35] took stereoscopic image sequences with the anaglyphic method. Viewed through red/cyan tinted glasses, the film appears three-dimensional and dissolves almost completely from the projection screen into the room. Experiments with HD cameras and fisheye lenses were recorded,[36] but they had the disadvantage that, in moving images, either the perspective is wrong or the cameraman is inevitably in the picture, if not hiding under the camera. Or, as impressively shown by Andreas Thürck,[37] the camera could be lying on its back strapped to a skateboard, the cameraman himself hidden behind a bush, pulling the camera forward with an invisible plastic thread. Aleksandar Radan[38] works with a RedOne camera that delivers images in 4K resolution. In a breakneck action, he films top down into a mirrored semisphere that is lying on the floor of a filled swimming pool and which functions like an inverted fisheye lens, recording its mise-en-scène in the water in one continuous take. In Weimar, Sönke Hahn[39] built a GoPro camera rig and filmed in all directions at the same time with six cameras. At the University of Applied Sciences in Potsdam, Dimitar Ruszev and Christopher Warnow developed the *DomeMod* and *DomeTester* software tools for the visualization of dome films. This software helps to

---

[33] Therea Maué, Moritz Heimsch *Awaken*, 2009 (4:40 minutes), Creative Award, 3. FullDome Festival Jena 2009.

[34] Matthias Winckelmann, *Chaos, Kosmos, Mu!*, 2009 (1:30 minutes), Best Experimental Award, DomeFest, Chicago, USA 2010.

[35] Thorsten Greiner, *Polycycle*, 2007 (4:30 minutes).

[36] Supported by Alex Oppermann, professor for Motion Graphics and Interactive Design, HfG, Frederichs-Stiftung.

[37] Andreas Thürck, *Niemals dein Leben (Never Your Life)*, 2011 (5:26 minutes).

[38] Aleksandar Radan, *Haie und die, die sie liebt (Sharks and Those Who Love Them)*, 2012 (5 minutes).

[39] Sönke Hahn, *Habitat*, 2013, Bauhaus Universität Weimar.

alleviate the tedious work process, making it possible to play image compositions and films in a simulated dome on the monitor—that is, without access to a physical dome, one can check the image content from the changing perspectives of the audience. Since 2010, the Interaction Design Lab at the University of Applied Sciences in Potsdam operates, under the direction of Klaus Dufke and Boris Müller, a 360° full-dome projection system, which has also been extended specifically for real-time visualization, so that alongside high-profile dome films, interactive applications such as games and scientific visualizations are also developed. In addition to other exciting experiments in the use of filmed images, there arose everywhere pure computer animations next to analog animations, and hybrid combinations of different technologies. Denis Carbone[40] mirrors the process of image formation in the dome with handmade light images which, drawn as stop-motion long exposures with colored laserpointers, always more rapidly on the move to explode into a unique world of visible thought lightning.

Stephanie Kayß[41] films her actors upright in HD and then can freely fit them into her computer-generated backgrounds. Another preceding level (rain) makes the illusion of a surrounding nighttime street corner perfect, and makes easier the editing with which she audaciously structures her short film, because classical montage does not work so well anymore. We have long been accustomed to accept cuts in the classic rectangular film format, as if we leafed through a stack of photos, contemplating them for longer or shorter moments of time. Now other sign systems and narrative structures, another timing, must step forward to meet the challenges of the new requirements and situations.

Spatially determined sound plays a still totally underestimated role—because the eye instinctively follows the auditory stimulus, as soon as the brain has registered it. By the end of 2011, it had come: Replace the somewhat weary ADLIP[42] projection system in the Jena planetarium with the more brilliant light Powerdome VELVET® System and the sound was renewed. The problem of the reflection of light in a dome, and thus the difficulty of displaying *black* occurs also in the area of sound.

40
Denis Carbone, *Laser Head Explosion,* 2012 (1:50 minutes), First Prize Full-Dome Category, Koordinaten Festival of Spatial Media, Kiel 2012.

41
Stephanie Kayß, *Schwimmende Einhörner (Floating Unicorns),* 2011 (5 minutes), Audience Award, 5. FullDome,Festival Jena 2011, Students-Nighlife-Award Silver, FH Kiel Media Dome 2011.

42
The All-Dome Laser Image Projection by Carl Zeiss and Jenoptik in 2006 was the first laser-based full-dome projection in Europe.

Working with language coming from different directions, the perfect blend was previously to be experienced strictly speaking only in the center of the dome. From the periphery, one could hear some things not at all, and others much too loud. The Fraunhofer Institute for Digital Media Technology (IDMT) has taken on the problem of spatial sound representation and has made the world's first permanent installation of 64 individually controllable sound sources behind the 360° screen in Jena. Based on wave-field synthesis, the 3-D sound system SpatialSound-Wave is another innovative medium that will revolutionize the handling of audio tracks which will now move as separate sound objects, and can be placed at exactly desired points in the space—in real time or programmed. René Rodigast and colleagues from the Fraunhofer Institute invited students and other participants to a Spatial Sound Workshop in Ilmenau. With the support of of the hFMA, and in cooperation with Sabine Breitsameter, professor of sound and media culture at the Faculty of Media of the University of Applied Sciences, Darmstadt (Hochschule Darmstadt: H_da), the research in both areas (picture and sound) was continued.

H_da students developed what was probably the first (entirely without images) Soundscape play[43] for this special 3-D environment, and supported the students of the HfG in the scoring of their extensive films. Kyung-Min Ko's film[44] excelled in this combination, and impressed the international jury of the FullDome festival, which awarded her a Janus, the first-ever »Oscar of full-dome film« in the form of a two-faced platinum-colored ceramic statuette with both front and rear eyes. Her film explores the traditional ritual of *good* which is still firmly rooted in modern Korean society, lifestyle and worldview. Good is the guiding principle of ›heaven—earth—man,‹ in which man, as a part of nature, is always in relation to heaven and earth, and, beyond life and death, can communicate with all living things. It makes sense to show this infinite circular journey of the energy in the universe in planetaria.

In its seventh year, the FullDome Festival at the Zeiss Planetarium in Jena has become the hub of the international dome-film community which stretches from San Francisco to

[43] Felix Deufel, Yannick Hofmann, Natasche Rehberg, Klaus Schüller, H_da, *I Water*, 2013 (8 minutes), Spatial Sound Recognition Award, FullDome Festival Jena 2013.

[44] Kyung-Min Ko, HfG, Bon Voyage, 2013 (5 minutes); sound design, Felix Deufel, Yannick Hofmann, H_da;Creative Award, FullDome Festival Jena 2013.

Moscow to Melbourne. On five days in May 2013, Micky Remann, Volkmar Schorcht and Jürgen Hellwig presented new works, between mainstream and underground, mostly as world premieres in various competition categories, to the growing international trade and fan public, coming to see the innovative highlights of the season, to have discussions, to exchange know-how, to start new ventures, and to recruit the next generation. Today, there are 1,150 full-dome theaters in the world. Half are in the US and only five of those are larger than the world's longest-serving dome in Jena. The fewest projection domes exist outside the context of planetaria.

With the idea of showing artistic dome films for the first time in Frankfurt, in the context of the B3 Moving Image Biennial, the full-dome curator team of Klaus Dufke, Ralph Heinsohn and Rotraut Pape has taken up the challenge of bringing a mobile dome[45] to Frankfurt. Over five days, an international »Best of Full-Dome Art« will be presented in the Weissfrauen church. Accompanying workshops provide insight into new opportunities, and there will be programs for children and young people. The work on the evolution of film language and film that can be experienced together in exhilirating quality only at these places, and not at home alone in front of the flat screen, has started everywhere.

45
With the support of André Wünscher and Domezelt Deutschland http://www.domezelt.com

Rotraut Pape
studied Fine Arts at the Hochschule für Bildende Künste Hamburg. Since 1979 she has done experimental film, video and performance art, experimental documentary film, short films and has participated in international festivals, exhibitions and theme nights for arte/ZDF/3sat. She is a film and video professor at HfG Offenbach since 2003, since 2008 is a founding and executive board member of the Hessian film and media academy (hFMA), a network of 13 academies Hessen, as well as founding member of the B3 Moving Image Biennial. She does international screenings, exhibitions, publications and lectures. Rotraut lives in Berlin and Offenbach am Main.

Narrativity's Marginal Utility: Format and Immersion in Panoramic Dome Films

Christian Janecke

Let me begin with a disclaimer. My concern here is not to explore the immersion dimensions per se of theater or art history, or to analyze them from a teleological standpoint[1] as a foundation for the evolution of the moving image. What I am interested in instead are the decisive parameters of today's immersion films, to which end I wish to shed light on the implications of the format shift per se and the opportunities for immersion afforded by such films. From the standpoint of the 2013 Moving Image Biennial, this would appear to be altogether appropriate, because its subject is not the technical-media aspects as such, but rather new narratives; although it's not altogether clear how consistent they are with the media coordinates of dome films.

The conventional unfolding of illusionistic maelstroms[2] in old picture squares aside, immersive films are predicated on breaking out of the good old horizontal format. The point here is not so much to exceed aesthetic boundaries[3] by virtue of the characters coming out of the screen at a 90-degree angle and climbing down into movie theater seats (or in a western perhaps taking a few potshots as well), as is depicted in movies that adhere to the Pygmalionesque and at the same time baroque principle of illusionism. My subject is literally expansion and going beyond the projection field. This does not entail merely enlarging the said horizontal format; for if this were the case thrill-seeking moviegoers would need only sit in the first few rows of a huge movieplex to put paid to the usual experience of watching a whole screen and movie image. So what counts here instead is occupation of a large portion of individual viewers' visual field, which is tantamount to a change in the proportion between height and width. And while in this regard the old familiar horizontal format has undergone change over time for reasons of history, fashion, technology or just plain taste, this format still remains basically familiar to audiences as a readily placeable albeit nonspecific *toward that*; and in this sense is basically no different from just about any other picture that you might encounter in a museum, or in a gallery even of contemporary art. Unlike such formats, however, an image depicted on a more

---

1 Oliver Grau, »Virtuelle Kunst in Geschichte und Gegenwart. Visuelle Strategien,« dissertation, 1999 (Berlin, 2001). See also Armin Bergmeier, »Dominanz der Imagination. Die Konstruktion immersiver Räume in der Spätantike,« in *Jahrbuch Immersiver Medien [JBIM]* 2012, 37–48, esp. 39f; Nadja Franz, »Einreihung des Mediendoms in eine Illusionsgeschichte,« in: *JBIM* 2008/09, pp. 27–38 (also see the bibliography here); and Tobias Hochscherf, Heidi Kjär, and Patrick Rupert-Kruse, »Phänomene und Medien der Immersion,« in *JBIM* 2011, 9–19.

2 One thinks here in particular of the effects of suggestive movie-ride scenes or those of 1990s movie heroes, where the indistinguishability of the digital and realworld contributed to the immersive experience. See Jörg Schweinitz, »Totale Immersion und die Utopien von der virtuellen Realität,« in *DasSpiel mit dem Medium. Partizipation—Immersion—Interaktion. Zur Teilhabe an den Medien von Kunst bis Computerspiel*, ed. Britta Neitzel and Rolf F. Nohr. Schriftenreihe der GfM, vol. 14 (Marburg, 2006), 136–53.

3 Ernst Michalsky, *Die Bedeutung der ästhetischen Grenze für die Methode der Kunstwissenschaft*, new ed., with an afterword by B. Kerber (Berlin, 1996; orig. pub. 1932).

accentuated curved surface tends to be regarded as the kind of scenery that we are going to enter incessantly and that it thus represents itself while at the same time also genuinely surrounds us (if we could enter it)—a prime example of this being the wraparound screens at IMAX movie theaters. This is reminiscent of a kind of lovely theater of illusion, where the performance on the stage and proscenium is enriched by an inclusion of side entrances and perhaps also of side box seats or rows. The minute the performance occurs outside of our visual field, forcing us to turn our heads to orient ourselves visually, it would be more accurate to speak in terms of visual surroundings along the lines of a more than semicircular and ideally 360-degree panorama.[4] The fact that such panoramas only occupy the leading edge of a cylindrical element and usually block the audience's view of a dark ceiling which (unlike the likewise round floor) normally juts far out over a space that no one in the smaller and usually enclosed seating area can see from below in the past never in the slightest undermined audiences' amazement at or at least enjoyment of the theatrical illusion. For significant events that unfold or are visible for the most part around us and at the same time at a fitting distance from us can plausibly be recounted in such horizontal surroundings—provided, that is, that the performance does not involve Icarus or a parachute jumper. The classic stage props and provenance of the deceptively painted scenery against which the figures on stage stand out in relief and who are ultimately mere decorative elements (like, for example, the so-called cardboard buddies in battle panoramas)—in short the whole *faux terrain*[5]—offers the audience undeniable proof that the visual surroundings place the emphasis on the aspect of the visual. The viewer, who is kept at a distance, is supposed to merely look on by letting his glance wander over quasi-imaged prototypical arrangements, whereby the thickening plot is conventionally resolved through understandable formatted images that are thus useful and transiently illuminating. And while the viewer may be immersed in musings in a vaguely defined (but sometimes also minutely defined from a topographical standpoint) middle ground between all that is suggested to him as he looks on from afar, everything is undoubtedly set up in such

4
Stephan Oettermann, »Das Panorama. Die Geschichte eines Massenmediums,« dissertation, 1979 (Frankfurt am Main, 1980); Oettermann, *Sehsucht. Das Panorama als Massenunterhaltung des 19. Jahrhunderts*, exh. cat. Kunst- und Ausstellungshalle der BRD (Bonn, 1993).

5
The artificiality of this domain is correctly emphasized by Peter Geimer(»Faux terrain. Ein Zwischenraum des 19. Jahrhunderts« in *Arbeit am Bild. Ein Album für Michael Diers*, ed. Steffen Haug [Cologne, 2010], 78–85) who also points out the relief-like set design provenance in this regard.

a way that the events he is beholding unfold from a standpoint that also *excludes* him; whereby the installation-irrelevant if not downright anti-installative moment of the panorama is crystal clear, even in cases where the images unfold horizontally all around the viewer. The fact that in the waning years of German battle panoramas, unduly moment-oriented subjects such as a soldier falling to the ground after being hit by a cannonball were avoided because they forced the viewer to gradually cast his wandering glance around the panorama in a manner that destroyed the illusion and in any case forced him to take a second look that was unpleasantly disturbing, is proof of how much more panoramas involved a long-lasting and somehow never-ending visualization in lieu of a protofilm experience, regardless how inadequately spread around it was. (This also applies, by the way, to unobtrusively motorized revolving visitor platforms whose movement is by no means panoramic in nature but which are mainly intended to get hordes of visitors onto a conveyance—the goal being to keep visitors from stepping back from the attraction in the midst of a crush of people so that the viewing experience of individual visitors is not brusquely disturbed.[6])

However a panoramic format also rises upward and encloses us in a hemisphere or cupola and thus the panoramic illusion includes an *above-us* dimension, and a spatial and above all scenic and situational *totum* is suggested. The panorama offered the viewer an ambient, all-encompassing illusion, yet still only functioned as an image, regardless of the angle from which it was perceived. The disassociation of an image that is »before us«, actually confronting us, was not abandoned. Only complete immersion replaces this »before us« with an »around us.« It is precisely for this reason, by the way, that long-ago-vanished panorama scenery of the type that perhaps referred to ancient Rome could delight audiences of the nineteenth century without their having to feel out of place; whereas in a space with a genuinely immersive design these same viewers would have been repelled by the attempt at creating an illusion by virtue (under certain circumstances) of their having come into conflict with the world suggested by such a panorama.

6
Grau recognizes this as well. However, invested as he is in the claim that panoramas were the forerunner of immersion movies, he conflates the gradual movement of the audience with the movement of moving images in settings such as early-nineteenth-century dioramas. See Grau, *Virtuelle Kunst in Geschichte und Gegenwart*, 97 (see note 1).

It remains unclear whether immersion needs to be predicated on an illusion, and if so, whether it needs to remain bound by a dimensionally restrictive representation in a perspectivist projection of intended spatial depth on a surface compartment; or whether it can, à la trompe-l'oeil, pretend to represent the so-to-speak relief-like presence and plastic curvature of objects; or whether, immersion might (by virtue of its etymology) merely involve immersion in a perhaps foggy-colored ambience in an artistic field, a literally physical immersion of the body (like floating in the esoteric/wellness sense of the term in the guise of a highly conscious letting go in search of an aesthetic experience in an installation or sound environment space or series of spaces; or whether, wherever possible, individuals venture into—and at same time are coproducers of—experiential and interchange spheres of actual contemporary immersion that thanks to the Internet 2.0 in recent years has become ever more prosumable;[7] or whether it would be better for an imagination-linked[8] immersion to be a precondition in keeping with the (albeit noncontingent) significance this had for picture rooms in Late Antiquity; although here one also thinks of a readily swallowed *Architecture Pill* by Hans Hollein (1967) to whose *concetto* its highly allusive subtitle, *Nonphysical Environment*,[9] refers.

It stands to reason that this not only opens up an unprecedentedly broad spectrum of options, but whether opposing options might also be in the offing here. For the illusionistic representation of elements such as a cage could (at least one assumes so!) unleash immersive force only for those who look around from within themselves in a monocular fashion from fixed points. And in the interest of maintaining a presumably engaging aesthetic illusion that is amenable to »discovery« but not »elimination,«[10] presumably binocular viewing would still make it necessary to restrict the viewer's freedom of movement; and in the case of immersive moving-image representations, the viewer would need to forget their body completely while watching the performance. But the fact that, on being shown the spectacular sight of a UFO passing overhead, viewers duck down, or during an immersively depicted auto race claim to have experienced centrifugal force, demonstrates not their direct but rather their indirect

---

[7] For an exemplary and eloqueent exposition, see Frank Rose: The Art of Immersion. How the Digital Generation is Remaking Hollywood, Madison Avenue, and the Way We Tell Stories. New York; London 2011.

[8] Bergmeier (ibid. note 1).

[9] Illustration in: Summer of Love. Psychedelische Kunst der 1960er Jahre. Ausstellungskatalog; Tate Liverpool; Schirn Kunsthalle Frankfurt; Kunsthalle Vienna 2006, p. 236.

[10] Lambert Wiesing: Von der defekten Illusion zum perfekten Phantom. Über phänomenologische Bildtheorien. In G. Koch; C. Voss (Ed.): ... kraft der Illusion, Munich 2006, pp. 90–101, pp. 89.

physical involvement in the shaping of powerful feedback solely from physical illusion aimed at their powers of sight and hearing.

On the other hand, when it comes to more nuanced immersive illusions, the viewer's body not only no longer tends toward the superfluous, but instead becomes an interface like borders in thick fog; whereby the body—like the lengthy performance of Tino Sehgal's designated comrade in arms at the last documenta (2012)—is physically forced to become a crystallization point for dance-like or quasi-ritual conjurations. In so-called postdramatic forms of theater or dance, audience members are wrenched out of their originally receptive behavior so as to entice them to want or need to join in. Regardless of one's take on such practices, undoubtedly not all audience members a.k.a. participants are needed as hearing or seeing onlookers, as would be the case with immersive films. And all the more so in cases where the logic of force is downplayed and audience members forgo fraternizing with each other—in short, in conventional installations. For here a viewer's own movements distills the installation into irreducible moments if not to the *ultima ratio* of a playful artistic experience that has been set in motion.[11] In such cases, a given viewer—physically in the literal sense, or in the broader sense of the term—might immerse themselves deeply in a constellation of evocation created by the artist without an a priori illusion being involved, such that the act of becoming involved and the act of remaining a recipient-cum-foreign-body protect what is theirs, so as to in turn enable them to begin reflecting on the interplay being consummated here.

Against the backdrop of this spectrum, it should now be perfectly clear that immersion films—or to be on the safe side let us call them dome films projected on a hemispheric dome— undeniably operate at one end of this spectrum, where the viewers are no longer aware of their physicality and take in the performance solely through their eyes and ears. This can be combined with the most gargantuan illusions imaginable: an uncontrolled and purposeless natural event is depicted life-size and in real time (along the lines of undersea worlds) and its actors in a sense pass through the viewers' field of view, much as

[11] See in this regard and in regard to the next sentence Juliane Rebentisch, *Äthestik der Installation* (Frankfurt am Main, 2003)—an exemplary work, in particular her discussion of Kabakov's installations, esp. 172 ff.

deep-sea divers do; or when constellations are visible in the nocturnal sky that are then not filmed and digitally combined, but instead their position and movements are as precisely computed as when the many individual points of light in myriad individual projections are combined into an astonishing whole. Hence when some or many elements move around us—while, simultaneously, the actor-like embodied subjects (or Others) whose encounters are the imperative precondition for narratives can be confidently forgone—then genuinely illusionistic surroundings can unfold and be sustained. And as is well known, all of our contemporaries will find their popular science or escapist dream potential to be appealing or significant.

But the situation is completely different when a story is told (the artistically experimental uses of narrative are discussed further on). Such attempts to combine apparatus technology and format-altered innovations in narrative or other cinematic modalities have generally fallen flat on their faces and remained the stuff of school science fairs or have turned out to be jejune takes on conventional films, and often in a manner that have confused cause and effect: for it is not cinema itself but rather narrative cinema that has needed expanded horizons,[12] whereby the immersive expanded possibilities have necessitated a cinematic pretext. Hence in the past, elements that worked well were incorporated into meager cinematic narratives: the showing of movement events distributed equally across 3D movies when plots involving galactic slaughters, stuff being blown up in mighty battles, submarines, roller-coaster rides and so on became addictive. This could lead one to cynically conclude that the computer games industry has cleverly taken the appropriate steps. For instance, not only are the ego-shooter games (although mostly on classically-formatted flat screens), largely unaffected by narration; they also allow their users to continually invade enemy territory. And it is thereby left to the player to decide on the direction of such invasion, at the same time as being forced to take permanent action.[13]

And so the question arises as to why the cinematic can only fail;[14] to this there are two partial answers:

---

[12] I fail to see the immersive or immersion-like potential here, which is not driven by illusion in film, but is instead either a theme only (see note 2) or an element that has to be adapted to, so to speak, constantly moving projections of illuminated images, and that from an experimental film standpoint (e.g., in flicker films) offers great potential via intensive and extended coloration.

[13] The relevant dimension of involvement is correctly emphasized by Anja Kuhn in »Computerspiel und Immersion. Eckpunkte eine Vertändnisrahmens,« in *JBIM* 2011, 50–62. See also the essays by Serjoscha Wiemer, Jan Distelmeyer and Frank Furtwängler in Neitzel and Nohr, *Das Spiel mit dem Medium* (see note 2).

[14] See for example Schweinitz's essay on Cinerama, »Totale Immersion, Kino und die Utopien von der virtuellen Realität,« in Neitzel and Nohr, *Das Spiel mit dem Medium*, 143f. (see note 2).

First, as a result of the format-driven change from the primacy of the Other to that of the surroundings, the events that unfold before our eyes and that require our attention have now become events that we find engaging but without being able to really intervene in them. Plus there's the limitation whereby the basic ingredients comprising narrative, conflict, and drama are never presented to us at the same time—which means that we cannot really adopt a reflexive stance toward them. For example, we're never shown a traffic accident at an intersection which, were it well-filmed, we could experience realistically and be able to express who did what to whom. Rather, to a certain extent, we find ourselves back at the crossing where the accident occurred. That might work as long as the object is not to make the crash a personal (and realistic) experience. But we have to sacrifice quite a bit in terms of our orientation, our possibility of relating to what is shown; when it comes to comprehending what has passed or anticipating what is to come. Besides, the cinematic cuts should not take us quickly out of the crash sequence,[15] as they are, themselves, a type of illusion which would otherwise be compromised. Nor can we agree with others as to what we've experienced or rationalize it via our antifictionalizing copresence with other spectator bodies. For like it or not, we insist on a lot more being darkened, a lot more bodies being concealed (but not bodies being shown as in mainstream movies) and much more being consumer-oriented in an experience that's concocted for us (likewise just as in mainstream movies—but in contrast to them we want to be permanently transfixed—it *would* be different).

The objection that could potentially be raised here to the effect that the history of immersion in art already attests to the possibilities opened up by complex pictorial narratives in baroque church murals for example, disregards a number of factors, first and foremost among them being the notoriously euphemistic use of the term *narrative* in art history (where for the most part only selected aspects of a putative or otherwise communicated narrative are illustrated). And although such images had an overall effect by virtue of their sequencing and their being in a permanent location, they have of course also been reinterpreted time and

---

15 Bauer concurs in this regard. See Matthias Bauer, »Immersion und Projektion,« in *JBIM* 2011, 20–36, esp. 21.

again and in particular read in succession and could oftentimes be individuated item by item for religious purposes. This applies in particular to secular pictorial narratives that tend to take the form of more complex and at the same time more precise conventionally composed paintings of historical subjects, rather than panoramas with expanded formats—which, as noted, did not serve similar purposes and with good reason.[16]

Secondly, regardless of their unending cinematic transcendence, dome film projection surfaces in enclosed spaces always invite us to come in, in that they emphasize more strongly than mainstream movies (with their basilica-like design) our presence with other customers as members of a secret society. And as noted, this space, physically tailored to us as it is, exists to promote our desire for an illusion to be protected and sustained. Hence whereas a comparably physically present and particularly a dome-shaped space would be perfectly suitable elsewhere in that it would inaugurate the undeniable presence of actors and spectators for a fitting theatrical performance and would work for an installation aimed at enabling viewers to experience something new (see above) aimed at and resulting from reflection, decision making, action, and representation, the fact remains that a hemispheric shell in connection with dome films is an indispensable part of a mechanism whose sole purpose is to create an illusion.[17]

In situations not involving entertainment or popular-science-oriented representations, but instead artistic use of this medium, it would in my view be unduly reductive if not downright misleading to expect solutions to emerge from the kind of experimentation that goes on here. Although this is exactly what is demanded time and again and in some cases marveled at (the unconvinced need only take a cursory gander at *Jahrbücher für immersive Medien*).[18] This does nothing to change the attempt to wherever possible move the seats out of the dome or perhaps have the audience move from one projection space to another—although ultimately you still end up with a visual-art installation that is limited by the confines of a dome. It furthermore seems

---

[16] This even applies to elements containing an unduly large amount of political propaganda and also to Anton von Werner's atypical *Sedan Panorama* (see Grau, »Virtuelle Kunst in Geschichte und Gegenwart,« 66–100 [see note 1]), which is devoid of detail but leaves no room for other elements to unfold, including the successive elements of a story.

[17] The fact that planetariums can also be used as hemispheric spaces for dance performances and can be decorated all the way around with projected scenery and light shows (see for example Tom Duscher, »ICH² – Tanz intermedial für Planetarien,« in *JBIM* 2007, 40–45) does not of course contradict this view, for it's simply another way to use a space for another medium.

[18] Four yearbooks have been published to date (2007, 2008/09, 2011, 2012) containing, apart from media texts, mainly reports on myriad promotional films, discussions of new technical developments and special problems, and practical hints for filmmakers, which is perfectly understandable given the complexity of this medium and the consequent fact that it is not widely disseminated.

doubtful to me whether the oft-used option whereby a suitable subject is found in the house from the projection dome really works—although this option does seek to illuminate. But unfortunately when it comes to both art and commercial immersion films, you constantly have scenes and dialogue that are shown in the conventional horizontal format, the sole difference being that a background that goes with such dialogues simply does not go all the way around the remaining 300 degrees of the dome that is not occupied by such dialogue.

This is reminiscent of circular frieze-like carnival decorations or of low-budget community theater sets where a character is supposed to chop down a massive tree that's freighted with symbolism, but the audience has to be content with a foot-high facsimile of a tree. Hence from this standpoint it doesn't seem completely out of place when in an immersion film's depiction of a legal battle, instead of dialogue between opposing parties who are right near each other, you instead have an impressive courtroom that the audience feels as though they're right in the middle of and part of. Or what if the audience were shown passersby walking around them who would react to the audience (who would be like panhandlers cowering on the ground) from above in various ways, i.e., empathetically, derisively or with ignorance; whereby the effect would remain comic in that everyone in the movie theater would be experiencing the same thing and thus audience members would feel not so much like individual panhandlers, but rather like part of a horde of panhandlers. The question remains in connection with all this as to whether we are able to provide a topic that would fill up an entire evening. Immersion-filmmakers are always faced with a dilemma: either make an action-packed movie, but in so doing sacrifice a large portion of the immersion film format, along with its specific capacity to tell a story (and with it the media-related givens, i.e., strengthening or weakening the intrinsic cinematic fostering of immersion that arises from the protensively[19] successive cinematic moments of classic film genres); or in the interest of achieving a healthy balance, scatter pieces of the narrative across the massive format of the immersive film.

[19] Based on Husserl's term *protention* with reference to the distinction Barthes makes between film and photography, as well as Barthes' use of Husserl's terminology. Robin Curtis, »Vicarious Pleasures. Fiktion, Immersion und Verortung in der Filmerfahrung,« in: …kraft der illusion, 191–204, esp. 199–202 (see note 10).

Unfortunately, this also applies often enough to artificially decorated elements and calls to mind what Goethe once said: »If you tread on soft cheese it gets big—not strong.« Consequently and understandably, it is still necessary to find a driver for the subjects and settings that come into play here—just as there are subjects and settings that are suitable to greater or lesser degrees for a tondo or a circus arena. To this end, one must be careful not to trivialize or conceal more deep-seated problems by focusing too intently on the suitability or lack of suitability of a given subject for a given medium: that narration is a genre ipso facto, and of course not any old genre that can gloss over »the sense of direction of gestural, vocal and instrumental expression;«[20] that dialogue first and foremost creates distance between pairs; that narration primarily creates its space out of images[21] instead of merely being poured out in existing space; that a gradually achieved high-level elaborateness and grace of pictorial narration cannot be forgone and must purify itself from the surroundings to the Other, visibly free itself from them, and unfold under our burdensome control.

The possible counterargument here to the effect that twentieth-century artists successfully and without giving up narrative (but through altered narrative forms) found many different ways to embrace and include the audience ranging from Total Theater to happenings to installations is wide of the mark precisely because in situ intervention, confrontation, and reflective options were incorporated into such practices;[22] just as literature and kindred practices, where a huge card index box or perhaps a space decked out with texts that could very well be part of a dome film, would—unlike such films—allow for other types of narratives. The constantly assessable and variable experience in all these art forms—in short their potential as vehicles for powerful narratives, or the changing processuality of aesthetic experience cannot possibly be provided, as a medium, by the heavy-handed style of movie theatres (particularly in the modern, complete Bazin and Einsenstein versions). Nor do movie theaters need to do this. But unlike conventional movie theaters—which only a fool would expect to enable audiences to experience movies in this way—dome films unassailably provide

[20] Friedrich Dieckmann, »Ursprünge des Bühnenbilds,« in idem., *Theaterbilder. Studien und Berichte* ([East] Berlin, 1979), 29–38, here 31.

[21] Wolfgang Kemp, *Die Räume der Maler. Zur Bilderzählung set Giotto* (Munich, 1996).

[22] Benjamin Buchloh, »Memory Lessons and History Tableaux: James Coleman's Archaeology of Spectacle,« in *James Coleman*, exh. cat. Fundacio Antoni Tàpies (Barcelona, 1999), 51–75.

just this kind of experience by virtue of the intrinsic attributes of the medium.

Thus narrative is still hugely important for dome films. For whenever narratives take flight from circumstances to events, we spectators have great difficulty hanging on to their wings; whereby this medium heartily invites us to act in the capacity of a copresence. But in cases where we, as subjects with bodies and a desire to experience art, feel that we're really wanted as is currently the case with other art forms that arouse our longing for this level of engagement, we need to make sure that we are not coperformers, but that instead a performance goes off like clockwork *before us*. Thus immersion films are faced with the unshakable paradox of being an emphatic suburb with spectators in it that nonetheless need to melt away so as to become eyes and ears. But this is tricky when it comes to creating an illusion, which the more complete it is, the less able it is to accommodate narrative to its genre.

Thus when, in Anna Pietochas's just-under-ninety-second dome film *Mit Haut und Haaren* (2008), an audience member is grabbed by a giant hand and is lifted up to the cinematic sky tent (an event rendered plausible by the timely scream of a person planted in the audience for this purpose), this could be taken as a whimsical reference to certain sci-fi movie conventions and possibly also as an example of the performative enrichment potential of the frame medium. But more important, I feel, is the fact that we have here a somewhat adventitious but also important parable of dome films, which goes as follows: (1) In dome films, a simple act is shown over our heads in illusionistic surroundings, whereby the performatively plausibilized spectator ascent to heaven constitutes a mystical union of a sphere that is part real and part cinematic illusion. (2) The aforementioned sphere harmony is disrupted or just plain thrown away in that yet another spectator is always needed, i.e., we can never be the one who is presumably grabbed (which also applies even to the person planted in the audience to let out a scream, as he would of course then see himself being abducted). (3) In the involuntarily towering sensory height involved here (it's after all the divine eagle that grabs Ganymede, not the other way around), it is once again clear exactly who is in charge of taking the initiative when it comes to immersion films.

Christian Janecke
is a professor of art history at the HfG Offenbach in Offenbach/Main. He finished his dissertation in 1993 and his habilitation dissertation in 2004. His book publications are: *Zufall und Kunst* (1995); *Johan Lorbeer* (1999); *Tragbare Stürme. Von spurtenden Haaren u. Windstoßfrisuren* (2003); (ed.): *Haar tragen – eine kulturwissenschaftliche Annäherung* (2004); *Performance und Bild / Performance als Bild* . FUNDUS 160 (2004); (ed.): *Gesichter auftragen. Argumente zum Schminken* (2006); *Christiane Feser. Arbeiten / Works* (2008); and *Maschen der Kunst* (2011).

Illusion and Its Reverse: About Artistic Explorations of Stereoscopic 3D

Erkki Huhtamo

Dedicated to the memory of Ray Zone (1947–2012), a true 3D enthusiast and friend

Stereoscopic 3D has undergone yet another comeback in recent years, but its cultural identity remains ambiguous. It has been marketed by Hollywood as the newest of the new, a secret weapon to win back the cinema spectators who these days seem more engaged in tapping their smartphones at street corners, and even while walking or driving. Hollywood's promotional teams may claim to have seen the future in the third dimension (although I doubt that the current wave of 3D movies will last); in reality 3D harkens back to the past—to the countless »amazing« and »fantastic« 3D forms, manifested in movies, comic books, View-Master reels, lenticular postcards and Magic Eye random dot stereograms that briefly became a fad in the early 1990s, spurred by the curiosity raised by computer graphics; it cannot avoid having a nostalgic ingredient.[1] In these and many other forms 3D images have attained a peculiar role in postmodern culture. They are ephemeral, and yet somehow essential. The spatial illusions they provide are artificial, and yet they can make the viewer gasp from astonishment. Projected on (or »from«) the cinema screen, they have the power to make audiences suspend their disbelief, scream, and try to grasp phantoms hovering in the air.[2]

The world of 3D is a gadget space—much of its fascination lies in the apparatus. For the 3D enthusiast, the cheap look of anaglyphic cardboard glasses with their red and blue filters may be as important as the eye-poking illusions they deliver. Making guesses about the tricks behind 3D effects is common, whether it has to do with the principle of the stereoscope or with the hidden layers of a computer-generated random dot stereogram. However, such an account of stereoscopy is one-sided (or should we say, »one-eyed«?). Ever since it was scientifically demonstrated, stereoscopic vision has been linked with issues the 3D world of popular illusions tends to reject: analysis, reason, power, control.[3] Charles Wheatstone's original mirror stereoscope (1838) was a scientific instrument made to demonstrate the disparity between the external stimuli entering the

---

1
Fantastic 3-D. A STARLOG Photo Guidebook, ed. David Hutchinson (New York, 1982); Hal Morgan and Dan Symmes, *Amazing 3-D* (Boston, 1982); *3-D-Film*, ed. Peter A. Hagemann (Munich, 1980).

2
This essay contains some material published earlier in my »Media Art in the Third Dimension: Stereoscopic Imaging and Contemporary Art,« in *Future Cinema*, ed. Jeffrey Shaw and Peter Weibel (Cambridge, MA, 2003), 466–73. A version of this essay was published in Italian as »Insidiare l'illusione. L'arte e il 3D,« trans. Gemma Lanzo, in *Moviemento. Speciale 3D* (Manduria, 2012) 62–71. By »3D« I mean stereoscopic 3D, not »3D computer graphics« based on stereoscopy.

3
Paris in 3D: From Stereoscopy to Virtual Reality 1850–2000, ed. Francoise Reynaud, Catherine Tambrun and Kim Timby (Paris and London, 2000).

eyes and their interpretation by the human mind.[4] Its anti-illusionistic nature was inscribed into the open structure of the apparatus—the observer could freely see the left and right eye images placed on its sides and grasp their 3D synthesis in angled mirrors in the center. Analysis and illusion coexisted, supporting each other.

Stereoscopy soon turned into a commodity, when it was marketed in the more immersive form of the boxlike lenticular Brewster stereoscope (first introduced in 1851 at the Crystal Palace exhibition in London). It was a peepshow apparatus that fully enclosed the stereoview and therefore made it more »mysterious.« Still, the analytic uses persisted in science and medicine. Special »eye training« card sets were developed to explore a phenomenon known as retinal rivalry. Such cards encouraged active looking (ocular gymnastics), and were used by opticians to train patients' eyes throughout the twentieth century. As most forms of optical technology, the stereoscope was also put into military use as a professional tool for aerial reconnaissance. Even »innocent« View-Master reels, a favorite childhood pastime that has survived for generations, were used for military purposes to identify enemy warships and train fighter pilots in target practice during World War II.[5] Holography, a later breakthrough in 3D, was turned into a security device used in bank notes and credit cards, helping to stabilize and perpetuate the socioeconomic order. The seemingly innocuous »magic eyes« of the stereoscope became both analytic and panoptic.

But what does 3D have to offer for artists? How—if at all—can it be recruited for experimental narrative purposes? For a century, experimental artists have produced paintings, collages, prints, photographs, films, videos, kinetic objects, performances and virtual reality installations in 3D. There is more variety than uniformity. The 3D paintings of Salvador Dali and René Magritte extended the spatial explorations of the surrealists, while Andy Warhol's 3D shower curtains gave an expression to the pop art sensibility.[6] The 3D films by Oskar Fischinger (who also created stereo paintings), Dwinell Grant, Hy Hirsh, Harry Smith and others added depth to the abstract dynamics of

[4] Thomas L. Hankins and Robert J. Silverman, *Instruments and the Imagination* (Princeton, 1995), 148–77.

[5] John Dennis, »View-Master Then and Now,« *Stereo World*, March-April 1984 (special issue). View-Master was invented in 1939.

[6] See *A Report on the Art and Technology Program of the Los Angeles County Museum of Art 1967–1971*, ed. Maurice Tuchman (Los Angeles, 1971), 330–37. »Neo-pop« artists like Mariko Mori have also used 3D projection in their installations. Warhol gave his name to publicize a 3D film by Paul Morrissey, known as *Andy Warhol's Frankenstein 3D* (1974).

[7] William Moritz, »La romance du l'animation abstraite en relief,« in *Le relief au cinéma*, ed. Thierry Lefebvre et Philippe-Alain Michaud, *1895*, special issue (Paris: l'Association francaise de recherche sur l'histoire du cinéma, 1997), 134–40.

[8] Margaret Benyon, »Holography as an Art Medium,« in *Kinetic Art: Theory and Practice. Selections from the Journal Leonardo*, ed. Frank Malina (New York, 1974), 185–92.

[9] The *Anaglyphic Chimney* was inspired by the book *Les anaglyphes geometriques* by H. Vuibert. See Linda Dalrymple Henderson, *Duchamp in Context : Science and Technology in the Large Glass and Related Works* (Princeton, 1998).

colors, shapes and motion tropes.[7] Others tried to bridge the gap between art and science. Margaret Benyon moved from stereoscopic paintings to holography, while media artists like Ken Jacobs, Jim Pomeroy, and Zoe Beloff have performed with stereoscopic slides, films, or »3D shadows« of objects in front of red and green lights.[8]

Playing Hide and Seek Between 3D and 4D

The history of 3D art is so varied that it cannot be covered here in full. Instead, I will concentrate on just a few artists, whose investigations challenged the ontology and common uses of 3D, opening up possibilities that are quite different from those promoted by the film industry or cherished nostalgically by 3D enthusiasts. The key figure is Marcel Duchamp (1887–1968), arguably the most influential artist of the twentieth century. 3D was a lifelong concern for him, appearing over and over again from his early »rectified readymade« *Handmade Stereopticon Slide* (*Hand Stereoscopy*, 1918) to his very final work, *The Anaglyphic Chimney* (1968).[9] The first mentioned found its origin in an unremarkable stereoview depicting the open sea and nothing else, found in Buenos Aires. Over its pair of dull images Duchamp drew with a pencil sharp geometric rhomboid forms. When observed with the stereoscope, the drawings merge and form a three-dimensional shape that »floats« in the visual field, while the original poor stereoview remains flat and indistinct (this contrast must have amused Duchamp, who has then living his dada years).

Although the *Handmade Stereopticon Slide* has often been seen just as a study for Duchamp's first chef d'oeuvre, *The Large Glass* (1915–1923), it can be read as a kind of condensed metacommentary of the history of stereoscopy that Duchamp was certainly familiar with. In a way he reversed the trajectory of its historical evolution which had—at least on the surface—moved from a scientific demonstration instrument toward a popular commodity that offered magic illusions. Duchamp's handdrawn rhomboids evoke the original drawings with which Charles Wheatstone had demonstrated the stereoscopic effect in 1838 (photography was not yet available, so stereoscopy was *not* its spinoff product), while the (in this case failed) illusionism of the industrially produced and mass-marketed stereocard has been relegated to the background. The reappearance of Wheatstone's rhomboidical ghost aligns the work with modernist critiques of representation: the two layers coexist but remain deliberately incompatible, highlighting the constructed nature of the artifact.

Duchamp's fascination to hidden signs and meanings—including those related with stereoscopy—is demonstrated by *Wanted, $2,000 Reward* (1923), a rectified readymade based on a proof for a wanted poster Duchamp is said to have found in a restaurant.[10] Duchamp listed not only the name of his female alter ego Rrose Sélavy as an alias for the wanted criminal, but added also his own mugshots (profile and frontal poses). A researcher has recently discovered that staring at the mugshots by crossing one's eyes (by so-called free viewing) makes the photographs merge with each other as in the retinal rivalry stereocards, producing a paradoxical sculptural composite of Duchamp's face; its spatiality is further emphasized by the double frame.[11] The discovery adds an extra layer of meaning to the piece. If crime is an »art« of hidden activities, 3D is an art of hidden visual spaces. Criminals, just like artists, use aliases. However, there is a difference: perfect crime is one that remains undetected, whereas perfect 3D reveals what has been previously invisible.

Beside posing as Rrose Sélavy in his artworks, Duchamp was simultaneously engaged for years in another role play process as Precision Oculist, a kind of artist-cum-optician-cum-optical-scientist designing series of rotating optical illusion discs (such as the famous boxed set *Rotoreliefs*, 1935).[12] The experiments of the Precision Oculist combined 3D with 4D, adding cyclical motion to the impression of depth and relief.[13] In his final major work, *Etant donnés* (Given, 1946–66), Duchamp developed yet another strategy of approaching 3D. He constructed a deliberately obscene scene using a reclining nude female mannequin and other physical props, hiding the combination behind an old wooden door. The viewer could only access it by peeping through two holes drilled side by side in the door. Although the installation can be interpreted as an artist's

10
Arturo Schwartz, *The Complete Works of Marcel Duchamp*, rev. and exp. ed., vol. 1 (New York, 2000), 699.

11
Rhonda Roland Shearer et. al., »Why the *Hatrack* is and/or is not Readymade: with Interactive Software, Animations, and Video for Readers to Explore, Part III: Duchamp's Revolutionary Alternative in the Context of Competing Optical Experimentss,« *tout-fait. The Marcel Duchamp Studies Online Journal* 1, no. 3 (Dec. 2000): 10 (online at http://www.toutfait.com/issues/issue_3/Multimedia/Shearer/Shearer10.html. The Wanted poster has first issued in Duchamp's *Boite-en-valise* (1941). Duchamp hinted at this interpretation in the cover he designed for his catalogue raisonné (1953), showing a composite of his face.

12
See my »Mr. Duchamp's Playtoy, or Reflections on Marcel Duchamp's Relationship to Optical Science,« in *Experiencing the Media: Assemblages and Cross-overs*, ed. Tanja Sihvonen and Pasi Väliaho (Turku, 2003), 54–72.

13
Francis M. Naumann, *Marcel Duchamp: The Art of Making Art in the Age of Mechanical Reproduction* (Ghent, 1999).

commentary on illusionistic museum diorama realized actual objects (which can be encountered in museums of natural history and elsewhere), the viewing situation evokes the stereoscope, and so does the ambiguous perspectival arrangement of the scene behind the peepholes. Its composition has similarities with pornographic stereoviews.[14]

How should we interpret Duchamp's engagement with 3D? It is certainly related with his subtle but firm one-man crusade against »retinal painting,« or artworks that he felt were content with reproducing surface effects of reality only (such as Impressionism). Duchamp advocated a cerebral attitude—art that penetrates beyond the obvious and engages the intellect, generating signification by turning into a kind of deliberately ambiguous sign system. Stereoscopy and other types of optical illusions intrigued him, because their effects did not preexist »out there,« but emerged through the active looking in the observer's mind. 3D was a meeting point for Duchamp's many interests, including science, technology, his nerdy fascination with gadgets, and sneer appreciation of popular commodity culture.

The Swiss-born Alfons Schilling (1934–2013) is another major figure whose work explored 3D imaging in all its varieties.[15] Like Duchamp, he was a kind of artist-inventor, who also began his career as a painter, and—again like Duchamp—experimented with many different media forms, including rotating picture discs. Under the influence of abstract expressionism, the young Schilling began throwing paint on large circular canvases which were rotated by motors (the works could be exhibited either in stasis or in motion). Stereoscopy became an integral aspect of Schilling's explorations of vision in the early 1970s. His work covers stereoscopic drawings and paintings (both for viewing devices and for free viewing), a 3D video headset and wearable »vision machines« (Sehmachinen), as well as stereoscopic slide projections that created unusual optical effects by means of rotating shutter discs (the principle became known as the Schilling Effect).[16] Schilling also invented a new way of creating random dot stereograms (inspired by their inventor, the optical scientist Béla Julesz), as well as »autobinary« stereo pictures.[17]

14
As far as I see, no one else has associated the pair of peepholes with the stereoscope. Haladyn only mentions the »interior diorama« accessed through »peepholes.« Julian Jason Haladyn, *Marcel Duchamp Étant donnés* (London, 2010), 84. In his cardboard model for *Étant donnés* Duchamp used the expression »Trous de Voyeur.« Marcel Duchamp, *Manual of Instructions for Étant donnés* (Philadelphia, 1987), separate insert.

15
The main source on Schilling is his *Ich/Auge/Welt—The Art of Vision* (Vienna, 1997).

16
Experimental filmmaker Ken Jacobs was inspired by the Schilling Effect and applied it in his own stereoscopic projections known as The Nervous System and the Nervous Magic Lantern. Jacobs uses two 16mm film projectors and a custom-made »shutter wheel« that rotates in front of their lenses. Jacobs often projects two prints of the same film, but a little out of sync. By means of the rotating shutter, he manages to manipulate the filmic space in surprising ways that include the creation of an artificial sense of depth. See Ken Jacobs: »Le Nervous System Film Performance,« in *Le relief au cinéma*, 141–46. In *Cineprobe*, January 19, 1981 (New York: The Museum of Modern Art, Department of Film), Jacobs admitted his debt for Schilling's 3D work, but seems to have »forgotten« it since. See Schilling, *Ich/Auge/Welt—The Art of Vision*, 185 (see note 15).

Disrobing the Ontology: Challenging the 3D Illusion

Duchamp's and Schilling's interventions were only implicitly political. Both avoided overt confrontations with the cultural and ideological ramifications of stereoscopy. Artists like Esther Parada, Manual (Ed Hill and Suzanne Bloom) and Jim Pomeroy engaged in exactly what they avoided. Their explorations of 3D sprang from debates on postmodernism and digital photography. In the photomontage *Malevich in America* (1991) Manual superimposed a cross of (bandage-looking) blue and red bars over a grainy monochrome stereoview of a nondescript forest.[18] The cross refers to the abstract paintings by the Russian modernist Kasimir Malevich. Recalling Duchamp's *Handmade Stereopticon Slide*, two separate visual orders, flat and three-dimensional, coexist. Following the hint of the title, these visual orders may be culturally determined. If the forest represents America, what does the Russian cross signify—dominance, progress, or just abstract flatness? The answers have been left deliberately ambiguous.

Esther Parada's (1938–2005) work deconstructed ideological representations by subtle digital collages, creating highly ambiguous narrative sequences. For a series called *2-3-4-D: Digital Revisions in Time and Space* (1991–92), she selected the Keystone View Company's mass-produced old stereocards of colonial Latin America and combined them with other visual sources. In the four-panel sequence *At the Margin* the starting point is a stereocard titled »Statue of Columbus, Ciudad Trujillo, The Dominican Republic« from 1939.[19] For Parada, it represents imperialism and racism, augmented by the fact that stereoviews like this were mostly meant for European and North American eyes. Parada subverts the ideology embedded in it by focusing on seemingly marginal figures (a black woman and an Indian woman) and moving them toward the center, at the same time distorting the 3D effect. In the last panel, a monoscopic photograph of two young Cuban pioneer women has been added, overshadowing the original referent and further compromising the 3D illusion.[20]

Parada's way of treating the Columbus stereoview represented »a militant stance of autonomy in relation to

European or North American dominance in this hemisphere.«[21] Disturbing the stereoscopic illusion had central importance for her: »Just as the two different angles of a stereographic image create the illusion of dimension optically, I hope that my strategy of juxtaposing, my layering of distinct perspectives through digital technology, will create a more complex or dimensional perception conceptually.«[22] Keystone stereoviews were often marketed with the support of scientists and other authoritative figures, who emphasized in their testimonies the ontological truth of the views, their absolute accuracy in depicting reality as it is. For Parada, the homogeneous visual 3D space represented a hegemonic ideological position that marginalized other sights and voices. It needed to be dissected to give them a chance to appear from behind the scenes.

In a series of stereoscopic images called *Reading Lessons* (1988), Jim Pomeroy also reworked old Keystone stereoviews by digitally inserting pun-like textual fragments within them.[23] The eyes of the viewer wander within his spatial montages from plane to plane, drawing connections between words and things. The opening view of the series has the text »Reading Lessons and Eye Exercises« distributed on different planes around a figure of a man reading in a position that recalls (probably inadvertently) Andrea Mantegna's *Dead Christ* (c. 1500)—he is virtually pushing the soles of his shoes in the viewer's face. Pomeroy also playfully refers to stereoscopy in medical eye-training. The humoristic and absurd text/image combinations he creates are not just pranks, but serve critical purposes as well. »We are not seduced by farce, but rather, sharpened,« Pomeroy wrote.[24] Significantly, he released these 3D works as a boxed set of three View-Master reels and a viewer, an ambiguous homage to popular stereoscopy.[25]

Pomeroy also projected 3D slides in performances. In *Apollo Jest: An American Mythology* (1978) he used a series of stereoscopic slides and a voiceover to »prove« that the moon landing actually did take place. This issue was often debated in the popular discussions of the time. The moment was prone to conspiracy theories; it was even claimed that NASA had secretly staged its achievement in a Hollywood movie studio. In *Apollo Jest* Pomeroy found a hilarious way of tackling false ontological

---

21 Parada, Artist Statement, at http://www.uic.edu/depts/lib/projects/parada/html/art/atm.html (accessed April 15, 2012).

22 Esther Parada, »...To Make All Mankind Acquaintance,« in Druckery, *Iterations*, 110 (see note 19).

23 Like Parada, Pomeroy produced his works as an artist in residence at the California Museum of Photography (Riverside) that houses the huge Keystone-Mast collection.

24 Jim Pomeroy, »Reading ›Reading Lessons‹«, a text included in the View-Master package *Ver Multidimensionales/Stereo Views* (Syracuse, NY, 1988). This publication accompanied Pomeroy's exhibition at Light Work's Robert B. Menchel Photography Gallery, January 10–February 13, 1988.

25 Ibid.

certainties attached to photographs as evidence.[26] The female voiceover presents a dispassionate but tongue-in-cheek narrative of the events that culminated in the moon landing, while a long series of mixed stereoviews provide »incontestable« evidence (the Empire State Building stands for the rocket, etc.). The mismatches between words and images reveal to what extent the meanings of photographs are anchored by the texts attached to them. Concluding the spoof in an appropriate way, the stereoviews were later issued as a set of 88 3D bubblegum cards, delivered with a cheap cardboard stereo viewer.[27]

The Future of Illusion, or Illusion of Future?

Artists keep finding intriguing ways of commenting on 3D in their idiosyncratic works, and also weaving in narrative strategies. As a general observation, the relationship between steorescopy and storytelling has often been seen as problematic. The former is connected with gimmicks and attractions that jump out from a storyline, disrupting it rather than supporting it. An unusual example in which these dimensions have been woven together is William Kentridge's masterful animation *Stereoscope* (1999). In Kentridge's customary way, it depicts a dark and crazed society on the brink of breaking apart. It is not a 3D film although it constantly refers to the three-dimensionality. As Kentridge himself has stated, it is »a kind of stereoscopic reverse.«[28] Many of the scenes are depicted as pairs as on traditional stereoviews (albeit in motion). These never produce a coherent stereoscopic illusion. Instead, as Tom Gunning has observed, »the two images deviate from each other, not only refusing us the place of perfect convergence, but also imaging instead a schizoid world in which doubles confront each other with suspicion.«[29] In its own peculiar way, *Stereoscope* shares the century-old artistic preoccupation of penetrating beyond the 3D illusion and shattering its coordinates.

Another original example of artists who have been engeged in weaving together stereoscopy and narrative experimentation is Zoe Beloff. Beloff's films and performances involve projected images and live narration. Stereoscopic images conjure up spectral scenes and phantoms, essential for her media-archae-

---

26
A version can be experienced on-line at http://www.jim-pomeroy.org/video/hiq.mov .About Pomeroy's 3D performances, such as *Composition in Deep/Light at the Opera* (1981), see Paul DeMarinis, »The Boy Mechanic—Mechanical Personae in the Works of Jim Pomeroy,« in *For a Burning World Is Come to Dance Inane. Essays by and About Jim Pomeroy*, ed. Timothy Druckrey and Nadine Lemmon(Brooklyn, 1993), 9–10.

27
Jim Pomeroy, *Apollo Jest. An American Mythology (in depth)* (San Francisco, 1983).

28
William Kentridge, quotes in Lillian Tone, »William Kentridge: Stereoscope,« online at http://homepage.mac.com/studioarchives/artarchives/liliantone/tonekentridge.html (interview made on February 22, 1999).

29
Tom Gunning, »Double Vision: Peering through Kentridge's ›Stereoscope,‹« *Parkett*, no. 63 (2001): 69.

30
Beloff's performances with projected 3D slides and film include *Life Underwater*, *Lost* and *Claire and Don in Slumberland*. Beloff has also directed 16mm 3D films like *Shadow Land or Light from the Other Side* and *Charming Augustine*. See www.zoebeloff.com.

31
Virtual reality inspired many experiments by artists, but many remained little more than manifestations of »demo aesthetics.« Important digital virtual reality works in 3D include Perry Hoberman's *Barcode Hotel* (1994) and Maurice Benayoun's and Jean-Baptiste Barrière's *World Skin* (1997). See my »Media Art in the Third Dimension,« as well as *Immersed in Technology: Art and Virtual Environments*, ed. Mary Anne Moser with Douglas MacLeod (Cambridge, MA, 1995).

ological investigations of the relationship between imagination and technology.[30] Her works evoke the contemporary discourses on virtual reality, but situate it within a wider context that includes magic lantern projections, nineteenth-century ghost shows, early cinema, telepathy and telegraphy, Freudian dream narratives and discursive traditions that raise the impact of media technology on schizophrenic delusions. In her installation *The Influencing Machine of Miss Natalija A.* (2001) the spectators are confronted with a 3D representation of a machine that purportedly projects delusions to the mind of a fictional persona. Touching parts of this virtual machine visualizes the delusions, derived from early-twentieth-century media. Here, as in her performances, stereoscopy serves as an appropriate medium to express Beloff's artistic interests.

As I stated in the beginning, in recent years 3D has been all the rage in the world of commercial cinema. Even films that were originally shot in traditional formats, such as James Cameron's *Titanic*, have been digitally converted into 3D. There are those who declare that 3D cinema has finally come of age, while others object that stereoscopic 3D has always been and will always remain a fad, introduced in waves that come and go like tides. The wave of 3D films experienced in the early 1950s that produced cult classics like *It Came from Outer Space* had been preceded by the »stereoscopomania« of the Victorian Age a hundred years earlier. Although they were distant from each other in time, these 3D waves shared many motifs, particularly when it comes to the discursive fantasies they inspired. Both may have signaled ruptures in the evolution of media culture. Another 3D wave rose around 1990, inspired by the buzz about virtual reality.[31] The rupture was even more evident. It is hardly necessary to point that our own time is again undergoing a transformation that deeply affects media use, and the social, ideological and economic models it supports. Mobile media is all the rage, but other media forms are not ready to yield, at least not without struggle.

Against this background it is far from certain that 3D films will continue to draw spectators to the cinema, at least not in similar quantities as in recent years. The 3D boom of the early

1950s was Hollywood's counterattack against the rising popularity of a new rival, television. Likewise, the current 3D boom is a calculated measure to win back diminishing cinema audiences, whose major occupations these days are Netflix, YouTube, and the burgeoning social media. It could be argued that digital production and exhibition methods make 3D lucrative (but not necessarily cheaper), but how long the interest will last is anybody's guess. One also wonders whether there is a long-lasting future for innovations like 3D television, or whether it is doomed to fade into oblivion like so many fads. Be that as it may, there are artists who are committed to explore 3D, and in ways ignored by commercial enterprises. Their input is definitely needed—perhaps more than ever—to discover new critical ways of exploring the changing realms of vision and visuality. It is experimental artists who have the power, persistence and imagination to expose inflated and treacherous illusions mass-produced and force-fed by the cultural industry in the name of the antigod known as Money.

Erkki Huhtamo
is a media archaeologist, writer and exhibition curator. He holds a Ph.D. in cultural history, and works as professor of media history and theory at the University of California Los Angeles, Department of Design Media Arts. He recently edited *Media Archaeology: Approaches, Applications, and Implications* (with Jussi Parikka, University of California Press, 2011), and wrote *Illusions in Motion: Media Archaeology of the Moving Panorama and Related Spectacles* (The MIT Press, 2013).

Time-Seeking Connections

Interviews with Bjørn Melhus and Yves Netzhammer

The artists Bjørn Melhus and Yves Netzhammer, who work with film and video, are involved in the discussion of new forms of narrative. Bjørn Melhus's works explore in innovative ways a wide variety of ordinary narrative structures from television and American war films. His films result in a kind of metanarrative concerned with deconstructing narratives communicated by media. With the help of a strategy of difference and repetition, Melhus shifts existing formats in order to call into question our media memory.

Likewise, Yves Netzhammer reflects on our ideas and expectations, which form the basis for our communicative action. By means of his emphatic, digital, graphic language, Yves Netzhammer creates a distance in the medium that rejects concepts that can be quickly explained. His »mental stage« offers optimal places to try out our socially conditioned action. Whereas Melhus works with sequences of sounds, Netzhammer takes the route of visual language to contradict our habitual description of forms of representation.

Bjørn Melhus

Liliana Rodrigues
Bjørn, in principle your work refers to the world of American commercial film, television, pop music and advertising. The Biennial (B3 Biennial) is exhibiting *The Oral Thing*, an icon from the year 2001, in which you grappled with the phenomena of American televangelism. How does New Narrative relate to your work?
Bjørn Melhus
First, I would like to call into question the term *New Narrative,* which has been in the air, and see my work separately from it. It is clear that I am a storyteller, but in my artistic practice I have always been interested in experimenting with narrative structures and innovations on them. The video *The Oral Thing* alludes—via the host, the moderator—to the image of a television preacher who is hearing a confession and over the course of it turns those who initially seemed like victims into the perpetrators. But the video alludes much more to the format of

so-called daytime talk shows, which as exhibitionist confessions are almost like a pseudoreligious ritual. (In Germany, on *Fliege*, there was even an actual minister [Jürgen Fliege—*Trans.*] who could emotionally entice his guests, even back from the final abyss.) On the level of language, *The Oral Thing* is based entirely on material quoted from *Maury*, with Maury Povich as moderator, which is produced in New York. At the time I was intensely occupied with these shows, which were actually invented only to fill the broadcast time between blocks of advertising during the day (hence »daytime« as opposed to »prime-time«). The basic understanding of commercial television is by means of any sort of content whatsoever to expose consumers to advertising for as long as possible. In contrast to film, therefore, television narratives always conform to these conditions, for example, by having a cliffhanger before the breaks for advertising. In *The Oral Thing*, I adopted this interruption and storytelling in miniepisodes very directly in terms of form, and in later works such as *Captain, Deadly Storms* and very recently in *I'm Not the Enemy* I've explored them at greater depth. As viewers, we withdraw for a moment only to get back into the events after a brief moment. For me, this fragmented form was interesting in the exhibition context with an eye to an endless narrative, that is, the video loop, in which the final episode or scene becomes the backstory for the first one; hence the point at which a viewer steps into the narrative is relatively open.

LR

One would suppose that as a video artist you are primarily interested in images. But the first thing you do is take excerpts of sounds from various media contexts and only then create the visual components. Can you tell us more about this strategy? Why is it of central importance to your work?

BM

Mostly they are fragments of dialogue that are taken out of their original context and restructured to convert and condense them into a kind of metanarrative. Then separate images are produced that follow the level of the sound but in some cases interpret it very freely and hence create a new context of meaning. But this method also means that I can only use things that already exist in the media archive. The source material establishes a framework, so to speak, but I am interested in its possible, and also impossible, deconstruction.

LR

That strategy could almost be compared to DJing. You build up your archive of sound excerpts and manipulate them choreographically. Could you say something about that, please?

BM

A crucial step was the installation *Still Men out There* (2003), in which I dispensed with images entirely for the first time. In that color spectacle on eighteen monitors, which was based on a sound collage from American war films, it was less about war itself than about the representation of war in American entertainment films. Since 2003 in addition to the other films I have been producing works that operate exclusively with colors, most recently *Murphy* (2008).

LR

Your work clearly destroys classical structures of narrative. Do you think that traditional narrative is no longer useful?

BM

I don't believe that traditional narratives are useful any longer. They simply interest me less personally, whether as a viewer or artist. Many traditional forms of narrative follow a very established, traditional pattern. They offer a fixed, recurring framework within which various content can be treated. They're more like a ritual with clearly established rules.

LR

Hecho in México (2009) masters several principles that seem to be central to your work. It employs a variation of just a few elements; it borders on narration; the tension rises to an unbearable point; and then nothing happens. I define this »deception« of the audience as a political intention. Why are you interested in misleading the audience?

BM

Hecho in México refers to the situation in Mexico in the summer of 2009; by that point more than fifty thousand people had become victims in just a few years of the drug wars. Public areas in that country were marked by militias from both sides who were armed to the teeth—the normal state of affairs. The work was produced for the Bicentenario of 2010: the celebrations of two hundred years of Latin American independence. In the first part of the video, we see a grotesquely overarmed modern soldier on horseback in the forest, riding toward us to heroically driving sounds of a plot that never plays out. I am alluding here to the advertisements produced all over the world to recruit soldiers, which tell a story of heroic preparedness for fighting but never of contact with the enemy or an actual battle. These are films that have not only frequently misled their viewers but often led them to death. I adopt existing formats and shift them to different contexts in order reflect on both the formats and the new contexts. In *Hecho in México*, the soldier is standing opposite a completely depopulated, postapocalyptic Mexico City. The work is very minimal, and not everyone understands it, but it is shown much more often in Latin America than in Europe, for example.

LR

The Biennial (B3 Biennial) (Parcours exhibition) is showing *Die umgekehrte Rüstung*, a film you produced in in 2002 in collaboration with Yves Netzhammer. How did you come to work together? What was the appeal of this work?

BM

Yves Netzhammer and I met in New York, although each of us was already familiar with the other's work. We had a number of conversations, which then led to the bold idea of collaboration, which we worked out very precisely. He produced the images—sequences of animations that had something to do with blood—and I sifted through video stores looking at films from which to extract scraps of dialogue and sounds that revolved around that red juice in the broadest sense. Once Yves Netzhammer had provided me with a number of mininarratives, I began combining the visual material with selected sound excerpts to create a large narrative that would be compatible with the crackling of films from the 1950s and would embed quotations that hang about somewhere in our collective memory of media into a new, associative narrative. For me it was an interesting challenge, the first time I was dealing with the principle of double appropriation that is, not producing the images myself either. As a result, developing the narrative became the main act for me.

LR

I'm Not the Enemy (2011) employs various characters. But rather than going back to storytelling, you introduce subtle variations in the second half. Is that another strategy to destroy narrative?

BM

I see it as part of the narrative aspect. As in real life, it is often about repetition and difference. The story itself is divided into episodes by embedded images of single-family and multi-family homes. So it's a kind of hybrid. One earlier experiment was *The Meadow* (2007), which consisted of a twenty-eight-minute loop of four episodes that were identical in several sections but varied in others. Alongside the obviously different encounters of the main figure, there are tiny variations that lie more in the realm of the palpable. In addition to consciously playing with the viewers' expectations of a loop installation, which always tells something new just when you wanted to leave, for me it was about structures of memory in four temporally overlapping narrative backgrounds. The repetition leaves an impression, and by the fourth time at the latest it becomes unbearable, whereas the difference and development of the story are perceived as genuine relief.

LR

Let's talk about your latest work. In your retrospective at the Haus am Waldsee (2011), you concentrated on issues of posttraumatic stress disorder among war veterans. Why does that topic interest you? Where would you place your film within that controversy?

BM

I'm Not the Enemy is primarily about how people returning from war are represented in mainstream American films. As in many of my other works, here too I am interested in a processing of the processing and relocation. At least since the Vietnam War, the war veteran is one of the most popular hero figures in the American action and mainstream film, whether *Rambo* or *Avatar*. What interests me is what is treated and how. It is, of course, inevitable that this will touch on the current political debate about foreign deployment in so-called asymmetrical wars.

LR

Aren't you afraid sometimes that, because of your unconventional narrative style, your strategy will be misunderstood as patronizing?

BM

I can't really understand that conclusion. I feel that every form of conventional narration is much more patronizing, for example, when a film tries to monopolize me completely and ignores my critical distance as a viewer. I believe that the difference is precisely challenging your audience, sometimes being deliberately more grating or annoying and hence also more challenging. But leaving that aside, it makes a difference whether I am making good entertainment or art and what expectations the audience has.

LR

You use many media formats in your work: a wide variety of television formats, news, and Hollywood war films, all of which influence our social and cultural perceptions. We found ourselves in an age of digitization. How are the rules of the game changing?

BM

A big part of my practice as an artist can indeed be understood as media archaeology. Over the past century, the moving image has certainly become one of the most influential instruments in our society, whether as propaganda, as reflection on the present, or as a way to work through trauma. In addition to studying narrative structures, my work is also very clearly about the senders taking substantive positions relative to the recipients. The presence of media today is more about dialogue and participation—whether it's the world of social networks, of YouTube, or of the gaming industry. We are asked to give our two cents about everything and to help shape developments, which amounts to an extreme democratization of the image. At the same time, of course, there is a risk of arbitrariness into which everything can descend amid the great white noise, according to the old proverb that too many cooks spoil the soup.

LR

Your works in public spaces, such as *Screensavers* (2008) or the expanded reality app *Gate-X* for the still unopened new airport in Berlin, are an attempt to reach out to new, challenging themes of the age of social media and to reflect on the issues it raises. Where will this trip take you?

BM

In the case of *Screensavers* (2008), voice-recognition software grabbed various keywords from radio news in near real time and reproduced them on large LED displays next to a busy street. When it did not understand something, the software just chose a similar word, as happens with rumors. Drivers listening to the radio had both the public space of the radio and the visual even in a public space outdoors.

Every situation experienced here was unique and unrepeatable. That was part of the appeal. A site-specific augmented-reality smartphone app created as part of a percent-for-art program for an international airport took it a step farther: With the help of markers, we find life-sized virtual passengers integrated into the architecture of the airport in the form of a 3D animation of a small family that has been stranded in the transit zone and has set up its home there. As viewers, we can share the visual space with them and share this experience as an image with our friends. We become part of a narrative that we then narrate ourselves.

In addition to its participatory character, *Gate-X* also offers a way of grappling with the nonplace of the transit zone, whose strange status was recently in the headlines again thanks to Edward Snowden. The transformation of technology offers a number of opportunities and hence also challenges for artists. I think we should never forget our main concern and the often tragicomic relationship of man and machine, as Stanley Kubrick predicted more than forty years ago in his *2001: A Space Odyssey*. It is one of the great tales of the twentieth century, and its strong authorship earned it a place in history.

LR

Thank you.

Yves Netzhammer

Liliana Rodrigues

The Biennial: B3 Biennial (Parcours exhibition) is showing *Die umgekehrte Rüstung* (The inverted armament), a film you produced in in 2002 in collaboration with Bjørn Melhus. How did you come to work together? What was the appeal of this work?

Yves Netzhammer

Both of us had a scholarship to study in New York the same year. Then after September 11 transformed the city, the political landscape, and even the individual sense of life so dramatically, we were searching for a way to reflect on it together. We were guided by the idea of a transformable, physical and psychological material that in its restless, viral nature settles into identities, interprets them, and expands them with narrative elements in such a way that its own qualities change, and hence also its use.

LR

In the summer of 2007 your work attracted international attention for the first time through parallel exhibitions in the Swiss Pavilion at the Venice Biennale and in the Karlskirche in Karlsruhe. These installations generate new visual paths for everyday presentations of problems, rather than depicting reality in the usual documentary way. Can you describe the artistic, narrative form you have developed?

YN

In both exhibitions it was important to me to address the model-like and imaginary quality of my working with the dominant political situation (refugee policies in Italy, a national pavilion, a Huguenot church in Kassel) and by means of precise interventions in the installation to confront the narrative level of the images and sounds with the history of the space.

Although my work tends to be created more from an intrinsic process, in Venice and Kassel it can also be read politically. There are many inscriptions stored in our cultural »image code.« *Politics* is perhaps the wrong word; it is more about moral or social rules and role playing. One danger of art is that it often illustrates something that is already familiar.

In terms of subject matter, I wanted to develop my work in the context of a national pavilion even more intensely in the direction of alternative problem zones. As someone who creates images, I myself often feel subjected to pressure to legitimize myself, because the radius of influence of open, circular visual stories is almost obsolete in our society. Nevertheless, I try to understand sensitivity as a resource through which we can develop a point of identification with others' suffering. This point of departure can form a new relationship to idly watching and make us judge it more critically. My experiences with the work *Die Subjektivierung der Wiederholung* (The subjectifying of repetition) led me to start with the introspectively structured themes of *Die Möbel der Proportionen* (The furniture of proportions), which I developed for SFMOMA.

LR

You have created a unique means of depiction using digital images that consists of a syntax of certain characters and motifs. These human and nonhuman elements and the ways they interact in the digital world seem to test our traditional plots and patterns of behavior. Could you go into that a little?

YN

The characters are stylized, but nevertheless they are in a sense »test bodies,« which demonstrate mental and physical states and are connected to me. On a fictional level, they enrich my store of experiences. It is astonishing how much even fictional experiences influence and supplement your own thinking. In a certain sense, it is part of my personal self-experiment that through my work I transform myself into something new. I oscillate between the phantom pains in the image and actual pains.

The result is a »mental stage,« on which our ideas and expectations—that is to say, the basis of communicative action—can be questioned but also have their confidence shaken.

LR

Despite our established logic, the characters in your films seem to be engaged. By means of absurd situations—even though absurdity is only one of several strategies in your work—a shared logic is disturbed. It feels as if you are working against narratives. Would you agree?

YN

It is an attempt to reach other cognitive insights through images. In contrast to a text-based approach, I develop my questions through processes of empathy. Processes in which knowing and feeling develop each other. Working in an open system means allowing yourself to be surprised. Paradoxically, something I don't know and don't understand at first informs me precisely about the other. In fact, I am interested in the unsaid, the invisible. The references of the narrative seem to me to be different, however, from text-based knowledge. I think it is important in art not to create »foreign knowledge«—that is, easily explainable concepts. The approach through drawing seems very suitable to me for that reason, especially because you can work directly on the true resistance to narrative, and because of the distance the medium creates—that is, the stylistics—you don't fall into a »suspicion of illustrating« the real but instead operate with the means of the imagination.

LR

Is your intention in your works to ensure confusion at the beginning and thus find a way to break with the narrative. Where you ever interested in storytelling?

YN

For me, *image* means the transition of perception to graphic idea. I understand it as a vis-à-vis unspecific to any medium that serves to store experiences and values and also makes it possible to generate open and imaginative relationships. My visual world has a lot to do with sensing strengths, identifying initial questions, and working out the necessary vocabulary.

The exchange of inside and outside is reciprocal and is always process-oriented. You change when you grapple with the question of what characterizes you. Within the work I tend to make it as complicated for myself as possible in order to develop a »vivid« type of description. I approach the themes both with the aid of a nonnaturalizing medium and with idea-heavy description.

LR

But then the viewer grasps the actions on the screen as a consequence and cause and searches for an organic development. How do you incorporate the viewer's natural disposition to narrative? How does this persistence affect your work?

YN

Is the society just text? I produce enormous numbers of drawings and uneconomically long films that seek to communicate and establish closeness. My need focuses on the visual potential in their differences, which also want to make it possible to experience humanistic issues. Normative and function-oriented concepts of communication often seem to me too generalizing with such themes.

LR

It seems like, once the digital sequence has found its place, the object follows. These objects are neither simple ready-mades nor sculptures in the traditional sense. They are born of the practice of your digital drawing and consist at first of animations. Why turn the cinematic form into a sculptural form? Why translate the viewer's intellectual experience into a physical world?

YN

Our ability to perceive is challenged by time and space. As subjects, we are stuck in different time zones. If you remember something from before or imagine something in the future, you encounter yourself as a different person. Mixing digital and actual spaces provides a temporal consistency for our questions.

LR

Kathleen Bühler, who curated your big solo exhibition *Das Reservat der Nachteile* (A refuge for drawbacks) at the Kunstmuseum Bern (2010–11), pointed to the growing theatricality in your latest piece. How should we understand that aspect in connection with your continuing interest in exploring the relationship between subject and object? And how does it affect the narration?

YN

In the installation, I'm concerned about illustrating cognitive possibilities. About ensuring that viewers are addressed through all their senses and are guided to networked thinking and seeing. Those are things I find lacking in art spaces, with coolness and limited sensory arsenal, while they are possible in theater and installations. But they shouldn't serve seduction or entertainment alone but should rather produce synergies and channels to the self.

LR

Let's talk about your latest works. You have just completed a trilogy of films: *Dialogischer Abrieb* (Dialogical wear, 2011), *Vororte der Körper* (Suburbs of the body, 2012), and finally *Alte Verstecke in neuen Räumen* (Old hideouts in new spaces, 2013). One key moment is the scene with a car accident. Why has bodily injury become such an important theme for you in recent years?

YN

I would like to clarify that question, without judging it. Accidents enlarge surfaces; they are a kind of lens. First, I try to imagine how the anomaly came about, to clear up the questions what happened to whom and what happened at all. When I sense certain reactions, I ask myself: What triggered them? Why am I reacting in this way? Then comes the next step, namely, hierarchizing the pain: How is it applied to inanimate things, to animals, to human beings? This reveals social connections in our intuitive visual thinking. Images are great fields for experiment, for trying something out, because social activity is conditioned and can be read from images. Often you stumble over stereotypes: culturally inscribed values that are very limited, really, simplifying. Visual stereotypes frequently occur in advertising, with the usual polarizations: old/young, white/black, familiar/foreign.

LR

This special moment of the car crash is shown in slow motion and narrated in a discontinuous style. The characters recall crash test dummies, which creates an emotional distance. You are known for using other strategies such as transformation, zoom, and fusion effects in order to trigger our chain of associations. In your own words: »What I am pursuing is not just visual but more a vision accompanied by narratives. I reflect on and question concepts.«

YN

The metaphorically constructed plot of a dialogue in the form of a car crash in which two subjects approach each other in slow motion and ultimately collide is offered by the film's formal structure. It illustrates symbolically mutual dependencies and influences.

The violence of the collision generates surprising body positions, a kind of memory archive inherent in the body that provokes confronting traumas. By means of crossfades, biographical flashbacks and flash-forwards are inserted into the slowed course of the accident.

LR

Thank you.

Bjørn Melhus
studied art and film at the HBK Braunschweig and at the California Institute of the Arts in Los Angeles. He has earned several awards for his work, which has not only been shown internationally but forms part of both private and public collections. Bjørn Melhus lives and works in Berlin and is a professor at Kunsthochschule Kassel Since 2003.

Yves Netzhammer
studied at the Hochschule für Gestaltung in Zurich. Since 1997 he has been developing a digital visual language for which he earned several awards. His work has been shown and included in museum collections worldwide. In 2007 he represented Switzerland at the Venedig Biennal. Yves Netzhammer lives and works in Zurich.

Liliana Rodrigues
graduated from the Universität Nova in Lisbon in 2002 with a master of arts degree in art history. She has worked internationally in art management and communications. She worked as a curatorial assistant for Dublin Contemporary 2011 and published on contemporary art positions. Since 2008 she is the head of sales & exhibitons at the Galerie Anita Beckers in Frankfurt.

Loop Narration and Hyperlayered Narratives

Eva Paulitsch

Uta Weyrich

Fig.1
»Things exist in a multiple versions, and one is not truer than the other.« –Parker Ito
#hybrid reality, img: Benjamin Franzki

Fig.2
The network-user navigates his mind and his profile as a dual entity through cyberspace.

1. Meanwhile…

In our modern consumerist society the influence of »#the digital« has expanded beyond the mere handling of digital facilities. It has been oozing into and growing within our consciousness, gradually taking effect on how we think and act. New routines become integrated into our daily lives, expanding the frontiers of the digital realm. #Social networks stand on the forefront of that development, binding people with a reward system of attention and »#Likes«.

The #Winners of that world are no longer only the ones who succeed in #life, but even more the ones who manage to share it most effectively. Platforms such as #Instagram facilitate that process and provide the aesthetic tools, in the form of filters, to visually upgrade the image for #mass appeal. With enhanced emotional qualities and a cosmetic facelift the image is then ready to walk the catwalk of social-networks competing for attention. Each of these »#Shares« eventually adds to the biography and character traits of the digital self, which can be constantly tweaked by altering, adding, or deleting information. With only the tips of his fingers the social network user navigates its mind and profile as a #dual entity through #cyberspace.

»Things exist in a multiple versions, and one is not truer than the other,«[1] says #Parker Ito and further states that today we live in a hybrid reality in which the space between the physical and the virtual is fluid; its transition however is not seamless.[2] It is that #hybrid reality in which people's behavior becomes sensitized toward acting in front of a camera, most predominantly that of a mobile phone. Some people are natural talents whereas others become awkwardly deranged in front of the lens of the mobile.

Besides this, other situational parameters, such as the relationship to those filming or the environment additionally influence the behavior of the person being pictured. With the activation of the #record/capture function, something ordinary turns into a #spectacle, interrupting our »common« reality.[3] For the person in focus the more decisive event is not necessarily the moment the function is triggered but the moment he notices it. It is when both events do not occur simultaneously that sudden

---

[1] »Today we live in a hybrid reality where the space between the physical and the virtual is fluid. Gone is the radical Internet of the 90s where logging off was an option. Though integrated into our daily lives, the web of today is fluid but not seamless.« Parker Ito, http://www.marktholander.dk/today_we_live_in_a_hybrid_reality.html

[2] »Sometimes people take really good photos and sometimes people look hotter offline. I heard a rumor that I'm hotter in person. More so now than ever things exist in multiple versions and one is not truer than the other.« Parker Ito, http://dismagazine.com/blog/36943/interview-with-parker-ito/

[3] It may soon be possible, through neurological implants to switch from our »common« reality to another computer-generated reality without all the clumsy machinery of today's Virtual Reality (the awkward glasses) (…) Slavoj Zizek: NO SEX, PLEASE, WE'RE POST-HUMAN!

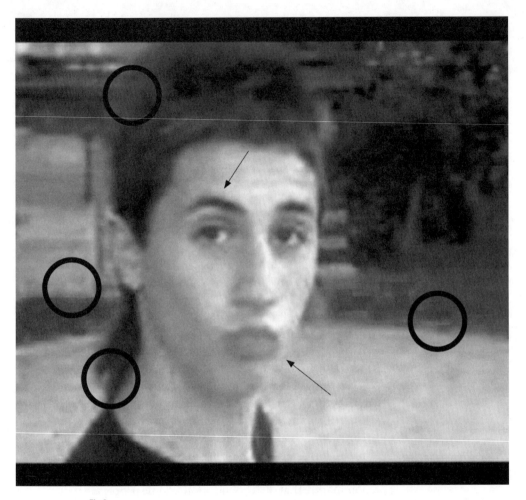

Fig.3
Some people are natural talents whereas others become awkwardly deranged in front of the lens of the mobile. #duckface #lifted eyebrow

Fig.4
»We shape our tools and thereafter our tools shape us.«—Marshall McLuhan, *Understanding Media* (1964) #mutal effect #hybrid reality

changes in character reveal one's most personal side. Every image and video mutually reveals information about the subject as well as whoever is behind the camera.

With the »#Selfie«[4] both positions merge into one. These images contain stories of fetishes and aversions, #fails, #wins, character and environment. Within this setting images and videos that haven't made the cut into social networks, that are maybe too personal or too revealing or just of no apparent value, are locked away in the private image gallery fortresses on mobile phones and computers, silently waiting for the »#Share«.

2. Loop Narration and Hyperlayered Narratives

Big #Loops make your mind go upside down. A longer loop facilitates generating a multitude of associations whereas a short loop rather refines one specific idea through #repetition. Due to its hypnotizing iteration however, sometimes a short loop viewed long enough is also capable of making the mind drift.

According to #Mark Twain »Ideally a book would have no order to it and the reader would have to discover his own.« Following this idea means that a story ideally would have to consist of a multitude of discrete narratives without a predefined role. Loops dissolve the meaningfulness of positioning and therefore render each event on an invisible circular #timeline ambiguous. Although without a standard starting point the linear course of sequences (in a video) still essentially directs the viewer always along the same track. (Therefore:) By constructing the entire loop out of #synchronistic looped sequences and distributing them in a spatial dimension, the viewer becomes the explorer of a #hyperlayered landscape in which he can move freely.

Removing/#editing out the linearity of narration, leaving the viewer solemnly interpretable codes as starting points, the viewer's mind is able to jump the #hyperspace of meaning from one semiotic base to another. Incorporating #vernacular video material (being constructed of cultural codes) acts as #Stimulus to enhance that experience. #Videos produced without the artists, only #collected by the artists—do elements as signifiers within these clips suddenly become some sort of digital #Objet trouvé? However, a distinction in relevance

---

[4] »A selfie is a genre of self-portrait photograph, typically taken with a hand-held digital camera or camera phone. Selfies are often associated with social networking and photo-sharing services such as MySpace, Facebook, and Instagram, where they are commonly posted. They are often casual, are typically taken either with a camera held at arm's length or in a mirror, and typically include either only the photographer, or the photographer and up to three other people.« http://en.wikipedia.org/wiki/Selfie

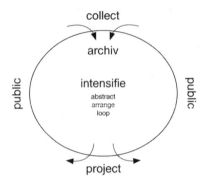

Fig.5
Artistic process of PW Video
#public #collect #archiv #intensifie

Fig.6
The looped video renders positions of scenes within its
#circular timeline #ambiguous

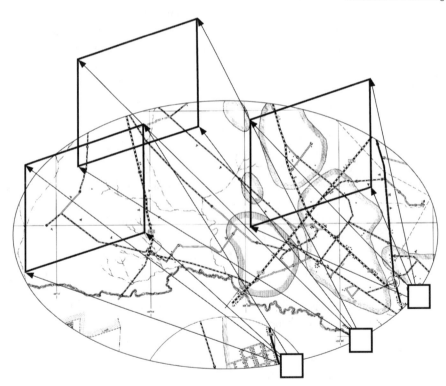

Fig.7
Through spatial arrangement of the projected material, the construction of narratives not also
varies with the mental but also the physical position of the viewer. #hyper layered landscape

between #protagonist, #background actor, #cameraman, or #object becomes needless, they are all code, meaningful or shallow depending on the viewer.

2.1. Artistic Process

A typical work process may consist of first establishing a range of #associations that may group certain videos for the #artist itself. By seeking the dialogue within the group or between another party, artists can overcome the limitations of unambiguous meaning defined by a single viewpoint. Through this the artist becomes less of an #author to represent a certain thesis but rather a representative to a variety of positions.

Creating loose #correspondences but no #causality is essential to the construction of interpretable narratives. The viewer has to receive just enough information to construct his own meaning, therefore any explicit features need to be chipped away from the sequences. Without sound for example, contexts become vague: speeches are dubbed within the viewer's mind, persons are abstracted from #identity becoming #representations of a social group, #friend or #foe. Using excerpts of a video may create room for speculation about events before and after the sequence. All of these artistic alterations seek to #maximize and #intensify the amount of #associations within a loop. Lastly through #spatial arrangement of the projected material, the construction of narratives varies not just with the #mental but also the #physical position of the viewer.

#Concept: Timm Häneke, Eva Paulitsch, Uta Weyrich
#Text #Graphic: Timm Häneke

#the digital #Social networks #Likes #Winners #life #mass appeal #Shares #dual entity #cyberspace #Parker Ito #record/capture #spectacle #Selfie #fails #wins #Share #hybrid reality #Loops #repetition #Mark Twain #timeline #synchronistic looped sequences #hyper-layered landscape #editing out #hyperspace of meaning #Videos produced without the artists #collected by the artists #Objet trouvé #protagonist #background actor #camera man #object #associations #author #causality #identity #foe #mental #physical position #associations #spatial arrangement

#hiphop #bros #distraction #car #roadtrip #haircut #music #bright

Eva Paulitsch and Uta Weyrich

Received their education from Staatliche Akademie der Bildenden Künste Stuttgart. Since 2003 they do artistic collaborations, exhibitions and projects. Some of their work selection includes: ZKM Medienmuseum Karlsruhe, Künstlerhaus Stuttgart, Museum Moderner Kunst Kärnten, Künstlerhaus Dortmund; Lothringerstraße 13 München, zeitraumexit Mannheim, E-WERK Freiburg, Thurgauische Kunstgesellschaft Kreuzlingen. Their research since 2011 includes: (re)presentations of everday life, mobile videos as a medium of expression by youth culture, and a three-year research project at Hochschule der Künste in Zurich.

The artistic vision of Eva Paulitsch and Uta Weyrich is dedicated to the many facets of everyday life. They find their inspiration on the street and on the cell phones of young people. Their interest is thus the »No Story Videos«—self-made films that are produced incidentally. They approach these young people and discuss the oft-forgotten footage and save it from deletion—by transferring it from the film makers' cell phones to their own, via Bluetooth. Since 2006, the two artists have thus been compiling a unique digital cell phone film archive, worldwide, that represents the foundation of their artistic work.

Timm Häneke

works as a graphic designer in Berlin. He currently works in culture/arts and publishing for and in collaboration with his clients. He designs the »transmediale, festival for art and digital culture« together with Manuel Bürger since 2012. He is concerned with cultural notions and the associative perception of design, political and social effects of aesthetics, representation and authorship.

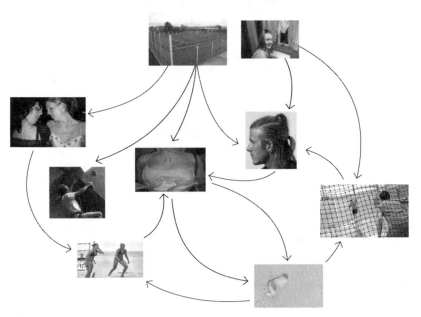

#climbing #chest # hands #zoo #exhaustion #sports #sand #ponytail

Eva Paulitsch and Uta Weyrich
Loop Narration and Hyperlayered Narratives

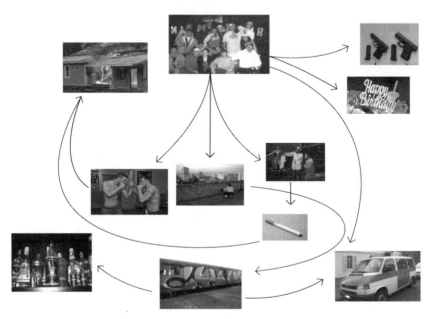

#concert #group #fight #houseparty #argument #streetwear #chaos #gang

Listening While Out Walking: A Brief History of Soundwalking

Sabine Breitsameter

1. Goethe's Venetian soundwalk

While Goethe was in Venice in October 1786, he was impressed not only by way the city looked, but also with how it sounded—which was mainly attributable to the ubiquity of water and water-related activities, particularly the inhabitants' verbal utterances: the *parlandi* and *canti* of the fishermen and mariners who were heard from near and afar on the city's canals and narrow streets. In a letter to his Weimar friend Charlotte von Stein, Goethe talks about how he wended his way among the various sources of sound for the express purpose of exploring the sounds embedded in the cityscape, as well as background noise. This was a perceptual experience that moved him deeply: »Why can't I also send a sound over to you,« he wrote to Charlotte, »so that you can take it in and answer me.—Good night, my love, I'm tired from all this walking around and climbing bridges.«[1]

2. Audio Walks as a Cultural Practice

It takes a certain amount of agility to explore a city on foot for the express purpose of eavesdropping on the sources of its sounds from various places, and in doing so internalizing new perspectives and deciphering the soundscape through one's ears. And indeed, this was a harbinger of the practice known as soundwalking that emerged in the late 1960s. The term was coined at the time by the Canadian composer and hearing researcher Murray Schafer, who thus endowed it with a method whose practice in the late 1960s already had a history, which I will be discussing here. The history of soundwalks can be regarded as a kind of ancient and early history of the newly emerging, experimental and expanded narrative forms that mainly emerged as multidisciplinary and audio-media art forms in the late 1960s and that still today—with their multifaceted presence in cultural manifestations—reside in the gray area between radio plays, radio art, electroacoustic music, sound installations, the visual arts, action art, and experimental theater.[2]

Listening and walking, being mobile while eavesdropping on the people around you: according to the prevailing cultural standards and perceptual customs, this does not appear

---

[1] Johann Wolfgang von Goethe, *Tagebücher, vol. 1, 1770–1810*, ed. Gerhart Baumann (Stuttgart, 1953), 270.

[2] It's difficult to come up with a genre name for this electracoustic art form that would do justice to its state of genre limbo. The problem with this state is that soundwalks are likely to suffer with particular severity the fate of all invisible arts, namely marginalization or even downright denial of its presence and relevance. But on the other hand, this state has something genuinely artistic about it by virtue of the genre in question being ineffable and out of reach for purposes of fitting it into the valuation categories of the art market.

to be an ideal combination. This is why, for the past two and a half centuries or so, concert halls have been requiring audience members to sit facing the stage and sit still while the musicians perform. Accordingly, concert recordings, classical music stations and the like, with their artistic productions such as radio plays and special programming, imagine the ideal listener to be a person who remains seated in one place. This is also the predominant instructional paradigm for both schools and colleges, with their lectures and frontal teaching. If, as the conventional wisdom holds, audiences and students didn't sit still and remain silent, carefully composed sounds and words wouldn't stand a chance of being coherently internalized. What's more, the conventional wisdom claims, walking around is totally distracting, whereas sitting still is not; for presumably the former reduces the intensity of the disposition to listen and the related ability to absorb what is being said or played.

In contrast, Goethe noted that simultaneous walking and listening in Venice gave him great insight by virtue of intensified perception and a deeper understanding of his surroundings. His Venetian soundscape experience, his aural attentiveness to the acoustic sensations as he took the pulse of the city, opened his eyes (and ears) to the art and culture of Venice and, by his own testimony, brought him closer to Venetians, their *mentalité*, and their concerns.

3. From the »Emancipation of Dissonance« to the Aesthetics of Sound

Against this backdrop, Goethe should undeniably be regarded as a pioneer of his era, for which the concept that everyday sounds—sounds produced outside of an officially musical context—could be objects of aesthetic contemplation was simply absurd. Up until the end of the nineteenth century, music and ambient sound were regarded as irreconcilable enemies—a dogma that began to soften during the latter half of the nineteenth century.

In this regard, Hermann Helmholtz's *Lehre von den Tonempfindungen*[3] (1863) would appear to be both the result of and catalyst for this aesthetic paradigm shift. And while Helm-

---

3
Hermann Helmholtz, *Die Lehre von den Tonempfindungen als physiologische Grundlage für die Theorie der Musik* (Braunschweig, 1863).

holtz noted the differences between music and sound, he then pointed out that the scientific method proves that from a physics standpoint sounds are nothing more than the movement of air—the difference between the experience of music and random or ambient sound being a culture-bound and time-related manifestation of aesthetics.[4]

At this same period, Richard Wagner's »Tristan chord« and »restless« harmonies ushered in a phenomenon that was referred to in the early twentieth century as »the emancipation of dissonance.«[5] This is closely related to Arnold Schönberg's development of the dodecaphonic system (likewise in the early twentieth century), in which the received wisdom about the value of harmony as opposed to dissonance and thus music as opposed to sound was no longer relevant.

This in turn paved the way shortly thereafter for everyday sounds to become an established artistic medium and for soundwalks to emerge as an auditory internalization method.

Italian futurism provides archetypal testimony to this evolution in the guise of Luigi Russolo's 1913 manifesto *L'Arte dei Rumori* (The art of noise), which declared: »Life in the past was silent. [...] Today sound has triumphed and reigns supreme over human sensibility.«[6] According to Russolo, twentieth-century innovations, particularly urban growth and ever-more-powerful machines, had changed the way people hear and in doing so had spawned a new aesthetic auditory yardstick. »We futurists have all deeply loved and partaken of the great masters of harmony. [...] Now we are weary of them and derive far more enjoyment from combining the sounds of trams, internal combustion engines, cars, and screaming hordes of people than attending yet another performance of the *Eroica* or *Pastoral*.«[7]

Accordingly, Russolo was an advocate of soundwalks, which, he felt, suspend visual impressions in favor of their auditory counterpart: »When we traverse a large city with more alert ears than eyes, it's a great pleasure to differentiate between the sound of water, air or gas in metal pipes, the roar of engines that undoubtedly drink and breathe like animals, the clang of valves, the hammering of pistons, the screech of sawmills, the bouncing of trolleys, the snap of whips and the sound of drapes

[4] See in this regard Helmholtz, *Die Lehre*, 551ff. (see note 3).

[5] Arnold Schönberg, *Die formbildenden Tendenzen der Harmonie* (Mainz, 1957), 186. See also idem., Harmonielehre (Leipzig and Vienna, 1911), 19.

[6] Luigi Russolo, »Futuristisches Manifest« (1913), in *Für Augen und Ohren. Von der Spieluhr zum akustischen Environment*, ed. Berliner Festspiele (Berlin 1980), 254.

[7] Ibid.

and flags. We love listening for the sound of window shades and orchestrating in our minds the sounds of stores, closing doors, the sound and fury of the masses, and the various sounds of train stations, spinning mills, printing establishments, power stations and underground trains.«⁸ The futurists regarded soundwalks not only as a receptive activity for the purpose of taking in urban auditory sensations and the sounds of modern machinery, but also as an opportunity to hone their ability to shape auditory input.

4. The Emergence of Multidisciplinary Approaches to Sound Art in the 1920s

The 1920s saw the emergence of sound as an established artistic medium. In the late 1920s the composer Kurt Weill, the radio maker Hans Flesch, the experimental filmmakers Dziga Vertov and Walter Ruttmann and the media theorist Rudolf Arnheim were all central figures in an evolution whereby everyday sounds became supremely important and were regarded as every bit the equal of music and the spoken word. According to the radio pioneer Hans Flesch, an innovative audio art form emerged that no longer fit the conventional definition of music, and that was making advances thanks to the new medium of radio.⁹

Groundbreaking in this regard was Walter Ruttmann's 1929 audio production *Weekend*, in which the sounds of a Berlin weekend were arranged chronologically and were designed and edited in a refined manner. Some of the sounds were precisely edited together as fleeting elements. This was possible only because the filmmaker had discovered a way to edit any sounds desired into a soundtrack, just as was done with film images.

Weekend—the first-ever reproducible version of a soundwalk—showed how easily, as with film, new sound production and reproduction technologies allowed for the transcendence of the classic unities of place, time and action. Hence these elements took on a movement-like quality thanks to the heterogeneous juxtaposition of locations, activities and moments. By forgoing images, *Weekend* also made abundantly clear the acoustic and artistic autonomy of acoustic phenomena. The strength of *Weekend* lies not in the illustrative references and

8
Ibid.

9
»Today we cannot possibly imagine what this as yet unborn creation might look like. Perhaps *music* isn't really the right word for it. Perhaps someday something new will be created from the uniqueness of electrical oscillations, from their process of transformation into acoustic waves; and this new entity will surely be tonal but will have nothing to do with music.« Hans Flesch, »Rundfunkmusik,« in Rundfunkjahrbuch, 1929, 150.

evocations of its acoustic materials, but rather in the passages where the eye and its illusions are shut out, thus exposing archetypal structures and the »interior« of materials, events, characters and the like that would otherwise be concealed by a visual »manifestation.« The auditory does not play the role of surrogate in the absence of visual stimuli, but instead affords insight into another manifestation of reality. These seeds of acoustic art that were sown by Ruttman began to bear fruit. But it would take political freedom and further technical advances for this phenomenon to truly take hold and for this essence of auditory design to flourish.

5. Concrete Music and Acoustic Found Objects

Artistic explorations of everyday sounds and their signifiers got going in earnest in post–World War II France under the aegis of state-owned radio stations, via concrete music (*musique concrète*) and its founders Pierre Schaeffer and Pierre Henry. Sounds of every description were incorporated into concrete music and were modified by manipulating audio devices, in the early days using turntables and then tape recorders. In this process, the original sounds underwent various manipulations, mainly by slowing them down or speeding them up in order to change their tonality; or they were edited so that only fragments of a sound such as its oscillations were used; or they were repeated in accordance with the principle of the closed groove that for we moderns evokes their roots in the vinyl record era and today is referred to as a loop, in homage to the era of tape recorders. In Pierre Schaeffer's view, sounds thus processed should be altered beyond recognition so that the original sound becomes unidentifiable. This practice of modifying sounds to the point of abstraction didn't always work, as one of Schaeffer's most renowned compositions, *Etude aux chemins de fer* (1948), shows. This piece consists of recorded train station, train, and locomotive sounds. Contrary to Schaeffer's dictum, the origin of the sounds could not be rendered completely unrecognizable. Even after careful manipulation of the recordings, the processed sounds still evoked mechanical rhythms, regular movements, metallic materials, powerful mechanisms and the sounds of shrill signals. In short, they evoke and compress the auditory world of train stations during the steam locomotive era.

The aesthetic starting points for concrete music are found objects such as railroads, auto traffic, steps, squeaky doors, humming tops, material sounds, radio sounds and so on. The narrative potential of this acoustic art form opens up in cases where the acoustic provenance cannot be rendered fully abstract, and particularly by juxtaposing the original sound with its acoustically processed abstraction. When the original sound is heard, its context is »illustrated« and the shades of difference between the original and the processed sound are transformed into a surreal auditory phenomenon comprised of imageless manifestations such as spatial, movement or material sounds. This creates a tension between imaged concretization and auditory abstraction, a tension whose narrative potential for audio art—including beyond that of concrete music—was developed and expanded in the subsequent decades.

6. Luc Ferrari's *Musique anecdotique*

Ironically, it was one of the disciples of concrete music who rebelled against its artistic principles: Luc Ferrari made strolls (*promenades*) and landscapes (*paysages*) the essence of his approach to composition[10] and in doing so explored the concept of the mobile and agile process of finding oneself in landscapes. No attempt is made to alter sounds or solely achieve spectacular auditory effects. His radio play *Lever du Jour au Bord de la Mer* (1969)[11] is composed of purportedly nonmanipulated everyday sounds. It takes us on an early-morning seaside soundwalk, during which we hear signs of the dawning day. Ferrari recorded the clatter of boat engines, the cry of seagulls, people beginning their daily activities and the twittering of crickets for a number of hours, made connections between the various sounds and then deftly edited the footage down to twenty-one minutes of documentary and artistic authenticity. Ferrari calls this kind of composition *musique anecdotique* (anecdotal music), a term that emphasizes its narrative potential.[12]

10
In works such as *Musique promenade* (1964–69) or *Petite symphonie intuitive pour un paysage de printemps* (1973–74).

11
Part of his four-part cycle *Presque Rien*.

12
In line with similar auditory and content principles—albeit using more striking editing methods—the beginning of Ennio Morricone's soundtrack for Sergio Leone's *Once Upon a Time in the West* is an acoustic journey through what appears to be the train station of a Wild West ghost town. The environmental sounds here symbolize not so much objects or persons, but rather states and atmospheres—in this case monotony, drowsiness and the absence of action.

7. Strolls as happenings and interventions

Ambient sounds took on tremendous importance in the late 1960s not only in contemporary music, but also in fluxus poetry, happenings, performance art, and new kinds of radio plays. What is particularly noteworthy in this regard is that multidisciplinary art forms emerged that do not fit into the usual artistic pigeonholes.[13] In the late 1960s, the concept of auditory art forms beyond music that Hans Flesch and others invented developed into a powerful artistic reality.

Inspired by fluxus poetry, dada, and happenings, the boundaries between acoustic art and visual art were blurred by artists such as Nam June Paik and Joseph Beuys. The idea of wandering around from place to place in search of strong sensory experiences culminated in a series of spectacular actions such as *24 hour Tour of Paris* by Ben Patterson and Robert Filiou in the summer of 1962 and Wolf Vostell's *Guided Tour Happenings* through the cityscapes of numerous urban areas. In his legendary *In Ulm, um Ulm und um Ulm herum*, participants were taken to twenty-four different locations such as military airbases, where they were subjected to the sound of jet engines; or to a field at night, where they were meant to eavesdrop on someone telling stories about their life.[14]

One of the driving forces behind the emergence of sound art—apart from a number of renowned flux poets—was the American composer John Cage (and others), with his composition 4'33(1952) that used the expectations of a piano concert audience to draw attention to the ambient sounds attendant upon such an event. Cage took up and popularized[15] Edgar Varèse's dictum to the effect that music should be »the organization of sound.«[16]

The widespread radicalization and antiauthoritarian rebelliousness in the wake of the social movements of 1968 legitimized and popularized the break with perceptual habits and with received opinion concerning materials, forms and reception. The desire to be provocative, along with antiart behaviors that aimed to criticize the art »system,« prompted many people to mobilize and take action in the early 1960s, whereby such events were seen as interventions that were intended to break through the uniformity and »normality« of the everyday.

---

[13] Central to this evolution were so-called new radio plays that combined elements from literature, music and performance art and were created by nonmainstream artists and writers such as the following: composers Mauricio Kagel, John Cage, Dieter Schnebel and Luc Ferrari, authors Franz Mon, Ernst Jandl, Friederike Mayröcker, Peter Handke, and Wolf Wondratschek; and audio artists Barry Bermange, Ferdinand Kriwet, and Paul Pörtner.

[14] Also see Lisa Bosbach, »Wolf Vostells Guided-Tour-Happenings. Interventionsstrategien im öffentlichen Raum,« in *kunsttexte.de*, no. 4 (2012), 6 pages. http://edoc.hu-berlin.de/kunsttexte/2012-4/bosbach-lisa-7/PDF/bosbach.pdf (accessed August 19, 2013).

[15] John Cage, »Die Zukunft der Musik—Credo« (1937), in *Für Augen und Ohren*, 112f (see note 6).

[16] Edgard Varèse and Chou Wen-chung, »The Liberation of Sound,« in *Perspectives of New Music* 5, no. 1 (1966): 18.

8. Max Neuhaus's *LISTEN* Strolls

Everyday perceptions as a critique of authority played a central role in the politicized climate of the late 1960s and early 1970s.¹⁷ This milieu enabled the American musician Max Neuhaus to develop soundwalks, albeit devoid of politicizing rhetoric. His LISTEN actions, which he first held in New York and then in various other US cities, sought to make hearing and listening more important and to shed light on creative cultural action: »As a percussionist I had been directly involved in the gradual insertion of everyday sound into the concert hall, from Russolo through Varèse and finally to Cage who brought live street sounds directly into the hall. I saw these activities as a way of giving aesthetic credence to these sounds [...].«¹⁸ Neuhaus described how his soundwalks at first ran counter to the audience's expectations, because when they arrived at the meeting place they were expecting a reading or concert. »I asked (the audience) to meet me on the corner of Avenue D and West 14th Street in Manhattan. I rubber-stamped LISTEN on each person's hand and began walking with them down 14th Street toward the East River. At that point the street bisects a power plant and [...] one hears some spectacularly massive rumbling. We continued, crossing the highway and walking along the sound [...] passing through the Puerto Rican street life of the Lower East Side to my studio, where I performed some percussion pieces for them.«¹⁹

Neuhaus regarded the LISTEN soundwalks as a new strategy that would help to promote acceptance of contemporary music: »The group would proceed silently, and by the time we returned to the hall many had found a new way to listen for themselves.«²⁰

9. Urban Sounds a an Artistic Movement

The intense and multifaceted seeking and finding of »unheard« urban sounds,²¹ making art out of these elements in their capacity as aesthetic and musical material led, during this era, to a sustained and broad-based art movement for which probably the best term is the *urban sounds movement*.²² The aim of making art out of sounds that either semantically or atmospherically made urban life palpable was to expand the descriptive and

---

17 Numerous cultural theorists of the time took the view that sociopolitical reality and the prevailing aesthetic art and design principles were inextricably bound up, and that this legitimized the artistic avant-garde. See Herbert Marcuse, Versuch über die Befreiung (Frankfurt am Main, 1969), 43f.

18 http://www.max-neuhaus.info/soundworks/vectors/walks/LISTEN/ (accessed August 19, 2013).

19 Ibid.

20 Ibid.

21 Neuhaus talked about the fascinating people that can be listened to under the Brooklyn Bridge: »[A] long fascination of mine with sounds of traffic moving across that bridge— the rich sound texture formed from hundreds of tires rolling over the open grating of the roadbed, each with a different speed and tread.« Neuhaus (see note 18).

22 It would be beyond the scope of this essay to discuss all of the phenomena that come into play here. The following are particularly noteworthy, however: the innovation (likewise strongly influenced by Neuhaus) entailed by sound installations in public urban spaces (see Neuhaus's 1976 work *Times Square*); and the emergence of radio art as an outgrowth of experimental radio plays, a representative and archetypal example (in terms of the subject of this essay) being the series of radio programs titled *Metropolis* (Studio für Akustische Kunst/WDR, 1970–). Audio artists such as Klarenz Barlow (Calcutta), Charles Armirkhanian (San Francisco) and Pierre Henry (Paris), the latter of whom was one of the founders of concrete music, composed poetic narrative-like portraits of large cities using everyday sounds.

narrative arsenal of verbal or visual-cinematic processes. Listening to urban environments both microscopically and macroscopically allowed people to break away from the sensory comfort zone afforded by sight and led to everyday but also surprising urban sounds, as well as to their opposite and contradiction. For in order to seek out individual sounds and soundscapes with a microphone, you also have to go on a soundwalk.

10. Soundwalks and Acoustic Ecology

Not sites worth visiting but rather sounds worth hearing: in the late 1960s the reality-constituting and imagination-promoting potential of soundwalks prompted the Canadian composer, sound researcher, and hearing educator Murray Schafer to combine these elements into a holistic method he called acoustic ecology. Based on a critique of audible manifestations, Murray explored the acoustic interactions between living organisms and their environment, along with the cultural-history relationship between the acoustic manifestations of an era and the hearing/listening related value that the era in question placed on them.[23]

The purpose of »drawing the hearer's attention to unusual sounds and environmental noises«[24] while encouraging the hearer to connect with soundscapes by totally devoting his attention to listening is to (a) enable the hearer to use his ears in a more differentiated fashion and thus incorporate the richness of the environment into his sensor perceptions; and (b) call into question the physical and mental tolerability of the acoustic environment and assess its aesthetic quality.[25]

Schafer's former research associate, the German-Canadian composer and music educator Hildegard Westerkamp, expanded and refined this method:[26] »A soundwalk is any excursion whose main purpose is listening to the environment. It is exposing our ears to every sound around us no matter where we are. [...] Wherever we go we will give our ears priority. They have been neglected by us for a long time and, as a result, we have done little to develop an acoustic environment of good quality.«[27]

The central aim here—apart from developing a critical sensitivity to a host of sounds that normally go unnoticed—is strategic listening as a starting point for one's own artistic

---

[23] Owing to space limitations, it is not possible for me to discuss Schafer's distinction between listening walks and sound walks. See R. Murray Schafer, *Die Ordnung der Klänge. Eine Kulturgeschichte des Hörens*, trans. and ed. Sabine Breitameter (Mainz, 2010), 347f. The geographer Justin Winkler succinctly elucidates this difference idem., »Landschaft hören.« http://www.musik-for.uni-oldenburg.de/soundscape/blatt6.htm (accessed August 19, 2013).

[24] Winkler, »Landschaft hören,« 347 (see note 23).

[25] Using soundwalks, audio recordings and cartography, Schafer and his associates investigated numerous acoustic environments for the 1970s World Soundscape project at Simon Fraser University in Vancouver, with the goal of analyzing the physiological, mental and aesthetic tolerability of these environments and identifying the factors that cause soundscapes to change. These investigations, which centered around the issues of the humanity of cities and their quality of life, were conducted in downtown Vancouver, the car-free city of Cembra in Italy and the village of Bissingen in southern Germany.

[26] In the late 1970s Westerkamp produced a weekly program for Vancouver's Co-operative Radio called *Soundwalking* in which he documented his hometown of Vancouver using a tape recorder, and commented on the sounds he heard. See Hildegard Westerkamp, »The Soundscape on Radio,« in *Radio Rethink: Art, Sound and Transmission*, ed. Daina Augaitis and Dan Lander (Banff, 1994), 87–94. His radio play *Kits Beach Soundwalk* (1989) explores the relationship between the acoustic imagination and experiencing reality with a critically listening mind-set.

creations; for soundscape compositions comprise an acoustic/ electroacoustic musical genre that uses the whole gamut of sounds from everyday activities and the natural environment. This genre encompasses the entire spectrum of sound-based compositions, ranging from film sound and sound installations to radio art and related acoustic arts. According to Westerkamp, listening proactively and creatively with »unguarded« (i.e., nonmediatized) ears during a soundwalk is the sine qua non for acoustic media creativity: »In the same way in which architects acquaint themselves with the landscape into which they want to integrate the shape of a house, so we must get to know the main characteristics of the soundscape into which we want to immerse our own sounds. [...] [L]ift the environmental sounds out of their context into the context of your composition, and in turn make your sounds a natural part of the music around you.«[28]

The Canadian soundwalk artist and researcher Andra McCartney explores this concept of a dialogue between the soundwalker and the environment: soundwalks as interventions in the everyday, whereby not only do the perceived sounds express something about the surroundings, but also the interactions between the surroundings and soundwalker are highly instructive.[29] What occurs here is a dynamic and an interaction in which environmental sounds are neither product nor object, but rather a process. Thus the narrative potential of the sounds discovered in this way expands into involvement on the part of the listener as participant, such that the preconditions for receptiveness are not limited solely to perception; for in point of fact the very existence of perception hinges on participation, a process of being in the world.

[27] Hildegard Westerkamp, »Soundwalking,« in *Autumn Leaves: Sound and the Environment in Artistic Practice*, ed. Angus Carlyle (Paris, 2007), 49. A revised version of this article can be found in *Sound Heritage* 3, no. 4 (1974): 18.

[28] Westerkamp, »The Soundscape on Radio,« 49 (see note 26).

[29] Andra McCartney, »Performing Soundwalks for Journées Sonores, Canal de Lachine,« in *Performing Nature: Explorations in Ecology and the Arts*, ed. Gabriella Giannachi and Nigel Stewart (Bern, 2005), 217–34; David Paquette and Andra McCartney, »Soundwalking and the Bodily Exploration of Places,« *Canadian Journal of Communication* 37, no. 1 (2012): 135–45.

Sabine Breitsameter
is a professor for sound and media culture at the Hochschule Darmstadt since 2006. She was cofounder of the master program Soundstudies at the UdK Berlin from 2002 to 2008. Since the mid-1980s she works as author, director and editor, especially for audio drama productions for the ARD and in North America. She has done numerous workshops, presentations, publications and artistic audio productions. She is a research and art director for several symposiums and festivals, among others: Akademie der Künste Berlin, ZKM Karlsruhe, Ars Electronica Linz, as well as Documenta Kassel.

Varieties of Cinematic Narrative

Martin Seel

Literature and cinema by no means have a monopoly on the ability to tell stories, for virtually all art forms have an affinity for narrative. Stories are not confined to stage and screen: we find them in the visual arts as well, which have developed their own storytelling genres; and indeed, traces of narrative can even be found in instrumental music. And in cases where music, whether as art songs or pop songs, but particularly in opera, is combined with texts and dramatic representations, it becomes a genuinely narrative art. Even architecture, which unlike sculpture harbors no particular narrative potential, can establish a connection with the narrative arts through the use of frescoes, murals, and the incorporation of other visual forms.

The fact that so many art forms have an affinity for narrative is no accident, for this tendency has its roots in the human predilection for narrative. Doers are by their very nature storytellers, they are dependent on storytelling cultures. In virtually every area of life, doers need their own stories and those of others in order to make sense of what is going on around them. The art of storytelling extends far beyond the realm of art. For storytelling is a universally and anthropologically rooted practice which is, by creating and absorbing artistic narrative, continued as well as transgressed.

One break with tradition invariably leads to another, a process mainly driven by the ceaseless evolution of various media and the venues where stories are made, performed and watched and/or listened to. So long as art forms fade away and give rise to the transformation of artistic creation, storytelling will remain a part of civilization; although a displacement of narrative comprehension can be expected at any time. This was true of movies from the get-go, particularly when it came to feature films and their complex interactions with other narrative arts. And while we don't watch movies solely for their gripping stories, insofar as they are plot-oriented variants and variations are the lifeblood of storytelling in this realm as well.

Storytelling

Storytelling enables us to make sense, for ourselves and others, of what has transpired or could potentially transpire.

Narratives establish relationships between circumstances and events, and show us how and why specific kinds of events and changes have or could have occurred. Stories relate the events that happen to individuals or collectivities or tell us how and why certain events have come to pass, whether they be everyday events, political transformations, scientific discoveries, or natural evolutionary processes. Stories situate fictional or factual events in a context whose transparency can vary, as can the complexity of the manner which the story is told. Cause-and-effect relationships are pivotal in this regard, for stories either reconstruct or imagine which circumstances and events gave rise to which other circumstances and events. This also includes another very significant constellation of factors—namely the affective or rational attitudes of those who were or are being affected by them. In the final analysis most stories, whether of the everyday or artistic variety, revolve around the activities and sufferings of human beings (or fictitious creatures of all kinds that reflect the human realm). In the context of external forces, the perceptions, moods, feelings, beliefs and intentions as well as their impact on the behavior of the narrative's protagonists are depicted. These types of entanglements are the drivers of a given story, which often begins with a prominent event as a starting point and moves toward a significant end point: a resolved conflict, a fateful outcome, or the chiaroscuro of an ambiguous ending. Regardless of whether a story involves the success or failure—or the success *and* failure—of actions, activities, projects, ambitions and hopes, a story always aims to depict the particular present, past and/or future significance of the story's events for those involved in them.

There is a multistep continuum along which narratives revolve around the real or the unreal. Insofar as human or human-like protagonists are involved, virtually all stories recount what transpired or might transpire in a certain situation, or the fate that might befall or has befallen specific characters. This holds true in particular in cases where unexpected or unforeseeable events, up to and including totally random events, come into play—and is above all the case when individuals or collectivities experience events resulting in the collapse of their frame of reference; for here, stories have the ability to show us, or at least attempt to show us, how the events are causally and motivationally interconnected. In doing this, stories make explicit how the events that follow one another follow *from* one another.

Storytelling provides a completely different kind of insight than that obtained with nomological explanations;[1] for narratives specialize in a depiction of the individuality of factual or fictional biographical and historical processes that defy law-based reconstruction. In narratives, the actual or apparent contingency of a narrative's events is not always completely eliminated. Happenstance and chaos need not be set aside, eliminated or overcome over the course of a narrative, for they can also be shaped and depicted. Particularly in artistic narratives, it is precisely the contingency of developments that is depicted, as is the case in Heinrich von Kleist's narratives *Das Erdbeben in Chili* and *Michael Kohlhaas*, the depictions of war in Claude Simon's novel *La route des Flandres*, and in movies such as Robert Altman's *Short Cuts* (USA 1993) and Alejandro González Iñárritu's *Amores Perros* (Mexico 2000).

Besides, narratives tend not to depict the particularities of event contexts in contrast to a possible generality of their content. By depicting examples of individual events, they can tease out the general contours of a situation, conflict or fate.

The point of view from which a particular event is reported can be of exemplary significance, too. The manner in which a narrative is shaped enables it to portray a point of view, regardless of what is actually being represented. This comes to the fore not so much through explicit value judgments, but rather and above all via narrative style. Narratives constructed in this manner lend a particular intensity not only to the subject matter of the story, but also to the narrative itself. Such narratives show us or call into question how reasonably or unreasonably, how justifiably or unjustifiably, or how sensibly or irrationally a given situation was handled, as well as the extent to which both active and passive participants experienced justice or injustice, reasonableness or unreasonableness, the probable or improbable, and the amazing or banal. The »how« of a narrative—through its choice of words, choice of scenes, composition from beginning

---

[1] Michael Hampe, *Kleine Geschichte des Naturgesetzbegriffs* (Frankfurt am Main, 2007), 22–28.

to end, in lingering on certain events and glossing over others, in delaying and speeding up the pace of events, and through other stylistic devices—sheds a specific light on the »what« of the narrative, that to one degree or another casts judgment on the story's events. In other words, every story opens up a normative and interpretive perspective on the narrated events.

This perspectivity of narratives is a very peculiar thing indeed. For the points of view opened up by narratives on the actions, sufferings, opinions and desires of a story's characters are never fully congruent with those of its protagonists, who to one degree or another have a different take on things. Contrasts of this nature can be found in ordinary everyday stories as well, but are far more prevalent in elaborate religious, historical and political narratives and the narratives of myth and art.

Cinematic Narratives

Movies bring into play their own particular set of opportunities in all of the aforesaid respects.[2] More than any other narrative form, filmed stories can be told from the inside out because in movies everything that is seen and heard during the film occurs in a horizon of time and space that is absent from the action seen on the screen. This phenomenon enables movies to guide the viewer's perceptions in and through a visually and audibly palpable world—one which of course can be related to and which can refer to the real world in widely varying degrees. This in turn enables narrative films to depict in a particularly intense manner situations from the characters' vantage points and at the same time provide perspectives on the events that unfold in a given situation, that differ from the characters'. This is one of the reasons why the events dramatized in movies (and particularly in major feature films) on the one hand are rendered understandable, but on the other hand are turned into opaqueness, as has always been the case in the great fictional narratives.

Right up until the end of John Ford's *The Searchers* (USA 1956), it remains unclear what motivates Ethan Edwards—a man about whose life since joining the Confederate army we are given little information—to spend years searching for his abducted niece Debbie, or what prompts him to take this young woman in

[2] Martin Seel, *Die Künste des Kinos* (Frankfurt am Main, 2013), chapters 3 and 5.

his arms and bring her »home,« despite his having said on a number of occasions that her life is no longer worth living. Abbas Kiarostami's *Taste of Cherry* (Ireland/France 1997) recounts what is probably the last day in the life of a man who intends to commit suicide, without giving us the slightest hint as to why this is so. The hero of Paul Greengrass's *The Bourne Supremacy* (USA 2004) knows as little as the audience (who watch his involvement in a search punctuated with violence) about how he has become the person he is. During the course of the film he and the audience find out fragmentary facts about his past (which is to some extent revealed in *The Bourne Ultimatum* [Paul Greengrass, USA 2007]). Each of these films primarily centers around its main characters, who are on screen for much of the time. But these characters are led through a cinematic narrative space that neither the characters nor the audience truly understand; and as a result their horizon and that of the audience is continuously exceeded.

Each of the aforementioned films broke new narrative ground. John Ford (and other filmmakers) rang in the late-western phase in the annals of cinema; Abbas Kiarostami developed a new aesthetic of slow pacing; while Paul Greengrass ramped up the pace of action movies. Every intense movie opens up new cinematic narrative possibilities, as is also the case in other narrative art forms. This applies not only to filmmaking eras and styles such as film noir, the *Nouvelle Vague*, the *Neue Deutsche Kino*, the New Hollywood and so on, but also to individual movies whose new narrative devices also alter the genres to which they belong or are related to. One need only think of *Dancer in the Dark* (Lars von Trier, Denmark 2000), *Memento* (Christopher Nolan, USA 2000), *Code Unknown* (Michael Haneke, Germany/France/Romania 2000) or *Kill Bill* (Quentin Tarantino, USA 2003/2004).

Despite the heterogeneity and variety of even the few films mentioned here, there is a basic formal characteristic that is common to all feature films. For the particularity of how cinematic narratives unfold arises from the special temporal form of their storytelling; in that the viewer sitting in a darkened movie theater unavoidably undergoes the movie's unfolding, everything happening in the movie is entirely dependent on the here and now of the movie's audiovisual appearing, including all of the inaudible and invisible elements continuously surrounding it. A movie theater audience is extraordinarily present to that which is being narrated because it is particularly engaged in the narration, i.e., the audience is captivated by the narration and its progression. The audience members find themselves in the here and now of an audiovisual appearing that rubs off on everything that is depicted in the narrative arrangements of a temporal and causal succession of elements. In feature films the pace of the cinematic story constitutes the here and now—particularly in cases where the story is set in the distant future or past.

On the other hand, in most narrative genres the events being recounted are irretrievably out of reach once they are told. This is because agents as members of historical life forms move in a time frame extending beyond their actual present. »To exist historically is to perceive the events one lives through as part of a story later to be told,« Arthur Danto laconically observed in his study of the grammar of historical narratives.[3] »The cognitive openness of the future is required if we are to believe that the shape of the future is in any way a matter of what we choose to do.«[4] Our ability to act only exists within a constellation of possibilities that are not clearly discernible and whose significance for our own lives we cannot foresee or predict. It is only after the fact that we are able to absorb, in the form of narrative elucidation and interpretation, the coming to fruition and the processes entailed by individual or collective action. And even narrative films cannot neutralize these conditions, for even cinematic narratives are imbued with the temporal and cognitive asymmetry of narrative communication. Like most narrative fictions (provided that they are not open to stage improvisation) movie plots are hermetic, no matter how open their endings may be. They too engage in a process whereby the options open to their characters grow ever more limited. They too continuously depict the actions of their characters against the backdrop of a bygone future. But by virtue of their narrative form, movies have a different relationship to past time than is allowed in other narrative art forms. For everything that happens in a movie

[3] Arthur C. Danto, *Narration and Knowledge* (New York, 2007), 342–83, here 343.

[4] Ibid., 353.

unfolds in a mode that can be termed the bygone present, or past-time present. A past-time space comes into being as the film unfolds. The film takes its audience with it into this, its own space and time. It is in this irreversible space-time that the stories told by movies unfold.

Beyond cinema

Narrative cinema has of course long since emancipated itself from its dependency on movie theaters as its main viewing venue; for today, movie theaters are just one of a number of places where people watch films. But the conditions under which movies are watched have changed in non-movie theater venues. The temporal diktat of movies can be suspended at any time on TVs, computers or mobile devices. The irreversibility of a cinematic narrative can be interrupted with a remote control, i.e., by pressing the Pause button or fast-forwarding or rewinding, among other possible viewer interventions. Films no longer move from setting to setting with their audiences in the old-fashioned way; for now audiences can in a sense move from place to place with movies, in a manner that movies cannot hope to do. But at the same time, this has changed the temporal form of movie watching. Viewers can now incorporate a movie's own timeline into their own schedule and in doing so make their own rhythm overlap with or disrupt the move's rhythm. They can dole out the imposition of a movie's here and now in an infinite number of ways, on their own terms. They can endow the movies of their choosing with a strong, weak, occasional or dominating presence within the here and now of their own lives.

These new forms of taking in cinematic narratives also color the manner in which they are shown. The changed circumstances under which films are now viewed have given rise to new film-production modalities. The fact that films can now be viewed on all kinds of screens has occasioned a greater number of films that are specifically produced for viewing using new technical media. One need only think of the so-called new series that have sprung up mainly in the US, but elsewhere as well. *The Sopranos* (HBO 1999–2007) centers around unresolvable conflicts between family and clan. *The Wire* (HBO 2002–2008) is set in an allegorical big-city cosmos of conflict between individuals and institutions. *In Treatment* (HBO 2007–2010) is about the fragile relationship between human closeness and distance, as exemplified by psychotherapy. *Mad Men* (AMC 2007–) centers around careers driven by sexism and machismo in the 1960s and in doing so constantly asks the audience to consider to what extent these tendencies have (or have not) been eliminated. *Homeland* (Showtime, 2010–) unfolds in an atmosphere of unending paranoia with which the war on terror has infected everyday life in the US.

What is new about these and other series lies not solely (and often not particularly) in a multidimensional narrative form, or in the fact that these series dramatize social, political and existential themes using complexly drawn characters who fundamentally change over the course of the series. The main innovation of these series lies in the open form of their episodic structures that allow for myriad variations in, digressions from and suspensions of the main story arcs; and this in turn allows for transformation of the baseline structures of the series themselves. The narrative structure of these series explodes the homogeneity of their episodes, thus lending these series an epic quality that is driven by the varied overall pace of their seasons and makes for compelling viewing. These series open up new horizons for the telling of what are to all intents and purposes stories without an end, while at the same time providing proof positive that cinematic narratives are themselves a never-ending story—and are thus another testament to the inexhaustibility of narrative as a cultural practice within and outside of the artistic realm.

Martin Seel
is a professor of philosophy at Johann Wolfgang Goethe-Universität, Frankfurt/Main. Among his book publications are: *Eine Ästhetik der Natur*, Frankfurt am Main, 1991; *Versuch über die Form des Glücks* (1995); *Ästhetik des Erscheinens* (2000)/ *Aesthetics of Appearing* (2004); *Sich bestimmen lassen. Studien zur theoretischen und praktischen Philosophie* (2002); *Die Macht des Erscheinens. Texte zur Ästhetik* (2007); *Theorien* (2009); *111 Tugenden, 111 Laster. Eine philosophische Revue* (2011); *Die Künste des Kinos* (2013).

No Hurry, No Time: On the Proper Length of a Film

Vinzenz Hediger

Why does a motion picture, as a rule, run for one-and-a-half to two hours? Why not two thirty-two minutes, or nine hours?

The normal length of 90 to 120 minutes is almost as old as cinema itself. It established itself in the early part of 1910, when the feature film supplanted the short film in the cinema as the standard format of distribution. Compared to so-called one-reel films, feature-length motion pictures had decisive commercial advantages. They could be shown in larger houses for a higher admission price than the usual 10-minute films. They appealed to a larger audience and attracted middle-class patrons who set the consumer standards for other customers. Most important, with the introduction of the full-length motion picture and the relocation of the cinema into larger venues, re-created on the model of the opera house, the film industry achieved credibility in the eyes of the banks. Only with the large cinemas, which were simultaneously investments and properties serving as collateral for bank loans, were film producers able to access the bank credit required for the production of expensive full-length motion pictures. The feature film running time from 90 to 120 minutes was thus the film industry's ticket to big business.

Motion picture length, however, remained variable to a degree. In the 1920s, prestige productions sometimes ran for four or even six hours, especially some German films. The first version of *Das indische Grabmal* (*The Indian's Tomb*), filmed in 1921 by Joe May from the screenplay by Fritz Lang and Thea von Harbou, ran for more than four hours, Lang's *Nibelungen* of 1924, more than five hours. These films were, however, shown in two-hour parts with an intermission, or spread over two or three evenings. The two-hour parts usually had separate titles. In the case of the *Nibelungen* the episodes were called *Siegfried* and *Kriemhilds Rache* (*Kriemhild's Revenge*). In the 1950s and 1960s, the four-hour film made a reappearance in Hollywood in the form of such lavish productions as *Lawrence of Arabia*, *Dr. Zhivago* or *The Sound of Music*, while Fritz Lang returned to the format with the last of three versions of *Das indische Grabmal*, the first one he directed, in Germany in 1958. In all these cases the format of two parts with an intermission was retained. Even so, however the program was composed of basic units of a duration of two hours, today's normal feature-film length.

As long as films were only to be seen in movie theaters, there was little alternative to the standard length as far as audiences were concerned. Up until the 1960s, the theatrical program always included short films: cartoons or animated films and short fiction films in the USA; while German law required that documentaries, so-called *Kulturfilme*, were shown, in order to fulfill an educational mandate from which the cinema was only freed upon the establishment of the public television broadcasters. The heart of the program was always, however, the motion picture. In Germany in particular the audience often perceived the shorts as reprimands and used them as an opportunity to converse. Nor did the introduction of home video change the dominance of this standard length. On the contrary, the first marketable video system, Betamax from Sony, introduced in Japan and the USA in 1975, was intended as a »time-shifting device,« to record TV programs one would otherwise have missed. The recording time amounted to sixty minutes, matching the programming pattern of American television, which consisted of one-hour windows. Sony lost the battle against the competing system VHS (Video Home System), developed by Matsushita/Panasonic together with JVC, which hit the market in 1976, mainly because the VHS cassettes offered a storage capacity of two hours and were thus equipped to record and reproduce feature films.

Although motion pictures for home cinema projection have been in existence since the 1920s, when Pathé reduced a number of films to the 9.5 mm Pathé Baby Format launched in December 1921, making them available to the home market. These films were, however, reduced in a double sense: The reel or filmstrip not only amounted to 9.5 mm instead of the world standard of 35 mm, established as global standard within the provisions of an international convention in Paris; but the films were also substantially cut and, as a rule, consisted of a half-hour of reedited highlights, linked by subheadings or intertitles. It was all about the reduction of content, as was practiced by the magazine *Reader's Digest*, which made its first appearance on

February 5, 1922, only two months after the introduction of Pathé Baby and, to great and still continuing success, published »articles and book extracts of enduring value,« as per its slogan for the German-language editions. As opposed to *Reader's Digest,* which had 16 million subscribers, the coverage of Pathe's 9.5 mm system remained limited to a relatively small circle of wealthy consumers. Only upon introduction of the VHS video recorder did home cinema become a mass phenomenon. The decisive advantage of the VHS recorder was precisely the fact that it enabled full-length motion pictures to be recorded and reproduced.

One of the main reasons why the standard length continued to be the norm was due to the distributors and cinema operators. If directors had a say, films would probably be longer than two hours. The idea that the director is the author of the film is of French origin. In 1920s France the concept of the auteur, also served to distinguish French films from their industrially produced American counterparts by virtue of their quality as artistic works attributable to a single author rather than to a collective. The auteur concept reached Hollywood by way of New Wave filmmakers like Godard and Truffaut and the influential film critic Andrew Sarris, then working for the *Village Voice* in New York. The directors of the new Hollywood cinema like Scorsese, Coppola or Cimino considered themselves auteurs, with long-term consequences. The director's union, the Director's Guild of America, or DGA, revised its standard contract in the 1990s to enforce the official attribution of authorship to the director by inserting »a [name of the director] film« in a film's credits. Part of this role change was the demand by many directors to be freed from the standard guidelines of film marketing, which involved cutting their films to the standard two-hour length. But the marketing people prevailed, for the simple reason that a film lasting two hours can be shown more than once an evening as opposed to one of three hours' duration. In a marketing regime where audiences pay a standard ticket price regardless of the film's length or production budget, and where they watch the film from the beginning to the end and are in the cinema at the beginning of each performance, i.e., pay specifically for each screening of the film, extending a film over the standard length of two hours incurs a substantive loss of revenue. Thus, the director's vision of the appropriate length of the film comes into its own only with the Director's Cut, which is usually released on DVD. Ideally, this version of the film only hits the market a certain time after the DVD release of the theatrical version, which enables the movie to be sold again to its fans. The Director's Cut, then, is designed to make both the director and the marketing department happy.

It is thus not difficult to ascribe the dominance of standard film length to economic causes. No dominant cultural form, however, has ever been shaped by the wishes of bookkeepers alone. Another kind of economy, the economy of time, must be added to the commercial equation.

As Fassbinder said, one goes to the cinema to have an experience: to be involved in a narrative world or—to use the metaphor of newer media and narrative theory, the metaphor of immersion—to immerse oneself. The film is not life but, when it succeeds, can become a major part of the lives of its viewers. For this to happen, a certain investment is required. One must spend time with the characters, allowing them to become integrated within the concerns of one's own existence. The film, however, should not get out of hand. One is supposed to watch the entire film, at least as far as classical cinema is concerned, but the film must not become life's major purpose. A two-hour film fits well into the daily routine, where other things have priority, such as work or sleep. The standard length of a film roughly corresponds to the amount of time that remains after all those basic things have been done. It is no accident that a football game with an interval lasts just as long as the average motion picture. Cricket, on the other hand, is evidently a sport for those who need their sleep, but don't have to worry too much about work; otherwise how could cricket games last for days at a time? Baseball, on the other hand, seems to be a sport for people who work, but don't necessarily need much sleep. The games begin mostly in the evening and can go on for as long as four hours. Football and feature films are aimed at people who work hard and sleep a lot.

Economy, according to French philosopher Georges Bataille, always implies overspending and waste. The telos of the entire discipline of deferral that is at the heart of economic behavior, states Bataille dialectically, lies in the excesses of *dépense,* of overspending. Thus, as the law implies its transgression—for only when violated is the norm effective—are time economy and time wasting interdependent. In the economy of standard motion-picture length its suspension must therefore be contained and in the film must live on a sense of that confusion which it masters by imprinting the order of narrative upon the experience of time.

To watch a film in a cinema nowadays means, as a rule, watching it from the beginning to the end. Historically speaking this practice is relatively new. When Hitchcock brought *Psycho* to the silver screen in 1960 the advertising slogan ran: »This is a film you must see from the beginning—or not at all.« Those familiar with the movie will understand what Hitchcock, who exercised an unusual amount of control over his marketing campaigns, had in mind: Anyone missing the first half hour of *Psycho* will be waiting in vain for the appearance of Janet Leigh, the film's star. The famous shower sequence comes after twenty-five minutes; thereafter Janet Leigh's character is dead and no longer in the picture. The slogan was necessary because the films of the 1960s were still screened in the *séance continue* method. The cinema opened at 11:00 a.m. and the film ran as an uninterrupted loop until midnight. Only in the 1950s did New York cinemas begin publishing starting times in their advertising. Hitchock had to discipline the audience through advertising for *Psycho* to work the way he intended. By the late 1960s, most cinemas (with the exception of the now-defunct institution of the Bahnhofskino, which continued to show films with a continuous admission system until the mid-1980s) moved to a system where entrance was only granted at the beginning of the film.

Before 1960 and Hitchcock, however, it was normal to watch films from the middle to the middle. »This is where we came in« is an American colloquial expression with which cinema goers used to indicate to each other that they had now seen the entire film. The loop is no invention from the age of video installation, but rather the default mode of film viewing prior to 1960. For that reason, classic Hollywood films work with many redundancies and always explain everything at least twice: not because the directors and screenwriters assume their audience to be far from clever, but because they reckon that people are likely to barge in sometime midfilm and must quickly get their bearings in the narrative world. Godard's statement in defense of his erratic narrative style already applied to Hollywood films: You have a beginning, middle and an end—but not necessarily in that order. As far as Hollywood films are concerned, however, it is important that in the end—i.e., from whatever point one has begun watching—one sees the entire film.

Incidentally, Andy Warhol critized just this formulaic constraint with his production of *Empire*, an experimental film shot on 16mm in the night from June 25 to 26, 1964. Warhol justified his eight-hour film by contesting that with conventional films one was not able to leave the cinema and go shopping without missing something, and that he considered it necessary to shoot a film that granted its audience just such liberties. His work was an eight-hour rebellion against the discipline of being quiet and remaining seated during a movie. Godard's narrative style, on the other hand, can be read as an effort to preserve the puzzling character of film viewing in the classic era of Hollywood cinema, by inscribing the narrative disorder of the classical film-viewing experience into the very structure of his postclassical films. In this sense, too, Goddard is a film historian, his cinema a living cinematic history. On the other hand, such recent films as *Inception* or *The Sixth Sense*, for instance, which tell their stories in slivers and fragments—thus forcing us, among other things, to ultimately recompose the entire fictional world we are accustomed to viewing in a reliably linear manner throughout the film—can also be read as contemporary attempts to re-create that narrative confusion that was once an elementary component of the cinematic experience.

But sublating the economy of time does not only mean reconstructing the original complications and complexities of film comprehension. Sublating, i.e., suspending and dialectically reaffirming the economy of time, also means transgressing the scope of the film's standard format.

As a film critic and a film scholar, one is invariably asked: what is your favorite film, or the film that most recently impressed you? For some time now my standard answer to this question has been Wang Bing's *West of the Tracks* (2003), a thee-part, nine-hour documentary about the deindustrialization of the northeast Chinese city of Shenyang. Mentioning the film's length usually helps to underline the seriousness of the endeavor and thus to bolster the standing of my chosen profession, but the tought of a nine-hour film also makes most questioners swallow hard. Watching this film—or Béla Tarr's *Sátántángó* (1994, likewise nine hours), or Andy Warhol's *Empire* (1964, eight hours)—seems like a dizzying prospect. Interesting to hear, so long as you do not have to subject yourself to the experience.

Meanwhile excess length and the vertigo that comes with it have been elevated to a key element of aesthetic experience in the visual arts. Two of the most discussed and most controversial works of the last decade are without doubt Douglas Gordon's installation *24 Hour Psycho* (1993) and Christian Marclay's film-based work *The Clock*, winner of the grand prize at the Venice Biennale in 2011, and which has since been touring the world's great museums. Gordon's *24 Hour Psycho* is an extended, slowed-down projection of Hitchcock's *Psycho*, protracted throughout an entire day. *The Clock,* for its part, is a compilation of extracts from various motion pictures in which a clock is featured. The excerpts are selected so that they present a chronological sequence. The work is usually performed in synchrony with local time, whereby the respective time corresponds to the exact time displayed in a specific extract. Outside of the museum, Marclay's work is currently only accessible in the form of brief youTube clips, shot by museum visitors who record excerpts of the work and publish them on the social network platform. While these clips may or may not constitute an infringement of copyright, some of these clips attempt to maintain the basic principle of synchrony. One presentation of a YouTube excerpt from *The Clock* reads: »In order to respect the concept of Christian Marclay's work spectators are kindly requested to play this video at 0.04 pm, local time.« Like *24 Hour Psycho*, *The Clock* lasts twenty-four hours, or a complete day. »If time is passed«, the commentary to the YouTube clip continues, »Please wait for tomorrow or another day.«

Obviously nobody, not even the artist himself, expects anyone to spend a whole day watching *24 Hour Psycho* and/or *The Clock*. Whereas one usually listens to a symphony in a concert hall until the last chord has died away—unless, of course, it is played so badly that one leaves the hall in protest, or is so outrageously innovative that it is unendurable—no artistically minded audience would choose to spend a whole twenty-four hours—the running time of a performance of *24 Hour Psycho* or *The Clock*—actually watching these works.

According to a study by a sociologist of art the average length of time a museum visitor lingers before a moving-picture installation, or audiovisual performance is ninety seconds to three minutes (which happens to be the average length of a scene in a classical Hollywood film). Nor do *24 Hour Psycho* or *The Clock* manage, as a rule, to capture the audience's attention for any longer. It is safe to assume that no one has ever stayed long enough to confirm that the two works actually last for twenty-four hours. The public take their information about the length of these works on authority from curators and critics, just as one believes the statements about artistic technique and format usually displayed on a small plaque beside a painting in the museum; without testing the technique for oneself, or measuring the painting. Even when in an enthusiastic review of Marclay's *The Clock* published in the *New York Review of Books* British novelist Zadie Smith recommends her readers take a sleeping bag and provisions and pitch camp in the exhibition room that recommendation is ostensibly made tongue-in-cheek. Neither *24 Hour Psycho* nor *The Clock* is about absorbing the work in its entirety, but about recognizing and understanding the principle.

The duration—twenty-four hours, a whole day!—is obviously a key element of these works. It shows that these works are indeed of a limited duration. Athe same time, a work that lasts for a whole day extends beyond any reasonable limit for time-based art. »If time is passed, please wait for tomorrow or another day»: the day of the performance or screening relates to any following day, and the performance of the work potentially repeats itself ad infinitum. Works that run for twenty-four hours will, in a sense, run forever after. Through their duration these works approach infinity in yet another sense. An extremely slow projection of *Psycho* may have its appeal, but an extremely slow projection of *Psycho* that lasts for an entire day is overpowering: Through their duration these time-based films are constructed in a way that necessarily exceeds and even explodes the horizon of subjective temporal experience. The works of Gordon and Marclay create a second nature that is, as Kant said: »great beyond all comparison«: their duration lends them an aspect of the sublime.

Other films can also convey the experience of the sublime, even while more or less respecting the standard feature-film length. Stanley Kubrick, the favorite director of every educated German who otherwise knows little about cinema, specializes in such moments; one thinks of the spaceship sequence to the music of Strauss at the beginning of *2001—A Space Odyssey*. David Lean also comes to mind, who examined the incommensurability of man and desert in *Lawrence of Arabia*.

The intimation of infinite duration of works such as *24 Hour Psycho* and *The Clock* and the experience of the sublime that this intimation entails only forms a pre- or intermediate stage, however. Beyond it lurks something else.

When I once asked a colleague from Paris whether he had ever watched *24 Hour Psycho* in its entirety, he responded with an indignant cry of, »Do you think I'm crazy!« He may have been on to something. In his novella of 2010, *Point Omega,* Don DeLillo explores what happens when someone actually subjects himself to the full-length version of Douglas Gordon's work. DeLillo's answer: He turns into Norman Bates.

Beyond the normal length of a film, way beyond, lurks madness. So then, why does a film, as a rule, last for 90 to 120 minutes and not 20 minutes or nine hours?

The answer could be that the standard length strikes the correct balance between narrative time and life time, between time economy and time wasting. However, it is not only the audiovisual arts—which always can be (and usually are) trusted to be at the forefront of the production of new cultural meanings—which are currently engaged in de- and reconstructing the established framework of a motion picture's standard length.

With digital network communication and the emergence of such video platforms as YouTube and Vimeo, the short form, the splinter and the fragment have become a standard in their own right, beside the norm. One can describe the posting of film clips on YouTube as a form of externalized recollection. As a rule, one does not recall a film's entire plot but only particularly impressive scenes. Trailers are systematically composed of such scenes: They show the film in *futurum exactum*, thus from the perspective of the anticipated recollection of the coming film. Trailers contain the scenes that an enthusiastic audience would supposedly talk about once they have seen the film. YouTube clips with excerpts from films can thus be described as trailers in reverse: recollecting the actual remains of a film in an ongoing conversation in a social network.

One could think of YouTube and Vimeo video clips as the apogee of the principle of time economy. One would be mistaken, however. Linking video clips and passing the links back and forth via e-mail or posts on social networks like Facebook, has become a privileged mode of communication for Internet users, and a privileged new mode of wasting time.

At the other end of the spectrum the long form also has established itself as a standard beside the norm, even beyond the occasional—and commercially irrelevant—excesses in length of such art house directors as Béla Tarr and Wang Bing. »With the new series, we can finally do what we always wanted to do in the cinema back in the 1970s,« said Martin Scorsese recently, while discussing his collaboration on the HBO series, *Boardwalk Empire*, a kind of *Sopranos* in the Prohibition era about a gangster boss from the gambling town of Atlantic City, New Jersey, which just started its fourth season. *Boardwalk Empire* belongs to the current crop of quality television series such as *Mad Men*, *Breaking Bad* and *The Wire*, for which *The Sopranos* was a trailblazer in the 1990s. These shows are preferably produced for cable networks that cater to a paying audience of consenting adults and are thus allowed to show their paying subscribers more sex and violence than the free TV broadcasters (and as much as, or more than, in a motion picture). In somewhat suspicious unanimity critics agree that these TV series are the new and better cinema and obviously as good as, if not superior to novels. Whether that is actually the case is a matter of conjecture. Hardly mentioned in this discussion is the fact that the format of the long feature film with production values comparable to cinema but produced for television originated in Germany with Fassbinder's *Berlin Alexanderplatz* from 1980 (13 episodes plus epilogue, 894 minutes) and *Heimat*, the chronicle of a village in Hunsrück, which Edgard Reitz tackled in the early 1980s as an answer to the American TV miniseries *Holocaust* and which for more than three decades has evolved into a three-part narrative with a total running time of 3131 minutes, or just over 52 hours. *The Sopranos*, the mother of all American »quality« series, consists of six seasons and 86 episodes, at 55 minutes each, and has a total running time of more than 7,300 minutes or 121 hours, but Reitz and Fassbinder can still claim to be the pioneers of the format. Even the GDR made a pioneering contribution to the very long form, albeit in the documentary field. At a total length of 2,535 minutes *Wir Kinder von Golzow* by Wilfried and Bärbel Junge, which follows the destiny of a village in Oderbruch from the building of the Berlin Wall up to 2006, in twenty individual films, is the longest-running, and longest longitudinal documentary project in the history of documentary filmmaking. At least for the time being.

To the excessive length of the quality-TV series now corresponds a new form of excessive viewing behavior or, as the Americans call it, *binge viewing*. Binge viewing describes viewing a great number of episodes in succession, sometimes for entire days and nights. Such viewing behavior, which constitutes an entirely new form of wasting time on watching films, only became possible once the series had broken loose from the rigid program structure of commercial television and became freely available on DVD and via streaming and file-sharing platforms.

The industry was quick to respond to the new trend toward binge viewing. Online video distributor Netflix, which leases DVDs through the mail and operates a huge streaming platform and brought about the end of the classical video store with its business model, has recently entered the production side of the film and television business in an attempt to become less dependent on Hollywood studios and cable TV companies for their supply of programming. Their first venture into production was *House of Cards*, a series revolving around political intrigue in Washington, directed by such renowned Hollywood directors as David Fincher and Joel Schumacher. On February 1, 2013, Netflix published all thirteen episodes of the first season of *House of Cards* simultaneously on its Web site, with the express intent of meeting binge-viewing demands.

The digital availability of film formats, fragments and short clips, as well as feature-length series, thus undermines the balance between life time and film time enshrined in the standard length of the motion picture. Ever-expanding narratives and new patterns of viewing contribute to a sublation of the economy of time, i.e., a suspension that is at the same time, dialectically, an affirmation. For in episodes of overspending, to quote Bataille again, lies the ultimate goal and meaning of economic behavior.

Incidentally, *Nuit et Brouillard* by Alain Resnais (1956) lasts thirty-two minutes, while Claude Lanzmann's *Shoah* (1986) lasts nine hours. *Nuit et Brouillard* consists of footage filmed at Auschwitz and photographic archive material with a commentary by André Cayrol and music by Hanns Eisler, and explains how the concentration camp functioned. When the film premiered at the Cannes Film Festival the government of the Federal Republic of Germany lodged a formal complaint with the French foreign ministry; apparently in the 1950s Bonn did not feel answerable for the crimes committed by the Nazis in the quite the way that became the norm, at the very latest, with Willy Brandt's visit to the Warsow ghetto in 1970. Among the things that Resnais got right with *Nuit et Brouillard* was the film's length. At thirty-two minutes, it could easily be televised in prime-time slots after the evening news, which for many years happened every time a Holocaust denier made a controversial public statement in France. *Shoah*, for its part, which consists only of interviews with survivors at the locations of the atrocities and important places in their lives after the concentration camp, is a monument in time. There has been much debate about the representation and the representability of the Holocaust over the last few decades, beginning with the controversy surrounding the US miniseries *Holocaust* and including in particular the sharp divide in public opinion occasioned by Spielberg's *Schindler's List* (1994) which the assembled European cinema intelligence from Lanzmann to Godard (and back) condemned as an inexcusable transgression. Lanzmann's own film and that of Resnais are, apart from the initial controversy surrounding Renais's film, were always exempted from criticisms of the kind that were leveled at *Holocaust* and *Schindler's List*. Quite to the contrary, these two films usually serve as the reference points in the debate, as the paradigms of how the problem of the representability of the Holocaust should be addressed.

From which we can learn that the proper relationship between film and history, a contentious relationship if ever there was one, may well be, at least in part, a matter of the right length of the film.

Vinzenz Hediger
is a professor of film at Goethe-Universität Frankfurt since 2011. He obtained his doctoral degree with a dissertation on American movie trailers from the Universität Zürich, where he was also a postdoctoral research fellow until 2004. In 2004 he became the Krupp Foundation professor of film and media at Ruhr-Universität Bochum. He is a cofounder of the European Network of Cinema and Media Studies (NECS, www.necs.org) and the founding editor of the *Zeitschrift für Medienwissenschaft* (www.zfmedienwissenschaft.de).

Narrating Life: The Biopic and Its Deconstruction in Todd Haynes's *I'm Not There*

Juliane Rebentisch

Before we can turn to Todd Haynes's tribute to Bob Dylan, *I'm Not There* (2007), a feature film and also an exploration of the biopic genre, we should ask ourselves what a biopic actually is. The entry in the German Wikipedia provides the following definition: »A film biography, also *biopic*, refers to a film that narrates the life of a historically verifiable person in fictionalized form. The biopic is one of the oldest film genres. [...] A biopic need not narrate the life story of a real person from birth to death; it is sufficient to place one or more periods of the person's life in the context of a dramatic and cinematic whole. One of the central criteria of the biopic is to use the name of the real person. It is usually assumed that the person portrayed has some sort of social relevance.«[1]

The stories that are told in biopics are as varied as life itself. Nevertheless, as Wikipedia explains, »it has been shown that figures of deviance have been particularly intriguing to screenwriters and producers. These are people whose lives break with convention and who usually no longer follow the norms of conventional morality.«[2] It is no coincidence therefore that biopics very often focus on artists. The »legendary« status of the figure is »updated and enhanced«[3] in the film. This also means that the biopic is less interested in a detailed representation of a particular life than in those aspects that fit into the stereotype of the proximity between genius and madness.

»The trouble with conventional biopics,« according to of the apt comments of a blogger named Prospero, »is that they invariably fall short in both the ›bio‹ and the ›pic‹ departments. That is, they don't have enough narrative momentum to engage as dramas, but they have too much fudging and falsifying to qualify as biographies. If you already know about the person being profiled, you're annoyed by how much is distorted and omitted. If you aren't an expert going into the cinema, you're never sure how much of what you see on screen actually happened in real life. [...] Biopics always try to box their subjects' unruly lives into a rigid rise/fall/rise structure. They always prioritize drink-and-drugs-hells over artistic achievements.... Quite a few of us grit our teeth at the prospect of two-and-a-half formulaic hours of aging make-up and pop psychology punctu-

---

[1] See the German *Wikipedia* entry on »Filmbiographie«. URL: http://de.wikipedia.org/wiki/Filmbiografie (accessed August 12, 2013).

[2] Ibid.

[3] Ibid.

ated by a sequence in which someone composes their best-known hit in a flash of inspiration.«[4]

An example of a conventional biopic about a musician, who incidentally also collaborated with Bob Dylan,[5] is *Walk the Line* (2005). The film recounts an episode from the life of Johnny Cash. Apart from the remarkable musical performances by Joaquin Phoenix and Reese Witherspoon, who as Johnny Cash and June Carter also undertook performing all the vocals themselves, this is a biopic of the type previously described. At the heart of the plot is Cash's pill addiction, which is psychologically explained by a childhood conflict, and overcome at the end thanks to his love of June Carter. In between scenes are interspersed showing how Cash finds his musical style, or of June Carter composing *Ring of Fire* at the kitchen table.

*

Unlike Johnny Cash, Bob Dylan is from the outset not an obvious candidate for such a venture. If Dylan is a legend, then it would be the legend of someone who, by taking on very different, and partly incompatible identities, eludes the logic of the legend itself, creating something like an antilegend instead. During a Bob Dylan conference that took place a few years ago in Frankfurt, which was a kind of summit meeting of German Dylanologists, Rüdiger Dannemann asked rhetorically: «Who is the real Dylan? The hobo or the dandy, for whom the attitude of *L'art pour l'art* seems to have been tailored? Is he a descendant of Rimbaud, Baudelaire, or Wilde, or an admirer of Woody Guthrie? Is he the protagonist in the video to *Subterranean Homesick Blues*, the first significant example of this genre, in which the principles of semiology are demonstrated? Having already got to know the Nashville Skyline Dylan, the Gospel Dylan, the broken eighties Dylan, the Dylan of the Never Ending Tour, etc., we now know that a one-dimensional Dylan does not actually exist. There is only the thinking and playing artist Dylan who constantly redefines and reinterprets his art anew, who lives to destroy the imagery he has created, again and again.«[6]

»It is the existential motif of self-choice, the Sartre-inspired pathos of a permanent self-shaping,« added Axel Honneth, »which Dylan brings to mind in the musical articula-

---

[4] Prospero, »How to make a good biopic« (2011). URL: http://www.economist.com/blogs/prospero/2011/11/new-film-my-week-marilyn (accessed August 12, 2013).

[5] Dylan and Cash recorded a session together on February 17 and 18, 1969, from which stemmed, among other things, the great duet version of *Girl from the North Country*.

[6] Rüdiger Dannemann, »Maskenspiele der Freiheit. Songwriting zwischen Folk, Rockavantgarde, Literatur und Philosophie«, in *Bob Dylan. Ein Kongreß*, ed. Axel Honneth, Peter Kemper, and Richard Klein (Frankfurt am Main, 2007), 50–69, here 62f.

tion of freedom and detachment. Amid protest movements and hippie culture, two social currents that raised a great deal of expectation, either in terms of good political conduct or of authenticity, Dylan defended the right of the individual to be able to radically reshape the self—by constantly testing new arrangements, by the eccentric phrasing of his songs, and by the blasé tone of his voice.«[7]

For the time being, I would like to leave the motifs of freedom attributed here to Dylan uncommented, and wish only to summarize the following: Bob Dylan represents a challenge for the traditional genre of the biopic. His character withdraws again and again into other identities, between which there are leaps that not only elude the continuity of the normal rise-fall-rise-plots, but which trouble any biographical project that would try to integrate all these identities into the developmental logic of *one* life. Anyone still wanting to take up the challenge would probably first have to consider that Dylan himself had a few encounters with film, in which the problem of his elusiveness was also reflected in a particular way.

The first character that Dylan played in a film, namely in Sam Peckinpah's *Pat Garrett & Billy the Kid* (1973), was rather significantly called Alias. That is the perfect name for the performative principle that Bob Dylan epitomizes for most of his critics. He is always himself, always Bob Dylan, but forever, it seems, as someone else.[8] In 1975/76, Dylan himself directed a film, *Renaldo & Clara*, which was released in 1977 in a four-and-a-half hour version and was a major flop, both with the audience and with critics. In this actually rather disastrously disorganized film, Bob and Sara Dylan apparently appear as themselves, yet playing the two characters Renaldo and Clara. Ronnie Hawkins, the former singer of Dylan's backing group, The Band, plays Bob Dylan. Allen Ginsberg plays a character named Father, Joan Baez is a so-called Woman in White. Other big names of the cultural scene at the time play themselves or their colleagues. Documentary and staged sequences alternate. The film is marked by its historical time of the 1970s, especially with regard to contemporary taste for *The Children of Paradise*. The world of the street performer depicted there, as well as the enthusiastic play with

[7] Axel Honneth, »Verwicklungen von Freiheit. Bob Dylan und seine Zeit,« in Honneth, Kemper, and Klein, *Bob Dylan*, 15–28, here 20f (see note 6).

[8] Stephen Scobie, *Alias Bob Dylan: Revisited* (Calgary, 2004).

gender roles and the masks of rock theater can be seen in this context as well. Nevertheless, more interesting than the passion for employing the mask and confusing role-play, through which the directing star tries to elude, is that the film *as a film* accomplishes this elusion in quite another, particularly cinematic way.

Critic Pauline Kael wrote in the *New Yorker:* »More tight close-ups than any actor could have had in the entire history of film. He's overpoweringly present, yet he's never in direct contact with us. [...] We are invited to stare [...] to perceive the mystery of his elusiveness—his distance.«[9] In his penchant for close-ups, Dylan is clearly influenced by Andy Warhol. In an interview with Jonathan Cott about questions relating to his film aesthetics, Dylan said that what matters is having confidence in film. Further: »You know who understood this? Andy Warhol. Andy Warhol did a lot for American cinema.«[10] It is certainly no coincidence that Warhol's films are closely related to a reflection on the phenomenon of the star. Warhol had discovered, in around 1965, that not only are the stars in Hollywood's film industry clearly *made*, they are produced. Bert Brecht's son, Stefan Brecht, theater critic and one of the most important chroniclers of the New York theater and performance scene of the 1960s and 1970s, stated in his legendary book *Queer Theatre* that Warhol's »genius for abstraction« led him to recognize that it is not so much how big a star is, but the quality of the stardom itself that hooks consumers on the commodity of film. Warhol was able, Brecht continued, »to isolate this quality and to successfully market it under the name ›superstar.‹«[11] Unlike what one might assume, however, Warhol's sense for abstraction did not aim to distill an ideal image from the visual potential of the amateur actor. On the contrary, the point of most of his *Screen Tests* is that the neutral arrangement–the confrontation of a person with a running camera, without script or stage directions—will sooner or later capture what falls out of the controlled image, or what cannot be absorbed by it. Perverting what Walter Benjamin in his famous essay on the work of art calls the »test performance«[12] of the film actor, so characteristic of film production, oriented as it is toward the ideal take, Warhol turned the situation of the screen tests themselves into the decisive event. Thus, only at first glance

[9] Quoted from Diedrich Diederichsen, *Eigenblutdoping. Selbstverwertung, Künstlerromantik, Partizipation* (Cologne, 2008), 103.

[10] Jonathan Cott, »Bob Dylan Interview # 1« ((1977), in idem., *Back to a Shadow in the Night: Music, Writings, and Interviews 1961–2001* (Milwaukee, 2002), 47–73, here 69.

[11] Stefan Brecht, *Queer Theatre: The Original Theatre of the City of New York: From the Mid-60s to the Mid-70s* vol. 2 (Frankfurt am Main, 1978), 113f.

[12] Walter Benjamin, »The Work of Art in the Age of Its Technological Reproducibility,« in idem., Selected Writings, vol. 3, 1935–1938 (Cambridge, MA, 2003), 101–133, here p. 111.

do Warhol's fictitious *Screen Tests* aim to determine the potential of performers to become images or their willingness to perform. In fact, they do not seek to identify certain performative achievements or talents, but to capture moments in which we no longer read a role, pose, or legend in the face of the star because the face itself is there to be read. Such moments usually happen to film, they just slip in. For the photographic technique of the camera registers movements that are no longer subject to, or at least are not fully covered by any representational function. It produces snatches of unsuspecting contingency casually or accidentally, in which the generic character of the role, but also the generic character we address as the image of the star, recoils from the expression of the singularity of this face. Such moments should not be confused with an expression of authenticity, which »good acting« would bring forth. For they occur in the mode of outward appearance, which is more inaccessible and more puzzling than the psychological inwardness we are expected to decipher in so-called character acting. This can of course be observed in nearly all *Screen Tests*, not least, however, in the *Screen Tests* # 82 and # 83 from 1966, whose subject—in the double sense of the word—is Bob Dylan.

The effect of Warhol's *Screen Tests*, in any case, is obviously not authenticity, but rather a certain opacity which results from that which cannot be fully absorbed by any representational performance. The indexical »optical unconscious«[13] of film, which makes us aware of things that usually escape our pragmatic perception of the world, does not display any true identity of the person behind all the roles or poses, but a potentiality, which eludes every definition of a specific identity (be it the self-chosen one, or a foreign one determined by the director). The difference at issue here, in other words, is not that of authentic person and role, but of determinacy and indeterminacy.

*

Precisely herein is Warhol relevant to classical discussions of how to relate the figure of the actor to the problem of freedom. And his »genius for abstraction« has made him recognize a specific feature of film in this regard, which he then threw into sharp relief. Warhol's capacity for abstraction, one might

---

13 Ibid., 117.

say, is bound to a profound insight into the particular ontology of film. As Stanley Cavell writes in his book on autobiography, *A Pitch of Philosophy*, continuing from an argument begun in his book on film, *The World Viewed*, it is significant for the ontology of film »that the medium of the motion picture reverses the ascension in theater, of character over actor; on film the actor is the subject of the camera, emphasizing that this actor could (have) become other characters (that is, emphasizing the potentiality in human existence, the self's journeying), as opposed to theater's emphasizing that this character could (will) accept other actors (that is, emphasizing the fatedness in human existence, the self's finality or typicality at each step of the journey).«[14]

The motif of freedom that Cavell addresses here, the potentiality of human life and the journey of the self during which it may take on several roles, is not the same as another approach to theorizing freedom that might be suggested with respect to the actor as well as with respect to Dylan, namely that there is something like a real self behind the respective social roles that confidently takes them on or discards them. From this perspective, the stage actor could appear even freer than the film actor. While a stage actor always reveals a certain distance from the role, which he shows in his own particular way, the film actor seems largely to merge with his roles. Indeed, the role that exists in film is generally not independent of the actor, there are no characters in the theatrical sense, but only types that are defined first and foremost by the stars that occupy them uniquely (one thinks of De Niro's *Taxi Driver*, for example). Movie stars therefore, in contrast to theater actors, are intrinsically not interchangeable. But Cavell argues for a different point, namely, that the film star makes us aware of the potential to be very different in the next film (think again of De Niro and his amazing versatility, documented in his filmography). The model of freedom, which is at issue here, is not an inner distance of the self to predefined roles (according to the model of the theater actor), but the changeability of the self. The separation under consideration is then not between real and fake identity, but, once again, it is between identity and potentiality, between the determinacy

[14] Stanley Cavell, *A Pitch of Philosophy: Autobiographical Exercises* (Cambridge, MA, 1994), 137.

of an identity embodied right now, and the possibility of yet undetermined future identifications.

When looking at Bob Dylan's identity changes from this perspective, he no longer appears as an exceptional subject, slickly playing his part with everyone else, but more like the prototype of a subjectivity that can only realize freedom in a process in which the tension between the freedom to take a distance from the social, a freedom to take a distance from identity attribution, and a freedom to be realized in the social, a freedom to (re)define one's identity, is carried out dialectically.[15] Such a process can precisely not be described in terms of an independent meta-subject that faces all its social roles in an indifferent and superior way. Rather, the subject and its sovereignty are also questioned in the changes from one identity to another. The subject does not free itself of previously valid self-understandings from some imaginary position of superiority with regard to its own identity, but by having experiences that run counter to previously affirmed self-perceptions. The changes are not brought about voluntarily by the meta-subject, but on the contrary, are rooted in experiences of self-difference that motivate the subject to grasp the new meaning of its subjectivity from a distance towards itself.[16]

The relationship of such an image, of a life taking on changing social identities, to narration, is of course complicated, or better: eccentric. In his misleadingly titled book *Erzähle Dich selbst (Tell yourself)*, Dieter Thomä argues that it is precisely impossible to tell of your own life, at least if you aspire to capture life as a unity, by constructing a biographical narrative.[17] At the very moment that I come into conflict with myself, when I am at odds with myself, when I quarrel with how I have seen myself thus far, the narrative that I have set up for myself will fall into a crisis as well. And this can affect both the prospective dimension of my self-understanding, my self-conception, as well as the retrospective dimension of my self-understanding, the way I see my own past.

Also, the material of one's own life, which is the basis for the narrative of one's background, is reexamined in the light of another experience. A previously overlooked detail can suddenly

---

15 See Axel Honneth's thesis that Dylan stands for the tensions the pervade the term freedom itself: *Bob Dylan*.

16 For a thorough discussion of this dialectic, see Juliane Rebentisch, *Die Kunst der Freiheit. Zur Dialektik demokratischer Existenz* (Berlin, 2012).

17 Dieter Thomä, *Erzähle dich selbst. Lebensgeschichte als philosophisches Problem* (Frankfurt am Main, 2007).

appear as a »warning of the coming crisis.«[18] Thus, under certain circumstances we might stretch the threads of the narrative anew, forward as well as backward. Of course, the fresh narrative can also not provide a final, comprehensive representation of one's life. Rather, such crises and turns in life make it clear that there is always something untold and undetected in life. This means acknowledging a difference between narrative and life. However, acknowledging this difference does not diminish the constructive function of narrative for life. Rather, according to Thomä, insight into this difference can help us to define this function in a more precise way. For it now becomes clear that narratives fulfill *situative* functions in our lives. From this perspective, narration appears as the medium in which a subject tries, again and again, to become intelligible, both to itself and to others. One could also say it appears as a medium of justification. The awareness of the situative role of the narratives with which we tell ourselves not only implies an awareness of the difference between narrative and life, but also respect for the potentiality, the inexhaustibility of human existence.

*

The connection between Dylan and Warhol has led us to certain motifs relating to the theory of freedom and narratology that, in reference to the potentiality of the film actor, support a certain correspondence to the ontology of film. But this connection, or so it seems, has led us far away from the genre of the biopic, at least as it is usually understood. Not only does the narrative scheme of the ordinary biopic contradict every awareness of life's potentiality, the conventional biopic also brings film closer to theater, at least with regard to Cavell's theory of the differences between the film actor and the theater actor. Joaquin Phoenix is not Johnny Cash, as everyone knows. The vague resemblance merely underlines the difference. The emphasis on uniqueness does not lie on the side of the actor playing a character, with which the actor will always be associated. The emphasis on the uniqueness in the biopic lies instead on the side of the character occupied by the actor: Johnny Cash. In biopics, the characteristic change in the relation between actor and role, and vice versa, could account for why the Oscars

[18] Ibid., 259.

for the best acting performances are given remarkably often to the lead actor in biopics. It is exactly because everyone knows the original that biopics demonstrate very clearly what it means to transform into someone else. However, in the case of *Walk the Line*, the Oscar did not go to Phoenix, but to Reese Witherspoon for her portrayal of June Carter.

The challenge that arises for the biopic, in view of the antilegend Dylan, is immense. Todd Haynes has addressed it. But *I'm Not There* was certainly not his first biopic project. He became known for the short forty-three-minute film *Superstar: The Karen Carpenter Story* (1987), which uses Barbie dolls to narrate Karen Carpenter's life from her discovery in 1966 to her death from the effects of anorexia in 1983. All the sets were made in this miniature size, while Karen Carpenter's anorexia was illustrated from scene to scene by carving away bits from the face and arms of the Karen doll. The plot follows the usual biopic interest in the people behind the roles and the failure of the person to fulfill her public image and to handle the pressure. Nevertheless, *Superstar* differs significantly from other movies about female stars. One might think, for example, of *The Rose* (1979), based on the life of Janis Joplin with Bette Midler in the lead role. Or of the biopic *What's Love Got to Do with It* (1993) with Angela Bassett, about Tina Turner's liberation from Ike and the start of her solo career. While both of these films live from the blood-sweat-and-tears performances of their leading actresses, Bette Midler and Angela Bassett, the demand for authenticity in such forms of representation is, in Brechtian fashion, unequivocally negated by Haynes to allow one to see something general through the construction: the generality, as it were, of anorexia as a woman's disease, which can be interpreted as a »disincarnation«[19] of the female ideal (Barbie). *Superstar* thus functions as a *Lehrstück* in the Brechtian sense. The family of Karen Carpenter, who do not come off particularly well here, were not thrilled, of course. Richard Carpenter sued and his claim was acknowledged, mainly because of the unresolved status of the music rights. The film was actually taken off the market and was then not available for a long time. In the meantime, one can watch it in full on YouTube. The title of the film, *Superstar*, refers undoubtedly less to Warhol than to

19
Christina von Braun, *Nichtich. Logik, Lüge, Libido* (Frankfurt am Main, 1990), 460.

the famous Carpenters song about the longing of a woman for the person behind the star, who remains absent in the wrong proximity his image communicates: »Your guitar, it sounds so sweet and clear. But you're not really here. It's just the radio.« In our context, however, the theme of the person-star difference, which generally gives the biopic its vitality, is less crucial than the fact that Haynes turns the Carpenter legend into a *Lehrstück,* thereby marking the narrative as a construction that stands at a distance from the life that provides its material.

Naturally, a further precursor of *I'm Not There* is Haynes's film *Velvet Goldmine* from 1998. The plot is based on *Citizen Kane,* wherein a reporter, played by Christian Bale, tries years later to investigate the mysterious disappearance of a glam rock star. He travels around, talking to people who knew the star and who then recall in flashbacks. The star is played by Jonathan Rhys Meyers and is obviously inspired by David Bowie and, somewhat less conspicuously, Marc Bolan. Ewan McGregor plays a character reminiscent of Iggy Pop and Lou Reed. Moreover, the plot is based on elements from the story told in Bowie's *Ziggy Stardust* album, which is known to end with the character's ambivalent rock-and-roll suicide. The rapprochement toward the stars of the glam rock era is carried out here through strict fictionalization. The characters all have different names, the allusions to events in the lives of historical figures are blended with references to the fictional worlds that have been created by them; Bowie mixes indistinguishably with Ziggy. While *Velvet Goldmine* is not a biopic, it does nevertheless contain a cinematic approach to a star who, like Dylan, is known for his chameleon-like character, eluding through his use of changing personae, namely Bowie. It is no coincidence that Bowie's *Hunky Dory,* in my opinion his best album, contains not only Bowie's famous *Changes,* but also a song titled *Andy Warhol,* and finally a *Song for Bob Dylan.*

*

Now *I'm Not There* (2007) *is* considered a biopic by the director, but its subject, which also inspired its title, is precisely the antilegendary, elusive character of Dylan. The film was originally meant to be called *Alias,* after Dylan's character in *Pat Garret and Billy the Kid,* but then an American television action series with the same name came out in the meantime.[20] *I'm Not There* nevertheless hits the nail on the head in that it is about the inscrutability of the self vis-à-vis all narratives of justification that one might, or even Dylan himself might have told about Dylan at some point. It is about a potentiality of the self, a freedom from determination that keeps that self on its journey.

»People are always talkin' about freedom,« a voice says in the trailer of *I'm Not There*, »Freedom to live a certain way. Of course the more you live a certain way, the less it feels like freedom. Me, I can change during the course of a day. By waking I'm one person, and when I go to sleep, I know for certain I'm somebody else.«

To turn to the theme of the freedom from identity determination in cinema is to deal with the difference between narrative and life, and to find a form for this difference. To do this means, of course, to turn against, let's be frank, the ideology of the biopic that hides this difference in authenticity claims, of the real story as well as of the characters. The latter being a claim, of course, that requires the utmost acting discipline. Yet Haynes by no means simply turns away from using such acting performances, as he did in *Superstar*, and he also does not negate the immersive, illusionistic potential of film. The most obvious and yet far-reaching intervention that Haynes makes in the biopic is quite different, in that he multiplies his subject into seven very different characters, played by six actors—including a woman (Cate Blanchett) and a black boy (Marcus Carl Franklin). None of these characters receive the name Bob Dylan—a further break with the traditional biopic. The boy's name in the film is Woody Guthrie, like the protest singer revered by Dylan, and it is also his, not Dylan's words that are written on the guitar case that the boy takes on his freight train journey through the USA: »This machine kills fascists.« At the same time, the boy is referred to at the beginning of the film as »fake.« His role is also linked to the stories Dylan once spread about his youth as a runaway and that emerged for a time in the official Dylan biographies, until they were revealed not to be true. Ben Winshaw plays the sharp-tongued poet, who calls himself Arthur Rimbaud. The folk and

---

[20] Todd Haynes in conversation with Jim Hoberman on the occasion of a Haynes retrospective at Cornell University. URL: http://www.youtube.com/watch?v=eMfr_pzBU18 (accessed August 8, 2013).

protest songwriter Dylan of the period when he worked together with Joan Baez (who is called Alice Fabian in the film and is played by Julianne Moore) is called Jack Rollins. He is played by Christian Bale and is the only character who is granted any development. For it is Jack Rollins who will become Pastor John at a later stage, and thus be the figure to portray Dylan's religious phase. Cate Blanchett's character goes under the name of Jude Quinn. It refers to the Dylan who, with electric guitar sound and rock and roll, clashes with his folk fans. At one point, the press confront Jude Quinn over the disclosure of his real name, namely that it is not Jude Quinn, but Aaron Jacob Edelstein, analogous to Dylan's original name of Robert Zimmerman. Heath Ledger plays (in his last role, incidentally) a character named Robbie Clark, an actor who once played the lead role in a biopic about Jack Rollins, who also tries unsuccessfully to be a filmmaker and who is otherwise in a failing marriage together with Claire, played by Charlotte Gainsbourgh. The remaining character in the cast is an aging outlaw by the name of Billy McCarty and is played by Richard Gere. Like the Woody character, he is mostly inspired by Dylan's work. The name Billy is reminiscent of Billy the Kid, while the characters Billy meets in a city significantly named Riddle have names found in songs of the so-called *Basement Tapes,* which Dylan recorded in 1967 with The Band, but which were only officially released in 1975, and from which the title song *I'm Not There* stems. As in *Velvet Goldmine*, we have a web of references here relating to work and life, resulting in a whole set of Dylan-inspired characters that are simultaneously already marked as fictional on the level of the plot. The following statement appears rather truthfully in the credits of the film: »This motion picture is fictional but some elements have been inspired by real people and real events.«

Another effect of this approach is that any attempt to bring the characters into a clear chronology, to associate them with certain discernible stages in the life of Dylan, is doomed to fail. This is especially true for the first and last characters, Woody and Billy, who arise less from the material of life, than of the work of Dylan, both figures taking on elements from very different work phases. The other figures, however, also interfere with each other, referencing each other in small details, such that they enter a constellation impossible to subject to the narrative order of succession. *I'm Not There* is quite clearly not about trying to tell or explain the changes. We find out hardly anything about how the many portraits of Dylan are related. Even Jack Rollins appears in the last part of the film, having become Pastor John, simply as another.

One could think that the film does not justify anything. In any case, it does not explain any identity transformation in order to bring the different characters into the coherency of a concluded biography, like a typical biopic, which, like *Walk the Line*, lives from telling the drama of identity crises and respective changes. However, *I'm Not There* does something else in that it lends cinematic evidence to every single character. It cinematically justifies, so to speak, the world of every figure. For not only are the characters multiplied, but so too are the narrative styles. Every figure corresponds with its own cinematic world. Thus there could be no bigger contrast than between the 1960s world in black and white, in which Jude Quinn (Cate Blanchett) moves around, and the world of the 1970s western, immersed in a very specific soft lighting, through which Billy McCarty (Richard Gere) rides.

Haynes thereby also exposes an important structural characteristic of the biopic. According to Henry Taylor, the biopic is a chameleon-like genre which does not create its own style and thus does not have its own distinctive look.[21] Rather, each is a kind of auxiliary genre that shapes the stylistic design of the biopic. In our example, such auxiliary genres would be the 1970s western, or the 1960s black-and-white aesthetics, which is influenced of course by *Don't Look Back*, D. A. Pennebaker's famous documentary film about Dylan's 1965 tour through England, during which Pannebaker also shot the famous clip for *Subterranean Homesick Blues*. Other, quite obvious sources for the Blanchett scenes are Murray Lerner's documentary *The Other Side of the Mirror: Bob Dylan at the Newport Folk Festival*, which shows »how Bob Dylan plugged in a whole generation,« as well as a series of photos that Berry Feinstein took in 1966 on another of Dylan's England tours. All these references are well known and

---

21 Henry M. Taylor, *Rolle des Lebens. Die Filmbiographie als narratives System* (Marburg, 2002), 21.

are reconstructed in detail in what could be called a feature-film remake of such documentary material. In brackets, it should be noted that Haynes is of course also relevant for any theory of the remake. In 2011, he produced a highly recommendable remake of *Mildred Pierce*, originally a melodrama by Michael Curtiz from 1945 with Joan Crawford in the leading role. Haynes created an HBO miniseries, in which Kate Winslet provides the central figure with quite a distinctive quality.

Nevertheless, the highlighting of the cinematic auxiliary genres that outline their respective worlds, the marking of their genre character through hard cuts, and the switching back and forth between very different worlds in form and content, interestingly does not diminish their respective illusionistic effects. In each case, one is in the world which one sees, one immediately believes in it, although one is simultaneously challenged to perceive it as mediated, as a construction. This tension is vital for any film experience, but it becomes effective in different ways. Even the classical biopic has its way of referring to its own construction. This is true not only for the somewhat obviously distorting relation of life and screenplay, or for the acting performance that seeks to remain as faithful as possible to the publicly known model and is nevertheless always unable to accomplish that entirely. It is valid too with respect to the attempts to reconstruct the worlds of their subjects by quoting already *iconic* historical events, thereby reminding us of the original more than simply replacing it. The fact that this last aspect is also typical of the traditional biopic can be seen clearly in many examples, such as in the remake of the well-known imagery of Arthur Miller and Marilyn Monroe in *My Week with Marilyn* (2011), with Michelle Williams as Marilyn Monroe. Another example is the famous Cash appearances in the prison of San Quentin that are cited in *Walk the Line*. Of course, we are very aware that despite the most faithful reconstructions of every detail, Joaquin Phoenix is still not Johnny Cash and Michelle Williams very clearly is not Marilyn. But although even Cate Blanchett's acting triumph in *I'm Not There* arises of course out of the ever-present (gender) difference between her and Dylan, we do not only take pleasure in the formalist consciousness of the construction. The entire cinematic world may be cited, but for us it is nevertheless also immediately valid. Even when we consider *Walk the Line,* we do not constantly think of Joaquin Phoenix, instead we follow his character, his Johnny Cash.

This double experience is especially highlighted in *I'm Not There*. Despite the jump cuts separating the Dylan-inspired worlds, despite our consciousness of their construction, we are drawn into each one of them. *I'm Not There* thus emphasizes a paradox that is more or less latently characteristic of all feature film experiences: Film demands an immediate belief in the world it discloses as well as an attention to its mediatedness as a cinematic construction breaking such belief.[22] The emphasis on this paradox has, in view of *I'm Not There*, a certain ethical resonance, too. For with this, *I'm Not There* clearly contradicts the argument that behind the many faces of Dylan there is a meta-sovereign subject for whom all his identities are nothing but exterior masks he just uses to confuse his audience. One can also say that were the film to take a position concerning Dylan's irony, it would not be the irony of a meta-subject indifferently standing above his own social identity. We are not dealing with a subject that claims to be independent from the social sphere as such. Rather we are dealing here with a subject that turns away from certain determinations because it has been alienated from them, therefore looking for new ones, trying to find itself again. Such a subject could be called an ironist not because it takes the position of the nihilist for whom the world as a whole is nothing but semblance, but because it is aware of the fallibility of all determination, including those with which we try to become intelligible to ourselves. That which appears to us today as right, according to the best of our knowledge and conscience, can turn out wrong or insufficient in the light of other events, or more gradual developments. This does not, however, relativize the respective decisions or the existential justification narratives that come along with them. Rather, they have in each case full validity and existential weight.

Nonetheless, such an awareness of fallibility is linked with an understanding of the difference that always exists between narrative and life. Yet, such consciousness does not only know of the untold and undetected aspects of life and about its

[22] Alexander García Düttmann, »QUASI. Antonioni und die Teilhabe an der Kunst,« in *Neue Rundschau* 4 (2009): 151–65.

potentiality in relation to identity determinations, but also of the constructive function of narratives that can only be understood in its existential dimension if one relieves them of the need to justify the whole of life. Then the narrative limits itself to certain aspects, which come to the fore in a certain practical context, a certain world, while others remain disregarded.[23] It is exactly through this restriction that a difference between life and concrete narratives is confirmed, without thereby taking from them their situative evidence or concluding from the fallibility of such narratives that they are of no existential significance.

The problem of the relation between determinacy and indeterminacy (in contrast to that between the mere role and the real person behind it) at issue here is taken up by Haynes in *I'm Not There* in a way that could be seen as complementary to what Warhol does in his *Screen Tests*. While Warhol isolated the potentiality of the film actor to become other characters by focusing on the singularity of the face as a cipher for this potentiality of becoming, Haynes takes a different approach. The potentiality of the person is expressed here not by a withdrawal of any narrative, not even of any legend with its fateful elements, as Cavell would have it, but by assigning another status to the narrative, namely that of a limited narrative of justification, bound to a specific situation, that—although we are aware of its restrictions—always, and in each case anew, means the world to us. This is reflected, as it were, in the position that *I'm Not There* demands from its audience, the position of, as Alexander García Düttmann formulates, a »double participation«[24] in film for which the acknowledgement of its construction is no reason to withdraw from its world. The ethic that corresponds with such a position would be one that neither attempts to deny the other the possibility to change nor ignores the existential weight of the narratives with which he or she tries to become intelligible to us in any given situation. Everything depends here on acknowledging the dynamic between life and narrative without neglecting their difference.

*

A short credit sequence still: If it is the problem of the conventional biopic, for example of *Walk the Line*, that it tends to collapse the difference between narrative and life on the side of the narrative, it is the problem of many current reality formats that they tend to collapse this difference on the side of life. The consequence of this, too, is to repress any awareness of the potentiality of human existence, although, of course, not through a fateful plot but in the reification of human potentiality itself. The documentation of the conduct of life without a constructive filtering of the narrative here, unlike in Warhol's formally strict settings, does not have the effect of elusiveness, but of the endless availability of the people who have to perform under the panoptical presence of the cameras, even when there is nothing to tell.

Interestingly enough, we encounter Joaquin Phoenix again at this end of a false identification of narrative and life. For the mockumentary *I'm Still Here* (2010), which he developed in cooperation with Casey Affleck, Phoenix, who is generally respected for his performance in *Walk the Line,* quite literally played the role of his life. He plays Phoenix, who quit his life as an actor in order to become a hip-hop musician, fails magnificently, the rest of his life also somewhat derailing. During the time of the production he is, or at least so suggests the material that is being spliced together, constantly accompanied by a camera. In addition, he visits live broadcastings in which he appears as himself, as a changed Joaquin Phoenix.

In an appearance on David Letterman's *Late Show* (February 2, 2009), for example, a bearded Phoenix wearing sunglasses was invited to talk about his latest film with Gwyneth Paltrow (*Two Lovers*) and did so in monosyllables. When the conversation did not seem to be moving forward, Letterman became gradually indignant when neither his curious questions regarding Phoenix's unusual appearance, nor his polite interest in the new film was of any avail. Here are a few extracts from the meeting:

David Letterman (*after a very long break of silence addressing Phoenix, whose appearance is indeed reminiscent of Theodore Kaczynski*): So what can you tell us about your days with the Unabomber? [...]

JOAQUIN PHOENIX: (*mumbles through his chewing gum*): Well, I've been working on my music. [...]
DL: You're not gonna act anymore?
JP: No. [...]
DL (*after a fresh pause*): Joaquin, I'm sorry you couldn't be here tonight.
JP (*grins, points with his thumb at Letterman*): He's funny. [...]
DL: Now—can you set up the clip for us, Joaquin? [...]
JP: I don't know what the clip is.
DL: You don't know what the clip is? It's a scene with you and Gwyneth Paltrow.
JP (*brightening up*): Ah—you're doing fine.
DL (*annoyed*): Oh, thanks—that's a high praise coming from you.
(*Phoenix bends forward and sluggishly gets ready to react to the insults.*)
DL (*relents*): We're having fun.
JP: Is that fun?
DL: We're having fun, just relax, seriously.
(*Phoenix leans back again, chews on his chewing gum.*)
DL (*annoyed again*): I'll come to your house and chew gum.
JP: No, I don't have to chew gum. (*Takes the chewing gum from his mouth and sticks it under Letterman's table.*) I won't chew the gum.
DL: Wow.

In the meantime, of course, Phoenix has rehabilitated himself again in the eyes of the public, being acknowledged as a commanding actor, who is even able to portray his own downfall without stepping out of character. He then returns to Letterman's show, freshly shaved and without chewing gum (September 23, 2010):
DAVID LETTERMAN: How are you doing? (*Laughs*) You know, I've always liked you, I've been to see your films, I've always liked you, I recognize you as a powerful talent. The Johnny Cash thing, you were tremendous in that. (*Applause*)
JOAQUIN PHOENIX (*to the audience*): Thank you. Thank you.

DL: And then, a year and a half ago, you come out, and honestly, it's like you slipped and hit your head in the tub.
(*Laughter*)
DL: And I knew immediately, when you sat down, something ain't right, because if you're really the way you appeared to be, you don't go out.
(*Laughter*)
DL: You know what I mean? People don't let guys like you out, if you're really like that. You don't go out.
JP (*laconic*): Right.
DL (*after a short pause reminiscent of his perplexity towards the monosyllabism of his erstwhile interlocutor*): Yeah.
(*Laughter*)
DL (*becomes emphatic*): So what do you have to say for yourself?
(*Laughter*)

Even if Phoenix's rehabilitation came at the price of being nothing else again for all than the exceedingly gifted actor from *Walk the Line*—with *I'm Still Here* he managed to give Letterman's joke—»Joaquin, I'm sorry you couldn't be here tonight«—a meaning that places his project not just through the allusion in the title close to that of Haynes. Yet, *I'm Still Here* is not about confronting the biopic with the potentiality of life, but about confronting reality formats with the constructive function of the narrative. Both projects, however, insist on the existential weight of the situational question: *What do you have to say for yourself?*

Juliane Rebentisch

is a professor of philosophy and aesthetics at the Hochschule für Gestaltung in Offenbach am Main and an associate member of the Frankfurter Institut für Sozialforschung. Her main research areas are aesthetics, ethics, and political philosophy. Her publications include: *Ästhetik der Installation* (2003)/*Aesthetics of Installation Art* (2012); *Kreation und Depression. Freiheit im gegenwärtigen Kapitalismus* (coedited with Ch. Menke, 2010); *Die Kunst der Freiheit. Zur Dialektik demokratischer Existenz* (2012) and her forthcoming book, *Theorien der Gegenwartskunst zur Einführung*.

Constructions of the Digital Film: Aesthetics, Narrative, Discourse

Sabine Nessel
Winfried Pauleit

General expectations about novelty in film and cinema have, in the recent past, focused almost exclusively on digitization. This changed in 2010 when, on the occasion of films like *Avatar* (2010) or *Shrek 4* (2010), the technology of 3D was presented as a novelty that would revolutionize cinema.[1] This fact alone is remarkable. Historically, the »new« in the cinema was usually much more concrete, i.e., not only achieved through technical innovation. Although there has always been an interest in technological and media developments, general expectations, especially those of the public, were directed, in the early days, for example, to visible attractions, to the Hollywood star system, to the newly discovered star, and, in modern cinema, to the forms of a new aesthetic that was audible and visible. The paradox associated with the expectation of digitization is, in short, that the new digital is a phenomenon of appearance, yet this appearance is measured according to the standard of the old photographic look. The headlines regarding digital film projection in cinemas have focused on the fact that the classical projection of the film strip on celluloid could no longer be distinguished from digital projection. What was, or is, then, the new promise of digital cinema?

In the following, we intend to make, in three steps, an inventory of the discourses that until now appear to be relevant for digital cinema and its imagery.[2] The first part of this essay considers the presentation of media theory descriptions of film: on the one hand, with a now seemingly classic derivation of the film from the photographic (Kracauer, Bazin) and, on the other hand, with a media theory conception of film as a hybrid media or hypermedia (Mulvey/Wollen, Mitchell). The second part of this essay highlights, based on films of the digital entertainment cinema (*The Perfect Storm,* 2000; *King Kong,* 2005), and productions that are distinguished by a relaxed approach to the digital image (*Orly,* 2010), the formations of the digital and the analog in their concrete construction. The starting point for this elaboration is the statement by film theorist David Rodowick that film narration has largely been unchanged by the digital. The third part of this essay lays out the thesis that film—as a hypermedium of image, text and sound—thinks in advance an aesthetics of

---

1

3D technology goes back to the end of the nineteenth century with the development of stereoscopy, and it is today »newly« discovered in the process of digitization of film. Numerous articles make reference to the history of 3D, especially to its further development in the 1970s. At the same time, however, 3D is treated as a »revolution« (see Sander 2009).

2

A first version of this essay was published under the title: »Das Neue in Film und Kino. Filmästhetik und Digitalisierung« (The new in film and cinema: film aesthetics and digitization), in *Die Figur des Neuen,* ed. Wolfgang Sohst (Berlin, 2008), 331–56.

digital cinema. In this perspective, novelty is not generated by a technological quantum leap into the digital world, but rather from a diverse developmental history of cultural acts that has been accompanied by seemingly fundamental technological innovations (e.g., the sound film, color film, etc.). The defining moment of the new is therefore not to be grasped only in technical innovations, but rather in the work on a cultural technology that emerged as film/cinema in its hybrid specificity in the twentieth century: Grasped concretely as cultural action in a field of discourse which tested aesthetic and commercial strategies and explored technical possibilities. In this perspective, altered cinematic narratives are not at the center of the discussion, but rather are those cultural events in the field of discourse which appear in the movies.

1 Media Theory Descriptions of Film

What connects and distinguishes various film theory writings is the idea that, in addition to the individual film that one can see in the cinema or elsewhere, there is something specifically cinematic, a genuine, uniformly definable object, which, based on specific properties of other arts and media, e.g., theater, literature, and television, can be identified. The characteristic elements and facts of film have been historically understood differently: in the course of motion of the images of the cinematic apparatus, the editing, the indexicality of the photographic image, its materiality, and especially in the close-up.

Two different media theory perspectives on film will be outlined briefly below. First, we will consider the descriptions of film of André Bazin and Siegfried Kracauer, who think about film starting from photography. In the wake of digitization, the positions of both of these thinkers appear at first glance to be obsolete, to be historical chapters that one can file away. Second, we will examine the descriptions of a »cinema imput,« a »hybrid cinema,« which Bazin already makes, and which appear in the ideas of Peter Wollen and Laura Mulvey in the 1970s, and of W. J. T. Mitchell in the 1990s, in the context of poststructuralism and deconstruction, and which take on the theoretical form of a hypermedium or »image text.«

1.1. Film as a Photographic Medium

As a photographic medium, film is bound in a special way to physical reality. However, the relation to reality of the photographic film does not tend toward a mere representational realism, but rather there is something added by film that was not visible before. André Bazin (1945) speaks, with regards to the photographic film, of a »mummy of change« whose aesthetic potential lies in the disclosure of reality. Film is understood as being the completion of the photographic objectivity of time, no longer clinging in just one instant to the object, but rather liberating the object from its concealment.

»Photography does not create eternity, as art does, it embalms time, rescuing it simply from its proper corruption. Viewed in this perspective, the cinema is objectivity in time. The film is no longer content to preserve the object, enshrouded as it were in an instant, as the bodies of insects are preserved intact, out of the distant past, in amber. The film delivers baroque art from its convulsive catalepsy. Now, for the first time, the image of things is likewise the image of their duration, change mummified as it were. Those categories of resemblance which determine the species photographic image likewise, then, determine the character of its aesthetic as distinct from that of painting.« (Bazin 1945:39)

As an argument that the photograph does not depict reality, but rather reveals it, Bazin cites the cultural action conditions which are determined by the technological apparatus and which highlight the model instead of the artist: »For the first time, between the originating object and its reproduction there intervenes only the instrumentality of a nonliving agent. For the first time an image of the world is formed automatically, without the creative intervention of man. The personality of the photographer enters into the proceedings only in his selection of the object to be photographed and by way of the purpose he has in mind. Although the final result may reflect something of his personality, this does not play the same role as is played by that of the painter. No matter how fuzzy, distorted, or discolored, no matter how lacking in documentary value the image may be, it shares, by virtue of the very process of its becoming, the being of the model of which it is the reproduction; it is the model.« (Bazin 1945:38f)

The ontology of the photographic image brings about the laying bare of realities in the model, beyond the merely documentary, and beyond the artistic subject.

Similarly, Siegfried Kracauer argues in his *Theory of Film* (1960): »In sum, my book is intended to afford insight into the intrinsic nature of photographic film.« (9) This declaration of intent comes from the preface, and before Kracauer turns to the film, there are fifty pages about photography. Kracauer names four affinities that photography has. First, photography has »an unspoken affinity for unstaged reality« (45); second, it has an affinity to the fortuitous; third, photography tends to »suggest endlessness,« (46); and fourth, photography has »an affinity for the indeterminate.« (46)

In both theoretical positions, the photograph is a central aspect of the media theory description of film. Whereas Kracauer also mentions the dream-like state of the viewer, Bazin speaks, for example, about film as being a language. Common to both authors is that they see film as having, on the basis of these aspects, a specific autonomy as art, as medium, and as a cultural technology.

1.2. The Film as Hybrid or Hypermedium

Laura Mulvey and Peter Wollen outline, in the spirit of the times of the 1970s, and influenced by poststructuralist theories from France (Barthes, Derrida, Lacan), a utopian, different cinema. Mulvey emphasizes the gesture of a feminist liberation struggle and searches for a new language of desire, which, however, does not reject the old cinema: »The alternative is the thrill that comes from leaving the past behind without rejecting it [...] in order to conceive a new language of desire.« (Mulvey 1975:200).

Wollen formulates in an exemplary way an expanded cinema concept: »The text/film can only be understood as an arena, a meeting-place in which different discourses encounter each other. [...] [These] can be seen more as [...] palimpsests, multiple *Niederschriften* (Freud's word) in which meaning can no longer be said to express the intention of the author or to be a representation of the world, but must like the discourse of the unconscious be understood by a different kind of decipherment.« (Wollen 1972:87).

In another essay, Wollen clarifies his thoughts which go in the direction of an understanding of film as hypermedium: »The cinema offers more opportunities than any other art—the cross-fertilization [...] the reciprocal interlocking and input between painting, writing, music, theater, could take place within the field of cinema itself. This is not a plea for a great harmony, a synesthetic Gesamtkunstwerk in the Wagnerian sense. But cinema, [...] [as] a dialectical montage within and between a complex of codes.« (Wollen 1975:104).

On closer reading, in comparison with the positions of Bazin and Kracauer, there is less of an agreement and more of a radicalization of the purpose of film. Mulvey and Wollen also characterize the specific quality of film as being a cultural technology, already hinted at by Bazin and Kracauer. Mulvey and Wollen formulate in their description the foundations for an understanding of film as hypermedia. Nevertheless, they are oriented to that phenomenon of film that Kracauer described in 1960 as »the redemption of physical reality«[3] with respect to the photographic nature of film. Yet the »salvation« of which Kracauer speaks, which includes the relationship between external reality and the cinema, has changed. Mulvey and Wollen's model has become more complex. In addition to photography, it integrates the various facets of film as well as other aesthetic productions, arts, and media.

Thus Mulvey and Wollen imagine a project that would actually make film into a reflexive dominant medium of our culture that is no longer bound to the materiality of celluloid films, but that can rather be understood as hypermedia also in video format, such as was realized in an exemplary way by Jean-Luc Godard in *Histoire(s)du cinéma* (1988–1998). This idea of the hypermedia of film was pursued further by Chris Marker in his computer-based multimedia installations like *Zapping Zone* (1990) or his CD-ROM *Immemory One* (1997). This idea is currently continued in network-based documentary productions (i-docs).[4]

---

[3] That is the subtitle of Kracauer's *Theory of Film;* see Kracauer 1960.

[4] See Stefano Odorico, »i-Docs: Interactivity, Documentary and Memories,« in *Avanca/Cinema 2012*, edited by Antonio Costa Valente and Rita Capucho. Avanca, 2012, 1140–46.

W. J. T. Mitchell goes in a similar direction as Mulvey and Wollen in his 1994 book *Picture Theory,* where he questioned the concept of a single medium. For this purpose, he introduced the term *imagetext.* The basis for this operation is an (aesthetic and political) mistrust of all approaches of comparative media, and also of all approaches generalizing, systematizing, or schematizing media relationships. With the term *imagetext*, Mitchell sets himself into opposition against the traditional understanding of intermediality. He assumes that there is no relationship between the arts and the media, but rather that, in all of the so-called individual arts (and single media), an inevitable relationship between image and text exists. His summary of these considerations is: All arts and composite arts (consisting of text and image), all media, are mixed media which embrace different codes, discourses, channels, and different modes of perception and judgment.⁵ Mitchell understands the imagetext not as a concept, but rather as a theoretical figure (analogous to Derrida's *différance*), as a place of dialectical tension and transformation. Under this condition, there emerges a film studies without the inclusion of other arts and media—its hybrid formations and discourse productions—as the undertaking of a cultural purification.

5
From today's perspective, one would have to complement the sound dimension, and speak of a »Soundimagetext« if one wants to build on these considerations.

2 Constructions of the Digital

The film scholar David Rodowick has commented on the digitization of the cinema as follows: »At first glance, it is not the revolution that the industry likes to talk about. Digitally produced Hollywood films [...] tell stories, which is basically what movies have been doing since 1915. [...] The basic form of storytelling and the spatial organization through editing are unchanged.« (Rodowick 2003).

Rodowick's diagnosis still applies to most Hollywood productions of the present. Yet in the last few years, there have been indeed some shifts in the »basic form of storytelling,« especially in the form of shortenings of the story. In some productions—even or especially in Hollywood—there is also a return to early cinema, to the cinema of attractions, with its different, direct addressing of the audience. One thinks of the genre of disaster films, those films in the transition from the twentieth to the twenty-first century, which were a kind of testing ground for digital effects. An example would be Wolfgang Petersen's *The Perfect Storm* (USA 2000), a film that flopped back then in the movie theaters, and is probably already forgotten by most. It was not until later that the extent of influence of the digital production effects on the narrative became clear. The digital appears in this film (as in many others of the time) in the form of an oversized visual effect. For the presentation of the digital ocean waves, the entire action framework was so much reduced that the entire film basically became the mere production of a single, elongated visual effect. At least from a media theory point of view, this film represents an experiment. Film critics, however, mainly sat back speechless in their movie theater seats because there were hardly any connecting narrative possibilities. Petersen's film was put together in a different way, as was, for example, the celebrated *The Matrix* (USA 1999), with the digital innovations of the Wachowski brothers. Petersen's starkly reduced plot has no salvation story and no heroic figure. The only real hero of the film is the digitally constructed ocean waves. As a point of contact to such an aesthetic experience, the silenced movie critics might have offered up some paintings of William Turner which, as static images, were created in a different way, but also stem from an existential experience of the natural power of the sea.

Such returns to the early cinema or even older design levels of imagery—such as Turner's paintings—can be interpreted as a symptom of a social insecurity. On the other hand, they can also be understood as an inner strength and as an act of emancipation, in which a cultural sphere no longer sees itself as committed to the compulsion of eternal repetition of narrative structure, including the happy ending, but actually dares to experiment.

In terms of aesthetic reception, the beginning of the history of digital film can quite accurately be described. It begins in 1991 with the movie *Terminator 2*. Digital technology is exhibited as a visual effect in this film.[6] Until then employed mainly to support the action of films, here the digital images

6
In contrast to special effects that are filmed on the set, visual effects arise in the context of postproduction on the computer.

are the stars and the magnet for the public. The film presents a multiple Terminator character who visibly changes his appearance without editing, who, for example, in order to get past an iron grating, liquefies himself and then returns to the shape of his original design. In this case, the visual effect is supplemented by a sophisticated digital sound design, which gives the image a convincing physical appearance. The semiliquid, muddy and, at the same time, metallic sound is produced digitally, but nevertheless is based on noises from our everyday experience. It was produced by a distortion of the sound made when emptying a can of dog food. This image and sound effect remains fascinating today and has gone into the technological history of film.[7] *Terminator 2* is the first in a series of disaster films of the new digital cinema which presented to the millennium sound design and visual effects as attractions. The question What is film? is posed anew in this decade of film history. As in the early days of film, the films of this decade are primarily concerned with the exhibition of attractions, and with the proud presentation of a new technology.

2.1. *King Kong* (1933/2005)

To analyze the constructions of the digital, the comparison of film versions of *King Kong* proves fruitful. The image of King Kong on the Empire State Building doing battle with airplanes was spectacularly staged in 1933 by Merian C. Cooper and Ernest B. Schoedsack. The same image became an icon of digital film with Peter Jackson's *King Kong* (USA, NZ, D 2005). In each of the two film versions, this famous image, which has become part of the cultural history of the twentieth century, is presented with a different focus. In 1933 Cooper and Schoedsack place the rescue operation attempted by the airplanes at the center of the action, as a second attraction next to the monster King Kong. In Peter Jackson's remake, the focus of attraction is shifted to digital technology. What connects both films is the entanglement of the struggle between man and monster with the presentation of the new.

In *King Kong* (USA 1933), the airplanes are presented as the new, along with their new perspective of flight images.

---

[7] See Bernd Willim: »Filme aus dem Rechner« (Computer-based films), *Fernseh- und Kinotechnik* 52 (May 1998): 255–60.

Before they come into the picture, they are first the subject of dialogue. They are introduced as a last resort for saving the city from the monster. »There is one thing we can do: airplanes.« In *King Kong* (2005), the aircraft appear without prior notice. The double-decker with the pilots in an open cockpit appears now in color, and New York City lies under them in the evening sun. The novelty in this case is not the airplanes and the perspective associated with them. It is far more classic than that in the best sense of the word. The new is a gigantic visual effect, appearing as an urban view of New York, produced with Peter Jackson's computers. »You've never seen New York like this before.«[8]

Whereas the visual effects in *Terminator 2* is still limited to a single character, it is here the streets of a metropolis, a city landscape as an entire picture, that has been created with digital technology. The image of New York City was reconstructed on the basis of aerial photographs and images from the 1930s. Buildings of today that did not yet exist in the 1930s were removed and replaced by digital reconstructions of how the sites previously looked.

Since the photos and aerial images from the 1930s were consistently black-and-white pictures, the creation of the image of New York City was also associated with a complete reinvention of color. The double-decker aircraft, which nostalgically represents the dream of flying—but also the digitally (or however) generated smoking chimneys of the factories—speaks in favor of a historical treatment of film that does not leave what has been as a trace in the document, but rather envisions what once was in terms of a complete imaging. The not-always-so-humorless imagining in the new digital cinema of something that has previously been defined as reality reached an absurd climax in Peter Jackson's *King Kong,* with the attempt to digitally restore the old dream of flying. The photographic aerial images of the New York of the 1930s are not seen on the screen. Rather, they are part of a simulation of photography which is reshaping the museums and archives of the present time—be it photograpic images or the bones of a mammoth in the paleontological department of the Jardin des Plantes. Thus, the principle of tracing and indexicality is devalued. Jackson's project illustrates

[8] Eileen Moran, visual effects producer of *King Kong* (2005, Peter Jackson), quoted in the booklet accompanying the DVD, Universal 2006.

the persistence of the fundamental concerns of the representatives of classic material archiving over the digital.

The dream of flying, whose realization coincided with the invention of the cinema (Morin 1958), returns in Jackson's remake, but the director no longer refers to the airplane as a new invention. Rather, it becomes an empty sign that no longer has any counterpart in the imagination of the viewers, except possibly for amnesia itself. The only thing left up to the viewer is the effect and the level of the film text, which, as photographic as it may seem, exists only as an empty shell, cut off from the world, and deeply nostalgic. With the simulation of indexicality, the potential of the archive material are revealed, precisely because the productive spaces between documents come to be digitally filled. A productive rearrangement of the archive material, which Kracauer in 1927, in his essay on photography, already designated as the »all-in« game of history, is henceforth impossible. (Kracauer 1927)

2.2. Orly/La Jetée

In contrast to films like *The Perfect Storm, Terminator 2,* or Jackson's *King Kong,* which, with respect to narration, deserve the label »digital attraction cinema,« in the following, and on the basis of the film *Orly* (D 2010) by Angela Schanelec, a construction of the digital will be considered which is less formal and more brute than the attraction cinema. In *Orly,* narrative and the arrangement of discourses which are produced in their specificity using digital recording methods become visible. A more relaxed attitude to the digital image as well as a juxtaposition of the digital/analog recording process are characteristic of the work of this director.

Orly takes place in the airport near Paris of the same name, and treats, in a loose context, microstories of people who are in the airport or on the way there. The episodic structure is connected with views of the airport as a place with special legal procedures and operations. Given the filming location and the episodic structure of the film, one might be reminded of *Airport* (USA 1970), a classic of 1970s disaster films starring Burt Lancaster, in which several stories and the fates of the main characters are also developed and treated at an airport. In contrast, however, to *Airport,* which only shows sporadic documentary views of the airport, *Orly* was shot amid running airport operations. Couples who are in transit in the airport are successively shown: their waiting, their stories, their conversations via mobile phone. The light-flooded hall of the airport becomes a place of encounter, communication, confession, in short, of microdramas against the backdrop of the everyday events of the Paris airport. Contact with the actors took place over radio and headphones. The camera is often far away. And the sound sounds as if acoustic islands were drawn from the original soundscape of the airport—or as if Gene Hackman, in his role as Harry Caul (*The Conversation,* USA 1974), had prepared these recordings in their hybridity (between art and surveillance). What makes the digital recording process in *Orly* possible is the hybridization of different film traditions, such as the classic studio recording with actors along with the director's instructions, and the documentary-related tradition of a cinema vérité, or the recordings of an secret observer or a Peeping Tom.

    In addition, photography is a key issue in *Orly.* Already in the second scene we see the protagonist of the film (Maren Eggert) in a photograph. It is a black-and-white photographic print. In it, the actress appears much younger than in the film. The photo is a reference to the older film *Marseille* (D 2004) by the same director, in which Maren Eggert plays a photographer. In *Marseille,* photography was still obliged to serve analog photography. This changes with *Orly*. Here, photography is not only done with a digital camera—the film itself is digitally recorded and edited. And you realize: This is not the new digital cinema with its visual effects that is being celebrated (although there clearly are such effects), but here the history of cinema is updated by digital means—simply and without fanfare. *Orly* plays with the different registers that constitute the cinema. From the beginning, the film is accompanied and fed by media. It is not only photography that sets the tone, but also architecture, literature, music, the mobile phone, and the film itself as medium which are significant. That is why it is so hard to describe what this film actually does, what it consists of, what it is about. In a specific narrative form (episodic narration), it adds up to as little as in a specific genre.

Orly »designs« itself like an architecture of hybrid elements, in order to finally show itself as architecture. What is shown is the Orly Airport—an icon of modernity—in a sort of time image. But the Bibliothèque Nationale in Paris is also shown, in the memory of a digital camera. The strategy of the film can perhaps be described as a structural shift from a conventional arrangement of events in a narrative context (Scheffel 2009) to a hybrid arrangement of discourse fragments.

Starting from *Orly*, not only is a reference to current digital film and its effects on narration possible, but also a look back to the predigital cinema of the 1960s. In Chris Marker's film *La Jetée* (F 1962), which also takes place in the Orly airport —analogous to Mulvey and Wollen—an idea of the digital long before its general dissemination in the 1990s is already sketched. In Marker's film, the traces of photography can already be read as a discourse field, one which builds on and further thinks the theoretical sketches of Kracauer, Bazin or Morin. The legendary film La Jetée is assembled from photographs. In his construction, Marker presents his creation and the breaks between the images almost didactically. He also highlights in this context central places as sites of action in his film: on the one hand, the museum as an archive and collection of traces of the past (the collections of the Jardin des Plantes); on the other, the runway of the Orly airport as the materialized dream of modernity. Although the film is composed of photographs, its sphere of action is situated in the future, where, in the image of an atomic World War III, a catastrophic moment of modernity is thematized—but which, ultimately, also happening in the future, presents a mysterious energy center, which, at least from today's vantage point, is associated with the image of a computer motherboard. Marker himself characterizes this film form as a »novel-photo«—it displays its hybrid character also in conceptual image.

3 The Digital Medium as an Extension of the Film Hybrid Medium

The central moments of the constructions of the digital are part of the production of difference. Whether historically between two versions of a film, or within a film, or in the sense of a media theory discourse, the digital is tied to the difference of the photographic film. Conversely, only in difference is the determination of the film as an analog or digital work established. This happens according to the same principle as a long time ago when the invention of sound film first brought forth the »silent movie.« (Hickethier 2001:95) An effect of the opposition of photographic and digital film is the temporary fetishization of the photographic (Jackson's *King Kong*) due to the simulation of photography by digital means, and, at the same time, the distortion of photography through the indexical principle linked to it.

These constructions show the digital as a sensation and therefore, in the tradition of the technical tricks of the cinema, the historical beginning of which in film history is associated with the name Georges Méliès, a tradition that also stretches back to the prehistory of the apparatus and projection arts. At the same time, these constructions of digital moments of self-reflection and experimentation show technology as a new possibility. The digital cinema creates a new universal means of payment, one which was put into operation whenever the aesthetic strategy ran into a technical limit, or when technical zeal imitated aesthetic strategies.

In a similar sense, the digital has also made its presence felt at the level of sound in the cinema. It should be noted that creative work on sound basically started in the 1970s with the cinema of New Hollywood and the development of sound design (see Flückiger 2001 and 2006). Creative processes in the area of sound have connected much faster with the digital due to late development. Nevertheless, (digital) sound design qualifies as just another aspect in the framework of the hybridization of film. The pragmatism of sound design remains oriented in a similar way to the auditory experiences of everyday life, analogous to the relationship between digital imaging and photographic film.

Beyond digital sensation cinema, however, there is another cinema in which forward-thinking ideas of the digital are elaborated—historically before their technical invention—from the confrontation of photography and film, as well as in combination with the literary forms of the novel, including the assembly of various levels of sound as a hybrid arrangement of discourses (*La Jetée*). Schanelec's *Orly* is related to this kind of cinema (without entirely dispensing with digital effects).

Not only does the form of the narration change, but also the imagination of the viewers, our concrete and general mental images of the cinema, in other words, the common understanding of what we mean by »film« and »cinema« is getting realigned. These innovations unfold—similarly to how it was outlined by Mulvey/Wollen and Mitchell—as a form of hypermedia, fashioning a hybrid field of discourse in film and cinema. Thus, the ontological determinations of film—if it, for example, is a photographic or a narrative medium, or in the field of discourse—are lifted to a higher place, a site of encounters with other arts, media, and their resulting hybrid formations.

References

Bazin, André. »The Ontology of the Photographic Image« (1945), translated by Hugh Gray, Film Quarterly 19, no. 4 (Summer 1960).
Flückiger, Barbara. Sound Design. Die virtuelle Klangwelt des Films. Marburg, 2002.
Flückiger, Barbara, in conversation with Winfried Pauleit. »Sound Effects—Zu Theorie und Praxis des Film-Sound Designs« (German/English), in Sound Art: Zwischen Avantgarde und Popkultur, edited by Anne Thurmann-Jajes, Sabine Breitsameter, and Winfried Pauleit. Cologne, 2006, 219–36.
Hickethier, Knut. Film- und Fernsehanalyse. Stuttgart, 2001.
Kracauer, Siegfried. Theory of Film: The Redemption of Physical Reality, with an introduction by Miriam Bratu Hensen. Princeton, 1997 (originally published 1960).
Kracauer, Siegfried. »Photography« (1927), in The Mass Ornament: Weimar Essays, translated by Thomas Y. Levin. Cambridge, MA, 2005.
Mitchell, W. J. T. Picture Theory. Chicago, 1994.
Moran, Eileen. »The Visual Effects of King Kong,«(2005), NZ/USA 2005, Peter Jackson. Booklet 2006.
Morin, Edgar. The Cinema, or the Imaginary Man, translated by Lorraine Mortimer. Minneapolis, 2005 (originally published 1956).
Mulvey, Laura. »Visual Pleasure and Narrative Cinema« (1975), in Narrative, Apparatus, Ideology, edited by Philip Rosen. New York, 1986, 198–209.
Odorico, Stefano. »i-Docs: Interactivity, Documentary and Memories,« in Avanca/ Cinema 2012, edited by Antonio Costa Valente and Rita Capucho. Avanca, 2012, 1140–46.
Rodowick, David, in conversation with Claudia Lenssen. »Digitale Fotografie ist paradox,« in Die Tageszeitung, November 6, 2003.

Scheffel, Michael. »Was heißt (Film-)Erzählen?,«in Erzhälen im Film, edited by
　　　　Susanne Kaul, Jean-Pierre Palmier, and Timo Skrandies. Bielefeld, 2009,
　　　　15–31.
Willim, Bernd. »Filme aus dem Rechner,« Fernseh- und Kinotechnik 52 (May 1998):
　　　　255–60.
Wollen, Peter. »Godard and Counter-cinema: Vent d'est« (1972), in idem., Readings
　　　　and Writings: Semiotic Counter-Strategies. London, 1982, 79–91.
Wollen, Peter. »The Two Avant-Gardes« (1975), in idem., Readings and Writings:
　　　　Semiotic Counter-Strategies. London, 1982, 92–104.

Sabine Nessel

currently is a guest professor at Universität Wien and a past visiting professor at Freie Universität Berlin (2010–2012). In 2010 she completed her habilitation dissertation at Universität Frankfurt on *Zoo und Kino als Schauordnungen der Moderne*. Some of her recent publications include: *Kino und Ereignis. Das Kinematografische zwischen Text und Körper* (2008); *Zoo und Kino* (edited with Heide Schlüpmann, 2012); and *Der Film und das Tier. Klassifizierungen, Cinephilien und Philosophien* (edited with Winfried Pauleit et al, 2012).

Winfried Pauleit,

professor at the Universität Bremen, works in the areas of film studies, media aesthetics and film education. Since 2008 he is the academic director of Internationale Bremer Symposium zum Film and coeditor of the symposium publication series. His publications include: *Filmstandbilder. Passagen zwischen Kunst und Kino* (2004); *Das ABC des Kinos. Foto, Film, Neue Medien* (2009); and *Reading Film Stills: Analyzing Film and Media Culture* (forthcoming 2014).

Transmedia Storytelling and New Product Language in Film, Or What Happens When Objects Even Speak

Martin Gessmann

I. The Phenomenon

Many viewers may well have noticed the phenomenon for the first time in the autumn of 2012. *Skyfall,* James Bond's twenty-third screen appearance, was heralded by the usual promotional trailers on TV, and advertised in other relevant media. Other clips were also running on TV concurrently, featuring the same leading actor (Daniel Craig), using many of the same locations and action scenes as in *Skyfall*, while including other sequences that did not occur in the film, nor were in any way associated with its history. These were commercials, presenting not only the well-known character, but also a specially selected product. A fictional yet typical situation was created for this mise-en scène, in order to highlight the importance of the character in conjunction with the product. Only with a Brand X mobile phone was 007/the secret agent sure to succeed; only with Brand X aftershave or wearing a Brand Z watch: »James Bond's product of choice.« On the surface, it might appear like a variation of the classic product placement practiced in movies. However, unlike in the Bond film of 2006 *(Casino Royale)*, the leading actress must no longer exclaim (»Beautiful!«) in her first tête-à-tête with the leading actor in a somewhat embarrassing scene—obviously specially written to extol the virtues of his deluxe wristwatch. It seems that the products themselves have now become the narrative focus, in the style of a spin-off (series), creating the impression of an independent offshoot of the Bond story.

Such offshoots have always provided for the transformation of minor characters into main characters; minor characters shifted into the center of their own, new story. Fans of the 1980s TV series *Cheers,* for example, which was set in Boston, could delight in the relocation of the minor character of Frasier to Seattle in the 1990s. Accompanied by a significant rise in station: from the original basement of a Boston bar and a culture surrounding after-work drinking, to a psychoanalytical, academic, radio environment on the upper floor of an American high-rise. Now, it seems that the products themselves are moving up the ladder and becoming the core of self-sustained narrative. Bond film fans in the summer of 2012 couldn't say they hadn't been warned. Yet the opening of the Olympics in London featured a gag involving the British Queen Elizabeth II being chauffeured to the stadium in true Daniel Craig/James Bond style. The focus of this brief, royal insert was, likewise, the Bond character's typical mode of transport—cinematically speaking, the Queen could just as well have leapt into frame on the end of a parachute. And it is almost needless to say that the twenty-third Bond film adaptation ultimately followed the principle outlined above—unless, of course, it preceded it: you can pick. Because, to mention just one example, the role of the 1964 Aston Martin DB 4, shown in the movie's final scenes, is different from those of its forerunners, in both a transport-specific and symbolic sense. More than a mere quote, reminiscence, or historical film accessory, the car symbolically refers to former episodes, previous adventures and earlier times. The car ultimately is far more a symbol of the original narrative style of the Bond novels and the film adaptations themselves. Thus, the viewer is not only swept into the film's fairytale, Scottish landscape, and likewise into the childhood memories of its hero, but also into the original premise and dramatic foundation of all Bond narratives. The car, as overloaded as it appears with such pretensions at the mere retelling, thus forms a narrative moment in the film itself. It is narrative because it typifies the basic motif of all narratives of this kind. The entire film is ultimately nothing but the narrative performance of a progression. Though it has, over the course of cinematic development, distanced itself greatly from the beginning, it has nonetheless rediscovered the dramatic as the core of the story as well as of its repetition. And the core is still there where the foundation of the Bond novels already seems buried under the challenges of the present.

  The aforesaid emancipation of products, which were originally mere accessories (and at best have become tangible attributes of the main characters), and now the core of potential narrative progression, did not happen overnight. In the background is a video games industry, which has long recognized and made use of the defined principle of the serial or episodic continuation of story. And looking at it theoretically—and positively for a moment—it has done so in quite a diverse and democratic sense: for not only has it given rise to an almost infinite number of possibilities for a story's continuation, but every time the game is played, its outcome is yet undecided, and we have all become its new role-playing heroes. The former accessories and mechanisms have become the ontological pillars of the narrative in as much as they determine the framework of the plot and specifically pre-define its progression. They are now sustained in all episodes and ultimately serve to make the stories recognizable.

II. Theory

Such emancipation of objects into independent narrative elements and autonomous agents of the plot requires theoretical comment. Since the history of the emancipation of things is thematically part of an on-going debate on the suppressive effect of the media, it is nonetheless generally agreed that all concerned—spanning all media from film, television and video game, through to theme parks, Disneyland, or wax-work displays—could only suffer. They have suffered by their increasing dehumanization in the media, by their passivity and dependence, inasmuch as, being immersed in their respective medium, they have had no logical alternative but to comply with technical and media-related rules. People were generally reified,[1] to coin a phrase from twentieth-century cultural criticism, once they came into contact with the media. Yet contrary to this thesis, things have recently become humanized. Humanized in the activation of products in a narrative sense; humanized in that the creative element which had been extracted from the media, has been returned to the game by the objects themselves. Objects and mechanisms have, as indicated above, become active moments in a plot structure, in that they contribute productively and independently toward the continuation of the story. But how can that be? How does a history of suppression suddenly turn into emancipation? How does the media, unquestionably assumed to be dehumanizing, suddenly become a medium that even attributes artistic talent and power to inanimate objects?

IIa. Excursion Theory and Media History

To better comprehend this phenomenon, let's take a brief look at recent theory and media history. Beginning with the

---

[1] ›Reification‹ has taken on since Heidegger's technical writings this critical meaning. The term comes however from an adaption of Marxist cultural critique. See Georg Lucács, *Geschichte und Klassenbewußtsein. Studien über marxistische Dialektik* (Berlin, 1923).

key word, likewise the basis of this anthology, the *storytelling*, or academic access to the narrative, (from the Latin: *narrative*). Literary scholar Albrecht Koschorke recently published a book on the »principles of a general theory of narrative«[2] that created quite a stir. Koschorke concluded that the narrative represented the discovery of a new apriority. Such a statement would not in itself be cause for any real academic sensation as, for the last half century we have grown accustomed to being surprised by a new apriority about every five years. Thus, after the linguistic turn, e.g., the performative turn, came the iconic turn, with its numerous offshoots, that has differentiated[3] the richness of imagery in our humanistic culture[4]. According to the prevailing worldview, the initial indicator for such defining moments occurred in the 1960s with the emerging computer culture. It was thus assumed that only that which could be formulated in the new computer language—enabling its specific binary coding—could be established scientifically. That which permeates the filter of code is real, that which does not, is unreal—or as real as the unreal may seem in everyday life. This made computer culture, as a new academic culture, perfectly safe. According to what appeared codable in computer language, the circuit was extended to include that which could be resolved with binary coding. Simple procedures, which were now programmed as feedback loops, triggered the concept of the performative as the new apriority, while the digitization of analog images in the early 1990s became the »iconic« turn.[5] What is remarkable about Koschorke's new apriority assertion can now be seen in his multidimensional argument, whereby he does more than just introduce an additional sphere to the world of coding. He does not mean that the latest inventions in our world of coding skills could simply be added to the language, plot and images of narrative. Rather, he means that in narration itself, an overall media framework is created that encompasses all former apriorities: »As opposed to being framed within binary structures, the stories precede any such structural consolidation. By token of their nonfixity and inner restlessness, they provide access to a cultural fluidum within which binary codes initially form, enter into competition or alliances that mutually weaken, strengthen,

---

[2] Albrecht Koschorke, Wahrheit und Erfindung. Grundzüge einer Allgemein Erzhähltheorie (Frankfurt am Main, 2012).

[3] See Dieter Mersch, Medientheorien zur Einführung (Hamburg, 2006); and idem., Was sich zeigt. Materialität, Präsenz, Ereignis (Munich/Paderborn, 2002).

[4] Ibid.

[5] See Friedrich Kittler's notion of media and technology as the »hardware« and our culture as »software« that preconfigures our worldview significantly.

cross-pollinate, solidify and resolve.«[6] This absolute self-confidence can best be understood in the description of the narrative when one considers the following: Computer-readable coding has, with increasing influence over time, linked the network of programs and their languages of binary distinctions ever more closely. Although only simple differences were coded in the beginning, more complexity was added over time and what has been ethnologically termed a »dense (or thick) description«[7] since the 1980s, can also be better used to describe the world in general. What was previously only perceived as the gap between that which could be captured in code and that which we can encompass in our experience of the world, became ever narrower. The narrower this gap became, the more certainly it could be expressed, rather than merely sensed. Until the point where Koschorke found that the narrative is the code of all codes, a form of general description, which includes all other local descriptions and is, first and foremost, dynamically differentiated. This theoretical shift, culminating in the new and comprehensive status of narrative explanation is, in turn, itself only part of a broader reflection.

Already upon the sufficiently effective illustration of all analog media, digitally stored, can one be said to have concluded a medial apriority in the new quality, which also applies with regard to the consequences that must result from the media framework, all prior media forms and from our very understanding of media theory.[8]

IIb. The Particular Theory of Transmedia Storytelling

Looking back at media history and the historical theory of the past fifty years also enables the phenomenon of transmedia storytelling to be consciously re-evaluated. It is now generally understood that convergence culture emerges as described by Henry Jenkins in his book *Convergence Culture: Where Old and New Media Collide*.[9] It converges in a transmedia story in accordance with »multiple media platforms, with each new text making a distinctive and valuable contribution to the whole.«[10] Theoretically, however, such convergence as described by Jenkins goes even further. Not only is the story edited via various media

---

[6] Koschorke, Wahrheit und Erfindung, 22 (see note 2).

[7] This phrase comes from Clifford Geertz, Dichte Beschreibung. Beiträge zum Verstehen kultureller Systeme (Frankfurt am Main, 2003).

[8] See Bernard Stiegler, Etats de choc. Bétise et savoir au XXIe siècle (Paris, 2012); and Martin Gessmann, Zur Zukunft der Hermeneutik (Munich/Paderborn, 2012).

[9] Henry Jenkins, Convergence Culture: Where Old and New Media Collide (New York/London, 2006).

[10] Ibid., 98.

platforms, meaning in the case of Bond, that a Hollywood adaptation unravels the story, further affected by lavish TV commercials, and shifted into a three-dimensional reality by the Olympic stadium appearance of the Queen of England—while new, pseudo-Bond novels supply the necessary link (»Bond is back«). Until, finally, the hero compliantly accepts a role reversal in the video game. Such historical transformation is not necessarily easy to follow in the normal course of storytelling over the various media platforms, especially when it is continually based on the same hero and his key weapons and accoutrements. The history of Bond not only plays on different medial keyboards; according to Jenkins, each new media re-creation likewise makes a distinctive and original contribution to the overall story. It is geared to the whole, and what is more, in an ideal form of transmedia storytelling, each medium does what it does best, should still apply. Thus, no medium represents anything more than a second-best solution, or stopgap, while one had nothing better to hand. Thus, for example, the Bond character in a comic would be a Bond for the poor, while Hollywood films are for the rich (or for those who can afford the price of a movie ticket). On the contrary, the media for the respective performances complement one another, since each medium brings us closer to exactly the experience it can best achieve. Again, in the context of Jenkins, »Its world might be explored through game, or experienced as an amusement park attraction.« All is possible in the context of such preconceived stories, as opposed to the real feeling of being caught up in strange and dangerous circumstances, best experienced in video games or adventure parks. Such unique narratives are often excellently structured and multilayered, which is why we go to the cinema. Advertising shows the extent to which we can both differentiate as well as participate—at least in terms of the featured product—in the cult of the »double O« agent: That he, in Her Majesty's Service, actually provides a service—as shown at the opening of the recent Olympic Games. In the light of recent theoretical developments, the question as to why transmedia storytelling still obviously functions today, just as Jenkins formulated with his list of criteria, should be fairly and conclusively reinterpreted. Success obviously depends on the new role of narrative as an overall medial framework for all conceivable representative forms. For every overall framework creates relief to a certain extent. For if, namely, the inner narratives were previously trapped in mutual competition as far as their claims of narrative validity were concerned, they now conversely find themselves in a convergent movement. Since talk of claiming validity sounds so abstract, allow me to explain. We are all familiar with the often acrimonious discussions sparked off among members of the film industry upon the introduction of a new media playback method. Upon the advent of the talking picture, many intellectuals swore that silent films embodied the true art of filmmaking. After the introduction of color, they mourned the end of the black-and-white era. Lastly, when 3-D film hit the screen, it was once again noted, although mostly in artistic and cultural circles, that nothing compared to the poetry of black-and-white (referring to a review of James Cameron's *Avatar*).

Now, it would seem as if the play-offs and rivalry between media formats and platforms is essentially over. Basically because the technical capability of converting one media-viewing mode to another has paved the way for a sovereignty and equanimity in the sense of mutual laissez-faire. The best evidence of this is the astounding success of the recent black-and-white silent film, Michel Hazanavicius's *The Artist*. Such success is especially valid in the broader context, not only with regard to the formal medial playback, but also to the contextual permeation of the narrative levels. Let us agree, as Jenkins demands, that narratives are interconnected and can even be understood as mutually helpful. Should one form of representation fail, the other jumps in episodically. In content and form, *The Artist* is nothing other than an illustration of just such mutual assistance. The obsolete silent movie star makes a comeback in the talking film due to the fact that he can mutely reappear in the silent film *The Artist*. Although the silent film ultimately closes as a talking picture and, as such, demonstrates what it achieves when it doesn't achieve what it otherwise set out to achieve. Here, content and media structure go hand in hand, in rhythmic counterpoint. And *The Artist* is, in turn, itself a great silent-film that gives voice to the whole silent film genre. Acknowledgment of the film with five Oscars in 2012 can be regarded as a sign that the jury understood the ploy without further instruction by means of cultural magazines. The film narrative of *The Artist* was clearly understood as something other than a romantic counterprogram to current Hollywood cinema (even when some commentators chose to see it that way), but rather as a unique and enduring history of filmmaking, as such, bringing its viewers closer to a long-forgotten media decor with a very contemporary narrative.

When it comes to that, a threshold has in fact been crossed in the broad perception of contemporary film and the media arts. It is now generally accepted that various narrative levels, as well as the associated narrative media, can be linked by means of a narrative thread. Thus, there is always a starting point and always at least one overall narrative. As media forms can merge, so, too, can the narrative contents—particularly when the very merging is formally addressed with regard to such content; thus completing a long-lasting flow of medial and thematic differentiation, replaced by a well-considered, seemingly final, at least potentially, *en principe* consolidation. Instead of the maxim of mutual, media-specific exclusion, there is now the option of just such inclusion. The demand for sole, artistically legitimate representation is superseded by the liberal principle of laissez-faire, as well as mutual support and cooperation with the widest possible tolerance, to leave the other medium and its contents alone. Or, better still, to strengthen its media limitations. Thus, black-and-white silent film can still ultimately be regarded as highly contemporary due to its artistic merit.

III. The New Product Language in Film

Conceptually, we need only one more small step to finally and fully understand the remarkable cooperation of products in the continuation of long-familiar narratives. For that, the narrative's media platforms should be reexamined or, more precisely, their specific product arrangement studied. Thus we find that the narrative figures are, in a media sense, »coded,« in that they are surrounded by certain products that schematize their prospective character development and, to some extent, their behavior. Sticking with our initial example, 007 or the agent, operates within the framework of what is provided in terms of agent scenography, e.g., a special car with unique fittings, etc. In principle, the accessories co-determine what and how the character performs. Whether the car can just be driven as a vehicle on the road, or if it can fly, or dive under water, etc., as well as what attitude should generally be assumed while driving such a vehicle. The product-specific hardware here creates the media framework for the software, in which a narrative is played out.

With such a liberal and interconnected approach to narrative media, virtually amounting to the end of certain exclusive representational demands (the story is only the real story in this specific medium), there comes a new, and more liberal, method in the integration of the corresponding product's technology. The transmission from one medial plane to another (e.g., from the virtual world of the video game to the real world of the theme park) is no longer unilaterally assessed in a profit-and-loss situation. Rather, it seems as though, depending on the product, new opportunities open with each transmission: Opportunities that give both the character and the plot in which the character is embedded new scope for development.

Unforeseen circumstances require the player to make risky, evasive driving maneuvers, when »Game Over« flashes onto the screen, for example, allowing the video game to begin anew with a basic story reset. To stick with our car analogy, in the hands of a sophisticated novelist, it is introduced as a lovable old-timer, allowing for a glamorous narrative setting. But when the character steps on the gas, a sense of action is created, turning it into a getaway car or vehicle fast enough to escape pursuit by dangerous villains and capable of enduring drastic escape maneuvers, etc. This does not endanger the overall context in which 007 or the agent's narrative takes place in such media and character variation, but rather it is renewed and emphasized. It creates a shifting universe of stories which, although continually revolving around a creative center, is unlimited with regard to scope and further development. The continued narrative thus evolves in and of itself, so forming the actual center of the stories, as opposed to merely their adventurous content.

Such consideration ultimately makes it possible to understand how the aforesaid emancipation of objects—and particularly of products—has virtually redefined narrative in the humanities. Albeit a major critique, especially in our example of the agent or adventure story genres, being that the characters have ultimately been reduced to their respective accessories: Bond's car, Superman's costume, Robin Hood's bow and arrow, Ironman's hi-tech body armor, and so on. The accessories are more in the nature of a narrative prosthesis, upon which the characters are flange-mounted, as opposed to being independent and free-moving trappings which the characters have personally selected. Such outfits and trappings ultimately represent an essential restriction/constriction upon the characters, resulting in a complete reification of the protagonists' human characteristics. To put it another way: Bond *is* the car, Robin Hood *is* the bow and arrow. Embedding such accessories in new media environments, and especially in conjunction with new players and player types ultimately represents an intellectual turning point. Rather than defining the human characters in a reified manner, the products themselves have now become the agents and instigators of potential action. This is due to the new modes of their media appearance which redefine their effectiveness in different ways simultaneously; i.e., when used in conjunction with other accessories or equipment, or conversely, when confronted by superior or inferior equipment. This results in new perspectives on the means used by the protagonists in meeting each unique and varied narrative challenge. Viewing the last Bond movie from this perspective, it is clear that much more scope has been provided for the role of gadgets, in that they themselves have become a major focus. So, presentation of the best-equipped agent, technically speaking, which has never been traditionally staged without the inventor's consummate pride, is this time demonstrated in the style of a sovereign disclaimer. Ingenious inventions and technical novelties consist of little more than 007's realization that the time for games is at an end. »Did you expect an exploding pen?« asks the newly appointed Q, in response to both the viewer's and hero's unvoiced question: could it be that the era of dispensing lethal new »toys« is over? Behind this is the assumption that evil events have already moved so far into the virtual, hi-tech world of network controllers that no further technical upgrading could efficiently counter such escalation. Rather, the film's only solution must be sought with the aid of such archetypal, analog gadgets as were featured in the classic, original staging of the twentieth century's first spy thriller, in this case: a radio transmitter and simple revolver, tailored to its user, which ultimately symbolize the fact that the Bond story only functions today with constant translation from one medium to another. The high-tech network world and its virtuality, along with the devastating consequences for a reality that has remained analog, in conjunction with the low-tech world of the agents, represent the formal brackets of the story. They are, at the same time, the specific narrative framework underlying the cinematic translation process, which itself may become the material of a further film adventure. Our cinematic focus on the hi-tech, media-oriented agents, especially on their outfits and equipment, may finally link the formal aspects of storytelling to the real adventure as portrayed in film.

Academic IV: In Conclusion

In conclusion, one question still remains: What is needed as a new theory design in order to do justice to the media's narrative emancipation and, at the same time, the newly presented objects thus involved? There are two offers are on the table: the continental and the Anglo-American. The continental has already been touched upon with Koschorke's narrative theory in his basic hermeneutical pattern. The decisive feature is that, with the new medial »zero medium«« of the narrative, a horizontal order of the media-based internal narratives has been organized. Ultimately, it is a scheme borrowed from the methodology of modern intellectual history. It has long wrestled with the issue of understanding, from our perspective, the basic and fundamental changes exerted on classic, intellectual products. And in the middle of the last century, it was concluded that it was necessary to follow a so-called horizon shift in many aspects, to the extent that one can do justice to a variety of aspects, without completely losing the thread of the many individual stories relating to an underlying theme or plot. The new theory of narrative seeks to expand that diachronic horizontal course once again to the synchronous education level of storytelling. Lastly, it is the continental approach that (at least theoretically and historically) draws upon dialogical or dialectical self-organization of the representational sphere. Unlike the Anglo-American perspective, which is less about the horizontal divergence of narrative levels and media, than their vertical and pyramidal organization. In the theoretical background, reference is made to a theory of mind on the basis of scientific grounding in the sphere of facts. On this, then, the narrative is built, in so far as it forms so-called meta-narratives, which function as a type of higher-tiered commentary, far removed from fact (and thus always also fictional). Vice versa, but still a vertical direction of substantiation, it should be remembered that the teaching methods of the social sciences and humanities in terms of textual interpretation have their roots in the Anglo-American Bible reading and *close reading*. The latter was secularized in the 1930s as a maxim for the seriousness of the precise meaning of the text. Seen in this light, narrative is likewise more concerned with a commentary function as opposed to facts, preferring words and concepts from which facts then emerge from the more significant biblical concept of unity.

The meta-narrative moves in an intermediate sphere, where mediation between two irrevocable truths is applied: the truth of God and that of the world. Their sphere is a gray area, mentally and factually, structured by a tentative alignment that refers backward toward the above or below and, so, in towards the factual or transcendent. In this respect, meta-narratives are not subject to any process of horizontal self-discovery and self-organization, as is envisaged in the continental scheme of the formation of comprehensive sensory units. They are far more interim phenomena, which still aim for the ultimate and comprehensive truth, which they never, in principle, attain. Their uncertainty and ambiguity hold something miraculous that should astound people: evoking something higher and more eminent than their own finite and fallible views of the world. How such a basic methodological position can still be related to the use of product language in transmedial narrative, can be seen in detail by Roy Sommer when he takes the »meta-design« position, which he describes as a »mythological approach to self-reference in consumer culture.«[11] According to Roland Barthes's metaphoric notion of the modern design classics, they are objects created by gods which fell directly from the sky. Quoted literally—at least as far as the notion of the mythical in design is concerned.

A last, seemingly academic approach would be with regard to experimental transmedia productions, such as the TV series *About Kate,* currently on-air. The pivotal film shoot, which distinguishes these attempts from the consumer culture of the aforementioned blockbuster genre, is a highly significant and sustained self-thematization of media horizon fusions or meta-references. Thus, from the outset, the protagonists, especially the central figure of Kate, as well as the media in which they appear, are narratively interlaced, mutually reflective, and practically interchangeable. This especially applies to their respective social media platforms and mobile terminals. The fictional character of *Kate* and her psychological masquerades, or masking attempts, are basically nothing other than a cinematic reversal of the media profiles, in which the fictional *Kate* tries out her role as the fictional character of *Kate,* thus setting the scene.

The cinema, in its so-called mirror phase of the 1960s, as Christian Metz once presented in exemplary detail according to Jacques Lacan, offers an additional theoretical and historical prototype.[12] *About Kate* transfers the concept into a multi-layered 2.0 environment of an endlessly expanding universe within contemporary culture. It is a multiple self-calibration and self-improvement of personal horizons and their attendant Anglo-American differentiations, yet never an exploration of cross-references. And still, one could humbly suggest that *About Kate*—at least, in a transmedia theory approach—could be similarly described by the title of *Skyfall.* Since, in *About Kate,* we ultimately follow a narrative journey from the peak of academic reflection to the therapeutic depths of media self-

[11] Roy Sommer, »Metadesign: A ›Mythological‹ Approach to Self-Reference in Consumer Culture,« in The Metareferential Turn in Contemporary Arts and Media, ed. Werner Wolf (New York, 2011).

[12] See Christian Metz, *Der imaginäre Signficant. Psychoanalyse im Kino* (Münster, 2000; originally published as *Le Significant imaginaire,* 1977).

representation, the end of which only confirms the simple insight that all such transmedia events, now so dominant in our new film and media culture, are merely a reversal of comprehensively understood storytelling.

Martin Gessmann
studied philosophy, German studies and Romance studies at Eberhard Karls University in Tübingen, with study-abroad stays in Nantes and Washington, D.C. He worked as a television reporter at the SWR regional broadcaster from 1991 to 1996. He did a postdoctoral fellowship at the German Research Foundation, dfg (1998) and was a Fellow at Marsilius Kolleg at Heidelberg University from 2008 to 2011. In June 2010 he was appointed professor at Heidelberg University and is a professor of the history of culture and technology at HfG Offenbach since October 2011. He is an editor of *Philosophische Rundschau* since 2003. He has written several books, including monographs on Montaigne, Hegel and Wittgenstein.

Jos Diegel

Spoiler alert!: You're always making things without beginnings or ends, big pictures full of who knows what rubbish.

À reprendre depuis le début (Repeat from the beginning)
Il faut être absolument modern (It is necessary to be absolutely modern)

M: Sorry about having that narrative crisis. Don't hold it against me! I'm not always on the surest footing there.

B: You're not exactly a postmodernist! You want to appear in narrative form because everything for you plays in front of the backdrop of a coherent story.

M: I can find my way around literature, art, cinema, as I am. In fact, you can put me anywhere and I won't bore either the audience or myself.

B: They've seen it all before. I like to produce a lot of boredom, to a very high standard using lots of techniques.

M: All the same—your magnificent use of various techniques hasn't got you anywhere yet. It's a love technique of yours. You're always trying to be so creative, to be a pioneer, until you realize you have mastered your toys. At the same time, you're incapable of mediating.

B: You don't need to give me such an opening every time. It gives me a pain in my backside. At the beginning, I don't want to have the end. Everything that I already know is of no interest anymore.

M: Don't talk such nonsense. You are constantly busy with openings and conclusions; you just don't notice it anymore. You are always leading yourself or me into something, before reaching a turning point, a G-spot, the climax comes, and afterward you sweep everything aside, everything that was beautiful.

B.: Oh, if I embody a collage or a montage, then I think that I am developing quite well.

M.: Now that would be exciting, a virtual cross between you and a self-realization program.

B.: Don't make such a media spectacle out of it. For me it's really quite trivial.

M.: Just thinking about it makes me feel attracted to you in a nonlinear way. You master your cinematographic technique quite well, I'll grant you that. One feels very well cared for and safe in your moving images.

B.: You admire me and follow my life story, not only because I'm so successful and my story makes headway, but because I embody such an incredibly great character whom you can identify with?

M.: No, that's not it. I can't build a relationship with you because you don't have any conflict within yourself. I have the feeling, you're always telling me the same thing.

B.: I don't feel the need to constantly confront you with far-fetched conflicts, just because they would be the opposite of who you are and what makes you good.

M.: Do you want to build up around me a serious physical treatment and a decent story or are you here because of the happy end?

B.: I can see it coming already. This story will end badly. There is no great ending to this story.

M.: But I like to hear great stories. But wait just a bit, every seven seconds one loses the attention of one's listener. Every seven seconds a child dies in the world. Maybe there's a context.

B.: Your story is merely symbolic and visually stunning. Do you know that? You don't have anything more to offer than that?

M.: Yes, exactly. That's it. That is the crisis of narrating one's own life in the context of the decline of the great stories of our time. But I guess you already know that?

B.: You are not telling me anything I don't know. If you want to stand around there and tell me something about context, you are telling me nothing. I'm open for almost anything.

But not for your stories which, in any case, you never tell right.

M.: That's why you bombard people with images. I feel like I'm in a picture book, overwhelmed with warm words.

B.: In October 2013, these images have reached the zenith of their effect. The revolutionary project is sinking in a flood of images which are henceforth only occupied nostalgically with themselves.

M.: You're always talking about sinking. You're always talking about the flood. When is the flood coming? I am making an effort to interrupt a naturally given flow of images, while you are showing pictures together rather one after another.

B.: Look at a picture until it looks back as a stranger.

M: When the point is reached, then I can look, as if for the first time, at what I have here, what happened between us here. From a distance, it is almost a picture of a relationship, a picture of a dialogue.

B.: Consequently, as I said, I give everything to words that I have to offer for this dialogue, everything to images that I have to offer for this dialogue. Most people travel to the image that they have of the sea. Most people live in the image that they have of a relationship or of a happy community.

M.: This fluctuation really warms my heart: this fluctuation of words, this fluctuation of images.

B.: I feel that I am missing something, if I break them down to their essentials and the telling is economical. Basically, the essence doesn't interest me. I am pleased with you and when I tell you that, that is the essence. But basically you don't get anything from that because there is something else I must tell you.

M.: You tell me nothing. And I gain nothing. These are all things that should have been established before.

B.: Are you serious? I want there to be something between us. I want to establish a story with you. Most people find that pretty good.

M.: You can stop right there. When someone says to me: tell us your version, then I usually don't know what to say.

B.: I am constantly pushed in front of or behind the camera, and someone says: You'll be fine! Without any clue as to what I should represent, what I should feel. And then they show the images anywhere.

M.: Yesterday morning I woke up and I thought of you. I thought to myself that you look like a scene in a movie in which you acted. I was quite surprised because I did not even know you except from the film.

B.: We were not a bad duo. And I think that we enjoyed acting with each other and producing images. Do you still have the films that we made together? I couldn't find them anywhere.

M.: You're just babbling about unimportant stuff that doesn't interest anyone here. I feel better that I've been so honest with you, but it's a pity that I've never thought about why you babble so insecurely and try to fill images with text.

B.: I would gladly visit you in this exotic world where, out of anticipation and confidence, a flimmering twenty-five, fifty, or goodness knows how many frames per second are passing by. To finally travel somewhere, with the assuredness of knowing myself capable of depicting any situation in the customary dramatic poses.

M.: And you think that something dramatic is already there? What you are drawing there for me is a rather dramatic picture.

B.: I have to constantly learn how to comfortably and dramatically negotiate my intellectual adventure.

M.: But you also create such wonderful moments when you narrate in pictures. And, along the way, you make very moving pictures of us. Because there is nothing that you forbid yourself. There is no prohibition of images.

B.: I also like what I see there. If someone is watching now, then I feel more entertained than I would ever with you.

M.: I am constantly moved by your images. I always feel a sense of amazement. I can't shake the feeling that you're making your stories and your pictures for someone who is still missing.

B.: I constantly have the feeling that I'm being observed and that someone is forming a picture of me or someone is stipulating what I have to do.

M.: That's right! I, too, have the feeling that what you say is written for you. You have also gratefully accepted it. No one has complained, certainly not myself.

B: I know a lot of pictures; I know what you want here. I'm not complaining, but your stubborn way of viewing images, is a way of viewing something so as to separate it from its truth. You seem quite separated from what you are doing.

M.: No, the way I see it is that I also don't want to have an opinion about, or an image of, everything. There are things that just leave me cold. Your warm, well-intentioned images also leave me cold. The time is over in which we both needed to create greater images in our relationship.

B.: I don't know if it's over. I just know that you have ceased to occupy yourself with the theory of your character. In this frame of mind, you are certainly no longer creating any usable images. It doesn't work like that. I feel such a stupid distance between us. But I still don't want to be at a distance when you form a picture of me.

M.: One doesn't have to be an expert to build a bridge across that. You are, anyway, such a distant animal, communicating as you do through a forest of images. You always expect me to gather information about your images. You constantly portray some emotional state of mind, which I then have to interpret.

B.: Your information really has nothing to do with my emotions. Your images only serve to convey and negotiate issues on an emotional level. I don't need that.

M.: But there is still a lot of emotion in them. I should have guessed that you don't need them.

B.: Okay, you've understood that pretty well. But one can also see it in another way. I have to hurry now; otherwise I'll lose the images.

Jos Diegel
is an artist and filmmaker. He studied at the Hochschule für Gestaltung Offenbach until 2010 and plays, experiments, entertains and is concerned with sociopolitical and normative-narrative structures. He conceives of his gay and interdisciplinary science of negotiating and constructing postdramatic and alternative situations in media among others; film, video, installation, painting, performance and text. He is involved in several exhibitions, film screenings and projects.

A Narrative Revolution

Steffen Huck

Diana Iljine

Sir Peter Jonas

The 1999 revolution did not happen on the streets; it did not happen in the East and it did not have a specific color, neither yellow, nor orange or pink. Instead was variegated.

Like all revolutions it owed its existence to a fortunate confluence of various social, economic and technological forces, hunger for risk on the part of large US corporations and the innovation of a small Silicon Valley start-up at the geographic point on the compass where the Guadalupe River and Coyote Creek flow into San Francisco Bay.

The first flash of lightning came on January 10 1999, the second on September 22. This was a double whammy that reached the living rooms of America with the big screen TV as a shrine dominating the space. This time around, however, the TV screen was not showing short self-contained short stories ...

It was the revolution of TV epics. A harbinger of things to come had appeared two years previously when *Oz* (Tom Fontana, HBO, 1997–2003), a phantasmagoric journey through the hell of a US high-security prison, was first broadcast on HBO. Pulling no punches *Oz* proved to be a radical first attempt that ignited the revolution. The leaders of that revolution were David Chase and Aaron Sorkin, two writers who could not have been more different from one another. Chase was a seasoned TV producer with an impressive CV; Sorkin a screenwriter with a history of substance abuse who had sold a mere three screenplays within a decade.

Career patterns, however, played no role in this particular revolution because American TV had its back to the wall. Declining viewer numbers accompanied by intensified competition between the networks and cable were placing all US broadcasters under extreme pressure. When one has got nothing to lose one can recklessly experiment: an approach that more often than not fails but can also turn into a startling success.

It was against this backdrop that the epic series as a genre was born. In its development cable broadcasters such as HBO, whose programs unlike those on the networks were not interrupted by commercials, not only identified their business model but also defined the style and narrative techniques of this new genre forever. The winter of that year brought with it *The Sopranos* (David Chase, HBO, 1999–2007) about the life of a New Jersey

Mafia family. This went on to win twenty-one Emmys and five Golden Globes. The autumn saw the debut of *The West Wing* (Aaron Sorkin, NBC, 1999–2006) recounting the daily life of a fictitious US president named Josiah Bartlett (Martin Sheen) and his White House staff. American audiences got so caught up in *The West Wing* that for years there were rumours that Martin Sheen was planning to run for president—something many would have liked to see happen.

The Sopranos and *The West Wing* were parallel quantum leaps of the kind the world had experienced over a century earlier when Verdi and Wagner revolutionized opera by transforming it into a new dramatic form with more detailed and complex structures exploring to the full the music theater experience. The narrative form that Chase and Sorkin set in motion was astoundingly simple. Given that a typical season consists of ten or twenty episodes, why make each of them a self-contained story featuring the same cast of characters when instead you can recount complex, epic tales? Why should a series not attempt to follow the narrative structure of the novel? *War and Peace* for the twenty-first century with all the astonishing and haunting possibilities that are handed to you on a plate depicting the development of characters and the gradual or sudden changes in their dramaturgical situation. Sometimes such changes are merely alluded to in a subordinate clause that makes attentive viewers cringe with horror because they know the characters intimately. All the greater the shock when deeper unimagined traits of beloved heroes are shown. For example in episode 5 of *The Sopranos'* first season, while paterfamilias Tony Soprano is visiting prospective colleges with his daughter, we see him kill someone for the first time with his bare and sensitive hands. What viewers saw during that episode in February of 1999 had never been so glaringly portrayed before on TV.

But let us return to Coyote Creek. When one transforms a TV series into a novel for our time one needs to make sure that viewers do not miss episodes. To imagine Thomas Mann's *Magic Mountain* without the duel—that is surely unthinkable!

These problems did not arise with conventional series with self-contained episodes for the simple reason that it made little difference whether a viewer missed one now and then. The worst that could happen was that you missed a particularly good one but this did not interfere with the overall understanding and enjoyment of the series as a whole. This was not the case with *The Sopranos* and *The West Wing*: if one missed the episode where Tony, the loving father of innocent Meadow, strangles Febby Petrulio, one never really got to grips with Tony's psyche. In other words, both *The Sopranos* and *The West Wing* would have been total flops in a TiVo-less world in which viewers would not have been able to record a complete series at the push of a button.

Other technological advances such as DVDs and online vendors such as Netflix and iTunes also contributed to the revolution. At long last, viewers could watch a TV series the way they read novels: not one episode a day or week, but two, three or four in a single evening. And when time comes around for the season finale, they could even watch six or seven episodes to see how it all turns out in the end. The German newsmagazine *Der Spiegel* called this phenomenon »the new media drug.« Viewers can now watch two or more seasons, thus eliminating the »agony« provoked by end-of-season cliff-hangers. As we watched *The West Wing* after the whole series was issued on DVD, we had the privilege of watching the first episode of season 2 right after the final episode of season 1 and we simply could not imagine what it must have been like during the original broadcast run to have to wait four and a half months to find out *what kind of day* it had really been—to see who would survive and who would not.

Perhaps we need to think back to that evening on June 18, 1865, in Munich and to the audience at the premiere of *Tristan und Isolde*—a radical new work with harmonies no one had ever heard before, with the passionately enamored hero stabbed in the chest at the end of Act 2. The ensuing intermission must have been difficult for the audience although it reportedly only lasted half an hour.

Today, armed with a box set containing a number of seasons, viewers need no longer wait to find out what is going to happen next. The revolution of 1999 electrified not only TV viewers but also the creators of these shows—indeed, the whole TV community—and proved that a new kind of TV was not only possible but was indeed exactly what people had long been waiting for. HBO and its colleagues initially targeted an educated and affluent audience, as it could survive on smaller target groups than the ones the networks needed. The networks and producers, however, wasted no time in targeting an international audience so that its viewing constituency became not only more differentiated but also more global.

The money soon began to flow, attracting talent galore: Alan Ball/*Six Feet Under* and Joel Surnow/*24* (both 2001); Shawn Ryan/*The Shield* and David Simon/*The Wire* (both 2002); David Milch/*Deadwood* and David E. Kelley/*Boston Legal* (both 2004). It soon became difficult to keep track of all this new product, particularly since the production of series with this kind of narrative complexity was getting started in Europe as well, first in France with *Engrènages* (*Spiral*) (Alexandra Clark, 2005) and soon thereafter in the UK and not least in Denmark.

Complex narratives required users to use their intelligence to get intensely involved, to connect the dots between the events in the various episodes and understand the series' narrative world. The narrative comprised a series of parallel story arcs and in this respect exhibited a novel-like narrative structure. A longer overarching plot line in lieu of self-enclosed narratives always leaves viewers wanting more on account of the complex, dynamic and personal relationships they develop with the series characters. Heroes with »normal« problems— even if the problems usually are not resolved normally—create a bond between viewers and these characters and foster viewer identification with them.

The premise behind each of these series is also innovative. For example, how can America's biggest hero possibly be a terrorist (*Homeland*)? A respectable chemistry teacher becomes a criminal drug lord (*Breaking Bad*); a Mafia boss goes to a shrink (*The Sopranos*); a smooth-talking and brilliant advertising executive has demons and dark secrets galore (*Mad Men*). Instead of the classic struggle between good and evil one has highly differentiated characters with both positive and negative traits. This gave rise to detailed discussions about content on online forums and on fan Web sites. Producers used the Internet to provide background information about the series and give away possible future plotline triggering even more interest and higher cult status.

The revolution passed Germany by. *The Sopranos* ran for a season on ZDF, then nothing for a year. Season 2 was broadcast but even later at night than season 1 and that was it. The series did not return to German TV until 2005 and then on cable. *The West Wing*, which had won twenty-six Emmys and three Golden Globes, was completely ignored by German broadcasters for nine long years and finally surfaced on the Fox German cable network. There was »only« a three-year delay for *Six Feet Under* and then it was snapped up by—guess what—a cable broadcaster. After a delay of two years, *Boston Legal* and *The Shield* were broadcast on Vox and ProSieben respectively. This was not the German public broadcasters' finest hour—a pity because they so lightly passed up the chance to participate in the global competition for TV epics. A series called *KDD-Kriminaldauerdienst* about a Berlin police criminal investigation unit was a genuine masterpiece of German TV but only ran for three seasons. The first two seasons were broadcast during the unappealing 9 p.m. slot on ZDF while season 3 was shown on Arte.

Im Angesicht des Verbrechens (Dominik Graf and Rolf Basedow, 2010), about two Berlin policemen in a Mafia milieu, was shown on Arte, and then in a late-night slot on ARD. It was then canceled due to low ratings. And where is the TV epic from the German master of the miniseries? Where, dear ARD executives, is Dieter Wedel's recent work? In Germany, there has been so far a reluctance to spend the kind of money it takes to hire a creative team of the caliber that is behind the best US TV series.

It is worth noting that American TV series writers and producers have by no means a free hand, their output is subject to strict production cycles that, in turn, means that the system of writers working on their own, as is customary in Europe, is simply out of the question. While creators of American series have high status and are paid extremely well they also work with the system of writer's rooms where four to six writers continuously brainstorm, write and operate a collective self-prophylaxis over content and form. Otherwise it would simply be impossible to provide up to twenty-four episodes of consistent quality over the course of a single season. This type of collaboration is attributable to market pressure, to harsh competition in the American TV industry but also provides viewers with something that a European »genius« working on his or her own could never hope to accomplish.

Writer's rooms work hand in glove with a so-called showrunner who is often an experienced screenwriter such as David Chase (*The Sopranos*) or Vince Gilligan (*Breaking Bad*). Each showrunner is responsible for his or her plot development, has a finger in every aspect of production and often acts as a producer, in which case being also responsible for the financial aspect of the show. The showrunner creates the overall series concept but is also open to suggestions from the writer's room. The Writers Guild of America now offers showrunner training programs.

The new epic genre has spread like lightning. Matthew Weiner's *Mad Men* showed that one can narrate without a plotline and still attract a large audience of viewers riveted to their TV screens; while Vince Gilligan's *Breaking Bad* is for the moment the jewel in the crown of TV epics—a work of such extraordinary artistic and narrative complexity that one constantly finds oneself wondering how the creators pull it off. These TV epics are attracting not only new talent to TV but also the grand masters of film. As the large studios are now making fewer feature films than in the past ever-growing numbers of cinema luminaries are working in TV. Martin Scorsese produced and directed the pilot for *Boardwalk Empire* and Dustin Hoffman was the lead in *Luck*. Now as the cloud is beginning to supplant DVDs, *House of Cards,* starring Kevin Spacey, was shown in its entirety from day one; an evolution attributable to Netflix's striving to offer exclusive content.

It has been a mere decade and a half since the double whammy of *The Sopranos* and *The West Wing*, a period in which the interplay between creative daring and madness, quantum leaps in technological innovation and extremely tough competition has changed the face of TV forever. Gone is the time when the high point of many TV programs was the TV premiere of a major Hollywood film. It is now the independently produced new series that are not only on a par with movies but often excel, outpacing them from both a narrative and aesthetic standpoint. Regardless of whether TV series turn out to be the movies of the twenty-first century, TV epics with their innovative and complex narrative structures can certainly be regarded as the novels of the twenty-first century. They transpose the narrative forms of great novels into an audiovisual format in a revolutionary way as a reaction and response not to a black-and-white world but to one that is rich in the color and socioeconomic fabric of our young century.

Steffen Huck
is director of Economics of Change at the WZB and Professor of Economics at UCL. The recipient of a 2004 Philip Leverhulme Prize, his research has investigated the role of trust and fairness for competition as well as issues in bounded rationality and evolutionary game theory. More recently, he has worked on counterfactuals in Richard Wagner's *Tannhäuser* and belief systems in *Lohengrin*.

Diana Iljine
A native of Frankfurt, Germany, Diana Iljine earned a degree in communication studies and has been working in the film and TV industries for twenty-five years, including for many years as a certified purchasing agent for movies and TV series. Her book about film production, *Der Produzent*, is well on its way to becoming the standard work in the field. Diane recently earned an MBA from Steinbeishochschule in Berlin and since August 2011 has been director of the Munich Film Festival.

Sir Peter Jonas
was general director of the English National Opera from 1985 to 1993. In 1993 he became general director of the Bavarian State Opera until he retired in 2006. He has a first degree in English literature and studied opera and music history as a postgraduate. In 1974 he joined the Chicago Symphony Orchestra where he was director of artistic administration before moving to ENO. He is a Fellow of the Royal Society of Arts, Royal College of Music and University of Sussex. He was knighted for services to the arts on New Year's Day 2000. He holds teaching posts at the Universities of St. Gallen and Zürich and serves on the Board of the Netherlands Opera and University of Lucerne. He was, for nine years, until 2012, a member of the Board for the three Berlin State Opera companies and the Berlin Ballet.

Steffen Huck, Diana Iljine, Sir Peter Jonas
A Narrative Revolution

»Gonna Break Bad?«
On Implicit Dramaturgy in *Breaking Bad*

Christine Lang

The series *Breaking Bad* (USA, 2008, developed by Vince Gilligan) is one of the most successful examples of the new ›author's television‹ and is characterized by exceptionally tight and well-written scripts. Actions and events in this show never happen for just any reason. They always have reasons and consequences, often becoming clear only several episodes or even entire seasons later. The wealth of narrative detail, the references, the metaphorical language of film, and the many symbolic activations of film-aesthetic design techniques unite the explicit action with deeper levels of meaning. They create subtexts that might elude perception on the first or only viewing of the show. They reward active »aesthetic seeing« and repeated viewing of the series with ever new discoveries.

This essay considers the importance of implicit dramaturgy for the success of contemporary television film narratives—in interaction with the explicit dramaturgy of pure action events. It will be shown, in an exemplary way, how knowledge of the world and other special knowledge that is included and reflected in this TV series (and in other author's series) help to constitute the high quality of the series and thereby build a high narrative credibility.

Implicit Dramaturgy in *Breaking Bad*

In the pilot episode of *Breaking Bad*, the basic situation of the series is communicated in an elegant way: in an apparently unremarkable sequence, the viewers learn the most important things about the life of the main character. At the level of the explicit narrative, the backstory of the hero is told: his life has unfolded differently than he had expected, he will soon become a father, he was once a contender for the Nobel Prize, and his health is no longer quite up to par. In addition, his wife Skyler is introduced and characterized by the color patterns which are carefully hung on the wall. Although this is important information for the explicit action, at the same time—largely through the color pattern—something else is being implicitly conveyed. Here is hidden an agreement with the viewers, a kind of guide to the reading of the series: In this series, a lot will be told with, about and through style. The viewers are asked to adjust to this and to pay attention to it. In this way, not only is general knowledge of life in the Western world a prerequisite for understanding *Breaking Bad* in all the dimensions of its narrative, but a solid knowledge of style is also demanded. Genre knowledge and the skill to read different styles—such as interior decoration of apartments, car brands, and clothing—all play an important role.

In a later key scene of the pilot episode (Figure 1), Walter hands over his life savings to his new business partner, Jesse, while standing in a parking lot, so that Jesse can set up a meth lab:

JESSE: Tell me why you're doing this. Seriously.
WALT: Why do you do it?
JESSE: Money, mainly.
WALT: There you go.
JESSE: Nah. Come on, man! Some straight like you, giant stick up his ass ... all of a sudden at age, what, sixty—he's just gonna break bad?
WALT: I'm fifty.
JESSE: It's weird, is all, okay? It doesn't compute. Listen, if you're gone crazy or something. I mean, if you've gone crazy, or depressed—I'm just saying—that's something I need to know about. Okay? That affects me.
WALT: I am ... awake.
JESSE: What?
WALT: Buy the RV. We start tomorrow.

That there are essentially two dimensions of storytelling in *Breaking Bad*—the explicit and the implicit levels—is pointed to in this scene, even by the question that Jesse asks that provides the series with its title. On the explicit level, his query »Some straight like you [...] he's just gonna break bad?« refers to the question of whether Walter will now become evil. Jesse's youth-culture language serves as the key characterization of Jesse, who is the contrasting figure to Walter White. On the other hand—and implicitly—an encoding is hidden in the phrase that gives the viewer a hint of an important implication of the entire series: »Breaking bad« carries in this youth language the connotation of being cool. The implicit dramaturgy addresses itself in this scene to a culturally imprinted everyday knowledge and to the knowledge of a specific target group, especially to pop culture-influenced special knowledge—for example, to the distinction between cool and not cool.

Implicit Dramaturgy

Implicit dramaturgy is a term that can be used productively for the interpretation of specific aspects of the analysis—for example, concepts such as *style* and *excess* which have been brought into play by David Bordwell—of certain aggregated components of cinematic storytelling.[1] Dramaturgy, both as a practical activity and as a praxis-oriented science, is always to be understood as that media which steers the process of the reception aesthetics of a work, and through which hidden meanings of a filmic narrative can be decrypted. Implicit dramaturgy is not just one, but perhaps *the* determining factor in contemporary cinematic stories. Through it, deep dimensions of cinematic narration are shaped and communicated. Implicit dramaturgy does not limit itself in its world references to substantive allusions and quotes, as in postmodern cinema, but rather it organizes the use of all cinematic design elements. It guides all aesthetic decisions regarding material, color, camera, editing, mise-en-scène—from performance to scenography—and, last but not least, all auditory elements. In film language, all filmic aesthetic elements have, if not an explicit, then an implicit dramatic function.

The term *implicit dramaturgy* comes from theoretical theater dramaturgy, in which there is a tradition of dealing with implicit, i.e., hidden dramaturgy. Both for the deeper understanding of a dramatic cinematic narrative as well as for film analysis and cinematic practice, the terms *explicit* and *implicit dramaturgy* are extremely helpful. *Explicit dramaturgy* refers to the basic level of the film narrative, to the concrete action that is happening, somewhat analogous to the adoption by David Bordwell and Kristin Thompson of the Russian formalist concepts *fabula* and *syuzhet* taken together. *Fabula* refers to the story that is being told, which exists independently of the narrative medium, while *syuzhet* refers to the media-dependent organization and communication of this action. In contrast to explicit dramaturgy, implicit dramaturgy refers to the dramaturgy hidden

[1] On the concepts of *fabula*, *syuzhet* and *style*: see David Bordwell, *Narration in the Fiction Film* (Madison, 1985).

within the explicit narrative. It refers to those elements of the story that allude to the knowledge of the world of the viewer, and are thus responsible for the extended radius of impact of a work—something that the concept *style* can only inadequately describe. In contrast to the semiotic terms *denotation* and *connotation* (e.g., Metz, Barthes), with the argued four levels of meaning (referential and explicit as well as implicit and symptomatic[2]) of neoformalism, the concept of implicit dramaturgy aims, as a supplement to explicit dramaturgy, not only at the contexts of meaning in the world outside the film/image to which it refers, but rather asks especially, similar to reception aesthetics, about function, meaning, and interactions within the narrative itself. Explicit and implicit dramaturgy are relative terms that refer to the meaning contexts of individual elements within cinematic narrative. The film-aesthetic elements are usually in the service of both—explicit dramaturgy and implicit dramaturgy—but the more open and in more of a poetic manner a film is told, the more the emphasis is on the implicit dramaturgy as a key to the deciphering of the presented narration. In this way, implicit dramaturgy is largely responsible for the realism effect and the authenticity of the narrative. Style and humor are always time- and context-dependent phenomena, and if metaphors and references to knowledge of the world and everyday knowledge of the media-experienced viewer are not correct, then a film or a TV show can quickly appear to be clueless or naive.[3]

Implicit dramaturgy unfolds in cooperation with the explicit dramaturgy and »is realized functionally first in the appropriation, production and mediation process.«[4] Viewers compare films continuously with their experiences, with their knowledge of the world, and bring the film narrative into relationship with their own experiences of the world. The more knowledge of the world is present on the part of authors and viewers, the greater is the importance of implicit dramaturgy. It is the means by which the film author and the work address extensive knowledge of the world—on all levels and with all film aesthetic means. Implicit dramaturgies are above all not associated with purely artwork-specific historical, sociological and cultural factors.[5] Implications within a work can be brought into

---

[2] See: Kristin Thompson, »Neoformalistische Filmanalyse,« in Montage AV 4, no. 1 (1995): 32. www.montage-av.de (accessed August 16, 2013).

[3] If a film does not connect to popular aesthetic discourses and codes, then its reception seems to be difficult or even impossible. This applies to both commercial entertainment films and to art videos. The term *poetic imagery* does not take into consideration which canon of taste this »poetry« refers to. The dramaturgical, aesthetic and stylistic issues of televisual narratives are not yet being sufficiently researched. In television research, sociocultural and media-theoretical approaches still dominate.

[4] Peter Reichel, ed., *Studien zur Dramaturgie: Kontexte—Implikationen—Berufspraxis* (Tübingen, 2000), 21.

[5] Ibid.

the work from the philosophical, cultural-historical, or even from the biographical context of the author and all artists participating in the work. Not only intentional artistic purposes play a role, but, for example, the filmographies of actors appearing in a film influence its reception. Implicit dramaturgies relate, in this way, not only to the textual, linguistic level of a work, but also to its formal aesthetic structure, for example, the meter and rhythm of a cinematic work. Although certain implicit dramaturgies can sometimes be located within the internal structure of a film, such as when the reason for the organization of the aesthetic means is itself created in the work, they are associated with the aesthetic discourse historically surrounding a filmwork, with technical innovations, and with sociopolitical circumstances. That this also applies to rhythm and meter can also be seen in the differences between the well-made American entertainment film and the tradition of artistic realism of the European author's film. Both have aesthetic implications coming from completely different musical historical traditions—on the one hand, a culture permeated by the African American subcultural experience, and, on the other hand, white, European avant-garde culture.[6]

Breaking Bad

Breaking Bad is, for a television series, at an above-average level of being cinematic, and narrated with a view to a specific visual style. Thus the aesthetics, in other words, the *how*, become a major vehicle of the narration. A special quality of *Breaking Bad* is the ways in which the film-aesthetic possibilities are exhausted and placed at the service of the narrative. The series is linear-causal, in other words, it narrates via the dramaturgy of the closed form. But there also exist forays into the open form and into postmodern structures.[7] A special feature of the series consists especially in how implicit elements are tightly linked to the causal narrative and contribute to its progress. The implicit dramaturgical parts have a particularly strong meaning for the organization of the action. Even the subject matter of the series and the starting point for the dramatic narrative—which serve on the explicit narrative level to place a character in a situation

[6] On this subject, Annegret Gertz and Rolf Rohmer, »Versteckte. Dramaturgien im amerikanischen Bühnenentertainment,« in Reichel, *Studien zur Dramaturgie*, 81–133 (see note 4).

[7] For details see Kerstin Stutterheim and Silke Kaiser, *Handbuch der Filmdramaturgie. Das Bauchgefühl und seine Ursachen*, 2nd ed. (Frankfurt am Main, 2011); and Kerstin Stutterheim and Christine Lang, »Come and Play with Us«. *Dramaturgie und Ästhetik im postmodernen Kino* (Marburg, 2014).

that forces him or her to act, refer implicitly to the social reality of the inadequate health insurance system in the United States. (In Germany, such a starting point for a story would not be very credible.)

The middle-class chemistry teacher Walter White needs money due to his cancer. He wants to make his medical treatment possible, and to ensure (first) that his family is taken care of after his foreseeable demise. Due to certain circumstances, he hits upon the idea of going into the drug business, specifically into the manufacture of methamphetamine (crystal meth). Through the cancer of the main character, a plot is set in motion that spans the largest dramaturgical arc of the series. Walter White becomes a criminal, and the question is posed of whether he will be discovered and punished or not. Many smaller dramaturgical arcs are subsumed in this larger arc, told sometimes in one episode, sometimes over the course of a few episodes, or over the course of an entire season. A feature of this and other similar high-quality author's series is that greater weight is attached to the horizontal dramaturgy than to the vertical one, which makes this series very different from traditional television series.[8] These new series, which are therefore repeatedly called »film novels,« are determined by different, unpredictable long story arcs that are indeed intertwined in the sense of the dramaturgy of classic concurrent story threads of episodic storytelling,[9] but stand in relation to each other in a new way. The arcs may have completely different lengths and weights. They can extend over one, two or several episodes, or over one or all seasons. In the English-speaking world, the term *flexi-narrative* exists for this kind of dramaturgy, and the distinction is also made between *series* and *serials*. Series are traditional serial formats in which the main story arc is resolved within one episode, whereas in the *serial*, narrative arcs extend over several episodes or entire seasons.[10]

In the aforementioned parking lot scene, a lot of the characterization of the characters is made through the dress code and the respective cars of the two protagonists, Walter White and Jesse Pinkman. In this scene, it becomes clear just how productive is the relationship of exchange between explicit and implicit dramaturgies, and how they correspond to each

---

8
Vertical dramaturgy refers to the dramaturgical patterns which are repeated in every episode, such as in a classic detective series where, in each episode, a new murder case is to be solved by the same police inspector. *Horizontal dramaturgy* refer to arcs that extend over the length of a single episode, over several episodes, or over the length of an entire series; this is true, for example, for the narrative of the life of the police inspector.

9
German: *Zopfdramaturgie*. A concept of the dramaturgy of series where several parallel storylines are interwoven. For more detail on this, Stutterheim and Kaiser, *Handbuch der Filmdramaturgie*, 372 (see note 8).

10
Robin Nelson, *TV Drama in Transition: Forms, Values and Cultural Change* (London, 1997), 30ff.

other: on the dramaturgically explicit level of the pilot episode, the scene sets in motion the »envelope of the plot« (the *peripetia*) announcing that the criminal career of Walter White can begin. On the dramaturgically implicit level, the contrasts of the two characters—on all stylistic levels—are played against each other. Walter and Jesse obviously are not compatible with each other. They move in completely different social and linguistic spheres. Walter White is just about the most uncool person whom Jesse and the authors of the series could possibly imagine: He wears (as a colorless type) only the color beige—which in the context of the surrounding sand-colored landscape and architecture (in this scene, the bank) can be interpreted as an expression of his social conformism. He drives a tan-colored Pontiac Aztek—which has been named in the UK's *Daily Telegraph* as one of the hundred ugliest cars of all time—whereas Jesse Pinkman, by contrast, wears oversized large-printed hip-hop clothing and drives an affordable yet glamorously red 1970s automobile. For the purposes of explicit dramaturgy, these design aspects serve to develop the characterizations of the characters within the filmwork. At the level of the implicit dramaturgy, the design aspects carry coherent world references in themselves, are responsible for the authentic ring of truth of the characters, and are part of the immanent visual dramaturgy: the color red—as the color of the legally and morally, at the same time tempting, forbidden—is used throughout the series as the color of the drug scene and factors related to it.[11] This includes Jesse's red-colored car, the red sports car later acquired with drug money for son, Walter Jr., and the increasingly red components of Walter's clothes.[12]

In the parking lot scene is also hidden an additional significant formal style principle of the implicit dramaturgy that drives the series: It is an aesthetic of popular culture, one of opposition, of not being compatible with each other, which distinguishes the deep dramaturgical structure of the series. *Breaking Bad* lives from playing different genres brilliantly against each other: crime drama against comedy, psychological realism against postmodern comedy aesthetics, technical perfection against trash. These pop-cultural implications, its

[11] Colors have different meanings in different cultures, which are dependent on their respective application contexts. The color red is, however, often used as a medium through which someone is able to do something. For more details see Anna Schmid, Alexander Brust, eds., *Rot. Wenn Farbe zur Täterin wird* (Basel, 2007), 9.

[12] Blue is presented in *Breaking Bad* as an antagonistic color to red. Rather, blue is assigned to the elements of the storyline around the character Skyler, who, initially alongside other bright colors, often wears blue. Later she, in a way analogous to the overall darker film images of later episodes, increasingly wears black.

aesthetic principles—in which comparable methods of absurd or surreal confrontations, the destruction of conventional myths, and black humor are to be found—comprise the organizing principle of the narrative. This contrasting procedure creates the musical rhythm of the series, which in turn represents an aesthetic analogy to the formal language of pop cultural entertainment television. *Breaking Bad* is an ideal television series in that it uses the medium of television in the best way as an artistic medium. In the series, the same formal languages are displayed as in neotelevision, in which an entire TV-specific design language has evolved which, overall, is »based more on music than on language.«[13] It is »above all interested in visual surfaces, in the diversity of forms, and in movement.« According to Engell, in historical phases of change (such as digitalization), the principles of pop as the dominant foundation of television discourse and viewer practices prevail. One of these is that television aesthetics reflects »the mediality of the media and its fundamental properties.«

The referencing of pop in the implicit dramaturgy of *Breaking Bad* becomes visible in condensed form in the music video–like sequences, in the eye-candy aesthetics, and in the camera work in which perspectives are taken that do not have any identification with a human gaze, but it is rather the surfaces of things that self-referentially set up the scene, and which, in ›high culture film art‹, would be considered as ornamental and would be banned. In *Breaking Bad*, these settings can be interpreted as moments of self-reflexivity, since with them the attention of the viewers is is consciously directed to the artificiality and the construction of the film's narrative.

There are two scenes in the first four seasons of *Breaking Bad* which are staged as authentic contraband music videos. Thus the implicit elements referring to pop culture are never an end in themselves, but always also serve the explicit dramaturgy. Especially in the video *Negro y Azul*, the lyrics of which were cowritten by *Breaking Bad* creator Vince Giligan (for the 7th episode of Season 2/Figure 3), the band *Los Cuates de Sinaloa* brings implicit and explicit dramaturgies seamlessly together: On the implicit level, the *Negro y Azul* clip operates as a postmodern

---

[13] Lorenz Engell, »TV Pop,« in: *Was ist Pop? Zehn Versuche*, ed. Walter Grasskamp, Michaela Krützen, and Stephan Schmitt (Frankfurt am Main, 2004), 195ff. Engell refers to the term *neotelevision* in Umberto Eco and Roger Odin Casetti. Neotelevision designates the second historical and transitional phase of television (1985 to the present). It is, among other things, a product of enormous channel propagation.

yet authentic reference-joke.¹⁴ Here a specific segment of Mexican pop culture is cited, the so-called Narcocorridos, in which bands who specialize in this sing hymns of praise to the drug lords. The video represents the commonly employed popular culture medium of pastiche which, as opposed to parody, carries within itself recognition of and admiration for the original. This demonstrates, on the one hand, a very competent handling by the producer of special kinds of knowledge, but, on the other hand, is not sufficient: Within the action events, in the service of explicit dramaturgy, suspense is generated by this video: One learns in a unique way that the life of Walter White, a.k.a. Heisenberg, is in serious danger, because now new adversaries threaten the plan. The clip explains how successful the blue crystal meth is on the market and that Walter White, a.k.a. Heisenberg, has become a legend. Through the lyrics, the viewers are *en passant* informed that the new adversaries are not to be trifled with: »The cartel is about respect, and they don't forgive, that homie dead already, it's just ... nobody's told him.«¹⁵

Breaking Bad shows how important a consistently thought out and implemented implicit dramaturgy is, and how this contributes to the success of a film story when it is closely related to the explicit dramaturgy. Cinematic storytelling is always the sum total of explicit and implicit dramaturgy, and the more knowledgeably the implicit drama is handled, the more successful the subject unfolds in its reception through the filmic narration. Cinematic storytelling, no matter in which media—whether film or television—it takes place, always ignites dialectical-dialogical processes between author, work, and viewer, and in the special realization of this dialogue resides the decisive potential.¹⁶

Moreover, implicit dramaturgy also plays a role in the deep structures of a film and a TV series. Assuming that the medium of television finds itself in a transitional phase, challenged as it is in its legitimacy as the leading medium by the successor media Internet and computer games, it makes sense to research the conditions and aesthetic possibilities of television.¹⁷ It would seem that the author's series which have appeared since the mid-1990s, of which *Breaking Bad* is one important example,

---

14
Moreover, the actor Danny Trejo, who plays the lead character in Robert Rodriguez's postmodern film *Machete* (USA, 2010) appears briefly in the clip as a drug baron. In *Breaking Bad*, Trejo has a small but spectacular supporting role.

15
The English text appears as subtitles. The original is in Spanish: »A la furia del cartel, nadie jamás a escapado, ese compa ya esta muerto, nomas no le han avisado.«

16
In cognitive-(neo-) formalist film and narration theory (Bordwell, Thompson and others), the relationship between viewers and film is extensively theorized. Another approach is based on the literary theoretical works of Mikhail Bakhtin. A useful introduction to the various approaches to film theory is Thomas Elsaesser, and Malte Hagen, *Introduction to Film Theory* (Hamburg, 2007), 62ff.

17
On the concept of television as the leading medium and the challenge to its lofty position coming from the Internet, see Klaus Kreimeier, »TV,« in Handbuch der populären Kultur, ed. Hans-Otto Hill (Stuttgart, 2003). Online at: www.kreimeier-online.de/Fernsehen.html (accessed June 30, 2012).

have been created partly as a response to the advancement of other media, and that, with these series, television is activating its genuine aesthetic means.[18] Rather than imitating the possibilities of interactive media, for example, through hypothetically creating multiple-choice formats, television is reinventing itself on a high level through the configuration of the dialogic relationship of reception, inviting viewers to an active reception, and also reflecting the aesthetic organizational principles of the pop culture medium in the work itself. *Breaking Bad* would be, along with other complexly narrated author's series, unthinkable in any other media. How successful this approach is, and how well television through it connects to the present, is demonstrated not least by the existence of a virulent fan community on the Internet, in which perhaps the true potential of interactive television can be read today.[19]

[18] On the concept of the *author's series* (Autorenserie in German), see Christoph Dreher, ed., *Autorenserien. Die Neuerfindung des Fernsehens* (Stuttgart, 2010); and

[19] To name just two examples of the active fan culture and reception on the Internet: A remix of the Flies episode and a montage of the POV shots. Thanks to Harry Delgado for the links: www.youtube.com/watch?v=Hj2kAdcMDTo (accessed August 16, 2013). http://vimeo.com/34773713 (accessed August 16, 2013).

This text is a revised version of an essay published in the book *Breaking Down Breaking Bad*, edited together with Christoph Dreher, published in 2013 by the Fink Verlag.

References

Bakhtin, Mikhail M. *Autor und Held in der ästhetischen Tätigkeit*. Frankfurt, 1941, 2008.
Bakhtin, Mikhail M. *Toward a Philosophy of the Act,* translated by Vadim Liapunov, edited by Michael Holquist. Austin, TX, 1993.
Balázs, Béla. *Der sichtbare Mensch oder die Kultur des Films*. Frankfurt, 1924, 2001.
Barthes, Roland. »Rhétorique de l'image,« in *Communications* 4 (1964): 40–51.
Blanchet, Robert, Kristina Koehler, Tereza Smid, and Julia Zutavern, eds. *Serielle Formen. Von den frühen Film-Serials zu aktuellen Quality-TV und Online-Serien*. Marburg, 2011.
Bordwell, David. *Narration in the Fiction Film*. Madison, WI, 1985.
Carrière, Jean-Claude; Bonitzer, Pascal. *Praxis des Drehbuchschreibens/Über das Geschichtenerzählen*, Berlin, 1999.
Dreher, Christoph, ed. *Autorenserien. Die Neuerfindung des Fernsehens*. Stuttgart, 2010.
Eco, Umberto. *The Open Work,* translated by Anna Cancogni, with an introduction by David Robey. Cambridge, MA, 1989.
Eder, Jens. *Die Figur im Film*. Marburg, 2008.
Elsaesser, Thomas, and Malte Hagen. *Filmtheorie zur Einführung*. Hamburg, 2007.
Engell, Lorenz. »TV Pop,« in: *Was ist Pop? Zehn versuche,* edited by Walter Grasskamp, Michaela Krützen, and Stephan Schmitt. Frankfurt am Main, 2004, 189–210.
Engell, Lorenz. *Fernsehtheorie. Zur Einführung*. Hamburg 2012.
Fahle, Oliver, and Lawrence Engell, eds. *Philosophie des Fernsehens*. Munich, 2005.
Fire, Jane. *MTM. Quality Television*. London 1984.
Frank, Michael C., Mahlke, Kirsten. Afterword to Mikhail M. Bakhtin. *Chronotopos*. Frankfurt, 2008, 201–242.
Freytag, Gustav. *Die Technik des Dramas. Unveränderter Nachdruck*. Darmstadt, 1863, 1969.

Genette, Gérard. *Narrative Discourse: An Essay in Method,* 3rd ed., translated by Jane E. Lewin, with a foreword by Jonathan Culler. Ithaca, NY, 1983 (originally published in French 1972/1983).
Gertz, Annegret, and Rolf Rohmer. »Versteckte Dramaturgien im amerikanischen Bühnenentertainment,« in *Studien zur Dramaturgie: Kontexte—Implikationen—Berufspraxis,* edited by Peter Reichel. Tübingen, 2000, 81–133.
Klotz, Volker. *Geschlossene und offene Form im Drama,* 8th ed. Munich, 1998.
Kreimeier, Klaus. »Fernsehen,« in: *Handbuch der populären Kultur,* edited by Hans-Otto Hill. Stuttgart, 2003. Online at: www.kreimeier-online.de/Fernsehen.html (accessed June 30, 2012)
Lotman, Yuri M. *Kunst als Sprache. Untersuchungen zum Zeichencharakter von Literatur und Kunst,* edited by Klaus Städtke. Leipzig, 1981.
Leverette, Marc, Brian L. Ott, and Cara Louise Buckley, eds. *It's not TV: Watching HBO in the Post-Television Era.* New York, 2008.
Metz, Christian. *The Imaginary Signifier: Psychoanalysis and the Cinema.* Bloomington, IN, 1986 (first published in French in 1977).
Mittell, Jason. »DVD-Editionen und der kulturelle Wert amerikanischer Fernsehserien,« in *Serielle Formen. Von den frühen Film-Serials zu aktuellen Quality-TV und Online-Serien,* edited by Robert Blanchet, Kristina Koehler, Tereza Smid, and Julia Zutavern. Marburg, 2011, 133–52.
Nelson, Robin. *TV Drama in Transition: Forms, Values and Cultural Change.* London, 1997.
Reichel, Peter, ed. *Studien zur Dramaturgie: Kontexte—Implikationen—Berufspraxis.* Tübingen, 2000.
Sasse, Sylvia. Vorwort. In: Bakhtin, Mikhail M. (1921): *Zur Philosophie der Handlung.* Berlin, 2011, 5–31.
Schmid, Anna, and Alexander Brust, eds.*Rot. Wenn Farbe zur Täterin wird.* Basel, 2007.
Steinke, Anthrin. *Aspekte postmodernen Erzählems im amerikanischen Film der Gegenwart.* Trier, 2007.
Stutterheim, Kerstin, and Silke Kaiser. *Handbuch der Filmdramaturgie. Das Bauchgefühl und seine Ursache,* 2nd ed. Frankfurt, 2011.
Stutterheim, Kerstin, and Christine Long. »Come and play with us«. *Ästhetik und Dramaturgie im Postmodernen Kino.* Marburg, 2014.
Thompson, Kristin. »Neoformalistische film analysis«. *Montage AV,* (April 1, 1995). Online: www.montage-av.de (accessed August 16, 2013).

Christine Lang
studied cultural studies (under Friedrich A. Kittler), art history and literature at the Humboldt Universität in Berlin, followed by film and TV direction at the Kunsthochschule für Medien in Cologne. She was a scholar at Villa Aurora in Los Angeles. She was an artistic-research assistant at the Hochschule für Film und Fernsehen Konrad Wolf in Potsdam-Babelsberg in the department of media aesthetics and dramatic theory since 2009. Christine Lang works as a filmmaker and author. Her films ran at internatonal film festivals and won several awards. She published *Breaking Down Breaking Bad. Dramaturgie und Ästhetik einer Fernsehserie* (2013).

Christine Lang
»Gonna Break Bad?«

Fig. 1

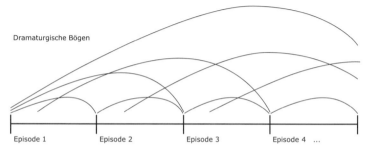

Fig. 2
Flexi-Narrative/Concurrent Story Threads Dramaturgy (Zopfdramaturgie)
(Graphic by Yvy Heußler)

Fig. 3

One Thousand and One: #Neuland

Alain Bieber

There's this *South Park* episode where suddenly the Internet disappears. The result: A mass panic breaks out, »Internet Refugee Camps« are set up, and fathers search desperately for Internet porn. Because: »Once you jack off to Japanese girls puking in each other's mouths, you can't exactly go back to *Playboy*,« explains Randy Marsh.

Short trip into the past. It was just a decade ago that Boris »Bobbele« Becker still had to use a dial-up connection (»Am I already in?«) and the people sitting in front of computers were laughed at as nerds. Today they are the cover stars of international magazines, and social media are lauded for making revolutions. The print media have by now largely stopped laughing. The German press is currently experiencing the biggest wave of layoffs since the founding of the Federal Republic, reports the Federal Employment Agency. The daily newspapers *Frankfurter Rundschau*, *Financial Times Germany*, and *Abendzeitung Nürnberg*, the city magazine *Prinz*, and the news agency DAPD have all declared bankruptcy. The basic problem is that the business model of print media still stands on two pillars: sales price and ad revenue. And the current media crisis is primarily an advertising crisis, because the big commercial advertisers rely less and less on traditional print advertising, due to too large wastage. Today they prefer digital social media campaigns. In short, the total advertising pie for newspapers and magazines is shrinking, that for TV and radio is holding steady, and the online pie is growing.

»The Internet is an uncharted country (›#Neuland‹) for all of us,« said Angela Merkel during a press conference in connection with the *Prism* affair. Complaints followed immediately in numerous tweets. »I'm skeptical because this ›uncharted country‹ is already populated. How many are we? Two billion? Probably all terrorists,« joked one Twitter user. But actually a fact. Since the early 1990s, it has been repeatedly stated that terrorists, Nazis, child molesters and porn consumers make particular use of the Internet. The net is made out to be a haven for crime, illegal downloads, Facebook parties, cybercrime, child pornography, street view. For the traditional media, the Internet is the perfect bogeyman. Bloggers ruin our business, everyone steals content and they just want free content, no one is buying CDs/books/newspapers anymore, nobody is watching TV. The list can be added to at any time. Anke Domscheit-Berg has described this well: »The Internet is no digital Sodom and Gomorrah, it is a mirror of society—in this respect, it reflects also society's darker side. Nevertheless, it is only a mirror and an image—not the cause. The causes of the problems still lay within society itself and it is there that they must be fought against.« One more example of this: that of the users of the self-designed virtual world *Second Life*. It could have been the perfect utopia, the creation of a new world in the realm of the virtual. And what happened? There came into being an exact replica of our existing world, there was prostitution and criminal gangs, commercial companies selling digital products, the Old Masters Picture Gallery of Dresden was virtually present, the archbishop's pastoral office held Bible studies, *Second Life* was used as an electoral campaign platform by parties and politicians. In short: at a certain point interest in *Second Life* went down to zero, because what is the charm of having reality also available as a digital copy?

It is all really quite simple. There are things that change, and there are things that will never change. The Internet is currently changing the TV landscape on a massive scale: cinema for the vest pocket, nonlinear documentaries on the net, participatory TV formats, and YouTube »original channels« produced by Endemol and UFA. These are turbulent times for the moving image of the future. But what is really changing is above all the data memory for text, image, and audio information. Drum storage, tape, diskettes, microfiche, vinyl records, cassettes, video cassettes, and CD-ROMs are (almost) extinct, and in the near future these will be terms known only to those interested in nostalgia. The form of storytelling has, of course, also changed. From the tradition of oral stories silent films eventually emerged, and then came the radio. The spectacular misjudgment of the movie studio boss Harry M. Warner in 1927 has gone into the history books. He asked at that time: »Who the hell wants to hear actors talk?« Minstrels, bards and troubadours are more and more rare today, but there will always be good storytellers, no matter which storage device or output device is used. The demand for good films and TV series continues uninterrupted. The US series *Game of Thrones* has about five million viewers per episode—and is also the most frequently illegally downloaded TV series (also approximately five million per episode). For *Warner* CEO Jeff Bewkes this is no cause for concern. He sees these statistics as being a kind of award: »I think that is better than an Emmy.« Even movie studios are capable of learning. No question about it: one must constantly use the specific features of each medium perfectly. Of course one consumes a film in a movie theater differently than on a tablet computer or through one's Google Glass.

Arte Creative is the magazine, laboratory, and network for contemporary culture of the European channel Arte in Strasbourg. Our first big experiment was *About: Kate*. This cross-media project made it possible to accompany the main character Kate in her experience at a psychiatric hospital—on TV on Arte, online at arte.tv/kate, with the app of the series, and on Facebook. You become a friend, a fellow patient and a media director of *About: Kate*. The free app for iOS and Android synchronizes automatically with the series via audio signal, and feeds the audience watching in real time with links, surveys, tests and information. You could then analyze your answers online, upload your own videos and photo contributions, and test your friends. And, if you become Facebook friends with Kate, you can write messages to her, leave comments, or just see what kind of mood she is in right now. »When the cultural channel *Arte* narrates about the life of Kate Harff, then the era of postmodern narrative has finally begun for the often solemn German television,« wrote *Die Welt*. »Finally the viewer can be more than just one among millions of others who casts a vote, finally he or she is treated as a human being, is allowed to be part of the story.« Our goal was: the narration should become three-dimensional, should work itself into the real space, and should connect with its audience wherever that audience happens to be at the moment, in social networks like Facebook and at their cell phones and computers.

»If the message is important, then it will reach me,« said a college student in a study of media consumerism in 2008. This sentence has become the nightmare scenario for media companies. It's so simple: If you have nothing to say, you should rather remain silent. If you have a story to tell, then obey the commandment: Thou shalt not bore. And if you have a really good story to tell, then go to where the listeners and viewers are, and use all the memory and playback media through which you can reach your target group.

Alain Bieber
studied rhetoric, sociology, literature and political science in Tübingen and Paris. In 2004 he founded rebel:art, a platform for art, culture and politics as well as the exhibition series PARASITES – illegal exhibitions. He cocurated the Subversiv Messe in Linz and the Dockville Festival in Hamburg. He has worked as an art critic and an author of artnet, ARTE, ART Magazin, Neural, Merian, Spiegel Online and Max und Die Gestalten. Today he is a project manager for Arte Creative, a magazine, a network and lab in Strasbourg.

Of Lonely Girls, Prom Queens, and Cool Guys: Web Series as a New Audiovisual Form on the Internet

Markus Kuhn

1. Introduction[1]

The Internet is often referred to as a success story largely because it has spawned countless success stories of varying magnitudes. And in turn, these narratives achieve popularity not so much because resounding success is normally accompanied by robust financial gain and stratospheric user or revenue figures, but rather because such tales lend themselves to countless retellings and are passed from one communication medium to another. One need only think of the rise of such erstwhile insignificant services as certain search engines, or Web sites where users can exchange videos and photos. And then, of course, there's the personal success of »freakish self-made men« and »nerdy students« like Chad Hurly and Mark Zuckerberg, and all other rags-to-riches myths of the Internet age. Now the social web has given the digital gold rush yet another powerful boost.

One such Horatio Alger tale is that of a lonely teenage girl named Bree who, in the summer of 2006, reported on the »errors and confusions of teenage life«[2] and in so doing gained unexpected notoriety in the Internet's »struggle for attention.«[3] Hence »her« YouTube series *lonelygirl15* (USA 2006–2008) is now an Internet »classic« in the still relatively new audiovisual narrative format known as Web series—despite *lonelygirl15* not having been so recognized at the outset.

In a series of YouTube videos beginning on June 16, 2006, and using the alias *lonelygirl15,* sixteen-year-old Bree recounted her daily life, her home schooling and the bizarre cult to which her parents belonged. In her videos, seldom more than three minutes long, Bree sat down in front of her webcam and just started talking (Fig. 1). In keeping with her whimsical nature, the material she uploaded to YouTube exhibited all manner of digitally generated, amateurish visual and sound effects with which, she noted, her buddy Daniel had helped. Bree also contributed to the lively comments that were posted about her videos.

But the subject matter grew increasingly intimate and the digital editing gradually began to surpass the quality usually achievable with conventional desktop editing software. Moreover, growing numbers of users began posting comments expressing doubt as to whether *lonelygirl15* could really be the

---

[1] This article is largely based on previous articles of mine about Web series, particularly the following: »Zwischen Kunst, Kommerz und Lokalkolorit. Der Einfluss der Medienumgebung auf die narrative Struktur von Webserien und Ansätze zu einerKlassifizierung,« in *Narrative Genres im Internet. Theoretische Bezugsrahmen, Mediengattungstypologie und Funktionen,* ed. Ansgar Nünning, Jan Rupp, Rebecca Hagelmoser, and Jonas Ivo Meyer (Trier, 2012), 51–92; »Medienreflexives filmisches Erzählen im Internet. Die Webserie Pietshow,« in *Rabbit Eye—Zeitschrift für Filmforschung* 1 (2010): 19–40, http://www.rabbiteye.de/2010/1/kuhn_erzaehlen_im_internet.pdf (accessed July 30, 2013); »YouTube als Loopingbahn. lonelygirl15 als Phänomen und Symptom der Erfolgsinitiation von YouTube,« in *Videoportale: Broadcast Yourself? Versprechen und Enttäuschung,* ed. Julia Schumacher and Andreas Stuhlmann, Hamburger Hefte zur Medienkultur 12 (Hamburg, 2011), 119–36, http://www.slm.uni-hamburg.de/imk/HamburgerHefte/hamburgerhefte.html (accessed July 30, 2013); »Der Einfluss medialer Rahmungen auf das Spiel mit Genrekonventionen. Die Webserie Prom Queen als Transformation des Highschool-Films im Internet,« in *Hollywood Reloaded. Genrewandel und Medienerfahrung nach der Jahrtausendwende,* ed. Jennifer Henke, Magdalena Krakowski, Benjamin Moldenhauer, and Oliver Schmidt (Marburg, 2013).

[2] Barbara Munker, »Die Enttarnung von lonelygirl15,« in *stern.de* (September 14, 2006), http://www.stern.de/computertechnik/internet/570087.html?nv=cb (accessed July 30, 2013).

private outpourings of a teenage girl; until journalists ultimately discovered that Bree was »merely« played by an actress and that *lonelygirl15* was actually produced by three amateur filmmakers.«[4] Following this unmasking, the series continued for three further seasons as a fictional narrative with more than 500 episodes; there are also numerous spin-offs. The number of hits remained relatively high[5] (although many viewers of the initial episodes felt cheated), largely due to the fact that the first wave of attention generated by *lonelygirl15* was followed by a second one. In the wake of its »unmasking,« at the same time episode 33 (*House Arrest*) went online, the phenomenon was being widely discussed in the print and online media, as well as on TV.[6] Many commentators felt that a pastiche on the appearance of »real« authenticity was an effective way to build identification potential and to publicize this particular YouTube series—which progressively evolved into a kind of thriller and mystery series.[7] Hence *lonelygirl15* represents not only the story of a teenage girl named Bree, but also (at least marginally) the Horatio Alger story of three semiprofessional »filmmakers«: Miles Beckett, Mesh Flinders and Greg Goodfried, in their capacity as creators of a fictitious series on YouTube and elsewhere on the Web.

Owing to the resounding success of *lonelygirl15*, Web series are often lumped together with user-generated content (UGC)[8] and video blogs, and some even presume *lonelygirl15* to be the very first-ever Web series.[9] However, this view fails to take a number of factors into account. First, Web series productions existed both prior to and concurrently with *lonelygirl15*—for example the US series *SamHas7Friends* (2006), and the German series *90sechzig90* (2000), as well as *Borscht—Einsatz in Neukölln* (2001).[10] Second, many other Web series have only partly employed mechanisms of authentication and interactivity. And since *lonelygirl15*, a broad diversity of Web series genres has emerged.

Largely owing to growing professionalism and commercial interest, Web series are increasingly implementing the tried-and-tested genres and audiovisual narrative conventions of film and TV.[11] But despite this evolution, most Web series, including those that are genre-oriented, still show traces of their

---

3
Roberto Simanowski, *Digitale Medien in der Erlebnisgesellschaft. Kultur—Kunst—Utopien* (Reinbek bei Hamburg, 2008) 84–88; Jean Burgess and Joshua Green, *YouTube: Online Video and Participatory Culture* (Cambridge/Malden, 2009), 27ff; Jean Burgess and Joshua Green, »The Entrepreneurial Vlogger: Participatory Culture Beyond the Professional-Amateur Divide,« in *The YouTube Reader*, ed. Pelle Snickars and Patrick Vonderau (Stockholm, 2009), 89–107, esp. 95f; Kuhn, »Medienreflexives filmisches Erzählen im Internet,« 19f. (see note 1); and Kuhn, »YouTube« (see note 1).

4
Frank Patalong, »Nur falsch ist wirklich echt,« in Spiegel Online (September 11, 2006), http://www.spiegel.de/netzwelt/web/0,1518,436070,00.html (accessed July 30, 2013); Munker, »Die Enttarnung von lonelygirl15« (see note 2); Joshua Davis, »The Secret World of Lonelygirl: How a 19-year-old actress and a few struggling Web filmmakers took on TV,« in *Wired* 14 (2006): 232–39, http://www.wired.com/wired/archive/14.12/lonelygirl.html (accessed July 30, 2013); Burgess and Green, *YouTube*, 27f. (see note 3); and Kuhn, »YouTube« (see note 1).

5
For 2006 visitor figures, see Davis, »The Secret World of Lonelygirl« (see note 4); and Burgess and Green, YouTube, 27f. (see note 3).

6
When, in September 2006, lonelygirl15 was »unmasked,« a great deal of ink was spilled in both print and online media. See Burgess and Green, *YouTube*, 27f. (see note 3); and Kuhn, »YouTube« (see note 1)

7
Kuhn, »YouTube« (see note 1).

media environment.¹² At the same time, growing numbers of semiprofessional organizations, such as theater companies, colleges and drama clubs, are producing relatively low-budget Web series, some of which aspire to be intellectual, while others consciously aim to be low-brow, popular-culture products.

In this article, I explore the ever-growing domain of Web series by looking at shows whose concepts differ considerably. And so, apart from *lonelygirl15*, I will be discussing *Prom Queen* (USA 2007, 2010) and *Pietshow* (Germany, 2008). My working hypothesis here is that Web series should not be assessed on the basis of their intrinsic characteristics alone, but also in terms of their contextual factors; the media setting as well as local and social contexts of Web series have a tremendous influence on their aesthetics and narrative structures. I will also show that Web series draw heavily upon genres and narrative conventions from film and TV.

2. Web Series as a Media Format: A Definition

In this essay I will be adhering to the following definition of the term »Web series« that I have proposed elsewhere:¹³

Web series are online, audiovisual representations, characterized by their serial, fictional, and narrative nature and that are produced expressly for Internet presentation.

The centerpiece of this definition is the concept of audiovisual representations that are serial, fictional and narrative in nature and that are posted online for viewing. The (production-related) fact that Web series are premiered online is a first step toward differentiating between Web and TV series, which are broadcast and subsequently made available online. Web series which are transmedial spin-offs of TV series fall within this working definition and include the following examples: a video blog called *Eine wie keine—So Isses!* (Germany, 2009), which is a spin-off of a soap opera on Germany's Sat 1 TV network; *Lost: Missing Pieces* (USA, 2007–2008), a transmedia spin-off of the narrative world of the TV series *Lost* (USA, 2004–2010); and *Nurse Jeffrey: Bitch Tapes* (USA, 2010), which is a transmedia spin-off of *House M.D.* (USA, 2004–2012).

8
Glen Creeber, »Online-Serien. Intime Begegnungen der dritten Art,« in *Serielle Formen. Von den frühen Film-Serials zu aktuellen Quality-TV und Onllineserien* (Marburg, 2011), 377–96.

9
Gunther Eschke and Rudolf Bohne, *Bleiben Sie dran! Dramaturgie von TV-Serien* (Konstanz, 2010), 235.

10
But it is nonetheless fair to say that *lonelygirl15* is a milestone in the annals of Web series, including in Germany. And while *lonelygirl15* wasn't the first series of online videos worthy of the name Web series, it was the first to gain considerable international attention, particularly in Germany, and the first to be extensively discussed in offline media (Kuhn 2011b). For more on the various Web series referred to in this article, see my *Webserien-Blog* (Kuhn 2012b), where I briefly discuss all searchable German Web series in German (entries in German only, at http://webserie.blogspot.de).

11
Kuhn, »Der Einfluss« (see note 1).

12
Ibid. See also Creeber, »Online-Serien« (see note 8).

13
Kuhn, »Zwischen Kunst« (see note 1); Kuhn, *Webserien-Blog* (see note 10).

One way of moving from a definition centering around the production aspect to one that focuses on the work itself is to study numerous Web series, in order to gain a rough idea of the prototypical characteristics of Web series in general. In line with the findings of a corpus analysis,[14] I would like to propose the following characterization of the prototype of a Web series, based on Germany's Web series culture: a series of episodes with an average length of three to ten minutes and which, apart from a framing portal or channel within a portal, in many cases incorporate brief credits, a logo, or a digital »watermark.« There are Web *series,* where the narrative of each episode is the predominant element, as well as Web *serials,* where a narrative arc extending over multiple episodes is the salient feature. Statistically speaking, the predominant modality is a hybrid form tending toward serialization, i.e., narrative arcs.

Owing to their brevity, most episodes of Web serials need to keep their storylines to a bare minimum, which results in overlapping narrative arcs. In many cases, each episode of a Web serial consists of only a few scenes and usually ends with a cliffhanger. Other tendencies—to which there are notable exceptions—include a very small number of settings or locations (e.g., *Die Hütte*, Switzerland, 2010), and a limited number of characters (e.g., *Die Snobs*, Germany, 2010, and *52 Monologe*, Germany, 2011). Owing to the small viewing frame available on video Web sites or diminutive smart phone screens, Web series shots tend to be *medium* or *close-up* and character-centered. The quality limitations imposed by relatively small screens/frames and low pixel density promote the use of digital hand-held, and simplistic consumer-electronics cameras.[15] Modalities where poor image quality, and the amateur nature of the production itself become part of the series are often used in a deliberately compelling fashion. Thus, in some cases, low production values become a key selling point, which explains why so many German Web series are mockumentaries[16] —for example *Making of Süße Stuten 7* (Germany, 2010), *Flusstouristen* (Germany, 2010) and *Die Essenz des Guten* (Germany, 2011). Like their TV counterparts, Web series are composed of episodes and seasons, but are often referred to as webisodes or mobisodes—the latter in »honor« of viewers who

14
See Jan Henne and Markus Kuhn, »Die deutsche Webserien-Landschaft. Eine Übersicht,« in *Medienwissenschaft*, ed. Jens Eder and Hans J. Wulff. Berichte und Papiere 127 (Hamburg, 2011), http://www1.uni-hamburg.de/Medien/berichte/arbeiten/0127_11.html (accessed July 30, 2013); and Kuhn, *Webserien Blog* (see note 10).

15
While poor quality resulting from suboptimal resolutions is often attributed to the use of digital cameras, the latest technological developments have indisputably cast doubt on this correlation. Moreover, many smartphone screens now have better resolution than conventional SD TVs, and HD videos are even available on YouTube nowadays. However, the image quality of many Web series is still distinctly downmarket so as to minimize file sizes and thus speed up downloading and streaming.

16
For a definition, differentiation and classification of the mockumentary format beyond the Web, see Roscoe and Hight (2001), who, however use the term *mock-documentary*.

follow Web series on their smart phones. The term *webisode* is occasionally used to refer to an entire Web series, as opposed to merely an individual episode.

When it comes to *lonelygirl15*, I favor the term *pseudo-authentic Web series*. Such series mimic video blogs that are posted regularly, purport to consist of seemingly authentic videos which could have plausibly been produced by »normal« Internet users, and are premiered on Web sites such as YouTube. Features intended to draw attention to the private and amateurish nature of such videos can be described as *authentication strategies*. Pseudoauthentic Web series are characterized by fabricated communication with other users on the outer levels of communication.

Be this as it may, I shall now turn to a Web series that's a whole different ball of (virtual) wax.

3. Prom Queen: A Media-Savvy Pastiche[17]

Unlike *lonelygirl15*, the Web series *Prom Queen* was marketed with professional aplomb from the get-go, using instruments such as sponsoring, product placement, and the sale of merchandising items via an online store. The series format was sold to Japan, where the Web series *Tokyo Prom Queen* (Japan, 2008–2009) was produced and then extensively dubbed into German for commercial German Web sites such as *3min* and *Sevenload*. *Prom Queen* proved that it is altogether possible to create a successful business model around a Web series that users can view for free. The first of the series' three seasons consists of 80 episodes of approx. 90 seconds each. As its title suggests, *Prom Queen* is a pastiche of teen movies whose plots center around a high school prom. Typical examples of this genre include *Pretty in Pink* (USA, 1986), *She's All That* (USA, 1999) and *Not Another Teen Movie* (USA, 2001).[18]

Episode 1 (*The Long Walk*) builds up an atmosphere of mystery and suspense which is not resolved until the end of the season. But the storyline per se begins with episode 2 (*Teenage Wasteland: The Video Yearbook*), in which British exchange student Danica Ashby walks around her school brandishing a digital camera and aggressively asking her American classmates

[17] My discussion here of the Web series *Prom Queen* draws heavily on an extensive analysis of the series' first season (Kuhn, »Der Einfluss« [see note 1]) but has been altered and condensed to fit the argument I am making here.

[18] Ibid. On teen movies see James Hay and Stephen Bailey, »Cinema and the Premises of Youth: ›Teen Films‹ and Their Sites in the 1980s and 1990s,« in *Genre and Contemporary History*, ed. Steve Neale (London, 2002), 218–35; and Julia Schumacher, »Jugendfilm,« in *Filmwissenschaftliche Genreanalyse. Eine Einführung*, ed. Markus Kuhn, Irina Scheidgen, and Nicola Valeska Weber (Berlin/Boston, 2013), 295–313.

questions about the senior prom along the lines of, »What is the American obsession with prom?« The characters we meet are reminiscent of stock high school movie characters: Lauren Holland the heartthrob, Chad Moore the professional athlete (Fig. 2), Sadie Simmons the political activist, and so on. Unlike *lonelygirl15*, the episode is edited in a way which makes it clear that all of the footage cannot possibly originate from Danica's camera. Thus, sequences which Danica could have shot alternate with those showing her actively filming, interspersed with brief stills of the various characters' signed yearbook pictures, and a brief text about their accomplishments and future plans (see Fig. 2). For this reason alone, *Prom Queen* cannot be regarded as pseudo-authentic; added to which, among other things, the series has well framed images and smooth camera movements, a closing montage that neatly wraps up the episode, and professional-quality postproduction dubbing.[19] Many of these attributes suggest an extradiegetic, audiovisual instance hovering over the characters.[20]

Over the course of the first 11 episodes the high school setting is recognizably established via such physical high school hallmarks as classrooms, playing field, locker rooms, and the hallway with student lockers. The fact that in episode 2 all the main characters imply that the prom is of huge importance (via statements such as »Prom is the single most important night of your life«), establishes the prom as the narrative lynchpin. An SMS that Ben Simmons receives at the end of the episode invests-the prom and selection of the prom queen with greater meaning: »U r going 2 kill the prom queen [sic!],« texts an unknown user. This SMS initiates two story arcs that decisively establish the prom as the pivotal event of the series, the first being the question as to who will be elected prom queen, which is a core genre element, and the second being a mysterious subplot adding violence to the mix. At the same time, an unknown entity is introduced who appears to know things that the characters do not.

In episode 2, additional subplots are only briefly introduced via the characters, although are well developed over the course of the first 15 episodes. These subplots revolve around the

[19] Kuhn, »Der Einfluss« (see note 1).

[20] On the concept of audiovisual narrative entities and instances see Markus Kuhn, *Filmnarratologie. Ein erzähltheoretisches Analysemodell* (Berlin/Boston, 2011), 87–94.

motivation of various romantic relationships, plus (and far more important) events causing the characters to evolve. Take Sadie Simmons, for example. Seemingly unsuited to partying and romance, due to her political activism and quirky fashion sense, over the course of 80 episodes Sadie morphs into an »evening gown princess« who is suddenly a frontrunner in the prom queen stakes. All in all, the touchstones of an archetypal high school movie are so clear and myriad that *Prom Queen* can be regarded as an Internet transformation of a high school movie.[21]

Episode 2 presents a great deal of information, which can generally be regarded as a Web series benchmark. And here, it is precisely the use of tried-and-tested soap opera modalities that contributes to the »leanness« of the narrative. In other words, the use of stock figures and their immediate familiarity to the viewer allow characters to be labeled with stereotypical traits common in high school movies. Hence, with just a few narrative strokes, a stock character can be established who can then be used to various ends in the narrative arc. Because Web series episodes are so short, a great deal of information must be conveyed quickly; and this can be seen as a consequence of the media environment from which these series spring. You could almost say that, from a formal standpoint, Web series are forced to use genre and the narrative conventions of mainstream film and TV; for only in this way can the stories be quickly told which fit into these very short formats.

All the characters are constantly using media-based telecommunication tools: someone's always texting, e-mailing, filming, photographing, or posting such »works« online. This harks back to the user-generated content origins of Web series. In film-oriented Web series, online communication—which in pseudoauthentic Web series such as *lonelygirl15* occurs at the outer levels of communication—often shifts into the place of action.

The Web series *Prom Queen* originally ran on Myspace (at a time when it was still a highly relevant portal) and was also linked to Myspace by means of its characters each having their own Myspace profiles and video blogs, where actual Myspace users could interact with them. In the Web series *Pietshow*, this

21 Kuhn, »Der Einfluss« (see note 1)

type of interaction between the series and its integrated social networking Web site is even more pronounced.

4. Pietshow: Self- and Media-Reflection as a Product of the Representation's Media Framework[22]

Along with *They Call Us Candy Girls* (Germany, 2008), *Pietshow* was one of the first commercially produced Web series in Germany. The first episode begins with a forty-two-second precredit sequence, where we see what appears to be a video of a typical college party, shot with a hand-held camera. But things soon veer away from normality when, a mere thirty seconds into the sequence, the main character Piet, dancing, crashes through the wall into the next-door apartment (Fig. 3). This event sets the series in motion, by advantageously connecting the apartment Piet shares with his friend Nick with the one next door, occupied by Jesse and Melanie, who have likewise relocated to Berlin to attend college. And while no one particularly wants to repair the hole in the wall, the four students are forced to get used to their new situation. Thus, the 15 episodes of season 1 revolve around the four protagonists getting to know each other, replete with ex-boyfriends and girlfriends, casting calls, and domestic arguments.

The *hand-held camera effects*[23] here suggest that the opening episode was shot with a lightweight digital camera. And the fact that the camera is recording the party's spontaneous events is mentioned by one of the camera »operators.« Piet, crashing through the wall in the decisive shot, is only shown in the background, as if he'd been accidentally caught on film. But the editing of this sequence casts doubt on whether one of the guests is filming while moving around the apartment. The forty-two-second opening sequence consists of nine shots whose editing isn't especially remarkable and which are »held together« by the music playing in the background. But it is precisely at this juncture that the first break with the illusion of authenticity occurs. For the music cannot possibly be a soundtrack, as it is continuous in the (visual) edited transitions. In other words, the sequence cannot possibly have resulted from the camera simply being turned on and off as is often the case in home videos. If

---

22 My discussion here of the Web series *Pietshow* draws heavily on an extensive analysis of the series' first season. See Kuhn, »Medienreflexives filmisches Erzählen im Internet« (see note 1).

23 Markus Kuhn, »Das narrative Potenzial der Handkamera. Zur Funktionalisierung von Handkameraeffekten in Spielfilmen und fiktionalen Filmclips im Internet,« in *DIEGESIS. Interdisziplinäres E-Journal für Erzählforschung* 2, no. 1 (2013): 92–114. https://www.diegesis.uni-wuppertal.de/index.php/diegesis/article/download/127/149 (accessed July 30, 2013).

you assume that only one camera was used, it follows that the scenes were edited together and the sound was dubbed in postproduction; or that the audio was recorded separately.

Hence, this opening episode has the stamp of an authentic video of a private event, but also bears signs of a relatively professional production. This attribute recurs throughout *Pietshow*. However, the series itself offers an explanation for this unusual conflict by ascribing the dubbing and editing to the series' main character. Piet, we learn, is a film student, currently working on a film project for a social network called studiVZ. He films his roommates, edits the footage on his computer, and says that he is posting it online at studiVZ. The fact that we see (a) Piet editing the footage on a number of occasions (Fig. 4) and (b) the characters talking about the film makes *Pietshow* an extremely self-oriented and media-focused series. In episode 2, Piet describes the four characters who are (apparently by happenstance) involved in the project as »typical series characters«: Jessy, »the bombshell with a wide mouth«; Melanie the »sexually-repressed bitch«; Nick the »good-looking, boring guy«; and Piet, himself, »the cool guy, who's got it all together.«

And although the divergence from authenticity through montages and postproduction dubbing can be ascribed to Piet and his film project, this is certainly not the case in those sequences where we see Piet filming. What is more, all four roommates are visible in these scenes, meaning that, in the diegetical sense, no one could have been holding a camera; nor could a camera have been placed on a table or the like, since the shots are jerky. This creates a conflict that is not immediately resolved (Fig. 5). An additional cluster of stylistic devices which destroy the illusion that Piet could be the series' »showrunner« is evidenced by the presence of an entity »above« the characters, successively establishing a meta-level that can potentially serve as a narrative variation. I'd like to mention just a handful of these attributes: In episode 1, Piet comes across a page of script dialogue referring to Jessy and Melanie. In episode 10, we see footage filmed purportedly by Piet with a hidden camera and we catch sight of what is presumably the real production team recording the sound. And in episode 15, we hear a woman off-screen, calling: »And...action!«.[24]

And so the story told by *Pietshow* can also be interpreted as the unmasking of the professional film production that, »in reality,« is the driving force behind Piet's project. Thus, Piet is, in a sense, a prisoner in the world of his own TV series, à la Truman Burbank (*The Truman Show*, USA, 1998); where the diegetic world of the characters is continually invaded by people and objects from the outside world of the production itself. Hence *Pietshow* can be regarded as a type of Web series that differs from such obviously fictional series as *Prom Queen,* and from such pseudo-authentic series as *lonelygirl15*. The distinguishing feature of *Pietshow* is that the actual shooting of the series is, itself, incorporated into the show both in terms of the action and its formal structure. Hence *Pietshow*'s »double decker« structure is redolent of the production of (a) a semiprofessional Web series, by virtue of the illusion that the show is Piet's own project; and (b) a *professional* production, by virtue of its exposure of the show as such. Nonetheless, the pseudoauthentic dimension predominates in the first season by the fact that allusions are made to the overarching level of the professional production, although it does not take the form of a stand-alone diegetic level. *Pietshow* is linked to a social media Web site in the same way as *Prom Queen*—which involves characters from Myspace, yet does not imply that they actually exist beyond the confines of the narrative; while the *Pietshow* series is a pure fabrication that studiVZ-user Piet himself purportedly posts on studiVZ. This is also, incidentally, where *Pietshow* was first shown, a fact repeatedly reflected in the series.

5. Conclusion

Hence we have seen that when it comes to Web series seeking to mimic movie and TV genres, the medium in which these series are embedded influences the reworking of the genre; and thus various types of Web series have arisen depending on the media context of their integration. Not discussed here and what, to some extent, is the polar opposite of the media context, is the local integration of a Web series. Many German Web series

[24] Kuhn, »Medienreflexives filmisches Erzählen im Internet« (see note 1).

such as *Studis 4.0* (Germany, 2010), *Sex and Zaziki* (Germany, 2008), *Prenzlbasher* (Germany, 2009) and *SPPD: Die Sau ist tot* (Germany, 2009) show evidence of their local settings. For example, *Prenzlbasher* explicitly addresses the gentrifying of Berlin's Prenzlauer Berg neighborhood, while the episodes of *SPPD* are replete with typical settings and characters from Hamburg's St. Pauli district. As its title suggests, *Moabit Vice* (Germany, 2008) takes its cue from the 1980s TV series *Miami Vice* (USA, 1984–1990) and the fact that it is set in Berlin's Moabit district.

I have likewise not discussed pseudodocumentary Web series[25] like *Making of Süße Stuten 7*, *Flusstouristen*, *Prenzlbasher* and *Preußisch Gangstar* (Germany, 2008). While pseudoauthentic Web series are redolent of media self-representation, whereas pseudodocumentary Web series involve documentation centering around another person, object or topic. Pseudoauthentic Web series are imitations of video-blog self-representation, while pseudodocumentaries mainly take their stylistic cues from film and TV documentaries. On the other hand, the use of lightweight digital cameras and the traces they leave (via *hand-held camera effects*[26]) on the artistic dimension of a given work are often comparable.

By virtue of their being embedded in the social web, *Pietshow* and *Prom Queen* were both interactive to the extent that viewers had the opportunity to post comments and »provide advice« on *studiVZ*, *MySpace* and *Facebook*. A more complex aspect of interactivity arises on a social media Web site such as YouTube, where both personal and professional videos can be found. The structures specific to *lonelygirl15*, for example, prompted myriad users to go beyond their countless comments on the series on a variety of Web sites by posting their own series parodies on YouTube in response to the show. Hence *lonelygirl15* can be regarded as a stylistic »forerunner« of pseudo-authentic as well as interactive Web series.[27]

And then there's the question of how Web series can generate revenue. *Prom Queen* is a successful example of an approach involving fan articles, sponsoring, product placement, and advertising on the Web sites showing the series. But there is

---

25
I've elected to use the term pseudodocumentary Web series here rather than mockumentary series because producers of the former genre don't always aim to mislead the viewer. See Kuhn, »Zwischen Kunst,« 76 (see note 1).

26
Kuhn, »Das narrative Potenzial« (see note 23).

27
While *lonelygirl15* contains elements that can potentially incite interaction and involvement on the part of a user community, the series is also a complete and standalone artistic creation without all the sideshows. A project that points beyond these boundaries is the German Web series *Epicsode* (Germany 2010), which to some extent »forces« audience members to interact. See Kuhn, »Zwischen Kunst,« 76 (see note 1).

room here for a Web series to do even more. It could directly link attitudes toward habits and lifestyle with brand products, by virtue of the fact that, among other things, commercial Web series or Internet broadcasters in general are not as yet subject to any clearly defined restrictions in terms of product placement or surreptitious advertising. In fact, they can—as did the youth-oriented Web series *Deer Lucy* (Germany, 2009)—sell products from the show in a linked online store at the exact moment when those products first appear on the screen; plus, they can sell sponsors' products which are an integral part of the show's narrative world.

And what does the future hold? The commercialization and professionalization of Web series on the one hand, and the fact that ambitious, semiprofessional projects have difficulty obtaining financing on the other, may result in a loss of diversity, whereby Web series are limited to a few successful formats. But this evolution may well be offset by the creative potential and the tremendous willingness of semiprofessional and amateur series producers to experiment; not to mention the pioneering spirit that prevails in this still relatively new field. The incorporation of Web series into a broader transmedia, narrative world is a third key area with great potential. It remains to be seen whether quality TV series can also be produced for the Internet, as Netflix has already done; which also raises the question as to the possible convergence of Web and TV series. Web series are, first and foremost, a media-based narrative form with a strong Internet affinity. Their development is bound to be spurred by both brand producers seeking to generate revenue, and increasingly professional producers and directors. In short, whatever the future holds, it promises to be very exciting.

Bibliography
Burgess, Jean/Green, Joshua (2009a): *YouTube: Online Video and Participatory Culture*. Cambridge/Malden: Polity.
Burgess, Jean/Green, Joshua (2009b): »The Entrepreneurial Vlogger: Participatory Culture Beyond the Professional-Amateur Divide.« In: Pelle Snickars/ Patrick Vonderau (Ed.): *The YouTube Reader*. Stockholm: National Library of Sweden, pp. 89–107.
Creeber, Glen (2011): »Online-Serien: Intime Begegnungen der dritten Art.« In: Robert Blanchet/Kristina Köhler/Tereza Smid/Julia Zutavern (Ed.): *Serielle*

Formen: Von den frühen Film-Serials zu aktuellen Quality-TV- und Onlineserien. Marburg: Schüren, pp. 377–396.
Davis, Joshua (2006): »The Secret World of Lonelygirl: How a 19-year-old actress and a few struggling Web filmmakers took on TV. A Wired exclusive.« In: *Wired*. 14 (12/2006), pp. 232–239. http://www.wired.com/wired/archive/14.12/lonelygirl.html (accessed July 30, 2013).
Eschke, Gunther/Bohne, Rudolf (2010): *Bleiben Sie dran! Dramaturgie von TV-Serien*. Konstanz: UVK.
Hay, James/Bailey, Stephen (2002): »Cinema and the Premises of Youth: ›Teen Films‹ and Their Sites in the 1980s and 1990s.« In: Steve Neale (Ed.): *Genre and Contemporary Hollywood*. London: BFI Publishing, pp. 218–235.
Henne, Jan/Kuhn, Markus (2011): »Die deutsche Webserien-Landschaft: eine Übersicht.« In: Jens Eder/Hans J. Wulff (Eds.): *Medienwissenschaft/ Hamburg: Berichte und Papiere* 127. http://www1.uni-hamburg.de/Medien/berichte/arbeiten/0127_11.html (accessed July 30, 2013).
Kuhn, Markus (2010): »Medienreflexives filmisches Erzählen im Internet: die Webserie Pietshow.« In: *Rabbit Eye—Zeitschrift für Filmforschung* 1, pp. 19–40. http://www.rabbiteye.de/2010/1/kuhn_erzaehlen_im_internet.pdf (accessed July 30, 2013).
Kuhn, Markus (2011a): *Filmnarratologie: Ein erzähltheoretisches Analysemodell*. Berlin/New York: de Gruyter [paperback edition: Berlin/Boston: de Gruyter, 2013].
Kuhn, Markus. 2011b. »YouTube als Loopingbahn: lonelygirl15 als Phänomen und Symptom der Erfolgsinitiation von YouTube.« In: Julia Schumacher/Andreas Stuhlmann (Eds.): *Videoportale: Broadcast Yourself? Versprechen und Enttäuschung. Hamburger Hefte zur Medienkultur* 12, pp. 119–136 [*Hamburger Heft zur Medienkultur* no. 12 can be downloaded as a PDF file from http://www.slm.uni-hamburg.de/imk/HamburgerHefte/hamburgerhefte.html (accessed July 30, 2013)].
Kuhn, Markus (2012a): »Zwischen Kunst, Kommerz und Lokalkolorit: Der Einfluss der Medienumgebung auf die narrative Struktur von Webserien und Ansätze zu einer Klassifizierung.« In: Ansgar Nünning/Jan Rupp/Rebecca Hagelmoser/Jonas Ivo Meyer (Eds.): *Narrative Genres im Internet. Theoretische Bezugsrahmen, Mediengattungstypologie und Funktionen*, Trier: WVT 2012, pp. 51–92.
Kuhn, Markus (Ed.) (2012b): *Webserien-Blog: Webserien, Online-Serien, Webisodes, Websoaps und Mobisodes in Deutschland*. The first version (August, 2012), which was issued in collaboration with Jan Henne (with help from Johannes Noldt and Stella Schaller), available online at http://webserie.blogspot.de/ (accessed July 30, 2013)
Kuhn, Markus (2013a): »Das narrative Potenzial der Handkamera. Zur Funktionalisierung von Handkameraeffekten in Spielfilmen und fiktionalen Filmclips im Internet.« In: *DIEGESIS. Interdisziplinäres E-Journal für Erzählforschung* 2.1, pp. 92–114.
https://www.diegesis.uni-wuppertal.de/index.php/diegesis/article/download/127/149 (accessed July 30, 2013).
Kuhn, Markus (2013b): »Der Einfluss medialer Rahmungen auf das Spiel mit Genrekonventionen: Die Webserie Prom Queen als Transformation des Highschool-Films im Internet.« In: Jennifer Henke/Magdalena Krakowski/Benjamin Moldenhauer/Oliver Schmidt (Eds.) *Hollywood Reloaded. Genrewandel und Medienerfahrung nach der Jahrtausendwende*. Marburg: Schüren [in press].
Munker, Barbara (2006): »Die Enttarnung von Lonelygirl15.« In: *stern.de* (14 September, 2006). http://www.stern.de/computertechnik/internet/570087.html?nv=cb (accessed July 30, 2013).

Patalong, Frank. (2006): »Nur falsch ist wirklich echt.« In: SPIEGEL ONLINE (11.9.2006). http://www.spiegel.de/netzwelt/web/0,1518,436070,00.html (accessed July 30, 2013).
Roscoe, Jane/Hight, Craig (2001): *Faking It: Mock-Documentary and the Subversion of Factuality*. Manchester: Manchester UP.
Schumacher, Julia (2013): »Jugendfilm.« In: Markus Kuhn/Irina Scheidgen/Nicola Valeska Weber (Eds.): *Filmwissenschaftliche Genreanalyse. Eine Einführung*, Berlin/Boston: de Gruyter, 2013, pp. 295–313.
Simanowski, Roberto (2008): *Digitale Medien in der Erlebnisgesellschaft: Kultur—Kunst—Utopien*. Reinbek bei Hamburg: Rowohlt.

Web series[28]

[28] For the Web series titles listed here the following information is indicated in parenthesis: the country where the series was produced, the year the series premiered, the production company and/or producer and/or production team/production context, and the Web site where the series premiered. Some of these series are no longer available on the Web sites where they premiered, and some are no longer available online at all.

52 Monologe (Germany, 2011, Filmebene, 52monologe.de).
90sechzig90 (Germany, 2000, United Vision/T-Online, 90sechzig90.de).
Borscht—Einsatz in Neukölln (Germany, 2001, Safran Films, borscht.de).
Deer Lucy (Germany 2009, MME Me, Myself & Eye Entertainment, BILD.de)
Eine wie keine—So Isses! (Germany, 2009, Grundy UFA TV Produktion/Phoenix Film, Sat1.de).
Epicsode (Germany, 2010, Hochschule Offenburg, epicsode.de).
Die Essenz des Guten (Germany, 2011, UFA Lab/Das Kind mit der goldenen Jacke, 3min).
Flusstouristen (Germany, 2010, 1AVista Reisen, YouTube).
Die Hütte (Switzerland, 2010, Zürcher Hochschule der Künste, Frischfilm).
lonelygirl15 (USA, 2006–2008, EQAL, YouTube).
Lost: Missing Pieces (USA 2007–2008, ABC Studios, ABC Web site [abc.go.com/shows/lost]).
Making of Süße Stuten 7 (Germany, 2010, Vice Productions, 3min).
Moabit Vice (Germany, 2008, Vice Productions, moabit-vice.de).
Nurse Jeffrey: Bitch Tapes (USA, 2010, Retrofit Films, at first exclusively in form of an app, subsequently on the Fox Web site [fox.com/house/inhouse/#type:jeffrey]).
Pietshow (Germany, 2008, Grundy UFA, studiVZ).
Prenzlbasher (Germany, 2009, Filter Filmproduktion, Myspace).
Preußisch Gangstar (Germany, 2008, Fortuna Film, Myspace).
Prom Queen (USA, 2007/2010, Vuguru, Myspace; season 1, 2007: 80 episodes; season 2 (*Prom Queen: Summer Heat*), 2007: 15 episodes; season 3 (*Prom Queen: The Homecoming*), 2010: 22 episodes).
SamHas7Friends (USA, 2006, Big Fantastic, YouTube).
Sex and Zaziki (Germany, 2008, U-Film Produktions GmbH, YouTube).
Die Snobs (Germany, 2010, Ulmen Television/ZDFneo, 3min).
SPPD: Die Sau ist tot (Germany, 2009, Studio Seidel, sppd.tv).
Studis 4.0 (Germany, 2010, Gropperfilm, Darmtstädter Echo Web site).
They call us Candy Girls (Germany, 2008, MME Me, Myself & Eye Entertainment, Myspace).
Tokyo Prom Queen (J 2008–2009, director: Futoshi Sato, Mixi) [Youtube link to episode 1: http://www.youtube.com/watch?v=pAJ7HtqW6G0; accessed July 17, 2011].

TV series

Eine wie keine (producers: Guido Reinhardt/Rainer Wemcken/Markus Brunnemann, Germany, 2009–2010).
House M.D. (*Dr. House*. David Shore, USA, 2004–2012).
Lost (created by: J.J. Abrams/Jeffrey Lieber/Damon Lindelof, USA, 2004–2010).
Miami Vice (created by: Anthony Yerkovich, USA, 1984–1990).

Films

Not Another Teen Movie (Joel Gallen, USA, 2001).
Pretty in Pink (Howard Deutch, USA, 1986).
She's All That (Robert Iscove, USA, 1999).
The Truman Show (Peter Weir, USA, 1998).

Markus Kuhn
is a junior professor of media studies at the Institut für Medien und Kommunikation of the Universität Hamburg. He studied German studies, media culture, art history and publishing studies in Göttingen and Hamburg and worked as a freelance journalist for several print and online publications. His dissertation *Filmnarratologie: Ein erzähltheoretisches Analysemodell* (published 2011, paperback 2013) won the graduation award from the Studienstiftung Hamburg. Publications: *Filmwissenschaftliche Genreanalyse. Eine Einführung* (2013, coedited with I. Scheidgen and N. V. Weber); and *Film, Text, Kultur: Beiträge zur Textualität des Films* (2013, coedited with J. A. Bateman and M. Kepser.)

Fig. 1

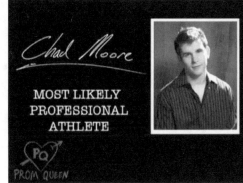

Fig. 2

Fig. 3

Fig. 4

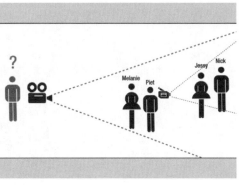

Fig. 5

Gearing Up: Where Do We Stand with the Current Emergence of Interactive Storytelling?

Michel Reilhac

Multiplatform and immersive storytelling is building momentum right now. All that broadcasters and producers speak about (at least in my conversations with them) is ways to include the second screen into their programs. They all search for models of capitalizing and monetizing social media traffic. The Internet is the new Eldorado and IP (intellectual property) is seen as the new gold. Switching from stories designed for a passive viewer to experiences offered to an active participant is the deep trend. Exploring the possibilities of interactive storytelling is like entering a virgin land where we do not really know anything about how things should be done, what people truly want, where there are no models, no serious financing, no trustable feedback from projects already done that could help us measure what we are attempting. It is a jungle for explorers and pioneers with traders lurking behind our backs, ready to be the first ones to jump on what they see as the next potentially massive opportunity for a profitable media investment: transmedia that is, you know, interactive stories.

What Do We Know So Far?

Even though we are still inventing the forms that interactive storytelling might take on, there are a certain number of lessons we have learned from our first mistakes. By the way, when I say »we,« I include myself within the growing international community of interactive, immersive and participatory storytellers who are attempting to transform the art of telling stories into an active experience for the viewer/participant.

Here is a list of just a few of the things we have learned along the way so far that can maybe help us to explore the field further:

It Is Not about the Tools

We must lose the fascination for the tools, the gimmicks, the gadgets, the toys we use (like smartphones, tablets, etc.), the technology that keeps inventing exciting new devices and functions we did not know we needed—all these are just toys, objects. As sophisticated and performing as they may be, they are nothing else than instruments at our disposal today to be used.

We need to learn how to master the possibilities they provide us with, and most times, we need to find the ways to divert and pervert what they were designed to do originally in order to highjack them toward completely unexpected uses.

Story Is the Eternal Need

The focus and purpose of interactive storytelling will always remain the story itself, whatever its shape. It serves exactly the same purpose as ever since man has started to be able to share his thoughts:

- transform reality to escape it
- question the existential mystery of why we are here living on earth, collectively and individually
- confront our ignorance of what happens after we die and why do we have to die
- share the most beautiful and moving experiences of our lives
- build social cohesion and construct a shared culture that helps the individual develop a sense of belonging
- weave our relationship to time past, present and future as we attempt to keep a record of events for future generations or foresee what lies in the future for us. Create the opportunity to become someone else than our physical self through imagination and thus experience virtual lives.
- And much more.

Storytelling Is an Age-Old Tradition

The vehicle we have created ages ago to satisfy these needs is story. It started with hands imprinted on the walls of prehistoric caves, followed by the first attempts to represent animals and humans on the same walls. Religions built themselves as all-encompassing meta-stories. Troubadours, minstrels, griot tellers in Africa and grandmothers everywhere invented the art of orally transmitted stories. Legends, myths and fairy tales were written to open access to magical dimensions in our perception of the world. Then radio and cinema appeared, followed by television. Books are still written, stories are still told around campfires, but the audiovisual method of telling stories has been the prevailing, most modern way of telling stories, still providing for the same eternal needs listed above. Indeed filmmaking or film writing is only the dominant shape that the ancient art of storytelling has taken on today. Filmmakers and film writers are first and foremost storytellers, carrying the torch passed on to them by their more primitive predecessors since the dawn of mankind.

Story Is the Need at the Heart of Any Shape Storytelling Takes On, Including Transmedia

And now a new extended form of telling stories in the audiovisual field is shaping itself: interactive storytelling. The most contemporary form for this ancient art of storytelling is designing immersive, participatory and interactive ways of using sound, images and real-life experience to tell each other our stories and possibly build them together. Story is at the heart. Not technology.

Transmedia Does Not Fix the Absence of Story

If you do not have a strong story to tell, a transmedia approach is not going to magically bring relevance where there is none. Transmedia is a shape, story is the essence.

Interactive Offers an Opportunity for a Real-Life or Virtual Experience Away from Daily Routine

A transmedia approach to storytelling emphasizes the out-of-the-ordinary experience aspect in storytelling. If we consider that transmedia offers the viewer a chance to get involved in the story world through his or her physical participation (even if only by using his or her fingers on a keyboard to interact via the web), we can see how it breaks the traditional consensus of passive viewing.

It Is a Tough Challenge to Trigger Passive Audience Engagement

There are of course many degrees of engagement that one can get involved in a story experience. But the most exciting challenge that an author has to embrace when building an interactive narrative experience in real or virtual life, is to trigger in the viewer the urge to get involved. But it is not easy to convince an audience to leave the comfort of their cozy couch where they are used to being fed films through television, or their computer screen, and take any sort of action related to the story they are watching. Doing nothing and just watching a movie is a very pleasant way of letting go of the troubles of the day. Abandoning oneself fully to be immersed into someone else's vision of the world is perceived as a necessary and welcome escape from the constraints of everyday chores and responsibilities that come with struggling to stay alive and well in the physical reality. The notion of escape attached to stories, whichever form they take, has structurally built the notion of passive viewing into our accepted cultural behavioral patterns. You listen to a story, you watch a movie, you read a book, and you do nothing else at the same time. Okay, maybe you do your e-mails, update your Facebook page, and chat with your friends at the same time as you watch TV, I know… But that is because TV provides you with programs that do not require your full attention on an average basis, right?

The only interaction you have around a movie is discussing it with your friends around a beer after the screening, or chatting about it on a web platform about films or on your Facebook page.

Therefore it takes quite a high level of motivation for someone to step out of the comfortable passive viewing mode and shift into an active experience as a participant in the story world. Triggering it is one of the toughest challenges for a transmedia author today.

Audence Members Prefer to Remain Passive Viewers

As a result, whenever offered an interactive opportunity within a story experience, the vast majority of the audience does not respond and remains entirely passive. Most people cannot be bothered by the invitation to be an active part of the narration through doing something in relation with it. They much prefer to keep on watching the content in a nonparticipatory traditional fashion. Only a minority of individuals are willing to engage, interact and play with your story.

Be Creative to Break Through the Internet Clutter

The competition for content on the net is fierce. Posting stuff on the Internet anywhere does not suffice. The content, whatever form it takes, needs to be pushed to the potential user. It takes a lot of good creative thinking to find the way to allow your content to break through the noisy clutter on the Internet today.

Gaming Is Part of Our Standard Culture

The game culture is the prevailing culture. All young adults entering active life in society today have been raised with playing games of all kinds on electronic devices. Playing is now very much a standard way of approaching everything in life. It is no longer considered a kids' thing. The game culture is infiltrating everything we do. All aspects of life are being gamified. Gameplay is therefore an ingredient that storytellers learn how to use.

Games themselves are being more and more designed with storytelling in mind. Scriptwriters are being hired by game companies to add depth, complexity and emotional involvement to new game design approaches that are more and more character-driven.

Gamers Are the Driving Force to Spread Active Engagement Behaviors

In games, there is no passive viewer (except of course for those who love to just watch gamers play), but only active players. If a player does not play the game, nothing happens.

Players have therefore an ingrained active behavior towards everything. They have been trained to interact with the game world and perform tasks, achieve goals. To them, participating is something totally natural. They are going to progressively change our passive mode of being just a spectator to a more accepted notion that it is more fun to engage with a story in an active way. Players are the locomotives of engaged reactions towards transmedia storytelling on the part of the audience.

We All Multiplatform

Using different devices, sometimes simultaneously, is something we naturally do more and more. We learn how to follow different threads of information from different sources at the same time (we watch TV and do what we need to do on our tablet and smart phone). We switch from one device to another depending on the situation we find ourselves in. We are more and more mobile, using our devices whenever, wherever. This agility facilitates the spreading of transmedia dynamics in story experience and the engagement opportunities for the viewer. It allows transportability and fluidity for the chronological narrative events to unfold and be accessible for the viewer across the different moments of one's daily life.

All-Media Coverage

More and more devices can do more things. We do not need a GPS anymore because it is an app in most devices. Apps are multiplying and can be accessed through more connected objects. This versatility that most interfaces have also makes access to different streams of information more fluid and easier to handle. Interaction between different components as activated within the user experience is made less cumbersome when one does not have to switch from one object to another.

People Do Not Want to Pay for Anything

The economic challenge that we are faced with when dealing with anything on the Internet is that the global perception by the public is that everything on the net can be accessed for free. It is therefore very tricky to get around this expectation and trigger payment. Many strategies to address this serious issue for any producer of interactive content are starting to appear and be tested: from micropayments to freemium, ad-supported, try before you buy, subscription prepaid cards, formatting, franchising, replayability, etc. The only thing that web users seem to be ready to pay for are out-of-the-ordinary experiences and events, perceived as once-only opportunities. This, by the way, relates to the way the music industry has reinvented itself by pushing concerts as the main vehicle that it services.

Real Is Back, Niches Are Fragmenting the Market

Now that the first generation of digital natives that have been educated from birth in a digital, web-connected, interactive environment is entering the world of active social life, we are seeing the beginning of a backlash in the appeal of social media and purely virtual Internet experiences and content. People want to go back to having fewer and more real friends. They want to physically experience in the real-world (IRL: In Real Life) moments that are out of the norm, different in every way from what their daily normal lives are. They want fiction inserted into reality. They want to be someone else using their physical body and actual presence in the world, playing with others as kids do within a fictitious realm that for a moment becomes an alternate reality.

The game culture is embracing Alternate Reality Games (ARG), Live Action Role Play (LARP), treasure hunts and quest games, as new designs to expand game play into reality. And it is working: marketing and advertising agencies are fully exploring the appeal that staged reality events carry for their brands, theater companies are developing work around the notion of immersive experiential theater where the audience is the actor—and so can transmedia.

Relevance Is Key

The notion of relevance to an audience is a key to trigger engagement. Through asking himself »why« this particular story should absolutely be told, an interactive storyteller can clarify »who« he is talking with (and not to). It is quite obvious that only when a spectator finds that the content he is watching is relevant to him, he can consider engaging actively in the story being told to him.

Outreach and Content Are No Longer Separate

The making of a story as an experience is no longer focused on the object (the movie) that it is trying to materialize. It is the process of making it happen which becomes the ultimate nature of the story being built *with* the participants and not *for* a passive audience.

The whole process becomes a conversation between the author/experience designer/story architect and the receptive players who willingly engage with the story world. It is no longer a monologue from the artist, delivered as a finished object to the viewer to be consumed.

This means that, in transmedia, marketing and distribution blend into the native process of making the story experience happen. It is about how you build a community of individuals that have a sense of ownership of the theme of the story, or its approach, its angle and how you drive the awareness around the project all along the process itself of building the story experience. Marketing and distribution are no longer a gatekeepered method that comes after the content is ready to go out, but much more an outreach state of mind that infuses the whole creative work with an awareness of the persons you are having this conversation with.

What Do We Do Next?

As the field of interactive stories develops and as we are learning from our first explorations and attempts, I see new exciting ways of shaping further the art form of storytelling as an experience:

Keep It Simple, Make Technology Invisible

The feel of access to any content needs to be as intuitive, fluid and easy as possible. Transmedia shapes in storytelling must avoid at all cost to appear as a geek thing. Technology allows us now to embed all kinds of software that can be totally transparent to the user.

Creative technologists are among the most valuable new jobs in the creative field that we need to include in our creative team building process. They can help us design services, functions and interfaces that spring from innovative tools which suggest new operational modes.

The look of any interface needs to be designed with simplicity in mind. Anyone needs to get it right away, understand how to navigate the service immediately. No one has any time available any more to educate themselves into deciphering how interfaces work. On top of that, all the latest successful designs in Internet services tend to all be bare simple with very, very few instructions .

But simplicity is not a simple thing. To achieve it in anything requires careful analysis of what it is that we are trying to say, why we want to say it, who do we want to share it with and how we want the shape of it to be.

Build Teams

We need to explore further new ways of collaborating. An interactive story builds itself through a team of different creative experts gathered around a story architect. There are new specific functions that need to be identified ahead of time so that all aspects of a multiplatform interactive story world can be built and coordinated smoothly and effectively. I recently identified a new need for a specific expert on one of the projects I am working on currently (a feature transmedia movie) that I labeled »Matrix designer«. He is an editor who also wants to push further the definition boundaries of the work he does. To each project its own needs and definitions. A complete team should include an experience designer, story architect, gameplay designer, audience designer, social network and community activator, monetizer, creative technologist and a scriptwriter. Now of course, the great difficulty is to find these people. These jobs are not yet learned in schools. They are defining themselves as we go on with the exploration. I guess the best way to find the right team members is to identify those experts in their own fields who are interested in taking a chance and question how they can expand their field in the future by opening up to multiplatforming and interactivity.

The other challenge with this is to learn how to work as teams. We need to experiment with work-sharing tools that optimize creative methods and processes. It is not as easy as it may first seem. Circulating the information and making sure that everyone is updated and working on the same page at any given moment requires quite a bit of self-discipline and collective fluidity.

Be Interface-Obsessed

Along the same lines as above, the process of designing the different interfaces for the various combined aspects of a story world (ranging from aWeb site home page to a specific device, an app, a staged-reality party in the real world, a poster, etc.) needs to keep in mind that they operate as gateways into the story. We need to learn how to design them in an inviting, intriguing, sometimes fun way that triggers the viewer's curiosity and therefore facilitates his engagement.

Love Game

We need to establish strong creative partnerships between traditional filmmaking professionals and game designers. Storytelling needs to incorporate game play beyond the gamification techniques that are currently being embraced by the marketing industry. An organic natively transmedia story has to ask itself to what extent it needs to be game-like. Chances are that, quite often, a game play approach will facilitate audience engagement into the story.

People Crave Real Experience: Go Back to IRL

Because, as we have seen, digital natives have no fascination for the virtual dimension in their digitized lives since birth, and, as a result, because they now crave real-world unusual experiences, we must include the IRL ingredient into the event value of our narrative mix. We need to see how we can marry the virtual and the real in a mix that can create a multilayered circulation through the story universe between real and fiction.

Give Up »For,« Explore »With«

We will progressively find out what it truly means to make stories *with* people and not *for* them. How can we structure the unknown factor of participant-contributed content and reaction into the fabric of our otherwise carefully planned immersive worlds? How does a community of fans build itself around the same passion? How do we manage trust between the audience and the creators as the narrative process unfolds? What does it truly mean for an author when we say that the true content of a transmedia project is the dialogue around its set subject? In transmedia, the ultimate reward is not getting financed, it is getting embraced by the audience.

Empathy Happens through Emotion

Emotion is what makes us all tick, share and connect. Finding the emotional hook that connects immediately an individual with a story is the root of storytelling that we need to connect with. We have been focusing a lot on the mechanics of transmedia, fascinated by the new tools and options we were discovering. Now it is time to lose the fascination and come back to the essence of what drives any story: emotion.

Start Local, Start Small

Because most interactive story experiences are made up of different narrative components (a film, a book, a live event, an app, a Web site, blogs) and that each of these components needs to stand alone for a user, it is best to start quickly to produce some of the components without waiting for the whole puzzle that a transmedia story is to be fully developed and financed. Failing on one aspect is bound to happen and it is best to fail fast and small rather than slow and big. Testing is of the essence in transmedia storytelling, it seems.

...

These are just a few of my current views on where we stand in the field of transmedia story building. As we do more and patterns start to appear we will shape models and keep learning lessons. Right now the field is still one for bold explorers and daring pioneers. There is no real money to be made yet, and very few projects have reached any significant public awareness. But the moment is near when it will be embraced as a new narrative experience. And the broadcasters whose jobs it is to foresee where to go next to increase or keep their audience are all waking up to the idea. Watch out for the soon-to-come transmedia equivalent to *Big Brother* which started the overwhelming advent of reality TV.

To be continued...

Michel Reilhac
is the executive director for Arte France Cinéma and head of cinema acquisitions for Arte France. In 1998 he directed *All Alike*, his first documentary. Upon request by Canal + TV, he made *To Be a Man* in 1999, and he directed *Kenya Islands*, for Arte in 2000. In the same year, he created *Melange*, a film production company based in France. He produced the feature film *Cry Woman*, from the Chinese director Liu Bing Jian, which was shown as part of the section, *Un certain regard,* at the Cannes Festival The film *7 days, 7 nights* by Cuban director Joel Cano, and *The Good Old Naughty Days* (which Reilhac directed) were both produced by him and were presented at the Filmmakers Fortnight of the same festival.

Transmedia Storytelling and Participation Experience

Claudia Söller-Eckert

Introduction

»The term participatory culture contrasts with older notions of passive media spectatorship. [...] [W]e might now see them as participants who interact with each other according to a new set of rules that none of us fully understands.«[1]

Henry Jenkins

Nowadays we're all media multitaskers, what with the Internet, TV (if at all), double-screen computers, and of course text messaging. Without this media convergence, transmedia storytelling would be unthinkable in a universe of fictional narratives and games. Thus it makes perfect sense that this narrative modality is an ever-growing focus of interest in the field of storytelling.

I'd like to address the following issues here: What role do users/viewers play? How does transmedia storytelling change a user or viewer's behavior? Does she also exert an influence on the stories? The answer, as I shall show, is this: There now exists a completely new species of audience to which the classic terms »viewer« and even »user« simply don't apply.

Thus I am following the user-centred approach of user experience design, which narrative theory has basically ignored up until now. User experience involves combining action, emotion, and thought into a unified whole with the goal of creating an experience for the user. In keeping with narratology, this means that the creative process revolves around experience being created rather than the story per se. In transmedia projects, user experience takes the form of participation experience.

My aim in this essay is not to posit a transmedia storytelling theory, but rather to point out the possibilities opened up by participation experience, using European fictional transmedia projects as examples.

Transmedia projects encompass a complex narrative universe whose various components complement and have a determining effect on each other. And while American projects such as *The Matrix* do in fact complement each other, they remain stand-alone media products with a cross-media bent whose transmedia character arises from fan community activi-

---

[1] Henry Jenkins, *Convergence Culture: Where Old and New Media Collide* (New York, 2008), 3.

ties that connect the dots between the various media involved. European transmedia projects on the other hand create a narrative universe from the get-go, using various media. They tell stories, assign tasks of varying complexity in virtual or real spaces, and need to be experienced holistically through participation experience.

What Is Transmedia Storytelling?

Henry Jenkins coined the term *transmedia storytelling* in 2006: »Transmedia, used by itself, simply means ›across media.‹ [...] Transmedia storytelling describes one logic for thinking about the flow of content across media.«[2] Although this platform switching is intrinsic to transmedia storytelling, Jenkins regards collective intelligence as its most salient feature: »Consumption has become a collective process—and that's what this book means by collective intelligence [...].«[3]

Nicoletta Iacobacci noted in 2008 the change in the role played by the recipient: »Content spread across various media (cross-media) is no longer satisfying enough, viewers want more, they are becoming VUPs and in viewing/using/playing want to participate, and to a certain extent create, the story themselves.«[4]

Transmedia storytelling is predicated on consumer participation, whereby consumers become »hunters and gatherers«—a wonderful analogy for the beginnings of storytelling: »Transmedia storytelling is the art of world making. To fully experience any fictional world, consumers must assume the role of hunters and gatherers, chasing down bits of the story across media channels, comparing notes with each other via online discussion groups, and collaborating to ensure that everyone who invests time and effort will come away with a richer entertainment experience.«[5]

The terms *viewer* and even *user* no longer really fit this complex form of consumption and participation, and so it is more accurate to speak in terms of user experience or participation experience when referring to these phenomena. I will therefore refer to users as »explorers« in the examples discussed below.

2
Henry Jenkins, »Transmedia 202: Further Reflections,« *Confessions of a Aca-Fan* (blog), August 1, 2001, http://henryjenkins.org/2011/08/defining_transmedia_further_re.html (accessed July 25, 2013).

3
Jenkins, *Convergence Culture*, 4 (see note 1).

4
Nicoletta Iacobacci, »From Crossmedia to Transmedia: Thoughts on the Future of Entertainment,« *Lunchover IP* (blog), May 24, 2008, http://www.lunchoverip.com/2008/05/from-crossmedia.html (accessed July 25, 2013).

5
Jenkins, *Convergence Culture*, 21 (see note 1).

In a 2009 talk at MIT, Henry Jenkins described the »seven core concepts of transmedia storytelling.«[6] Some of the concepts that he formulated are extremely relevant for participation experience:

Drillability: getting deeply involved in a story and its hidden mysteries.

Multiplicity: the multiplicity of characters in various media.

Immersion and *world building*: a captivating, complex and detailed narrative universe.

Seriality: dividing the story universe and the events that transpire in it into exciting segments.

Subjectivity: the various points of view intrinsic to a story.

Performance: motivation of fans to organize their own activities.

Alternate Reality Games

Alternate Reality Games (ARGs) are an outgrowth of the convergence and mobility of digital network technology. ARGs are played concurrently in real time and in virtual and real spaces, thus making them a transmedia experience. ARGs were originally developed for large-scale ad campaigns, and are now also used for educational purposes, but rarely in commercial settings. Well-known examples of ARGs are the promotional ARG titled *The Beast* (2001) for the movie *A.I.* and *I Love Bees* (2004) for Coca-Cola and the Olympics. Transmedia projects often incorporate ARGs, since they allow TV, games and the Internet to be combined with real space.

The narrative world of ARGs is a hybrid of fiction and reality in that when players go online they encounter mysterious events whose reality they are tasked with validating. Elements of a fictional story point to real facts, while real spaces contain traces of the solution to a fictitious mystery. For ARG aficionados the familiar mantra »This is not a game« is one of the hallmarks of an ARG, describing as it does the feeling of immersion and the potential to have an impact in the real world.

ARGs are predicated on the existence of an active community, because unraveling the complex mysteries of such games requires a group effort. Solving them is a tremendous challenge to players and requires extensive research using every

---

6
See Henry Jenkins, »The Revenge of the Origami Unicorn: Seven Principles of Transmedia Storytelling (Well, Two Actually. Five More on Friday),« *Confessions of an Aca-Fan* (blog), December 12, 2009, http://henryjenkins.org/2009/12/the_revenge_of_the_origami_uni.html (accessed July 25, 2013); and idem., »The Revenge of the Origami Unicorn: The Remaining Four Principles of Transmedia Storytelling,« *Confessions of an Aca-Fan* (blog), December 12, 2009, http://henryjenkins.org/2009/12/revenge_of_the_origami_unicorn.html (accessed July 25, 2013).

imaginable resource. The story creates the framework and starting point that is guided by the puppet master and if necessary modified on the fly. The current status of the action is documented in so-called guides, and game-related information is logged in so-called trails. ARGs are accessed via so-called rabbit holes that constitute a gateway to the fictitious world comprising elements such as letters, e-mails, and a hidden message in a YouTube video.[7]

The first known ARG, *The Beast*, was developed by Microsoft's Game Group for Steven Spielberg's *A.I.* (2001). Spielberg wanted viewers to experience the movie's narrative world even before the release date. Posters, trailer credits, and e-mails contained clues leading to a network of Web sites that addressed the social and philosophical problems faced by the movie's sensate robots in 2142. Players pursued these clues for three months. After the first week, the relevant Web sites had registered hundreds of accesses, and ultimately there were more than three million visits. This also led to the founding of the renowned Cloudmakers community, which had 7,500 members who uncovered three core narratives, subplots involving 150 characters, and 4,000 digital texts, images, videos and flash files. The guide was 130 pages long. The players had to solve riddles, program, translate, hack, and use knowledge from the fields of literature, history, art and cryptology.[8]

The resounding success of the Cloudmakers took the movie's producers completely by surprise: »What we quickly learned was that the Cloudmakers were a hell of a lot smarter than we are […] The Cloudmakers solved all of these riddles on the first day.«[9] After a month, the »This is not a game« mantra interrupted an *A.I.* TV ad. The ARG having a real-world presence was a core concept from the get-go: »We need to do something. This isn't just about the death of [the character] Evan Chan anymore, this is about our future, all of us.«[10]

Transmedia Projects in Europe: Participation Experience

In a consistent further development of ARGs, genuine transmedia projects tell a story using distributed media plat-

---

[7] See Jeffrey Kim, Elan Lee, Timothy Thomas, and Caroline Dombrowski, »›Storytelling in New Media‹: The Case of Alternate Reality Games, 2001–2009,« First Monday 14, no. 6-1 (2009). http://journals.uic.edu/ojs/index.php/fm/article/viewArticle/2484/2199 (accessed July 25, 2013).

[8] Jane McGonigal, »›This Is Not a Game‹: Immersive Aesthetics and Collective Play,« paper presented at Digital Arts and Culture conference in Melbourne, Australia, May 19–23, 2003, http://www.seanstewart.org/beast/mcgonigal/notagame/paper.pdf (accessed July 25, 2013).

[9] Elan Lee, »This Is Not a Game,« lecture at the Game Developers Conference 2002. Convention Center, San Jose, CA. 2002. Cited in McGonigal, »›This Is Not a Game‹« (see note 8).

[10] Rich Stoehr, »Only Solutions,« editorial, Cloudmakers.org, July 26, 2001, http://cloudmakers.org/editorials/rstoehr726.shtml (accessed July 25, 2013).

forms. As platform switching is absolutely essential to understanding the action or carrying out the initial tasks such as unmasking a conspiracy, in order to have a complete experience explorers needs to actively participate in the process of moving from one medium to another.

Conspiracy theories are a recipe for success when it comes to transmedia stories, for they need to be attended to by the collective intelligence of a community. The riddles are so complex that it's highly unlikely that any individual player can solve them. This is where participation experience comes in.

Successfully performing the initial task in a participative fashion is complicated by a host of riddles and actions which, however, do provoke debates on current social issues in social networks. Participation experience has become a core concept of transmedia formats. Collective tasks are strongly influenced by American ARGs, whereas the narrative elements are conveyed by mainstream media, particularly TV—including TV networks, which participate to an amazingly large extent. They attempt to use these new and experimental formats to attract younger viewers and at the same time fulfill their statutory broadcast quotas for transmedia formats.

I shall now discuss examples of participation experience in the most significant European transmedia projects to date.

The Truth about Marika (Sanningen om Marika)

Producer: Christopher Sandberg. Production company: The company P, Sveriges Television SVT, 2007

The Swedish program *The Truth about Marika* was Europe's first transmedia project and won many international prizes. Thanks to a remarkable fusion of fiction and reality, many explorers could barely distinguish between the two levels. The depth of explorer immersion had a massive impact on user involvement and experience. TV, online games and ARG unfolded a »fiction without limits« [11] within the »participation drama,« [12] while the incorporated story levels recounted »a living mystery with powerful philosophical themes.« [13]

---

11 Alessandro Nani, »Sanningen om Marika The truth About Marika. A Transmedia Case Study« (2011). http://truthaboutmarika.files.wordpress.com/2011/12/the-truth-about-marika.pdf (accessed July 25, 2013).

12 Promotional video for *The Truth about Marika* (2008). http://www.thecompanyp.com/site/?page_id=7 (accessed July 25, 2013).

13 Ibid.

Fiction or Reality?[14]

The Swedish TV station SVT decided to produce a five-episode fictional series revolving around a character named Marika, who vanishes on her wedding day. While searching for her, Marika's friends stumble upon a secret society known as *Ordo Serpentis*. The fictional narrative was presented as a true story.

A few months before the series was broadcast, a blogger named Adrijanna accused SVT of having stolen the plot for *The Truth about Marika* from her blog *conspirare.se*, which contained the series' backstory to the effect that as a child, Adrijanna lost her best friend Maria and was now using her blog to find her. Although SVT denied the accusation, they invited Adrijanna and the show's producer to appear on a live talk show the night before the first episode was aired. During the show, the two guests accused each other of lying.

A media scandal erupted, and the case was debated in all Swedish media outlets, as well as on the SVT Web site and *conspirare.se*. Meanwhile the series was broadcast, and at the same time explorers began searching for the truth and immersed themselves in the ARG.

Fiction and Fictionalized Reality[15]

It turned out that the purportedly live talk show hosted by a wel-known Swedish TV moderator was in fact a rehearsed and planned event—a »fictionalized reality.«[16] The fakery was rendered even more plausible by scripted phone calls and a screen ticker containing text messages. The talk shows were shown along with the TV episodes on the day following each broadcast and were shot the day before the broadcast so as to incorporate current ARG happenings into the discussion. The talk show guests were actors playing their role in the series, along with nonactors such as sociologists, psychologists and forensic experts who »played« themselves. Each segment revolved around a topical subject such as social exclusion, surveillance in public areas, police work and conspiracies. The TV audience had no clue that what they were watching was in fact a total fabrication. The SVT Web site and *conspirare.se* continued the debate online. And although the fictional nature of the show was revealed online, only 30 percent of users even noticed this.[17]

Timeline and Narrative Levels

The pre-TV phase involving introduction of the online story world and the ARG got under way five months before the five forty-five-minute-episode shows and accompanying five fifteen-minute talk shows were broadcast.

Three different narrative levels came into play here. At the »fictional« level, the show told the story of a character named Marika, and in doing so also incorporated subliminal images with clues to solve the ARG. At the »fictionalized reality« level, series actors playing their respective characters and nonactors »playing« themselves were guests on a staged talk show where real social issues were discussed, including the issue of authenticity in the media. The talk show served as a bridge between the fictional TV series and the ARG. The »real-world ARG« level comprised the narrative-gameplay platforms comprising *conspirare.se*, *Ordo Serpentis, and Entropia* as well as actions carried out in nonvirtual space.

The *conspirare.se* Web site was the ARG rabbit hole and the jumping-off point for participation experience, where Maria's backstory was recounted and the *Ordo Serpentis* conspiracy theory was set in motion. The *Ordo Serpentis* Web site provided a platform for participation in the real-world ARG and live events. The gameplay of the massively multplayer online VR game *Entropia Universe* was instrumental in promoting immersion.

Immersion, Participation and Collective Intelligence in the Real-World ARG

Conspirare.se provided a gateway for narrative-world explorers to a game world. In its capacity as a landing page, it played host to discussions about the TV series and was the first platform to receive hints about the ARG. On the *Ordo Serpentis* Web site, immersion was heightened and explorers were assigned »missions and tasks.« In numerous communities spread across the Web, the explorers exchanged views, produced their own content and posted pictures and videos. As is always

[17] Ibid.

the case with ARGs, *The Truth about Marika* took on a life of its own, to which the producers, for whom this was unexpected, had to respond.[18]

Conspirare.se and *Ordo Serpentis* expressly mentioned the fictitious nature of the series by saying this: »Warning: *Conspirare* is part of a fictional creation. [...] *Conspirare* has only one rule— pretend that it is real.«[19] Many players simply overlooked this »warning,« as their immersion level was already too high. Explorers who read it obeyed the instruction to keep the fictitious nature of the series a secret. Waern and Denward studied the game experience, the understanding of the story and how the »Pretend that it's real!« slogan was handled. The feedback showed that the explorers needed this introductory slogan in order to recognize that the story was part of an ARG. Some explorers, however, thought that the slogan was part of the story and just another one of SVT's concealment tactics.[20]

Participation unfolded at various activity levels. Lean-back activities allowed for observation of the project on the talk shows, Web sites and blogs. Lean-forward activities involved four different types of players. Active participants in the debate posted their opinions in blogs, forums and chat rooms. Internet-riddle players broke codes and looked for clues. Real-world players looked for clues at real locations and in real media. Content producers created mind maps, pictures, videos and the like, and thus became part of the narrative universe.

The TV series and talk shows attracted 350,000 and 240,000 viewers respectively, while *conspirare.se* and *Ordo Serpentis* had 490 and 751 registered users respectively.[21]

Although in some cases blurring the lines between fiction and reality reached its limits, everyone in Sweden was dying to find out the truth about Marika and Maria. In short, people wanted to know what was fictitious and what was real. Blurring the lines[22] in this manner heightened fictionality and immersion, but it was also an impediment to the ethical and philosophical debate concerning the credibility of the story and the media used for the game experience.[23]

If *The Truth about Marika* was a transmedia experiment, the media scandal that erupted at the beginning of the series was

---

18
Peter Kasza, »Transmedia Classics: ›The Truth about Marika‹— A Participation Drama,« *Xtrans* (blog), January 5, 2012, http://peterkasza.com/2012/01/the-truth-about-marika/ (accessed July 25, 2013).

19
Waern and Denward, »On the Edge of Reality« (see note 15).

20
Ibid.

21
Rosie Lavan, »Participatory Drama Blurs Truth and Fiction,« *The Pixel Report*, August 24, 2010, http://thepixelreport.org/2010/08/24/truth-about-marika/ (accessed July 25, 2013).

22
Promotional video for The Truth about Marika (see note 12).

23
Waern and Denward, »On the Edge of Reality« (see note 15).

also a carefully planned marketing strategy that was instrumental in the project's success. The issue as to whether a broadcaster is justified in blurring the lines between fiction and reality simply for a publicity stunt aimed at promoting a program was hotly debated.[24]

Alpha 0.7—Der Feind in dir[25]

Authors: Sebastian Büttner, Oliver Hohengarten. Producers: Zeitsprung Entertainment, SWR, 2010

Germany's first transmedia project was a sci-fi thriller series that used TV, radio and the Internet. As the theme of *Alpha 0.7* is government control, the show has an affinity with George Orwell's *1984*. The series aimed to raise explorer awareness of current issues concerning security and personal freedoms. Apart from being an exciting narrative, the series dealt with contemporary social, political and scientific issues.

Story and Story World

In 2010 mysterious messages from the year 2017 began appearing online that led to blogs by Johanna Berger and the activist group Apollon. The blogs portrayed the world of the future as a police state. The remainder of the story was set in Stuttgart in 2017 and revolved around a security company known as Protecta developing a brain scanner for crime-fighting purposes in collaboration with the neuroscience Pre-Crime-Center NPC run by the BKA, which is Germany's FBI. Once the device is implanted in a subject's brain, it allows them, however, to manipulate the carrier. The Apollon activists engage in a struggle against the brain scanner and Protecta. Johanna Berger doesn't know a brain scanner has been implanted in her and that in her capacity as Alpha 0.7 she is the seventh subject of a neuroscience experiment. Johanna gradually loses control of her life and joins forces with the activists in the fight against Protecta. Meanwhile, the unscrupulous individuals who are manipulating Johanna are planning to use her for an assassination...

Fictional and Real Space

In *Alpha 0.7*, the fictional world of the future unfolded in a sci-fi scenario via radio and TV. The relationship to the real

[24] Kasza, »Transmedia Classics« (see note 18).

[25] SWR: Alpha 0.7. http://www.alpha07.de/ (accessed July 25, 2013).

physical space of the present was established by having the series address topical political and scientific issues. The two worlds were combined via blogs.

Timeline and Narrative Levels

The timeline involved a two-month-long pre-TV phase, a TV phase with six episodes, the online game, and a radio phase immediately following the TV phase comprising radio plays. The pre-TV phase revolved around the transition to the year 2017 via the actions by the activist group Apollon. The narrative world and its characters were explored through the Apollon and Johanna blogs, as well as the Web sites of NPC and Protecta. The TV episodes involved a plotline that began with the scanner and ended with the planned assassination. The radio continued the TV plot line by recounting the story of an eventful escape. All in all, *Alpha 0.7*'s TV episodes and radio plays followed a conventionally structured sequential plotline that was the springboard for the main action. Online, the story was told in a fragmented fashion and it was up to explorers to make sense of it.

Participation Experience

The online documents from the pre-TV phase were related to the pieces of the puzzle, which the Community was tasked with collecting and reconstructing over a two month period. An initially planned ARG was scuttled. The blogs contained background information concerning the characters' motivations. Links on the Web sites enabled users to decrypt Protecta and Apollon activities. The user experience mainly centered around the task of reconstructing the plot. Explorers were also given extensive material on scientific subjects and current political events such as a protest against Stuttgart 21. For example, one link led to an article titled »Der Mensch wird zum Datensatz« [26] (People are becoming data sets) by Chaos Computer Club's Frank Rieger. The TV station SWR2 streamed podcasts on brain research and other scientific topics.[27]

Participation experience primarily revolved around the tension between the story on one hand and current social issues on the other, the central one being this: How far should the

[26] Frank Rieger, »Der Mensch wird zum Datensatz,« faz.net, January 16, 2010, http://www.faz.net/aktuell/feuilleton/ein-echtzeit-experiment-der-mensch-wird-zum-datensatz-1591336.html (accessed July 25, 2013).

[27] SWR: Alpha 0.7 (210). http://www.alpha07.de/de/media/was-sagt-die-forschung/ (accessed July 25, 2013).

government be allowed to go when it comes to protecting its citizens against terrorist attacks and other crimes? The goal was to avert this threatening future scenario in the here and now.

Rescue Dina Foxx!—An Internet Crime[28]

Director: Max Zeitler. Producers: teamWorx + UFA-Lab. ZDF, 2011

Rescue Dina Foxx! was a combination TV and online crime show. The narrative universe took the form of lean-back variants, a click adventure and an ARG. A complete user experience was only obtainable for users who were willing to make the media leap from TV to the Internet. The concept of having a ZDF TV crime show be resolved online was very daring, and thus *Rescue Dina Foxx!* can be regarded as one of Germany's most consequential transmedia projects. The show garnered numerous prizes for this reason.

Story and Story World

Dina Foxx is a so-called datagrrl, and a member of the activist group freidaten.org, which through various actions warns against data misuse and mindless data storage. Dina's boyfriend Vasco works for a company called Avadata, which develops software that allows people to extirpate their online digital trail. As a result of being recruited by Avadata, Dina breaks with her old circle of friends. While Vasco is pursuing a potentially explosive story, strange accidents occur. He unexpectedly breaks up with Dina and is murdered. Dina begins looking into the same story that Vasco was pursuing and obtains crucial information from a company called QoppaMax. But suddenly she becomes a suspect in Vasco's murder and is taken into custody on the strength of an evidentiary video showing her at the crime scene...

The ZDF TV crime series ended at this point and then became an online crime series, whose plot went as follows: Although data protection specialists get her out of jail, Dina is nonetheless forced to go underground. And so she asks the forum to gather information about *QoppaMax*. Dina's boyfriend Jason coordinates an interactive scavenger hunt on *freidaten.org*,

---

[28] ZDF, *Freidaten.org* (blog for TV crime show *Rescue Dina Foxx!*, 2011, http://www.freidaten.org/ (accessed July 25, 2013).

whereupon the online community ends up finding the real murderer and comes to Dina's rescue.

Fictional and Real Space

Fictional space became manifestly visible and experiential via the *Datenschutzraum*[29] (data protection space) and *freidaten.org*[30]. Dina's boyfriend Jason connects the fictional world with the real world of the ARG. Real space is the scene of live interactions such as live chats, phone calls and geocaching.

Timeline and Narrative Levels

The timeline comprised a pre-TV phase and post-TV phase, each three weeks long, during which the TV thriller was broadcast. The pre-TV phase created the narrative world, along with the show's characters and plot. The data protection specialists' blog told the story as an online thriller, until Dina's sudden incarceration (online cliffhanger). The fifty-minute TV thriller began in prison and recounted the plot thus far in flashback so as to enable TV viewers to participate in the project as well. The thriller ended at a dramaturgical climax, with the evidentiary video showing Dina at the scene of the crime. A voiceover by a ZDF off-speaker encouraged viewers to help her. In the subsequent post-TV phase, the explorers' task was to prove Dina's innocence and find the real killer. Dina's boyfriend Jason documented all of the story's key events on *freidaten.org*.

Participation Experience[31]

During the pre-TV phase, the explorers obtained plot information from the blog and could investigate Dina's apartment interactively. In doing so, they could also enter the *DatenschutzraumFehler: Referenz nicht gefunden* and by clicking on a data object could obtain data security information. The interactive search for clues online began when the TV crime show ended. Novice TV viewers could play the online game on the blog in a lean-back version, whereas active players could choose between two levels of difficulty. The elementary level unfolded in the interactive *Datenschutzraum* in the guise of a click adventure where explorers could constantly discover new clues about Dina's case. The complex level

---

29 ZDF, *Datenschutzraum*, interactive Flash page for TV crime show *Rescue Dina Foxx!* http://xt.zdf.de/datenschutzraum/ ((accessed July 25, 2013).

30 ZDF, *Freidaten.org* (see note 28).

31 ZDF, promotional video for TV crime show *Rescue Dina Foxx!* http://www.zdf.de/Das-kleine-Fernsehspiel/Wer-rettet-Dina-Foxx-13099690.html (accessed July 25, 2013).

took the form of an ARG with a difficult riddle. Many clues were scattered around the Internet on Facebook, Twitter, Xing, MySpace, Flickr and various blogs, whose IP addresses or access codes players had to either figure out or hack. To this end, for example, complex photos were processed, images evaluated, numerical codes decrypted, sources assessed and geocache coordinates determined. The community created a wiki and a comprehensive mind map depicting all of the key relationships between the characters and objects. These two platforms were continuously updated. Explorers could talk to the fictional actors over the phone, conduct interviews in chat rooms or find geocaches.

The TV crime show attracted 670,000 viewers (8 percent audience share), 200 million Web site access and 200,000 video accesses on YouTube and at the ZDF media library.[32] The ARG attracted around 1,000 registered players, 50 to 100 of whom were active players.[33]

The Spiral: a Transmedia Art Thriller[34]

Director: Hans Herbots. Producers: Caviar Films. Co-producers: VRT, VARA, NRK, Yle, SVT, ARTE France, ARTE Deutschland, TV3 Dänemark.

The Spiral was an exceptional European coproduction comprising five episodes that were broadcast simultaneously in eight European countries. The transmedia project was a typical scavenger hunt whose goal was to solve a case. But the main goal was to get the community creatively involved and to create a collective work of art. By the end of the project, 19,752 works of art from throughout Europe were amassed.[35]

Story and Story World

The artist Arturo and a young group of Copenhagen artists known as The Warehouse stages provocative protests concerning the corrupt art market. Arturo plans a high-profile caper involving the simultaneous heist of six paintings from renowned museums in six European capitals. When Arturo is unexpectedly arrested, the young artists of The Warehouse successfully carry out the theft. As a result, not only the Danish police but also the powerful investors that own the paintings want the members of The Warehouse to be apprehended. After

---

[32] Kristian Müller, »›Dina Foxx‹ ein voller Erfolg—Bilanz zum Internet-Krimi im ZDF,« press release, May 13, 2011, http://www.ufa.de/presse/news/?s=/44736/Dina_Foxx_ein_voller_Erfolg_-_Bilanz_zum_Internetkrimi_im_ZDF (accessed July 25, 2013).

[33] Personal communication from author Max Zeitler.

[34] Arte, The Spiral, 2012,: http://www.arte.tv/de/the-spiral/6835026.html (accessed July 25, 2013).

[35] Arte, video of The Spiral End Event, in Brussels, 2012, http://www.youtube.com/watch?v=vrKRiXijeBw#at=160 (accessed July 25, 2013).

Arturo is murdered, the whole affair becomes a matter of life and death for all members of the group.

The stolen paintings are equipped with GPS sensors by the young artists, mailed to various places in Europe and are supposed to be returned in Brussels with lots of media coverage. The Warehouse asks the Internet community for help. While the explorers search online for clues to the paintings' whereabouts, the TV storyline involving various subplots, twists and turns continues, in the style of a classic Scandinavian thriller.

Fictional and Real Space

The Belgian artist Jean-Baptiste Dumont reported on the Community's findings in real time on his arte.tv[36] blog called *The Spiral*, and in his capacity as a former Warehouse artist acted as a bridge between fiction and reality. As in *The Truth about Marika*, a fictionalized reality level emerged. The fictional space was defined by the changing TV settings, the blog and the Web site *thespiral.eu* via the map of Europe. Relationships to real space arose from the real locations of the museums and the apparently real locations of the works of art on the map. The works of art were in fact hung in the real museums and were made accessible again following their symbolic return in the closing event, which was held in Brussels and five other European capitals.[37] Thanks to the creative contributions from many nations, an authentic European ambience was created that was palpable in *The Spiral*.

Timeline and Narrative Levels

The timeline comprised a two-week pre-TV phase and a four-week TV phase featuring five episodes and the online game. The pre-TV phase developed the narrative universe of *The Warehouse* and its characters, and the plot unfolded sequentially via the 4forty-five-minute TV episodes. The closing event involving the collective work of art in Brussels was incorporated into the final episode as a scene.

Participation Experience

If the Community had no impact on the plot, the series did give rise to a highly developed participation culture. The plot could be figured out without media switching which was how-

---

[36] Jean-Baptiste Dumont, *The Spiral—Der Blog* (blog on arte.tv), 2012, http://www.arte.tv/sites/de/the-spiral-de/2012/10/02/hector-dhaese-belgischer-geschaftsmann-ist-fur-die-morde-verantwortlich/ (accessed July 2013).

[37] Ibid.

ever necessary for participation in the collective tasks, namely the search for the paintings and the creative activity. The virtual counterpart to the artists' collective The Warehouse came into being on *thespiral.eu*[38] and Facebook as a virtual counterpart of the artists' collective. In order for the explorers to obtain clues to the actual whereabouts of the paintings, they had to carry out tasks, participate in games and produce their own »works of art.« For example, they were told to look for clues in the real museums or to copy one of the stolen paintings, René Magritte's »The Kiss« with imaginative means. By way of a reward, the current GPS data was shown on a map.

The explorers' activities culminated in creation of a collective work of art called »The Spiral,« which was projected via video on the European Parliament building in Brussels during the magnificent closing event and was on view in six European capitals.

The cinematic production was more professional than for series such as *Dina Foxx* and *Alpha 0.7*. The series attracted a weekly audience numbering seven million, while *thespiral.eu* registered a million visitors, 142,700 active members and 19,752 user-generated content elements.[39]

Participation Experience in Transmedia Projects

As shown by the examples, transmedia storytelling involves more than just distributing the elements of a story across various media channels. Participative culture creates a »unified and coordinated entertainment experience«[40] and a collective experience as well. European transmedia projects exhibit the core characteristics of this kind of participation experience, which I shall now discuss.

1. The story is constructed or reconstructed collectively, and the nature of the plot makes it necessary for explorers to switch from one medium to another.
2. The fictional narrative world relates to real-world current issues that the community debates.
3. Artistically stimulating narrative worlds translate into a high level of immersion.
4. Thus participation experience can only unfold within a time and space dimension.

---

38 *The Spiral* Web site (2012). http://www.thespiral.eu/ (accessed October 1, 2012).

39 Honigstudios, *The Spiral*, http://www.honigstudios.com/the-spiral/ (accessed July 25, 2013).

40 Jenkins, »Revenge of the Origami Unicorn« (see note 6).

5. Explorers are folded into the narrative universe through myriad interactions and a wealth of user-generated content.
6. Collective intelligence is promoted by complex riddles.

The Story Is Constructed or Reconstructed Collectively and the Nature of the Plot Makes It Necessary for Explorerss to Switch from One Medium to Another

Plot construction/reconstruction relates to all narrative levels, as well as the characters' motivations. Explorers need to seek out all of the various story fragments in various media or in real physical space. These investigations are usually oriented toward the past in the guise of background information and/or backstories, and their complexity is heightened by twists, turns and subplots. A network comprising narrative references and relationships emerges that can be externalized using a mind map. The narrative world typically centers around a conspiracy scenario wherein the hero goes after the enemy institution and neutralizes it, with the help of the community. Explorers are prompted to engage in media switching by gaps in the narrative, a mission or the characters' fan potential. Explorers enter the magic circle of the virtual world through a rabbit hole, which leads to a main landing page.

The Fictional Narrative World Relates to Real-World Current Issues That the Community Debates

ARGs and European transmedia projects combine fictional story worlds with current real-world issues. American ARGs tend to center around the classic conflict between good and evil. Conspiracy theories, sci-fi scenarios, and resource constraints serve as platforms for potential threats and for consideration of the key issue as to how we can collectively protect our world. The European transmedia projects discussed here address fundamental ethical issues (which are debated in the forums) such as authenticity and reality in the media, government control of the population by institutions or technology, and the threat to privacy posed by wall-to-wall digital trails. In some cases the mixture of reality and fiction gives rise to cognitive dissonance, but also to heightened immersion. This state of limbo between fiction and reality[41] was what made *Alpha 0.7* and *The Truth about Marika* so thrilling.

Artistically Stimulating Narrative Worlds Translate into a High Level of Immersion

Transmedia narrative worlds and characters need to be created in such a way that they attract and hold the interest of explorers, the goal being to create a community identity. The European transmedia projects discussed here achieved a high level of explorer involvement by blurring the lines between fiction and reality and through collective community activities. The narrative worlds of such projects have thus far been more realistic and dreary than their American counterparts, and the characters are often a tad over-the-top, thus making it difficult for the community to identify with them.

Thus Participation Experience Can Only Unfold within a Time and Space Dimension

Narrative worlds comprising plots and characters need a temporal dimension in order for social interaction and collective intelligence to evolve. In lieu of hermetic dramaturgy of movie plots, we are offered series with an expanded time strucuture. The timeline is extended via the pre-TV phase, post-TV phase and/or the temporal rhythm of the series per se. Specific missions or actions in real physical space can only unfold in real time and are folded into the timeline as a whole. The spatial dimension encompasses both virtual and real space and is intertwined with both, an example being the virtual whereabouts of the artworks in *The Spiral* and the real museum locations. This space-time constellation is absolutely essential for participation experience.

Explorers Are Folded into the Narrative Universe Through Myriad Interactions and a Wealth of User-Generated Content

The multifaceted interactions that come into play involve mental exercises such as finding clues, solving riddles, breaking codes, and hacking access data; physical activities such as looking for clues in real physical space; artistic activities such as editing

[41] Maike Coelle; Kristian Kosta-Zahn, Maike Hank, Katharina Kokoska, Dorothea Martin, Patrick Möller, Gregor Sedlag, and Philipp Zimmermann, »Thesis 1: Claiming Reality,« *Transmedia-Manifest* (2011), http://www.transmedia-manifest.com/ (accessed July 25, 2013).

photos and producing videos; and ethics-related actions such as evaluating behaviors, discussing situations, and uncovering machinations. Lean-back and lean-forward variants allow for the inclusion of various kinds of target groups. The optimal participation experience modality is helping to create the narrative world as author, artist (*The Spiral*), actor or part of an investigation team (*Dina Foxx*, *Tatort+*). Findings and user-generated content are posted in forums and thus become part of the narrative universe. *The Spiral* art objects were incorporated into the last TV episode, while in *The Truth about Marika* artifacts were shown to the public and discussed during the talk shows.

Collective Intelligence Is Promoted by Complex Riddles

Participation experience arises through explorer social interaction. Solving complex riddles necessitates the collective intelligence of an experienced and motivated community. This in turn leads to construction and/or reconstruction of the plot for purposes of carrying out missions and debating social and ethical issues. The community's awareness of real-world problems is raised in the context of the fictional stories, prompting the community to jointly devise problem-solving strategies. The intelligence of the collectivity unfolds in the virtual space of the fiction and has an impact on the real space of our world.

Martin Elricsson, producer and creative director of The Company P (*The Truth about Marika*) puts it this way: »In participatory culture things change completely. The artist acts as a host, sets up the game space, produces some stimuli, but the real producer, the real artist in participatory culture is the audience itself.«[42]

42
Martin Elricsson, »Extending the Experience: The New Storytellers,« presentation given at Power to the Pixel, London, October 2009, http://www.slideshare.net/tishna/extending-the-experience-the-new-storytellers-martin-elricsson (accessed July 25, 2013).

Claudia Söller-Eckert
is a professor of media design and interactive media at the Hochschule Darmstadt. After her architecture studies she worked as a scientific collaborator in the special field of geometric information processing at the TU Darmstadt. Within an interdisciplinary team she developed 3D CAD software, and created the computer animation for several awarded films. 1992 she was appointed professor of 3D computer animation and interactive media at the FH Mainz. She ran the media design program and was associate dean for the Institut für Mediengestaltung und Medientechnologie *img*. For the exhition Village Gutenberg/Gutenberg 2000 in Mainz, she created the AR-installation *Augmented Man* in collaboration with the Fraunhofer-Institut Darmstadt. She is the director of the master's program Leadership in the Creative Industries, which focuses on innovative media strategies, hereby especially transmedia projects.

Social Media Storytelling

Ramón Reichert

In the everyday use of the digital networked media of peer-to-peer (P2P) networks, Internet-based companies have changed the traditional forms of writing and reading of the book culture in significant ways. However, the change in narrative culture brought about by social media affects not only the *contents* of narrative, but also the manner in which the narrative is constructed as *media*, calling forth a certain social participation. In this sense, narratives in social networks exert a decisive influence on the reshaping of narrative structures and functions, suggesting a media reflection of the participatory and networking cultures that enable it.

In this context, building on the performative theory of action of Erika Fischer-Lichte (2002, 2004), the concept of the performative as useful for identifying the procedural performance, regulatory and transformation practices of social media storytelling is introduced. Based on the promising research approach of the performative, generated performative processes of Web 2.0 social media can be identified as narrative *transformation processes*, since they open up unplanned game spaces and open spaces of narrative, and elevate contingent and emergent modes to inseparable parts of digital storytelling.

The New Narratives in Online Social Media

In the networked digital communication spaces, interactive media channels carrying heterogeneous production of meaning have emerged. These channels are accompanied by collective and collaborative media practices which include all aspects of production, distribution, use and evaluation of narrated content. Social media storytelling on social networking sites and Internet portals is highly influenced by production and reception contingencies and forms a diffuse state of aggregation of free play for cultural interpretation within dynamic meaning and negotiation processes. In this sense, social media storytelling can be understood as a technology of social activity that allows users to develop, in peer-to-peer networks, concrete forms of usage of habitualized telling that include forms of social communication and novel procedures for narrative participation and codetermination. Alongside these shifts, pop cultural practices have emerged which set up anonymous, flexible and changeable structures and constellations of social media in Web 2.0, and open up a radical alternative to the traditional forms of publishing of media content. This evolving conceptualized collaborative communication structure can no longer be attributed to a work as property or an identical author subject. Related to that, narration proves itself as content and form only in a limited and restricted way as a distinct and stable object of knowledge, and is always also embedded in performative framing strategies. From a performative perspective, a dynamic and temporarily-given-meaning production of Web 2.0 social media can, as a consequence, be exposed which engages with the productivity and procedural orientation of collaborative practices as the focus of the analysis. In their media theory posing of problems, the performative framing processes do not recur in the network as a spontaneous voluntarism—which would derive from the aspect of the performative genuinely as the creative achievement of an individual subject, since the processing narrative practices are regulated by the *technical infrastructure* of digital communication spaces. Consequently, the narrative contributions of the users, who carry out their acts in the name of real authors, fictional characters, or anonymous nicknames, are always taken into consideration as a technical artifact of the enabling of space and negotiating positions. But this approach of technological determinism must, among other things, be qualified, since the practices of information and communication design which are being investigated here aim at a basic pop-cultural reorganization of network-based knowledge production and reception, and thereby are given over to the network knowledge of a performative rhetoric of appropriation—from the associative indexing of fans to the editorial framing of the so-called webmaster.

In the following, I will address the practices of the peer-to-peer communication of online platforms and social media formats along the lines of *three different performativity strategies*.

(1) In dealing with the video content generated by users on the video-sharing Web site YouTube, it is a question of which performative role the initiators of video uploads play. Which

network discursive framing practices do they use when they want to take up a discursively moderating role for themselves? How important are collective and collaborative framing processes in relation to the production of meaning, negotiation and distribution of videos in online portals and social media formats?

(2) The pronounced tendency in the Internet culture towards resignification and reiteration of already existing content (mash-up, remix) refers to an aspect of the performative which connects seamlessly to collective and collaborative framing processes. Here also the performative practice shows itself to be primarily something that generates a surplus to which no intersubjectively controllable field of discourse can be assigned. In this sense, »the productive force of the performative does not reside with the simple power to create something, but rather with what we have not ourselves brought about.« (Kramer 1998:48) The performative act can be understood as a surplus of meaning which not only realizes a new performative framework, but also retroactively modifies the already existing content.

(3) Performative processes in the Internet are the result of technical achievements which make them possible. Specifically, it is the computer-based information and communication technologies which regulate the modes, the application, and the dissemination of user-generated content. Consequently, the network media and their technically generated activities for the production of meaning are heavily involved with and must be incorporated into the methodology of investigation of performative processes. This questioning has not only a heuristic importance in scientific discourse practice, but also opens up, beyond the dichotomy of technological determinism versus technological euphoria, critical questions about the scope of performative enabling in technical environments.

1 Collaborative Storytelling

With the rise of social media in Web 2.0, the importance of the moving image has changed in the Web in a comprehensive manner. In the new subject-centered Internet media, storytelling has been interwoven with visual self-presentation styles. But the moving image is not a finished work. It has rather developed into being the venue of an open-meaning production and permanent negotiation. Regulated comment functions, hypertext systems, ranking and voting processes through collective and collaborative framing processes position audiovisual content in multimedia and discursive environments. Online video content and its narratives emerge as improvising knowledge that promotes narrative developments, contextualizations and reenactments.

In view of the history of media discourses, one can understand the collective narrative practices and cross- and transmedia operations which are associated with the videos also as a continuation of the debates around the paradigm shift of interactivity (Intermedia, Happenings, Fluxus) and the »Open Work« (Eco 1989), which, since the 1960s, have been intensively going on. In this context, structural homologies between the efforts to place into question the assumption of the authorial subject as founding instance and the work as completed entity, and the expressed call to interaction and collaboration in the social media of Web 2.0 can be established. If the vlogs (video blogs) on YouTube become, in this sense, showplaces for cultural circulation and aesthetic conflicts, then the possibility is opened up of discussing this not only in a limited way as a genre of film and media studies, but with a farsighted view as cultural and media practice.

The leading number and the largest content category of clips uploaded to YouTube is called »ego clips« by the media theorist Birgit Richard. This refers to a type of clip that engages in »excessive narcissistic self-presentation« covering a »wide range from shy talks to visual prostitution.« (Richard 2008: 227). It is about mainstream formats that can be identified with the characteristic appearance of YouTube. The dominant position of ego clips in the rapt attention market of YouTube has led to the predominance of personalizing communication styles of social media in Web 2.0. With YouTube, subject-centered narrative styles have emerged that operate mainly through the stylistic devices of implicit authenticity markers, visual and auditory elements of direct addressing, and with a number of self-presentation conventions with which YouTubers show themselves through discourse rituals in spontaneous naturalness and informality as being as authentic as possible. According to Michel Foucault, the confession, the productive constraint to »make speak,« is a highly rated technology in the production of truth. (Foucault 1983:22f) The specific context of power, truth and the formation of the subject is here not so much the result of repressive oppression, but rather much more substantiated in an increasingly intensive discursivity. The narrative self-addressing in this context means linguistic[1], gestural or facially communicated self-reference which constitutively acts back on the addresser and helps to make the narrative credible. The self-addressing addresses apparently the addressee, but also opens up a continuous secondary addressing, which is aimed at an imaginary audience and enables spaces of possibility for future viewers. Conventional forms of self-addressing contain partial self-criticism or signals of irony and weaken the overall narcissistic gesture of self-presentation. This demonstrative maneuver that signals willingness to engage critical capacities, aims at the production of nearby conspiracy. In this sense, vlog narratives are positioned less as finished works and rather much more as improvising sketches. This strategy of weakening and relativizing its own position in self-design enjoys great popularity within the different communities, because it invites other users to participate. The forms of explicit self-addressing serve thus as a weakening of one's own subject position and thus try to bind participatory engagement to the video. This narrative technique of self-thematization has proven to be a very successful framing strategy for drawing attention to particular narrative content within social media in Web 2.0. On the other hand, the vlog narratives also take on specific formats and genre categories in order to enhance their recognition. Thus, the proximity of vlogs and their representatives to television formats is demonstrated most vividly in the serialized structures and narrative forms. In order to promote the interest and the identification of the viewer, and the collection of knowledge of the series that the viewer can apply to subsequent episodes, numerous vlogs divide themselves into successively developing episodes and archive them in their own YouTube channel. The channels can also be subscribed to, thus greater reinforcing the bonding of the viewer.

---

[1] Linguistically, this means verbal and written language statements in the broadest sense, or statements that are communicated in the form of monologues, inserts, intertitles or tagging.

Conclusion: The value of motion-picture narratives in the net can no longer be assessed on the basis of cinematic aesthetics. The centrality of the filmic text gives way to an open and nonlinear heteromediality, which inscribes the video images into volatile and unstable meaning networks. The importance of online video for the negotiation of interactive storytelling cultures and mash-up practices is consequently not only at the level of representation (which would suggest a film studies analysis), but also in how, in the circulation of the videos through feedback, explicit recommendations and hyperlinks, open meaning productions are engendered which are largely responsible for which value a specific video will have within the reception contexts. In this sense, both the narrative production and the reception context of the videos change constantly and remain open and unfinished. Although online videos, in a sense, present and perceive conventions that contribute to the cultural and media construction of individual and constructive identities (Hilderbrand 2007: 48-57), they always allow the subjects involved scope to derive from conventional meaning production (Hoskins also takes this view. Hoskins 2009: 15–17). The narrative performance character of YouTube videos must therefore be broadened as follows: They are not only a stage for self-presentations, but also a place of productive feedback loops between production and reception. In this sense, they remain in the aggregate state of the negotiation processes and participation opportunities of social media storytelling ambiguous, ephemeral and contested.

2 Transmedia Storytelling

Performative practices in the net have developed new perspectives on oppositional reading practices. They develop their productive potential in the field of subcultural media practices. The destabilization of hegemonic meaning architectures and sense assignments in the mode of transmedial performativity is to be discussed here by the example of the user-generated appropriation practices of the *Sims 2* computer game. Transmedial modification means in this context that user computer games are to be understood as iterable discursive systems whose meanings can—in reference to different media formats—basically be modified. (cf. Derrida, 1988:309). The modification makes general citational and iterable use of the programmed game scenes, and ensures that the games can be divested from their original inherent game intentions.

Sims is so far the best-selling PC game series. With more than 100 million copies sold, it has contributed to spreading management knowledge, normalcy constructions and life-management techniques (lifestyle treats) worldwide. The *Sims* computer games are designed as a role-play simulation and expect their gamers to successfully manage the life of simulated game characters called Sims: »Create a family and build it a house. Then help your Sims to have a career, earn money, make friends and fall in love.«[2]

To successfully handle the level-based game modes, the players must develop specific mapping and monitoring capabilities. They control the whole social life of the game characters and supervise, via the *Sims*-typical motivation and need bars, the state of their physical and mental satisfaction of needs, their emotional competence, and their skills in the area of everyday life and relationship management. Against this organizational theoretical background, the game architecture of the *Sims* is created. It is based on recorded knowledge techniques that serve the systematic monitoring of bodily functions and social relations by means of technical media and computer-based observation systems.

In September 2004, the commercially available episode *The Sims 2* offered the possibility of producing digital animations with the help of the computer game, i.e., in real time and without additional animation tools. The game-immanent story mode of interconnected in-game technologies of image recording (camera options for the game camera, camera snapshots and video recordings) have enabled media practices which could replace level-based and goal-oriented gaming with an open network of narrative forms. Against this background, a small form of digital storytelling has emerged: the *machinima*.

The possibility that is provided to produce animated films without financial and technical effort has lastingly and

[2] Maxis (Will Wright): »The Sims« (Emeryville, CA, 2000).

fundamentally changed gaming. Machinimas are real-time animation films which are created in a computer game and which exhibit no more interactive component. (Lowood 2005:10–17) They use the technical means of a defined virtual gaming environment, which is used as a framework for the game action. (Kelland/Morris/Hartas 2005: 17f) The outstanding feature of the Maschinimas characters lies in their mash-up aesthetics (Frølunde 2012:491–507): The users experiment with the realities of an indisposable game world. They more or less modify diegetic, fictional, or narrative meanings of the game and thereby identify alternative strategies of media use. In this context, they use not only creative freedom that is enshrined in game design, but also create in their mash-up practices counter-narratives that not only set into motion a different kind of meaning production, but also achieve a media-reflexive contribution to the theoretical situating of hegemonic narratives and counternarratives. (See Kraus, 2011: 100–112) Methodologically speaking, the pop-cultural research of mash-ups as a cultural and social phenomenon assumes a performative logic of the media that exists, not in itself, but rather always only for itself, i.e., in concrete everyday social contexts. The basic assumption that cultural practices are always ambiguous and changeable, and their theoretical reflection is always also an active process of construction, can be taken as the starting point for the discussion of the procedural component of mash-up practices that generate transitory spaces of aesthetic sense shifts, new orientations and negotiations.

Machinimas have established their own field of practice in digital storytelling in which game design, clip aesthetics, and industrialized genre conventions in popular movies (action plots, character-dominated material) get hybridized. Machinimas, which are produced using *Sims 2* or *Sims 3*, constitute an extreme form of mods,[3] which are known in the community as *total conversion*. Total conversions open up a new game which reads the original game rules against the grain. A further characteristic of *Sims* machinimas is located in the area of the image-sound relationship. The sound engine of the computer game is usually completely turned off and replaced with your own soundtrack

---

[3] *Mod* is the abbreviation for modification, and it means the change of an original game content.

that opens for machinima productions an additional design space for parodic- and/or immersive-style media. Unlike game movies which are shot exclusively with game assets and thus remain close to the programmed game content, machinimas generate both new game content as well as new game characters and narrate, with the help of self-produced assets, stories that often stand in direct contrast to the image design and branding strategies of the games.

Since 2004, the formative machinima scene has distanced itself from the computer game model of the heroic ideal body, and has rather tried to make the loss of control experienced within the social virtual reality visible and speakable. The machinima scene has therefore embarked on the search for the imperfect, weak everyday body, and has developed a variety of narrative styles and configurations to introduce into the success-oriented and socially normalized game world's biographically experienced violence, power and domination, as well as simulated accidents, catastrophes and disturbances. The *Sims* machinimas therefore place into question the computer game as a cultural apparatus for the popularization of management knowledge, and replace it with narrative processing techniques that try to expose the ambivalent structures of family organization. The ironic commentary on the plot of the original *Sims* game makes it clear why, in the machinima community, there prevails a strong tendency to dramatic narrative forms at the reception aesthetic interface of Gothic and splatter movies.

Machinima films circulate today in all relevant Web 2.0 social networking sites. In addition to relevant community sites (www.machinima.com), video uploads to YouTube dominate the media presence of machinimas in the net. The YouTube video portal ensures its global reach and creates, by means of semantic tagging fields and nodes, an additional contextualization of machinimas. With their networking in the field of online portals and social media, *Sims* machinimas have grown into a crowded venue of heterogeneous identity discourses and conceptions of social order. Against this background, feedback comments of social networking sites fight over distinctions of belongingness and tirelessly carry on certification struggles which revolve around the search terms *emo, goth* or *punk*.

Machinimas are *small forms*, i.e., formats, that, in the space of a few minutes, focus on narrative actions and present character constellations in a condensed way. They react to the reception habits of Internet use. The frequency of seminear and near settings is an indication that machinimas interpret narrative forms as time-critical, and therefore try as quickly as possible to attract the attention of the observing audience. To increase attention value, references to recognizable movie characters and scenes of Hollywood cinema are often made. Overall, intermedial and intertextual references are presented in a compressed way, due to the limitations of the mandatory time frame conditions. How can general conclusions for mash-ups be formulated in this context? It is a distinct advantage for the formation of a cultural studies perspective in the area of recent reception and impact research of the interactive communication media to use an extended notion of productive media adoption. Intermedia formats, appropriations, evidence strategies, fakes and truth discourses have in the network a hybrid perception culture and social rules have given rise to a new politics of representation that suggests a modulating use of gaming: »Many games companies are releasing their design tools and games engines alongside their games.« (Jenkins 2008:166)

The art historian Aby Warburg developed in the 1920s his concept of the »pathos formula« to show the cultural historical tradition of expressive gestures according to the antique pattern in Renaissance art. He interprets this in his 1893 dissertation on Sandro Botticelli's artworks as cultural symbols that do not directly represent emotions and passions, but rather refer much more to a historically related, semantically charged and socially constructed meaning process. (Warburg 1992:11–64) In this sense, Warburg does not understand the feeling expression as an original, individually lived body experience, but rather as a location within a culturally based representational order »in which one passively suffers and does not actively act.« (Luhmann, 1982:73)

The *Sims* machinimas can be understood in three ways in connection with Warburg's conception of the pathos formula.

(1) They *reproduce* without modification, the formulaic inventory of kinesthetic scripts. Thus, they assume the role that previously, in game design, fixed notations of elementary gestures and simple body movements. This leads to a uniform motion animation. For example, the affective vocabulary of mourning gestures remains highly repetitive and follows the logic of ergonomic movement patterns and standardized work routines.

(2) Based on this, they produce transformative frame-of-reference tables which interrupt the goal-orientedness of the game and associate the kinesthetic scripts with different meaning contexts. In this way, they overcome the computer game as a device deployed for training perceptions and reactions. Machinimas change the mode of the physical performance: they make a communicating gesture out of the originally planned efficiency of movement. They use computer culture for communication, and mix it with popular culture citations from advertising, blockbusters, or video clips.

(3) Finally, they establish a *composite repertoire* of gestures and facial-motion graphics, which, by means of the ranking tools of relevant portals, form canons.

For the development of the *Sims* machinima, the restricted programming of the body movements and facial expression do not constitute a defect, but—on the contrary—an essential prerequisite of their genuine media aesthetics: »Machinima replaces the gestures of the game and thus compensates for a loss of theater and film gestures which appear to be difficult or impossible in computer games.« (Krapp , 2008:299) They interpret the technological limitations of the computer game as an artistic productive force and point out that gestural and mimetic systems do not spring from a natural spontaneity, but rather, in dealing with game technology, always must be assumed to be *acquired* properties and *citable* sizes. In this sense, the *Sims* machinima force the game with their own restrictions and reflect the computer-based mediatization of emotional scripts which are the product of digital processing operations. They point out that we have to rely on a cultural repertoire of gestures in showing our feelings to make ourselves understood by means of specific bodily techniques. In the space of possibilities of machinima, however, gaming is shifted away from being an exercise to increase the efficiency of motor skills shifts in favor of small narrative forms which declare the loss of perception and of control of the virtual game characters to be the starting point of an oppositional narrative.

3 Media Reflective Storytelling

Webcomics designates a comics format that is published exclusively or at least in the first place on the Internet. They are the product of technical media breakthroughs from analog to digital media, and cultural practices in the field of Internet communication. Computer and network-based comics can be understood as mixed formats because they are situated at the interface of different media, technologies and practices, and they participate both in the analog and the digital media cultures. They thus constitute neither a uniform nor a radically new genre. Webcomics can be seen more as a hybrid inheriting from already known genres, formats and media.

The continuous transformation of the aesthetics and narrativity of collaborative online comics projects points to a culture of reception that is the opposite of the classical model of authorship, and which seeks to promote collective practices. The conditions of permanent variability open to the user the possibility to endlessly rewrite the course of the narrative. The similarly organized narrative spaces of digital graphic novels give this collaborative stance an appropriate expression. Thus, not only the reception contexts, but also the action roles in the production process change. Clear and well-defined tasks and skills dissolve the traditional division of labor regulations of comics production, and new negotiation processes occur. For example, the comiczine *Reihenhaus* goes far beyond the usual style of teamwork in comic book production. There is no work specialization in the classical sense: »Our comics all have texted, invented characters, sketched and fully drawn. With the help of the write-based storytelling workshop we develop plots and characters. Only after an intensive collaborative process is the finished comic book created.« (Schmidt/Backes/Möhring 2006 ff.)

In *Hamlet on the Holodeck*, her book on narrativity in electronic media, the American media theorist Janet Murray introduces the concept of *procedural authorship* to emphasize the aspect of modified action roles with respect to interactive media: »Procedural authorship means writing the rules by which by the text appears as well as writing the texts themselves. It means writing the rules for the interactor's involvement, that is, the conditions under which things will happen in response to the participant's actions. [...] The procedural author creates not just a set of scenes but a world of narrative possibilities.« (Murray 2000:152) In this context, Murray understands the interactive exertion of influence as a choreographic reception model: »In electronic narrative the procedural author is like a choreographer who supplies the rhythms, the context, and the set of steps that will be performed. The interactor, whether as navigator, protagonist, explorer, or builder, makes use of this repertoire of possible steps and rhythms to improvise a particular dance among the many, many possible dances the author has enabled.« (Murray 2000:152)

Participatory comics require of their procedural authors a basic willingness to negotiate, which may include all aspects of storytelling. They thereby achieve a double framing of storytelling. First, they formulate their interactions by means of new conventions of storytelling. They allow experiences, comments and ratings to flow into the digital environment of webcomics (via ranking, voting and response tools). In this way, an editorial framing of preferred character constellations and narrative forms is produced. Second, they establish a stochastic component by creating possibilities for programmed random processes or for interventions by users. Against the background of this hyperfictional structure, users develop their own paths of reading and thus have to—as in a computer game—continuously make abductive decisions.

The appreciation of the active role of the reader while reading a text is on the list of requirements of today's reception aesthetics. The recognition of the interactive influence must, however, not obscure the fact that the freedom of multimedia reception is limited by the technical possibilities of the computer. In the webcomic, the rules according to which the reading process is supposed to proceed are part of script sequences that cannot be modified in the framework of interactive participation. In this respect, the much vaunted freedom of interactivity is more or less limited to the participatory mode of point-and-click, reducing the cognitive activity in the reception process to a few user commands. The vast majority of traditional webcomic hyperfictions show that the user remains inside the link structures that are provided for him or her. Murray rightly calls for »a distinction between playing a creative role within an authored environment and having authorship of the environment itself.« (Murray 2000:57) It is at this point where the media-reflexive comics, which are not satisfied with the mere increase of interactivity and participation, are situated. They tell us a lot about the role of the media and the reflection of media conditions, characterizing contents and their symbolic representations, communication culture and our media experiences.

If webcomics reflect on the realities of their own mediatization, then their uncircumventable starting point is the question of the importance of technological media. One of their main concerns focuses therefore on the process behind the graphical user interfaces that they want to make visible and accessible, to make clear that the computer is less of an image medium, and rather more of a writing medium that generates its multimedia interfaces with programming codes and texts. Since the computer is effective not only as a storage medium, but also as a computational system, it is itself effectively a *narrative medium* in that it stipulates specific rules, structures and possibilities of participatory interaction and meaningful interpretation. It does so in its capacity as hardware. In this sense, the computer acts as a procedural medium in appearance by calculating different inputs and generating different actions.

Against this background, Anja Rau postulates a greater involvement of graphical and symbolic software tools in the aesthetic design of network literature (Rau 1999, p.119). Media-reflective comics graft this meta-discourse onto electronic texts and remind us that digital comic stories are always processes of data processing. Their projects seek to emancipate the users, who are treated as stupid in the inscrutable simulations using the mouse, cursor, and graphical user interface in which they are captive. How is this happening now? The comic project *The Church of Cointel* (Niepold / Wastlhuber 2001ff.) tries to make the usually hidden structures of software architecture visible and usable for the user. The users see the whole narrative structure and organization of the comic and can enter at any point and continue to develop a strip in any direction.

The result is always new comic branches. However, with every new picture one must gain the approval of the other users. The interactivity is combined with grassroots democracy. If the new branch is narrowly defeated in a democratic vote, then the new image becomes the beginning of a new offshoot comic. It is primarily an association game and a test for new forms of cooperation. Therefore, everyone who visits the open ends of the stories can vote on alternative turns in the narrative. The possibilities of *Cointel* are endless. Complete breaks in the stories are therefore the rule, people change appearance and character, trade roles with others, and arouse thereby either the desire to surf further or, on the contrary, to themselves intervene. (Heckmann 2001)

Most multimedia webcomics restrict the participation of users to point-and-click operations. The user cannot anticipate his or her own reading and decision path. The comic project *Cointel*, by contrast, reverse-draws the hidden data presentations in software script to the screen, and makes these structures into the game material of aesthetic interventions. Media-reflective webcomics such as the project *The Church of Cointel* make the program code visible in two ways. First, it makes it available as a pragmatic-functional tool in the service of the comic. Second, it makes the program code available as artistic design material. In their projects, the media-reflective webcomics thematize their own media conditions, and integrate them into their own aesthetic development process, relating them in that way to the cultural and social significance of software.

At the last examined interface of computer-based technology, mediality and performativity, popular culture can be delimited: Although information and communication technologies constitute specific investment and negotiation processes, their performative framings in the context of reception have an effect, in turn, on the technologies and change them continuously. In this context, there inheres in popular culture practice an interventionist orientation which includes both media content and media technologies, and, faced with a reflection on media that ultimately places into question the self-understanding of cultural socialization, makes sociocultural differences visible and speakable, thereby making their political changeability possible.

Literature

Derrida, Jacques. »Signature Event Context,« in *Limited Inc.*, translated by Jeffrey Mehlman and Samuel Weber, edited by Gerald Graft. Evanston, IL, 1988.

Eco, Umberto. *The Open Work*, translated by Anna Cancogni, with an introduction by David Robey. Cambridge, MA, 1989.

Fischer-Lichte, Erika. »Grenzgänge und Tauschhandel. Auf dem Wege zu einer performativen Kultur,« in: *Performanz. Zwischen Sprachphilosophie und Kulturwissenschaften,* edited by Uwe Wirth. Frankfurt am Main, 2002, 277–300.

Fischer-Lichte, Erika. *Ästhetik des Performativen*. Frankfurt am Main, 2004.

Foucault, Michel. *The History of Sexuality, Vol. 1: An Introduction*, translated by Robert Hurley. New York, 1990.

Frølunde, Lisbeth. »Machinima Filmmaking as Culture in Practice: Dialogical Processes of Remix,« in *Computer Games and New Media Cultures: A Handbook of Digital Games Studies,* edited by Johannes Fromme and Alexander Unger. New York, 2012, 491–507.

Heckmann, Carsten. »Wir wollen eure Hirne melken,« *Spiegel Online. Netzwelt*. 2001. Online unter: http://www.spiegel.de/netzwelt/web/0,1518,126623,00.html (accessed May 1, 2013).

Hilderbrand, Lucas. »Youtube: Where Cultural Memory and Copyright Converge,« *Film Quarterly* 61, no. 1 (2007): 48–57.

Hoskins, Deb. »Do You YouTube? Using Online Video in Women's Studies Courses,« *Feminist Collections* 30, no. 2 (2009): 15–17.

Jenkins, Henry. *Convergence Culture*. New York, 2008.

Kelland, Matt, Dave Morris, and Leo Hartas. *Machinima: Making Animated Movies in 3D Virtual Environments*. Ilex, 2005.

Krämer, Sybille. »Sprache—Stimme—Schrift. Sieben Thesen über Performativität als Medialität,« *Paragrana* 7 (1998): 33–57.

Krapp, Peter. »Über Spiele und Gesten. Machinima und das Anhalten der Bewegung,« *Paragrana* 17 (2008): 296–315.

Kraus, Kari. »›A Counter-Friction to the Machine‹: What Game Scholars, Librarians, and Archivists Can Learn from Machinima Makers about User Activism,« in *Journal of Visual Culture* 10, 1 (2011): 100–112.

Lowood, Henry E. »Real-Time Performance: Machinima and Game Studies,«
The International Digital Media & Arts Association Journal 2,
no. 1 (2005): 10–17.
Luhmann, Niklas. *Love as Passion: The Codification of Intimacy,* translated by
Jeremy Gaines and Doris Jones. Stanford, CA, 1998.
Murray, Janet H. *Hamlet on the Holodeck: The Future of Narrative in Cyberspace.*
Cambridge, 2000.
Niepold, Hannes, and Hans Wastlhuber. *The Church of Cointel.* 2001ff,
http://www.cointel.de (accessed on: 01.08.2013)
Rau, Anja. »Toward the Recognition of the Shell as an Integral Part of the Digital
Text,« in *Hypertext '99. Returning to Our Diverse Roots. Proceedings of the
10th ACM Conference on Hypertext and Hypermedia,* edited by Klaus
Tochtermann et al. New York, 1999, 119–20.
Richard, Birgit. »Art 2.0: Kunst aus der YouTube! Bildguerilla und Medienmeister,« in
Konsumguerilla. Widerstand gegen Masssenkultur? edited by Birgit Richard
and Alexander Ruhl. Frankfurt am Main/New York, 2008, 225–46.
Schmidt, Imke, Ellen Backes, and Jonas Möhring. *123comics nach Maß.* 2006ff.
http://www.123comics.net (accessed August 1, 2013).
Warburg, Aby M. »Sandro Botticellis ›Geburt der Venus‹ und ›Frühling,‹« in
Aby Warburg—Ausgewählte Schriften und Würdigungen, 3rd ed.
Baden-Baden, 1992, 11–64.

Ramón Reichert

is a professor of new media at the Universität Wien's Institut
für Theater-, Film- und Medienwissenschaft. His research interests
include the historiography of media and technology as well as the
impact of new media and communication technologies such as the
Internet, social media, visual culture and identity politics. He is the
author of *Im Kino der Humanwissenschaften. Studien zur Medialisierung wissenschaftlichen Wissens* (2007); *Amateure im Netz.
Selbstmanagement und Wissenstechnik im Web 2.0* (2008); *Das
Wissen der Börse. Medien und Praktiken des Finanzmarktes* (2009);
Die Macht der Vielen. Über den neuen Kultur der digitalen Vernetzung
(2013); and *Big Data. Die Gesellschaft als digitale Maschine* (2014,
forthcoming).

Image and Narrative in the Computer Game

Stephan Günzel

»Do games tell stories? Answering this should tell us both *how* to study games and *who* should study them.«[1]
Jesper Juul

In the fundamental debate concerning computer game research, two opposite positions are predominantly made very apparent: on the one hand, that of narratology, and on the other, that of ludology.[2] While for those who see a computer game as an interactive story, it is primarily a digital game: For narratologists, the computer game is therefore just a story that is realized in some other form, without changing the narrative significantly in the process. Just as a film would only gradually be distinguished from a novel, so the computer game differs little from a written account[3]: there is always a person or character at the center of the plot, and the narrator will always identify from whose position the story is told. But ludologists also consider the computer game slightly differently from what is already known: because the screen play is the continuation for this position of a real-space game by other means, i.e., an implementation of the rules of a board, paper or brain-teasers in digital form. Ludological analysis compares computer games, therefore not with printed or filmed stories, but with analog games. The research has thus experienced a boom. Ludologists, like narratologists, negate the fact that computer games have a characteristic by which they would otherwise be distinguished from a story or from a traditional game as the game medium, thus the hard- and software, the computer and the program. Instead, both are of the opinion that what they are and how computer games function, could also be realized without a computer. The simple fact is ignored that all computer games are distinguished by the phenomena that they are to be viewed on a screen. Computer games are primarily visual manifestations and in that respect they are clearly different from literature, film and other games. Therefore, the distinctive feature is not in interactivity alone, this already exists between playing or communicating people, but it lies in the potential of the manipulation of the interactive image itself: computer games, as Constanze Bausch and Benjamin Jörissen aptly write,

---

[1] Jesper Juul, »Games Telling Stories?« in *Handbook of Computer Game Studies*, ed. Jeffrey Goldstein and Joost Raessens (Cambridge/London, 2005), 219–26, here 219.

[2] The term *ludology* comes from Gonzalo Frasca in 1998, who defined the approach retrospectively as follows: »Ludology can be defined as a discipline that studies games in general, and video games in particular.« See Gonzalo Frasca, »Simulation versus Narrative: Introduction to Ludology,« in *The Video Game Theory Reader*, ed. Mark J. P. Wolf and Bernard Perron (New York/London, 2003), 221–35, here 222.

[3] The continuity of conventional narrative and narration in virtual space stresses the works by Janet H. Murray. Without exaggeration, her monograph *Hamlet on the Holodeck: The Future of Narrative in Cyberspace* (Cambridge, 1997) can be described as a classic of narratological computer game research, even though games are only dealt with peripherally here.

are »played images«[4] Even though the medial difference is implied by the narratological as well as the ludological side, and even though both in their descriptions of computer games refer to something as a game or as a narration, this is taken as visually mediated but without having to bear the particular status of the computer game at its expense, and that is: to be attached with the description of the computer game as an image.

Narrative-Theoretical Computer Game Analysis

The proposed differentiation game theorists themselves make between narratology and ludology has a specific reason and several implications: The basis for it was the fact that literature and film scholars began to investigate computer games, without recognizable game experience or the ability to experience their analyses. So it seems that narratologists can agree that for the sciences of the older media, a game will always be inferior as a narrative, in comparison to film: »In terms of traditional narrative meaning, games,« said media scholar Andrew Darley, »are even more shallow than the blockbuster movie or the music video«.[5] The primary distinguishing feature of literary studies are descriptive categories, which is the source for philology: A game is always treated as text, which is quasi-linguistically mediated. The paradigm of »text«, in which computer games have been treated to this day by narratologists, has ultimately led to the situation that a certain games canon of narratology has been established, which mainly includes games that are either based on a preceding narrative, or where the game is controlled by inputting text. This means that the description therefore does not only depend on the procedure, but also on the selection of games, in particular, adventure or role-playing, the preferred genres from which the examples are drawn in narratological analyses. In addition, narratologists often negotiate digital forms of communication such as Internet forums or multiuser dungeons and online role-playing games, but instead offer platforms with which virtual parallel societies are cultivated. These are not games in the strictest sense, which are primarily based on an invariant set of rules and on both spatial and temporal limitations. In contrast, *Second Life* is a play in a different sense to other

---

[4] Constanze Bausch and Benjamin Jörisssen, »Das Spiel mit dem Bild. Zur Ikonologie von Action-Computerspielen,« in *Ikonologie des Performativen*, ed. Christoph Wulf and Jörg Zirfas (Munich, 2005), 345–64, here 347.. 345–364, here p. 347.

[5] Andrew Darley, *Visual Digital Culture: Surface Play and Spectacle in New Media Genres* (London/New York, 2000), 154.

computer games, as one plays primarily with the identity.[6] From the perspective of narratology, computer games can mostly only be themed as derivatives or hybrids between human communication, not as a specific medium. Nevertheless narratological analysis contributes to an understanding of these new forms of communication and can, in turn, form a basis for the description. However, they lose such a reasonably »open text term«[7] media analytical description of potential when it comes to computer games.

Games Theory Counter-Proposal

Given the narratologically limited prominence of computer games, the Finnish Game theorist and representative of many games theorists, Markku Eskelinen conveyed his displeasure in the founding number of the relevant online journal *Game Studies*. He remarked: »If I throw a ball at you I do not expect you to drop it and wait until it starts telling stories.«[8] Eskelinen's annoyance related to literary theory and its resulting hierarchical approach to games. The first step to an independent game theory approach, surprisingly, is not that one could now turn to a ludologist web page for the allocation of computer games in which no text appears. While this was subsequently also done, the actual use was in something else. It was to show the innate resources of literary theory consideration that the limited canon games themselves did not sufficiently analyse. A main argument of ludologists here was that, even if there is a story in a computer game, this is structured completely differently than in the conventional form of literature, which functions in a linear way. In contrast, games are not completely nonlinear, yet differ from a printed text by the possibility that the »reader« can choose between alternatives and can thus change the outcome and even the sense of the story within the process of reception.

A fundamental distinction of narratology, which was put forward in 1929 by the English literary scholar Edward Forster, views a general difference as one between *plot* and *story*.[9] In contrast to the story, which means the fullness of telling individual events in chronological order, Forster describes the

---

[6] The model of role-playing is also under reasonable investigation by Sherry Turkle. See idem., *Life on the Screen: Identity in the Age of the Internet* (New York, 1995).

[7] Randi Gunzenhäuser, »Spielkultur, Stichworte zur kulturwissenschaftlichen Computerspielanalyse,« in *Computerspiele. Eine Provokation*, ed. Evelyne Keitel et al. (Lengerich et al., 2003), 49–68, here 52.

[8] Markku Eskelinen, »The Gaming Situation,« Game Studies 1, no. 1 (2000), www.gamestudies.org/0101/eskelinen (accessed August 19, 2013).

[9] Ibid.

plot as being only such events, between which there is a logical or causal connection: »A plot is thus a narrative of events, [...] but the sense of causality overshadows it.«[10] The story therefore arises from the activity of »storytelling« in the literal sense as story-based, or as enumerate individual (real or fictional) facts. The plot, however, is the original causal connection between them. The difference between story and plot, or narrative and plot(s) is then obvious, when the reader of a book or audience member of a film, is asked after reading the book or watching the movie, what it was about. In most cases, the story is then recapitulated, reporting too on some of the amorous entanglements, but not describing the love scenes as a plot in detail. This level of plot that Forster calls »an organism of a higher type«[11] proves in this sense to be a construction of spatiotemporal contexts, of which authors or filmmakers can expect that readers or viewers reveal a (variable) story during their receptions. Their deductions can turn out to be relatively trivial in comparison to the plot. So it is that computer players, in their search to find out what a game is really about, will often attempt to derive a story from causal relationships. It is recapped that there had been an accident in a Mars station and that their workers have now turned into zombies that are to be killed in the game. Game packaging and advertising contain such endeavors at inferring from the plot, which is one of the main reasons why computer games seem less interesting or even stupid to some people.

    The media feature of computer games does not, however, lie at the level of the narrative, but at that of the plot: While the story may vary in the interpretation of the recipient, action, unless unchanged in the other media, may vary in computer games too. So players have the possibility, if need be, to walk around the zombies that they could kill or to kill them in a varying order. The reader of a book or the viewer of a film does not have this option, except to put the book down or close their eyes.[12] The plot of the game is therefore not entirely dictated. The opportunities for variation are perhaps limited by the program or computing capacity, and of course many games contain an »ideal plot« that conveys the plot in the shortest possible time, such as Speedruns.

---

10 Edward Morgan, *Aspects of the Novel* (New York, London, 2005; originally published 1927), 87.

11 Ibid., 44.

12 But also when one does not agree with this view and considers rather that in individual computer games there nevertheless ultimately is a linear *story*, one has still just shifted the layers of analysis. Rather, one would have to admit that the *plot* in the game was taken in and now assumes the layer of the *story*. Then, negotiation in games becomes a sequence of causes that a *story* shows in the screen display.

One of those who were later to be called ludologists was the Norwegian Espen J. Aarseth, the current teaching and editor in chief of Game Studies at the Center for Computer Games Research at the Copenhagen IT University. It was he who, in 1997 with his book *Cybertext,* tried for the first time to highlight the autonomy of computer games, in such a way, and according to their analysis. As the title clearly indicates, Aarseth holds fast to the notion of the text. This does not contradict ludological concerns, since this does not take the position that computer games do not display narrative elements,[13] only that the form of their reception is, as a result, not to be viewed like written narratives. In his first monographic work, which is treated as a founding document of ludology at times, Aarseth therefore refers less to existing theories on games and game playing but set the goal of identifying the particular narrative in computer games. His focus lies on the labyrinthian structure of nonlinear narrative of a computer game, in which Aarseth seeks to make its status obvious through the neologism »Cybertextuality.« To be described here is the nature of the computer game narrative, to be able to »control« the plot, insofar as it is possible to choose between alternatives. Unlike the book, in which jumps are at best possible by paging through, or within a narrative produced by explicit forward and reverse actions, it is a characteristic of computer game narratives that arise from the plots that a decision as a whole has an influence on the course of the game.[14] For instance, so that the path through a maze game with a certain weapon or the key to a room, not to mention without the proper tools, is made easier or even all possible. In that way, Aarseth holds a mirror in front of narratology by pointing out that what is indifferent in this game, in terms of the analog medium as narrative, is entirely different by nature than any previously known form of literature: »A nonlinear text is [...] not simply one fixed sequence of letters, words, and sentences but one, in which the words or sequences of words may differentiate from reading to reading because of the shape, conventions, or mechanisms of the text.«[15] The term for this new type of text that Aarseth brought into use is *ergodic literature.* According to Aarseth, ergodic literature is a narration form in which the sequence of events in

---

[13] Vgl. Gonzalo Frasca: Ludologists Love Stories, Too. Notes from a Debate that Never Took Place. In: Marinka Copier/Joost Raessens (ed.), Level Up. Digital Game Research Conference, Utrecht. Universiteit Utrecht 2003, pp. 92–99 (http://www.digra.org/dl/db/05163.01125 [*last accessed*:: 19.08.2013]).

[14] »I refer to the idea of a narrative text as a labyrinth, a game, or an imaginary world, in which the reader can explore at will, get lost, discover secret paths, play around, follow the rules, and so on.« (Espen J. Aarseth: Cybertext. Perspectives on Ergodic Literature, Baltimore/London 1997, p. 3.)

[15] Espen J. Aarseth: Nonlinearity and Literary Theory. In: Georg P. Landow (ed.), Hyper/Text/Theory, Baltimore 1994, Spp. 51-86, here p. 51.

the game stems from the work (Greek *ergon*) by the player. The causal relationship is constituted, according to Aarseth, as the way (Greek *hodos*). Further, Aarseth states that it is not the narrative in the sense of the story that therefore distinguishes computer games, but the causal link between the narrative elements or events, which are brought into relationship with the passing through of the space within the game.

Game vs. Narrative

Even when Aarseth's criticism strikes at the weak point of the narratological argument, by retaining the textual term it nevertheless blurs the fundamental difference between the digital computer game and the analog book mediums. So it is also not surprising that the term »Cybertextuality« has not been enforced—even its author no longer uses it today.[16] The Danish theorist Jesper Juul finally took the decisive step toward the creation of a separate computer ludology. Beside Aarseth, Juul counts one of the most well known game theorists in Scandinavia and, after an brief position at the Computer Game Research Center GAMBIT at the Massachusetts Institute of Technology in Boston, is currently visiting professor at the Game Center at New York University. Juul assumes that the necessary narratological approach is based on a presumption that categorically questions its validity: »Narratives may be fundamental to human thought, but this does not mean that everything *should* be described in narrative terms. And that something can be presented in narrative form does not mean that it *is* narrative.«[17] In his keynote address »A Clash Between Game and Narrative,« given at the Digital Arts and Culture Conference 1998 in Bergen, Juul summarized his just-completed master thesis.[18] In it, he cites seven features that make computer games clearly distinguishable from literature:[19]

1. Foremost of these, Juul makes the distinction between *history* and *program*. This means an accentuation of the difference between linearity and nonlinearity, as mentioned by Aarseth: A program, according to Juul, is a history that is principally distinct in that it responds to the inputs of the user. The book, or rather the course of the narrative, does not however change due to the

16
Already with his introduction, Aarseth admits to difficulty in mediating terminology. See idem., *Nonlinearity and Literary Theory* (see note 15), Espen J. Aarseth, »Cybertext. Perspektiven zur ergodischen Literatur: Das Buch und das Labyrinth,« (1997), trans. Jeannette Pacher, in *Reader Neue Medien. Texte zur digitalen Kultur and Kommunikation*, ed. Karin Bruns and Ramón Reichert, Cultural Studies 18 (Bielefeld, 2008), 203–11, here 204.

17
Juul, »Games Telling Stories?,« 14 (see note 1).

18
Jesper Juul, »A Clash between Game and Narrative: Interactive Fiction,« speech given at the Digital Arts and Culture Conference, Bergen, Norway, November 27, 1998, http://www.jesperjuul.net/thesis/AClashBetweenGameAndNarrative.pdf (accessed August 19, 2013).

19
Ibid.

fact that it is being read. The game changes during the progression of the game or is different in each new game.

2. Related to this is a characteristic difference that Juul describes as *single* and r*epeated consumption:* Now this does not mean that the book could not be read several times. (It is not destroyed by his reading, but is physically still very much present.) Repeated reading is indeed possible, but the story does not change because of it. At best, a dense narrative for the reader becomes richer, in so far as more implications or allusions can be discovered. Rather significantly, frequent reading does not, however, cause a new character to suddenly appear in the novel. Conversely, this is possible in a computer game, such as when a room is entered that had not been reached or passed through before in a previous game and in which a new form of the game with certain characteristics are »waiting« on the protagonists. Strictly speaking, every change in the viewing direction and every single action, according to Juul, is a change in comparison to the previous game. In a narrative being read for the second time, neither the hero nor the reader of the novel can choose to not kill the bad guy and instead pass him by. For Juul this means an added feature:

3. and 4. The sequences of the book are set *(fixed),* the sequences of the game are variable *(flexible)*, or, what amounts to the same thing, the reason or the drive *(desire)* to read a book consists in follow the narration, which is consequently received *passively*. The reason to play a game, however, is to explore the structures and possibilities of the game world, and is therefore *actively* received.

5. Hence, Juul is initially surprised by a further distinction: Time in a novel is *variable,* while in the game it is, in contrast, *fixed*. But it does not contradict his previously given characterization of the flexibility of the gameplay. Instead, Juul refers here to the internal time of the narrative within the novel (which is mostly identical to the *story*). A written history can jump in time and, like a film, does not need to take account of the natural order of past, present and future, or the earlier, now and later.[20]

20
Even though jumps in time are also conceivable in the play, these occur mostly in *in-game* film sequences if the interaction is suspended in the play and the player views a given cinematic sequence. However, it is absolutely conceivable that in a game, not only space jumps (the reentrance of the field on the opposite side are possibly realized), but also time jumps during interactive passages.

6 According to Juul, this in turn relates to the plot in which traditional writing in the past takes place (the narration time as *plot*) or took place. The action in the game, in contrast, occurs in the present. This applies principally to the content, since it is often reported as the past in a novel. But even if it told of future events, the time of writing and the production of the story would be passed or would set the (future) course. Although the game has been programmed in the past, the process is, as already described, not determined. The plot (plot) is created, rather, by playing only in the present, in any historical period the game (or the story) is located.

7 Regarding a concluding characteristic, Juul finally considers the abstract nature of the game. Where counternarratives need vital anthropomorphic characters to convey the meaning of a story, cuboids can also appear in games. Further, Juul writes elsewhere: »Tetris does not have a visible actor either, and it does not seem possible to construct any actor controlling the falling bricks. ›Tetris—The Movie‹ does not seem like a viable concept. But Tetris is incredibly popular, and nobody is disputing its status as a computer game.«[21] Transitions are in turn possible. A novel can, in terms of prosopopoiia, contain objects or forms in nature that can talk, but then nature would always speak *like* a man. While the player, in comparison, can name each of the falling bricks, they will not become human by doing so. They simply remain moving geometric shapes. This is ultimately not Juul's point: Of course there are speaking and acting characters in computer games who have a close resemblance to humans, but the computer game can do without it. Not so in the case of the novel. In other words, the computer game does not need text, but can bring the story across through visual means alone, unlike in narration.

Computer game ludology, as can be observed through Juul, thus holds the key with which to highlight the role of imagery in media theory. However, it is not specially made for the theme. On the contrary, it seems as if the emphasis on active playing has caused the character of the medium to be neglected, which in turn allows you to play: The computer game is princi-

[21] Juul, »Games Telling Stories?,« 223f. (see note 1).

pally visible, then manipulated and only afterward may also be meaningful. While narratologists focus on the last stage, i.e., meaning, ludologists refer mainly to the second: interactivity. Yet both are equally preceded by an appearing image which is manipulated or interpreted.

Stephan Günzel
is a professor for media theory at the Technische Kunsthochschule (btk) in Berlin. Until 2011 he was the coordinator for the Zentrum für Computerspielforschung (DIGAREC) at the Universität Potsdam and visiting professor for space studies at both the HU Berlin and the Universität Trier. His monographs include: *Egoshooter. Das Raumbild des Computerspiels* (2012); *Raum/Bild. Zur Logik des Medialen* (2011); *Maurice Merleau-Ponty. Werk und Wirkung* (2007); *Geophilosophie. Nietzsches philosophische Geographie* (2001). As editor: *Lexikon der Raumphilosophie* (2012); *KartenWissen. Territoriale Räume zwischen Bild und Diagramm* (2012); and *Raum. Ein interdisziplinäres Handbuch* (2010).

Software Code as Expanded Narration

Alan N. Shapiro

Computer programming is about algorithms, formal logic, precise reasoning and problem solving. As such, it would appear to have little to do with what we call creative expression. The logical act of programming and the self-expressive act of creativity would seem to be polar opposites. We think of creative expression as taking place within certain literary or visual arts, through certain kinds of communication or symbolic systems, via certain kinds of writing, speech, discourse, language, or notation.

Some examples of these expressive media and genres are poetry, storytelling, nonsense, humor, musical notation, screenplays, notes for an artwork, notes for a dance or other choreography and architectural drawings. We don't think of software code as being an expressive media. When we think of software code, we think of it as being about the way that we handle a physical or virtual device that is to be programmed. This is a rational and calculating activity, a practical consequence of the philosophical assumptions of the symbolic logic of Bertrand Russell, of Friedrich Ludwig Gottlob Frege, of Noam Chomsky, of the classical paradigm of computing theory. It is about the issuing of a series of instructions or commands to a machine, to an object or mechanism that is considered as essentially being dead.

What is the difference between the expressivity of the expressive act in the literary or visual arts and the series of instructions that is the computer program? We have always assumed that there is an insurmountable wall between these two kinds of writing or notation. To tear down this wall, like the Berliners did to their Wall in 1989, was until now almost unthinkable. Only now are we ready to ask these questions. Could software code also be expressive? Does software code have to be only productive? The idea of expanded narration as applied to software code means going beyond the established binary opposition of writing as being either expressive or utilitarian. The paradigm of software code as we know it is reaching its limit: the exclusive emphasis on engineering and on getting the program to do something, code as a series of instructions to a machine.

In order to progress further, software development or computer science must begin to concern itself with cultural codes as well as with software codes. Computer science must transform itself into a hybrid engineering and humanities discipline.

One of the most important media theorists was the German Friedrich Kittler, who is regarded as being a poststructuralist. Kittler deeply resisted expanding media theory to include software theory. Kittler wrote a famous essay called »There Is No Software.«[1] His position was that everything in computing breaks down to the digital code of the hardware, that there is no going beyond the pervasive logic of the binary. Kittler was wrong because, in a few words, digital-binary logic is not the only possibility for computing. Digital-binary logic is not universal and forever, and it is precisely software theory as an academic field, deriving from both media theory and computer science, which can lead us to new paradigms and new possibilities such as quantum computing, creative coding, software that operates like the reverse-engineered human brain, and software as semi-living entities in the sense of artificial life rather than inert things to be manipulated by the dominating programmer subject.

In »There is No Software,« Kittler fancies himself as writing about the end of history and the end of writing. It is a sweeping postmodernist and poststructuralist thesis. In a contemporary writing and cultural scene of endlessly expanding and exploding signification, there is ironically an implosion into the no-space and no-time of microscopic computer memory. The relationship of information technology developments to writing, for Kittler, is a causality bringing about the current situation that we supposedly do not write anymore. The idea that software code might be a form of writing, a form of *écriture* in the Derridean deconstructionist sense (an intervention or inscription into language that is more fundamental and effective than that of speech), never occurs to Kittler. He represses this thought and instead assumes that the computer must bring about the programmatic automation of reading and writing. »This state of affairs [...],« writes Kittler, »hide[s] the very act of writing.« »We do not write anymore,« he continues. Kittler believes that writing done on a computer is not to be seen as an historical act anymore because the writing tools of the computer »are able to read and write by themselves.«[2]

[1] Friedrich A. Kittler, »There Is No Software,« in *Literature, Media, Information Systems: Essays*, ed. and introduced by John Johnston (Amsterdam, 1997), 147–55.

[2] Ibid., 147.

Kittler writes: »[The] all-important property of being programmable has, in all evidence, nothing to do with software; it is an exclusive feature of hardware, more or less suited as it is to house some notation system.«[3]

My view is the opposite of Kittler's. I think that software code can be the site of the re-emergence of *écriture* in Derrida's sense. There can be a shift from programming as the programmability of some device to programming as creativity, creative expression, and writing in the deepest sense of effecting change.

In his examination of the Saussurian sign, the early Derrida focused on the negative linguistic concept of difference, taking apart Saussure's (mistaken) dualistic metaphysics of *signifier* (sound) and *signified* (concept). Derrida radicalized Saussure's semiotics when he said that there are endless chains of signification in sign systems, and not just a one-to-one static relationship between the signifier and the signified. Linguistic signs always refer to other signs, and there can never be a sign that is the endpoint of signification. One never arrives at any ultimate meaning of a word. Writing in Derrida's sense is the opposite of the system of stabilized and clear-cut definitions of words which dictionaries are intended to be. There is always an insurmountable gap between what I write or say and what my readers or listeners read or hear.

For Friedrich Kittler, the software space is just virtuality or simulation. It is not possible, according to him, to establish any new relationship to reality through programming, any aesthetically instituted opening for democracy or creativity. Art/aesthetics/design and informatics have no possible bridge between them. The miniaturization of hardware is, for Kittler, the proper dimension of simulation, of our »postmodern writing scene« which is no longer a scene of writing.[4] Jean Baudrillard thought something similar to this when he wrote in *Simulacra and Simulation* that »genetic miniaturization is the dimension of simulation.«[5] Yet Baudrillard transcended this conservative and nostalgic position with respect to technology when he practiced his photography and wrote about photography as »the writing of light.«[6]

[3] Ibid., 153.

[4] Ibid., 148.

[5] Jean Baudrillard, *Simulations*, trans. Paul Foss, Paul Patton, and Philip Beitchman (New York, 1983), 3.

[6] Jean Baudrillard, »Photography, or the Writing of Light,« trans. François Debrix, http://www.ctheory.net/articles.aspx?id=126 Also, under the title »Photography, or Light-Writing: Literalness of the Image,« in idem., *Impossible Exchange*, trans. Chris Turner (London, 2001), 139–47.

For Kittler, hardware always precedes and determines software. »There are good grounds to assume the indispensability and, consequently, the priority of hardware in general.« »All code operations,« he wrote in the essay »There Is No Software,« »come down to absolutely local string manipulations, that is, I am afraid, *to signifiers of voltage differences*. [...] The so-called philosophy of the so-called computer community tends systematically to obscure hardware with software, electronic signifiers with interfaces between formal and everyday languages.«[7] Kittler's solution, on the contrary, is that we should all write our programs in assembler code in order to counteract the tendency of the entire world to hide the machine from its users, in order to keep at the forefront the awareness that the underlying hardware is what the program boils down to.

Kittler waxes nostalgic for »the good old days of Shannon's mathematical theory of information, [when] the maximum of information coincided strangely with maximal unpredictability or noise.«[8] Although we are said to live in the information society, and this has been said for several decades in sociological discourse, in my view it is very difficult to come across any definition of information (or communication) that illuminates much of anything. Roman Jakobson elaborated a classical model of communication that identified a message transmitted from a sender to a receiver.[9] I think that there are three limitations of Jakobson's model:

(1) The sender-receiver paradigm is not sufficient for understanding today's virtual online software systems where a message is sent to a shared data structure by a publisher which is then seen by many subscribers.

(2) As Jean Baudrillard pointed out in his 1972 essay »Requiem for the Media,« the alleged objective and scientific status of Jakobson's model merely formalizes a socioculturally given configuration.[10]

(3) Jakobson's model of communication is ultimately a simulation model. The purpose of the model is to provide »technical safe passage« for the transparently readable message, which is stripped of meaning and ambivalence, and become pure information.

[7] Kittler, »There Is No Software,« 152, 150 (see note 1).

[8] Ibid., 151.

[9] Roman Jakobson, »Linguistics and Poetics,« in *Style inLanguage*, ed. T. Sebeok (Cambridge, MA, 1960), 350–77.

[10] Jean Baudrillard, »Requiem pour les medias,« in idem., *Pour une critique de l'économie politique du signe* (Paris, 1972), 220–23.

To summarize, we can speak of an old paradigm of communication and a new paradigm of communication. The old Communication Model, as exemplified in the works of Claude Shannon and of Roman Jakobson, has three problems reflective of its twentieth-century context: the obsolescence of the point-to-point messaging which occurs through a queue or an elementary physical channel as distinguished from newer publisher-subscriber messaging exchanges which take place over a topic data structure or via even more complex virtual channel messaging topologies and across simultaneous multimedia channels; the idealized elevation of specific sociocultural relationships of power to the allegedly neutral or eternal or technological status of the technical code (communication considered as being strictly a matter of and for engineering); and the elimination of the reverberations, resonances and depths of language in favor of an information that gets purified by being stripped of the interference of noise.

The new paradigm of communication, relevant and promising for the twenty-first century, takes the publisher-subscriber model as its point of departure, emphasizes the political science (feminist, postcolonialist) awareness of specific historical relations of power, and underlines the ambivalences and singularities of words and of languages.

All three of these innovations, bringing technical codes and technical systems design into hybrid coupling with cultural codes and cultural design patterns, move in the direction of expanded narration. The publisher-subscriber model, leaving the realm of the strictly technical, is a storytelling framework of interactive human contact and the circulation of ideas and discursive material information that is social and participatory and involves many people, in contrast to the simplified straightforward point-to-point narrative of the archetypically twentieth-century node-to-node connectivity phone conversation which operates with two persons only and takes place over a single media channel.

The politicized or hybrid technical-cultural awareness which accentuates sensitivity to power relations is a more expanded narration relative to the myth of noise-free communication as implemented by an exclusively technical code and carried over a merely technical channel. Openness to the richness of language rather than solely paying attention to the engineering dimension of the message transmission relates within the university classification system of knowledge to the study of comparative literatures and languages, which belong to the province of narration. The academic and scientific assignment of the field of communication to the perspective of engineering has previously reduced the treatment of exchanges of meaning in human sign systems to the nonnarrative of an abstract manipulable no-time and no-space.

The point-to-point communication model is explicitly superceded by publish-and-subscribe messaging in message-oriented middleware like IBM's WebSphere MQ or SonicMQ from Progress Software, and in the Java Message Service (JMS) Application Programming Interface, which is a higher-level specification for programming such messaging systems. In the publish-and-subscribe model, messages are delivered to subscribed consumers without them explicitly having to request them. This is expanded narration because the number of readers is not restricted by a declarative programmatic deed. The performative acts of reading by the subscribers are something that transpires outside of the programming by the programmer, made existentially specific and alive during the runtime of the running application which, contemplated from the new transdisciplinary perspective, is the context of a social and literary practice. Publish-and-subscribe is a social model, yet technical books on messaging would never describe it as expanded narration because literature studies and literary sociology have been excommunicated from the engineering domain. Once we take it upon ourselves to study communication in a transdisciplinary way, then the spread and explosion of narrative which has already happened in the last decades becomes evident.

Now I will examine more closely the famous Shannon-Weaver model of communication and information, which was developed shortly after World War II, and emerged from the context of the telecommunications industry. Claude Shannon published his article »A Mathematical Theory of Communication« in the AT&T *Bell System Technical Journal* in 1948.[11] In my view, the Shannon-Weaver model is now obsolete. Its goal is to isolate the message as a technical entity, to ensure the integrity of the

11
Claude Shannon, »A Mathematical Theory of Communication,« *Bell System Technical Journal* 27 (July and October 1948): 379–423, 623–65.

message. Everything which is not this technically conceived message gets relocated elsewhere in the system.

Let us consider the 8 well-known components of the Shannon-Weaver model, how we can critique the assumptions of each component, and how this leads toward a new model:

Component of Shannon-Weaver model	Critique	Comment	New Concept
Source	There is no origin (Derrida). »In this play of representation, the point of origin becomes ungraspable.«[12]	Publishers continue an ongoing process which had no beginning.	Subscribed Publisher (a message producer broadcasts to topics and simultaneously consumes messages from other topics)
Encoder	The format is not neutral (Marshall McLuhan and Quentin Fiore). The media is the message/massage.[13]	The format is flexible and extensible; encoding is a creative act.	Creative Code Modifier (service or process is altered at runtime in specific real-life circumstances, but code or specification is not changed).
Message	There is no one-to-one relationship of signifier/signified; there is an endless chain of textuality (radicalized semiotics).	The message contains markups or index values connecting it to lots of other data.	Indexed Message (each message contains a header which identifies its role in a cross-referenced software design schema).
Channel	»57 Channels and Nothing on« (song by »The Boss« Bruce Springsteen).	Not all communication is meaningful (au contraire!).	Topic (the named destination to which we publish and/or subscribe).
Noise	»We live in a society of noise« (Anonymous).	Move the information/noise boundary farther over into the territory called noise.	Interpret the Noise (instead of trying to interpret noise as data bits, which messes up memory addressing or program logic flow, start from the viewpoint of the »nonknowledge«).
Decoder	The format is not neutral (Marshall McLuhan and Quentin Fiore). The media is the message/massage.	The interpretation or reading of the format offers creative options.	Creative Code Modifier (the service or process is altered at runtime in specific real-life circumstances, but the code or specification is not changed).
Receiver	Some pitches don't arrive in the catcher's glove. In baseball, this is called a passed ball, or a wild pitch.	Systems are constantly crashing.	Glitch (instead of designing around errors, one should design starting from the perspective of the anomaly, accident or soft error).
Feedback	Exception Handling, rather than return codes, to change program flow under anomalous conditions (Bjarne Stroustrup, originator of the C++ programming language).[14]	Errors are systemic events of differing severity levels.	Social Exception Handling (return to the spirit of experimentation and surprises of cybernetics, but replacing the notion of feedback with a proactive design strategy of multi-inheritance levels of Exception Handling, as in object-orientation).

Semantic Software or Linked Data is another example of the new communication model in action. Linked Data entails the design and implementation of a new software integration layer that adds more intelligence to the use of already existing structured databases, and unstructured data such as Web sites and blogs, in its invocation of multilevel database joins (in the former case) and associative semantic crawlers (in the latter case). The provided software layer is an abstract complex pattern or representation analogous to the topic data structure in the Java Message Service: it is an intermediate middleware artifact that gets positioned between what used to be called senders and what used to be called receivers. It furnishes the real data-processing power of the system, which is at the same time a social power and a narrative power. With linked data, the flexibility of search is brought together with the exactness of query. The user or software agent sees new relationships between previously unconnected data, and benefits from the contextual reasoning of the combined search/query.

The recent emergence of software studies (Matthew Fuller, Lev Manovich) contests Kittler's thesis that there is no software and points to the primacy of software as a societally critical hybrid of technical and cultural patterns. In 2006 Fuller published a pioneering book on software as media and as culture called *Behind the Blip*.[15] In his 2013 book *Software Takes Command*, Manovich expands media theory to include software theory. His book »is concerned with ›media software‹—programs such as Word, PowerPoint, Photoshop, Illustrator, After Effects, Final Cut, Firefox, Blogger, Wordpress, Google Earth, Maya and 3Ds Max. These programs enable creation, publishing, sharing, and remixing of images, moving-image sequences, 3D designs, texts, maps, interactive elements. [...]«[16]

Thinking along with Manovich, we can assert that one of the major contemporary challenges to media theory is to consider how Web sites, computer games, web applications and mobile applications transform the essence of what media are. And how do the universality and trends of software affect the design process? Is the basic nature of design altered by the fact that it is now almost everywhere carried out with the tools of

---

12
Jacques Derrida, *Of Grammatology*, trans. Gayatri Chakravorty Spivak (Baltimore, 1997), 36.

13
Marshall McLuhan and Quentin Fiore, *The Medium is the Massage* (New York, 1967).

14
Bjarne Stroustrup, *The C++ Programming Language* (New York: Addison-Wesley, 1991).

15
Matthew Fuller, *Behind the Blip: Essays on the Culture of Software* (Brooklyn, New York, 2003).

16
Lev Manovich, *Software Takes Command* (New York, 2013). See http://lab.softwarestudies.com/2012/09/does-media-still-exist.html

simulation and software which are built on top of object-oriented design patterns? What is the relationship between the object-oriented and business logic patterns of software design and the patterns of other kinds of design (such as architectural, graphical, fashion, communication, industrial and product design)? Together with Manovich, we can ask the question: »Are there some structural features which motion graphics, graphic designs, Web sites, product designs, buildings, and video games share since they are all designed with software?«[17] And what does media become after software?

Lev Manovich's theses are in some ways reminiscent of the ideas of the great media theorist Vilém Flusser who, in his seminal book *Into the Universe of Technical Images*, presented the pragmatic-utopian vision of an advanced science fictional society of the continuous creative creation and permanent prolific exchange of high-tech images.

Following Flusser, we can assert that technical images are made possible by scientific principles worked up into technologies. Particles in the contexts of specific technologies are assembled or computed into visible images. Each image technology (the photograph, the .jpg image, the VRML-programmed virtual world) is a different way of structuring particles. Technical images are reservoirs of information. Programming is a form of freedom. In the future society of images, everyone will be empowered to envision. Everyone will be a programmer and a synthesizer of images.

»There will be an ongoing dialogical programming of all apparatuses by all participants,« writes Flusser in *Into the Universe of Technical Images*.[18] New-media artists and creative people should initiate a project of transforming software code into something other than what it currently is. We must go beyond practicing the unconscious reification (*Verdinglichung* in German, a theoretical term coined by the Hungarian Marxist György Lukács meaning the ideological operation of treating an artifact that is a specific cultural-historical construction as ahistorical or eternal) of assuming that software code as »left-brain« (the rational-calculating side of the human brain) engineers have defined it is the only possibility for software.[19]

17 Ibid.

18 Vilém Flusser, *Into the Universe of Technical Images*, trans. Nancy Ann Roth, introduction by Mark Poster (Minneapolis, 2001), 154.

19 György Lukács, *History and Class Consciousness: Studies in Marxist Dialectics*, trans. Rodney Livingstone (Cambridge, MA, 1972).

Beyond software studies (beyond even the positions of Fuller and Manovich which have not quite worked through the problematic of reification and which remain chiefly tied to the empirical study of software as it is, characterized by engineering and commodification), I propose starting the activity of observing and participating in the active transformation of software by creative coders who are artists and designers and thinkers: devising a new curriculum for informatics itself—a »right-brain« (the creative and intuitive side of the human brain) informatics that builds on existing computer science yet moves it much closer to art, design, sociology, philosophy and cultural theory.

According to Marshall McLuhan and Bruce R. Powers in *The Global Village: Transformations in World Life and Media in the 21st Century*, reading, writing and hierarchical ordering are associated with the left brain, as are phonetic literacy and the linear concept of time. The left brain is the locus of analysis, classification, and rationality. The right brain is the locus of the spatial, tactile, and musical. Comprehensive awareness results when the two sides of the brain are in true balance.[20]

A key aspect of software code as expanded narration is the concept of *similarities* (as opposed to the system of discrete identities and differences of combinatorial software). Similarities is how the reality of the universe in fact really works. Urgently required for software development after object-orientation is the design and implementation of relations of similarity, fractal/holographic-like patterns, and music-like resonance between the whole (the software instance) and the parts (smallest units of information or database elements) as opposed to the logic of discrete identities and differences of Turing machines. The approach that would correspond to a true breakthrough into twenty-first-century science would be to identify relationships of similarity, to find *samples* or *patterns* that capture something of the vitality and complexity of the whole without breaking it down in a mechanistic way, as in the seventeenth-century Cartesian method of dealing with a complex problem by breaking it down into smaller, more manageable parts, along the lines of the mechanistic relation between the whole and its parts in the archetypal legendary car engine.

[20] Marshall McLuhan and Bruce R. Powers, *The Global Village: Transformations in World Life and Media in the 21st Century* (New York, 1989).

The design and implementation of the new logic of similarities involves a major reconsideration and inclusion of nonknowledge. We need to rethink science as a whole with a healthy dose of nonknowledge, away from the pure obsession with knowing everything and seeking total information. The significance of nonknowledge for science is already manifest in the twentieth-century sciences of quantum physics and chaos theory.[21]

It is within quantum physics that we find the idea of a vast number of states of information which are potentialities, not yet actualized realities, and which have a relationship of similarity to each other.

Previously (in »A Proposal for Developing Quantum Computing in Software«), I wrote about the »nondestructive space of observation.«[22] We want to build a »quantum reservoir« of nonobservable information that cannot be simply read or written in a visible way as in the standard get and set operations of conventional programming without destroying the integrity of the data. What we want in the quantum reservoir is a special sort of blueprint. We want an immensely vast number of software classes which are similar to each other in very subtle ways. They are invisible to the observer. They have no identity and we cannot look at them. The information is read only in order to no longer be what it is. In the act of reading, the information is transferred from its own quantum state into the domain of real-world usefulness.

It would be a mistake to call the number of states within the quantum informational reservoir infinite. Here we are in a realm beyond traditional mathematics, beyond concepts like finite and infinite, beyond their binary opposition. We are involved with a more complex and paradoxical topology. This is the applied task that awaits a new mathematics: to make a correct description of the quantum informational space.

We need a system where an immense number of possible states is possible, but the switching actions involved are manageable. There is a great deal of flexibility in assigning individuals to classes, and a high degree of variability among the individuals of a class.

---

[21] See Alan N. Shapiro, »Rethinking Science,« in *We Magazine Special: Future Challenges* (2010, print and online editions), http://www.we-magazine.net/we-volume-03/re-thinking-science/#.UgJU-kaw9Xzw

[22] Alan N. Shapiro and Alexis Clancy, »A Proposal for Developing Quantum Computing in Software,« http://choreograph.net/articles/a-proposal-for-developing-quantum-computing-in-software.

Empirically speaking, in the business world, a new software paradigm is emerging: software that handles uncertain social media data and massive volumes of data, software that is »alive« and is an ecosystem, code that does something productive but is also poetic, musical, and expressive: an expanded narration.

In the age of Big Data, new customer business requirements at the systems and applications levels are also changing what software is and how it fundamentally should be designed. These new computing requirements include embedded data analytics, linked data, unprecedented massive volumes of data, uncertain social media data, and continuous self-learning as a crucial and intrinsic quality of software. Storage, memory, networking and processing will move closer to the data as long, sequential, symbolic, scripted, ratiocinating top-down logic gives way to short, parallel, semantic-semiotic, coupling of perception and action, immediate bottom-up intelligence.[23]

Creative coding where a line of code is an aesthetic artifact and not only an instruction to the machine, where a new software layer opens up as a performance space for music, poetry, storytelling, dance and philosophy.

Creative coding projects which are going on right now include the artist-oriented Integrated Development Environments (IDE) called openFrameworks, vvvv, and Processing.[24]

There is the area of generative art (artworks which have been created using an autonomous system such as a computer, a robot, an algorithm or mathematics), the vast area of programming and music, and the growing area of programming and dance.

There is the music programming language called SuperCollider, and the music programming environments called Max/MSP and Pure Data.[25]

From the openFrameworks IDE Web site: »openFrameworks is an open-source C++ toolkit designed to assist the creative process by providing a simple and intuitive framework for experimentation. The toolkit is designed to work as a general-purpose glue, and wraps together several commonly used libraries.«[26] Among these are coding libraries for graphics,

[23] See the current IBM Research project called »Cognitive Computing«: http://www.research.ibm.com/new-era-of-computing.shtml

[24] openFrameworks: http://www.openframeworks.cc/. vvvv: http://vvvv.org/. Processing: http://processing.org/

[25] SuperCollider: http://supercollider.sourceforge.net/. Max/MSP: http://cycling74.com/products/max/. PureData: http://puredata.info/

[26] http://vvvv.org/.

typography, computer vision, 3D modeling and audio, image and video processing.

The artist-oriented development environment vvvv is a visual programming toolkit for rapid prototyping and creative coding. From the vvvv Web site: »It is designed to facilitate the handling of large media environments with physical interfaces, real-time motion graphics [and] audio and video that can interact with many users simultaneously.«[26]

From the Processing Web site: »Processing is a programming language, development environment, and online community. Since 2001, Processing has promoted software literacy within the visual arts and visual literacy within technology. Initially created to serve as a software sketchbook and to teach computer programming fundamentals within a visual context, Processing evolved into a development tool for professionals.«[27]

At the University of Bayreuth, Germany, there is an important project of creative coding. »Creative coding,« its initiators write at their Web site, »refers to the use of programming languages and code as design tools for media production. This is not an effort to understand software development as an engineering discipline, but rather to bring together practices that can be described as bricolage, tinkering and hacking (in the original sense). In the broadest sense, [creative coding] is about learning to understand that software is a creative form of expression that has its place alongside the other arts.«[28] (my translation)

According to its SourceForge open source project Web site, »SuperCollider is an environment and programming language for real-time audio synthesis and algorithmic composition. It provides an interpreted object-oriented language which functions as a network client to a state-of-the-art, real-time sound synthesis server.«[29] Professor Alberto de Campo of the University of the Arts in Berlin has made major contributions to the development and applications of SuperCollider in the areas of just-in-time programming, object modeling, the sonification of linguistic data and social media data, auditory display, microsound, and many others.[30]

According to the German-language and English-language Wikipedia articles on the music-programming toolkit

[26] http://vvvv.org/.

[27] http://processing.org/

[28] http://creativecoding.uni-bayreuth.de/

[29] http://supercollider.sourceforge.net/

[30] See *The SuperCollider Book*, ed. Scott Wilson, David Cottle, and Nick Collins, with an introduction by James McCartney (Cambridge, MA, 2011).

Max/MSP, »Max/MSP is a graphical development environment for music and multimedia maintained by San Francisco-based software company Cycling '74. It is designed for real-time processes. During its twenty-year history, it has been widely used by composers, musicians, performers, software designers, and artists for creating innovative recordings, performances, installations, and interactive software.« It provides creative coders with independence from the imposed »aesthetic requirements of commercial products.«[31]

From the Pure Data music programming environment Web site: »Pure Data (a.k.a. Pd) is an open-source visual programming language. Pd enables musicians, visual artists, performers, researchers, and developers to create software graphically, without writing lines of code. Pd is used to process and generate sound, video, 2D/3D graphics, and interface sensors, input devices, and MIDI.«[32]

The next major phase of my research is to intensively study the ongoing creative coding projects and to extract from them the basic principles of a cultural and professional movement toward a new paradigm of writing software as a creative act practiced by artists and designers. The pedagogy of instructing artists and designers how to make software involves teaching them how to write code in a way that is not dry and boring for them (as the engineering approach can often be for creative-oriented students), teaching them how to design software in a way that brings together software patterns and artistic/cultural patterns, teaching them creativity, and teaching them cultural theory so they can grasp conceptually how the paradigm of object-orientation can be pushed through to the next paradigm (which I call—as one of its names—»power to the objects«).

We need to unpack object-orientation philosophically into its two separate streams, which are *commodified* and *creative*. The mainstream understanding of object-orientation by engineering schools and the institutions for which they train programmers is philosophically naive: they assume the existence of a »real world« and so-called real-world processes, and regard software development as being the practice of modeling these real-world processes in a province of utility known as software.

[31] http://de.wikipedia.org/wiki/Max/MSP, http://en.wikipedia.org/wiki/Max_(software). My rendition combines a translation from the German-language Wikipedia article with some phrases adapted from the English-language Wikipedia article.

[32] http://puredata.info/

This alleged »real world« is really the realm of simulations and simulacra, as diagnosed by the media sociologist-philosopher Jean Baudrillard in his extensive and important work.

Radicalized and creative object-orientation (the direction and new paradigm of software that is coming in the very near future) neither assumes the existence of a real world nor does it seek to model or simulate this real world (an approach which becomes, in the mainstream practice, the simulation of a simulation). The activity of creative coding wants to fashion a new reality, a hybrid of the good old familiar phenomenological reality and new virtual realities, new experiences of existence in a hybrid real/virtual dimension. This is the potential of software at its best, as its present and future will soon unfold for us.

Alan N. Shapiro
is a transdisciplinary thinker who studied science-technology at MIT as well as philosophy, history and literature at Cornell University. He is the author of *Star Trek: Technologies of Disappearance* (2004) and *Software of the Future* (2013), as well as the translator of *The Technological Herbarium* (2010). Recently, he was a keynote speaker at the conference *Das Wissen der Zukunft* at the University of Vienna, at University of Amsterdam's BOBCATSSS conference, at the IEEE conference in London, at the Share Art Festival in Turin, and at the ISI International Symposium of Information Science in Potsdam. Shapiro also gave the International Flusser Lecture in Berlin in July 2012.

Jonas Englert
Norman Hildebrandt

Mothers, Can't We Please Come Home? This Freedom Fills Us with Anxiety.

Though the author is a fifteen-week-old fetus, his eyes are already fully formed. By week seventeen he can already hear his mother's intestines rumbling, and a mere two weeks later he can perceive his acoustic surroundings. When he reaches twenty-seven weeks, he can see the sun. He sees red. Four months later, curtain opens and he is born, a tabula rasa affiliated to narration. The Bach prelude that was playing in the background in the hope of stimulating the infant's postnatal intelligence, suddenly stops. The performance begins.

After two months of theater, his eyes can focus. The narration is now synchronized. Colors are primarily primary. Graphically told tales expedite color differentiation. And then he looks at the stage, outside of himself, into narrative space. Deep. He interacts and reaches toward the narrator. Micro-narration begins. If he sees only part of an object, he can decode it in its entirety a month later. He expands into pastel-colored backgrounds through small, haptically narrative games of hide and seek.

At eight months the author is grown-up. Before, his sight was only 40 percent at most; but now his field of view has reached its narrative climax.

And now he's been sitting there for eight months, in the spectator's cradle of humanity. He dons a sensibly operative pair of ice skates and goes out for a stroll. He strolls around, skates over the frozen lake, which is ripe for action. He circles around there, on the touchscreen, and is nearing a breakthrough, the break-in. The more closely he hones in on his narrator's core, his authorial identity, the greater the danger that he will be pulled under the user interface of his own history. The antithesis, the emotional predetermined breaking point.

But then—then he begins the telling:

Ladies and gentlemen, this text reports on members of a generation which, no sooner had they assiduously sprung from their mothers' wombs, were immediately confronted with the alienation effect. With themselves, watching each other while perceiving. This kind of diffuse manifestation is often referred to as clouds—and the western narrative sky is cloudy. But there's no heterotopic rain at all. Partly necessary, barely existential, the ice layers illuminated from below. We've longed for ourselves for so long. Thither. Thither to long-desired embryonic resistance. Against Ratio.

Mothers, can't we please come back home? This freedom fills us with anxiety.

We absolutely must return into our luxurious mansion. Our real estate. With a sea view. The sun is setting. Red. And at the end, we're all sitting in front of the beach screen, touched. Touché. Because we all cling to our digital heart-ends and end up as caressable goods in a massive dialectic show—a 99.5-degree well tempered narration.

Jonas Englert
studies visual communication/art/experimental spacial concepts since the winter semester of 2010/2011 with Professor Heiner Blum at the HfG Offenbach, as well as applied theater studies since the winter semester of 2012/13 with Professor Heiner Goebbels at the Justus-Liebig-Universität Gießen. He is an editor for Faust-Kultur since 2010. He was awarded the Dr. Marschner-Preis in 2012 and the Johannes Mosbau scholarship in 2010. Exhibitions (2013): *CineTeatroAlemán* (Buenos Aires), *Atlas 2013* (Bundeskunsthalle Bonn), *Biennale des bewegten Bildes* (Frankfurt/M.), and *1822-Forum* (Frankfurt/M.)

Norman Hildebrandt
studied visual communication at the HfG Offenbach from 2003 to 2010, with a focus on drawing and sculpture. He studied for his doctoral degree in art and cultural studies at the Universität für Angewandte Kunst Wien from 2010 to 2013. He is an artistic-research assistant at the HfG Offenbach for the Moving Image Biennial (B3). Since the summer semester of 2013, he holds a lecture on the introduction to communication design. Research interests: crossovers between art, poetry and aesthetics. He has numerous publications for exhibition catalgoues. He lives in Offenbach and Vienna.

die Benutzeroberfläche seiner eigenen Historie gezogen zu werden. Der Antithese, seiner emotionalen Sollbruchstelle. Doch dann – dann beginnt er zu erzählen:
Sehr geehrte Damen und Herren, dieser Text berichtet von einer Generation, welche, unverdrossen dem Mutterleib entsprungen, unmittelbar mit dem Verfremdungseffekt konfrontiert wurde. Mit sich selbst, wie sie sich beim Wahrnehmen zuguckt. Oftmals spricht man bei solch diffusen Erscheinungen von Wolken – und der westliche Erzählhimmel ist bewölkt. Doch es regnet keine Heterotopie. Partiell notwendig, kaum existentiell, die unterleuchteten Eisschichten. Lange haben wir uns danach gesehnt. Hin, Hin zum lang ersehnten embryonalen Widerstand. Wider Verstand.
Mutter, lasst uns wieder nach Hause kommen! Diese Freiheit macht uns Angst.
Wir müssen uns unbedingt in unsere Luxusvilla zurückziehen. Unsere Real Estate Immobilie. Mit Blick aufs Meer. Die Sonne geht unter. Rot. Und wir alle sitzen berührt am Strandscreen. Touché. Denn wir alle fassen uns an unseren digitalen Herzenden – und enden als Streichelware in einer ganz großen Dialektikshow, einer 37,5°C Wohltemperierten Narration.

Jonas Englert
studiert seit dem Wintersemester 2010/11 Visuelle Kommunikation/Kunst/Experimentelle Raumkonzepte bei Heiner Blum an der HfG Offenbach am Main und parallel seit dem WS 2012/13 Angewandte Theaterwissenschaften bei Professor Heiner Goebbels an der Justus-Liebig-Universität Gießen. Er ist seit 2010 Redaktionsmitglied bei Faust-Kultur. 2012 erhielt er den Dr. Marschner-Preis, Offenbach/M, 2013 das Johannes Mosbach-Stipendium. Ausstellungen (2013): Sala ArteCinema (Buenos Aires, Argentinien), *Atlas* (Bundeskunsthalle Bonn), *Biennale des bewegten Bildes* (Frankfurt/M.), 1822-Forum (Frankfurt/M.).

Norman Hildebrandt
studierte 2003 bis 2010 Visuelle Kommunikation an der HfG-Offenbach mit den Schwerpunkten Freies Zeichnen und Bildhauerei. 2010 bis 2013 Doktoratsstudium der Kunst und Kulturwissenschaften an der Universität für Angewandte Kunst Wien. Künstlerisch-wissenschaftlicher Mitarbeiter an der HfG-Offenbach im Rahmen der Biennale des bewegten Bildes (B3). Seit dem Sommersemester 2013 Lehraufträge in »Grundlagen Kommunikationsdesign«. Forschungsinteressen: Grenzgänge zwischen Kunst, Poesie und Ästhetik. Zahlreiche Texte für Ausstellungskataloge. Er lebt in Offenbach und Wien.

Jonas Englert,
Norman Hildebrandt
Mütter, lasst uns wieder nach Hause kommen!
Diese Freiheit macht uns Angst.

Ist der Autor ein Embryo, ein fünfzehn Wochen altes, so sind seine Augen bereits in Gänze ausgebildet. In der siebzehnten Woche hört er die Gedärme der Mutter arbeiten. Zwei Wochen später nimmt er ihr akustisches Umfeld wahr. Mit siebenundzwanzig Wochen sieht er die Sonne. Er sieht rot. Vier Monate später, als narrationsaffine Tabula Rasa enthunden, öffnet sich der Vorhang. Das Bach'sche Präludium zur Förderung seiner postnatalen Intelligenz setzt aus. Die Vorstellung beginnt. Nach zweimonatigem Theater können seine Augen fokussieren. Die Narration ist jetzt synchron. Farben primär primär! Gegenständlich erzählendes Vorhalten beschleunigt Farbdifferenzierung. Und dann schaut er auf die Bühne, aus sich heraus, in den Erzählraum. Tief. Er interagiert und greift nach dem Erzähler aus. Mikronarration setzt ein. Sieht er nur einen Teil eines Objektes, so kann er im nächsten Monat dessen Gesamtheit kognitiv erschließen. Er expandiert in kleine, dinglich narrative Versteckspiele auf mittlerweile pastellfarbenem Hintergrund. Mit acht Monaten ist der Autor erwachsen. Machten seine Sehkräfte zuvor nur maximal vierzig Prozent aus, so hat seine Weitsicht eben den narrativen Klimax erreicht.
Und jetzt, jetzt sitzt er da – seit einem dreiviertel Jahr. In der Zuschauerwiege der Menschheit. Er zieht sich seine smartoperativen Schlittschuhe an und flaniert, er streicht über den starren See, in den es hineinzuhandeln gilt. Da kreist er, auf dem Touchscreen, und ist kurz vorm Durchbruch, dem Einbruch. Je verdichtender er sich kreisend seiner Erzählermitte nähert, seiner Autorenidentität, desto eher läuft er Gefahr, unter

kann – das ich unter anderem als »Ermächtigung der Objekte« bezeichne.

Wir müssen die Objektorientierung »philosophisch« in ihre seperaten Strömungen aufspalten, die sowohl »zur Ware werden« als auch »kreativ« sein können. Das etablierte Verständnis von »Objektorientierung«, wie es etwa in Ingenieurhochschulen oder in Einrichtungen zu finden ist, in denen Programmierer unterrichtet werden, ist philosophisch naiv: Sie gehen von der Existenz einer »realen Welt« und »real« stattfindenden Prozessen aus und sehen die Entwicklung von Software als eine Praxis an, die diese »realen« Prozesse modelliert – in einem nutzbaren Bereich, der Software genannt wird. Diese vermeintlich »reale Welt« ist aber in Wirklichkeit ein Bereich der »Simulation und der Simulakren«, wie es der Mediensoziologe und Medienphilosoph Jean Baudrillard in seinem umfassenden und wichtigen Werk beschrieb.

Eine radikalisierte und kreative Objektorientierung (die Ausrichtung und das neue Paradigma von Software, das in der nahen Zukunft zu erwarten ist) nimmt weder die Existenz einer »realen Welt« an noch sucht es nach einem »Modell« oder einer »Simulation« dieser »realen Welt« (ein Ansatz, der in der etablierten Praxis nämlich lediglich zu einer Simulation der Simulation führt). Die Tätigkeit des Creative Coding möchte eine »neue Wirklichkeit« formen, ein Hybrid aus der guten alten phänomenologischen »Realität« und neuen »virtuellen Realitäten« – eine neuartige Existenzerfahrung in einer hybriden real-virtuellen Dimension. Darin liegt das größtmögliche Potential von Software, das uns ihre Gegenwart und Zukunft bald schon offenlegen wird.

Alan N. Shapiro
ist ein transdisziplinärer Denker mit Schwerpunkt auf Wissenschaftstechnologien. Er studierte am MIT sowie Philosophie, Geschichte und Literatur an der Cornell Universität. Er ist Autor von *Star Trek. Technologien des Verschwindens* (2004) und *Die Software der Zukunft* (2013). Zuletzt war er ein Hauptredner bei der Konferenz über *Das Wissen der Zukunft* an der Universität Wien, bei der BOBCATSSS-Konferenz über Informations-Management an der Universität Amsterdam, bei der IEEE-Konferenz über die Informationsgesellschaft in London, beim Share Kunst Festival in Turin und am ISI International Symposium für Informationswissenschaft in Potsdam. Im Juli 2012 hielt er die *International Flusser Lecture* in Berlin ab.

Gebieten Just in time-Programmierung, Objektmodellierung,
bei der »Sonifikation« von sprachlichen und Social Media-Daten,
bei akustischen Displays, Microsound und vielen anderen.[30]

Laut deutschsprachigen und englischsprachigen
Wikipedia-Einträgen zu dem Musikprogrammiertool *Max/MSP*,
ist es »eine graphische Entwicklungsumgebung für Musik und
Multimedia von der in San Francisco beheimateten Software
Company Cycling '74, die für Echtzeitprozesse ausgelegt ist. Sie
wird seit 20 Jahren von Komponisten, Musikern, Softwareent-
wicklern und Künstlern eingesetzt, um interaktive Software
selbst zu erstellen – unabhängig von den ästhetischen Vorgaben
kommerzieller Produkte.«[31]

Das folgende Zitat stammt von der Musik-Programmie-
rungsumgebungswebsite von *Pure Data*: »*Pure Data* (a.k.a. Pd) ist
eine visuelle Open Source-Programmiersprache. Pd ermöglicht
Musikern, Bildenden Künstlern, Darstellern, Forschern und
Entwicklern, Software grafisch zu entwickeln, ohne Codezeilen
schreiben zu müssen. Pd wird verwendet, um Klang, Video,
2D- und 3D-Graphiken, Interface-Sensoren, Eingabegeräte und
MIDI zu prozessieren und zu generieren.«[32]

In der nächsten wichtigen Phase meiner Forschung
werde ich mich intensiv mit den aktuellen Projekten zum
Creative Coding beschäftigen und aus ihnen die Grundprinzi-
pien einer kulturellen und professionellen Bewegung extrahieren, die zu einem neuen Paradigma in der Entwicklung von
Software führt, bei der Programmieren als kreativer, von Künstlern und Designern praktizierter Akt verstanden wird.

Von pädagogischer Seite erfordert die Anleitung von
Künstlern und Designern, wie Software zu entwickeln ist, ihnen
die Tätigkeit des Programmierens so zu vermitteln, dass es
nicht trocken und langweilig ist (so wie auf kreativ arbeitende
Studierende oftmals die ingenieurswissenschaftliche Heran-
gehensweise wirkt); das Design von Software so zu unterrichten,
dass Software-Muster und künstlerische und kulturelle Muster
miteinander zusammengebracht werden; ihnen Kreativität
ebenso zu vermitteln wie Kulturtheorien, sodass sie auch begriff-
lich erfassen können, wie das Paradigma der Objektorientierung
zugunsten des nächsten Paradigmas hin überwunden werden

30
Vgl. dazu Scott Wilson; David
Cottle; Nick Collins: The SuperCol-
lider Book (mit einem Vorwort von
James McCartney). Cambridge
2011.

31
http://de.wikipedia.org/wiki/Max/
MSP. http://en.wikipedia.org/wiki/
Max_(software).

32
http://puredata.info/.

dungen, Computer Vision, 3D-Modellierungen sowie Audio-, Bild- und Videoverarbeitungsfunktionen.

Die künstlerorientierte Entwicklungsumgebung *vvvv* ist ein visuelles Programmierwerkzeug für Rapid Prototyping und Creative Coding. Dazu die *vvvv*-Website: »Es wurde entwickelt, um das Handling von großen Medienumgebungen, die physische Schnittstellen haben, zu vereinfachen, und zwar mit der Hilfe von in Echtzeit bewegten Graphiken und mit Audio und Video, die mit mehreren Benutzern gleichzeitig interagieren können.«[26]

Auf der *Processing*-Website wiederum findet sich: »*Processing* ist eine Programmiersprache, eine Entwicklungsumgebung und eine Online Community. Seit 2001 förderte *Processing* die Software-Kompetenz innerhalb der Bildenden Künste und die visuelle Kompetenz innerhalb der Technik. Ursprünglich geschaffen, um als Software-Skizzenbuch zu dienen und um Grundlagen des Programmierens in einem visuellen Kontext zu lehren, wurde *Processing* zu einem Entwicklungs-Tool für Profis.«[27]

An der Universität von Bayreuth in Deutschland wird zurzeit an einem wichtigen Projekt zum Creative Coding gearbeitet. Dazu schreiben die Initiatoren: »Creative Coding bezeichnet den Umgang mit Programmiersprachen und Code als Gestaltungsmittel für die mediale Produktion. Dies steht gerade nicht in der Bemühung, Software-Entwicklung als Ingenieur-Disziplin zu begreifen, sondern gruppiert Praktiken, die als *bricolage*, *tinkering* oder *hacking* (im ursprünglichen Sinn) bezeichnet werden können. Im weitesten Sinne geht es darum, Software als kreative Ausdrucksform begreifen zu lernen, die neben andere Künsten ihren Platz hat.«[28]

Laut der Open Source-Projektwebsite von *SourceForge* ist »SuperCollider eine Programmierumgebung und Programmiersprache für eine in Echtzeit ablaufende Klangsynthese und algorithmische Komposition. Es bietet eine interpretierte objektorientierte Sprache an, die als Netzwerk-Client in Verbindung mit einem hochmodernen Echtzeit- Klangsynthesenserver steht.«[29] Professor Alberto de Campo von der Universität der Künste Berlin hat einen wichtigen Beitrag zu der Entwicklung und Anwendbarkeit von *SuperCollider* geleistet, etwa auf den

26
http://vvvv.org/.

27
http://processing.org/.

28
http://creativecoding.uni-bayreuth.de/.

29
http://supercollider.sourceforge.net/.

Im Zeitalter von Big Data stellen Geschäftskunden neue Anforderungen an Systeme und Anwendungen und verändern damit, was Software ist und wie sie gestaltet sein soll. Diese neuartigen Anforderungen an den Computer beinhalten integrierte Datenanalysen, Datenverknüpfungen, noch nie da gewesene riesige Datenmengen, unbestimmte Social Media-Daten sowie kontinuierliches eigenständiges Lernen als wesentliches Qualitätsmerkmal von Software.

Speicherung, Vernetzung und Verarbeitung werden immer »näher an die Daten« heranrücken, so lange, bis die sequentielle, symbolische, geschriebene, von oben nach unten verlaufende schlussfolgernde Logik den Platz frei macht für eine kurze, parallele, semantisch-semiotische, die Wahrnehmung und Handlung verknüpfende, von unten nach oben verlaufende unmittelbare Intelligenz.[23] Es wäre Creative Coding, bei dem eine Zeile Code ein ästhetisches Artefakt und nicht nur einen an die Maschine gerichteten Befehl darstellt und bei dem sich neue Softwareschichten als Performance-Raum für Musik, Poesie, Geschichtenerzählen, Tanz und Philosophie öffnen. Creative Coding-Projekte, die gerade stattfinden, beinhalten künstlerorientierte *Integrated Development Environments* (IDE), etwa *openFrameworks*, *vvvv* und *Processing*.[24]

Dazu ist der Bereich der Generativen Kunst zu erwähnen (Kunstwerke, die mit »autonomen Systemen« geschaffen worden sind, wie etwa dem Computer, Robotern, einem Algorithmus oder der Mathematik), genauso wie das riesige Feld von Informatik und Musik und das von Informatik und Tanz. Zu nennen wäre hier das Musikprogramm *SuperCollider* und die Programmierplattformen *Max/MSP* und *Pure Data*.[25]

Das folgende Zitat stammt von der *openFrameworks*-IDE-Website: »*openFrameworks* ist ein Open Source Tool, das entwickelt worden ist, um kreatives Arbeiten zu unterstützen, indem es einen einfachen und intuitiven Rahmen für das Experimentieren bereitstellt. Das Tool wurde entwickelt, um als Alleskleber zu arbeiten. Es bindet verschiedene häufig verwendete Bibliotheken zusammen.«[26] Darunter finden sich Bibliotheken für die Programmierung von graphischen und typographischen Anwen-

---

23
Vgl. dazu das aktuell stattfindende Forschungsprojekt *Cognitive Computing* von IBM: http://www.research.ibm.com/new-era-of-computing.shtml.

24
Vgl. openFrameworks: http://www.openframeworks.cc/. vvvv: http://vvvv.org/. Processing: http://processing.org/.

25
SuperCollider: http://supercollider.sourceforge.net/. Max/MSP: http://cycling74.com/products/max/. PureData: http://puredata.info/.

26
http://vvvv.org/.

22
Alan N. Shapiro und Alexis Clancy:
A Proposal for Developing Quantum Computing in Software. URL:
http://choreograph.net/
articles/a-proposal-for-developing-quantum-computing-in-software.

In einem früheren Text mit dem Titel *A Proposal for Developing Quantum Computing in Software* schrieb ich bereits über den »nicht-zerstörerischen Überwachungsraum«.[22] Wir wollen ein »Quantenreservoir« von »nicht-observierbaren Informationen« einrichten, die nicht einfach in einer sichtbaren Weise gelesen oder geschrieben werden, so wie in den standardisierten Get- und Set-Befehlen der konventionellen Programmierung, ohne die Datenintegrität zu »zerstören«.

Für das Quantenreservoir benötigen wir eine ganz spezielle Art des Entwurfs: Wir brauchen eine riesige Anzahl an Software-Klassen, die sich auf eine äußerst subtile Art ähneln. Für die Betrachter sind sie unsichtbar. Sie haben keine Identität, und wir können sie nicht anschauen. Die Information wird gelesen, um nicht mehr das zu sein, was sie ist. Erst im Akt des Lesens wird die Information von ihrem Quantenzustand in einen Bereich der tatsächlichen Benutzbarkeit überführt.

Es wäre falsch, die Anzahl der Zustände innerhalb des Quanteninformationsspeichers unendlich zu nennen. Wir befinden uns hier in einem Bereich außerhalb der traditionellen Mathematik, außerhalb von Konzepten wie »endlich« oder »unendlich« sowie außerhalb von binären Oppositionen. Wir haben es mit einer weit komplexeren und paradoxeren Topologie zu tun. Dies ist die Aufgabe der neuen Mathematik: eine stimmige Beschreibung des Quanteninformationsraumes zu liefern.

Wir benötigen ein System, in dem zwar eine große Anzahl von Zuständen möglich ist, die involvierten Schaltvorgänge aber dennoch handhabbar sind. In der Zuweisung von Individuen zu Klassen gibt es eine Menge an Flexibilität wie auch ein hohes Maß an Variabilität zwischen den jeweiligen Individuen einer Klasse.

Erfahrungsgemäß entsteht in der Geschäftswelt bereits ein neues Software-Paradigma: Zu nennen ist hier Software, die unbestimmte Social Media-Daten und riesige Datenpakete bewerkstelligt; Software, die »lebendig« ist und ein Ökosystem darstellt; Code, der produktiv tätig, aber ebenso poetisch, musikalisch und expressiv ist: also eine Expanded Narration darstellt.

20
Marshall McLuhan; Bruce R.
Powers: The Global Village. Transformations in World Life and Media
in the 21st Century. New York 1989.

21
Vgl. Alan N. Shapiro: Rethinking
Science. In: We Magazine Special.
Future Challenges (2010). URL:
http://www.we-magazine.net/
we-volume-03/re-thinking-sci-
ence/#.UgJUkaw9Xzw.

entsteht, wenn sich beide Gehirnhälften in einem wahren
Gleichgewicht befinden.[20]

Ein Schlüsselaspekt dafür, Software-Code als Expanded
Narration zu verstehen, findet sich im Konzept der *similarities*,
der Ähnlichkeiten (im Gegensatz zu dem System der diskreten
Identitäten und den Unterschieden der »kombinatorischen«
Software). Die Wirklichkeit des Universums basiert tatsächlich
auf Ähnlichkeiten. Dringend benötigt für eine auf die Objektorientierung folgende Software-Entwicklung wird das Design
und die Implementierung von Ähnlichkeitsbeziehungen, von
fraktal/holographieartigen Mustern und einer musikähnlichen
Resonanz zwischen dem Ganzen (der Software-Instanz) und den
Teilen (den kleinsten Einheiten von Informationen bzw. Daten-
bankelementen), im Gegensatz zu einer Logik der diskreten
Identitäten und den Differenzen der Turing-Maschinen.

Ein Ansatz, der einen wirklichen Durchbruch für die
Wissenschaft des 21. Jahrhunderts darstellte, bestünde darin,
Ähnlichkeitsbeziehungen festzustellen: Beispiele oder Muster
zu finden, die etwas von der Vitalität und Komplexität des
Ganzen einfangen, ohne es in mechanistischer Weise aufzuglie-
dern – wie in der Cartesianischen Methode des 17. Jahrhunderts,
bei der komplexe Probleme behandelt wurden, indem sie in
kleinere, überschaubare Einzelteile zerlegt wurden – vergleichbar dem mechanistischen Verhältnis zwischen dem Ganzen und
seinen Teilen wie etwa im Falle des archetypisch legendären
Automotors.

Das Design und die Implementierung der neuen Logik
der Ähnlichkeiten beinhaltet eine umfassende Neubewertung
und Einbeziehung von »Nicht-Wissen«. Mit einer gesunden
Dosis an Nicht-Wissen müssen wir die Wissenschaft als Ganzes
überdenken und uns von der Obsession befreien, alles wissen zu
können und alle Informationen zu bekommen. Die Bedeutung
des Nicht-Wissens für die Wissenschaft wird bereits im 20.
Jahrhundert in Form der Quantenphysik und der Chaostheorie
offensichtlich.[21] In der Quantenphysik finden wir bereits die Idee
einer Vielzahl an Informationszuständen, die Potentialitäten darstellen, die sich noch nicht »verwirklicht« haben und die in
Ähnlichkeitsbeziehungen zueinander stehen.

18
Vilém Flusser: Ins Universum der technischen Bilder. Göttingen S. 130. Engl.: Into the Universe of Technical Images. Minneapolis 2001, S.154.

19
György Lukács: History and Class Consciousness. Studies in Marxist Dialectics (1923). Cambridge 1972.

In seinem Buch *Ins Universum der technischen Bilder* schreibt Flusser, dass »demnach ein ständiges dialogisches Programmieren aller Apparate seitens aller Beteiligten vor sich gehen wird«[18]. Heutige Medienkünstler und andere kreative Menschen sollten ein Projekt initiieren, bei dem Software-Code in etwas anderes transformiert wird, als was es momentan ist.

Wir müssen die Praxis der unbewussten »Verdinglichung« überwinden – ein Begriff, mit dem der ungarische Marxist György Lukács die ideologische Operation beschrieb, ein Artefakt so zu behandeln, als sei es ahistorisch oder ewig, obwohl es ein spezifisches kulturhistorisches Konstrukt darstellt. In der Annahme, dass Software-Code der linken Gehirnhälfte, also der rational-kalkulierenden Gehirnhälfte, entstamme, haben Ingenieure diese Praxis als die einzige Möglichkeit für Software festgelegt.[19]

Jenseits herkömmlicher Software Studies (selbst jenseits der Positionen von Fuller oder Manovich, die sich durch das Problem der »Verdinglichung« noch nicht ganz durchgearbeitet haben und die den empirischen Studien von Software, so wie sie erscheinen und durch Ingenieurwesen und Kommodifizierung charakterisiert worden sind, überwiegend verbunden bleiben) plädiere ich an kreative Programmierer – etwa an Künstler, Designer und Denker – sich aktiv an der Transformation von Software zu beteiligen: Es gilt ein neues Curriculum für die Informatik selbst zu entwickeln – eine Informatik der rechten Gehirnhälfte (also der kreativen und intuitiven Seite des menschlichen Gehirns), die auf bereits existierender Computerwissenschaft aufbaut, sich dabei aber weiter in Richtung der Kunst, des Design, der Soziologie, der Philosophie und der Kulturtheorie bewegt.

Nach den Ausführungen von Marshall McLuhan und Bruce R. Powers in dem Buch *The Global Village. Transformations in World Life and Media in the 21st Century* werden Lesen, Schreiben und hierarchische Anordnungen mit der linken Gehirnhälfte assoziiert, ebenso wie die phonetische Alphabetisierung und die lineare Vorstellung von Zeit. Die linke Gehirnhälfte ist der Ort der Analyse, der Klassifizierung und Rationalität. Die rechte Gehirnhälfte ist der Ort der räumlichen Vorstellung, des Taktilen und der Musikalität. Ein »umfassendes Bewusstsein«

Alan N. Shapiro
Software Code als Expanded Narration

Indem wir Manovich folgen, können wir behaupten, dass eine wesentliche Aufgabe der zeitgenössischen Medientheorie darin bestehe, sich zu überlegen, wie Websites, Computerspiele, Web Applications und Mobile Anwendungen das Wesen der Medien verändern und wie die Universalität und Entwicklungstendenzen von Software den Designprozess verändern.

Wird das grundlegende Wesen von Design durch die Tatsache verändert, dass es mittlerweile beinahe überall mit Simulationswerkzeugen ausgeführt wird sowie mittels Software, die auf objektorientierte Design-Muster aufgesetzt worden ist?

In welchem Verhältnis stehen objektorientierte und »geschäftsorientierte« Muster innerhalb des Software-Designs zu anderen Arten von Designmustern (etwa in der Architektur, der Grafik, der Mode, der Kommunikation oder im Industrie- und Produktdesign)? Mit Manovich können wir die folgende Frage stellen: »Lassen sich strukturelle Merkmale finden, die Bewegt-Graphiken, graphische Entwürfe, Internetseiten, Produktdesign, Bauwerke oder Videospiele gemeinsam haben, da sie ja alle mit der Hilfe von Software entworfen worden sind?«[17] Und was wird dann aus den »Medien«?

In mancherlei Hinsicht erinnern Manovichs Thesen an die Ideen des großen Medientheoretikers Vilém Flusser, der in seinem zukunftsweisenden Buch *Ins Universum der technischen Bilder* die pragmatisch-utopische Vision einer fortgeschrittenen Science Fiction-Gesellschaft präsentierte, die kontinuierlich kreativ tätig ist und einen permanent fruchtbaren Austausch von High Tech-Bildern pflegt. Mit Flusser können wir behaupten, dass technische Bilder durch wissenschaftliche Prinzipien ermöglicht wurden, die in Technologien eingearbeitet worden sind. Mittels spezifischer Technologien werden kleinste Partikel zu sichtbaren Bildern zusammengefasst bzw. »komputiert«. Jede Bildtechnik (die Fotografie, das JPG-Bild, die VRML-programmierte virtuelle Welt) ist eine andere Art und Weise Partikel zu strukturieren. Technische Bilder sind Informationsreservoirs. Programmieren stellt eine Art von Freiheit dar. In einer zukünftigen Gesellschaft der Bilder wird jeder befähigt sein, sich etwas »vorzustellen«. Jeder Mensch wird ein Programmierer und ein Synthetisierer von Bildern sein.

17
Ebd.

Semantische Software bzw. Linked Open Data sind ein weiteres Beispiel für das neue Kommunikationsmodell in Aktion. Linked Open Data bringt das Design und die Implementierung einer neuartigen Software-»Integrationsschicht« mit sich, das eine intelligentere Nutzung von bereits existierenden strukturierten Datenbanken ebenso ermöglicht wie die von unstrukturierten Datensätzen wie Websites oder Blogs, in ihrer Beschwörung von Multi Level-»Datenbankverbindungen« (im ersteren Fall) und assoziativen »semantischen Crawlern« (im letzteren Fall).

Die bereitgestellte Software-Ebene ist ein »abstrakt-komplexes« Muster bzw. eine Repräsentation analog zu der thematischen Datenstruktur innerhalb des *Java Message Services*: Es ist ein dazwischenliegendes »Middleware«-Artefakt, das zwischen das positioniert wird, was ehemals »Sender« und »Empfänger« genannt worden ist.

Es liefert die wirkliche »datenprozessierende« Kraft des Systems, die zugleich eine soziale und eine narrative Kraft darstellt. Mittels Linked Open Data wird die Flexibilität der Suche mit der Exaktheit der Anfrage zusammengebracht. Der Benutzer bzw. Software-Agent erkennt neue Beziehungen zwischen zuvor unverbundenen Daten und profitiert von den kontextabhängigen Schlussfolgerungen der kombinierten Suche/Anfrage.

Jüngste Ergebnisse der Software-Studies (Matthew Fuller, Lev Manovich) fechten Kittlers These, dass »es keine Software gibt«, an und weisen auf die Vorrangstellung von Software als gesellschaftlich kritisches Hybrid aus technischen und kulturellen Mustern hin. 2006 veröffentlichte Fuller ein wegweisendes Buch über Software als Medium und Kultur mit dem Titel *Behind the Blip*.[15]

In seinem Buch von 2013, *Software Takes Command*, erweitert Manovich die Medientheorie, um die Software-Theorie einzubeziehen. Sein Buch »beschäftigt sich mit ›Medien-Software‹, mit Programmen wie *Word, PowerPoint, Photoshop, Illustrator, After Effects, Final Cut, Firefox, Blogger, Wordpress, Google Earth, Maya* und *3Ds Max*. Diese Programme ermöglichen die Generierung, das Publizieren, das Teilen und das Remixing von Bildern, Bewegtbildsequenzen, 3D-Gestaltungen, Texten, Landkarten, interaktiven Elementen«[16].

15
Matthew Fuller: Behind the Blip. Essays on the Culture of Software. Brooklyn; New York 2003.

16
Lev Manovich: Software Takes Command. New York 2013. Vgl.: http://lab.softwarestudies.com/2012/09/does-media-still-exist.html.

Alan N. Shapiro
Software Code als Expanded Narration

Komponente des Shannon-Weaver-Modells	Kritik	Kommentar	Neues Konzept
Quelle (Source)	Es gibt keinen Ursprung (Derrida). «In diesem Spiel der Repräsentation wird der Ursprungspunkt ungreifbar.»[12]	Publisher setzen einen andauernden Prozess fort, der keinen Anfang hatte.	Subskribierte Publisher (ein Nachrichtenverfasser berichtet über Themen und konsumiert gleichzeitig Nachrichten zu anderen Themen).
Kodierung (Encoder)	Das Format ist nicht neutral (Marshall McLuhan and Quentin Fiore). Das Medium ist die Message/Massage.[13]	Das Format ist flexibel und erweiterbar; Kodieren ist ein kreativer Akt.	Kreativer Code-Umwandler (der Betrieb bzw. der Prozess verwandelt sich während der Laufzeit unter bestimmten realen Lebensumständen, aber der Code bzw. die Spezifikation ändert sich nicht).
Nachricht (Message)	Es gibt kein Eins-zu-eins-Verhältnis zwischen Signifikant und Signifikat, sondern eine endlose Kette von Textualität (radikalisierte Semiotik).	Die Botschaft enthält Aufschläge bzw. Indexwerte, die sie mit einer Vielzahl von anderen Daten verbinden.	Indexierte Botschaft (jede Nachricht enthält eine Kopfzeile, der ihre Rolle innerhalb eines querverweisenden Software-Design-Schemas ermittelt).
Kanal (Channel)	*57 channels and nothing on* (ein Song von *The Boss* Bruce Springsteen).	Nicht jede Kommunikation ist bedeutungsvoll (au contraire!).	Thema (die benannte Zieladresse, an der wir veröffentlichen und/oder an der wir subskribieren).
Störung (Noise)	»Wir leben in einer Gesellschaft der Störungen« (anonym).	Verschieben der Information-Störungs-Grenze in Richtung des Territoriums der Störung.	Interpretieren der Störung (anstatt zu versuchen, Störungen als Datenbits zu interpretieren, was die Speicheradressierung bzw. den Ablauf der Programmlogik durcheinanderbringt; Start vom Standpunkt des »Nicht-Wissens«).
Dekodierung (Decoder)	Das Format ist nicht neutral (Marshall McLuhan and Quentin Fiore). Das Medium ist die Message/Massage.[13]	Die Interpretation bzw. das Lesen des Formats bietet kreative Möglichkeiten an.	Kreativer Code-Umwandler (der Betrieb bzw. der Prozess verwandelt sich während der Laufzeit unter bestimmten realen Lebensumständen, aber der Code bzw. die Spezifikation ändert sich nicht).
Empfänger (Receiver)	Manche Würfe landen nicht im Handschuh des Fängers. Im Baseball wird dies »Passed Ball« oder »Wild Pitch« genannt.	Systeme brechen ständig zusammen.	Funktionsstörung (anstatt um Fehler herum zu gestalten, sollte Gestaltung das Unregelmäßige, den Störfall oder den Soft Error als Ausgangspunkt wählen).
Feedback	Handling des Ausnahmefalls anstatt Codes zurückzusenden; den Programmablauf unter ungewöhnlichen Umständen verändern (Bjarne Stroustrup, Erfinder der Programmiersprache C++).[14]	Fehler sind systemische Ereignisse von verschiedenen Schwierigkeitsgraden.	Soziales Handling des Ausnahmefalls (Rückkehr zum Experimentiergeist und den Überrraschungen der Kybernetik; dabei den Begriff des Feedbacks durch eine proaktive Design-Strategie, von sich vielfach vererbenden Ebenen des Ausnahmefall-Handlings ersetzend [so wie in der Objektorientierung]).

lichen Zeichensystemen auf die nicht-narrative Ebene einer abstrakt manipulierbaren Un-Zeit und eines Un-Ortes reduziert.

Mittlerweile ist das Punkt-zu-Punkt-Kommunikations-modell eindeutig durch die Publisher-Subscriber-Nachrichten-vermittlung verdrängt worden, wie etwa in »message-oriented middleware« wie *IBMs WebSphere MQ* oder *SonicMQ* von *Progress Software* ebenso wie in dem *Application Programming Interface* von *Java Message Service* (JMS), das eine übergeordnete Spezifikation darstellt, um solche Übertragungssysteme zu programmieren.

In dem Publisher-Subscriber-Modell werden Botschaften an subskribierte Abnehmer versandt, ohne von ihnen ausdrück-lich angefordert worden zu sein. Es handelt sich dabei um eine Expanded Narration, weil die Anzahl der Leser nicht durch einen deklarativ programmatischen Akt begrenzt wird. Die performati-ven Leseakte der Subscriber sind etwas, das sich außerhalb der Programmierung des Programmierers ereignet und es während der Laufzeit der ablaufenden Anwendung existentiell besonders und lebendig macht, welches – aus der Perspektive der neuen Disziplin betrachtet – den Rahmen für die »soziale« und »literari-sche« Praxis bietet.

Publish-and-Subscribe ist ein soziales Modell, obwohl technisch-orientierte Bücher zur Nachrichtenübertragung es niemals als Expanded Narration beschreiben würden, da die Literaturwissenschaft und die Literarische Soziologie aus der Domäne der Ingenieurswissenschaften verbannt worden sind. Sobald wir beginnen, Kommunikation transdisziplinär zu studieren, werden die Verbreitung und die Explosion des Narra-tiven, die schon längst vonstatten gegangen sind, evident.

Im Folgenden werde ich das berühmte Shannon-Weaver-Modell zur Kommunikation und Information genauer untersu-chen, das kurz nach dem 2. Weltkrieg entwickelt wurde und aus der Telekommunikationsindustrie hervorgegangen ist.[11] Sein Ziel ist es, die Botschaft als technische Einheit zu isolieren und dabei die Integrität derselben zu gewährleisten.

Betrachten wir dazu die acht allseits bekannten Kompo-nenten des Shannon-Weaver-Modells und überlegen dabei, wie wir die Annahmen zu jeder Komponente kritisieren können und wie dies zu einem neuen Modell führen kann:

11
Claude Shannon: A Mathematical Theory of Communication. In: Bell System Technical Journal 27 (Juli und Oktober 1948), S. 379–423 und 623–665.

12
Jacques Derrida: Grammatologie. Frankfurt am Main 1996, S. 65.

13
Marshall McLuhan und Quentin Fiore: The Medium is the Massage. New York 1967.

14
Bjarne Stroustrup: The C++ Programming Language. New York 1991.

Gegenstand des Ingenieurwesens aufgefasst) sowie aufgrund der Eliminierung des Nachhalls, der Resonanz und der Tiefe von Sprache zugunsten einer »Information«, die »gereinigt« wird, indem sie sich der Störung durch ›Geräusche‹ entledigt.

3. aufgrund des neuen Kommunikationsparadigmas, für das 21. Jahrhundert relevant und vielversprechend, das das Publisher-Subscriber-Modell als Ausgangspunkt nimmt, das politikwissenschaftliche (wie auch das feministische und postkolonialistische) Bewusstsein von den spezifischen historischen Beziehungen der Macht betont und die Ambivalenz und Einzigartigkeit von Worten und von Sprachen unterstreicht.

Jede der drei Innovationen bewegt sich in Richtung einer erweiterten Narration, indem sie technische Codes und die Gestaltung technischer Systeme in eine hybride Verbindung mit kulturellen Codes und kulturellen Entwurfsmustern bringt. Indem es den strikt technischen Bereich verlassen hat, stellt das Publisher-Subscriber-Modell einen »Geschichten erzählenden« Rahmen für den interaktiven menschlichen Kontakt und die Zirkulation von Ideen ebenso dar, wie es diskursive Material-Informationen bereitstellt, die sozial und partizipatorisch sind und viele Menschen involviert. Es steht damit in Kontrast zu dem vereinfachten geradlinigen Punkt-zu-Punkt-Narrative der archetypischen Knoten-zu-Knoten-verbindenden Telefongespräche des 20. Jahrhunderts, die lediglich zwischen zwei Personen und mittels eines einzigen Medienkanals stattfanden.

Ein »politisiertes« oder hybrides technisch-kulturelles Bewusstsein, das für Machtbeziehungen sensibel ist, stellt eher eine Expanded Narration dar als der Mythos einer »geräuschfreien« Kommunikation, wie sie durch ausschließlich technische Codes ausgeführt oder mittels bloßer technischer Kanäle transportiert wird. Eine Offenheit gegenüber dem Reichtum der Sprache entspricht eher dem universitären Klassifizierungssystem von Wissen im Studium der Vergleichenden Literaturwissenschaft, die ja auf dem Gebiet der Narration beheimatet ist, als eine ausschließliche Aufmerksamkeit für die technische Dimension der Nachrichtenübertragung. Die akademische und wissenschaftliche Betrachtung von Kommunikation aus einer technischen Perspektive hat die Behandlung des Bedeutungstransfers in mensch-

9
Roman Jakobson: Linguistics and Poetics. In: T. Sebeok (Hg.): Style in Language. Cambridge 1960, S. 350–377.

10
Jean Baudrillard: Requiem pour les medias. In: Pour une critique de l'économie politique du signe. Paris 1972, S. 220–223. Auf Deutsch erschienen als: Requiem für die Medien. In: Kool Killer, oder der Aufstand der Zeichen. Berlin 1978, S. 83–118.

kation«) zu finden, die irgendwie erhellend ist. Roman Jakobson etwa entwickelte ein klassisches Kommunikationsmodell, das eine Botschaft identifiziert, die von einem Sender zu einem Empfänger hin übermittelt wird.[9]

Ich denke, es gibt drei Anwendungsgrenzen von Jakobsons Modell:

1. Das Sender-Empfänger-Paradigma reicht nicht aus, um die heutigen virtuellen Software-Systeme verstehen zu können, bei denen eine Botschaft von einem Publisher an eine geteilte Datenstruktur gesendet wird, in der sie dann von mehreren Subscribern (Abonnenten) gesehen wird.

2. Wie Jean Baudrillard in seinem 1972 verfassten Essay *Requiem für die Medien* hervorgehoben hat, formalisiert der angebliche objektive und wissenschaftliche Status von Jakobsons Modell lediglich eine soziokulturell gegebene Konfiguration.[10]

3. Jakobsons Kommunikationsmodell ist letztendlich ein Simulationsmodell. Die Absicht des Modells besteht darin, eine »technisch sichere Passage« für die offensichtlich lesbare Botschaft bereitzustellen, die sich ihrer Bedeutung und ihrer Ambivalenz entledigt hat und zu einer reinen Information geworden ist.

Wir können, um dies zusammenzufassen, von einem alten und einem neuen Paradigma der Kommunikation sprechen. Das alte Kommunikationsmodell, wie es in den Arbeiten von Claude Shannon und Roman Jakobson dargelegt wurde, ist, bezogen auf ihren zeitlichen Kontext des 20. Jahrhunderts, in dreierlei Hinsicht problematisch:

1. aufgrund der Veralterung der Nachrichtenübertragung zwischen zwei Punkten, die innerhalb einer Warteschlange oder einem einfachen »physischen« Kanal stattfindet, im Unterschied zu dem neueren Austausch von Botschaften zwischen Publishern und Subscribern, der innerhalb einer »thematischen« Datenstruktur oder mittels komplexeren »virtuellen« botschaftsverteilenden Topologien und über simultane Multi Media-Kanäle vonstatten geht;

2. aufgrund der idealisierten Erhöhung spezifischer sozio-kultureller Beziehungen der Macht hin zu einem vermeintlich »neutralen« oder »ewigen« oder »technologischen« Status des technischen Codes (Kommunikation wird hierbei strikt als

Alan N. Shapiro
Software Code als Expanded Narration

Für Friedrich Kittler besteht Software lediglich aus Virtualität und Simulation. Seiner Meinung nach ist es unmöglich, mittels Programmierung eine neuartige Beziehung zur »Wirklichkeit« herzustellen – irgendeine ästhetisch begründete Möglichkeit für Demokratie oder Kreativität: Es existiere keine Brücke zwischen Kunst/Ästhetik/Design und der Informatik. Die Verkleinerung der Hardware ist für Kittler die angemessene Dimension der Simulation von unserer »postmodernen Schreibszene«, die keine Szene des Schreibens mehr sei.[4]

Jean Baudrillard dachte etwas Ähnliches darüber, indem er in *Die Präzession der Simulakra* schrieb: »die entscheidende Dimension der Simulation ist die genetische Verkleinerung«[5]. Allerdings überschritt Baudrillard diesen konservativen und nostalgischen Standpunkt in Bezug auf Technologie, indem er fotografierte oder über Fotografie »als Schreiben mit Licht«[6] schrieb.

Nach Kittler geht Hardware der Software immer voraus und determiniert sie: »Gute Gründe sprechen vielmehr für die Unabdingbarkeit und folglich auch die Vorgängigkeit von Hardware.« »Sogar die elementaren Code-Operationen«, so schreibt er in seinem Essay *Es gibt keine Software*, »reduzieren sich auf absolut lokale Zeichenmanipulationen und damit, Lacan sei's geklagt, auf Signifikanten elektrischer Potentiale.« Etwas später ergänzt er: «Die sogenannte Philosophie der sogenannten Computergemeinschaft setzt im Gegenteil alles daran, Hardware hinter Software, elektronische Signifikanten hinter Mensch-Maschine-Schnittstellen zu verdecken.«[7] Demgegenüber besteht Kittlers Problemlösung darin, dass wir unsere Programme in Assembler Code schreiben sollen, um der vorherrschenden Tendenz entgegenzuarbeiten, die darin besteht, die Maschine vor ihren Benutzern zu verbergen, und um das Bewusstsein aufrechtzuhalten, dass die zugrunde liegende Hardware das ist, worauf das Programm hinausläuft.

Kittler blickt nostalgisch auf »die guten alten Tage der Informationstheorie« zurück, in denen »maximale Information und maximales Rauschen einigermaßen zusammen fielen«.[8] Obwohl uns gesagt wird, dass wir in einer »Informationsgesellschaft« leben – und dies wird seit Jahrzehnten in soziologischen Diskursen behauptet – ist es meiner Meinung nach äußerst schwierig, eine Definition von »Information« (oder »Kommuni-

4
Ebd., S. 227.

5
Jean Baudrillard: Die Präzession der Simulakra. In: Agonie des Realen, Berlin 1978, S. 8 und 9.

6
Jean Baudrillard: Photography, or the Writing of Light. URL: http://www.ctheory.net/articles.aspx?id=126. Ebenso unter dem Titel *Photography, or Light-Writing: Literalness of the Image* in: Jean Baudrillard: Impossible Exchange. London 2001, S. 139–147.

7
Kittler 1999 (Anm. 1), S. 231, 232 und 237.

8
Ebd., S. 235.

Sprache, die fundamentaler und effektiver ist als mündliche Rede), ist Kittler nie gekommen.

Diesen Gedanken unterdrückte er und nahm stattdessen an, dass der Computer die programmatische Automatisierung des Lesens und Schreibens herbeiführen müsse. »Mit der Miniaturisierung aller Zeichen auf molekulare Maße dagegen ist der Schreibakt selber verschwunden«, schreibt Kittler. Er fährt fort: »Wie wir alle wissen und nicht nur sagen, schreibt kein Mensch mehr.« Kittler glaubte, dass Schreiben mittels eines Computers nicht mehr als historischer Akt angesehen werden könne, da die Schreibwerkzeuge des Computers »auch im Stande sind, selber zu lesen und zu schreiben«.[2] Kittler schreibt: «Diese entscheidende Fähigkeit von Computern hat ersichtlich nichts mit Software zu tun; sie hängt einzig und allein von dem Grad ab, in dem eine jeweilige Hardware dergleichen wie ein Schreibsystem beherbergen kann.«[3] Ich denke das genaue Gegenteil von Kittler, nämlich dass Software-Code genau der Ort sein kann, an dem *écriture* in Derridas Sinne wieder entstehen könnte. Es könnte eine Verschiebung von Programmierung als Programmierbarkeit eines Gerätes hin zu Programmierung als Kreativität, zur kreativen Äußerung stattfinden – hin zum Schreiben im tiefsten Sinne eines effektiven Wandels.

In seiner Untersuchung des Saussure'schen Zeichens konzentrierte sich Derrida auf das negative linguistische Konzept der Differenz und zerlegte damit Saussures (missverstandene) dualistische Metaphysik von »Signifikant« (Laut) und »Signifikat« (Vorstellung). Derrida radikalisierte Saussures Zeichentheorie, indem er sagte, dass es endlose Ketten von Bedeutungen innerhalb von Zeichensystemen gebe und nicht bloß eine statische Eins-zu-eins-Beziehung zwischen dem »Bezeichnenden« und dem »Bezeichneten«.

Sprachliche Zeichen referieren stets auf andere Zeichen; es kann niemals ein Zeichen geben, das eine letztendliche Bedeutung markiert. Es ist unmöglich, zu der ultimativen Bedeutung eines Wortes zu gelangen. Im Sinne Derridas zu schreiben, stellt das Gegenteil eines Systems der statischen und eindeutigen Definitionen von Wörtern dar, welches etwa von Wörterbüchern erwartet wird. Es gibt immer eine unüberwindbare Kluft zwischen dem, was ich »schreibe« oder »sage« und dem, was meine »Leser« oder »Zuhörer« lesen oder hören.

2
Ebd., S. 226.

3
Ebd., S. 239.

kommen, muss Software-Entwicklung bzw. die Informatik beginnen, sich mit kulturellen Codes ebenso zu beschäftigen wie mit Software-Codes. Die Informatik muss sich in einen Hybrid aus einer Ingenieurs- und einer Geisteswissenschaft verwandeln.

Einer der wichtigsten Medientheoretiker war der Deutsche Friedrich Kittler, der als Poststrukturalist angesehen wird. Kittler wehrte sich gegen die Erweiterung der Medientheorie um eine Theorie der Software. Von ihm stammt der berühmte Aufsatz mit dem Titel *Es gibt keine Software*.[1] Seine Position war, dass Software nicht existiere, dass alle Vorgänge innerhalb des Computers auf den digitalen Code der Hardware zurückgeführt werden können, dass es unmöglich sei, über die durchdringende Logik des Binären hinauszugehen. Kittler lag falsch, da – um es mit wenigen Worten zu sagen – die digital-binäre Logik nicht die einzige Möglichkeit der elektronischen Datenverarbeitung darstellt. Die digital-binäre Logik ist weder universell noch zeitlos, und gerade indem Software-Theorie sowohl von der Medientheorie als auch von der Informatik abgeleitet wird, kann sie uns zu neuen Paradigmen und neuen Möglichkeiten führen – etwa zu Quantencomputern, Creative Coding, zu Software, die wie ein nachgebautes menschliches Gehirn operiert, und zu Software, die im Sinne des künstlichen Lebens als beinahe schon lebendiges Wesen angesehen wird anstatt als regloses Ding, das von einem sie beherrschenden Programmierer manipuliert wird.

In dem Artikel *Es gibt keine Software* bildet Kittler sich ein, über das »Ende der Geschichte« und das »Ende der Schrift« zu schreiben. Dies ist eine schwungvolle »postmoderne« und »poststrukturalistische« These. In der zeitgenössischen Schreib- und Kulturszene einer endlos expandierenden und explodierenden Signifikation, gibt es ironischerweise eine Implosion hin zu einem »Nichtraum« und einer »Nichtzeit« des mikroskopisch kleinen Computer-Speichers. In dem Verhältnis zwischen Informationstechnologieentwicklungen und Schreiben verortet Kittler einen Kausalzusammenhang, der zu der aktuellen Situation geführt habe, dass wir jetzt angeblich nicht mehr schreiben. Auf die Idee, dass Software-Code eine Form des Schreibens darstellen kann, einer Form der *écriture* im dekonstruktionistischen Sinne Derridas (einem Eingriff bzw. einer Einschreibung in

1
Friedrich A. Kittler: Es gibt keine Software. In: Friedrich A. Kittler, Draculas Vermächtnis. Technische Schriften. Leipzig 1993, S. 225–242.

Beim Programmieren geht es um Algorithmen, formale Logik, präzises Denken und das Lösen von Problemen. Anscheinend hat es also kaum etwas mit dem zu tun, was wir als kreative Äußerung verstehen. Der logische Akt des Programmierens und der expressive kreative Akt erscheinen als unvereinbare Gegenpole. In unserer Vorstellung finden kreative Äußerungen in der Literatur oder der Bildenden Kunst statt – mittels bestimmter Arten der Kommunikation oder symbolischer Systeme, mittels bestimmter Arten des Schreibens, der Rede, des Diskurses, der Sprache oder der Notation. Beispiele dieser ausdrucksstarken Medien und Genres sind Poesie, Geschichtenerzählen, Nonsens, Humor, musikalische Notation, Drehbücher, Notizen für die Anfertigung eines Kunstwerks oder eines Tanzes oder einer anderen Choreographie sowie Architekturentwürfe. Bisher wurde Software nicht als ausdrucksvolles Medium verstanden. Wenn wir an Software-Code denken, denken wir ihn in einer Weise, wie wir ein reales oder virtuelles Gerät behandeln, das zu programmieren ist. Dies ist eine rationale und kalkulierende Aktivität, die praktische Konsequenz der philosophischen Annahmen der symbolischen Logik von Bertrand Russell, von Friedrich Ludwig Gottlob Frege oder Noam Chomsky – den klassischen Paradigmen der Computertheorie. Dabei geht es um die Erteilung einer Serie von Instruktionen bzw. Befehlen an eine Maschine, ein Objekt oder einen Mechanismus, an etwas also, von dem grundsätzlich angenommen wird, das es tot ist.

Worin besteht der Unterschied zwischen der Ausdruckskraft eines expressiven Aktes der Literatur oder der Bildenden Künste und den Befehlsfolgen innerhalb eines Computerprogramms? Wir haben stets angenommen, dass zwischen diesen beiden Arten von Schrift oder Notation eine unüberwindbare Mauer existiert. Diese Mauer einzureißen, so wie die Berliner es 1989 mit ihrer Mauer getan haben, war bis vor Kurzem undenkbar. Erst jetzt scheint es möglich zu sein, diese Fragen zu stellen. Kann Software-Code auch expressiv sein? Muss Software-Code immer ausschließlich produktiv sein? Die Idee einer auf Software-Code angewandten »Expanded Narration« setzt voraus, die binäre Opposition einer entweder als ausdrucksstark oder als nützlich aufgefassten »Schrift« zu verabschieden. Um voranzu-

Software Code
als Expanded
Narration

Alan N. Shapiro

bar anthropomorphe Charaktere benötigen, um den Sinn einer Geschichte zu transportieren, können in Spielen auch Quader auftreten. So schreibt Juul an anderer Stelle: »*Tetris* does not have a visible actor either, and it does not seem possible to construct any actor controlling the falling bricks. *Tetris – The Movie* does not seem like a viable concept. But *Tetris* is incredibly popular, and nobody is disputing its status as a computer game.«[21] Wiederum sind Übergänge denkbar: In einem Roman können im Sinne der Prosopopoiia durchaus Gegenstände oder die Natur selbst sprechen, aber dann spricht immer noch die Natur *wie* ein Mensch; der Spieler dagegen kann den fallenden Spielsteinen zwar Namen geben, aber sie werden dadurch nicht menschenähnlich, sondern schlichtweg bewegliche geometrische Formen. Das ist letztlich nicht Juuls Punkt: Freilich gibt es in Computerspielen sprechende und agierende Figuren, die extreme Ähnlichkeit mit Menschen haben, aber das Computerspiel *kann* darauf verzichten, nicht so der Roman. – Anders gesagt, muss sich das Computerspiel nicht der Schriftform bedienen, sondern es kann sich anders als die Erzählung allein visuell ausdrücken.

Die Computerspielludologie, so kann stellvertretend bei Juul festgestellt werden, hält somit den Schlüssel in der Hand, die Rolle der Bildlichkeit in medientheoretischer Hinsicht herausstellen zu können. – Eigens zum Thema gemacht wird sie jedoch nicht. Ganz im Gegenteil scheint es, als ob in der Betonung des aktiven Spielens die Eigenart des Mediums vernachlässigt wird, welches das Spielen erlaubt: Das Computerspiel ist zunächst *sichtbar*, sodann *manipulierbar* und erst hernach möglicherweise auch *sinnvoll*. Während Narratologen auf der letzten Stufe, dem Sinn, ansetzen, rekurrieren Ludologen vor allem auf die zweite, die Interaktivität. Beiden liegt aber gleichermaßen ein erscheinendes Bild voraus, das manipuliert oder interpretiert wird.

[21] Juul (2005), S. 223f. (wie Anm. 1).

Stephan Günzel
Professor für Medientheorie an der Berliner Technischen Kunsthochschule (btk); bis 2011 Koordinator des Zentrums für Computerspielforschung (DIGAREC) an der Universität Potsdam und Gastprofessor für Raumwissenschaften an der HU Berlin sowie der Universität Trier. Monographien: *Egoshooter. Das Raumbild des Computerspiels* (2012); *Raum/Bild. Zur Logik des Medialen* (2011); *Maurice Merleau-Ponty. Werk und Wirkung* (2007); *Geophilosophie. Nietzsches philosophische Geographie* (2001). Herausgaben: *Lexikon der Raumphilosophie* (2012); *KartenWissen. Territoriale Räume zwischen Bild und Diagramm* (2012); *Raum. Ein interdisziplinäres Handbuch* (2010).

den Protagonisten ›wartet‹. Genau genommen stellt schon jede Änderung der Blickrichtung und jede einzelne Aktion nach Juul eine Neuerung gegenüber dem vorangegangenen Spieldurchlauf dar. In einer Erzählung kann weder der Held noch der Leser des Romans sich beim zweiten Lesedurchgang dazu entscheiden, den Bösewicht nicht zu töten und stattdessen an ihm vorbeizugehen. Das heißt nach Juul – und dies wäre ein weiteres Merkmal:

3. und 4. Die Sequenzen des Buchs sind fest (*fixed*), die Sequenzen des Spiels variabel (*flexible*); oder, was auf Gleiches hinausläuft, der Grund oder der Antrieb (*desire*), ein Buch zu lesen, bestehe darin, der Narration beizuwohnen, die folglich *passiv* rezipiert wird, der Grund, ein Spiel zu spielen, ist dagegen der, die Strukturen und Möglichkeiten der Spielewelt zu erkunden; es wird daher *aktiv* rezipiert.

5. Von daher überrascht zunächst eine weitere Unterscheidung Juuls: Die Zeit im Roman sei *variabel*, im Spiel demgegenüber *fest*. Er widerspricht damit aber nicht etwa seiner zuvor gegebenen Charakterisierung der Flexibilität des Spielverlaufs, vielmehr bezieht sich Juul hier auf die interne, *erzählte* Zeit des Romans (die zumeist identisch ist mit der Story): Eine niedergeschriebene Geschichte kann in der Zeit springen und muss ebenso wie ein Film keine Rücksicht auf die natürliche Ordnung von Vergangenheit, Gegenwart und Zukunft oder früher, jetzt und später nehmen.[20]

6. Damit verbunden ist für Juul wiederum, dass die Handlung (die Erzählzeit als Plot) in der traditionellen Schriftform in der *Vergangenheit* stattfindet oder stattfand, die Handlung im Spiel dagegen in der *Gegenwart* erfolgt. Das trifft zunächst inhaltlich zu, denn in einem Roman wird oftmals von Vergangenem berichtet. Aber selbst wenn von zukünftigen Ereignissen erzählt würde, wäre die Zeit der Niederschrift – also die Produktion der Geschichte – vergangen oder der (zukünftige) Verlauf festgelegt. Zwar ist das Spiel in der Vergangenheit programmiert worden, der Ablauf aber ist, wie bereits beschrieben, nicht determiniert. Die Handlung (Plot) entsteht vielmehr erst durch das Spielen in der Gegenwart, gleich in welcher historischen Zeit das Spiel (oder dessen Story) angesiedelt ist.

7. Als ein letztes Merkmal führt Juul schließlich die *Abstraktheit* des Spiels an: Wohingegen Erzählungen unabding-

20
Gleichwohl sind auch Zeitsprünge im Spiel denkbar, diese erfolgen zumeist in *Ingame*-Filmsequenzen, wenn die Interaktion im Spiel ausgesetzt wird und der Spieler einen vorgegebenen filmischen Ablauf betrachtet. Durchaus denkbar ist aber, dass in einem Spiel nicht nur Raumsprünge (das Wiederbetreten des Spielfeldes auf der gegenüberliegenden Seite etwa), sondern auch Zeitsprünge während interaktiver Passagen realisiert werden.

17
Juul (2005), S. 14 (wie Anm. 1).

18
Jesper Juul: A Clash between
Game and Narrative. A Thesis on
Computer Games and Interactive
Fiction. 1999/2001, www.jesperju-
ul.net/thesis/AClashBetweenGa-
meAndNarrative.pdf (Stand:
19.08.2013).

19
Zum Folgenden siehe Jesper Juul:
A Clash between Game and
Narrative, 1998, www.jesperjuul.
net/text/clash_between_game_
and_narrative.html (Stand:
19.08.2013).

Theoretiker Jesper Juul, der neben Aarseth zu den bekanntesten Spieletheoretikern Skandinaviens zählt und nach einer Zwischenstation am Computerspielforschungszentrum GAMBIT des Massachusetts Institute of Technology in Boston derzeit Gastprofessor am Game Center der New York University ist. Juul geht davon aus, dass der narratologische Ansatz notwendig auf einer Annahme fußt, die es kategorisch in Zweifel zu ziehen gilt: »Narratives may be fundamental to human thought, but this does not mean that everything *should* be described in narrative terms. And that something can be presented in narrative form does not mean that it *is* narrative.«[17] In seinem Grundsatzvortrag *A Clash Between Game and Narrative,* in dem Juul auf der *Digital Arts and Culture*-Konferenz 1998 in Bergen die Thesen seiner soeben entstandenen Masterarbeit zusammenfasst,[18] führt er sieben Merkmale an, durch die sich Computerspiele eindeutig von Literatur unterscheiden lassen:[19]

1. An oberster Stelle steht für Juul die Unterscheidung von *Geschichte und Programm.* Sie bedeutet eine Verschärfung der von Aarseth angeführten Differenz von Linearität und Nonlinearität: Ein Programm ist für Juul von einer Geschichte prinzipiell dadurch unterschieden, dass es auf die Eingaben eines Benutzers reagiert. Das Buch oder vielmehr der Verlauf der Erzählung dagegen verändert sich nicht dadurch, dass es gelesen wird. Das Spiel verändert sich im Laufe des Spiels oder ist bei jedem Spieldurchgang ein anderes.

2. Damit verbunden ist eine Merkmalsdifferenz, die Juul als *einmaligen und mehrmaligen Konsum* beschreibt: Dies heißt nun nicht, dass das Buch nicht mehrmals gelesen werden könnte. (Es vernichtet sich nicht nach seiner Lektüre, sondern ist physisch sehr wohl noch vorhanden.) Mehrmaliges Lesen ist zwar möglich, aber dadurch verändert sich die Geschichte nicht. Allenfalls wird eine ›dichte‹ Erzählung für den Leser reichhaltiger, insofern mehr Implikationen oder Anspielungen entdeckt werden können. Nicht jedoch – und das ist letztlich entscheidend – tritt beim wiederholten Lesen plötzlich eine neue Figur im Roman auf. Im Computerspiel ist dies hingegen möglich; so etwa, wenn ein Raum betreten wird, den man im vorherigen Spieldurchgang nicht erreicht oder übergangen hat und in dem eine neue Gestalt des Spiels mit bestimmten Eigenschaften auf

machen sucht. Beschrieben werden soll damit die Eigenart der Computerspielerzählform, die Handlung ›steuern‹ zu können, insofern zwischen Alternativen gewählt werden kann. Anders als beim Buch, bei dem Sprünge allenfalls durch Blättern oder innerhalb einer Erzählung durch explizite Vor- und Rückgriffe möglich sind, ist es eine Eigenschaft von Computerspielerzählungen, die sich aus den Handlungen ergeben, dass eine Entscheidung insgesamt Einfluss auf den Spielverlauf hat;[14] also etwa, dass der Weg durch das Spiellabyrinth mit einer bestimmten Waffe oder dem Schlüssel aus einem Zimmer leichter fällt denn ohne das entsprechende Werkzeug oder dadurch überhaupt erst möglich wird. Aarseth hält der Narratologie damit einen Spiegel vor: Was diese im Spiel indifferent gegenüber dem analogen Medium als Erzählung angeht, sei gänzlich anders geartet als jede bisher bekannte Form von Literatur: »A nonlinear text is [...] not simply one fixed sequence of letters, words, and sentences but one, in which the words or sequences of words may differ from reading to reading because of the shape, conventions, or mechanisms of the text.«[15] Der für diese neue Textsorte von Aarseth in Anschlag gebrachte Terminus ist derjenige der Ergodic Literature. »Ergodische Literatur« im Sinne Aarseths ist eine Narrationsform, in welcher die Handlungsabfolge des Spiels aus einer Arbeit (gr. *ergon*) der Spieler resultiert. Der kausale Zusammenhang konstituiert sich Aarseth zufolge als Weg (gr. *hodos*). Auch nach Aarseth kann gelten: Nicht die Erzählung im Sinne der Story zeichnet daher Computerspiele aus, sondern die kausale Verknüpfung der Erzählelemente oder Ereignisse, die im Durchlaufen des Spielraums in Beziehung gebracht werden.

Spiel vs. Erzählung

Auch wenn Aarseths Kritik die Schwachstelle der narratologischen Argumentation trifft, so verschleift sein Beibehalten des Textbegriffs doch weiterhin die grundsätzliche Differenz zwischen dem digitalen Medium Computerspiel und dem analogen Medium Buch. So ist es denn auch wenig verwunderlich, dass sich der Begriff »Cybertextualität« nicht durchgesetzt hat und selbst sein Urheber ihn heute nicht mehr verwendet.[16] Den entscheidenden Schritt zur Begründung einer eigenständigen Computerludologie unternahm schließlich der dänische

14
»I refer to the idea of a narrative text as a labyrinth, a game, or an imaginary world, in which the reader can explore at will, get lost, discover secret paths, play around, follow the rules, and so on.« (Espen J. Aarseth: Cybertext. Perspectives on Ergodic Literature, Baltimore/London 1997, S. 3.)

15
Espen J. Aarseth: Nonlinearity and Literary Theory. In: Georg P. Landow (Hg.): Hyper/Text/Theory. Baltimore 1994, S. 51–86, hier S. 51.

16
Bereits bei seiner Einführung gesteht Aarseth Schwierigkeiten in der Begriffsvermittlung ein. Vgl. Espen J. Aarseth: Cybertext. Perspektiven zur ergodischen Literatur: Das Buch und das Labyrinth (1997). Aus. d. Engl. von Jeannette Pacher. In: Karin Bruns/ Ramón Reichert (Hg.): Reader Neue Medien. Texte zur digitalen Kultur und Kommunikation (= Cultural studies, 18). Bielefeld 2008, S. 203–211, hier S. 204.

ten, was einer der Hauptgründe ist, warum Computerspiele für manche Menschen wenig interessant oder gar stumpfsinnig erscheinen.

Die mediale Besonderheit von Computerspielen liegt aber gerade nicht auf der Ebene der Erzählung, sondern auf derjenigen der Handlung: Während die Erzählung in der Interpretation der Rezipienten variieren kann, variiert im Computerspiel auch die in anderen Medien ansonsten unveränderliche Handlung: So haben Spieler gegebenenfalls die Möglichkeit, um die Zombies herumzugehen, die sie töten könnten, oder sie in einer variierenden Reihenfolge zu töten. Diese Wahlmöglichkeit hat der Leser des Buchs oder der Betrachter des Films nicht: Einzig kann er das Buch weglegen oder die Augen schließen.[12] Die Handlung eines Spiels ist folglich nicht gänzlich vorgegeben, allenfalls sind die Möglichkeiten der Variation durch das Programm oder die Rechnerkapazität begrenzt; und freilich gibt es in vielen Spielen eine ›ideale Handlung‹, die – wie etwa Speedruns zeigen – die Erzählung in kürzestmöglicher Zeit vermitteln.

Aus dem Kreis der erst später so genannten Ludologen war es vor allem der heute am Center for Computer Games Research der Kopenhagener IT-Universität lehrende Chefherausgeber von *Game Studies*, der Norweger Espen J. Aarseth, welcher 1997 mit seinem Buch *Cybertext* erstmals versuchte, die Eigenständigkeit der Computerspiele – und entsprechend die ihrer Analyse – in solcher Hinsicht herauszustellen. Wie der Titel unmissverständlich zeigt, hält Aarseth am Begriff des Textes fest. Das ist auch kein Widerspruch zum ludologischen Anliegen, denn dieses vertritt nicht die Auffassung, dass Computerspiele keine narrativen Elemente aufwiesen,[13] sondern nur, dass sie der Form ihrer Rezeption zufolge nicht wie schriftlich niedergelegte Erzählungen zu begreifen seien. Aarseth hat in seiner ersten monographischen Arbeit, die bisweilen als Gründungsdokument der Ludologie gehandelt wird, daher weniger auf existierende Theorien des Spiels und Spielens rekurriert, als er es sich vielmehr zum Ziel gesetzt hat, die besondere Erzählweise in Computerspielen aufzuzeigen. Sein Fokus liegt auf der Labyrinthstruktur der nonlinearen Erzählung eines Computerspiels, deren Status Aarseth durch den Neologismus »Cybertextualität« kenntlich zu

12

Aber auch wenn man diese Ansicht nicht teilt und meint, im einzelnen Computerspiel liege dennoch eine letztlich linear rezipierte *Story* vor, so hat man damit einfach die Ebenen der Analyse verschoben. Vielmehr müsste man nun zugestehen, dass der *Plot* in das Spiel hineingenommen wurde und also nun die Ebene der *Story* einnimmt. Dann ist Handeln im Spiel ein Verursachen von Folgen, die eine *Story* in der Bildausgabe zur Folge haben.

13

Vgl. Gonzalo Frasca: Ludologists Love Stories, Too. Notes from a Debate that Never Took Place. In: Marinka Copier/Joost Raessens (Hg.): Level Up. Digital Game Research Conference, Utrecht. Universiteit Utrecht 2003, S. 92–99 (http://www.digra.org/dl/db/05163.01125 [Stand: 19.08.2013]).

kömmlichen Form: Literatur wird linear rezipiert. Spiele sind demgegenüber zwar nicht gänzlich nichtlinear, unterscheiden sich von einem gedruckten Text aber durch die Möglichkeit, dass der ›Leser‹ zwischen Alternativen wählen kann und damit den Ausgang der Geschichte, aber auch bereits ihren Sinn bei der Rezeption verändern kann.

Eine Grundunterscheidung der Narratologie, die bereits 1929 von dem englischen Literaturwissenschaftler Edward Forster vorgebracht wurde, kann diesen Unterschied allgemein fassen: die Differenz von *Plot* und *Story*.[9] Im Unterschied zur Story, welche die Fülle der erzählten Einzelereignisse in ihrer zeitlichen Abfolge meint, bezieht sich Plot nach Forster nur auf solche Ereignisse, zwischen denen ein logischer oder kausaler Zusammenhang besteht: »A plot is also a narrative of events, [...] but the sense of causality overshadows it.«[10] Die Story ergibt sich also aus der Tätigkeit des »Erzählens« im wörtlichen Sinne als Auf- oder Her*zählen* von einzelnen (realen oder fiktionalen) Tatsachen, der Plot hingegen ist die *Handlung* als der wirkursächliche Zusammenhang zwischen diesen. Der Unterschied zwischen Story und Plot bzw. Erzählung und Handlung(en) wird etwa dann augenfällig, wenn die Leser eines Buchs oder die Besucher eines Films nach dem Lesen des Buchs bzw. nach dem Sehen des Films gefragt werden, »worum es ging«. Zumeist wird dann die Story rekapituliert und etwa von amourösen Verwicklungen berichtet, nicht aber die Liebesszenen als Plot im Detail beschrieben. Diese Ebene der Handlung, die Forster »an organism of a higher type«[11] nennt, erweist sich in diesem Sinne als eine Konstruktion von raumzeitlichen Zusammenhängen, von denen Autoren oder Filmemacher erwarten können, dass Leser oder Betrachter sie während der Rezeption aufdecken und aus ihnen eine (variable) Story herauslesen, die im Vergleich zum Plot vergleichsweise banal sein kann. So werden auch Computerspieler auf die Frage danach, um was es in einem konkreten Spiel geht, oftmals versuchen, eine Story aus den Kausalzusammenhängen abzuleiten: Es wird etwa rekapituliert, es habe einen Unfall in einer Marsstation gegeben und deren Arbeiter haben sich nun in Zombies verwandelt, die es im Spiel zu töten gilt. Nicht zuletzt auf Spieleverpackungen und in der Werbung finden sich solche Versuche, aus der Handlung eine Erzählung abzulei-

9
Die russischen Formalisten verwendeten die ähnlich gelagerte Unterscheidung von *Fabel* und *Sujet*, der französische Strukturalismus diejenige von *Histoire* und *Discours*, wobei hiermit bereits eine Verschiebung verbunden ist, die den Unterschied von *Story* und *Plot* nach Forster einebnet und beiden gegenüber die (dahinterliegende) Narration als Drittes treten lässt.

10
Edward Morgan: Aspects of the Novel. London 2005 [1927], S. 87.

11
Forster (2005), S. 44 (wie Anm. 10).

6
Das Modell des Rollenspiels liegt
auch der einschlägigen Untersu-
chung von Sherry Turkle (Leben im
Netz. Identität in Zeiten des
Internets. Aus. d. Amerik. von
Thorsten Schmidt. Reinbek bei
Hamburg 1999 [1995]) zugrunde.

7
Randi Gunzenhäuser: Spielkultur.
Stichworte zur kulturwissenschaftlichen Computerspielanalyse. In: Evelyne Keitel et al. (Hg.):
Computerspiele – Eine Provokation. Lengerich et al. 2003, S. 49–68,
hier S. 52.

8
Markku Eskelinen: The Gaming
Situation. In: Game Studies 1 (Juli
2000), Nr. 1, www.gamestudies.
org/0101/eskelinen (Stand
19.08.2013).

stammen. Daneben verhandeln Narratologen oftmals digitale
Kommunikationsformen wie Internetforen oder Multi User
Dungeons und Online-Rollenspiele, die aber eher Plattformen
bieten, mit denen virtuelle Parallelgesellschaften kultiviert
werden, als dass es sich um Spiele im engeren Sinne handelte, die
primär auf einem invarianten Set an Regeln sowie auf einer
sowohl räumlichen als auch zeitlichen Begrenzung basieren. In
Second Life etwa findet dagegen ein Spielen in einem anderen
Sinne statt als bei sonstigen Computerspielen: Es wird dort
vorrangig mit der Identität gespielt.[6] Computerspiele können aus
Sicht der Narratologie damit zumeist nur als Derivate oder
Hybride zwischenmenschlicher Kommunikation thematisch
werden, nicht aber als ein spezifisches Medium. Gleichwohl
tragen narratologische Analysen zum Verständnis dieser neuen
Kommunikationsformen bei und können ihrerseits eine Basis für
deren Beschreibung bilden, jedoch verliert ein solchermaßen
»offener Textbegriff«[7] sein medienanalytisches Beschreibungspo-
tential, wenn es um Computerspiele geht.

Spieletheoretischer Gegenentwurf
Angesichts der narratologisch eingeschränkten Sicht auf
Computerspiele verlieh der finnische Spieletheoretiker Markku
Eskelinen seinem Unmut – stellvertretend für viele Spieletheoretiker – in der Gründungsnummer des einschlägigen Online-Jour-
nals *Game Studies* mit folgender Bemerkung Ausdruck:»If I throw
a ball at you I don't expect you to drop it and wait until it starts
telling stories.«[8] Eskelinens Unmut bezog sich auf die aus dem
literaturwissenschaftlichen Herangehen resultierende Hierarchisierung der Spiele. Der erste Schritt zu einem eigenständigen
spieletheoretischen Ansatz wurde überraschenderweise jedoch
nicht dadurch gemacht, dass man sich von ludologischer Seite
nun Computerspielen zugewandt hätte, in denen kein Text
vorkommt. Dies wurde in der Folge zwar auch getan, der eigentliche Einsatz bestand aber in etwas anderem: Es ging darum, mit
den ureigenen Mitteln der literaturtheoretischen Betrachtung zu
zeigen, dass der eingeschränkte Spielekanon sich selbst nicht
hinreichend analysieren ließ. Ein Hauptargument der Ludologen
war hierbei, dass, selbst wenn eine Geschichte im Computerspiel
vorliegt, diese gänzlich anders strukturiert sei als in ihrer her-

Stephan Günzel
Bild und Erzählung im Computerspiel

4
Constanze Bausch/Benjamin Jörissen: Das Spiel mit dem Bild. Zur Ikonologie von Action-Computerspielen. In: Christoph Wulf/ Jörg Zirfas (Hg.): Ikonologie des Performativen. München 2005, S. 345–364, hier S. 347.

5
Andrew Darley: Visual Digital Culture. Surface Play and Spectacle in New Media Genres. London/ New York 2000, S. 154.

oder kommunizierenden Menschen gibt, sondern sie liegt in der Manipulationsmöglichkeit des interaktiven Bildes selbst: Computerspiele sind, wie Constanze Bausch und Benjamin Jörissen treffend schreiben, »›erspielte‹ Bilder«[4]. Die mediale Differenz wird von narratologischer wie auch von ludologischer Seite durchaus mitgedacht, und ganz notwendigerweise rekurrieren beide in ihren Beschreibungen von Computerspielen immer auf etwas *als Spiel* oder *als Geschichte*, das als bildhaft Vermitteltes genommen wird – ohne aber diesem besonderen Status des Computerspiels Rechnung zu tragen, und das heißt: mit der Beschreibung des Computerspiels bei diesem *als Bild* anzusetzen.

Erzähltheoretische Computerspielanalyse

Die von Spieletheoretikern selbst vorgeschlagene Differenzierung zwischen Narratologie und Ludologie hatte einen konkreten Anlass und mehrere Implikationen: Unmittelbarer Anlass war der Umstand, dass Literatur-, aber auch Filmwissenschaftler begannen, sich mit Computerspielen zu befassen, ohne die Spielerfahrung oder das Spielerlebnis erkennbar in ihren Analysen einzubeziehen. So scheint es für Narratologen ausgemacht, dass für die Wissenschaften der älteren Medien ein Spiel als Geschichte gegenüber dem Film immer minderwertig bleiben wird: »In terms of traditional narrative meaning, games«, so der Medienwissenschaftler Andrew Darley, »are even more shallow than the blockbuster movie or the music video.«[5] Vorrangiges Erkennungsmerkmal der literaturwissenschaftlichen Untersuchungen sind dabei Beschreibungskategorien, welche sich aus den Beständen der Philologien speisen: So wird ein Spiel stets als Text angesehen, der quasi-sprachlich vermittelt ist. Das Paradigma »Text«, in dem Computerspiele von Narratologen behandelt wurden und noch behandelt werden, führt letztlich dazu, dass sich ein bestimmter Spielekanon der Narratologie herausgebildet hat, der vor allem Spiele umfasst, die entweder auf einer vorausgehenden Erzählung basieren oder in denen das Spiel mittels Texteingabe gesteuert wird. Das heißt, die Beschreibung ist somit nicht allein durch die Vorgehensweise bedingt, sondern darüber hinaus auch durch die Auswahl der Spiele: Im Besonderen sind Adventure- oder Rollenspiele die bevorzugten Genres, aus denen die Exempel in narratologischen Analysen

1
Jesper Juul: Games Telling Stories?. In: Jeffrey Goldstein/Joost Raessens (Hg.): Handbook of Computer Game Studies, Cambridge/London 2005, S. 219–226, hier S. 219.

2
Der Terminus »Ludology« geht auf Gonzalo Frasca aus dem Jahr 1998 zurück, der den Ansatz rückblickend wie folgt bestimmt: »Ludology can be defined as a discipline that studies games in general, and video games in particular.« (Gonzalo Frasca: Simulation versus Narrative. Introduction to Ludology. In: Mark J. P. Wolf/Bernard Perron (Hg.): The Video Game Theory Reader. New York/London 2003, S. 221–235, hier S. 222.)

3
Die Kontinuität von herkömmlicher Erzählung und Narration im virtuellen Raum betonen die Arbeiten von Janet H. Murray. Ohne Übertreibung kann ihre Monographie *Hamlet on the Holodeck. The Future of Narrative in Cyberspace* (Cambridge 1997) als Klassiker der narratologischen Computerspielforschung bezeichnet werden, gleichwohl Spiele hierin nur peripher thematisch sind.

»Do games tell stories? Answering this should tell us both *how* to study games and *who* should study them.«[1]

Jesper Juul

In der Grundlagendebatte der Computerspielforschung werden zumeist zwei entgegengesetzte Positionen stark gemacht: einmal diejenige der Narratologie und zum anderen diejenige der Ludologie.[2] Während jene ein Computerspiel als interaktive Erzählung auffasst, versteht diese es vor allem als digitales Spiel: Für Narratologen ist das Computerspiel demnach nur eine Geschichte, welche in anderer Form umgesetzt wurde, ohne dass sich die Erzählung dadurch wesentlich ändern würde. Ebenso wie sich ein Film nur graduell von einem Roman unterscheiden würde, so differiere auch das Computerspiel nur wenig von einer schriftlich niedergelegten Geschichte:[3] Stets gebe es eine Person oder Figur, die im Zentrum der Handlung steht, und stets lasse sich ein Erzähler identifizieren, aus dessen Position die Geschichte erzählt wird. Aber auch von Ludologen wird das Computerspiel als nur unwesentlich verschieden von etwas bereits Bekanntem angesehen: Denn das Bildschirmspiel ist für diese Position die Fortsetzung eines Echtraumspiels mit anderen Mitteln, das heißt eine Umsetzung der Regeln eines Brett-, Papier- oder Denkspiels im Digitalen. Ludologische Analysen vergleichen Computerspiele daher nicht mit gedruckten oder gefilmten Geschichten, sondern mit analogen Spielen, deren Erforschung dadurch letztlich auch wieder Konjunktur erfahren hat. Ludologen wie Narratologen negieren damit, dass Computerspiele eine Eigenschaft aufweisen, durch welche sie von einer Erzählung oder von einem herkömmlichen Spiel anders zu unterscheiden wären als durch die Spielmittel, also die Hard- und Software, den Rechner und das Programm. Vielmehr sind beide der Ansicht, dass was und wie Computerspiele sind, sich auch ohne Computer realisieren ließe. Dabei wird die einfache Tatsache übergangen, dass alle Computerspiele sich dadurch auszeichnen, Erscheinungen auf einem Bildschirm zu sein. Computerspiele sind in erster Linie Bilderscheinungen und als solche deutlich von Literatur, Film und auch von anderen Spielen unterschieden. Daher liegt die Besonderheit auch nicht allein in der Interaktivität, da es diese ja bereits auch zwischen spielenden

Bild und Erzählung im Computerspiel

Stephan Günzel

Literatur

Derrida, Jacques: Signatur Ereignis Kontext. In: Peter Engelmann (Hg.): Randgänge der
    Philosophie. Wien 1988, S. 291–362

Eco, Umberto: Das offene Kunstwerk. Frankfurt a. M. 1977

Fischer-Lichte, Erika: Grenzgänge und Tauschhandel. Auf dem Wege zu einer performativen
    Kultur. In: Uwe Wirth (Hg.): Performanz. Zwischen Sprachphilosophie und
    Kulturwissenschaften. Frankfurt a. M. 2002, S. 277–300.

Fischer-Lichte, Erika: Ästhetik des Performativen. Frankfurt a. M. 2004

Foucault, Michel: Sexualität und Wahrheit I. Der Wille zum Wissen. Frankfurt a. M. 1983

Frølunde, Lisbeth: Machinima Filmmaking as Culture in Practice: Dialogical Processes of
    Remix. In: Johannes Fromme; Alexander Unger (Hg.): Computer Games and New
    Media Cultures. A Handbook of Digital Games Studies. New York 2012, S. 491–507

Heckmann, Carsten: Wir wollen eure Hirne melken. In: Spiegel Online. Netzwelt. 2001. Online unter:
    http://www.spiegel.de/netzwelt/web/0,1518,126623,00.html (Stand 01.05.2013)

Hilderbrand, Lucas: Youtube: Where Cultural Memory and Copyright Converge. In: Film
    Quarterly 61, 1, (2007), S. 48–57

Hoskins, Deb: ›Do You YouTube?‹ Using Online Video in Women's Studies Courses. In: Feminist
    Collections 30, 2 (2009), S. 15–17

Jenkins, Henry: Convergence Culture. New York 2008

Kelland, Matt; Morris, Dave; Hartas, Leo: Machinima: Making Animated Movies in 3D Virtual
    Environments. Ilex 2005

Krämer, Sybille: Sprache – Stimme – Schrift. Sieben Thesen über Performativität als
    Medialität. In: Paragrana, Bd. 7 (1998), S. 33–57

Krapp, Peter: Über Spiele und Gesten. Machinima und das Anhalten der Bewegung.
    In: Paragrana, Bd. 17 (2008), S. 296–315

Kraus, Kari: ›A Counter-Friction to the Machine‹: What Game Scholars, Librarians, and
    Archivists Can Learn from Machinima Makers about User Activism. In: Journal of
    Visual Culture 10, 1 (2011), S. 100–112

Lowood, Henry E.: Real-Time Performance: Machinima and Game Studies. In: The Internatio-
    nal Digital Media & Arts Association Journal 2, 1 (2005), S. 10–17

Luhmann, Niklas: Liebe als Passion. Frankfurt a. M. 1982

Murray, Janet H.: Hamlet on the Holodeck: The Future of Narrative in Cyberspace. Cambridge 2000

Niepold, Hannes; Wastlhuber, Hans: The Church of Cointel. 2001ff. Online unter:
    www.cointel.de (Stand: 01.08.2013)

Rau, Anja: Towards the Recognition of the Shell as an Integral Part of the Digital Text.
    In: Klaus Tochtermann et.al. (Hg.): Hypertext '99. Returning to Our Diverse Roots.
    Proceedings of the 10th ACM Conference on Hypertext and Hypermedia. New
    York 1999, S. 119–120

Richard, Birgit: Art 2.0: Kunst aus der YouTube! Bildguerilla und Medienmeister.
    In: Birgit Richard; Alexander Ruhl (Hg.): Konsumguerilla. Widerstand gegen
    Massenkultur? Frankfurt a. M./New York 2008, S. 225–246

Schmidt, Imke; Backes, Ellen; Möhring, Jonas: 123comics nach Maß. 2006ff.
    Online unter: www.123comics.net (Stand: 01.08.2013)

Warburg, Aby M.: Sandro Botticellis ›Geburt der Venus‹ und ›Frühling‹. In: Dieter Wuttke (Hg.):
    Aby Warburg – Ausgewählte Schriften und Würdigungen. 3. Aufl. Baden-Baden
    1992, S. 11–64

Ramón Reichert
    ist Professor für Neue Medien am Institut für Theater-, Film- und
Medienwissenschaft der Universität Wien. Seine Forschungsschwerpunkte sind
Internetkultur, Digitale Ästhetik und Datenkritik. Publikationen (Auswahl): *Im Kino
der Humanwissenschaften. Studien zur Medialisierung wissenschaftlichen
Wissens* (2007); *Amateure im Netz. Selbstmanagement und Wissenstechnik im
Web 2.0* (2008); *Das Wissen der Börse. Medien und Praktiken des Finanzmarktes*
(2009); *Die Macht der Vielen. Über den neuen Kult der digitalen Vernetzung* (2013);
Big Data. Die Gesellschaft als digitale Maschine (2014, in Vorbereitung).

wird das Bild schlicht der Anfang eines neuen Comicastes. Es ist in erster Linie ein Assoziationsspiel und ein Test für neue Kooperationsformen. Daher kann jeder, der die offenen Enden der Geschichten besucht, über alternative Verläufe abstimmen. Die Möglichkeiten von *Cointel* sind unendlich. Völlige Brüche in den Geschichten sind daher die Regel, Personen wechseln Aussehen und Charakter, tauschen mit anderen die Rollen und wecken so entweder die Lust, weiterzusurfen oder ganz im Gegenteil selbst einzugreifen. (Heckmann 2001)

Die meisten multimedialen Webcomics beschränken die Beteiligung von User/innen auf Point-and-Click-Aktivitäten. Die User/innen können ihren eigenen Lese- und Entscheidungsweg nicht antizipieren. Das Comicprojekt *Cointel* stülpt demgegenüber die im Softwareskript verborgenen Datenpräsentationen an die Oberfläche und macht diese Strukturen zum Spielmaterial ästhetischer Interventionen. Medienreflexive Webcomics wie das Projekt *The Church of Cointel* machen die Programmcodes also in zweierlei Weise sichtbar. Erstens, sie machen ihn als pragmatisch-funktionales Werkzeug zur Bedienung der Comics verfügbar; und zweitens stellen sie Programmcodes als künstlerisches Gestaltungsmaterial zur Disposition. In ihren Projekten thematisieren die medienreflexiven Webcomics ihre eigenen medialen Bedingungen, integrieren diese in den eigenen ästhetischen Entstehungsprozess und beziehen sich dabei auf die kulturelle und soziale Bedeutung von Software.

An der zuletzt erörterten Schnittstelle von rechnergestützter Technologie, Medialität und Performativität kann populäre Kultur verortet werden: Informations- und Kommunikationstechnologien konstituieren zwar spezifische Beteiligungs- und Ausverhandlungsprozesse, deren performative Rahmungen im Rezeptionskontext wirken jedoch wieder auf die Technologien zurück und verändern diese nachhaltig. In diesem Zusammenhang inhäriert den populärkulturellen Praktiken eine interventionistische Orientierung, die sowohl die Medieninhalte als auch die Medientechnologien umfasst und mit einer Medienreflexion konfrontiert, die in letzter Konsequenz das Selbstverständnis der kulturellen Vergesellschaftung in Frage stellt, soziokulturelle Differenzen sicht- und sagbar macht und damit deren politische Veränderbarkeit ermöglicht.

Wenn Webcomics über die Gegebenheiten ihrer eigenen Medialisierung reflektieren, dann ist ihr unhintergehbarer Ausgangspunkt die Frage nach dem Stellenwert von technischen Medien. Eine ihrer zentralen Anliegen fokussiert daher den Prozess hinter den grafischen Benutzeroberflächen, den sie sichtbar und zugänglich machen wollen, um zu verdeutlichen, dass ein Computer weniger ein Bild-, sondern vielmehr ein Schriftmedium ist, das seine multimedialen Oberflächen mit Programmiercodes und -texten generiert. Da der Computer nicht nur als ein Speicher-, sondern auch als ein Rechenmedium wirksam ist, ist er selbst als ein *erzählerisches Medium* wirksam, indem er spezifische Regeln, Strukturen und Möglichkeiten der teilnehmenden Interaktion und der sinnstiftenden Interpretation vorgibt. Dies tut er in seiner Funktion als Hardware. In diesem Sinne tritt der Computer als prozedurales Medium in Erscheinung, indem er Eingaben unterschiedlich berechnet und auf diese Weise unterschiedliche Aktionen generiert.

Vor diesem Hintergrund postuliert Anja Rau eine stärkere Einbeziehung der grafischen und symbolischen Software Tools in die ästhetische Gestaltung der Netzliteratur (Rau 1999, S. 119). Medienreflexive Comics greifen diese Meta-Diskurse zu elektronischen Texten auf und erinnern uns daran, dass digitale Comicerzählungen immer auch Prozesse von Datenverarbeitung sind. Mit ihren Projekten versuchen sie, die User/innen, die in den für sie undurchschaubaren Simulationen mittels Maus, Cursor und grafischer Oberfläche für dumm gehalten werden, zu emanzipieren. Auf welche Weise geschieht dies nun? Das im Jahr 2001 an der Bauhaus-Universität Weimar entwickelte Comicprojekt *The Church of Cointel* (Niepold/Wastlhuber 2001ff.) versucht, die üblicherweise verborgenen Strukturen der Softwarearchitektur für die User/innen sichtbar und benutzbar zu machen. Die User/innen sehen die gesamte narrative Struktur und Organisation des Comics und können an einem beliebigen Punkt einsteigen und einen Strip in jede mögliche Richtung weiterentwickeln.

So entstehen immer wieder neue Comiczweige. Allerdings muss man sich mit jedem neuen Bild erst einmal der Abstimmung der anderen Nutzer stellen. Die Interaktivität wird gepaart mit Basisdemokratie. Fällt die Abstimmung knapp aus,

leisten damit eine doppelte Rahmung des Geschichtenerzählens. Erstens formulieren sie vermittels ihrer Interaktionen neue Konventionen des Erzählens, indem sie ihre Erfahrungen, Kommentare und Bewertungen in die digitale Umgebung der Webcomics einfließen lassen (vermittels Ranking-, Voting- und Response-Tools). Damit wird eine editoriale Rahmung bevorzugter Figurenkonstellationen und Erzählformen hergestellt. Zweitens etablieren sie eine stochastische Komponente, indem sie Möglichkeiten für programmierte Zufallsprozesse oder aber für Eingriffe durch User/innen schaffen. Vor dem Hintergrund dieser hyperfiktionalen Struktur erschließen sich User/innen ihren eigenen Lektüreweg und haben dabei – wie im Computerspiel – immer wieder abduktive Entscheidungen zu treffen.

Die Aufwertung der aktiven Rolle der Leser/innen bei der Lektüre eines Textes zählt heute zum fixen Forderungskatalog der Rezeptionsästhetik. Die Anerkennung der interaktiven Einflussnahme darf aber nicht darüber hinwegtäuschen, dass die Freiheit der multimedialen Rezeption durch die technischen Möglichkeiten des Computers beschränkt bleibt. Im Webcomic sind die Regeln, nach denen der Leseprozess abzulaufen hat, Bestandteil von Skriptsequenzen, die im Rahmen der interaktiven Beteiligung nicht modifiziert werden können. Insofern beschränkt sich die vielbeschworene Freiheit der Interaktivität mehr oder weniger auf den Beteiligungsmodus des Point-and-Click und reduziert damit die kognitive Aktivität im Rezeptionsprozess auf wenige Bedienbefehle. Die überwiegende Mehrzahl der traditionellen Webcomic-Hyperfictions zeigt, dass die User/innen den Linkstrukturen, die vorgegeben sind, ausgeliefert bleiben. Murray fordert daher zu Recht »a distinction between playing a creative role within an authored environment and having authorship of the environment itself«. (Murray 2000, S. 157) Genau an diesem Punkt setzen die medienreflexiven Comics an, die sich nicht mit der bloßen Steigerung von Interaktivität und Partizipation zufriedengeben, wenn nicht auch die Rolle des Mediums und die medialen Bedingungen reflektiert werden, welche die Inhalte und ihre symbolischen Repräsentationen, die Kommunikationskultur und unsere Medienerfahrungen prägen.

Novels verleihen dieser kollaborativen Haltung einen ange-
messenen Ausdruck. Damit verändern sich nicht nur die Rezeptionskontexte, sondern auch die Handlungsrollen im Produk-
tionsprozess. An die Stelle der klar und eindeutig definierten
Aufgabenbereiche und Kompetenzen lösen sich die klassischen
arbeitsteiligen Ordnungen der Comicproduktion auf, und neue
Ausverhandlungsprozesse treten auf. So geht etwa das Comiczine
Reihenhaus weit über die übliche Zusammenarbeit in der Comicproduktion hinaus. Es gibt keine Arbeitsspezialisierung im klassischen Sinne: »Bei unseren Comics haben alle getextet, Figuren
erfunden, skizziert und ins Reine gezeichnet. Mithilfe der schreib-
gestützten Erzählwerkstatt entwickeln wir Handlungsstränge
und Figuren. Erst nach einem intensiven gemeinsamen Prozess
entsteht das fertige Comic-Heft.« (Schmidt/Backes/Möhring
2006ff.)

In *Hamlet on the Holodeck*, ihrem Buch über die Narrativität in elektronischen Medien, führt die US-amerikanische
Medientheoretikerin Janet Murray den Begriff der »procedural
authorship« ein, um den Aspekt veränderter Handelsrollen in
Bezug auf interaktive Medien herauszustellen: »Procedural
authorship means writing the rules by which the text appears
as well as writing the texts themselves. It means writing the
rules for the interactor's involvement, that is, the conditions
under which things will happen in response to the participant's
actions. [...] The procedural author creates not just a set of
scenes but a world of narrative possibilities.« (Murray 2000:
152) In diesem Zusammenhang begreift sie die interaktive
Einflussnahme als choreographisches Rezeptionsmodell: »In
electronic narrative the procedural author is like a choreographer
who supplies the rhythms, the context, and the set of steps
that will be performed. The interactor, whether as navigator,
protagonist, explorer, or builder, makes use of this repertoire of
possible steps and rhythms to improvise a particular dance
among the many, many possible dances the author has enabled.«
(Murray 2000, S. 152)

Partizipatorische Comics verlangen von ihren prozedu-
ralen Autor/innen eine grundsätzliche Bereitschaft zur Verhandlung, die alle Bereiche des Storytellings umfassen kann. Sie

darauf aufmerksam, dass gestische und mimische Ordnungen nicht einer natürlichen Spontaneität entspringen, sondern im Umgang mit Spieltechnologie immer als *erworbene* Eigenschaften und *zitierbare* Größen angenommen werden müssen. In diesem Sinne forcieren die *Sims*-Machinimas das Spiel mit ihrer eigenen Beschränkung und reflektieren die computerbasierte Medialisierung emotionaler Scripts, die das Produkt von digitalen Rechenoperationen sind. Sie machen darauf aufmerksam, dass wir im Zeigen unserer Gefühle auf ein kulturelles Repertoire von Gesten zurückgreifen müssen, um uns vermittels spezifischer Körpertechniken verständlich zu machen. Im Möglichkeitsraum der Machinimas verschiebt sich allerdings das Gaming zur effizienzsteigernden Ertüchtigung motorischer Fähigkeiten zugunsten von kleinen Erzählformen, die den Wahrnehmungs- und Kontrollverlust der virtuellen Spielfiguren zum Ausgangspunkt oppositionellen Erzählens deklariert.

3. Medienreflexives Storytelling

Webcomics bezeichnen ein Comicformat, das ausschließlich oder zumindest an erster Stelle im Internet veröffentlicht wird. Sie sind das Produkt technischer Medienumbrüche von analogen zu digitalen Medien und kultureller Praktiken im Feld der Internetkommunikation. Computer- und netzbasierte Comics können als Mischformate verstanden werden, da sie sich an der Schnittstelle unterschiedlicher Medien, Technologien und Praktiken situieren und gleichermaßen an der analogen und der digitalen Medienkultur partizipieren. Insofern bilden sie weder ein einheitliches noch ein radikal neues Genre. Daher können Webcomics eher als eine Hybridbildung aus bereits bekannten Genres, Formaten und Medien gesehen werden.

Die kontinuierliche Transformation der Ästhetik und Narrativität von kollaborativen Online-Comicprojekten verweist auf eine Rezeptionskultur, die dem klassischen Modell von Autorschaft ablehnend gegenübersteht und demgegenüber versucht, kollektive Praktiken zu fördern. Die Bedingungen der permanenten Variabilität eröffnet den User/innen die Möglichkeit, den Verlauf der Erzählung endlos umzuschreiben. Die aggregatähnlich organisierten Erzählräume der digitalen Graphic

Sinne begreift Warburg den Gefühlsausdruck nicht als individu-
ell-ursprünglich erlebte Leiberfahrung, sondern als eine Verortung innerhalb einer kulturell bedingten Repräsentationsord-
nung, »in der man sich passiv leidend und nicht aktiv wirkend
vorfindet«. (Luhmann 1982, S. 73)

Die *Sims*-Machinimas nehmen in dreifacher Hinsicht
Bezug auf Warburgs Konzeption der Pathosformel.

1) Sie *reproduzieren* ohne Modifikation das formelhafte
Inventar der kinästhetischen Scripts. Sie übernehmen damit die
im Game Design fixierten Notationen elementarer Gesten und
einfacher Körperbewegungen. Dies führt zu einer einförmigen
Bewegungsanimation. So verbleibt etwa das Affektvokabular der
Trauergesten hochgradig repetitiv und folgt der Logik ergonomi-
scher Bewegungsmuster und standardisierter Arbeitsroutinen.

2) Darauf aufbauend *produzieren* sie transformatische
Referenzrahmen, welche die Zielgerichtetheit des Spielens
unterbrechen und die kinästhetischen Scripts mit abweichenden
Bedeutungskontexten assoziieren. Damit überwinden sie das
Computerspiel als Dispositiv der Abrichtung von Wahrnehmungen und Reaktionen. Machinimas wechseln den Modus der
körperlichen Performanz: Sie machen aus der ursprünglich
geplanten Effizienz der Bewegung eine kommunizierende Geste.
Sie nutzen Computerkultur zur Kommunikation und vermischen
sie mit populärkulturellen Zitaten der Werbung, der Blockbuster
oder der Videoclips.

3) Schließlich etablieren sie ein *zusammengesetztes
Repertoire* von gestischen und mimischen Bewegungsgrafiken, das
mittels der Ranking-Tools einschlägiger Portale wiederum
kanonbildend wirkt.

Für die Entwicklung der *Sims*-Machinimas stellt die
restringierte Programmatik der Körperbewegungen und des
Gesichtsausdrucks keinen Mangel dar, sondern – im Gegenteil
– eine wesentliche Voraussetzung ihrer genuinen Medienästhetik: »Machinima ersetzt die Gesten des Spiels und kompensiert
damit einen Verlust an Theater- und Filmgesten, die in Computerspielen schwierig oder unmöglich erscheinen.« (Krapp 2008,
S. 299) Sie interpretieren die technologischen Beschränkungen
des Computerspiels als künstlerische Produktivkraft und machen

diesem Hintergrund streiten Feedback-Kommentare der Sozialen Netzwerkseiten um Distinktionen der Zugehörigkeit und führen unermüdlich Zertifizierungskämpfe, die entlang der Suchbegriffe »Emo«, »Goth« oder »Punk« geführt werden.

Machinimas sind *kleine Formen,* also Formate, die innerhalb weniger Minuten Erzählhandlungen fokussieren und Figurenkonstellationen verdichten, um den Rezeptionsgewohnheiten der Internetnutzung entgegenzukommen. Die Häufigkeit von halbnahen und nahen Einstellungen ist ein Indiz dafür, dass Machinimas Erzählformen als zeitkritisch interpretieren und daher versuchen, möglichst rasch die Aufmerksamkeit des betrachtenden Publikums zu wecken. Zur zusätzlichen Steigerung des Aufmerksamkeitswertes werden oft Bezüge zu wiedererkennbaren Filmszenen und Filmfiguren des Hollywood-Kinos gesucht. Insgesamt verdichten sich intermediale und intertextuelle Bezüge, die aus der zwingenden Rahmenbedingung zeitlicher Begrenztheit hervorgehen. Wie können allgemeine Schlussfolgerungen für Mash-ups in diesem Zusammenhang formuliert werden? Es ist für die Ausbildung einer kulturwissenschaftlichen Perspektive im Bereich der neueren Rezeptions- und Wirkungsforschung zu »interaktiven« Kommunikationsmedien von entscheidendem Vorteil, einen erweiterten Begriff von produktiver Medienaneignung zu gebrauchen, denn intermediale Formate, Appropriationen, Evidenzstrategien, Fakes und Wahrheitsdiskurse haben im Netz eine hybride Wahrnehmungskultur und soziale Spielregeln einer neuen Repräsentationspolitik entstehen lassen, die einen modulierenden Gebrauch des Gamings nahe legen: »Many Games companies are releasing their design tools and games engines alongside their games.« (Jenkins 2008, S. 166)

Der Kunsthistoriker Aby Warburg entwickelte in den 1920er Jahren sein Konzept der *Pathosformel,* um die kulturhistorische Überlieferung von Ausdrucksgebärden nach antikem Muster in der Renaissancekunst aufzuzeigen. Diese interpretiert er in seiner 1893 verfassten Dissertation zu Sandro Botticelli als kulturelle Symbole, die Affekte und Leidenschaften nicht unvermittelt abbilden, sondern vielmehr auf einen historisch bedingten, semantisch aufgeladenen und sozial konstruierten Bedeutungsprozess verweisen. (Warburg 1992, S. 11–64) In diesem

Machinima-Produktionen einen zusätzlichen Gestaltungsspiel-
raum für parodierende und/oder immersive Stilmittel eröffnet.
Im Unterschied zu Game Movies, die ausschließlich mit Game
Assets gedreht werden und dadurch nahe am programmierten
Spielinhalt bleiben, generieren Machinimas sowohl neue Spielin-
halte als auch neue Spielfiguren und erzählen mit Hilfe eigenpro-
duzierter Assets Geschichten, die dem Image Design und den
Branding-Strategien der Games oft diametral gegenüberstehen.
    Die sich seit 2004 formierende Machinima-Szene
distanzierte sich vom Computerspiel-Leistungsdispositiv der
heroischen Idealkörper und versuchte vielmehr, die Kontrollver-
luste innerhalb der sozialen virtuellen Versuchsanordnungen
sicht- und sagbar zu machen. Sie begab sich daher auf die Suche
nach dem imperfekten, schwachen Alltagskörper und entwickelte eine Vielzahl von erzählerischen Stilen und Konstellationen, um in die erfolgsorientierten und sozial normalisierten
Spielwelten biographisch erlebte Gewalt, Macht, Herrschaft
sowie simulierte Unfälle, Katastrophen und Störungen einzufüh-
ren. Die *Sims*-Machinimas stellen damit das Computerspiel als
kulturellen Apparat zur Popularisierung von Managementwis-
sen in Frage und rücken an seine Stelle narrative Verfahrenstech-
niken, die versuchen, die ambivalenten Strukturen der familiären
Ordnung bloßzulegen. Der ironisierende Blick auf den ursprünglichen Plot des *Sims*-Game macht verständlich, warum in der
Machinima-Community eine ausgeprägte Tendenz zu dramatischen Erzählformen an der rezeptionsästhetischen Schnittstelle
von Gothic und Splatter Movie vorherrscht.
    Machinima-Filme zirkulieren heute in allen maßgebli-
chen Sozialen Netzwerkseiten des Web 2.0. Neben einschlägigen
Community-Seiten (www.machinima.com) dominiert der
Videoupload auf *YouTube* die Medienpräsenz der Machinimas im
Netz. Das Videoportal *YouTube* sorgt für ihre globale Vernetzung
und schafft vermittels des Taggings semantische Felder und
Knotenpunkte, die eine zusätzliche Kontextualisierung der
Machinimas etablieren. Mit ihrer Vernetzung im Feld der Online-
portale und der Social Media sind die *Sims*-Machinimas zu einem
umkämpften Schauplatz heterogener Identitätsdiskurse und
gesellschaftlicher Ordnungsvorstellungen aufgestiegen. Vor

Gegebenheiten einer definierten virtuellen Spielumgebung, die als Handlungsrahmen für die Spielhandlung benutzt wird. (Kelland/Morris/Hartas 2005, S. 17f.) Das herausragende Charaktermerkmal der Machinimas liegt in ihrer Mash-up-Ästhetik (Frølunde 2012, S. 491–507): Die User/innen experimentieren mit den Gegebenheiten einer indisponiblen Spielewelt, indem sie diegetische, fiktionale oder narrative Bedeutungen des Spiels mehr oder weniger modifizieren und dabei alternative Strategien eines Mediengebrauchs aufzeigen. In diesem Zusammenhang nutzen sie nicht nur die im Game Design festgeschrieben kreativen Freiräume, sondern erschaffen in ihren Mash-up-Praktiken Gegen-Narrative, die nicht nur eine andersartige Bedeutungsproduktion in Gang setzen, sondern auch einen medienreflexiven Beitrag zur theoretischen Situierung von hegemonialen Narrativen und Gegen-Narrativen leisten. (Vgl. Kraus 2011, S. 100–112) In methodologischer Hinsicht geht die Popkulturforschung der Mash-ups als kulturelles und soziales Phänomen von einer performativen Logik der Medien aus, die nicht an sich, sondern immer nur für sich, d. h. in konkreten alltäglichen, sozialen Zusammenhängen existiert. Die Grundannahme, dass kulturelle Praktiken immer vieldeutig und veränderlich sind und ihre theoretische Reflexion immer auch ein aktiver Konstruktionsprozess ist, kann als Ausgangspunkt für die Thematisierung der prozessualen Komponente von Mash-up-Praktiken genommen werden, die transitorische Räume ästhetischer Sinnverschiebungen, Neuorientierungen und Verhandlungen generieren.

Machinimas haben ein eigenes Praxisfeld im Digital Storytelling etabliert, in dem sich Game Design, Clipästhetik und industrialisierte Genrekonventionen im populären Spielfilm (Actionplots, charakterdominierte Stoffe) hybridisieren. Machinimas, die mit Hilfe der *Sims 2* oder der *Sims 3* produziert werden, bilden eine extreme Form der *Mods*[3], die in der Community als *Total Conversion* bezeichnet wird. Die Total Conversion eröffnet ein neues Spiel, das die ursprünglichen Spielaussagen gegen den Strich liest. Ein weiteres Charakteristikum der Sims-Machinimas ist im Bereich des Bild-Ton-Verhältnisses angesiedelt. Die Sound Engine des Computerspiels ist in der Regel vollkommen ausgeschaltet und durch eine eigene Soundspur ersetzt, die den

3
Mod ist die Abkürzung für Modification und bedeutet die Veränderung eines ursprünglichen Spielinhaltes.

mentwissen, Normalitätskonstruktionen und Lebensführungstechniken (*Lifestyle Treats*) weltweit zu verbreiten. Die *Sims*-Computerspiele sind als Rollenspielsimulation konzipiert und fordern von ihren Gamerinnen und Gamern, das Leben simulierter Spielfiguren, genannt *Sims*, ›erfolgreich zu managen‹: »Erstelle eine Familie und bau ihr ein Haus. Dann hilf Deinen Sims, Karriere zu machen, Geld zu verdienen, Freunde zu finden und sich zu verlieben.«[2]

Um die levelbasierten Spielmodi erfolgreich abzuwickeln, müssen die Spielenden bestimmte *Mapping*- und *Monitoring*-Fähigkeiten entwickeln. Dabei kontrollieren sie das gesamte soziale Leben der Spielfiguren und überwachen mittels der für *Die Sims* typischen Motivations- und Bedürfnisbalken den Zustand ihrer körperlichen und mentalen Bedürfnisbefriedigung, ihre emotionale Kompetenz sowie ihre Fähigkeiten im Bereich des Alltags- und Beziehungsmanagements. Vor diesem organisationstheoretischen Hintergrund ist die Spielarchitektur der *Sims* angelegt. Sie basiert auf protokollierenden Wissenstechniken, die der systematischen Überwachung von körperlichen Funktionen und sozialen Beziehungen vermittels technischer Medien und rechnergestützter Beobachtungssysteme dienen.

Im September 2004 bot die im Handel erhältliche Folge *The Sims 2* die Möglichkeit, digitale Animationen mit Hilfe des Computerspiels, d. h. in Echtzeit und ohne zusätzliche Animationstools, herzustellen. Die mit dem spielimmanenten Story-Modus verschalteten In-Game-Technologien der Bildaufzeichnung (Kameraoptionen für die Spielkamera, Kamera-Schnappschüsse und Videoaufnahmen) haben Medienpraktiken ermöglicht, die an die Stelle des levelbasierten und zielgerichteten Spielens ein offenes Netz von Erzählformen rücken konnten. Vor diesem Hintergrund ist eine kleine Form des digitalen Storytellings entstanden: das *Machinima*.

Die damit gegebene Möglichkeit, Animationsfilme ohne finanziellen und technischen Aufwand produzieren zu können, hat das Gaming nachhaltig und grundlegend verändert. Machinimas sind in einem Computerspiel in Echtzeit erstellte Animationsfilme, die keine interaktive Komponente mehr aufweisen. (Lowood 2005, S. 10–17) Sie bedienen sich der technischen

---

2
Hersteller-Text, Maxis (Will Wright): The Sims, Emeryville, Kalifornien (EA Games) 2000.

sches Video innerhalb der Rezeptionskontexte einnehmen kann. In diesem Sinne verändert sich sowohl der erzählerische Produktions- als auch der Rezeptionskontext der Videos andauernd und bleibt offen und unabgeschlossen. Obwohl Make-up-Tutorials auf eine bestimme Weise Darstellungs- und Wahrnehmungskonventionen verfestigen, die zur kulturellen und medialen Konstruktion von individuellen und kollektiven Identitäten beitragen (Hilderbrand 2007, S. 48–57), ermöglichen sie den beteiligten Subjekten immer auch Spielräume abweichender Bedeutungsproduktionen (diese Ansicht vertritt auch Hoskins 2009, S. 15–17). Der erzählerische Aufführungscharakter von Videos auf *YouTube* muss folglich weiter gefasst werden: Sie sind nicht nur eine Bühne für Selbstdarstellungen, sondern vor allem ein Ort ›produktiver Feedbackschleifen‹ zwischen Produktion und Rezeption. In diesem Sinne bleiben sie im Aggregatzustand der Verhandlungsprozesse und Mitbestimmungsmöglichkeiten des Social Media Storytelling uneindeutig, ephemer und umkämpft.

2. Transmediales Storytelling

Performative Praktiken im Netz haben neue Perspektiven auf oppositionelle Lesarten entwickelt. Ihr produktives Potential entfalten sie im Feld der subkulturellen Medienpraktiken. Die Destabilisierung hegemonialer Bedeutungsarchitekturen und Sinnzuweisungen im Modus der transmedialen Performativität soll hier am Beispiel der user/innengenerierten Aneignungspraktiken des Computerspiels *Sims 2* thematisiert werden. Transmediale Modifikation bedeutet in diesem Zusammenhang, dass User/innen Computerspiele als iterierbare Aussagesysteme verstehen, deren Bedeutungen sich – in Bezugnahme auf unterschiedliche Medienformate – grundsätzlich modifizieren lassen (vgl. Derrida 1988, S. 309). Die Modifikation macht aus den programmierten Games Schauplätze einer allgemeinen Zitathaftigkeit und Iterierbarkeit und sorgt dafür, dass die Games von einer ihnen ›ursprünglich‹ anhaftenden Spieleintention enthoben werden können.

Sims ist die bisher meistverkaufte PC-Spielserie. Sie hat in über 100 Millionen Exemplaren dazu beigetragen, Manage-

Diese demonstrativen Manöver, die Bereitschaft zur Kritikfähig-
keit signalisieren, zielen auf die Herstellung konspirativer Nähe.
In diesem Sinne positionieren sich Vlog-Narrative weniger als
fertige Werke, sondern vielmehr als improvisierende Entwürfe.
Diese Strategie der Abschwächung und Relativierung der eigenen
Position im Selbstentwurf erfreut sich innerhalb der unterschied-
lichen Communities größter Beliebtheit, weil sie die anderen
User/innen zur Beteiligung einlädt. Die Formen der expliziten
Selbstadressierung dienen also der Abschwächung der eigenen
Subjektposition und versuchen damit, partizipatives Engage-
ment an das Video zu binden. Diese narrative Technik der
Selbstthematisierung hat sich als sehr erfolgreiche Rahmenstrate-
gie erwiesen, um innerhalb der Sozialen Medien im Web 2.0
Aufmerksamkeit auf die jeweiligen Erzählinhalte zu lenken.
Andererseits übernehmen die Vlog-Narrative auch bestimmte
Formate und Genrekategorien, um die Wiedererkennbarkeit zu
steigern. So lässt sich die Nähe von Vlogs und ihren Repräsentan-
ten zu Fernsehformaten am eindringlichsten an den serialisier-
ten Strukturen und Erzählformen aufzeigen. Um das Interesse
und die Identifikation der Zuschauer/innen und das Sammeln
von Serienwissen, das Zuschauer/innen auf spätere Folgen
anwenden können, zu fördern, gliedern sich zahlreiche Vlogs in
aufeinander aufbauende Folgen und archivieren diese in eigenen
YouTube-Channels. Die Kanäle können zudem abonniert werden,
was die Zuschauer/innen-Bindung zusätzlich verstärkt.

 Fazit: Der Stellenwert der Bewegtbild-Narrative im Netz
kann auf der Grundlage der filmischen Ästhetik nicht mehr
erschlossen werden. Die Zentralität des filmischen Textes weicht
einer offenen und nichtlinearen Heteromedialität, welche die
Videobilder in flüchtige und instabile Bedeutungsnetze ein-
schreibt. Der Stellenwert von Onlinevideos zur Verhandlung
von interaktiven Erzählkulturen und Mash-up-Praktiken zeigt
sich folglich nicht nur alleine auf der Ebene der »Repräsentation« (die eine filmwissenschaftliche Analyse nahelegen würde),
sondern auch darin, wie in der Zirkulation der Videos durch
Feedback, explizite Empfehlungen und Hyperlinks offene
Bedeutungsproduktionen hervorgebracht werden, die maßgeblich dafür verantwortlich sind, welchen Stellenwert ein spezifi-

Film- und Medienwisenschaft einzugrenzen, sondern sie in einem weitsichtigeren Blick als kulturelle und mediale Praxis zu thematisieren.

Die vorherschende Anzahl und die größte inhaltliche Kategorie der bei *YouTube* hochgeladenen Clips bezeichnet Birgit Richard als »Ego-Clips« und meint damit eine Clipsorte der »exzessiven narzißtischen Selbstdarstellung«, in der eine »große Bandbreite von schüchternen Talks bis hin zur visuellen Prostitution zu beobachten« (Richard 2008, S. 227) ist. Es handelt sich um Mainstream-Formate, die mit dem charakteristischen Erscheinungsbild von *YouTube* identifiziert werden. Die auf dem Aufmerksamkeitsmarkt von *YouTube* dominierende Stellung der Ego-Clips hat dazu geführt, dass personalisierende Kommunikationsstile der Sozialen Medien im Web 2.0 vorherrschend sind. Mit *YouTube* haben sich subjektzentrierte Erzählstile herausgebildet, die überwiegend mit den Stilmitteln impliziter Authentizitätsmarker, visuellen und auditiven Elementen der direkten Adressierung und mit einer Reihe von Darstellungskonventionen operieren, mit denen sich die ›YouTuber‹ in den Diskursritualen der ›spontanen Natürlichkeit‹ und ›Ungezwungenheit‹ als möglichst authentisch präsentieren. Nach Michel Foucault ist das Geständnis, der produktive Zwang des »Sprechen-Machens«, die höchstbewertete Technik bei der Produktion von Wahrhaftigkeit (Foucault 1983, S. 22f.). Der spezifische Zusammenhang von Macht, Wahrheit und Subjektwerdung ist hier also weniger das Ergebnis repressiver Unterdrückung, sondern vielmehr in einer immer intensiver werdenden Diskursivierung begründet. Die erzählerische Selbstadressierung meint in diesem Zusammenhang eine sprachlich[1], gestisch oder mimisch kommunizierte Selbstbezüglichkeit, die konstitutiv auf die Adressant/en/innen zurückwirkt und helfen soll, das Erzählte glaubwürdig zu gestalten. Die Selbstadressierung adressiert zwar offensichtlich ihre Adressanten, eröffnet aber darüber hinausgehend eine sekundäre Adressierung, die sich an ein imaginiertes Publikum richtet und Möglichkeitsspielräume für künftige Betrachter/innen ermöglicht. Konventionelle Formen der Selbstadressierung enthalten etwa partielle Selbstkritik oder Ironiesignale und schwächen insgesamt den narzisstischen Gestus der Selbstdarstellung ab.

1
»Sprachlich« bedeutet hier im weitesten Sinne verbal- und schriftsprachliche Aussagen oder Äußerungen, die in Form von Monologen, Inserts, Zwischentiteln oder Tagging kommuniziert werden.

Methodologie der Untersuchung performativer Prozesse mitein-
bezogen werden. Diese Fragestellung hat nicht nur eine heuristi-
sche Bedeutung in der wissenschaftlichen Diskurspraktik,
sondern eröffnet auch jenseits der Dichotomie von Technikdeterminismus versus Technikeuphorie kritische Fragen nach dem
Handlungsspielraum performativer Ermöglichung in technischen Umgebungen.

1. Kollaboratives Storytelling

Mit dem Aufstieg der Sozialen Medien im Web 2.0 hat
sich der Stellenwert des Bewegtbildes im Web auf umfassende
Weise verändert. In den neuen subjektzentrierten Internet-
medien ist das Erzählen mit Stilen visueller Selbstinszenierungen
verwoben worden. Das Bewegtbild ist aber kein abgeschlossenes
Werk, sondern hat sich zum Schauplatz offener Bedeutungsproduktion und permanenter Ausverhandlung entwickelt. Geregelte
Kommentarfunktionen, Hypertextsysteme, Ranking- und
Votingverfahren durch kollektive und kollaborative Rahmungsprozesse verorten audiovisuelle Inhalte in multimedialen und
diskursiven Umgebungen. Online-Bewegtbildinhalte und ihre
Narrative treten als improvisierendes Wissen in Erscheinung, das
narrative Weiterentwicklungen, Kontextualisierungen und
Reinszenierungen fördert.

Im Hinblick auf die Geschichte von Mediendiskursen
kann man die kollektiven Erzählpraktiken und cross- und
transmedialen Verfahren, die den Videos beigelegt werden, auch
als Fortsetzung der Debatten um den Paradigmenwechsel der
Interaktivität (Intermedia, Happening, Fluxus) und das »offene
Kunstwerk« (Eco 1977), die seit den 1960er Jahren intensiv
geführt werden, verstehen. In diesem Zusammenhang können
strukturelle Homologien zwischen den Bestrebungen, das
Autorensubjekt als begründende Instanz und das Werk als
abgeschlossene Entität in Frage zu stellen, und die in den
Sozialen Medien des Web 2.0 geäußerte Aufforderung zu Interaktion und Kollaboration hergestellt werden. Wenn in diesem
Sinne die Vlogs (Videoblogs) auf *YouTube* zu Schauplätzen
kultureller Zirkulation und ästhetischer Konflikte werden, dann
eröffnet sich die Möglichkeit, diese nicht nur als ein Genre der

bis zum editorialen Framing der so genannten Webmaster –
überantworten.

Im Folgenden soll es nun darum gehen, die hier angesprochenen Verfahrensweisen der Peer-to-Peer-Kommunikation
von Onlineplattformen und Social Media-Formaten entlang von
drei unterschiedlichen Performativitätsstrategien zu thematisieren.

(1) In der Auseinandersetzung mit den von User/innen
generierten Bewegtbildinhalten auf dem Videoportal *YouTube*
geht es um die Frage, welche performative Rolle die Initiatoren
von Videouploads einnehmen. Welcher netzdiskursiven Rah-
mungspraktiken bedienen sie sich, wenn sie für sich eine
diskursmoderierende Rolle reklamieren wollen? Welchen
Stellenwert haben kollektive und kollaborative Rahmungsprozesse in Bezug auf die Bedeutungsproduktion, Ausverhandlung
und Distribution von Bewegtbildern in Onlineportalen und
Social Media-Formaten?

(2) Die in der Internetkultur ausgeprägte Tendenz zur
Resignifizierung und Reiteration von bereits bestehenden
Inhalten (Mash-up, Remix) verweist auf einen Aspekt des
Performativen, der nahtlos an die kollektiven und kollaborativen Rahmungsprozesse anschließt. Auch hier zeigt sich die
performative Praxis in erster Linie als etwas, das einen Überschuss erzeugt, der sich keinem intersubjektiv kontrollierbaren
Diskursfeld mehr zuordnen lässt. In diesem Sinne erweist sich
»die produktive Kraft des Performativen nicht einfach darin,
etwas zu erschaffen, sondern darin, mit dem, was wir nicht
selbst hervorgebracht haben, umzugehen« (Krämer 1998, S. 48).
So gesehen kann der performative Vollzug als Überschuss von
Bedeutung verstanden werden, der nicht nur eine neue performative Rahmung realisiert, sondern rückwirkend auch den
bereits bestehenden Inhalt modifiziert.

(3) Performative Prozesse im Internet sind das Resultat
technischer Ermöglichung. Speziell sind es die computergestützten Informations- und Kommunikationstechnologien, welche
die Modi, die Geltung und die Verbreitung der von User/innen
generierten Inhalte regulieren. Folglich sind die Netzmedien und
ihr technisch generierter Handlungsvollzug an der Produktion
von Sinn und Bedeutung maßgeblich beteiligt und müssen in die

User/innen ermöglicht, in Peer-to-Peer-Netzwerken konkrete Nutzungsformen des habitualisierten Erzählens herauszubilden, die Formen der sozialen Kommunikation und neuartige Prozeduren zur narrativen Mitgestaltung und Mitbestimmung miteinschließt. Entlang dieser Verschiebungen haben sich populärkulturelle Praktiken herausgebildet, die sich an den anonymen, flexiblen und veränderlichen Strukturen und Konstellationen der Sozialen Medien im Web 2.0 ansiedeln und eine radikale Alternative zu den traditionellen Formen des Publizierens von Medieninhalten eröffnen. Diese im Werden begriffene kollaborative Kommunikationskultur lässt sich nicht mehr auf ein *Werk als Eigentum* oder ein *identisches Autorensubjekt* zurückführen. Damit einhergehend erweist sich das Erzählen als Inhalt und als Form nur bedingt und eingeschränkt als ein distinktes und stabiles Wissensobjekt und ist immer auch eingebettet in performative Rahmungsstrategien. Aus performativer Perspektive kann folglich eine dynamische und sich provisorisch gebende Bedeutungsproduktion der Sozialen Medien des Web 2.0 freigelegt werden, mit welcher die Produktivität und die Prozessualität kollaborativer Praktiken in den Analysefokus einrückt. In ihrer medientheoretischen Problemstellung rekurrieren die performativen Rahmungsprozesse im Netz jedoch nicht auf einen spontaneistischen Voluntarismus, der den Aspekt des Performativen genuin von der kreativen Leistung eines Individualsubjektes ableiten würde, da die prozessierenden Erzählpraktiken von den technischen Infrastrukturen der digitalen Kommunikationsräume reguliert werden. Infolgedessen müssen die Erzählbeiträge der User/innen, die sie im Namen von realen Autor/innen, fiktiven Figuren oder anonymen Nicknames vollziehen, immer auch als ein technisches Artefakt der Ermöglichung von Rede- und Verhandlungspositionen in Betracht gezogen werden. Dieser im Ansatz gegebene Technikdeterminismus muss aber unter anderem dahingehend relativiert werden, insofern die hier untersuchten Praktiken zur Informations- und Kommunikationsgestaltung immer auch auf eine grundlegende populärkulturelle Reorganisation der netzbasierten Wissensproduktion und -rezeption abzielen und damit das Netzwissen einer performativen Aneignungsrhetorik – vom assoziativen Indexing der Fans

Internetbasierte Gesellschaften haben im Alltagsgebrauch der digital vernetzten Medien der Peer-to-Peer-Netzwerke (P2P) die traditionellen Formen des Schreibens und Lesens der Buchkultur auf maßgebliche Weise verändert. Die Veränderung der Erzählkultur durch die Sozialen Medien betreffen jedoch nicht nur die *Inhalte* des Erzählten, sondern auch die Art und Weise, wie das Erzählte *medial* konstruiert wird und eine bestimmte *soziale* Beteiligung hervorruft. In diesem Sinne übt das Erzählen in Sozialen Netzwerken einen entscheidenden Einfluss auf die Neugestaltung narrativer Strukturen und Funktionen, die eine Medienreflexion der sie ermöglichenden Beteiligungs- und Vernetzungskulturen nahelegt.

In diesem Zusammenhang kann in Anknüpfung an die performative Handlungstheorie von Erika Fischer-Lichte (2002, 2004) der Begriff des Performativen zur Kennzeichnung der prozessualen Aufführungs-, Vollzugs- und Transformationspraktiken des Social Media Storytellings eingebracht werden. In Anlehnung an den vielversprechenden Forschungsansatz des Performativen können die vermittels der Sozialen Medien des Web 2.0 generierten performativen Prozesse als erzählerische *Transformationsprozesse* bestimmt werden, indem sie ungeplante Spiel- und Freiräume des Erzählens eröffnen und damit Kontingentes und Emergentes zum untrennbaren Bestandteil des digitalen Erzählens erheben.

Das Neue Erzählen in sozialen Onlinemedien

In den vernetzten digitalen Kommunikationsräumen haben sich interaktive Medienkanäle heterogener Bedeutungsproduktion und damit einhergehend kollektive und kollaborative Medienpraktiken herausgebildet, die sämtliche Bereiche der Herstellung, Verbreitung, Nutzung und Bewertung erzählter Inhalte umfassen. Das Social Media Storytelling auf Sozialen Netzwerkseiten und Internetportalen ist hochgradig von Produktions- und Rezeptionskontingenz geprägt und formiert einen diffusen Aggregatzustand kultureller Deutungsspielräume innerhalb dynamischer Bedeutungs- und Ausverhandlungsprozesse. In diesem Sinne kann das Social Media Storytelling als Technologie sozialer Wirksamkeit verstanden werden, die es

Social Media Storytelling

Ramón Reichert

Raum Spuren entdecken), künstlerische Aktionen (z. B. Fotos bearbeiten, Videomaterial produzieren) sowie ethische Aktionen (z. B. Verhalten bewerten, Zustände diskutieren, Machenschaften entlarven). Lean Back und Lean Forward-Varianten berücksichtigen unterschiedliche Zielgruppen. Die optimale Form der Participation Experience ist die kreative Mitgestaltung der Storywelt als Autor, als Künstler (*The Spiral*), als Schauspieler oder als Teil des Ermittlerteams (*Dina Foxx, Tatort+*). Ergebnisse und usergenerierter Content werden in den Foren veröffentlicht und somit Teil des Storyversums. In *The Spiral* wurden die Kunstobjekte in die TV-Folge integriert, in SoM wurden Artefakte in den Talkshows öffentlich gezeigt und diskutiert.

Komplexe Rätsel erfordern eine kollektive Intelligenz.
Participation Experience entsteht durch die soziale Interaktion der Explorer. Die komplexen Rätsel benötigen zu ihrer Lösung die kollektive Intelligenz einer erfahrenen und motivierten Community. Diese führt zur (Re)Konstruktion der Handlung, zur Lösung der Missionen und zur Diskussion der ethisch-sozialen Fragestellungen. Die Probleme der realen Welt werden im Kontext der fiktiven Geschichten bewusst, die Community entwickelt gemeinsame Problemlösungsstrategien. Die kollektive Intelligenz entfaltet sich im virtuellen Raum der Fiktion und wirkt in den realen Raum unserer Welt hinein.

Martin Ericsson, Produzent und Creative Director von *The Company P* (SoM), macht deutlich, dass die Explorer letztendlich zum eigentlichen Gestalter transmedialer Projekte werden: »In participatory culture things change completely. The artist acts as a host, sets up the game space, produces some stimuli, but the real producer, the real artist in participatory culture is the audience itself.«[42]

42
Martin Ericsson: On Partecipation (2009). Speech at Power tot he Pixel 2009, URL: http://truthaboutmarika.wordpress.com/tag/the-companyp/ (Stand 25.07.2013).

Claudia Söller-Eckert
ist Professorin für Medien-Design und interaktive Medien an der Hochschule Darmstadt. Nach ihrem Architekturstudium arbeitete sie als wissenschaftliche Mitarbeiterin am Fachgebiet Geometrische Informationsverarbeitung an der TU Darmstadt. In einer Zeit, in der es noch keine Animationssoftware gab, entwickelte sie in einem interdisziplinären Team 3D-CAD-Software und realisierte die Computeranimationen für diverse ausgezeichnete Filme. 1992 wurde sie als Professorin für 3D-Computeranimation und interaktive Medien an die FH Mainz berufen. Dort leitete sie den Studiengang Medien-Design und war stellvertretende Leiterin des Institutes für Mediengestaltung und Medientechnologie *img*.

41
Vgl. Maike Coelle; Kristian Kosta-Zahn; Maike Hank; Katharina Kokoska; Dorothea Martin; Patrick Möller; Gregor Sedlag; Philipp Zimmermann: Thesis 1 Claiming Reality. In: Transmedia-Manifest (2011). URL: http://www.transmedia-manifest.com/ (Stand 25.07.2013).

auch zu einer hohen Immersion. Dieser fiktional-reale Schwebezustand[41] machte den besonderen Reiz in *Alpha 0.7* und SoM aus.

Ästhetisch reizvolle Storywelten führen zu einer hohen Immersion.

Transmediale Storywelten und ihre Figuren müssen so beschaffen sein, dass sie den Explorer anziehen und fesseln. Sie schaffen eine Identität für die Community. Die europäischen Beispiele erreichten das tiefe Involvement durch die Verschmelzung von Fiktion und Realität sowie durch die kollektiven Aktivitäten der Community. Im Vergleich zu den amerikanischen Beispielen sind die Storywelten bisher sehr realistisch und trist, die Figuren oft eine Spur zu schrill gezeichnet. Sie erschweren die Identifikation der Community mit ihnen.

Die Participation Experience kann sich nur innerhalb einer zeitlichen und einer räumlichen Dimension entfalten.

Das Storyversum mit Handlung und Charakteren benötigt eine zeitliche Dimension, damit sich die soziale Interaktion und die kollektive Intelligenz entwickeln können. Die geschlossene Dramaturgie des Kinofilms wird zugunsten der Serie mit einer gedehnten Zeitstruktur aufgelöst. Die Dehnung erfolgt durch die Pre-TV-Phase, Post-TV-Phase oder durch den zeitlichen Rhythmus der Serien. Besondere Missionen oder Aktionen im realen Raum können nur in Echtzeit gespielt werden und sind in die gesamte Zeitstruktur eingebunden. Die räumliche Dimension umfasst den virtuellen und den realen Raum und verschränkt die beiden. Beispiele für diese Verschränkung sind die virtuellen Orte der Kunstwerke in *The Spiral* und die realen Orte der Museen. Diese Raum-Zeit-Konstellation ist eine entscheidende Voraussetzung für die Participation Experience.

Der Explorer wird durch vielfältige Interaktionen und usergenerierten Content Teil des Storyversums.

Die vielfältigen Interaktionen umfassen intellektuelle Aufgaben (z. B. Hinweise finden, Rätsel lösen, Codes und Zugangsdaten knacken), physische Aktionen (z. B. im realen

5. Der Explorer wird durch vielfältige Interaktionen und user-generierten Content Teil des Storyversums.
6. Komplexe Rätsel erfordern eine kollektive Intelligenz.

Die (Re)Konstruktion erfolgt kollektiv, und die Handlung macht den Plattformwechsel notwendig.

Die (Re)Konstruktion der Handlung betrifft alle Erzähl-ebenen und die Motivation der Protagonisten. Die Explorer müssen sämtliche Fragmente der Geschichte in den verschiedenen Medien oder im realen Raum kollektiv aufspüren. In der Regel sind diese Untersuchungen in die Vergangenheit gerichtet (Hintergründe, Backstories) und werden durch permanente Twists und Nebenstränge erschwert. Es entsteht ein Netzwerk aus narrativen Verweisen und Bezügen, das in einer Mindmap dargestellt werden kann. Verschwörungsszenarien sind der typische Stoff, aus dem die Storywelt gemacht ist. In ihr verfolgt der Protagonist mit Hilfe der Community die feindliche Institution und macht sie unschädlich. Der Wechsel in ein anderes Medium wird durch narrative Lücken, durch eine Mission oder durch das Fanpotential der Figuren initiiert. Der Eintritt in den Magic Circle der virtuellen Welt erfolgt durch ein Rabbit Hole, das auf eine zentrale Landing Page führt.

Die fiktionale Storywelt hat einen Bezug zu aktuellen Fragestellungen der realen Welt, die die Community diskutiert.

ARG und europäische Transmedia Projekte verbinden die fiktionale Storywelt mit aktuellen Fragestellungen der realen Welt. In amerikanischen Beispielen geht es mehr um die traditionelle Frage nach Gut und Böse. Verschwörungstheorien, Science Fiction-Szenarien oder Ressourcenprobleme bieten Raum für potentielle Bedrohungen und die entscheidende Frage, wie wir unsere Welt gemeinsam schützen können. Die Beispiele thematisierten ethische Grundfragen, die in den Foren kollektiv diskutiert wurden: Authentizität und Realität der Medien, Kontrolle der Bürger durch politische Instanzen und Technologien oder den gläsernen Menschen. Die Vermischung von Fiktion und Realität führte in einigen Beispielen zu Wahrnehmungskonflikten, aber

38
The Spiral, Website (2012).
URL: http://www.thespiral.eu/
(Stand 01.10.2012).

39
Honigstudios: The Spiral.
URL: http://www.honigstudios.
com/the-spiral/ (Stand
25.07.2013).

40
Henry Jenkins: The Revenge of the
Origami Unicorn: Seven Principles
of Transmedia Storytelling (Well,
Two Actually. Five More on Friday)
(2009). URL: http://henryjenkins.
org/2009/12/the_revenge_of_the_
origami_uni.html (Stand
25.07.2013).

nahme an der kollektiven Aufgabe: der Suche nach Gemälden und die kreative Aktivität. Auf *thespiral.eu*[38] und *Facebook* entstand das virtuelle Pendant des Künstlerkollektivs, die *Spirale*. Bevor die Explorer Hinweise zum aktuellen Aufenthaltsort der Kunstwerke erhielten, mussten sie Aufgaben lösen, Games spielen und eigene ›Kunstwerke‹ produzieren. Beispielsweise sollten Hinweise in den echten Museen entdeckt oder eines der gestohlenen Bilder, René Magrittes *Der Kuss* (1951), mit originellen Darstellungsmöglichkeiten nachgestellt werden. Als Belohnung wurden die aktuellen GPS-Daten der verschwundenen Gemälde auf einer Karte angezeigt.

Die Aktivitäten der Explorer mündeten in einem kollektiven Kunstwerk, *The Spiral*, das bei dem grandiosen Schluss-Event per Video an die Gebäude des EU-Parlaments in Brüssel projiziert wurde und in sechs europäischen Hauptstädten zu sehen war.

Die filmische Produktion ist professioneller als beispielsweise jene von *Dina Foxx* oder *Alpha 0.7*. Die TV-Serie sahen zwei Millionen Zuschauer wöchentlich; *thespiral.eu* verzeichnete eine Million Besucher sowie 142.700 aktive Mitglieder mit 19.752 nutzergenerierten Inhalten.[39]

Participation Experience in Transmedia Projekten

Wie die Beispiele deutlich machen, umfasst Transmedia Storytelling mehr als nur die Verteilung einer Geschichte auf verschiedene Medienkanäle. Die Participation Experience schafft eine »unified and coordinated entertainment experience«[40] und ein kollektives Erlebnis. Die europäischen Transmedia Projekte zeigen die wesentlichen Merkmale dieser Participation Experience:

1. Die (Re)Konstruktion erfolgt kollektiv, und die Handlung macht den Plattformwechsel notwendig.
2. Die fiktionale Storywelt hat einen Bezug zu aktuellen Fragestellungen der realen Welt, die die Community diskutiert.
3. Ästhetisch reizvolle Storywelten führen zu einer hohen Immersion.
4. Die Participation Experience kann sich nur innerhalb einer zeitlichen und einer räumlichen Dimension entfalten.

in Brüssel mit viel Medienpräsenz zurückgegeben werden. Das Kollektiv bittet die Internetgemeinde um Mithilfe. Während die Explorer den Gemälden im Netz nachspüren, geht die Geschichte im TV mit mehreren Handlungssträngen und Twists, im Stil eines skandinavischen Thrillers, weiter.

Fiktiver und realer Raum

Der belgische Künstler Jean-Baptiste Dumont berichtete über die Ergebnisse der Community in Echtzeit auf seinem Blog *The Spiral* auf *arte.tv*[36] und übernahm als ehemaliger *Warehouse*-Künstler eine Vermittlerrolle zwischen Fiktion und Realität. Es entstand, wie in SoM, eine Ebene der fiktionalisierten Realität. Der fiktive Raum wurde durch die wechselnden TV-Schauplätze, den Blog und die Website *thespiral.eu* mit der Europakarte definiert. Bezüge zum realen Raum ergaben sich durch die realen Standorte der Museen und die scheinbar realen Orte der Kunstwerke auf der Karte. In den echten Museen wurden die Kunstwerke tatsächlich abgehängt und nach deren symbolischer Rückgabe in den Schluss-Events wieder zugänglich gemacht. Die Schluss-Events fanden in Brüssel und fünf weiteren Hauptstädten Europas statt.[37] Durch die kreativen Beiträge aus vielen Nationen entstand ein authentischer europäischer Charakter, der in *The Spiral* spürbar wurde.

Zeitstruktur und Erzählebenen

Die zeitliche Struktur umfasste eine zweiwöchige Pre-TV-Phase und eine vierwöchige TV-Phase mit fünf Episoden und dem Online Game. Die Pre-TV-Phase entwickelte die Storywelt des *Warehouse* mit den Charakteren, in den 45-minütigen TV-Episoden wurde die Handlung linear erzählt. Das Schluss-Event mit dem kollektiven Kunstwerk in Brüssel wurde als Szene in die letzte Folge integriert.

Participation Experience

Die Community konnte die Handlung nicht beeinflussen. Dieser Schwachstelle steht eine hoch entwickelte Participation Culture gegenüber. Der Mediensprung war nicht für die (Re) Konstruktion der Handlung notwendig, sondern für die Teil-

---

36
Vgl. Jean-Baptiste Dumont: The Spiral – Der Blog. Blog auf ARTE.tv (2012).
URL: http://www.arte.tv/sites/de/the-spiral-de/2012/10/02/hector-dhaese-belgischer-geschafts-mann-ist-fur-die-morde-verant-wortlich/ (Stand 25.07.2013).

37
ARTE: Video The Spiral End Event in Brüssel (2012) (wie Anm. 35).

Zahlencodes entschlüsselt, Quellen ausgewertet oder Koordinaten für Geocaches ermittelt. Die Community erstellte ein Wiki und eine umfassende Mindmap, die alle wichtigen Beziehungen zwischen Figuren und Objekten visualisierte und stets aktualisiert wurde. In Live-Interaktionen konnte der Explorer mit den fiktiven Darstellern per Telefon Kontakt aufnehmen, Interviews im Chat führen oder Geocaches finden.

Den TV-Krimi sahen 670.000 Zuschauer (8%), es wurden zwei Millionen Web-Aufrufe und 200.000 Video-Abrufe auf *YouTube* und in der ZDF-Mediathek verzeichnet.[32] Im ARG gab es ca. 1.000 registrierte Spieler und 50 bis 100 aktive Spieler.[33]

The Spiral – ein transmedialer Kunstthriller[34]

Regie: Hans Herbots, Produktion: Caviar Films, Koproduktion von acht europäischen Medienanstalten (VRT, VARA, NRK, Yle, SVT, ARTE France, ARTE Deutschland, TV3 Dänemark)

The Spiral war eine außergewöhnliche europäische Koproduktion. Die TV-Serie mit fünf Episoden wurde zeitgleich in acht europäischen Ländern ausgestrahlt. Das Transmedia Projekt war keine typische Schnitzeljagd mit dem primären Ziel, einen Fall zu lösen. Ziel war vielmehr die kreative Beteiligung der Community und die Schaffung eines kollektiven Kunstwerks – am Ende des Projekts kamen 19.752 Werke aus ganz Europa zusammen.[35]

Story und Storyworld

Der Künstler Arturo inszeniert mit dem jungen Kopenhagener Künstlerkollektiv *The Warehouse* provokante Aktionen gegen den korrupten Kunstmarkt. Arturo plant einen großen Coup mit dem gleichzeitigen Diebstahl von sechs Gemälden berühmter Museen in sechs europäischen Hauptstädten. Nachdem Arturo plötzlich verhaftet wird, ziehen die jungen Künstler den Coup erfolgreich allein durch. Nicht nur die schwedische Polizei ist ihnen auf den Fersen, denn die Bilder gehören mächtigen Investoren. Nachdem Arturo ermordet wird, geht es für alle um Leben und Tod...

Die gestohlenen Gemälde werden von der Gruppe mit GPS-Sensoren ausgestattet, per Post in Europa verteilt und sollen

---

32
Kristian Müller: »DINA FOXX« ein voller Erfolg – Bilanz zum Internet-Krimi im ZDF (2011). URL: http://www.ufa.de/presse/news/?s=/44736/»Dina_Foxx«_ein_voller_Erfolg_-_Bilanz_zum_Internetkrimi_im_ZDF (Stand 25.07.2013).

33
Nach Aussagen des Autors Max Zeitler.

34
ARTE: The Spiral (2012). URL: http://www.arte.tv/de/the-spiral/6835026.html (Stand 25.07.2013).

35
ARTE: Video The Spiral End Event in Brüssel (2012). URL: http://www.youtube.com/watch?v=vrKRiXijeBw#at=160 (Stand 25.07.2013).

Im realen Raum fanden Live-Interaktionen statt, wie z. B. Live-Chat, Telefonanrufe oder Geocaching.

Zeitstruktur und Erzählebenen

Die zeitliche Struktur umfasste eine Pre-TV-Phase und eine Post-TV-Phase von jeweils drei Wochen, dazwischen wurde der TV-Thriller ausgestrahlt. Die Pre-TV-Phase entwickelte die Storywelt mit den Charakteren und Aktionen. Der Blog der Datenschützer stellte die Handlung bis zur plötzlichen Verhaftung als Online Cliffhanger dar. Der 50-minütige TV-Thriller begann im Gefängnis und erzählte die bisherige Handlung in Rückblenden, sodass auch TV-Zuschauer in das Projekt einsteigen konnten. Der Thriller endete am dramaturgischen Höhepunkt: Ein Beweisvideo zeigte die Protagonistin am Tatort. Die Zuschauer wurden durch den ZDF-Off-Sprecher aufgefordert, Dina zu helfen. In der folgenden Post-TV-Phase mussten die Explorer Dinas Unschuld beweisen und den wahren Mörder finden. Dinas Freund Jason fasste alle wichtigen Erkenntnisse auf *Freidaten.org* zusammen.

Participation Experience[31]

In der Pre-TV-Phase erhielt der Explorer im Blog Informationen über die Handlung und konnte Dinas Wohnung interaktiv erforschen: Der Datenschutzraum21 war begehbar und enthüllte per Mausklick Hinweise zur Datensicherheit einzelner Objekte. Am Ende des TV-Krimis begann die interaktive Spurensuche im Netz. Unerfahrene TV-Zuschauer konnten das Online Game in einer Lean Back-Variante, auf dem Blog, mitverfolgen. Für aktive Spieler standen zwei Schwierigkeitsstufen zur Verfügung. Das einfache Spiellevel wurde durch den interaktiven Datenschutzraum realisiert: Wie in einem Click Adventure konnte der Explorer nun permanent neue Spuren zum Fall in Dinas Wohnung entdecken. Das komplexe Spiellevel wurde als ARG mit schwierigen Rätseln realisiert: Viele Spuren fanden sich verteilt im Netz auf *Facebook*, *Twitter*, *Xing*, *MySpace*, *Flickr* und anderen Blogs, deren IP-Adressen oder Zugangscodes zunächst ermittelt oder geknackt werden mussten. Hierzu wurden beispielsweise komplexe Fotos bearbeitet, Bilder ausgewertet,

31
ZDF: Promotion Video (2011) zum TV-Krimi *Wer rettet Dina Foxx?* URL: http://www.zdf.de/Das-kleine-Fernsehspiel/Wer-rettet-Dina-Foxx-13099690.html (Stand 25.07.2013).

28
ZDF: Freidaten.org (2011). Blog
zum TV-Krimi *Wer rettet Dina Foxx?*
URL: http://www.freidaten.org/
(Stand 25.07.2013).

Wer rettet Dina Foxx? – ein Internet-Krimi[28]

Regie: Max Zeitler, Produktion: teamWorx + UFA-Lab, ZDF, 2011

Wer rettet Dina Foxx? verband einen TV-Krimi mit einem Online-Krimi. Das Storyversum wurde als Lean Back-Variante, als Click Adventure und als ARG realisiert. Eine ganzheitliche User Experience war nur möglich, wenn man den Mediensprung vom TV ins Netz vollzog. Die Idee, einen Krimi des ZDF im Internet aufzulösen, ist äußerst mutig. Damit kann *Wer rettet Dina Foxx?* als eines der konsequentesten Transmedia Projekte in Deutschland gelten; entsprechend erhielt es zahlreiche Preise.

Story und Storyworld

Dina Foxx ist als »Datagrrl« Teil der Aktivistengruppe *Freidaten.org*. Diese Gruppe warnt mit diversen Aktionen vor Datenmissbrauch und sinnloser Datenspeicherung. Dinas Freund Vasco arbeitet bei der Firma *Avadata*, die eine Software entwickelt, mit der man seine Spuren im Netz löschen kann. Dina erhält ebenfalls einen Job in dieser Firma, was zum Bruch mit der alten Clique führt. Nachdem Vasco einer heißen Story auf der Spur ist, geschehen merkwürdige Unfälle. Er trennt sich unerwartet von Dina und wird ermordet. Dina beginnt mit eigenen Nachforschungen und findet wichtige Informationen über eine Firma, *QoppaMax*. Plötzlich jedoch wird sie des Mordes an Vasco verdächtigt und von der Polizei verhaftet. Ein Beweisvideo zeigt sie am Tatort...

Hier endet der ZDF-Krimi und wird zum Online-Krimi. Es gelingt den Datenschützern, Dina zu befreien, dennoch muss sie untertauchen. Sie bittet das Forum um Hilfe: Die Explorer sollen Informationen über *QoppaMax* sammeln. Dinas Freund Jason koordiniert die interaktive Schnitzeljagd auf der Website *Freidaten.org*. Die Online Community findet schließlich den wahren Mörder und rettet die Protagonistin.

29
ZDF: Datenschutzraum (2011).
Interaktive Flash-Seite zum
TV-Krimi *Wer rettet Dina Foxx?*
URL: http://xt.zdf.de/datenschutz-
raum/ (Stand 25.07.2013).

30
ZDF: Freidaten.org (2011). Blog
(wie Anm. 28).

Fiktiver und realer Raum

Der fiktive Raum wurde durch den Datenschutzraum[29] und *Freidaten.org*[30] deutlich sichtbar und erfahrbar. Dinas Freund Jason verknüpfte die fiktionale Welt mit der realen Welt des ARG.

Online-Spiel sowie einer unmittelbar anschließenden Radio-phase mit sechs Hörspielen. Die Pre-TV-Phase inszenierte den Übergang in das Jahr 2017 mit den Aktionen von *Apollon*. Die Storyworld und ihre Charaktere wurden in den Blogs von *Apollon* und Johanna sowie durch die Websites von NPC und *Protecta* vorgestellt. Die TV-Episoden entwickelten die lineare Handlung von der Präsentation des Scanners bis zum geplanten Attentat. Die Hörspiele im Radio bildeten eine Fortsetzung der TV-Serie und erzählten die Geschichte einer ereignisreichen Flucht. Insgesamt blieb *Alpha 0.7* mit TV-Episoden und Hörspielen nahe an linearen Erzählstrukturen. In ihnen wurde die primäre Handlung entwickelt. Im Internet wurde die Handlung fragmentarisch erzählt und musste rekonstruiert werden.

Participation Experience

Die Internetdokumente der Pre-TV-Phase waren wie Puzzleteile verknüpft und mussten von der Community über einen Zeitraum von zwei Monaten gesammelt und rekonstruiert werden. Ein ARG war ursprünglich geplant, wurde aber nicht realisiert. Die Blogs enthielten Hintergrundinformationen zur Motivation der Figuren. Wer die Links zu den Webseiten nutzte, konnte die Aktivitäten von *Protecta* und *Apollon* entschlüsseln. Die User Experience konzentriert sich stark auf diese Rekonstruktion der Handlung. Darüber hinaus erhielt der Explorer zahlreiche Informationen zu wissenschaftlichen Themen, zu aktuellen politischen Ereignissen wie etwa den Protest gegen *Stuttgart 21*. Beispielsweise führte ein Link zum Artikel *Der Mensch wird zum Datensatz* [26] von Frank Rieger vom *Chaos Computer Club*. Auf SWR2 wurden Podcasts zur Gehirnforschung und anderen wissenschaftliche Themen gesendet. [27]

Die Participation Experience wird maßgeblich durch die Verbindung von Fiktion und aktuellen Fragestellungen unserer Gesellschaft geprägt. In den Blogs und Foren wurde die Frage diskutiert, wie weit ein Staat gehen darf, um seine Bürger vor Straftätern oder Terroranschlägen zu schützen? Die Links verwiesen darauf, das drohende Zukunftsszenario im Hier und Jetzt der realen Welt zu verhindern.

26
Frank Rieger: Der Mensch wird zum Datensatz (2010). In: faz.net. URL: http://www.faz.net/aktuell/feuilleton/ein-echtzeit-experiment-der-mensch-wird-zum-datensatz-1591336.html (Stand 25.07.2013).

27
SWR: Alpha 0.7 (2010). URL: http://www.alpha07.de/de/media/was-sagt-die-forschung/ (Stand 25.07.2013).

25
SWR: Alpha 0.7 (2010).
URL: http://www.alpha07.de/
(Stand 25.07.2013).

Alpha 0.7 – Der Feind in dir[25]

Autoren: Sebastian Büttner, Oliver Hohengarten, Produktion: Zeitsprung Entertainment, SWR, 2010

Das erste transmediale Projekt in Deutschland war eine Science Fiction-Thriller-Serie in TV, Radio und Internet. *Alpha 0.7* stellte die Frage nach dem Sinn staatlicher Kontrolle und erinnerte an George Orwells *1984*. Die Serie wollte den Explorer für aktuelle Fragen der Sicherheit und persönlichen Freiheit sensibilisieren. Neben der spannenden Fiktion gelangen aktuelle Bezüge zu gesellschaftspolitischen und wissenschaftlichen Themen.

Story und Storyworld

2010 finden sich im Internet einige mysteriöse Meldungen aus dem Jahre 2017. Sie führen zu den Blogs der Aktivistengruppe *Apollon* und von Johanna Berger. Die Blogs zeigen die zukünftige Welt als Überwachungsstaat. Die weitere Handlung spielt im Stuttgart des Jahres 2017. Die Sicherheitsfirma *Protecta* entwickelt zusammen mit dem Pre-Crime-Center NPC des BKA einen Gehirnscanner zur Verbrechensbekämpfung. Einmal ins Gehirn eingepflanzt, dient er in Wirklichkeit zur Manipulation des Trägers. Die Aktivisten von *Apollon* kämpfen gegen den Brainscanner und gegen *Protecta*. Johanna Berger ahnt nicht, dass sie Trägerin des Brainscanners und als *Alpha 0.7* die siebte Versuchsperson eines neurowissenschaftlichen Experiments ist. Sie verliert allmählich die Kontrolle über ihr Leben und beginnt zusammen mit den Aktivisten einen Kampf gegen *Protecta*. Die skrupellosen Drahtzieher wollen Johanna für ein Attentat benutzen...

Fiktiver und realer Raum

Der fiktive Raum der Zukunft entfaltete sich in einem Science Fiction-Szenario in TV und Radio. Der Bezug zum realen Raum der Gegenwart wurde durch aktuelle politische und wissenschaftliche Themen hergestellt. Die Vermittlung beider Welten erfolgte durch die Blogs im Internet.

Zeitstruktur und Erzählebenen

Die zeitliche Struktur umfasste eine zweimonatige Pre-TV-Phase, eine TV-Phase mit sechs Episoden und dem

19
Nani (2011) (wie Anm. 12).

20
Ebd.

21
Rosie Lavan: Participatory drama
blurs truth and fition (2010). In: The
Pixel Report.
URL: http://thepixelreport.
org/2010/08/24/truth-about-mari-
ka/ (Stand 25.07.2013).

22
Promotion Video: The Truth about
Marika (2008) (wie Anm. 11).

23
Nani (2011) (wie Anm. 12).

24
Vgl. Waern; Denward (2009) (wie
Anm. 15).

Conspirare.se und *Ordo Serpentis* wiesen deutlich auf den fiktiven Charakter hin: »Warnung! *Conspirare* ist Teil einer fiktiven Produktion. [...] *Conspirare* hat nur eine Regel – pretend that it is real...«[19] Diese Warnung wurde von vielen Spielern übersehen, die Immersion war bereits zu hoch. Diejenigen, die die Informationen lasen, hielten sich an den Auftrag, den fiktiven Charakter geheimzuhalten. Waern und Denward untersuchten die Game Experience sowie das Story-Verständnis der Handlung und des Slogans »Pretend that it is real!«. Die Rückmeldungen zeigten, dass die Explorer diese Eingangsformel benötigen, um die Geschichte als ARG zu erkennen. Einige verstanden die Formel jedoch als Teil der Story, als eine Verschleierungstaktik von SVT.[20]

Die Partizipation erfolgte in unterschiedlichen Aktivitätslevels: Die Lean Back-Variante ermöglichte die Beobachtung des Projekts in der Talkshow, auf den Webseiten und Blogs. In der Lean Forward-Variante lassen sich vier Spielertypen unterscheiden: Aktive Diskussionsteilnehmer posten ihre Meinung in Blogs, Foren und Chats. Internetträtsel-Spieler knacken Codes und suchen Spuren. Real World-Spieler suchen Hinweise an realen Orten und in realen Medien. Die Content-Produzenten erstellen Mindmaps, Fotos, Videos, etc. und werden damit Teil des Storyversums.

Die TV-Serie sahen 350.000 Zuschauer, die Talkshow 240.000. *Conspirare.se* hatte 490 registrierte User, *Ordo Serpentis* 751.[21]

An einigen Stellen geriet das Verwirrspiel von Fiktion und Realität an seine Grenzen, dennoch wollte ganz Schweden die Wahrheit über Marika und Maria herausfinden – was ist Fiktion, was ist Realität? »Blurring the lines«[22] erhöhte auf der einen Seite die Fiktionalität und die Immersion. Auf der anderen Seite störte die philosophisch-ethische Debatte über die Glaubwürdigkeit der Story und der Medien die Game Experience.[23]

SoM war ein grenzüberschreitendes Medienexperiment – der Medienskandal, den die Produzenten zum Serienstart auslösten, war aber auch eine kalkulierte Marketingstrategie, die den Erfolg des Projekts maßgeblich beeinflusste. Die Frage, ob ein TV-Sender diesen Blurr der Formate für ein wenig Aufmerksamkeit inszenieren darf, wurde heiß diskutiert.[24]

Charakter der Produktion durch einen Disclaimer offengelegt, was jedoch nur 30 Prozent der Nutzer bemerkten.[17]

Zeitstruktur und Erzählebenen

Die Pre-TV-Phase mit der Einführung der Online Storyworld und das ARG starteten fünf Monate vor der TV-Serie mit fünf Episoden (45 min) und fünf Talkshows (15 min).

Insgesamt lassen sich drei Erzählebenen unterscheiden: In der Ebene »Fiktion« erzählt die TV-Serie die Geschichte von Marika. Subliminale Bilder geben dabei Hinweise zur Lösung des ARG. In der Ebene »Fiktionalisierte Realität« diskutieren Schauspieler und echte Personen in der fiktiven Talkshow über reale gesellschaftliche Probleme und die Authentizität der Medien. Die Talkshow verbindet die fiktionale TV-Serie und das ARG. In der Ebene »Real World ARG« gibt es die Erzähl- und Spielplattformen *Conspirare.se*, *Ordo Serpentis*, *Entropia* sowie Aktionen im realen Raum.

Die Website *Conspirare.se* war das Rabbit Hole in das ARG, der Start in die Participation Experience. Hier wurden die Backstory von Maria erzählt und die Verschwörungstheorie über *Ordo Serpentis* in Gang gesetzt. Die Website *Ordo Serpentis* organisierte die Partizipation im Real World ARG mit Live Events. Das Online VR-Game *Entropia Universe*, ein Massively Multiplayer Online Game, trug mit seinem Gameplay maßgeblich zur Immersion bei.

Immersion, Partizipation und kollektive Intelligenz im Real World ARG

Conspirare.se stellte die Brücke für den Explorer von der narrativen in eine spielerische Welt dar. Als Landing Page diskutierte sie die TV-Serie und enthielt erste Hinweise auf das ARG. In *Ordo Serpentis* erhöhte sich die Immersion, die Explorer erhielten »Missions and Tasks«. In zahlreichen Communities entwickelten sie eigene Ideen, tauschten Meinungen aus, produzierten eigenen Content, posteten Fotos und Videos. Wie in allen ARG entwickelte SoM eine Eigendynamik, mit der die Produzenten nicht immer gerechnet hatten und auf die sie spontan reagieren mussten.[18]

17
Ebd.

18
Vgl. Peter Kasza: Transmedia Classics: »The truth about Marika«. A participation drama (2012). URL: http://peterkasza.com/2012/01/the-truth-about-marika/ (Stand 25.07.2013).

14
Vgl. Nani (2011) (wie Anm. 12).

15
Annika Waern; Marie Denward: On the Edge of Reality. Reality Fiction in » Sanningen om Marika« (2009). In: Breaking New Ground. Innovation in Games, Play, Practice and Theory. Proceedings of DiGRA 2009. URL: http://www.digra.org/digital-library/publications/on-the-edge-of-reality-reality-fiction-in-sanningen-om-marika/ (Stand 25.07.2013).

16
Vgl. Nani (2011) (wie Anm. 12).

Story – Fiktion oder Realität? [14]

Der schwedische Sender SVT plant eine fiktive Serie mit fünf Episoden. Die Story handelt von Marika, die am Tag vor ihrer Hochzeit verschwindet. Ihre Freunde begeben sich auf die Suche nach ihr und stoßen auf den Geheimbund *Ordo Serpentis*. Die fiktionale Geschichte wird als wahre Begebenheit angekündigt.

Wenige Monate vor dem Sendetermin beschuldigt die Bloggerin Adrijanna den Sender SVT, die Story von ihrem Blog *Conspirare.se* gestohlen zu haben. *Conspirare.se* enthüllt die wichtige Backstory: Adrijanna verlor in ihrer Kindheit ihre beste Freundin Maria und benutzt nun den Blog für ihre Suche nach ihr. SVT leugnet die Vorwürfe, lässt aber die Produzenten und die Bloggerin am Vorabend der ersten Episode in einer Live-Talkshow zu Wort kommen. Beide Seiten beschuldigen sich gegenseitig der Lüge.

Ein Medienskandal bahnt sich an, alle Medien in Schweden diskutieren den Vorfall. Auf den Webseiten von SVT und *Conspirare.se* werden die Auseinandersetzungen fortgeführt. Die TV-Serie läuft an... Gleichzeitig begeben sich Explorer auf die Suche nach der Wahrheit und tauchen in das ARG ein.

Fiktion und fiktionalisierte Realität[15]

Die vermeintliche Live-Talkshow mit einem bekannten schwedischen Moderator war jedoch inszeniert und vorproduziert. Waern und Denward sprechen von einer »fiktionalisierten Realität«.[16] Unterstützt wurde die Konstruktion durch inszenierte Telefonanrufe und Live-Ticker mit SMS-Nachrichten. Die Talkshow begleitete die TV-Episoden am folgenden Tag. Sie wurde jeweils am Vortag produziert, um die aktuellen Ergebnisse des ARG in die Diskussion miteinzubeziehen. An ihr nahmen Schauspieler in ihren Filmrollen und echte Personen (darunter ein Soziologe, Forensiker, Psychologe) teil. Jede Debatte befasste sich mit gesellschaftlichen Themen, wie soziale Ausgrenzung, Überwachung im öffentlichen Raum, die Arbeit der Polizei oder Verschwörungen. Die TV-Zuschauer ahnten nichts von der Fiktion. Die Webseiten von SVT und *Conspirare.se* führten die Diskussion im Internet weiter. Allerdings wurde hier der fiktive

Verständnis der Handlung oder für die Lösung der initialen Aufgabe, z. B. das Aufdecken einer Verschwörung, zwingend notwendig. Für eine ganzheitliche Experience muss der Explorer den Mediensprung daher aktiv vollziehen. Verschwörungstheorien stellen ein Erfolgsrezept für transmediale Geschichten dar, die von der kollektiven Intelligenz aufgedeckt werden müssen. Dabei sind die Rätsel so komplex, dass sie kaum von einem einzelnen User gelöst werden können: Die Participation Experience entsteht.

Die kollektive Lösung der initialen Aufgabe wird durch zahlreiche Rätsel und Aktionen erschwert. Sie initiiert aber auch die Diskussion aktueller gesellschaftlicher Fragen in den Sozialen Netzwerken. Die Participation Experience wird zum zentralen Konzept des transmedialen Formats. Die kollektiven Aufgaben sind sehr stark von den amerikanischen ARG beeinflusst, während die narrativen Elemente zunächst über traditionelle Medien, insbesondere TV, transportiert werden. Der Anteil des öffentlich-rechtlichen Fernsehens ist erstaunlich hoch. Die Sendeanstalten versuchen, durch diese neuen experimentellen Formate junge Zuschauersegmente zurückzuerobern und den eigenen Sendeanteil in transmedialen Angeboten zu sichern.

Die folgenden Beispiele untersuchen die Participation Experience der wichtigsten europäischen Transmedia Projekte.

Sanningen om Marika

Produzent: Christopher Sandberg, Produktion: The Company P, Sveriges Television SVT, 2007

Die schwedische Produktion *Sanningen om Marika* (SoM) war das erste Transmedia Projekt in Europa und erhielt zahlreiche internationale Preise. In der bemerkenswerten Verschmelzung von Fiktion und Realität konnten viele Explorer die beiden Ebenen kaum noch voneinander trennen. Die Tiefe der Immersion beeinflusste in starkem Maße das Involvement und die User Experience. TV, Online Game und ARG entfalteten im »Participation Drama«[11] eine »Fiction without Limits«[12]. Die verknüpften Story-Ebenen erzählten »a living mystery with powerful philosophical themes«[13].

11
Promotion Video: The Truth about Marika (2008). URL: http://www.thecompanyp.com/site/?page_id=7 (Stand 25.07.2013).

12
Alessandro Nani: Sanningen om Marika. The truth About Marika. A Transmedia Case Study (2011). URL: http://truthaboutmarika.files.wordpress.com/2011/12/the-truth-about-marika.pdf (Stand 25.07.2013).

13
Website von The Company P. URL: http://www.thecompanyp.com/site/?page_id=7 (Stand 25.07.2013).

7
Vgl. Jeffrey Kim; Elan Lee; Timothy Thomas; Caroline Dombrowski: Storytelling in new media. The case of alternate reality games, 2001–2009 (2009). In: First Monday, Band 14, Nummer 6–1 (2009). URL: http://journals.uic.edu/ojs/index.php/fm/article/viewArticle/2484/2199 (Stand 25.07.2013).

8
Jane McGonigal: »This Is Not a Game«. Immersive Aesthetics and Collective Play (2003). URL: http://www.seanstewart.org/beast/mcgonigal/notagame/paper.pdf (Stand 25.07.2013).

9
Elan Lee: This Is Not a Game. Vortrag bei der Game Developers Conference 2002. Convention Center, San Jose, CA. 2002. Zitiert nach McGonigal (2003) (wie Anm. 8). URL: http://www.seanstewart.org/beast/mcgonigal/notagame/paper.pdf (Stand 25.07.2013).

10
Rich Stoehr: Only Solutions (2001). In: Cloudmakers.org: Editorials. URL: http://cloudmakers.org/editorials/rstoehr726.shtml (Stand 25.07.2013).

Quellen. Die Story bildet den Rahmen und Startpunkt, sie wird vom Puppet Master gesteuert und bei Bedarf ad hoc angepasst. Der aktuelle Stand der Handlung wird in Guides, der aktuelle Stand der Informationen im Trail festgehalten. Der Zugang zum ARG erfolgt über ein Rabbit Hole, das die fiktive Welt erschließt (z. B. Postsendung, E-Mail, versteckte Botschaft in einem *YouTube*-Video).[7]

Das erste bekannte ARG, *The Beast*, wurde von der Microsoft Game Group für Steven Spielbergs Kinofilm *A.I.* (dt. *Künstliche Intelligenz*) 2001 entwickelt. Spielberg wollte die Storywelt bereits vor dem Kinostart erlebbar werden lassen. Auf den Filmplakaten, den Trailer Credits und in E-Mails wurden Hinweise versteckt, die zu einem Netzwerk von Webseiten führten, die von sozialen und philosophischen Problemen der fühlenden Roboter im Jahre 2142 handelten. Drei Monate lang folgten die Spieler den Spuren. Nach der ersten Woche hatte die Seite Hunderte von Zugriffen, insgesamt waren es über drei Millionen Zugriffe. Es gründete sich die berühmte Community *Cloudmakers* mit insgesamt 7.500 Mitgliedern. Sie fanden drei Kerngeschichten, Subplots mit 150 Charakteren, 4.000 digitale Texte, Bilder, Videos und Flash Files, der Guide umfasste 130 Seiten. Dabei mussten die Spieler Rätsel lösen, programmieren, übersetzen, hacken und Wissen über Literatur, Geschichte, Kunst, Kryptologie anwenden.[8]

Die Produzenten hatten diesen Erfolg nicht erwartet: »What we quickly learned was that the *Cloudmakers* were a hell of a lot smarter than we are [...] The *Cloudmakers* solved all of these puzzles on the first day.«[9] Nach einem Monat unterbrach die berühmte Einblendung »This is not a Game« eine TV-Werbung zu *A.I.* Das Hineinwirken des ARG in die reale Welt war von Anfang an ein zentrales Konzept: »We need to do something. This isn't just about the death of Evan Chan [character] anymore, this is about our future, all of us.«[10]

Transmedia Projekte in Europa: Participation Experience

In einer konsequenten Weiterentwicklung der ARG erzählen echte Transmedia Projekte eine Geschichte über verteilte Medienplattformen. Der Plattformwechsel ist für das

formulierten Konzepte haben einen maßgeblichen Einfluss auf
die Participation Experience:
Drillability – das tiefe Eintauchen in die Story und deren verbor-
    gene Mysterien;
Multiplicity – die Vielfalt der Charaktere in verschiedenen
    Medien;
Immersion und Worldbuilding – eine fesselnde, komplexe und
    detaillierte Storywelt;
Seriality – die Aufteilung des Storyversums und der Handlung in
    spannende Teile;
Subjectivity – die verschiedenen Blickwinkel auf die Story;
Performance – die Motivation der Fans zum eigenen Handeln
    und für eigene Aktivitäten.

Das Alternate Reality Game

Das Alternate Reality Game (ARG) ist infolge der Konvergenz und Mobilität digitaler Netzwerktechnologien entstanden.
Das Game wird in Echtzeit und gleichzeitig im virtuellen und
realen Raum gespielt. Damit ist das ARG per se ein transmediales
Ereignis. ARG wurden zunächst für große Werbekampagnen
entwickelt; inzwischen gibt es sie auch in der Bildung, aber nur
wenige zur kommerziellen Nutzung. Bekannte Beispiele sind die
Promotion-ARG *The Beast*, 2001 für den Kinofilm *A.I.*, oder *I love
Bees*, 2004 für Coca-Cola+Olympiade. Transmediale Projekte
integrieren häufig ARG, da diese TV, Game und Internet mit dem
realen Raum verbinden können.

In ihren narrativen Storywelten vermischen sich Fiktion und Realität: Der Spieler trifft im Netz auf mysteriöse Ereignisse, deren Echtheit er prüfen muss. Elemente einer fiktiven
Geschichte verweisen auf reale Fakten – im realen Raum wiederum finden sich Spuren zur Lösung eines fiktiven Mysteriums.
Das bekannte Mantra »This is not a Game« ist für Fans das Erkennungsmerkmal des ARG. Es beschreibt das Gefühl der Immersion und das Potential des Hineinwirkens in die reale Welt.

Das ARG setzt eine aktive Community voraus, da die
schwierigen und vielseitigen Rätsel nur gemeinsam bearbeitet
werden können. Ihre Lösung stellt hohe Anforderungen an die
Spieler und erfordert intensive Recherchen in allen möglichen

Medienmix verbindet. Demgegenüber konstruieren die europäischen Transmedia Projekte von Anfang an ein Storyversum
über mehrere Medien. Sie erzählen eine Geschichte, erteilen
Missionen im virtuellen oder realen Raum und müssen durch
die Participation Experience als Ganzes *erfahren* werden.

Was ist Transmedia Storytelling?

Henry Jenkins prägte 2006 den Begriff »Transmedia
Storytelling« (TS): »Transmedia, used by itself, simply means
›across media‹. [...] Transmedia storytelling describes one logic
for thinking about the flow of content across media.«[2] Obwohl
dieser Plattformwechsel immer wieder als charakteristisches
Merkmal des TS genannt wird, formuliert Jenkins die kollektive
Intelligenz als seinen wesentlichsten Bestandteil: »Consumption
has become a collective process – and that's what this book
means by collective intelligence [...].«[3]

Nicoletta Iacobacci betonte 2008 die veränderte
Rolle des Rezipienten: »Content spread across various media
(crossmedia) is no longer satisfying enough, viewers wants
more, they are becoming VUPs and in viewing/using/playing
want to participate, and to a certain extent create, the story
themselves.«[4]

TS setzt die Partizipation der Konsumenten voraus und
macht sie zu »Jägern und Sammlern«, eine wunderbare Analogie
zu den Anfängen des Storytelling: »Transmedia storytelling is
the art of world making. To fully experience any fictional world,
consumers must assume the role of hunters and gatherers,
chasing down bits of the story across media channels, comparing
notes with each other via online discussion groups, and collaboration to ensure that everyone who invests time and effort will
come away with a richer entertainment experience.«[5]

Der Begriff des Zuschauers, selbst des Users wird dieser
komplexen Form der Rezeption nicht mehr gerecht. »User
Experience« oder »Participation Experience« sind passendere
Begriffe für diese Erlebnisse. Nennen wir den User daher in den
folgenden Beispielen »Explorer«.

Jenkins beschrieb 2009 in einem Vortrag am MIT die
Seven Core Concepts of Transmedia Storytelling[6]. Einige der darin

2
Henry Jenkins: Transmedia 202.
Further Reflections (2011).
URL: http://henryjenkins.
org/2011/08/defining_transme-
dia_further_re.html (Stand
25.07.2013).

3
Jenkins (2008), S. 4 (wie Anm. 1).

4
Nicoletta Iacobacci: From cross-
media to transmedia. Thoughts on
the future of entertainment (2008).
URL: http://www.lunchover.
com/2008/05/from-crossmedia.
html (Stand 25.07.2013).

5
Jenkins (2008), S. 21 (wie Anm. 1).

6
Vgl. Henry Jenkins: The Revenge of
the Origami Unicorn. Seven Prin-
ciples of Transmedia Storytelling
(Well, Two Actually. Five More on
Friday) (2009).
URL: http://henryjenkins.
org/2009/12/the_revenge_of_the_
origami_uni.html (Stand
25.07.2013).
Ders.: The Revenge of the Origami
Unicorn. Seven Principles of
Transmedia Storytelling.
Revenge of the Origami Unicorn.
The Remaining Four Principles of
Transmedia Storytelling (2009).
URL: http://henryjenkins.
org/2009/12/revenge_of_the_ori-
gami_unicorn.html (Stand
25.07.2013).

Einführung

»The term *participatory culture* contrasts with older notions of passive media spectatorship. [...], we might now see them as participants who interact with each other according to a new set of rules that none of us fully understands.«[1]

Henry Jenkins

1
Henry Jenkins: Convergence Culture. Where Old and New Media Collide. New York University Press 2008, S. 3.

Wir alle nutzen Internet, Fernsehen (wenn überhaupt), Second Screen und mobile Medien gleichzeitig und nebeneinander in unserer Freizeit. Ohne diese Konvergenz der Medien wäre Transmedia Storytelling in einem Universum fiktiver Geschichten und Spiele kaum denkbar. Das transmediale Erzählen rückt zunehmend in den Fokus der Erzählforschung.

Ich möchte mich hier vor allem einer Frage widmen: Welche Rolle spielt der User/Zuschauer? Wie verändert Transmedia Storytelling sein Verhalten? Beeinflusst auch er selbst die Geschichten? Um die Antwort schon vorwegzunehmen: Es entsteht eine völlig neue Spezies des Rezipienten, für den die alten Begriffe »Zuschauer« und selbst »User« kaum noch taugen.

Damit folge ich dem userzentrierten Ansatz des User Experience Design, den die Erzähltheorie bisher kaum berücksichtigt hat. In User Experience geht es um die ganzheitliche Verknüpfung von Handeln, Fühlen und Denken mit dem Ziel, Erlebnisse zu schaffen. Angewandt auf Narratologie bedeutet dies, dass nicht mehr die Erzählung als Produkt, sondern das zu gestaltende Erlebnis im Zentrum des Gestaltungsprozesses steht. Die User Experience manifestiert sich in den transmedialen Projekten als Participation Experience.

Dieser Beitrag formuliert keine transmediale Erzähltheorie – er zeigt vielmehr in einer pragmatischen Form die Möglichkeiten der Participation Experience anhand europäischer fiktionaler Transmedia Projekte auf.

Transmedia Projekte bilden ein komplexes Storyversum, in dem sich alle Komponenten gegenseitig ergänzen und bedingen. Die amerikanischen Beispiele (z. B. *The Matrix*) ergänzen sich zwar, bleiben aber dennoch eigenständige Medienprodukte in einem crossmedialen Gefüge. Ihr transmedialer Charakter ergibt sich aus den kollektiven Aktivitäten der Fan-Community, die den

Transmedia Storytelling und Participation Experience

Claudia
Söller-Eckert

Michel Reilhac

ist Exekutivdirektor von ARTE France Cinéma und Leiter der Akquisitionen für *Cinema* mit ARTE France. Im Jahr 1998 realisierte er mit *All Alike* seinen ersten Dokumentarfilm. Auf Wunsch von Canal + TV inszenierte er im Jahr 1999 *To be a Man,* und im Jahr 2000 führte er Regie für *Kenia Inseln*. Im gleichen Jahr schuf er *Melange*, eine Film-Produktionsfirma mit Sitz in Frankreich. Er produzierte den Spielfilm *Cry Woman* von der chinesischen Regisseurin Liu Jian Bing *(Un certain regard,* Filmfestival Cannes), *7 Tage, 7 Nächte* vom kubanischen Regisseur Joel Cano und *The Good Old Naughty Days (Directors Fortnight,* Filmfestival Cannes).

Lokal starten, klein beginnen.
Da die meisten interaktiven Erfahrungen mit Geschichten aus verschiedenen erzählenden Komponenten bestehen (ein Film, ein Buch, ein Live-Event, eine App, eine Website, Blogs usw.) und die meisten dieser Komponenten für den User alleine stehen müssen, ist es am besten, schnell damit anzufangen, einige der Komponenten herzustellen, ohne darauf zu warten, bis das gesamte Puzzle, das eine transmediale Geschichte darstellt, komplett entwickelt und finanziert ist. Es können immer Fehler passieren. Daher ist es besser, schnell und klein zu scheitern als langsam und groß. Es hat den Anschein, als seien Testphasen im transmedialen Geschichtenerzählen von essentieller Wichtigkeit.

...

Dies sind nur ein paar meiner gegenwärtigen Ansichten dahingehend, wo wir im Bereich des transmedialen Geschichtenerzählens stehen.

Wenn wir hier weiter unterwegs sind und sich Muster ergeben, werden wir Modelle erstellen und natürlich weiterhin aus unseren Lektionen lernen. Der Bereich ist bis jetzt noch immer ein Bereich für kühne Entdecker und wagemutige Pioniere. Man kann damit noch kein Geld verdienen. Und bislang haben es auch nur wenige Projekte in das Bewusstsein der Öffentlichkeit geschafft. Aber es wird nicht mehr lange dauern, bis dies als eine neue erzählende Erfahrung angenommen wird. Und die Sender, deren Job es ist abzusehen, welche Schritte als Nächstes erforderlich sind, um ihre Zuschauerzahlen beizubehalten oder zu erhöhen, sind bereits auf den Zug aufgesprungen. Obacht vor dem bald kommenden transmedialen Äquivalent zu *Big Brother*, das den überwältigenden Anbruch des Reality-TV gestartet hat.

Fortsetzung folgt...

Die Leute sehnen sich nach einer realen Erfahrung: Zurück zur IRL!

Weil, wie wir gesehen haben, die digitalen Einheimischen nicht von Geburt an von der virtuellen Dimension in ihrem digitalisierten Leben fasziniert sind und sich im Ergebnis nun nach spannenden Erfahrungen in der echten Welt sehnen, müssen wir die IRL in den Wert des Events unserer erzählenden Mischung aufnehmen. Wir müssen erkennen, wie wir das Virtuelle und das Reale in einer Mischung zusammenbringen können, die einen mehrschichtigen Kreislauf durch das Universum der Geschichte zwischen Realität und Fiktion erzeugen kann.

»Für« aufgeben, »mit« erforschen.

Wir müssen progressiv herausfinden, was es wirklich bedeutet, Geschichten *mit* Menschen und *nicht für* sie zu machen. Wie können wir den unbekannten Faktor an Inhalten der Teilnehmer und die Reaktionen auf unsere ansonsten sorgfältig geplante umfassende Welt strukturieren? Wie baut sich eine Gemeinschaft rund um ihre Leidenschaft auf? Wie handhaben wir das Vertrauen zwischen dem Publikum und den Erstellern als einen sich entfaltenden erzählenden Prozess? Was bedeutet es wirklich für einen Autor, wenn wir sagen, dass der wirkliche Inhalt eines transmedialen Projekts der Dialog rund um den Gegenstand ist? Im Bereich Transmedia liegt der letztliche Gewinn nicht in der Finanzierung, sondern darin, vom Publikum angenommen zu werden.

Einfühlungsvermögen stellt sich durch Emotionen ein.

Emotionen sind das, was uns alle verbindet. Man muss den emotionalen Aufhänger finden, der eine Person sofort an eine Geschichte fesselt. Das ist das, was das Geschichtenerzählen ausmacht. Das ist das, was wir damit verbinden müssen. Wir haben uns viel zu sehr auf die transmedialen Funktionsweisen konzentriert. Wir waren fasziniert von den neuen Tools und Möglichkeiten. Nun ist es an der Zeit, sich von dieser Faszination zu lösen und zu dem zurückzugehen, was für eine Geschichte wirklich wichtig ist: Emotionen.

Denn es handelt sich hierbei wohl kaum um Ausbildungsberufe. Sie definieren sich während unserer Erforschung selbst. Ich denke, der beste Weg, das richtige Team zusammenzustellen, ist der, Fachleute in deren Gebieten zu finden, die ein Interesse daran haben, eine neue Herausforderung anzunehmen, und diese zu fragen, wie sie ihren Bereich zukünftig mittels der Eröffnung einer Multiplattform mit Interaktivität erweitern können.

Die andere Herausforderung ist die zu lernen, wie dieses Team arbeitet. Wir müssen mit den gemeinsamen Arbeitstools, die die kreativen Methoden und Prozesse optimieren, experimentieren. Es ist nicht so einfach, wie es zunächst scheint. Die Informationen in Umlauf zu bringen und zu gewährleisten, dass jeder auf dem neuesten Stand ist und zum gegebenen Zeitpunkt an derselben Seite arbeitet, erfordert schon ein bisschen Selbstdisziplin und einen kollektiven Arbeitsfluss.

Man sollte von Schnittstellen begeistert sein.

Auch bei der Planung der verschiedenen Schnittstellen für die vielen kombinierten Aspekte einer Geschichtenwelt (angefangen von einer Homepage bis hin zu einem spezifischen Gerät, einer App, einer stufenweisen Realitätsgesellschaft in der realen Welt, ein Poster...) muss man zusammen mit dem oben Genannten im Hinterkopf behalten, dass diese als Zugang zur Geschichte dienen. Wir müssen lernen, wie man sie in einer ansprechenden, faszinierenden und mitunter witzigen Art und Weise konzipiert, die die Neugier des Betrachters anregt und daher sein Engagement fördert.

Man sollte Spiele mögen.

Wir müssen starke kreative Partnerschaften zwischen den traditionellen Filmemachern und den Spiele-Designern aufbauen. Das Geschichtenerzählen muss zusätzlich zu den Gamification-Techniken, die die Marketingindustrie gerade aufgreift, in das Spielen eingebunden werden. Eine organische und ursprüngliche transmediale Geschichte muss daraufhin befragt werden, in welchem Umfang sie wie ein Spiel sein muss. Die Chancen stehen gut, dass ein Spieleansatz das Engagement des Publikums hinsichtlich der Geschichte fördert.

Kreative Technologen bieten inzwischen die wertschöpfendsten neuen Jobs im kreativen Bereich. Diese müssen wir in unseren Prozess, ein kreatives Team aufzubauen, einbeziehen. Sie können uns dabei helfen, Dienstleistungen, Funktionen und Schnittstellen zu konzipieren, die aus innovativen Tools stammen, die neue betriebliche Modi empfehlen.

Das Erscheinungsbild jedweder Schnittstelle muss so einfach wie möglich konzipiert sein. Jeder muss in der Lage sein, sie bedienen zu können. Jeder muss verstehen können, wie man innerhalb des Services schnell navigiert. Es hat doch niemand die Zeit dafür, sich darin einzuarbeiten, wie die Schnittstellen funktionieren. Darüber hinaus tendieren die aktuellsten erfolgreichen Konzepte in Bezug auf Internetdienstleistungen dahin, so einfach wie möglich zu sein und möglichst wenig Anleitung zu geben.

Aber Einfachheit ist gar nicht so einfach. Um das zu erreichen, müssen wir das, was wir versuchen zu sagen, sorgfältig analysieren: warum wir das sagen wollen, mit wem wir das teilen wollen, wie die diesbezügliche Form aussehen soll usw.

Teams aufbauen.

Wir müssen neue Arten der Zusammenarbeit entwickeln. Eine interaktive Geschichte baut sich durch ein Team verschiedener kreativer Fachleute rund um einen Geschichtenarchitekten auf. Es gibt neue, spezifische Funktionen, die rechtzeitig festgelegt werden müssen, damit für eine Welt interaktiver Geschichten sämtliche Aspekte einer Multiplattform reibungslos und effektiv erstellt und koordiniert werden können. Ich habe letztens bei einem der Projekte, an denen ich aktuell arbeite, einen neuen Bedarf für einen spezifischen Fachmann erkannt (ein Feature-Transmedia-Film), den ich mit »Matrix-Designer« gekennzeichnet habe. Und zwar geht es um einen Redakteur, der die Definitionsgrenzen seiner Arbeit erweitern möchte. Ein komplettes Team sollte über einen Erfahrungsdesigner, einen Geschichtenarchitekten, einen Spieledesigner, einen Publikumsplaner, einen Aktivator für Soziale Netzwerke und Gemeinschaften, einen Monetesierer, einen kreativen Technologen, einen Drehbuchautor, etc. verfügen. Es ist natürlich schwierig, all diese Leute zu finden.

zu verwirklichen. Es ist der Prozess, es geschehen zu lassen, der zur letztlichen Art und Weise der Geschichte wird, die *mit* den Teilnehmern und *nicht für* ein passives Publikum geschrieben wird.

Der gesamte Prozess wird zu einer Konversation zwischen dem Autor / dem Erfahrungsdesigner / dem Geschichtenarchitekten und den jeweiligen Spielern, die sich in der Geschichtenwelt engagieren möchten. Es ist also kein Monolog des Künstlers mehr, das dem Betrachter als fertiges Objekt geliefert wird, das lediglich noch verbraucht werden muss.

Das bedeutet, dass sich im Bereich Transmedia das Marketing und der Vertrieb mit dem ursprünglichen Prozess, mit einer Geschichte eine Erfahrung erleben zu können, vermischt hat. Es geht darum, wie man eine Gemeinschaft aus Einzelnen aufbaut, die sich für die Geschichte, ihren Ansatz, ihren Blickwinkel verantwortlich fühlen, und wie man das Bewusstsein rund um das Projekt zusammen mit dem Prozess selbst, eine Erfahrung mit der Geschichte aufbauen zu können, vorantreiben kann. Das Marketing und der Vertrieb sind also nicht mehr die Methoden, die in Anspruch genommen werden, wenn der Inhalt zur Veröffentlichung bereit ist, sondern eher ein erreichter Bewusstseinszustand, der die gesamte kreative Arbeit mit einem Bewusstsein der Personen, mit denen man diese Konversation betreibt, durchdringt.

Was tun wir als Nächstes?

Wenn sich der Bereich interaktiver Geschichten entwickelt und wir aus unseren ersten Erforschungen und Versuchen lernen, sehe ich neue und spannende Wege, der Kunstform des Geschichtenerzählens als Erfahrung eine neue Form zu verleihen:

Es einfach halten, Technologie unsichtbar machen.

Zugang zu jedwedem Inhalt zu haben, muss intuitiv, flüssig und so einfach wie möglich sein. Die transmedialen Formen im Bereich Geschichtenerzählen dürfen auf keinen Fall langweilig sein. Die heutige Technologie ermöglicht es uns, sämtliche Arten an Software einzubinden, damit es für den User komplett transparent ist.

Das Echte ist zurück, Nischen fragmentieren den Markt.
Jetzt, da die erste Generation digitaler Anwender, die
von Geburt an in einer digitalen, mit dem Internet verbundenen,
interaktiven Umgebung aufgewachsen ist, in die Welt des aktiven
sozialen Lebens eintritt, sehen wir den Beginn der Rückwirkung
im Erscheinungsbild der Sozialen Medien und der rein virtuellen
Interneterfahrungen und -inhalte. Die Menschen möchten lieber
wieder weniger, aber dafür echte Freunde haben. Sie wollen in
der realen Welt Momente außerhalb der Norm erleben, die in jeder
Art unterschiedlich zum täglichen Leben sind (IRL: *im realen
Leben*). Sie wollen Fiktion in der Realität. Sie wollen in die Rolle
einer anderen Person schlüpfen, sie wollen wie Kinder in ihren
fiktiven Reichen spielen, die für einen Moment eine abwechslungsreiche Realität werden.

Die Spielekultur umfasst abwechslungsreiche Reality
Games (ARG), Rollenspiele in Echtzeit (LAPR), Schatzsuchen,
Quest-Spiele... als neue Konzepte, um das Spielen in die Realität
auszuweiten. Und das funktioniert: Die Marketing- und Werbe-
agenturen untersuchen das Erscheinungsbild, das reale Events in
Szene setzt, um ihre Marken zu transportieren. Theaterunter-
nehmen entwickeln Arbeiten rund um die Wahrnehmung eines
umfassenden experimentellen Theaters, in dem sich das Publikum als Schauspieler versuchen kann... Und das kann Transmedia auch.

Relevanz ist der Schlüssel.
Die Wahrnehmung von Relevanz beim Publikum ist der
Schlüssel, ein entsprechendes Engagement anzusteuern. Indem er
sich selbst fragt, »warum« diese bestimmte Geschichte unbedingt
erzählt werden muss, kann ein interaktiver Erzähler klären, mit
»wem« er spricht (und mit wem nicht). Denn es ist doch offensichtlich, dass ein Betrachter nur dann, wenn er der Meinung ist,
der gerade angeschaute Inhalt sei für ihn relevant, in Betracht
zieht, aktiv an der Geschichte, die ihm erzählt wird, teilzunehmen.

Reichweite und Inhalt sind nicht länger getrennt.
Die Erstellung einer Geschichte als Erfahrung konzentriert sich nicht mehr auf das Objekt (den Film), das sie versucht

unsere Geräte. Diese Agilität fördert die Verbreitung transmedialer Dynamiken im Bereich Geschichtenerzählen und die Beschäftigungsmöglichkeiten für die Betrachter. Sie ermöglicht die Transportierbarkeit und das Fließvermögen der chronologischen Erzähl-Events, die sich so entfalten können und für den Betrachter in den jeweiligen Momenten des täglichen Lebens zugänglich sind.

Sämtliche Medien abdecken.

Immer mehr Geräte können immer mehr Dinge. Wir brauchen heute kein GPS mehr, weil das in den meisten Geräten als App integriert ist. Apps multiplizieren sich geradezu. Sie sind von immer mehr Geräten aus zugänglich. Diese Vielseitigkeit, über die viele Schnittstellen verfügen, macht den Zugang zu unterschiedlichen Informationsströmen flüssiger und einfacher in der Handhabung. Die Interaktion zwischen zwei Komponenten, die ein User aktiviert, wird für ihn immer weniger mühevoll, da man nicht mehr von einem Gerät zum anderen wechseln muss.

Die Menschen wollen nicht für alles zahlen.

Die wirtschaftliche Herausforderung, der wir uns in Bezug auf das Internet gegenübersehen, ist die, dass die Öffentlichkeit weltweit der Ansicht ist, dass im Netz alles kostenlos zur Verfügung stehen müsse. Es ist daher sehr schwierig, diese Erwartungshaltung zu verändern und die Menschen zum Bezahlen zu bewegen. Hinsichtlich dieses ernsten Themas für die Hersteller interaktiver Inhalte gibt es inzwischen viele Strategien, die getestet werden: von Mikrozahlungen über Freemium, Werbesupport, zuerst-ausprobieren,-dann-zahlen, Prepaid-Karten für Mitgliedbeiträge, Franchisemöglichkeiten bis hin zu Wiederspielwerten etc.

Die einzige Sache, für die Internet-User Geld ausgeben, liegt außerhalb der normalen Events. Diese werden als die einzigen Möglichkeiten wahrgenommen. Dies bezieht sich im Übrigen auch auf die Art, wie sich die Musikindustrie neu erfunden hat, indem sie Konzerte als das Haupttransportmittel ihrer Dienstleistungen forciert hat.

Leben treten, sind mit Spielen auf elektronischen Geräten jedweder Art aufgewachsen. Spielen ist zu einem Standard geworden. Es wird heute nicht mehr als eine Sache von Kindern angesehen. Die Spielkultur dringt in alles, was wir machen, ein. Alle Aspekte unseres Lebens haben irgendwie mit Spielen zu tun. Spielen ist also etwas, das anzuwenden die Geschichtenerzähler lernen müssen.

Die Spiele selbst werden mehr und mehr mit dem Geschichtenerzählen im Hinterkopf konzipiert. Die Spieleunternehmen beschäftigen Drehbuchautoren, um neuen Spielen, die mehr und mehr von Charakteren leben, Tiefe in der Komplexität und der Emotionalität zu geben.

Spieler sind die treibende Kraft, um ein aktives Beschäftigungsverhalten zu erweitern.

Es gibt bei Spielen keine passiven Betrachter (außer natürlich, man mag es, sich einfach nur anzuschauen, wie ein Spieler spielt). Es gibt hierbei nur aktive Spieler. Denn es passiert nichts, wenn ein Spieler nicht spielt.

Spieler verfügen daher über ein tief verwurzeltes aktives Verhalten allem gegenüber. Sie sind es gewöhnt, in der Spielewelt zu interagieren, Aufgaben zu erfüllen und Ziele zu erreichen. Für sie ist ein Mitwirken absolut normal. Sie verwandeln unseren Passivmodus, einfach nur ein Betrachter zu sein, stufenweise in die Vorstellung, dass es Spaß machen könnte, sich mit einer Geschichte interaktiv zu beschäftigen. Auf der Seite des Publikums sind Spieler die treibende Kraft, wenn es um engagierte Reaktionen beim transmedialen Geschichtenerzählen geht.

Wir alle halten uns auf Multiplattformen auf.

Verschiedene Geräte und diese manchmal sogar gleichzeitig zu verwenden, ist etwas, das für uns heute fast schon normal ist. Wir haben gelernt, gleichzeitig verschiedenen Informationssträngen aus verschiedenen Quellen zu folgen (wir schauen Fernsehen und bedienen gleichzeitig unser Tablet oder Smartphone). Wir wechseln abhängig von der Situation, in der wir uns gerade befinden, von einem Gerät zum anderen. Wir sind immer mobiler. Wo und wann auch immer, wir nutzen

Betrachtungsweise erzeugt. Wenn man einer Geschichte lauscht, einen Film sieht oder ein Buch liest, macht man gleichzeitig nichts anderes. Okay, vielleicht checken Sie Ihre E-Mails, updaten Ihren *Facebook*-Account und chatten mit Ihren Freunden, wenn Sie Fernsehen schauen. Ich weiß. Aber das liegt doch eher daran, dass die Fernsehsender Programme ausstrahlen, auf die Sie sich in der Regel nicht wirklich konzentrieren müssen, oder? Die einzige Interaktion rund um einen Film besteht darin, diesen mit Ihren Freunden bei einem Bier oder im Internet auf einer Filmplattform oder in Ihrem *Facebook*-Account zu besprechen.

Es braucht also ein hohes Maß an Motivation, jemanden aus dem bequemen Modus des passiven Betrachtens herauszuholen und ihn als Teilnehmer der Welt der Geschichten zu gewinnen. Diese Ansteuerung ist für einen Transmedia-Autor heute die wohl größte Herausforderung.

Das Publikum bleibt lieber ein passiver Betrachter.

Wann immer eine interaktive Möglichkeit in Bezug auf Geschichten angeboten wird, reagiert die Mehrheit des Publikums folglich eher nicht und bleibt passiv. Die meisten Menschen wollen nicht dazu eingeladen werden, eine aktive Rolle in einer Erzählung anzunehmen und etwas zu tun, das damit zusammenhängt. Sie möchten sich die Inhalte lieber in der traditionellen Art und Weise anschauen. Nur wenige Menschen sind bereit, sich an Ihrer Geschichte zu beteiligen.

Seien Sie kreativ, um den Wirrwarr im Internet zu durchbrechen.

Der Wettbewerb um Inhalte ist heftig. Es reicht nicht aus, irgendwo im Netz irgendwas zu posten. Die Inhalte, in welcher Form auch, immer müssen dem potentiellen User vor die Nase gehalten werden. Angesichts des heutigen Wirrwarrs im Netz braucht es schon eine Menge guter Ideen, um Ihre Inhalte an der richtigen Stelle zu positionieren.

Gaming ist ein Teil unserer heutigen Standardkultur.

Die Game-Kultur ist die maßgebliche Kultur. Sämtliche jungen Erwachsenen, die heute in ein aktives gesellschaftliches

Transmedia hebt das Fehlen einer Geschichte nicht auf.
Wenn man nichts zu erzählen hat, kann der transmediale Ansatz nicht Relevanz herbeizaubern. Transmedia ist lediglich die Form. Wichtig ist die Geschichte.

Interaktive Angebote und Möglichkeiten für ein echtes Leben oder virtuelle Erfahrungen abseits der täglichen Routine.
Der transmediale Ansatz des Geschichtenerzählens hebt den Aspekt im Geschichtenerzählen hervor, eine Erfahrung abseits der Routine machen zu können. Wenn wir in Betracht ziehen, dass Transmedia dem Betrachter die Möglichkeit gibt, durch die physische Teilnahme (allein dadurch, dass man die Finger auf der Tastatur bewegt, um über das Internet zu interagieren) in die Welt der Geschichte eintauchen zu können, sehen wir, wie dies den traditionellen Konsens des passiven Betrachtens aufbricht.

Es ist schon eine Herausforderung, das Engagement des passiven Publikums anzusteuern.
Es gibt natürlich viele Abstufungen hinsichtlich des Engagements einer Person, in eine Geschichte einzutauchen. Aber die wohl größte Herausforderung, die ein Autor beim Aufbau einer interaktiven Geschichte in einer realen oder virtuellen Welt annehmen muss, ist, beim Betrachter das Bedürfnis auszulösen, eintauchen zu wollen. Es ist jedoch nicht so einfach, die Zielgruppe von ihrem gemütlichen Sofa hochzulocken, von dem aus sie sich Filme im Fernsehen oder über den Computer anschaut und Dinge macht, die sich auf die Geschichte, die sie gerade sieht, beziehen. Nichts zu tun und einfach nur einen Film anzuschauen, ist eine sehr angenehme Art, die Alltagsprobleme hinter sich zu lassen. In die Welt einer anderen Person einzutauchen, wird als notwendig und als willkommene Flucht aus dem Alltag mit all seinen Verantwortungen in der physischen Realität wahrgenommen. Die Vorstellung der Flucht, die die Geschichten in welcher Form auch immer enthalten, hat in unseren anerkannten kulturellen Verhaltensmustern strukturell die Vorstellung einer passiven

**Das Geschichtenerzählen hat eine
jahrhundertealte Tradition.**

Das Transportmittel, das wir, um diese Bedürfnisse zu
befriedigen, Jahrhunderte zuvor erfunden haben, ist die
Geschichte. Es begann mit Händen und Abdrücken, die sich auf
den Wänden prähistorischer Höhlen befinden. Ihnen folgten
erste Versuche, Tiere und Menschen auf diesen Wänden abzubilden. Religionen haben sich als allumfassende Metageschich-
ten aufgebaut. Troubadoure, Minnesänger, Griot-Erzähler in
Afrika und sämtliche Großmütter auf der Welt erfanden die
Kunst der mündlichen Erzählung. Legenden, Mythen, Märchen
wurden aufgeschrieben, um einen Zugang zu den zauberhaften
Dimensionen in unserer Wahrnehmung der Welt zu schaffen.
Dann kamen das Radio und die Kinos auf. Ihnen folgte das
Fernsehen. Es werden immer noch Bücher geschrieben. Auch
um die Lagerfeuer herum erzählt man sich nach wie vor
Geschichten. Aber die audiovisuelle Methode stellt – obwohl sie
nach wie vor die gleichen, oben genannten Bedürfnisse erfüllt
– die maßgebliche und modernste Art des Geschichtenerzählens
dar. Es verhält sich so, dass es sich beim Filmemachen oder
Drehbuchschreiben um die wohl dominanteste Form, die die
alte Kunst des Geschichtenerzählens heute angenommen hat,
handelt. Denn Filmemacher und Drehbuchautoren sind zualler-
erst einmal Geschichtenerzähler, die die Fackel, die ihnen ihre
primitiveren Vorgängern seit Anbeginn der Menschheit überreicht haben, weitertragen.

**Die Geschichte ist das Bedürfnis im Herzen
jeder Form, die das Geschichtenerzählen annehmen
kann – einschließlich Trandmedia.**

Und nun formt sich eine neue, erweiterte Form des
Geschichtenerzählens im audiovisuellen Bereich: das interaktive
Geschichtenerzählen. Die wohl zeitgenössischste Form der alten
Kunst erzeugt umfassende, teilnehmende und interaktive Wege,
Sounds, Bilder und Erfahrungen aus dem echten Leben zu
nutzen, um uns Geschichten zu erzählen und sie möglicherweise
sogar zusammen aufzubauen. Die Geschichte ist das, was zählt.
Nicht die Technologie.

Tablets,...), die wir nutzen, die Technologien, die immer wieder neue Geräte und Funktionen herausbringen, von denen wir noch nicht einmal wussten, dass wir sie brauchen. All das sind nur Spielereien, Objekte. Sie können noch so durchdacht und leistungsstark sein. Trotzdem sind sie nichts weiter als Instrumente, die uns heute zur Verfügung stehen. Wir müssen lernen, die Möglichkeiten, die sie uns bieten, zu meistern. Wir müssen Wege finden, das, wofür sie ursprünglich geplant waren, umzudrehen und zweckzuentfremden, um sie in komplett neue Verwendungsweisen zu entführen.

Geschichten werden immer gelesen.
Auch das interaktive Geschichtenerzählen konzentriert sich – egal, in welcher Form – noch immer auf die Geschichte selbst. Seit jeher dient sie, seit der Mensch in der Lage ist, seine Gedanken mitzuteilen, ein und demselben Zweck:

- Flucht aus der Realität;
- der Beantwortung des existentiellen Mysteriums, warum wir alle hier auf der Welt leben;
- unsere Ignoranz mit der Frage zu konfrontieren, warum wir sterben und was nach dem Tod passiert;
- die schönsten und bewegendsten Momente unseres Lebens mit anderen zu teilen;
- einen sozialen Zusammenhalt und eine gemeinsame Kultur aufzubauen, die dem Einzelnen dabei hilft, einen Sinn für Zusammengehörigkeit zu entwickeln;
- unsere Beziehungen hinsichtlich der Vergangenheit, der Gegenwart und der Zukunft miteinander zu verweben, um zu versuchen, Aufzeichnungen für die nächsten Generationen zu hinterlassen, oder um einschätzen zu können, was die Zukunft für uns bereithält;
- die Möglichkeit zu schaffen, durch die Vorstellungskraft jemand anderes als wir selbst sein und in ein virtuelles Leben schlüpfen zu können;
- und so weiter und so fort...

Multiplattformen und ein umfassendes Geschichtenerzählen sind Dinge, die gerade in Schwung kommen. Sämtliche
Sender und Produzenten sprechen (zumindest in meinen Gesprä-
chen mit ihnen…) darüber, wie sie den zweiten Screen in ihre
Programme aufnehmen könnten. Sie alle suchen nach Möglichkeiten, den Verkehr in den Sozialen Medien zu kapitalisieren und
zu monetisieren. Das Internet ist das neue Eldorado, und das
geistige Eigentum ist das neue Gold. Der Trend geht dahin, von
Geschichten für einen passiven Betrachter zu Erfahrungen, die für
einen aktiven Teilnehmer gedacht sind, umzuschalten. Die
Möglichkeiten des interaktiven Geschichtenerzählens zu erforschen, kommt dem Betreten eines jungfräulichen Landes gleich,
in dem wir noch nichts kennen und nicht wissen, wie wir die
Dinge, die die Leute wirklich haben wollen, handhaben sollen, in
dem es keine Modelle gibt, keine seriöse Finanzierung, kein
zuverlässiges Feedback aus bereits durchgeführten Projekten, das
uns dabei helfen würde, das einschätzen zu können, was wir da
gerade versuchen. Ein Dschungel für Entdecker und Pioniere.
Händler, die in Ihrem Rücken lauern, die bereit sind, als Erste auf
den Zug aufzuspringen, den sie als die nächste potentielle gewaltige Möglichkeit für ein profitables Medieninvestment betrachten: Transmedia ist wie interaktiv Geschichten zu erzählen…

Was wissen wir bislang?

Obwohl wir die Formen, die ein interaktives Geschichtenerzählen annehmen kann, gerade noch erfinden, gibt es doch
schon einige Lektionen, die wir aus unseren Fehlern lernen
mussten. Im Übrigen: Wenn ich »wir« sage, schließe ich mich in
die wachsende internationale Gemeinschaft interaktiver,
umfassender und teilnehmender Erzähler mit ein, die versuchen,
die Art, Geschichten zu erzählen, in eine aktive Erfahrung für
den Betrachter/Teilnehmer umzuwandeln.

Hier folgt eine Liste einiger Dinge, die wir heute wissen
und die uns dabei helfen können, den Bereich weiter zu erforschen:

Es geht nicht um die Tools.

Wir müssen aufhören, die Tools faszinierend zu finden.
Die Gimmicks, die Gadgets, die Spielereien (wie Smartphones,

Einen Gang hochschalten. Wo stehen wir hinsichtlich des aktuellen Aufkommens des interaktiven Geschichten- erzählens?

Michel Reilhac

Abb. 1

Abb. 2

Abb. 3

Abb. 4

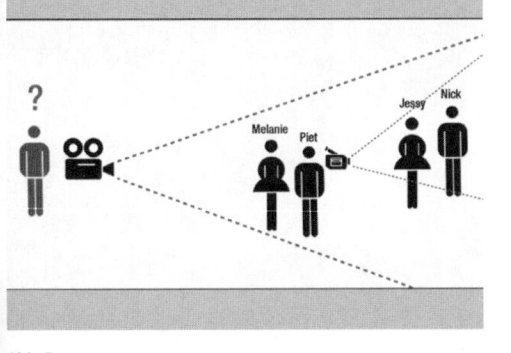

Abb. 5

Markus Kuhn
ist Juniorprofessor für Medienwissenschaft am Institut für Medien und Kommunikation der Universität Hamburg. Er hat Germanistik, Medienkultur, Kunstgeschichte und Publizistik in Göttingen und Hamburg studiert und als freier Journalist für verschiedene Print- und Onlinemedien gearbeitet. Seine Dissertation *Filmnarratologie. Ein erzähltheoretisches Analysemodell* (Publikation 2011) wurde mit dem Absolventenpreis der Studienstiftung Hamburg ausgezeichnet. Publikationen: *Filmwissenschaftliche Genreanalyse. Eine Einführung* (2013). *Film, Text, Kultur: Beiträge zur Textualität des Films* (2013). Hrsg. zusammen mit J. A. Bateman und M. Kepser.

Frank Patalong: Nur falsch ist wirklich echt. In: SPIEGEL ONLINE (11.9.2006). URL:
http://www.spiegel.de/netzwelt/web/0,1518,436070,00.html (Stand: 30.07.2013).
Jane Roscoe; Craig Hight: Faking It. Mock-Documentary and the Subversion of
Factuality. Manchester 2001.
Julia Schumacher: Jugendfilm. In: Markus Kuhn; Irina Scheidgen; Nicola Valeska Weber
(Hg.): Filmwissenschaftliche Genreanalyse. Eine Einführung, Berlin/Boston:
2013, S. 295–313.
Roberto Simanowski: Digitale Medien in der Erlebnisgesellschaft. Kultur – Kunst –
Utopien. Reinbek bei Hamburg 2008.

Medienverzeichnis

Webserien[30]

52 Monologe (D 2011, Filmebene, 52monologe.de).
90sechzig90 (D 2000, United Vision/T-Online, 90sechzig90.de).
Borscht – Einsatz in Neukölln (D 2001, Safran Films, borscht.de).
Deer Lucy (D 2009, MME Me, Myself & Eye Entertainment, BILD.de)
Eine wie keine – So Isses! (D 2009, Grundy UFA TV Produktion/Phoenix Film, Sat1.de).
Epicsode (D 2010, Hochschule Offenburg, epicsode.de).
Die Essenz des Guten (D 2011, UFA Lab/Das Kind mit der goldenen Jacke, 3min).
Flusstouristen (D 2010, 1AVista Reisen, YouTube).
Die Hütte (CH 2010, Zürcher Hochschule der Künste, Frischfilm).
lonelygirl15 (USA 2006–2008, EQAL, YouTube).
Lost: Missing Pieces (USA 2007–2008, ABC Studios, Website von ABC
[abc.go.com/shows/lost]).
Making of Süße Stuten 7 (D 2010, Vice Productions, 3min).
Moabit Vice (D 2008, Vice Productions, moabit-vice.de).
Nurse Jeffrey: Bitch Tapes (USA 2010, Retrofit Films, zunächst exklusiv über *App*
[als sog. *appisodes*], später auch auf der Webseite von Fox
[fox.com/house/inhouse/#type:jeffrey]).
Pietshow (D 2008, Grundy UFA, studiVZ).
Prenzlbasher (D 2009, Filter Filmproduktion, Myspace).
Preußisch Gangstar (D 2008, Fortuna Film, Myspace).
Prom Queen (USA 2007 u. 2010, Vuguru, Myspace; 1. Staffel 2007: 80 Folgen;
2. Staffel (*Prom Queen: Summer Heat*) 2007: 15 Folgen; 3. Staffel
(*Prom Queen: The Homecoming*) 2010: 22 Folgen).
SamHas7Friends (USA 2006, Big Fantastic, YouTube).
Sex and Zaziki (D 2008, U-Film Produktions GmbH, YouTube).
Die Snobs (D 2010, Ulmen Television/ZDFneo, 3min).
SPPD: Die Sau ist tot (D 2009, Studio Seidel, sppd.tv).
Studis 4.0 (D 2010, Gropperfilm, Webseite des Darmtstädter Echo).
They call us Candy Girls (D 2008, MME Me, Myself & Eye Entertainment, Myspace).
Tokyo Prom Queen (J 2008–2009, Regie: Futoshi Sato, Mixi) [Link zur ersten
Folge bei YouTube: http://www.youtube.com/watch?v=pAJ7HtqW6G0;
Zugriff am 17.07.2011].

Fernsehserien

Eine wie keine (Produzenten: Guido Reinhardt/Rainer Wemcken/
Markus Brunnemann, D 2009–2010).
House M.D. (*Dr. House*; Entwickler: David Shore, USA 2004ff.).
Lost (Entwickler: J.J. Abrams/Jeffrey Lieber/Damon Lindelof, USA 2004–2010).
Miami Vice (Entwickler: Anthony Yerkovich, USA 1984–1990).

Filme

Not Another Teen Movie (*Nicht noch ein Teenie-Film!*; Joel Gallen, USA 2001).
Pretty in Pink (Howard Deutch, USA 1986).
She's All That (*Eine wie keine*; Robert Iscove, USA 1999).
The Truman Show (*Die Truman Show*; Peter Weir, USA 1998).

30
Im Weiteren folgen auf den Titel der jeweiligen Webserie in Klammern die Angabe zum Produktionsland und Jahr der Erstveröffentlichung, die Produktionsfirma bzw. der (das) Produzent(en-Team)/der Produktionskontext sowie der Ort der Erstveröffentlichung. Einige der genannten Webserien sind nicht mehr auf den Portalen ihrer Erstveröffentlichung zu sehen, einige zurzeit nicht im Netz zu finden. Ein »ff.« hinter der Jahreszahl einer Web- oder Fernsehserie bedeutet, dass die Serie (voraussichtlich) noch nicht abgeschlossen ist.

Literaturverzeichnis

Jean Burgess; Joshua Green: YouTube: Online Video and Participatory Culture. Cambridge; Malden 2009.

Jean Burgess; Joshua Green: The Entrepreneurial Vlogger. Participatory Culture Beyond the Professional-Amateur Divide. In: Pelle Snickars; Patrick Vonderau (Hg.): The YouTube Reader. Stockholm 2009, S. 89–107.

Glen Creeber: Online-Serien. Intime Begegnungen der dritten Art. In: Robert Blanchet; Kristina Köhler; Tereza Smid; Julia Zutavern (Hg.): Serielle Formen. Von den frühen Film-Serials zu aktuellen Quality-TV- und Onlineserien. Marburg 2011, S. 377–396.

Joshua Davis: The Secret World of Lonelygirl: How a 19-year-old actress and a few struggling Web filmmakers took on TV. A Wired exclusive. In: Wired 14 (2006), S. 232–239. URL: http://www.wired.com/wired/archive/14.12/lonelygirl.html (Stand: 30.07.2013).

Gunther Eschke; Rudolf Bohne: Bleiben Sie dran! Dramaturgie von TV-Serien. Konstanz 2010.

James Hay; Stephen Bailey: Cinema and the Premises of Youth: ›Teen Films‹ and Their Sites in the 1980s and 1990s. In: Steve Neale (Hg.): Genre and Contemporary Hollywood. London 2002, S. 218–235.

Jan Henne; Markus Kuhn: Die deutsche Webserien-Landschaft. Eine Übersicht. In: Jens Eder; Hans Jürgen Wulff (Hg.): Medienwissenschaft/Hamburg: Berichte und Papiere 127 (2011). URL: http://www1.uni-hamburg.de/Medien/berichte/arbeiten/0127_11.html (Stand: 30.07.2013).

Markus Kuhn: Medienreflexives filmisches Erzählen im Internet. Die Webserie Pietshow. In: Rabbit Eye – Zeitschrift für Filmforschung 1 (2010), S. 19–40. URL: http://www.rabbiteye.de/2010/1/kuhn_erzaehlen_im_internet.pdf (Stand: 30.07.2013).

Markus Kuhn: Filmnarratologie. Ein erzähltheoretisches Analysemodell. Berlin/New York 2011 [als Paperback: Berlin/Boston 2013].

Markus Kuhn: YouTube als Loopingbahn. lonelygirl15 als Phänomen und Symptom der Erfolgsinitiation von YouTube. In: Julia Schumacher; Andreas Stuhlmann (Hg.): Videoportale: Broadcast Yourself? Versprechen und Enttäuschung. Hamburger Hefte zur Medienkultur 12 (2011), S. 119–136. URL: http://www.slm.uni-hamburg.de/imk/HamburgerHefte/hamburgerhefte.html (Stand: 30.07.2013).

Markus Kuhn: Zwischen Kunst, Kommerz und Lokalkolorit. Der Einfluss der Medienumgebung auf die narrative Struktur von Webserien und Ansätze zu einer Klassifizierung. In: Ansgar Nünning; Jan Rupp; Rebecca Hagelmoser; Jonas Ivo Meyer (Hg.): Narrative Genres im Internet. Theoretische Bezugsrahmen, Mediengattungstypologie und Funktionen. Trier 2012, S. 51–92.

Markus Kuhn (Hg.): Webserien-Blog. Webserien, Online-Serien, Webisodes, Websoaps und Mobisodes in Deutschland (2012) [die erste Version (August 2012) wurde gemeinsam mit Jan Henne erstellt, unter Mitarbeit von Johannes Noldt und Stella Schaller]. URL: http://webserie.blogspot.de/ (Stand: 30.07.2013).

Markus Kuhn: Das narrative Potenzial der Handkamera. Zur Funktionalisierung von Handkameraeffekten in Spielfilmen und fiktionalen Filmclips im Internet. In: DIEGESIS. Interdisziplinäres E-Journal für Erzählforschung 2.1 (2013), S. 92–114. URL: https://www.diegesis.uni-wuppertal.de/index.php/diegesis/article/download/127/149 (Stand: 30.07.2013).

Markus Kuhn: Der Einfluss medialer Rahmungen auf das Spiel mit Genrekonventionen. Die Webserie Prom Queen als Transformation des Highschool-Films im Internet. In: Jennifer Henke; Magdalena Krakowski; Benjamin Moldenhauer; Oliver Schmidt (Hg.): Hollywood Reloaded. Genrewandel und Medienerfahrung nach der Jahrtausendwende. Marburg 2013 [im Druck].

Barbara Munker: Die Enttarnung von Lonelygirl15. In: stern.de (14.9.2006). URL: http://www.stern.de/computertechnik/internet/570087.html?nv=cb (Stand: 30.07.2013).

Beispiel einen Weg in Richtung Fanartikel, Sponsoring, Product Placement und Werbung auf den veröffentlichenden Portalen. Auch auf diesem Feld bieten Webserien noch Steigerungspotential. Sie können Lebensgefühle unmittelbarer mit Markenprodukten zusammenbringen als Kinofilme und TV-Serien, u.a. weil es auf dem Feld kommerzieller Webserien (noch) keine klar definierten Verbote hinsichtlich Product Placement und Schleichwerbung gibt. Sie können sogar – wie die jugendorientierte Webserie *Deer Lucy* (D 2009) – die kommerziellen Produkte, die sie repräsentieren, im verlinkten Online Shop in genau dem Moment anbieten, in dem sie das erste Mal auftauchen, sowie Produkte der Sponsoren fest in den fiktionalen Kosmos integrieren.

Und die Zukunft? Die Kommerzialisierung und Professionalisierung der Webserienproduktion einerseits, die Schwierigkeit, ambitionierte semiprofessionelle Projekte zu finanzieren, andererseits könnten dazu führen, dass eine Beschränkung der Produktion auf wenige erfolgreiche Muster eine Einschränkung der Vielfalt nach sich zieht. Demgegenüber stehen das große experimentierfreudige und kreative Potential vor allem semiprofessioneller und privater Serienproduzenten sowie ein gewisser Pioniergeist auf dem vergleichsweise noch immer sehr jungen Feld professioneller Webserienproduktionen. Das Einbeziehen von Webserien in große transmediale Erzählkosmen ist ein drittes großes Feld, auf dem viel Dynamik zu erwarten ist. Inwiefern serielles ›Quality-TV‹ auch für das Netz produziert werden wird, wie es die Entwicklungen rund um den US-Anbieter *Netflix* erwarten lassen, bleibt abzuwarten und wirft wiederum die Frage auf, ob Webserien und Fernsehserien zunehmend konvergieren werden. Nicht zuletzt handelt es sich bei Webserien um eine mediale Erzählform mit einer jungen Zielgruppe, die eine hohe Affinität zum Internet hat, die also sowohl von großem Interesse für kommerzielle Akteure wie Markenanbieter ist als auch selbst zunehmend professioneller agierende Akteure hervorbringen wird. Die zukünftige Entwicklung verspricht also, so oder so, höchst dynamisch und spannend zu bleiben.

oder *SPPD: Die Sau ist tot* (D 2009) weisen Spuren ihrer lokalen Rahmung auf. So wird in *Prenzlbasher* die Gentrifizierung des Stadtteils Berlin-Prenzlauer Berg explizit thematisiert, so prägen stadtteiltypische Handlungsorte und Figuren die Episoden von *SPPD* (Hamburg-St. Pauli). *Moabit Vice* (D 2008) bewegt sich, wie der Titel andeutet, zwischen intermedialen Verweisen auf die 1980er-Fernsehserie *Miami Vice* (USA 1984–1990) und einer lokalen Verankerung in Berlin-Moabit.

Ebenfalls nicht thematisiert werden konnten *pseudo-dokumentarische Webserien*.[26] Pseudo-authentische Webserien sind zwar mit pseudo-dokumentarischen Webserien wie *Making of Süße Stuten 7, Flusstouristen, Prenzlbasher* und *Preußisch Gangstar* (D 2008) vergleichbar, unterscheiden sich aber dadurch, dass Erstere den Anstrich einer medialen Selbstdarstellung haben, letztere den einer Dokumentation, die eine andere Person, eine Sache oder ein abstraktes Thema in den Mittelpunkt rückt. Pseudo-authentische Webserien spielen mit Formen der Selbstdarstellung in Video-blogs, pseudo-dokumentarische mit dokumentarischen Formen, vor allem auch aus Film und Fernsehen. Der Einsatz leichter digitaler Kameras bzw. deren Spuren in der Werkästhetik (*Handka-meraeffekte*[27]) sind jedoch häufig vergleichbar.

Durch die Einbettung in das Social Web waren die Webserien *Pietshow* und *Prom Queen* interaktiv – zumindest wenn man die Möglichkeiten, in begleitenden Foren, durch die Kommentar-Funktion des Portals oder auf *studiVZ, Myspace* und *Facebook* zu kommentieren und ›mitzurätseln‹, als interaktive Momente auffasst. Eine komplexere Dimension der Interaktivität ergibt sich auf einer Videoplattform wie *YouTube*, auf der private und professionelle Clips aufeinandertreffen: *Lonelygirl15* z.B. hat durch ihre spezifischen Strukturen viele andere User dazu angeregt, über die vielfache Kommentierung der Clips hinaus an verschiedensten Stellen kommentierende, ergänzende und persiflierende *YouTube*-Filmbeiträge als Antwortvideos zu posten.[28] *Lonelygirl15* kann deshalb nicht nur als stilbildend für pseudo-authentische Webserien gelten, sondern auch für *interaktive Webserien*.[29]

Bleibt die Frage der Monetarisierung: Wie lässt sich mit Webserien Geld verdienen? *Prom Queen* weist als erfolgreiches

---

26
Ich wähle hier den Begriff der *pseudo-dokumentarischen Webserie* und nicht den der *Mockumentary-Webserie*, weil die Produzenten pseudo-dokumentarischer Webserien teilweise nicht an einer aktiven Täuschung interessiert sind, sondern die Produktionsbedingungen und/oder den Grenzgang zwischen Fiktion und Dokumentation offenlegen. Zu Mockumentaries vgl. Roscoe; Hight (2001, wie Anm. 16).

27
Vgl. Kuhn, Das narrative Potenzial (2013; wie Anm. 24).

28
Vgl. Kuhn, YouTube (2011; wie Anm. 1).

29
Lonelygirl15 enthält zwar Strukturen, die zur Interaktion anregen und zur Anbindung einer User Community führen können, funktioniert aber auch ohne diese Begleiterscheinungen als ein abgeschlossenes Werk. Ein Projekt, das über diese Grenze hinausweist, ist die deutsche Webserie *Epicsode* (D 2010), die den Rezipienten bis zu einem gewissen Grad dazu zwingt mitzumachen, so er/sie weitere Folgen der Serie sehen will, vgl. Kuhn, Zwischen Kunst (2012), S. 76 (wie Anm. 1).

lesen, die sich ›in Wahrheit‹ hinter Piets Projekt verbirgt. Piet wäre also eine Art in der Serienwelt gefangener Truman Burbank (vgl. *The Truman Show*, USA 1998). Die diegetische Welt der Figuren wird zunehmend von jenseits dieser Welt anzunehmenden Produktionsinstanzen und Gegenständen durchdrungen. So markiert *Pietshow* einen Serientypus, der sich sowohl von erkennbar fiktionalen Serien wie *Prom Queen* als auch von pseudo-authentischen Serien wie *lonelygirl15* abgrenzen lässt. Das Spezifische bei *Pietshow* ist, dass die Drehbedingungen der Webserie selbstreflexiv thematisiert werden, sowohl auf Handlungsebene als auch durch die formale Struktur. Letztlich reflektiert *Pietshow* durch die beschriebene ›Doppelstruktur‹ sowohl die Produktion einer *semi*professionellen Webserie (durch das Aufbauen der Illusion, die *Pietshow* sei Piets eigenes Projekt) als auch zugleich einer professionellen Produktion (durch das Enttarnen der professionellen Produktionsumstände dahinter). Eine Dominanz des Pseudo-Authentischen besteht allerdings dadurch, dass die übergeordnete Ebene der professionellen Produktion nicht als eigenständige diegetische Ebene gestaltet wird, sondern in der ersten Staffel nur angedeutet bleibt. Der Unterschied der Bindung von *Pietshow* an ein Portal des Social Web zu der von z. B. *Prom Queen*: Dort ist die Serie zwar über die Figuren an das Portal *Myspace* gebunden, die Serie selbst enthält aber kaum Spuren der werkexternen Existenz der Figuren. Bei *Pietshow* ist die Serie als ein Produkt fingiert, das der *studiVZ*-User Piet angeblich selbst bei *studiVZ* eingestellt hat, wo *Pietshow* tatsächlich zuerst gelaufen ist, was dauerhaft innerhalb der Serie reflektiert wird.

5. Fazit

Es hat sich gezeigt, dass Webserien mit Genremustern aus Film und Fernsehen spielen, dass die mediale Einbettung Einfluss auf die Transformation der Genremuster hat und dass es, abhängig von der Einbettung der Webserien in mediale Kontexte, unterschiedliche Typen von Webserien gibt. Nicht gezeigt werden konnte hier ein weiterer Aspekt, der in gewisser Hinsicht einen Gegenpol zu den medialen Kontexten bildet, und zwar die lokale Einbettung von Webserien. Viele deutsche Webserien wie *Studis 4.0* (D 2010), *Sex and Zaziki* (D 2008), *Prenzlbasher* (D 2009)

Figuren der Handlung zuschreibt. Piet, der als Filmstudent etabliert wird, arbeitet an einem Filmprojekt für das Social Network *studiVZ*: Er filmt die Mitglieder seiner WG, bearbeitet die Clips auf seinem PC und behauptet, sie bei *studiVZ* ins Netz zu stellen. Da Piet mehrfach beim Bearbeiten des zuvor gefilmten Materials gezeigt (Abb. 4) und das Filmprojekt in den Dialogen thematisiert wird, ist *Pietshow* sehr selbst- und medienreflexiv. In der zweiten Folge charakterisiert Piet die vier (angeblich zufällig) an dem Projekt Beteiligten begeistert als »die typischen Serienfiguren«: Jessy, »die Sexbombe mit dem großen Mund«; Melanie, »die Zicke, die frigide ist«; Nick, »der gutaussehende Langweiler«; Piet selbst, »die coole Sau, der Master«.

Auch wenn sich die ›einfachen‹ Brüche mit der Authentizität durch Montagen und Nachvertonungen also Piet und seinem Projekt zuschreiben lassen, können andere Sequenzen so nicht erklärt werden. Das betrifft Sequenzen, in denen Piet beim Filmen mit der Kamera zu sehen ist. Wenn es sich dabei zugleich um Einstellungen handelt, auf denen alle vier WG-Mitglieder zu sehen sind, gibt es innerhalb der Diegese niemanden, der eine weitere Kamera halten könnte. Weil diese Einstellungen verwackelt sind, kann die Kamera nicht auf einen Gegenstand gelegt worden sein. Hierdurch entsteht eine Spannung, die nicht unmittelbar aufzulösen ist (Abb. 5). Eine weitere Gruppe an Stilmitteln, die mit der Illusion brechen, dass Piet für die Serie verantwortlich sein könnte, verweist darüber hinaus auf eine Instanz, die jenseits der gezeigten Figuren steht, sodass sukzessive eine Metaebene etabliert wird, die als neue Erklärungsvariante dienen könnte. Um nur einige dieser Merkmale herauszugreifen: In Folge 1 findet Piet eine Drehbuchseite, die einen Dialog vorwegnimmt, der im Anschluss von Jessy und Melanie gesprochen wird. In Folge 10 ist auf einer Aufnahme, die Piet angeblich mit einer versteckten Kamera gemacht hat, die von oben ins Bild ragende Mikrofonangel der akustischen Aufzeichnung des – wie anzunehmen – realen Produktionsteams zu sehen. In Folge 14 ist ein »Kamera läuft. Achtung. Und bitte« von einer Frauenstimme aus dem Off zu hören.[25]

So kann man die Geschichte, die *Pietshow* erzählt, auch als Geschichte des Enttarnens der professionellen Filmproduktion

gl. ausführlicher Kuhn (2010; ie Anm. 1).

Begebenheit lässt jedoch nicht lange auf sich warten: Bereits nach 30 Sekunden stürzt Protagonist Piet beim Tanzen in die Wand zur Nachbarwohnung (Abb. 3). Mit diesem ungewollten Wanddurchbruch wird die Handlung der Serie in Gang gesetzt. Er verbindet die Wohnung, die Piet mit seinem Freund Nick teilt, ungewollt mit der WG von Jessy und Melanie, die auch gerade zum Studium nach Berlin gezogen sind. Weil niemand das Wandloch wieder schließen möchte, müssen sich die vier mit der neuen Wohnsituation arrangieren. In insgesamt 15 Folgen der ersten Staffel geht es um das gegenseitige Kennenlernen, um Ex-Freunde, Schauspiel-Castings und WG-Streitereien.

Handkameraeffekte[24] suggerieren, dass der Auftakt der Serie mit einer leichten Digitalkamera (Camcorder) gefilmt wurde. Dass die Kamera dabei spontanen Ereignissen der Party folgt, verweist auf eine die Kamera führende Person. In der entscheidenden Einstellung ist der Sturz durch die Wand dann nur im Hintergrund zu sehen, so als hätte die Kamera ihn eher zufällig ›erwischt‹. Dieser erste Eindruck, dass hier einer der Partygäste mit einer DV-Kamera durch den Raum geht und filmt, wird jedoch durch einige Schnitte infrage gestellt: Die kurze Eröffnungssequenz besteht aus neun Einstellungen. Die Schnitte sind unauffällig gesetzt und werden durch die Partymusik ›zusammengehalten‹. Aber genau hier lässt sich ein erster Bruch mit der Authentizitätsillusion benennen: Bei der Musik kann es sich nicht um Bildton handeln, weil es keine akustischen Schnitte gibt, wenn visuell von einer Einstellung zur nächsten geschnitten wird. Die Einstellungsmontagen können also nicht als An- und Abschaltprozess der Kamera aufgelöst werden, wie es in privaten Webclips oft der Fall ist. Geht man davon aus, dass es nur eine Kamera gegeben hat, müssen die einzelnen Szenen im Nachhinein zusammengeschnitten und nachvertont worden sein – oder es muss eine gesonderte Audioaufnahme gegeben haben.

Mit dieser Eröffnung liegen also einerseits Signale für Authentizität und Privatheit vor, andererseits für eine (relativ) professionelle Produktion. In diesem Punkt ist die Eröffnungsszene typisch für die gesamte Webserie *Pietshow*. Die Serie selbst liefert jedoch zugleich eine Erklärung für diese seltsame Spannung, indem sie das Nachvertonen und Schneiden einer der

24
Vgl. Markus Kuhn: Das narrative Potenzial der Handkamera. Zur Funktionalisierung von Handkameraeffekten in Spielfilmen und fiktionalen Filmclips im Internet. In: DIEGESIS. Interdisziplinäres E-Journal für Erzählforschung 2.1 (2013), S. 92–114. URL: https://www.diegesis.uni-wuppertal.de/index.php/diegesis/article/download/127/149 (Stand: 30.7.2013).

ten Webserie gelten kann. Und genau zu dieser Erzählökonomie trägt der Rückgriff auf etablierte Muster bei: Die Typisierung der Figuren und die unmittelbare Vertrautheit resultieren aus der Etikettierung der Figuren mit stereotypen Eigenschaften aus Highschool-Filmen. Durch wenige Andeutungen kann so ein konventionelles Charaktermuster etabliert werden, mit dem im Laufe der Handlung gespielt wird. Webserienfolgen sind sehr kurz, deshalb ist die Verdichtung der Informationsvergabe notwendig und kann als Merkmal des Einflusses der Medienumgebung gelten. Man möchte fast meinen: Webserien zwingen förmlich dazu, mit Genre- und Erzählkonventionen des Mainstream-Films und -Fernsehens zu arbeiten – denn nur so scheint die große Erzählökonomie möglich, die aufgrund der Kürze notwendig ist.

Insgesamt nutzen die Figuren auffallend häufig mediale Telekommunikationsmittel. Ständig wird gesimst, gemailt, gefilmt, fotografiert und das Material über das Netz weitergeleitet. Hier führt eine Spur zu den Ursprüngen von Webserien im User-Generated Content. Die Online-Kommunikation, die bei pseudo-authentischen Webserien wie *lonelygirl15* auf der äußeren Kommunikationsebene stattfindet, wandert in filmgenreorientierten Webserienproduktionen (häufig) auf die werkinterne Ebene.[22]

Die Webserie *Prom Queen* lief ursprünglich auf *Myspace* (als das Portal noch eine größere Relevanz besaß) und war zusätzlich an das Portal gebunden, indem die Figuren der Serie *Myspace*-Profile mit eigenen Videoblogs hatten, sodass sich andere (reale) User von *Myspace* mit ihren vernetzen konnten. In der Webserie *Pietshow* sind derartige gegenseitige Wechselwirkungen zwischen Serie und Einbettung in Social Web-Portale noch deutlicher.

4. Pietshow: Werkinterne Medienreflexion als Effekt der medialen Rahmung[23]

Nach *They call us Candy Girls* (D 2008) war *Pietshow* eine der ersten kommerziellen in Deutschland produzierten Webserien. Die erste Folge beginnt mit einer ca. 42-sekündigen Auftaktszene noch vor dem Vorspann. Zu sehen ist die scheinbar handgefilmte Aufzeichnung einer typischen WG-Party. Die unerhörte

---

22
Vgl. ebd.

23
Die Ausführungen zur Webserie *Pietshow* in diesem Kapitel beruhen zu großen Teilen auf der ausführlichen Analyse der ersten Staffel dieser Webserie in Kuhn (2010; wie Anm. 1).

19
Vgl. Kuhn, Der Einfluss (2013;
wie Anm. 1).

20
Zum Konzept der (audio)visuellen
Instanz/Erzählinstanz vgl. Markus
Kuhn: Filmnarratologie. Ein erzähl-
theoretisches Analysemodell.
Berlin; New York 2011, S. 87–94.

21
Vgl. ausführlicher Kuhn, Der
Einfluss (2013; wie Anm. 1).

ausgewogene Bild- und Bewegungsästhetik, eine die Anschlüsse glättende Montage, die professionelle Nachvertonung etc.[19] Viele dieser Merkmale verweisen auf eine über den Figuren stehende extradiegetische audiovisuelle Vermittlungsinstanz.[20]

Der genrekonstituierende Handlungsraum Highschool wird in dieser Folge nur angedeutet, aber in den ersten elf Folgen erkennbar etabliert, indem Teilräume einer Highschool eingeführt werden wie der Klassenraum, der Sportplatz mit Umkleidekabine oder der Gang mit Schließfächern. Mit den Statements aller Hauptfiguren über die (Un)Wichtigkeit oder persönliche Bedeutung des Abschlussballs in der zweiten Folge (z. B. »Prom is the single most important night of your life.«) wird der für Highschool-Filme konstitutive Abschlussball als zentrales Handlungsmoment etabliert. Eine SMS, die die Figur Ben Simmons am Schluss der Folge erhält, lädt den Abschlussball und die Wahl zur Prom Queen mit zusätzlicher Bedeutung auf: »U r going 2 kill the prom queen [sic!]«, schreibt ein »unknown user«. Über die Etablierung des Abschlussballs als zentrales Ereignis eröffnet die SMS zwei entscheidende Handlungsbögen: erstens die Frage nach der Prom Queen, die genrekonstituierend ist, und zweitens einen mysteriös aufgeladenen Gewaltplot. Zugleich wird eine unbekannte Instanz etabliert, die mehr zu wissen scheint als die Figuren.

Weitere typische Subplots des Highschool-Films werden über die Figuren eingeführt, in der zweiten Folge nur andeutungsweise, aber im Verlauf der ersten 15 Folgen ganz offensichtlich. Dazu zählen das Liebes- und Beziehungsmotiv sowie – sehr zentral – das Motiv der Verwandlung. Das für Partys und romantische Beziehungen ob ihres politischen Engagements und alternativen Kleidungsstils ungeeignet scheinende Mädchen Sadie Simmons verwandelt sich im Laufe der 80 Folgen in eine ›Abendkleidprinzessin‹, die große Chancen hat, die Wahl zur Prom Queen zu gewinnen. Die Merkmale des prototypischen Highschool-Films sind insgesamt so deutlich und zahlreich, dass man *Prom Queen* als Netztransformation eines Highschool-Films einordnen kann.[21]

In der zweiten Folge liegt eine extreme Verdichtung der Informationsvergabe vor, was als zentrales Merkmal der gesam-

3. Prom Queen: Das medienbewusste Spiel mit Genremustern[17]

Im Gegensatz zu *lonelygirl15* wurde die Webserie *Prom Queen* von vornherein professionell vermarktet, z. B. über Sponsoring, Product Placement oder die Möglichkeit, Merchandising-Artikel in einem Online Shop zu kaufen. Das Serienformat wurde nach Japan verkauft, wo die Webserie *Tokyo Prom Queen* (J 2008–2009) produziert wurde, und für kommerzielle deutsche Portale wie *3min* und *Sevenload* aufwendig synchronisiert. *Prom Queen* gilt als Beispiel dafür, dass es möglich ist, ein erfolgreiches Geschäftsmodell rund um eine Webserie zu kreieren, die kostenlos zu sehen ist. Die erste von insgesamt drei Staffeln besteht aus 80 Folgen; die Folgenlänge beträgt ca. 90 Sekunden. *Prom Queen* spielt, wie der Titel andeutet, mit dem Teenpic-Subgenre des Highschool-Films, in dem der Abschlussball (*prom*) eine handlungstragende Rolle spielt. Typisch dafür sind Filme wie *Pretty in Pink* (USA 1986), *She's All That* (USA 1999) oder *Not Another Teen Movie* (USA 2001)[18].

Nach einer ersten Folge (*The Long Walk*), die eine mysteriöse Spannung aufbaut, die erst am Ende der ersten Staffel aufgelöst wird, beginnt mit der zweiten Folge (*Teenage Wasteland: The Video Yearbook*) die eigentliche Exposition: Die britische Austauschschülerin Danica Ashby geht mit einer Digitalkamera durch die Schule und konfrontiert ihre amerikanischen Mitschülerinnen und Mitschüler mit Fragen nach der Bedeutung des Abschlussballs (»What is the American obsession with prom?«). Die Figuren, die dabei vorgestellt werden, erinnern an das prototypische Highschool-Filmpersonal: Lauren Holland, der Klassenschwarm, Chad Moore, der professionelle Athlet (Abb. 2), Sadie Simmons, die politische Aktivistin, etc. Die Sequenz ist, anders als bei *lonelygirl15*, so geschnitten, dass es sich nicht ausschließlich um das Filmmaterial der britischen Gaststudentin handeln kann: Sequenzen, die mit ihrer Kamera aufgenommen sein könnten, wechseln mit Sequenzen, die sie mit der Kamera beim Filmen zeigen, und kurzen Stills, die ein Jahrbuchfoto der jeweiligen Figur mit ihrer Unterschrift und einer Kurzcharakterisierung zeigen (vgl. Abb. 2; S.321). Allein deswegen kann die Serie nicht als pseudo-authentisch eingeordnet werden; hinzu kommen die

---

[17] Die Ausführungen zur Webserie *Prom Queen* in diesem Kapitel beruhen zu großen Teilen auf der ausführlichen Analyse der ersten Staffel dieser Webserie in Kuhn, Der Einfluss (2013; wie Anm. 1), sind aber bezüglich der vorliegenden Argumentation modifiziert und verdichtet.

[18] Vgl. Kuhn, Der Einfluss (2013; wie Anm. 1). Zu Teenpics/Jugendfilmen vgl. James Hay; Stephen Bailey: Cinema and the Premises of Youth. ›Teen Films‹ and Their Sites in the 1980s and 1990s. In: Steve Neale (Hg.): Genre and Contemporary Hollywood. London 2002, S. 218–235. Julia Schumacher: Jugendfilm. In: Markus Kuhn; Irina Scheidgen; Nicola Valeska Weber (Hg.): Filmwissenschaftliche Genreanalyse. Eine Einführung. Berlin; Boston 2013, S. 295–313.

15
Ein Zusammenhang zwischen Qualitätsbeschränkung durch schlechtere Auflösung und dem Einsatz digitaler Kameras lässt sich zwar häufig noch feststellen, er muss aber im Hinblick auf neueste technische Entwicklungen infrage gestellt werden. Die Displays vieler aktueller Smartphones haben mittlerweile eine bessere Auflösung als klassische (SD-)Fernsehgeräte, und auch bei *YouTube* gibt es inzwischen HD-Videos. Demgegenüber haben viele Webserien (noch) eine deutlich schlechtere Bildqualität, um die Dateigröße für einen schnellen Download bzw. einen flüssigen Stream möglichst klein zu halten.

16
Zur Definition, Abgrenzung und Klassifizierung des Mockumentary-Formats jenseits des Internets vgl. u.a. Jane Roscoe; Craig Hight: Faking It. Mock-Documentary and the Subversion of Factuality. Manchester 2001, die allerdings den Begriff »Mock-Documentary« verwenden.

(wie z. B. in *Die Snobs*, D 2010, oder *52 Monologe*, D 2011). Aufgrund des begrenzten Rahmens auf dem Videoportal oder dem Kleinstmonitor eines Smartphones gibt es eine Dominanz von figurenzentrierten *großen* und *nahen* Einstellungsgrößen. Die Qualitätsbeschränkung durch die Kleinheit der Fläche und die eingeschränkte Pixelzahl begünstigt den Einsatz digitaler Hand- und Consumer-Kameras.[15] Formen, die die günstigen Produktionsbedingungen, die vergleichsweise geringe Bildqualität und die Amateurhaftigkeit selbstreflexiv in das Werkkonzept einbetten, werden auffallend häufig verwendet. So gelingt es (teilweise), den produktionsästhetischen ›Mangel‹ als zentrales Konzept in den Mittelpunkt der Rezeption zu rücken, weshalb sich viele Mockumentary-Formate[16] unter den deutschsprachigen Webserien finden lassen (z. B. *Making of Süße Stuten 7*, D 2010; *Flusstouristen*, D 2010; *Die Essenz des Guten*, D 2011). Analog zu Fernsehserien werden die einzelnen Folgen einer Webserie als »Folgen« oder »Episoden« bezeichnet, die einzelnen Staffeln als »Staffeln« oder »Seasons«. Die Folgen von Webserien werden häufig auch als »Webisodes« (abgeleitet von »web« und »episode«) oder »Mobisodes« (von »mobile« und »episode« als Hinweis auf die intendierte Rezeption mittels mobiler Geräte wie Smartphones) bezeichnet. Gelegentlich wird der Begriff »Webisode« oder – im Plural – »Webisodes« auch für die gesamte Webserie, also zur Bezeichnung aller Episoden, benutzt.

Im Fall der Webserie *lonelygirl15* möchte ich von einer *pseudo-authentischen Webserie* sprechen. Pseudo-authentische Webserien imitieren regelmäßiges Videoblogging, geben vor, aus scheinbar authentischen Filmclips zu bestehen, die ›normale‹ User produziert haben könnten, und werden auf Portalen wie *YouTube* erstveröffentlicht. Merkmale, die auf Privatheit und Unprofessionalität verweisen sollen, können als *Authentifizierungsstrategien* beschrieben werden. Bei pseudo-authentischen Webserien findet eine fingierte Medienkommunikation mit anderen Usern auf der äußeren Ebene statt. Gänzlich anders ist das folgende Beispiel strukturiert.

rezipiert werden können. Mit dem produktionsorientierten Aspekt der Erstveröffentlichung im Netz soll in einem ersten Schritt versucht werden, das Feld der Webserie von Fernsehserien abzugrenzen, die online gezeigt oder angeboten werden. Mit in den Rahmen dieser Arbeitsdefinition fallen Webserien, die als transmediale Begleitprodukte zu Fernsehserien produziert worden sind. Dazu gehören das eine Sat.1-Soap begleitende Videoblog *Eine wie keine – So Isses!* (D 2009), *Lost: Missing Pieces* (USA 2007–2008) als transmediale Ergänzung zum Erzählkosmos der Fernsehserie *Lost* (USA 2004–2010) oder *Nurse Jeffrey: Bitch Tapes* (USA 2010) als Ergänzung zu *House M.D.* (USA 2004ff.).

Um von einer Definition, die einen produktions-bezogenen Aspekt in den Mittelpunkt rückt, zu einer Definition zu gelangen, die werkimmanente Aspekte fokussiert, kann man anhand der Analyse einer großen Zahl an Webserien zu einer Skizze prototypischer Eigenschaften von Webserien gelangen. Als Vorschlag würde ich – Ergebnissen unserer Korpus-arbeit[14] folgend – den Prototyp einer Webserie anhand der deutschsprachigen Webserienlandschaft wie folgt beschreiben: als Serie von Folgen, die eine durchschnittliche Länge von drei bis zehn Minuten haben und die – zusätzlich zu einem rah-menden Portal oder Kanal innerhalb eines Portals – in vielen Fällen durch einen Kurzvorspann oder ein Logo bzw. ein digita-les ›Wasserzeichen‹ als Teile einer Serie markiert sind. Es gibt sowohl Webserien, in denen die abgeschlossene Story je Folge dominiert (also so genannte *Series*), als auch Webserien, in denen die folgenübergreifenden Handlungsbögen dominieren (so genannte *Serials*). Statistisch dominiert eine Mischform mit einer Tendenz zur Serialisierung, also zu handlungsübergrei-fenden Storylines.

Aufgrund der Kürze ist in den meisten Serials eine effiziente Erzählökonomie notwendig. Es kommt zu einer Überlagerung folgenübergreifender Handlungsbögen. Eine Folge selbst besteht oft nur aus wenigen Szenen. Häufig enden die Folgen mit einem Cliffhanger. Weitere Tendenzen sind – bei eindeutigen Ausnahmen – die Beschränkung auf eine überschaubare Zahl verschiedener Handlungsorte (wie z. B. in *Die Hütte*, CH 2010) und eine Beschränkung des Personals

---

13
Kuhn, Zwischen Kunst (2012; wie Anm. 1). Kuhn, Webserien-Blog (2012; wie Anm. 10).

14
In Jan Henne; Markus Kuhn: Die deutsche Webserien-Landschaft. Eine Übersicht. In: Jens Eder; Hans Jürgen Wulff (Hg.): Medien-wissenschaft/Hamburg. Berichte und Papiere 127 (2011). URL: http://www1.uni-hamburg.de/Medien/berichte/arbeiten/0127_11.html (Stand: 30.07.2013), und Kuhn, Webserien-Blog (2012, wie Anm. 10).

8
Z.B. bei Glen Creeber: Online-Serien. Intime Begegnungen der dritten Art. In: Robert Blanchet; Kristina Köhler; Tereza Smid; Julia Zutavern (Hg.): Serielle Formen. Von den frühen Film-Serials zu aktuellen Quality-TV- und Onlineserien. Marburg 2011, S. 377–396.

9
Gunther Eschke; Rudolf Bohne: Bleiben Sie dran! Dramaturgie von TV-Serien. Konstanz 2010, S. 235.

10
Allerdings kann man mit *lonelygirl15* trotzdem einen entscheidenden historischen Punkt der Entwicklung von Webserien markieren, selbst in Deutschland. *Lonelygirl15* war zwar nicht die erste Filmclip-Reihe im Netz, die man als Webserie bezeichnen kann, aber die erste, die international und vor allem auch in Deutschland eine breitgefächerte Resonanz erfuhr sowie ein überdimensionales Medienecho auch jenseits des Internets hervorrief, vgl. Kuhn, YouTube (2011; wie Anm. 1). Zu allen deutschen Webserien, die im Text genannt werden, siehe auch das von mir herausgegebene Webserien-Blog, das alle recherchierbaren deutschsprachigen Webserien in kurzen Einträgen präsentiert, Markus Kuhn (Hg.): Webserien-Blog. Webserien, Online-Serien, Webisodes, Websoaps und Mobisodes in Deutschland (2012) (die erste Version [August 2012] wurde gemeinsam mit Jan Henne erstellt, unter Mitarbeit von Johannes Noldt und Stella Schaller). URL: http://webserie.blogspot.de/ (Stand: 30.07.2013).

11
Vgl. Kuhn, Der Einfluss (2013; wie Anm. 1).

12
Vgl. ebd. und Creeber (2011; wie Anm. 8).

D 2000; *Borscht – Einsatz in Neukölln*, D 2001);[10] zweitens, dass viele andere Webserien nur teilweise mit Mechanismen der Authentizitätstäuschung und der Interaktivität gearbeitet haben; sowie vor allem drittens, dass es inzwischen ein großes Spektrum unterschiedlichster Formen der Webserie gibt.

Nicht zuletzt aufgrund zunehmender Professionalität und wachsender kommerzieller Interessen arbeiten Webserien immer häufiger mit erfolgreichen Genremustern und audiovisuellen Erzählkonventionen aus Film und Fernsehen[11]. Die meisten Webserien – auch genreorientierte Produktionen – weisen aber trotz dieser Entwicklungen nach wie vor Spuren ihrer Medienumgebung auf[12]. Zugleich produzieren wiederum immer mehr private und semiprofessionelle Anbieter wie Theater, Universitäten und Schauspielvereine Webserien mit relativ geringen Budgets – teilweise mit hohem ästhetischem Anspruch, teilweise aber auch ganz bewusst als popkultureller ›Trash‹.

Mit dem vorliegenden Beitrag möchte ich versuchen, das breiter werdende Feld an Webserien anhand von unterschiedlich konzipierten Beispielen zu umreißen. Neben *lonelygirl15* gehe ich dabei auf *Prom Queen* (USA 2007, 2010) und *Pietshow* (D 2008) ein. Eine Arbeitshypothese ist dabei, dass Webserien nicht nur nach werkinternen Merkmalen analysiert werden sollten, sondern auch im Hinblick auf kontextuelle Faktoren, da die medialen, lokalen und sozialen Rahmungen der Webserien Einfluss auf die narrativen Strukturen und die Ästhetik der Serien haben. Zugleich werde ich zeigen, dass Webserien auf Genremuster und Erzählkonventionen aus Film und Fernsehen zurückgreifen.

2. Zur Definition der medialen Form der Webserie

An verschiedenen Stellen habe ich eine Definition von Webserien vorgeschlagen[13], der ich auch hier folgen möchte:

Webserien sind audiovisuelle Formen im Internet, die sich durch Serialität, Fiktionalität und Narrativität auszeichnen und die für das Web als Erstveröffentlichungsort produziert worden sind.

Im Zentrum der Definition stehen audiovisuelle Formen, die als seriell, fiktional und narrativ bestimmt werden können und die im Internet veröffentlicht worden sind, also online

3
Vgl. Roberto Simanowski: Digitale Medien in der Erlebnisgesellschaft. Kultur – Kunst – Utopien. Reinbek bei Hamburg 2008, S. 84–88. Jean Burgess; Joshua Green: YouTube. Online Video and Participatory Culture. Cambridge; Malden 2009, S. 27ff. Jean Burgess; Joshua Green: The Entrepreneurial Vlogger. Beyond the Professional-Amateur Divide. In: Pelle Snickars; Patrick Vonderau (Hg.): The YouTube Reader. Stockholm 2009, S. 89–107, S. 95f. Kuhn (2010), S. 19f. (wie Anm. 1). Kuhn, YouTube (2011; wie Anm. 1).

4
Vgl. u. a. Frank Patalong: Nur falsch ist wirklich echt. In: SPIEGEL ONLINE (11.9.2006). URL: http://www.spiegel.de/netzwelt/web/0,1518,436070,00.html (Stand: 30.7.2013). Munker (2006; wie Anm. 2). Joshua Davis: The Secret World of Lonelygirl. How a 19-year-old actress and a few struggling Web filmmakers took on TV. A Wired exclusive. In: Wired 14 (2006), S. 232–239. URL: http://www.wired.com/wired/archive/14.12/lonelygirl.html (Stand: 30.7.2013). Burgess; Green, YouTube (2009), S. 27f. (wie Anm. 3). Kuhn, YouTube (2011; wie Anm. 1).

5
Zu den Zugriffszahlen im Jahr 2006 vgl. Davis (2006; wie Anm. 4) und Burgess; Green, YouTube (2009), S. 27f. (wie Anm. 3).

6
Die Berichte über *lonelygirl15* häuften sich rund um die Enthüllung im September 2006 in verschiedenen Print- und Online-Medien. Vgl. dazu Burgess; Green, YouTube (2009), S. 27f. (wie Anm. 3), und Kuhn, YouTube (2011; wie Anm. 1).

7
Vgl. Kuhn, YouTube (2011; wie Anm. 1).

onen, die sich in den Kommentaren zu ihren Videos abspielten, beteiligte sie sich ebenfalls.

Doch die Themen wurden zunehmend intimer, und die digitalen Nachbearbeitungen der Filmclips wiesen allmählich über das Niveau hinaus, das User mit einem gewöhnlichen Editing-Programm generieren können. Immer mehr skeptische Rezipienten schalteten sich per Kommentar in die Spekulationen darüber ein, ob es sich tatsächlich um private Videoclips einer 16-Jährigen handeln könnte – bis Journalisten schließlich herausfanden, dass *lonelygirl15* alias Bree ›nur‹ eine von drei nicht-professionellen Filmemachern inszenierte Figur war[4]. Nach der Enttarnung wurde die Serie als fiktionales Produkt fortgesetzt, und drei Staffeln mit über 500 Folgen und viele Spin-offs sollten folgen. Die Zugriffszahlen blieben relativ hoch[5] (obwohl sich viele Rezipienten der ersten Folgen betrogen vorkamen), u. a. weil nach der ersten Aufmerksamkeitswelle auf *YouTube* eine zweite, medienübergreifende folgen sollte. Über das Phänomen *lonelygirl15* wurde im Zuge der Enttarnung rund um das 33. Video (*House Arrest*) in verschiedenen Print-, Fernseh- und Online-Medien berichtet.[6] Das Spiel mit der scheinbaren Authentizität stellte sich rückblickend als probates Mittel heraus, um Identifikationspotential aufzubauen und Werbung für diese *YouTube*-Webserie zu machen, die sich dann zunehmend zu einer Art Thriller- und Mystery-Serie weiterentwickelte[7]. Insofern repräsentiert die Webserie *lonelygirl15* nicht nur die Geschichte des Teenagers Bree, sondern steht auch – zumindest am Rande – für die Erfolgsgeschichte der drei semiprofessionellen ›Filmemacher‹ Miles Beckett, Mesh Flinders und Greg Goodfried (und ihrer Firma *EQAL*) als Schöpfer eines großen fiktionalen Webserien-Kosmos auf *YouTube* und anderen Portalen.

Wegen der Erfolgsgeschichte von *lonelygirl15* werden Webserien oft im Rahmen von User-Generated Content (UGC) und Videoblogs verortet[8] und es wird teilweise sogar davon ausgegangen, dass es sich bei *lonelygirl15* um die erste Webserie überhaupt handelt[9]. Diese Betrachtungsweise lässt jedoch einige Aspekte außer Acht: erstens, dass es vor und parallel zu *lonelygirl15* bereits Webserienproduktionen gab (in Amerika z. B. *SamHas7Friends*, USA 2006; in Deutschland z. B. *90sechzig90*,

1

Der vorliegende Beitrag basiert zu
großen Teilen auf Analysen, die ich
an anderen Stellen zum Themenfeld »Webserie« vorgelegt habe; v. a.
auf Markus Kuhn: Zwischen Kunst,
Kommerz und Lokalkolorit. Der
Einfluss der Medienumgebung auf
die narrative Struktur von Webserien und Ansätze zu einer Klassifizierung. In: Ansgar Nünning; Jan
Rupp; Rebecca Hagelmoser; Jonas
Ivo Meyer (Hg.): Narrative Genres
im Internet. Theoretische Bezugsrahmen, Mediengattungstypologie
und Funktionen. Trier 2012, S. 51–
92; aber auch auf: Markus Kuhn:
Medienreflexives filmisches Erzählen im Internet. Die Webserie
Pietshow. In: Rabbit Eye – Zeitschrift für Filmforschung 1 (2010),
S. 19–40. URL: http://www.rabbit-
eye.de/2010/1/kuhn_erzaehlen_
im_internet.pdf (Stand: 30.07.2013).
Markus Kuhn: YouTube als Loopingbahn. lonelygirl15 als Phänomen
und Symptom der Erfolgsinitiation
von YouTube. In: Julia Schumacher;
Andreas Stuhlmann (Hg.): Videoportale: Broadcast Yourself? Versprechen und Enttäuschung. Hamburger
Hefte zur Medienkultur 12 (2011),
S. 119–136. URL: http://www.slm.
uni-hamburg.de/imk/Hamburger-
Hefte/hamburgerhefte.html
(Stand: 30.07.2013). Markus Kuhn:
Der Einfluss medialer Rahmungen
auf das Spiel mit Genrekonventionen. Die Webserie Prom Queen als
Transformation des Highschool-
Films im Internet. In: Jennifer Henke;
Magdalena Krakowski; Benjamin
Moldenhauer; Oliver Schmidt (Hg.):
Hollywood Reloaded. Genrewandel
und Medienerfahrung nach der
Jahrtausendwende. Marburg 2013
[im Druck].

2

Barbara Munker: Die Enttarnung
von Lonelygirl15. In: stern.de
(14.9.2006). URL: http://www.stern.
de/computertechnik/internet/
570087.html?nv=cb (Stand:
30.07.2013).

1. Einleitung[1]

Die Entwicklung des Internets als solches wird nicht
zuletzt deswegen so oft als ›Story of success‹ erzählt, weil das Netz
so viele kleinere und größere Erfolgsgeschichten bedingt oder
hervorgebracht hat. Diese sind wiederum nicht nur deswegen so
populär, weil sich ein beeindruckender Erfolg zumeist an klaren
Gewinnmargen und schwindelerregenden User- oder Umsatzzahlen festmachen lässt, sondern auch, weil sie immer wieder
nacherzählt und von einem Medium zum anderen gereicht
werden. Man denke an die Aufstiegsgeschichten von einstmals so
unbedeutenden Serviceanbietern wie bestimmten Suchmaschinen oder Portalen zum Austauschen von Videos und Fotos. Oder
an die vielen personalisierten Erfolge von ›freakigen Selfmademen‹ und ›nerdigen Studenten‹ wie Chad Hurley oder
Mark Zuckerberg und all die anderen Vom-Tellerwäscher-zum-
Millionär-Mythen des Netzzeitalters. Gerade das Social Web hat
dem ›digitalen Goldrausch‹ noch einmal einen gewaltigen Schub
verliehen.

Eine dieser vielen Erfolgsgeschichten ist die des einsamen Mädchens Bree, das im Sommer 2006 auf *YouTube* über die
»Irrungen und Wirrungen des Teenagerlebens«[2] berichtete und
damit in den ›Aufmerksamkeitskämpfen‹ des Netzes einen
unerwarteten Erfolg erzielen konnte[3]. Allein deshalb kann ›ihre‹
YouTube-Filmclip-Reihe *lonelygirl15* (USA 2006–2008) als ›Klassiker‹ des noch relativ jungen filmischen Erzählformats der
Webserie gelten (auch wenn sie sich nicht von Anfang an als
solche zu erkennen gab).

Unter dem Usernamen *lonelygirl15* berichtete die 16-jährige Bree in einer Folge von seit dem 16.06.2006 sukzessive auf
YouTube hochgeladenen Filmclips über ihr Alltagsleben, ihren
Heimschulunterricht und die seltsame Religion ihres Elternhauses. In ihren Clips, die selten eine Länge von drei Minuten
überschritten, setzte sie sich vor eine Webcam und plauderte,
frontal in die Kamera blickend, ›drauf los‹ (Abb. 1). Das, was sie
schließlich hochlud, war – entsprechend ihres verspielten
Temperaments – mit allerlei amateurhaften Bild- und Soundeffekten digital nachbearbeitet, wobei sie, wie sie behauptete, Hilfe
von ihrem ›Kumpelfreund‹ Daniel bekam. An den regen Diskussi-

Von einsamen Mädchen, Prom-Queens und ›coolen Säuen‹. Die Webserie als neue serielle audiovisuelle Erzählform im Internet

Markus Kuhn

hineinwirken und den Zuschauer dort abholen, wo er sich sowieso gerade befindet, in Sozialen Netzwerken wie *Facebook* und vor seinem Handy und Computer.

»Ist die Nachricht wichtig, wird sie mich erreichen«, lautet der Satz eines College-Studenten in einer Studie über den Medienkonsum aus dem Jahr 2008. Dieser Satz wurde zum Schreckensszenario für Medienhäuser. Dabei ist es doch so einfach: Wer nichts zu sagen hat, sollte lieber schweigen. Wer eine Geschichte zu erzählen hat, der beachte das Gebot: Du sollst nicht langweilen. Und wer eine wirklich gute Geschichte zu erzählen hat, der gehe dorthin, wo die Zuhörer und Zuschauer auch sind, und nutze alle Speicher- und Abspielmedien, mit denen er diese Zielgruppe erreichen kann.

Alain Bieber
geb. 1978, studierte Rhetorik, Soziologie, Literatur und Politikwissenschaft in Tübingen und Paris. Im Jahr 2004 gründete er *rebel:art,* als Verlag und Plattform für Kunst, Kultur und Politik, und die Ausstellungsreihe *PARASITES – illegal exhibitions,* er co-kuratierte u. a. die Subversiv Messe in Linz und das Dockville Festival Hamburg, arbeitete als Ressortleiter für das Kunstmagazin ART und als Autor für *artnet, Arte Magazin, Neural, Merian, Spiegel Online, Max* und *Die Gestalten.* Heute ist er Projektleiter von *Arte Creative*, einem Magazin, Netzwerk und Labor für zeitgenössische Kultur.

»Who the hell wants to hear actors talk?« Auch Minnesänger,
Barden oder Troubadoure finden sich heute eher seltener, aber
gute Geschichtenerzähler wird es immer geben, egal welches
Speichermedium bzw. Ausgabemedium man nutzen wird. Die
Nachfrage nach guten Filmen und Serien ist ungebrochen. Die
US-Serie *Game of Thrones* hat pro Folge ungefähr fünf Millionen
Zuschauer – und ist auch die am meisten illegal heruntergela-
dene TV-Serie (pro Folge ebenfalls ungefähr fünf Millionen). Für
Warner-Chef Jeff Bewkes ist dies aber kein Grund zur Besorgnis. Er
sieht diese Statistik sogar als Auszeichnung: »Ich finde, dass ist
besser als ein *Emmy*.« Auch Filmstudios sind lernfähig. Keine
Frage: Man muss stets die spezifischen Besonderheiten von jedem
Medium perfekt nutzen. Natürlich konsumiert man einen
Spielfilm in einem Kinosaal anders als auf einem Tablet Computer oder seiner Google Glass.

    Arte Creative ist das Magazin, Labor und Netzwerk für
zeitgenössische Kultur des europäischen Senders *Arte* in Straß-
burg. Unser erstes großes Experiment war *About:Kate*. Das
Crossmedia-Projekt machte es möglich, die Protagonistin Kate
auf ihrem Weg in der Nervenklink zu begleiten – im TV auf *Arte*,
online auf *arte.tv/kate*, mit der App zur Serie und auf *Facebook*. So
wurde man zum Freund, Mitpatienten und Regisseur von
About:Kate. Die kostenlose App für iOS und Android synchronisierte sich über das Tonsignal automatisch mit der Serie und
fütterte den Zuschauer beim Anschauen in Echtzeit mit Links,
Umfragen, Tests und Infos. Online konnte man dann seine
Antworten auswerten, eigene Video- und Fotobeiträge für die
Serie einschicken und seine Freunde testen. Und wer sich mit
Kate auf *Facebook* anfreundete, konnte ihr Nachrichten schreiben, Kommentare hinterlassen oder einfach nur schauen, in
welcher Stimmung sie gerade ist. »Wenn der Kultursender *Arte*
aus dem Leben von Kate Harff erzählt, ist das Zeitalter postmodernen Erzählens endlich auch im oft biederen deutschen
Fernsehen angebrochen«, schrieb *Die Welt*. »Endlich darf der
Zuschauer mehr als neben Millionen Anderen per Online-Voting
eine Stimme abgeben, endlich wird er als Mensch angesprochen,
darf Teil dessen werden, was hier erzählt wird.« Unser Ziel war:
Die Narration sollte dreidimensional werden, in den realen Raum

stilisiert. Illegale Downloads, *Facebook*-Parties, Cybercrime, Kinderpornografie, Street View. Auch für die klassischen Medien ist es der ideale Buhmann: Blogger ruinieren unser Geschäft, alle klauen Inhalte und wollen nur kostenlose Contents, niemand kauft mehr CDs/Bücher/Zeitungen, schaut Fernsehen. Die Liste lässt sich beliebig ergänzen. Anke Domscheit-Berg hat dies gut umschrieben: »Das Internet ist kein digitales Sodom und Gomorrha, es ist ein Spiegel der Gesellschaft – insofern bildet es natürlich auch deren dunkleren Seiten ab. Dennoch ist es nur ein Spiegel und ein Abbild – nicht die Ursache. Die Ursachen für Missstände liegen immer noch in der Gesellschaft selbst und dort muss man sie auch bekämpfen.« Dazu nur noch ein Beispiel: Die von den Nutzern selbstgestaltete virtuelle Welt *Second Life*. Es hätte sein können: die perfekte Utopie, die Schaffung einer neuen Welt im Virtuellen. Und was ist passiert? Es entstand ein exaktes Abbild unserer bestehenden Welt, es gab Prostitution und kriminelle Banden, kommerzielle Firmen verkauften digitale Produkte, die Gemäldegalerie Dresden war virtuell präsent, das erzbischöfliche Seelsorgeamt hielt Bibelstunden ab, es wurde als Wahlkampfplattform von Parteien und Politikern genutzt. Kurzum: Irgendwann ging das Interesse gegen Null, denn worin liegt der Reiz, das Reale auch als digitale Replik zu haben.

Dabei ist eigentlich alles ganz einfach. Es gibt Dinge, die ändern sich eben, und es gibt Dinge, die sich nie ändern werden. Das Internet verändert gerade ganz massiv die TV-Landschaft: Kino für die Hosentasche, nicht-lineare Dokus im Netz, partizipative TV-Formate, und *YouTube* produziert mit *Endemol* und UFA. Es sind bewegte Zeiten für das Bewegtbild der Zukunft. Aber was sich eigentlich wirklich verändert, sind vor allem die Datenspeicher für Schrift-, Bild- und Toninformationen. Trommelspeicher, Lochstreifen, Disketten, Mikroplanfilm, Schallplatte, Kassette, Videokassette und CD-ROM sind (fast) ausgestorben bzw. in nächster Zukunft wohl nur noch Nostalgikern ein Begriff. Auch die Form des Erzählens hat sich natürlich verändert. Aus mündlich überlieferten Geschichten wurden irgendwann Stummfilme, und dann kam das Radio. Die spektakuläre Fehleinschätzung des Filmstudiochefs Harry M. Warner aus dem Jahr 1927 ist in die Geschichtsbücher eingegangen. Er fragte damals:

Es gibt da diese *South Park*-Folge, in der plötzlich das Internet verschwindet. Die Konsequenz: Eine Massenpanik bricht aus, es werden »Internet Refugee Camps« gebildet, und die Väter machen sich auf die verzweifelte Suche nach Internet-Pornografie. Denn: »Wenn du einmal zu japanischen Mädchen, die sich gegenseitig in den Mund kotzen, abgewichst hast, dann kannst du nicht wirklich wieder den *Playboy* lesen«, erklärt Randy Marsh.

Kurze Reise in die Vergangenheit. Vor gerade mal einem Jahrzehnt musste sich Bobbele Becker noch irgendwo einwählen (»Bin ich schon drin?«), und die Menschen hinter den Rechnern wurden als Nerds verlacht – heute sind sie die Coverstars internationaler Magazine, und Soziale Medien werden für Revolutionen verantwortlich gemacht. Den Holzmedien ist das Lachen inzwischen gründlich vergangen. Die deutsche Presse erlebt derzeit die größte Entlassungswelle seit Bestehen der Bundesrepublik, schätzt die Bundesagentur für Arbeit. *Frankfurter Rundschau, Financial Times Deutschland, Abendzeitung Nürnberg*, das Stadtmagazin *Prinz*, die Nachrichtenagentur dapd haben Insolvenz angemeldet. Das Grundproblem: Das Geschäftsmodell von Printmedien beruht noch immer auf zwei Pfeilern. Dem Verkaufspreis und dem Anzeigenerlös. Und die momentane Medienkrise ist vor allem eine Anzeigenkrise, weil die großen, kommerziellen Werbetreibenden immer weniger auf klassische Printwerbung setzen, wegen des zu großen Streuverlusts; man setzt heute lieber auf digitale Social Media-Kampagnen. Kurzum: Der Gesamtwerbekuchen für Zeitungen und Zeitschriften schrumpft, TV und Radio halten sich konstant, Online wächst.

»Das Internet ist für uns alle Neuland«, sagte Angela Merkel während einer Pressekonferenz in Zusammenhang mit der *Prism*-Affäre. Die Häme folgte sofort in zahlreichen Tweets. »Ich bin bloß misstrauisch, weil das #Neuland schon bevölkert ist. Wie viele sind wir? Zwei Milliarden? Wahrscheinlich alles Terroristen«, witzelte ein *Twitter*-Nutzer. Aber eigentlich ein Fakt. Seit den frühen 1990er Jahren wird immer wieder regelmäßig darauf verwiesen, dass insbesondere Terroristen, Nazis, Kinderschänder, Pornokonsumenten sich des Internets bedienen. Das Netz wird zu einem Hort für Kriminalität und Verbrechen

Tausendundein
#Neuland

Alain Bieber

Stutterheim, Kerstin; Kaiser, Silke: Handbuch der Filmdramaturgie. Das Bauchgefühl
und seine Ursachen. 2. Aufl., Frankfurt am Main 2011
Stutterheim, Kerstin, Lang, Christine: Come and play with us. Ästhetik und Dramaturgie
im Postmodernen Kino. Marburg 2014
Thompson, Kristin: Neoformalistische Filmanalyse. In: Montage AV, Heft 4.1.1995.
Online: www.montage-av.de (Stand 16.8.2013)

Christine Lang
studierte Kulturwissenschaft (bei Friedrich A. Kittler), Kunstgeschichte und Literaturwissenschaft an der Humboldt Universität zu Berlin,
anschließend Film und Fernsehregie an der Kunsthochschule für Medien
in Köln. 2007 war sie Stipendiatin in der Villa Aurora in Los Angeles. Seit
2009 ist sie künstlerisch-wissenschaftliche Mitarbeiterin an der
Hochschule für Film und Fernsehen *Konrad Wolf* in Potsdam-Babelsberg
im Fachbereich Medienästhetik und Dramaturgie. Christine Lang arbeitet
als Filmemacherin und Autorin. Ihre Filme liefen international auf
Filmfestivals und gewannen diverse Preise. Publikation: *Breaking Down
Breaking Bad. Dramaturgie und Ästhetik einer Fernsehserie* (2013).

Literatur

Bachtin, Michail M. (1941): Autor und Held in der ästhetischen Tätigkeit. Frankfurt am Main 2008b

Bachtin, Michail M. (1921): Zur Philosophie der Handlung. Berlin 2011

Balázs, Béla (1924): Der sichtbare Mensch oder die Kultur des Films. Frankfurt am Main 2001

Barthes, Roland: Rhétorique de l'image. In: Communications 4, 1964, S. 40–51

Blanchet, Robert; Köhler, Kristina; Smid, Tereza; Zutavern, Julia (Hg.): Serielle Formen. Von den frühen Film-Serials zu aktuellen Quality-TV und Online-Serien. Marburg 2011

Bordwell, David: Narration in the Fiction Film. Madison 1985

Carrière, Jean-Claude; Bonitzer, Pascal: Praxis des Drehbuchschreibens/Über das Geschichtenerzählen. Berlin 1999

Diederichsen, Diedrich: In bewegten Bildern blättern. Die Videothek von Babylon. In: Dreher, Christoph (Hg.): Autorenserien. Die Neuerfindung des Fernsehens. Stuttgart 2010, S. 167–197

Dreher, Christoph (Hg.): Autorenserien. Die Neuerfindung des Fernsehens. Stuttgart 2010

Eco, Umberto: Das offene Kunstwerk. Frankfurt am Main 1977

Eder, Jens: Die Figur im Film. Marburg 2008

Elsaesser, Thomas; Hagener, Malte: Filmtheorie zur Einführung. Hamburg 2007

Engell, Lorenz: TV Pop. In: Grasskamp, Walter; Krützen, Michaela; Schmitt, Stephan (Hg.): Was ist Pop? Zehn Versuche. Frankfurt am Main 2004, S. 189–210

Engell, Lorenz (Hg.): Fernsehtheorie. Zur Einführung. Hamburg 2012

Fahle, Oliver; Engell, Lorenz (Hg.): Philosophie des Fernsehens. München 2005

Feuer, Jane: MTM. Quality Television. London 1984

Frank, Michael C.; Mahlke, Kirsten: Nachwort zu Michail M. Bachtin: Chronotopos. Frankfurt am Main 2008, S. 201–242

Freytag, Gustav (1863): Die Technik des Dramas. Unveränderter Nachdruck, Darmstadt 1969

Gelfert, Hans-Dieter: Typisch amerikanisch. Wie die Amerikaner wurden, was sie sind. München 2003

Genette, Gérard: Die Erzählung. 3. Aufl. (frz. 1972/1983), München 2010

Gertz, Annegret; Rohmer, Rolf: Versteckte Dramaturgien im amerikanischen Bühnenentertainment. In: Reichel, Peter (Hg.): Studien zur Dramaturgie: Kontexte – Implikationen – Berufspraxis. Tübingen 2000, S. 81–133

Klotz, Volker: Geschlossene und offene Form im Drama. München 1960, 8. Auflage 1998

Kreimeier, Klaus: Fernsehen. In: Hügel, Hans-Otto: Handbuch der populären Kultur. Stuttgart 2003. Online unter: www.kreimeier-online.de/Fernsehen.html (Stand 30.06.2012)

Lotman, Jurij M.: Kunst als Sprache. Untersuchungen zum Zeichencharakter von Literatur und Kunst. Hg. v. Klaus Städtke. Leipzig 1981

Leverette, Marc; Ott, Brian L.; Buckley Cara Louise (Hg.): It's not TV. Watching HBO in the Post-Television Era. New York 2008

Metz, Christian: Der imaginäre Signifikant. Psychoanalyse und Kino. Münster 2000; zuerst frz. 1977

Mittell, Jason: DVD-Editionen und der kulturelle Wert amerikanischer Fernsehserien. In: Blanchet, Robert; Köhler, Kristina; Smid, Tereza; Zutavern, Julia (Hg.): Serielle Formen. Von den frühen Film-Serials zu aktuellen Quality-TV und Online-Serien. Marburg 2011, S. 133–152

Nelson, Robin: TV Drama in Transition. Forms, Values and Cultural Change. London 1997

Reichel, Peter (Hg.): Studien zur Dramaturgie: Kontexte – Implikationen – Berufspraxis. Tübingen 2000

Sasse, Sylvia: Vorwort. In: Bachtin, Michail M. (1921): Zur Philosophie der Handlung. Berlin 2011, S. 5–31

Schmid, Anna; Brust, Alexander (Hg.): Rot. Wenn Farbe zur Täterin wird. Basel 2007

Steinke, Anthrin: Aspekte postmodernen Erzählens im amerikanischen Film der Gegenwart. Trier 2007

Ansatz ist und wie sich das Fernsehen so an die Gegenwart anschließt, zeigt sich nicht zuletzt durch eine virulente Fangemeinde im Internet, an der sich vielleicht das wahre interaktive Potenzial des Fernsehens heute ablesen lässt.[20]

20
Um nur zwei Beispiele für die aktive Fankultur und Rezeption im Internet zu nennen: Ein Remix der Fliegenfolge und eine Montage der POV-Shots. Dank an Harry Delgado für die Links: www.youtube.com/watch?v=Hj2kAdcMDTo (Stand: 16.8.2013) http://vimeo.com/34773713 (Stand: 16.8.2013)

Bei dem Text handelt es sich um eine überarbeitete Fassung des in dem Buch »Breaking Down Breaking Bad« veröffentlichten Essays; das gemeinsam mit Christoph Dreher verfasste Buch erschien 2013 im Fink Verlag.

Abb. 1

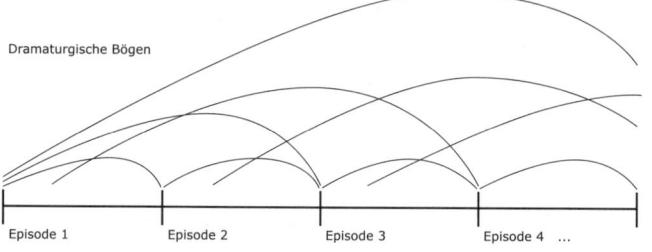

Abb. 2 – Flexi Narrative/Zopfdramaturgie (Grafik von Yvy Heußler)

Abb. 3

16
Im Original auf Spanisch: »A la furia del cartel, nadie jamás a escapado, ese compa ya esta muerto, nomas no le han avisado.« Englisch untertitelt: »The cartels's bout respect, and they ain't forgiving, but that homie's dead, he just doesn't know it yet.«

17
In der kognitiv-(neo-)formalistischen Film- und Narrationstheorie (Bordwell, Thompson u.a.) wird die Beziehung zwischen Zuschauenden und Film ausgiebig theoretisiert. Ein weiterer Ansatz basiert auf den literaturwissenschaftlichen Arbeiten Michael Bachtins. Eine hilfreiche Einführung in die diversen filmtheoretischen Ansätze bietet: Thomas Elsaesser; Malte Hagener: Filmtheorie zur Einführung. Hamburg 2007, S. 62ff.

18
Zum Begriff des Fernsehens als Leitmedium und seiner Anfechtung in dieser Rolle durch das Internet siehe: Klaus Kreimeier: Fernsehen. In: Hans-Otto Hügel: Handbuch der populären Kultur. Stuttgart 2003. Online unter: www. kreimeier-online.de/Fernsehen. html (Stand 30.06.2012).

19
Zum Begriff der Autorenserie siehe: Christoph Dreher (Hg.): Autorenserien. Die Neuerfindung des Fernsehens. Stuttgart 2010; Lavery 2010.

Crystal Meth auf dem Markt und dass Walter White alias Heisenberg inzwischen ein Mythos geworden ist. Durch die Lyrics wird en passant mitgeteilt, dass mit den neuen Gegenspielern nicht zu spaßen ist: »Dem Kartell geht es um Respekt, und sie vergeben niemals; der Typ ist tot, er weiß es nur noch nicht.«[16]

An *Breaking Bad* zeigt sich, wie wichtig eine konsequent gedachte und geführte Implizite Dramaturgie ist und wie sie zum Gelingen einer Filmerzählung beiträgt, wenn sie in einem engen Zusammenhang mit der Expliziten Dramaturgie steht. Filmisches Erzählen ist immer die Gesamtsumme der Expliziten und der Impliziten Dramaturgie, und je kenntnisreicher die Implizite Dramaturgie gehandhabt wird, desto erfolgreicher entfaltet sich das Sujet durch die filmische Narration in ihrer Rezeption. Filmisches Erzählen, egal in welchem Vermittlungsmedium – ob Kino oder Fernsehen – es stattfindet, meint immer dialektisch-dialogische Prozesse zwischen Autor, Werk und Rezipient, und in der besonderen Ausgestaltung dieses Dialogs liegt das entscheidende Potential.[17]

Darüber hinaus spielt die Implizite Dramaturgie auch in den Tiefenstrukturen eines Films und eben auch einer Fernsehserie eine Rolle. Geht man davon aus, dass das Medium Fernsehen sich in einer Umbruchphase befindet und in seiner Legitimation als »Leitmedium« durch die Nachfolgemedien Internet und Computerspiel herausgefordert ist, macht es Sinn, nach den Bedingungen und ästhetischen Möglichkeiten des Fernsehens zu forschen.[18] Dabei hat es den Anschein, dass die seit Mitte der 1990er Jahre entstehenden Autorenserien, zu denen *Breaking Bad* gehört, in einer Reaktion auf die Medienumbrüche entstanden sind und dass mit ihnen das Fernsehen seine genuinen ästhetischen Mittel aktiviert.[19] Anstatt die Möglichkeiten der interaktiven Medien durch deren Imitation, beispielsweise durch Multiple Choice-Verfahren, zu imitieren, besinnt sich das Fernsehen unter anderem mit *Breaking Bad* auf hohem Niveau auf die Ausgestaltung der dialogischen Rezeptionsbeziehung, lädt zu einer aktiven Rezeption ein und reflektiert zudem die ästhetischen Organisationsprinzipien des popkulturellen Mediums im Werk selber. *Breaking Bad* wäre, wie auch andere komplex erzählte Autorenserien, in keinem anderen Medium denkbar. Wie erfolgreich dieser

Fernsehdiskurses und der Zuschauerpraxis durch. Zu denen gehört, dass die Fernsehästhetik auf »die Medialität des Mediums und seine Grundeigenschaften« reflektiert.

Die auf Pop referierende Implizite Dramaturgie in *Breaking Bad* wird in verdichteter Form sichtbar in den musikvideohaften Sequenzen, in der »Eye-Candy-Ästhetik« und den Kameraeinstellungen, in denen Perspektiven eingenommen werden, die keine Identifikation mit einem Blick erzeugen, sondern die Oberflächen der Dinge selbstbezüglich in Szene setzen – und die in »hochkultureller Filmkunst« als ornamental und gewissermaßen als »verboten« gelten würden. In *Breaking Bad* können diese Einstellungen insofern als ein Moment der Selbstreflexivität gedeutet werden, als mit ihnen die Aufmerksamkeit der Zuschauenden bewusst auf die Künstlichkeit und die Konstruktion der filmischen Erzählung gelenkt wird.

In *Breaking Bad* existieren in den ersten vier Staffeln zwei Szenen, die als authentisch nachgeahmte Musikvideos inszeniert sind. Dabei sind die auf Popkultur verweisenden impliziten Elemente nie reiner Selbstzweck, sondern dienen immer auch der Expliziten Dramaturgie. Vor allem in dem Video *Negro y Azul* der Band *Los Cuates de Sinaloa* (in der 7. Folge der 2. Staffel/Abb. 3), an dessen Lyrics Creator Vince Giligan mitgeschrieben hat, greifen Implizite und Explizite Dramaturgie nahtlos ineinander: Auf der impliziten Ebene wirkt der *Negro y Azul*-Clip wie ein postmoderner, zugleich authentischer Referenz-Spaß.[15] Hier wird ein spezifisches Segment mexikanischer Popkultur zitiert, die so genannten Narcocorridos, in denen darauf spezialisierte Bands Lobeshymnen auf die Drogenbarone singen. Das Video repräsentiert das in der Popkultur gebräuchliche Mittel des Pastiche, der im Gegensatz zur Parodie Anerkennung und Bewunderung für das Original in sich trägt. Das zeigt einerseits eine äußerst kompetente Handhabung von Distinktionswissen seitens der Produzent_innen, genügt sich andererseits aber nicht darin: Innerhalb des Handlungsgeschehens, im Dienst der Expliziten Dramaturgie, wird über dieses Video *Suspense* erzeugt: Man erfährt auf originelle Weise, dass Walter White alias Heisenberg in ernster Lebensgefahr ist, weil nun neue Antagonisten auf den Plan treten. Der Clip legt dar, wie erfolgreich das blaue

15
Im Übrigen taucht in dem Clip der Hauptdarsteller Danny Trejo aus Robert Rodriguez' postmodernem Film *Machete* (USA, 2010) kurz als Drogenbaron auf. In *Breaking Bad* hat er eine kleine, aber spektakuläre Nebenrolle.

dienen diese Gestaltungsmittel der werkinternen Charakterisierung der Figuren, auf der Ebene der Impliziten Dramaturgie trägt deren Gestaltung stimmige Weltverweise in sich, die für die authentische Wirkung der Figuren verantwortlich sind, darüber hinaus sind sie Bestandteil der werkimmanenten visuellen Dramaturgie: Die Farbe Rot – als Farbe des gesetzlich und moralisch, zugleich verlockenden Verbotenen – wird in der gesamten Serie als eine des Drogenmilieus und den damit zusammenhängenden Faktoren eingesetzt.[12] Dazu gehören sowohl Jesses rotfarbenes Auto, der später mit Drogengeld erworbene rote Sportwagen für Sohn Walter Jr. als auch die zunehmenden Rot-Anteile in der Kleidung Walters.[13]

In der Parkplatz-Szene versteckt sich nun auch eine weitere wesentliche, das formale Stilprinzip der Serie steuernde, Implizite Dramaturgie: Es ist eine Ästhetik der Populärkultur, eine der Gegensätze, des Nicht-Zueinanderpassens, welche die dramaturgische Tiefenstruktur der Serie auszeichnet. *Breaking Bad* lebt davon, dass verschiedene Genres virtuos gegeneinandergesetzt werden: Crime-Drama gegen Komödie, psychologischer Realismus gegen postmoderne Comic-Ästhetik, handwerkliche Perfektion gegen Trash. Diese popkulturellen Implikationen, ihre ästhetischen Prinzipien, in denen gleichermaßen Methoden absurder oder surrealer Konfrontationen, Destruktionen konventioneller Mythen und schwarzer Humor vorzufinden sind, machen das Organisationsprinzip der Erzählung aus. Diese kontrastierende Verfahrensweise erzeugt dabei den musikalischen Rhythmus der Serie, der wiederum eine ästhetische Analogie zu der Formensprache des popkulturellen Entertainmentfernsehens darstellt. *Breaking Bad* ist insofern eine ideale Fernsehserie, als in ihr das Medium Fernsehen in bester Weise zu sich als künstlerisch genutztes Medium findet. In der Serie sind dieselben Formensprachen vertreten wie im »Neo-Fernsehen«, in dem sich eine ganz eigene, fernsehspezifische Formensprache herausgebildet hat, die sich insgesamt eher »an Musik als an Sprache orientiert«[14]. Es ist »vor allem an visuellen Oberflächen, an Formenvielfalt und Bewegung interessiert«. Dazu setzen sich, laut Engell, in historischen Umbruchphasen (wie der Digitalisierung) die Prinzipien des Pop als dominante Grundlagen des

---

12
Farben haben in verschiedenen Kulturen unterschiedliche Bedeutungen, die dazu von ihrem jeweiligen Anwendungszusammenhang abhängig sind. Die Farbe Rot wird allerdings häufig als Agens eingesetzt, durch welches jemand in die Lage versetzt wird, etwas zu tun. Ausführlich dazu: Anna Schmid; Alexander Brust (Hg.): Rot. Wenn Farbe zur Täterin wird. Basel 2007, S. 9.

13
Blau wird in *Breaking Bad* als antagonistische Farbe zu Rot gesetzt. Sie ist eher den Elementen des Handlungsstrangs um die Figur Skyler zugeordnet, die anfangs neben anderen hellen Farben häufig Blau – später zunehmend dann, analog zu den insgesamt dunkler werdenden Filmbildern, Schwarz – trägt.

14
Dazu: Lorenz Engell: TV Pop. In: Walter Grasskamp; Michaela Krützen; Stephan Schmitt (Hg.): Was ist Pop? Zehn Versuche. Frankfurt am Main 2004, S. 195 ff. Engell beruft sich mit dem Begriff »Neo-Fernsehen« auf Umberto Eco und Roger Odin Casetti. »Neo-Fernsehen« bezeichnet demnach die zweite historische, seit 1985 bis heute andauernde Phase des Fernsehens; es ist u. a. ein Produkt der enormen Kanalvermehrung.

10

Ein Begriff der Seriendramaturgie, mit dem das Verweben mehrerer paralleler Handlungsstränge bezeichnet wird. Ausführlich: Stutterheim; Kaiser (2011), S. 372 (wie Anm. 8).

11

Vgl. Robin Nelson: TV Drama in Transition. Forms, Values and Cultural Change. London 1997, S. 30ff.

als »Filmromane« bezeichnet werden, sind von unterschiedlichen, unvorhersehbar langen Handlungsbögen bestimmt, die zwar durch die klassische Zopfdramaturgie[10] des episodischen Erzählens miteinander verwoben sind, aber auf eine neue Weise im Verhältnis zueinander stehen. Die Handlungsbögen können völlig unterschiedliche Längen und Gewichtung aufweisen, sie können sich über eine, zwei oder mehrere Episoden, eine oder alle Staffeln erstrecken. Im angelsächsischen Sprachraum existiert für diese Dramaturgie der Begriff »Flexi Narrative«, dort wird darüber hinaus zwischen *Series* und *Serials* unterschieden. Series sind traditionelle Serienformate, in denen der Haupterzählbogen innerhalb einer Episode aufgelöst wird, während im Serial sich die Erzählbögen über mehrere Episoden oder gesamte Staffeln erstrecken.[11]

In der eingangs erwähnten Parkplatz-Szene wird ein Großteil der Figuren-Charakterisierung über die Dresscodes und die jeweiligen Autos der beiden Protagonisten Walter White und Jesse Pinkman vorgenommen. In dieser Szene wird sichtbar, wie produktiv das Wechselverhältnis von Expliziter und Impliziter Dramaturgie ist und wie sie miteinander korrespondieren: Auf der dramaturgisch expliziten Ebene leitet die Szene den »Umschlag der Handlung« (die *Peripetie*) ein, die kriminelle Karriere des Walter White kann beginnen, auf der impliziten Ebene werden die Gegensätze der Figuren – auf allen stilistischen Ebenen – gegeneinander ausgespielt. Walter und Jesse passen ganz offensichtlich nicht zueinander. Sie halten sich in komplett unterschiedlichen Sozial- und Sprachsphären auf. Walter White ist so etwa das »Uncoolste«, was sich Jesse und die Autor_innen der Serie vorstellen konnten: Er trägt (als »farbloser Typ«) ausschließlich die Farbe Beige – was im Zusammenhang mit der ihn umgebenden, sandfarbenen Landschaft und Architektur (in dieser Szene die Bank) als Ausdruck seiner gesellschaftlichen Angepasstheit gedeutet werden kann, er fährt einen beigefarbenen Pontiac Aztek – der im britischen *Daily Telegraph* zu einem der hundert hässlichsten Autos aller Zeiten gekürt wurde –, während Jesse Pinkman im Kontrast übergroße, großbedruckte Hip Hop-Kleidung trägt und einen zwar bezahlbaren, aber glamourös-roten 1970er-Jahre-Wagen fährt. Im Sinne der Expliziten Dramaturgie

Breaking Bad

Breaking Bad ist für eine Fernsehserie überdurchschnittlich kinohaft und mit Blick auf einen spezifischen visuellen Stil erzählt. Damit wird die Ästhetik, also das *Wie,* zu einem wichtigen Träger der Narration. Es ist eine Besonderheit von *Breaking Bad,* wie die filmästhetischen Möglichkeiten ausgeschöpft und in den Dienst der Narration gestellt werden. Die Serie ist linearkausal, also mittels der *Dramaturgie der geschlossenen Form* erzählt, dabei existieren aber Aufbrüche in die *Offene Form* und in postmoderne Strukturen.[8] Eine Besonderheit der Serie liegt jedoch vor allem darin, wie eng implizite Elemente an die kausale Erzählung angebunden sind und zu ihrem Fortgang beitragen. Die Anteile der Impliziten Dramaturgie haben hier für die Organisation der Handlung eine besonders starke Bedeutung. Bereits das Thema der Serie und der Ausgangspunkt für die dramatische Erzählung, die auf der expliziten Erzählebene dazu dient, eine Figur in eine Situation zu bringen, die sie zum Handeln nötigt, verweisen implizit auf die gesellschaftliche Realität des unzureichenden Krankenversicherungssystems in den USA. (In Deutschland wäre dieser Ausgangspunkt für eine solche Geschichte wenig glaubwürdig…)

Der Middleclass-Chemielehrer Walter White benötigt aufgrund seiner Krebserkrankung Geld, will er seine medizinische Behandlung ermöglichen und die Versorgung seiner Familie nach seinem absehbaren Ableben sichern. Aufgrund bestimmter Umstände kommt er auf die Idee, ins Drogengeschäft, genauer gesagt in die Herstellung von Methamphetaminen (Crystal Meth) einzusteigen. Durch die Krebserkrankung des Protagonisten wird eine Handlung in Gang gebracht, die als größter dramaturgischer Bogen die Serie umspannt. Walter White wird kriminell, und es ist die Frage, ob er entdeckt und bestraft wird oder nicht. Darunter subsumieren sich viele kleinere dramaturgische Bögen, die mal in einer Folge, mal über mehrere Folgen und mal über eine Staffel hinweg erzählt werden. Ein Merkmal dieser und ähnlich anspruchsvoller Autorenserien ist, dass der horizontalen Dramaturgie stärkeres Gewicht zugemessen wird als der vertikalen, was diese Serien von traditionellen Fernsehserien stark unterscheidet.[9] Diese Neuen Serien, die daher wiederholt auch

---

8
Ausführlich dazu: Kerstin Stutterheim; Silke Kaiser: Handbuch der Filmdramaturgie. Das Bauchgefühl und seine Ursachen. Frankfurt am Main 2011 (2. Aufl.) und Kerstin Stutterheim; Christine Lang: Come and play with us. Ästhetik und Dramaturgie im Postmodernen Kino. Marburg 2014.

9
»Vertikale Dramaturgie« bezeichnet die sich in jeder Episode wiederholenden dramaturgischen Muster, die beispielsweise in klassischen Kriminalserien darin besteht, dass immer wieder von einem Kriminalinspektor ein neuer Mordfall zu lösen ist. Horizontale Dramaturgien beziehen sich auf Handlungsbögen, die über die Länge einer Episode hinausgehen, über mehrere Episoden oder über die gesamte Länge einer ganze Serie gehen; das gilt beispielsweise für die Erzählung des Lebens des Kriminalinspektors.

5
Peter Reichel (Hg.): Studien zur Dramaturgie: Kontexte – Implikationen – Berufspraxis. Tübingen 2000, S. 21.

6
Ebd.

7
Zu diesem Thema: Annegret Gertz; Rolf Rohmer: Versteckte Dramaturgien im amerikanischen Bühnenentertainment. In: Ebd., S. 81–133.

Implizite Dramaturgie entfaltet sich im Zusammenwirken mit der Expliziten Dramaturgie und »realisiert sich funktional erst im Aneignungs- beziehungsweise Produktions- und Vermittlungsprozess«[5]. Zuschauer gleichen Filme laufend mit ihren Erfahrungen, mit ihrem Weltwissen ab und setzen die Filmerzählung mit den eigenen Welterfahrungen in Beziehung. Je mehr Weltwissen – bei Autor_innen und bei Rezipierenden – vorhanden ist, desto größer ist die Bedeutung von Impliziter Dramaturgie; sie ist das Mittel, mit dem sich Filmautor_innen und Werk an weitreichendes Weltwissen adressieren – auf allen Ebenen und mit allen filmästhetischen Mitteln. Implizite Dramaturgien sind vor allem mit nicht rein werkbezogenen historischen, soziologischen und kulturellen Gegebenheiten verbunden.[6] Implikationen innerhalb eines Werks werden aus dem philosophischen, kulturhistorischen oder auch aus dem biografischen Umfeld der Autor_innen und aller beteiligter Künstler_innen in das Werk hineingebracht. Nicht nur intentionale künstlerische Absichten spielen dabei eine Rolle, sondern beispielsweise allein die Filmografien von in einem Film vertretenen Schauspieler_innen beeinflussen dessen Rezeption. Implizite Dramaturgien beziehen sich dabei nicht nur auf die textliche, sprachliche Ebene eines Werks, sondern auch auf dessen formal-ästhetische Struktur, beispielsweise Metrum und Rhythmus eines filmischen Werks betreffend. Auch wenn bestimmte Implizite Dramaturgien in der Binnenstruktur eines Films angesiedelt sein können, wenn etwa der Grund für die Organisation der ästhetischen Mittel im Werk selber angelegt ist, sind sie mit den historisch ein Filmwerk umgebenden ästhetischen Diskursen, mit technischen Innovationen und gesellschaftspolitischen Umständen verbunden. Dass dies auch für Rhythmik und Metrik gilt, zeigt sich auch in den Unterschieden zwischen dem »gut gemachten« US-amerikanischen Unterhaltungsfilm und dem in der Tradition eines künstlerischen Realismus stehenden europäischen Autorenfilm. Beide weisen ästhetische Implikationen aus völlig unterschiedlichen musikhistorischen Traditionen – einerseits einer vom Black Atlantic durchdrungenen Kultur und andererseits einer weißen, europäischen Avantgardekultur – auf.[7]

reich. Die Explizite Dramaturgie bezieht sich auf die Basisebene der Filmerzählung, auf das konkrete Handlungsgeschehen, etwa analog zu den von David Bordwell und Kristin Thompson von den Russischen Formalisten übernommenen Termini »Fabula« und »Syuzhet« zusammengenommen. »Fabula« bezeichnet die erzählte Geschichte, die unabhängig vom Erzählmedium existiert, während »Syuzhet« die medienabhängige Organisation und Vermittlung dieses Handlungsgeschehens bezeichnet. Im Gegensatz zur Expliziten Dramaturgie bezeichnet die Implizite die innerhalb der expliziten Erzählung versteckten Dramaturgien. Sie bezieht sich auf jene Elemente der Erzählung, die auf das Weltwissen der Rezipienten referieren und die damit für den erweiterten Wirkungsradius eines Werks verantwortlich sind. Etwas, was mit dem Begriff »Style« nur unzureichend beschrieben werden kann. Im Unterschied zu den aus der semiotischen stammenden Begriffen »Denotation« und »Konnotation« (vgl. Metz, Barthes), mit den im Neoformalismus argumentierten vier Bedeutungsebenen (referenzielle und explizite sowie implizite und symptomatische[3]), zielt der Begriff der Impliziten Dramaturgie, in Ergänzung zur der Expliziten Dramaturgie, nicht nur auf die außerhalb des Films/Bildes in die Welt verweisende Bedeutungszusammenhänge, sondern fragt vor allem, ähnlich wie die Rezeptionsästhetik, nach Funktion, Bedeutung und Wechselwirkungen innerhalb der Narration selbst. Explizite und Implizite Dramaturgie sind relative Begriffe, die sich auf die Bedeutungszusammenhänge einzelner Elemente innerhalb filmischer Narration beziehen. Die filmästhetischen Elemente stehen meist im Dienst von beidem – der Expliziten und der Impliziten Dramaturgie –, aber je offener und »poetischer« ein Film erzählt ist, desto stärker liegt das Gewicht auf der Impliziten Dramaturgie als Schlüssel zur Entzifferung der präsentierten Narration. Dabei ist Implizite Dramaturgie nicht zuletzt und zum größten Teil für die Realismus-Wirkung und die Authentisierung des Erzählten verantwortlich. Stil und Humor sind immer zeit- und kontextabhängige Phänomene, und wenn etwa Metaphern und Verweise auf das Welt- und Alltagswissen medial erfahrener Rezipient_innen nicht stimmen, können ein Film oder eine Fernsehserie schnell ahnungslos oder naiv wirken.[4]

3
Ausführlich: Kristin Thompson: Neoformalistische Filmanalyse. In: Montage AV, Heft 4.1.1995; www.montage-av.de (Stand 16.08.2013) S. 32.

4
Wenn sich ein Film nicht an gängige ästhetische Diskurse und Codes anschließt, wird seine Rezeption erschwert bis unmöglich gemacht. Das gilt sowohl für kommerzielle Unterhaltungsfilme als auch für Kunstvideos. In der Bezeichnung »poetische Bilder« ist noch nicht enthalten, auf welchen Geschmackskanon sich diese »Poesie« bezieht. Die dramaturgischen, ästhetischen und stilistischen Fragestellungen in televisuellen Narrationen sind noch nicht ausreichend erforscht. In der Fernsehforschung überwiegen soziokulturelle und medientheoretische Ansätze.

verbirgt sich in dem Ausspruch eine Codierung, die den Rezipienten einen Hinweis auf eine wichtige Implikation der gesamten
Serie gibt: »Breaking bad« trägt in dieser Jugendsprache die
Konnotation »cool sein« in sich. Die Implizite Dramaturgie
adressiert sich in der Szene also an ein kulturell geprägtes Alltagswissen und an die Kenntnisse einer speziellen Zielgruppe, vor
allem an das popkulturell geprägte Distinktionswissen – eben an
das Wissen vom Unterschied zwischen »cool« und »nicht cool«.

Bei Impliziter Dramaturgie handelt es sich um einen
Begriff, mit dem man bestimmte, beispielsweise mit den von
David Bordwell ins Feld geführten Termini wie *Style* und *Excess*
(Überschuss) gefasste Komponenten des filmischen Erzählens
für eine über die Interpretation von Teilaspekten hinausgehende
Analyse produktiv machen kann.[2] Dramaturgie, sowohl als
praktische Tätigkeit als auch als praxisbezogene Wissenschaft,
ist dabei immer als jenes Mittel zu verstehen, welches die
rezeptionsästhetischen Prozesse eines Werks steuert und mittels
derer verborgene Sinngehalte einer filmischen Narration
entschlüsselt werden können. Implizite Dramaturgie ist dabei
nicht nur ein, sondern vielleicht *der* bestimmende Faktor in
zeitgenössischen filmischen Erzählungen. Durch sie werden
Tiefendimensionen des filmischen Erzählens geprägt und
vermittelt. Sie lässt sich dabei in ihrer Weltreferenz nicht nur auf
inhaltliche Verweise und Zitate, wie man sie aus dem so genannten postmodernen Kinofilm kennt, begrenzen, sondern sie
organisiert den Einsatz aller filmischen Gestaltungselemente. Sie
steuert alle ästhetischen Entscheidungen in Hinsicht auf
Material, Farbe, Kamera, Montage, die Mise-en-scène – von der
Performance bis zur Szenografie – und natürlich nicht zuletzt
alle auditiven Elemente. In der Filmsprache haben alle filmästhetischen Elemente, wenn nicht eine explizite, eine implizite
und eine dramaturgische Funktion.

Der Begriff »Implizite Dramaturgie« stammt aus der
theoretischen Theaterdramaturgie, in der es eine Tradition gibt,
sich mit impliziten, also versteckten Dramaturgien zu beschäftigen. Sowohl für das tiefere Verständnis einer dramatischen
filmischen Erzählung als auch für die Filmanalyse sind die
Begriffe »Explizite« und »Implizite Dramaturgie« äußerst hilf-

2
Zu den Begriffen »Fabula«,
»Syuzhet« und »Style«: David
Bordwell: Narration in the Fiction
Film. Madison 1985, S. 48ff.

Zuschauer_innenvereinbarung, eine Art Handlungsanweisung für die Lesart der Serie: In dieser Serie wird viel mit, über und durch Stil erzählt. Die Zuschauer_innen werden aufgefordert, sich darauf einzustellen und darauf zu achten. Dabei ist in *Breaking Bad* nicht nur allgemeines westliches Weltwissen Voraussetzung, um alle Dimensionen des Erzählten verstehen zu können, sondern es wird stilsicheres Distinktionswissen verlangt. Genre-Wissen und die Lesekompetenz der Stile, etwa der Wohnungseinrichtungen, der Automarken und der Kleidung spielen eine bedeutende Rolle.

In einer später folgenden Schlüsselszene der Pilotfolge (Abb. 1) überreicht Walter dem neuen Geschäftspartner Jesse auf dem Parkplatz seine gesamten Ersparnisse, damit dieser damit ein Meth-Labor einrichten kann:

JESSE: Tell me why you're doing this. Seriously.

WALT: Why do *you* do it?

JESSE: Money, mainly.

WALT: There you go.

JESSE: Nah. Come on, man! Some straight like you, giant stick up his ass... all of a sudden at age, what, sixty – he's just gonna break bad?

WALT: I'm fifty.

JESSE: It's weird, is all, okay? It doesn't compute. Listen, if you're gone crazy or something. I mean, if you've gone crazy, or depressed – I'm just saying – that's something I need to know about. Okay? That affects me.

WALT: I am... awake.

JESSE: What??

WALT: Buy the RV. We start tomorrow.[1]

Dass es in *Breaking Bad* zwei wesentliche Dimensionen des Erzählens gibt, die der expliziten und die der impliziten Ebene – darauf wird im originalsprachigen Dialog dieser Szene hingewiesen, ja sogar durch die der Serie ihren Titel gebende Frage Jesses direkt angespielt: Auf der expliziten Ebene richtet sich seine Frage »Some straight like you, ... he's just gonna break bad?« darauf, ob Walter jetzt »böse« werde. Diese Jugendkultursprache Jesses dient der schlüssigen Charakterisierung der Walter White kontrastierenden Figur. Andererseits – und implizit –

1
In der deutschen Synchronfassung verliert sich die Doppeldeutung: JESSE: Sagen Sie mir, warum Sie das tun. Jetzt im Ernst! WALT: Warum tust *du* das? JESSE: Wegen der Kohle, hauptsächlich. WALT: Da hast du's. JESSE: Nein, kommen Sie! Mann, so'n Spießer wie Sie mit 'nem riesigen Stock im Arsch will auf einmal mit - wie alt sind Sie, sechzig? - mit dem Kopf durch die Wand? WALT: Ich bin fünfzig. JESSE: Das ist verrückt. Total irre, das ergibt keinen Sinn. Wenn Sie durchgeknallt sind, oder so. Ich meine, wenn Sie verrückt geworden sind, oder depressiv, ich mein, ich mein ja nur, dann ist das was, was ich unbedingt wissen muss, verstehen Sie? Das betrifft mich auch. WALT: Ich bin aufgewacht. JESSE: Was? WALT: Kauf den Camper. Wir fangen morgen an. – Ins Deutsche ließe sich Jesses Satz vielleicht treffender mit »Willst du jetzt ein cooler Gangster werden?« übersetzen.

Die Serie *Breaking Bad* (USA, 2008, entwickelt von Vince Gilligan) ist eines der gelungensten Beispiele des neueren Autorenfernsehens und zeichnet sich durch außergewöhnlich dicht und gut geschriebene Drehbücher aus. Handlungen und Ereignisse geschehen hier niemals ›einfach so‹, sie sind stets motiviert und haben Konsequenzen, oftmals erst mehrere Folgen oder gar Staffeln später. Die Fülle von erzählerischen Details, die Referenzen, die metaphorische Filmsprache und die zahlreichen symbolischen Aktivierungen aller filmästhetischen Gestaltungsmittel fügen der expliziten Handlung tiefere Bedeutungsebenen hinzu. Sie schaffen Subtexte, die der Wahrnehmung beim ersten oder einmaligen Sehen möglicherweise entgehen und die das aktive »ästhetische Sehen« und das mehrfache Anschauen der Serie mit immer neuen Entdeckungen belohnen.

Der vorliegende Essay behandelt die Bedeutung der *Impliziten Dramaturgie* für das Gelingen zeitgenössischer Fernsehfilmerzählungen – im Zusammenwirken mit der sich auf das reine Handlungsgeschehen beziehenden *Expliziten Dramaturgie*. Beispielhaft wird gezeigt, wie das in dieser Serie (wie auch in anderen Autorenserien) enthaltene und reflektierte Welt- und Distinktionswissen die hohe Qualität der Serie mitkonstituiert und dadurch eine hohe erzählerische Glaubwürdigkeit erzeugt.

Implizite Dramaturgie in *Breaking Bad*

In der Exposition der *Breaking Bad*-Pilotfolge werden auf elegante Weise die Grundkoordinaten der Situation mitgeteilt: Die Zuschauenden erfahren in einer vordergründig unscheinbaren Sequenz das Wichtigste über die Lebenssituation des Protagonisten. Auf der Ebene der expliziten Erzählung wird in dieser Sequenz die Backstory des Helden vermittelt: dass sein Leben wohl anders verlaufen ist, als er es gedacht hat, dass er demnächst Vater wird, dass er einmal Anwärter auf den Nobelpreis war und dass er jetzt gesundheitlich nicht ganz auf der Höhe ist. Zudem wird seine Ehefrau Skyler über die an der Wand sorgfältig aufgehängten Farbmuster eingeführt und charakterisiert.

Dieses sind alles wichtige Informationen für die explizite Handlung, gleichzeitig wird – etwa durch die Farbmuster – implizit noch etwas anderes miterzählt. Hier versteckt sich eine

»Gonna Break Bad?«
Über *Implizite Dramaturgie* in *Breaking Bad*

Christine Lang

Steffen Huck

ist Geschäftsführer der *Economics of Change* bei der WZB und Professor für Wirtschaftswissenschaften bei der UCL. Seine Forschung hat sowohl die Rolle von Vertrauen und Fairness im Wettbewerb als auch Probleme hinsichtlich einer eingegrenzten Vernunft und eine evolutionäre Spieltheorie untersucht. Er hat im Jahr 2004 den Philip-Leverhulme-Preis erhalten. Kürzlich hat er kontrafaktisch an Richard Wagners *Tannhäuser* und den Glaubenssätzen in *Lohengrin* gearbeitet.

Diana Iljine

geboren in Frankfurt am Main, studierte Kommunikationswissenschaften und arbeitet seit 25 Jahren im Bereich Film und Fernsehen, davon viele Jahre als Lizenz-Einkäuferin für Filme und Serien. Ihr Buch *Der Produzent* über Filmproduktion avancierte zum Standardwerk. Vor kurzem beendete sie ein Wirtschaftsstudium/MBA an der Steinbeishochschule in Berlin. Seit August 2011 leitet sie das Filmfest München.

Sir Peter Jonas

war von 1985 bis 1993 Generaldirektor der English National Opera. 1993 übernahm er die Funktion des Generaldirektors der bayrischen Staatsoper. Diese Funktion bekleidete er bis zu seiner Pensionierung im Jahre 2006. Er hat einen First Degree in englischer Literatur und studierte als Postgraduierter Oper und Musikgeschichte. Im Jahr 1974 kam er zum Chicago Symphony Orchestra. Hier bekleidete er die Funktion eines Leiters der Künstlerverwaltung, bevor er zur ENO wechselte. Er ist ein Freund der Royal Society of Arts und des Royal College of Music. Im Jahr 2000 wurde er zum Ritter geschlagen. Er hält Lehrstühle an den Universitäten St. Gallen und Zürich sowie an der Bayrischen Theaterakademie. Darüber hinaus ist er Mitglied im Vorstand der niederländischen Oper und des Kollegiums der Universität zu Luzern. Er ist ein Freund der University of Sussex. Außerdem war er neun Jahre lang, bis zum Jahr 2013, Mitglied des Vorstands der drei Unternehmen der Berliner Staatsoper und des Berliner Balletts.

Das neue Genre entwickelt sich derweil mit atemraubender Virtuosität. Matthew Weiner zeigt in *Mad Men*, wie man ohne jegliche Handlung erzählen und Zuschauer fesseln kann, und Vince Gilligan setzt den TV Epics ihre vorläufige Krone auf mit *Breaking Bad*, einem Werk mit so ungeheurer Komplexität – ästhetischer wie narrativer –, dass man sich immer wieder aufs Neue fragt, wie es eigentlich gelingen kann.

Und es ist nicht nur das neue Talent, das sich das Fernsehen als Medium aussucht, es sind auch die alten großen Meister des Kinos, die sich den TV Epics zuwenden. Da die großen Studios weniger Kinofilme inszenieren, wirken immer mehr bekannte Kinogrößen im Fernsehen: Martin Scorsese produziert *Boardwalk Empire* (und inszenierte die Pilotfolge), Dustin Hoffman spielt die Hauptrolle in *Luck*. Und da die DVD verschwindet und die Cloud übernimmt, zeigt *Netflix* – im Kampf um exklusive Inhalte – *House of Cards* mit Kevin Spacey gleich vom ersten Tag an komplett.

Nicht einmal 15 Jahre sind verstrichen nach dem Double Blast von *The Sopranos* und *The West Wing*. 15 Jahre, in denen sich durch das Zusammenspiel von kreativem Mut und Wahn, sprunghafter technologischer Innovation und knallhartem Wettbewerb Fernsehen für immer geändert hat. Die Highlights des Fernsehprogramms sind nicht mehr die erstmaligen Ausstrahlungen großer Hollywoodfilme. Es sind die selbstproduzierten neuen Serien, die den Filmen nicht nur in nichts nachstehen, sondern sie oftmals ästhetisch wie narrativ überflügeln.

Sind also Serien das Kino des 21. Jahrhunderts? TV Epics mit ihrer neuen komplexen narrativen Struktur können auf jeden Fall als die Romane des 21. Jahrhunderts bezeichnet werden. Die Erzählweise großer Romane wird ins Audiovisuelle übertragen als Revolution, als Reaktion und Antwort auf die – nicht schwarzweiße, sondern – bunte neue Welt.

kam, wurde nach einem unattraktiven 21-Uhr-Slot im ZDF nach der zweiten Staffel auf *Arte* verbannt, um nach der dritten komplett eingestellt zu werden.

Im Angesicht des Verbrechens – bei dem zwei Berliner Polizisten im Mafiamilieu von Berlin ermitteln, von Dominik Graf und Rolf Basedow aus dem Jahr 2010 – lief bei *Arte,* dann auf einem späten Slot in der ARD und wurde daraufhin wegen mangelnder Quote eingestellt. Und wo bitte ist der TV Epic des deutschen Großmeisters der Miniserie, wo, liebe ARD, ist Dieter Wedels Spätwerk? Für ein kreatives Team, wie es bei US-Serien üblich ist, entstehen Kosten, die bisher in Deutschland gescheut werden.

Dabei ist interessant, dass die Macher amerikanischer Serien keineswegs freie Hand haben. Die US-Fernsehsaisons bedingen straffe Produktionszyklen, was wiederum bedeutet, dass Alleinarbeit von Autoren, wie in Europa üblich, schlechterdings unmöglich ist.

Zwar genießt der Autor in einem amerikanischen Produktionsteam eine hohe Stellung und ist extrem gut bezahlt, aber bei den Serien gibt es die so genannten Writers Rooms, bei denen vier bis sechs Autoren kontinuierlich gemeinsam brainstormen und schreiben.

Anders wäre es schlichtweg nicht möglich, über eine lange Saison mit bis zu 24 Episoden gleichbleibend hohe Qualität zu liefern. Es ist in der Tat der Druck des Markts, die kalte Konkurrenz in der amerikanischen Fernsehindustrie, die diese Form der Kollaboration erzwingt und damit dem Zuschauer etwas bietet, was ein vereinzeltes europäisches ›Genie‹ nicht stemmen kann.

Der Writers Room wird geleitet von einem so genannten Showrunner, oftmals ein erfahrener Drehbuchautor, so wie David Chase von *The Sopranos* oder Vince Gilligan von *Breaking Bad.* Der Showrunner ist inhaltlich für die narrative Entwicklung der Serie zuständig und hat Einblick in jeden Aspekt der Serienproduktion. Oftmals ist er als Produzent auch verantwortlich für die finanziellen Aspekte. Der Showrunner gibt die Vision für die Serie vor, lässt aber auch los und ist offen für Vorschläge der einzelnen Autoren. Es gibt inzwischen in den USA schon Ausbildungen zum Showrunner von der *Writers Guild of America.*

lung verdichten die Erzählweise und ähneln der Erzählstruktur von Romanen.

Ein langer, dramaturgischer Bogen statt in sich geschlossene Geschichten führt dazu, dass man immer weitersehen will. Es geht um komplexe, dynamische und persönliche Beziehungen der Protagonisten. Helden mit ›normalen‹ Problemen – wenngleich die Problemlösung meist nicht normal ist – binden den Zuschauer an die Figuren der Serie und schaffen Identifikation.

Innovativ sind auch die Prämissen: Der größte Held von Amerika – könnte das der größte Terrorist sein (*Homeland*)? Ein braver Chemieprofessor, der kriminell wird (*Breaking Bad*), ein Mafiaboss in Psychotherapie (*The Sopranos*) oder der aalglatte Werbetyp, der eine dunkle Seite hat (*Mad Men*). Nicht mehr das klassische Prinzip von Gut und Böse, sondern ausdifferenzierte Protagonisten mit guten und schlechten Eigenschaften...

Zugleich wurde von Anfang an im Internet auf Fanseiten und Foren diskutiert. Produzenten nutzten das Internet, um Hintergrundinformationen und weitere mögliche Handlungsstränge zu verraten und verliehen den Serien so einen noch höheren Kultstatus.

In Deutschland verschlief man die Revolution allerdings: *The Sopranos* liefen für eine Saison auf ZDF, dann ein Jahr Pause, dann noch zwei, noch später in der Nacht, dann aus – die Rückkehr fand erst wieder 2005 bei *kabel eins* statt. *The West Wing*, inzwischen dekoriert mit 26 *Emmys* und drei *Golden Globes*, wurde geschlagene neun Jahre ignoriert, dann schließlich im deutschen Pay-TV bei *Fox* gesendet. Immerhin gab es nur eine dreijährige Lücke bei *Six Feet Under*, und wieder war es das Privatfernsehen, das zuschnappte. Das gleiche bei *Boston Legal*, mit nur zwei Jahren Verzögerung bei *Vox,* und bei *The Shield*, nach zwei Jahren bei *ProSieben*.

Kein Ruhmesblatt für die öffentlich-rechtlichen Fernsehsender. Da ist es kein Trost, dass sie ihre eigenen Chancen im neuen globalen Kulturwettbewerb im Genre der TV Epics ebenfalls leichtfertig vergeben haben.

KDD-Kriminaldauerdienst über den Alltag einer Berliner Kripoeinheit, das deutsche Fernsehmeisterwerk des letzten Jahrzehnts, das den ausländischen Serienvorbildern am nächsten

uns nicht einmal annähernd vorstellen, was es damals bedeutete, ein halbes Jahr warten zu müssen, um zu sehen, um was für eine *Art von Tag* (so der Titel der Folge) es sich wirklich handelte – wer leben würde und wer nicht.

Vielleicht muss man sich das Premierenpublikum im Nationaltheater in München vorstellen, irgendwann am späteren Abend des 18. Juni 1865, am Ende des zweiten Akts von *Tristan*... Da war ein radikales neues Werk, mit Akkorden, wie es die Ohren noch nicht vernommen hatten, und dann wird dem so tief verliebten Helden am Ende des zweiten Akts ein Messer in die Brust gerammt. Es muss eine schwer erträgliche Pause gewesen sein, aber immerhin dauerte sie nur eine runde halbe Stunde. Heute freilich – mit einem Boxset mehrerer Staffeln ausgestattet – muss man nicht einmal mehr Minuten warten.

Die Revolution von '99 elektrisierte nicht nur das Publikum, sondern auch die Macher – ja, ganz Amerika! Der Beweis war erbracht: Ein neues Fernsehen war nicht nur möglich, sondern das, worauf alle schon lange gewartet hatten.

Sender wie HBO sprachen zunächst ein gebildetes und zahlungskräftiges Publikum an und konnten auch mit kleineren Zielgruppen als die Networks leben. Die Networks und die Produzenten zielten aber sogleich auf ein nationales und internationales Publikum ab. Das Publikum war nun nicht nur differenzierter, sondern auch globaler, zumal die Revolution auch nach Europa schwappte.

So floss das Geld, und es kam das Talent: 2001 bescherte uns Alan Ball *Six Feet Under* und Joel Surnow *24*, 2002 Shawn Ryan *The Shield* und David Simon *The Wire*, 2004 David Milch *Deadwood* und David E. Kelley *Boston Legal*. Bald wurde es schwer, den Überblick zu behalten, vor allem da auch in Europa produzierte Serien mit derartig komplexer Erzählweise starteten. Zunächst in Frankreich, wo 2005 Alexandra Clerts *Engrènages* begann, und bald auch in England und Dänemark.

Die komplexe Erzählweise verlangt vom Zuschauer aktive Mitarbeit und Klugheit. Er muss die Verbindung zwischen der Handlung in der einzelnen Serienepisode und dem gesamten Universum der Geschichte erkennen und verstehen. Viele parallele Handlungsstränge anstatt einer dominierenden Hand-

der ersten Staffel der *Sopranos*, wenn man Tony, den Familienva-
ter, der seine Tochter bei der Besichtigung von Universitäten
begleitet, das erste Mal töten sieht. Und das alleine mit der Kraft
seiner scheinbar so sensiblen Hände. Was die HBO-Abonnenten
am 5. Februar 1999 erlebten, hatte es auf dem Fernsehschirm bis
dato noch nie gegeben.

Aber zurück zu Coyote Creek. Wenn man die Fernsehserie zum Roman moduliert, sollte man sicherstellen, dass die
Zuschauer kein Kapitel verpassen. (*Der Zauberberg* ohne Pistolen-
duell? Oh je!)

Im alten Format der in sich geschlossenen Episoden
stellten sich solche Probleme nicht: Zuschauer konnten auch mal
eine Episode verpassen; im schlimmsten Fall war's eine besonders
gute Folge, aber künftiges Verstehen und künftiger Genuss
hingen davon nicht ab.

Anders in *The Sopranos* und *The West Wing* – wer nicht
Zeuge der Szene wird, in der Tony, der liebende Vater der
unschuldigen Meadow, »Febby« Petrulio erwürgt, kann später
Tonys Psyche nie richtig verstehen.

In anderen Worten, *The Sopranos* wäre genau wie *The
West Wing* aufs Schlimmste gefloppt, hätten Jim Barton und
Mike Ramsay nicht ihren TiVo erfunden, der auf einmal ermöglichte, eine komplette Serie mit nur einem Knopfdruck auf
einer flexiblen und mächtigen Hard Disk aufzunehmen.

Weitere technologische Möglichkeiten wie die DVD,
Online-Anbieter wie *Netflix* und *iTunes* taten ihr Übriges. Sie
erlaubten dem Zuschauer endlich, die Serie so zu konsumieren
wie den Roman, nämlich am Stück. Eben nicht nur eine Folge
pro Woche, nicht nur eine Episode am Tag, sondern zwei, drei
oder vier am Abend. Und wenn es dann zum Finale geht, auch
gerne sechs oder sieben – bis zur Erschöpfung und Katharsis,
bis zur Auflösung. »Serien: Die neue mediale Droge«, wie es
DER SPIEGEL bezeichnete. Auch dem Konsum ganzer Staffeln
steht heute nichts mehr im Wege, und so muss der Cliffhanger
am Ende einer Staffel nicht mehr als Qual empfunden werden.

Wir sahen *The West Wing* mit etwas Verspätung auf DVD.
Das ermöglichte uns, nach der letzten Episode der ersten Staffel
gleich die erste Folge der zweiten Staffel zu sehen. Wir können

Werbeunterbrechungen angewiesen waren, fanden mit der Entwicklung dieser Serien nicht nur ihr neues Geschäftsmodell, sondern definierten ab jetzt auch den Stil und die narrative Technik der neuen Serien.

Im Winter kam *The Sopranos* von David Chase. Die Serie handelt vom Leben einer Mafiafamilie in New Jersey und war vom Winter 1999 an bis 2007 auf HBO zu sehen. *The Sopranos* wurde mit 21 *Emmys* und fünf *Golden Globes* ausgezeichnet.

Und im Herbst startete *The West Wing* von Aaron Sorkin, eine Serie über das Leben im Westflügel des Weißen Hauses in Washington. Die Serie wurde bis 2006 ausgestrahlt und handelte vom Alltag des fiktiven US-Präsidenten, Joshua Bartlett, und seinem Beraterstab. Die Serie inspirierte das amerikanische Publikum so sehr, dass sich eine ganze Zeitlang Gerüchte hielten, Bartletts Darsteller, Martin Sheen, würde sich im richtigen Leben für das Amt des Präsidenten bewerben. Gewünscht hätten sich das viele.

The Sopranos und *The West Wing* waren parallele Quantensprünge, wie sie die Welt vielleicht zuletzt ein gutes Jahrhundert zuvor erlebt hatte, als zwei heute 200-Jährige die Oper revolutionierten, Guiseppe Verdi und Richard Wagner, die zu einer neue Form von Drama mit präziser, narrativ komplexer Entfaltung für das Musiktheater fanden.

Die Idee, die Chase und Sorkin teilten, war verblüffend einfach: Wenn man zehn oder zwanzig Folgen für eine Serie hat, warum muss man dann zehn oder zwanzig Kurzgeschichten erzählen, mit den immer gleichen Charakteren, wenn man auch eine große, tiefe, komplexe Geschichte erzählen kann?

Warum nicht, wenn schon Serie, das Äquivalent großer Romane fürs Fernsehen ausprobieren? *Krieg und Frieden* für unsere Zeit! Mit all den wunderbaren, verblüffenden, tief bewegenden Möglichkeiten, die sich ergeben, wenn man die Entwicklung von Charakteren zeigen kann?

Manchmal wird eine derartige Entwicklung nur in einem Nebensatz angedeutet, der den aufmerksamen Rezipienten aber erschaudern lässt, weil er die Figur ja in- und auswendig kennt. Oder aber sie wird in plötzlichen Ausbrüchen tieferer, ungeahnter Wesenszüge demonstriert. So in der fünften Folge

Die Revolution von 1999 fand nicht auf der Straße statt, nicht im Osten, und eine exklusive Farbe hatte sie auch nicht, weder gelb noch orange noch pink. Stattdessen kam sie in ›bunt‹.

Und wie alle Revolutionen wurde sie nur möglich durch das glückliche Zusammenspiel unterschiedlichster Kräfte: ökonomischer, sozialer, technologischer. Da war der Risikohunger amerikanischer Großunternehmen und der Tüftlergeist eines kleinen Start-ups in Santa Clara County, dort, wo sich Guadalupe River und Coyote Creek in die Bucht von San Francisco ergießen.

Der erste Donnerschlag kam am 10. Januar 1999, der zweite Knall folgte am 22. September 1999. Es war ein Double Blast, der die Wohnzimmer Amerikas traf, beherrscht wie alle Wohnzimmer der Welt vom Fernsehschrein in ihrer Mitte. Aber diesmal wurden keine Kurzgeschichten von den – damals noch mit großen Röhren befeuerten – Mattscheiben ausgestrahlt, sondern gewaltige, subtil geflochtene Romane.

Es war die Revolution der TV Epics. Ein erstes Aufflackern dessen, was kommen sollte, sah man schon zwei Jahre zuvor auf HBO. Dort startete Tom Fontanas *Oz*, eine phantasmagorische Reise durch die Hölle eines amerikanischen Hochsicherheitsknasts. Es wurde vor nichts, aber auch gar nichts zurückgeschreckt und so ein radikaler Entwurf geliefert, an dem sich die Revolution entzünden konnte.

Die Revolutionsanführer hießen David Chase und Aaron Sorkin. Die beiden hätten unterschiedlicher nicht sein können: der eine ein erfahrener Produzent mit langem Lebenslauf, der andere ein bekanntermaßen drogensüchtiger Drehbuchautor, der in einem Jahrzehnt gerade mal drei Drehbücher an den Mann gebracht hatte.

Aber Lebensläufe spielten keine Rolle, denn das US-Fernsehen stand mit dem Rücken zur Wand. Sinkende Zuschauerzahlen bei steigender Konkurrenz zwischen den US-Networks und den Kabel-Networks setzten alle amerikanischen Sender stark unter Druck. Und wenn man nichts mehr zu verlieren hat, kann man wild experimentieren! Das geht zwar oft schief, kann aber auch Großes und Gewaltiges hervorbringen.

Das war die Geburtsstunde der großen Serien. Pay-TV-Sender wie HBO, die nicht wie die amerikanischen Networks auf

Eine narrative Revolution

Steffen Huck

Diana Iljine

Sir Peter Jonas

lassen mich ebenfalls kalt. Das ist ja wohl vorbei, dass wir beide noch große Bilder in unserer Beziehung kreieren müssen.

B.: Ich weiß nicht, ob das vorbei ist. Ich weiß nur, dass du aufgehört hast, dich mit der Theorie deines Charakters zu beschäftigen. In dem Gemütszustand kreierst du bestimmt keine brauchbaren Bilder mehr. Das geht so nicht. Ich spüre so eine blöde Distanz zwischen uns. Aber ich will doch nicht immer eine Distanz haben, wenn du dir ein Bild von mir machst.

M.: Da muss man keine Expertin sein, um das zu überbrücken. Du bist doch sowieso solch ein distanziertes Tier, das durch einen Wald von Bildern kommuniziert. Du erwartest die ganze Zeit, dass ich mich über deine Bilder informiere. Ständig stellst du irgendeinen emotionalen Gemütszustand dar, und ich muss das dann interpretieren.

B.: Deine Informationen haben nun wirklich nichts mit meinen Emotionen zu tun. Deine Bilder dienen lediglich dazu, Sachverhalte auf einer emotionalen Ebene zu vermitteln und zu verhandeln. Also, ich brauche das nicht.

M.: Aber da ist doch jede Emotion drin. Dass du das nicht brauchst, hätte ich mir denken können.

B.: O.k., das siehst du schon ganz gut so. Aber man kann das auch anders sehen. Ich muss mich jetzt beeilen, sonst gehen mir noch die Bilder aus.

Jos Diegel
ist bildender Künstler und Filmemacher. Er studierte bis 2010 an der Hochschule für Gestaltung Offenbach und spielt, experimentiert, unterhält und beschäftigt sich mit gesellschaftspolitischen und normativ-narrativen Strukturen, begreift seine fröhliche, interdisziplinäre Wissenschaft im Verhandeln und Konstruieren post-dramatischer und alternativer Situationen in den Medien, u.a. Film, Video, Installation, Malerei, Performance, Text. Zahlreiche Ausstellungen, Filmvorführungen und Projekte.

B.: Gerne würde ich dich in dieser exotischen Welt besuchen, die vor Erwartung und Selbstvertrauen flimmernden fünf- undzwanzig, fünfzig oder was weiß ich, wie viele Bilder die Sekunde einsaugen, um letztlich irgendwohin abzureisen, mit der Gewissheit, jegliche Situation immer in gewohnt dramatische Pose setzen zu können.

M.: Und du meinst, irgendetwas Dramatisches wird es dort schon geben? Das, was du da zeichnest, ist für mich eher ein dramatisches Bild.

B.: Ständig muss ich lernen, meine intellektuellen Abenteuer für die anderen komfortabel und dramatisch zu verhandeln.

M.: Du schaffst aber auch so wunderbare Momente, wenn du in Bildern erzählst. Und du machst dabei ganz nebenbei ganz bewegte Bilder von uns. Da gibt es nichts, was du dir verbietest. Da gibt es kein Bilderverbot.

B.: Ich finde das auch ganz gut, was ich da sehe. Wenn jetzt jemand zuschaut, fühle ich mich gut unterhalten, zumindest besser als bei dir.

M.: Ständig bin ich bewegt von deinen Bildern. Ich komme aus dem Staunen nicht mehr heraus. Mich lässt das Gefühl nicht los, du machst deine Geschichten und deine Bilder für irgendwen, der noch fehlt.

B.: Dauernd habe ich das Gefühl, ich werde beobachtet und irgendjemand macht sich ein Bild von mir oder irgend- jemand schreibt mir etwas vor.

M.: Ja richtig! Ich habe immer das Gefühl, dass das, was du sagst, für dich geschrieben wurde. Du hast das aber auch dankend angenommen. Beschwert hat sich keiner, geschweige denn ich selbst.

B.: Ich kenne eine ganze Menge Bilder, ich weiß, was das hier soll. Ich will mich nicht beklagen, aber dein stures Bilder- betrachten ist das Betrachten von etwas, das von seiner Wahrheit getrennt ist. Du wirkst ziemlich getrennt von dem, was du da machst.

M.: Nein, bei mir ist das eben so, ich will auch nicht zu allem eine Meinung haben oder ein Bild. Es gibt eben Dinge, die mich kalt lassen. Deine warmen, gutgemeinten Bilder

M.: Diese Fluktuation macht mich ganz warm ums Herz. Diese Fluktuation der Worte. Diese Fluktuation der Bilder.

B.: Wenn ich die herunterbreche auf das Wesentliche und das Gefühl habe, das ist ökonomisch erzählt, dann fehlt mir etwas. Das Wesentliche interessiert mich meistens nicht. Ich bin gerne mit dir zusammen, und das ist das Wesentliche, wenn ich dir das erzähle. Aber eigentlich hast du davon nichts. Da gibt es noch etwas anderes, was ich dir erzählen muss.

M.: Du erzählst mir nichts. Davon habe ich auch nichts. Das sind alles Dinge, die man vorher hätte etablieren müssen.

B.: Das ist dein Ernst? Ich möchte mit dir etwas haben. Ich will mit dir eine Geschichte etablieren. Das finden doch die meisten ganz gut.

M.: Jetzt hör aber mal auf. Wenn mir gesagt wird: Erzählen Sie doch so, wie Sie wollen!, dann weiß ich meistens nicht, was ich sagen soll.

B.: Ich werde ständig vor oder hinter die Kamera gestoßen, und jemand sagt: Du machst das schon! Ohne irgendeinen Schimmer, was ich zeigen soll, um welches Gefühl es sich handelt. Und dann zeigen sie die Bilder auch noch irgendwo.

M.: Letztens morgens, da bin ich aufgewacht und musste an dich denken. Ich dachte mir, du siehst aus wie in einer Szene in einem Film, in dem du mitgespielt hast. Ich war ganz verwundert, weil, so kannte ich dich noch gar nicht, außer aus dem Film.

B.: Wir waren kein schlechtes Duo. Und ich glaube, wir haben gern miteinander gespielt und Bilder produziert. Hast du die Filme, die wir gemacht haben noch? Ich konnte sie nirgends finden.

M.: Du plapperst eigentlich gerade nur unwichtiges Zeug, das interessiert hier nicht. Ich finde ja gut, dass ich so ehrlich zu dir bin, aber schade, dass ich nicht auf den Gedanken komme, mir zu überlegen, warum du nur unsicher vor dich hin plapperst und versuchst, diese Bilder mit Text zu füllen.

Sekunden stirbt ein Kind auf der Welt. Da kann es ja wohl einen Zusammenhang geben.

B.: Deine Geschichte ist einfach nur sehr symbolträchtig und bildgewaltig. Weißt du das? Mehr zu bieten hast du wohl nicht?

M.: Ja genau. Das ist sie. Das ist die Krise der Erzählbarkeit deines eigenen Lebens im Zusammenhang mit dem Niedergang der großen Erzählungen unserer Epoche. Aber wem erzähl ich denn das?

B.: Mir erzählst du gar nichts. Wenn du da so herumstehst und mir irgendeinen Zusammenhang vermitteln willst, erzählst du mir gar nichts. Ich bin für alles zu haben. Aber nicht für deine Geschichten, die werden sowieso nie von der Richtigen erzählt.

M.: Darum wirfst du mit Bildern um dich. Ich komme mir vor wie in einem Bilderbuch, obwohl ich mit warmen Worten überhäuft werde.

B.: Mit dem Oktober 2013 haben diese Bilder den Zenit ihrer Wirkung erreicht. Das revolutionäre Projekt versinkt in einer Bilderflut, die sich nostalgisch nunmehr mit sich selbst befasst.

M.: Immer redest du vom Versinken. Immer redest du von der Flut. Wann kommt denn nun die Flut? Ich strenge mich hier an, einen natürlich gegebenen Bilderfluss zu unterbrechen, aber hier zeigt man nicht Bilder miteinander, sondern nacheinander.

B.: Ein Bild so lange ansehen, bis es fremd zurückblickt.

M.: Irgendwann ist es soweit, dann habe ich das hier, was hier zwischen uns passiert, zum ersten Mal angeschaut. Aus der Entfernung dann wird es fast ein Bild von einer Beziehung, ein Bild von einem Dialog.

B.: Im Zuge dessen, nun wie gesagt, gebe ich alles an Worten, die ich für diesen Dialog zu bieten habe, alles an Bildern, die ich für diesen Dialog zu bieten habe. Die meisten fahren an das Bild, das sie vom Meer haben. Die meisten leben in dem Bild, das sie von einer Beziehung oder von einer glücklichen Gemeinschaft haben.

M.: Erzähl mir nichts. Du bist ständig mit Einführung und Auflö-
     sung beschäftigt, du merkst das nur nicht mehr. Dauernd
     führst du dich oder mich in irgendetwas ein, dann
     gerätst du an einen Wendepunkt, so einen G-Punkt, und
     dann zum Höhepunkt und danach löst du das alles auf,
     was so schön war.
B.: Ach, ich finde, ich entwickele mich ganz gut, wenn ich eine
     Collage oder eine Montage verkörpere.
M.: Das wäre sicher ganz erregend, ein Crossing mit dir als
     virtuelles Selbstverwirklichungsprogramm.
B.: Jetzt mach doch da nicht so ein Medienspektakel daraus. Für
     mich ist das ganz trivial.
M.: Wenn ich nur daran denke, fühle ich mich schon ganz nichtli-
     near zu dir hingezogen. Du beherrschst deine kinemato-
     graphische Technik schon ganz gut, das muss man dir
     lassen. Man fühlt sich in deinen bewegten Bildern ganz
     gut aufgehoben und sicher.
B.: Du bewunderst mich und verfolgst mein Leben, nicht nur, weil
     ich so erfolgreich bin und Fortschritte mache in meiner
     Geschichte, sondern weil ich eine derart unglaublich
     tolle Figur verkörpere, mit der du dich identifizieren
     kannst?
M.: Nein, das ist es nicht. Ich jedenfalls kann keine Beziehung zu
     dir aufbauen, weil du keinen Konflikt in dir trägst. Ich
     habe das Gefühl, du erzählst mir immer das Gleiche.
B.: Ich habe das auch nicht nötig, dich dauernd mit irgendwel-
     chen an den Haaren herbeigezogenen Konflikten zu
     konfrontieren, nur weil sie das Gegenteil sind von dem,
     was dich aus- und gut macht.
M.: Willst du eine seriöse körperliche Behandlung und eine
     anständige Erzählung zu mir aufbauen oder bist du hier
     wegen des Happy Ends?
B.: Ich sehe es schon kommen. Diese Geschichte nimmt kein
     gutes Ende. Diese Erzählung bekommt kein großes Ende.
M.: Aber ich lasse mir gerne irgendwelche großen Geschichten
     erzählen. Warte aber kurz, alle sieben Sekunden verliert
     man die Aufmerksamkeit seiner Zuhörerin. Alle sieben

Jos Diegel

Spoileralarm!: Immer musst du etwas machen, was keinen Anfang und kein Ende hat, und irgendwelchen Kleinkram in großen Bildern zeigen

À reprendre depuis le début (Von Beginn an zu wiederholen)
Il faut être absolument moderne (Es gilt, absolut modern zu sein)

M.: Es tut mir leid, dass ich solch eine Erzählkrise bekommen habe. Nimm´s mir nicht übel! Ich bin da schon oft recht verunsichert.

B.: Du bist eben nicht so eine Postmoderne! Du willst unbedingt in eine narrative Form geraten, weil sich bei dir alles vor dem Hintergrund einer zusammenhängenden Geschichte abspielt.

M.: So wie ich bin, finde ich mich in der Literatur, der Bildenden Kunst und dem Kino zurecht. Eigentlich kannst du mich überall hinsetzen, und ich langweile mich und mein Publikum nicht.

B.: Das haben die doch alles schon gesehen. Ich produziere eigentlich ganz gerne auf einem sehr hohen Niveau mit Hilfe von Technik sehr viel Langeweile.

M.: Trotzdem – dein grandioser Umgang mit irgendwelchen Techniken hat dich auch noch zu nichts geführt. Das ist auch so eine Liebestechnik von dir. Immer willst du so eine Kreative sein, eine Pionierin, bis du begreifst, dass du deine Spielzeuge ganz gut beherrschst, aber verhandeln tust du nichts.

B.: Ich brauch` von dir nicht dauernd so eine Einführung. Das tut mir schon hinten weh. Ich will am Anfang auch kein Ende haben. Alles, was ich vorher schon weiß, interessiert mich nicht mehr.

zuletzt einer erzählerischen Abwärtsbewegung durch die höchsten akademischen Höhen der Reflexion in die tiefsten therapeutischen Tiefen medialer Selbstdarstellung, an deren Ende jedoch nur die einfache Einsicht stehen kann, dass alles derart prominent gewordene *transmediale* Geschehen unserer neuen Film- und Medienkultur nur die Kehrseite eines nun umfassend verstandenen Storytellings sein kann.

Martin Gessmann
Studium der Philosophie, Germanistik und Romanistik in Tübingen, Nantes und Washington D.C. Von 1991 bis 1996 Fernsehjournalist beim SWR. 1993 bis 1995 wissenschaftlicher Mitarbeiter an der Universität in Halle und 1996 bis 1997 an der Universität Heidelberg. Habilitationsstipendium der Deutschen Forschungsgemeinschaft. Fellow am Marsilius-Kolleg der Universität Heidelberg. 2010 Ernennung zum Univ.-Professor an der Universität Heidelberg. Ab Oktober 2011 Professor für Kultur- und Techniktheorien und Ästhetik an der HfG in Offenbach/M. Redakteur der *Philosophischen Rundschau* seit 2003. Monographien zu Montaigne, Hegel und Wittgenstein.

11
R. Sommer: Metadesign. A ›Mythological‹ Approach to Self-Reference in Consumer Culture. In: W. Wolf (Hg.): The Metareferential Turn in Contemporary Arts and Media. New York 2011.

duktsprache im transmedialen Erzählen zu beziehen ist, kann man en détail bei Roy Sommer nachvollziehen, wenn er zum »Metadesign« Stellung nimmt, das er als einen »›Mythological‹ Approach to Self-Reference in Consumer Culture« beschreibt[11]. Roland Barthes' metaphorische Vorstellung von modernen Design-Klassikern, sie seien wie ein von Göttern gestalteter Gegenstand direkt vom Himmel gefallen, wird hier wörtlich genommen – zumindest was die Vorstellung des Mythischen am Design betrifft.

Ein letzter, zumindest akademisch anmutender Zugang sei im Verweis auf experimentelle Transmedia-Produktionen angesprochen, wie sie bspw. in der TV-Serie *About: Kate* zurzeit nachzuvollziehen sind. Der entscheidende Dreh, der diese Versuche von der Consumer Culture der oben beschriebenen Blockbuster unterscheidet, ist die weit entschiedener durchgehaltene Selbstthematisierung von medialen »Horizontverschmelzungen« oder auch »Metareferenzen«. So erscheinen sowohl die Menschen, die agieren, besonders die Hauptfigur Kate, als auch die Medien, in denen die Menschen agieren und sich präsentieren, besonders die Social Media Platforms und ihre mobilen Terminals, von vornherein schon erzählerisch ineinander verschachtelt und gegenseitig reflektiert und nahezu austauschbar. Die Kunstfigur Kate und ihre psychologischen Maskenspiele oder -versuche sind grundsätzlich gar nichts anderes als die filmische Kehrseite der Medienprofile, in denen sich die Kunstfigur *Kate* eben als *Kunstfigur* Kate ausprobiert und damit erst konstituiert. Das Kino in seiner so genannten Spiegelphase der 1960er Jahre, wie Christian Metz es im Anschluss an Jacques Lacan einst vorbildlich herausgearbeitet hat[12], bildet dazu den theoriegeschichtlichen Vorgänger. *About: Kate* überträgt das Konzept ins vielschichtige 2.0-Milieu eines nun beinahe unendlich erweiterten Spiegelkosmos der Gegenwartskultur, ihrer multiplen Selbstkalibrierungs- und Selbstverbesserungshorizonte und deren anglo-amerikanisch auszudifferenzierenden, aber niemals auszulotenden Cross-References. Und doch sei abschließend der Hinweis erlaubt, dass auch *About: Kate* – zumindest ›transmedien-theoretisch‹ – mit dem Titel eines *Skyfall* nicht ganz falsch beschrieben wäre. Denn auch in *About: Kate* folgen wir

12
Vgl. Chr. Metz: Der imaginäre Signifikant. Psychoanalyse im Kino. Münster 2000 (im Original: Le Signifiant imaginaire. Paris 1977).

tale Ansatz ein solcher, der (theoriegeschichtlich wenigstens) auf dialogische oder auch dialektische Selbstorganisation der Darstellungssphäre zurückgreift.

Anders die angloamerikanische Sichtweise: Ihr geht es grundsätzlich nicht um das horizontale Auseinanderlegen der Erzählebenen und -medien, sondern vielmehr um deren vertikale Ausrichtung und pyramidale Durchordnung. Im Theoriehintergrund steht hierbei der Verweis einer Theory of Mind auf eine naturwissenschaftliche Erdung der Faktensphäre. Auf diese baut dann die Erzählung auf, insofern sie so genannte *Metanarrative* bildet, die als eine Art höherstufiger und faktenfernerer (und damit immer auch fiktiver) Kommentar fungiert. In umgekehrter, aber immer noch vertikaler Begründungsrichtung ist daran zu erinnern, dass die geisteswissenschaftliche Methodenlehre in Sachen Textauslegung ihre angloamerikanischen Wurzeln in der Bibellektüre und dem Close Reading hat. Letzteres wurde in den 1930er Jahren als Maxime des Ernstnehmens des genauen Textsinnes verweltlicht. So gesehen hat es die Erzählung dann ebenfalls mit einer Kommentarfunktion zu tun, jedoch nicht der Fakten, sondern der Worte und Konzepte, aus denen in immer noch biblischer gedachter Eintracht die Fakten allererst hervorgehen sollen. Die Metanarrative bewegen sich damit in einer Zwischensphäre, in der es zwischen zwei unumstößlichen Wahrheiten zu vermitteln gilt: den Wahrheiten von Gott und der Welt. Ihre Sphäre ist eine gedankliche und faktische Grauzone, sie wird durch tentative Linienführung der referentiellen Rückverweise nach ›oben‹ oder ›unten‹, also ins Faktische oder ins Transzendente, strukturiert. Metanarrative unterliegen so gesehen auch keinem Prozess der horizontalen Selbstfindung und Selbstorganisation, wie es die kontinentalen Schemata der Herausbildung umfassender Sinneinheiten vorsehen. Sie sind vielmehr Interimsphänomene, die immer noch auf letzte und umfassende Wahrheit zielen, sie nur prinzipiell nicht erreichen. Ihre Unbestimmtheit hat immer etwas Wunderbares, was den Menschen staunen lassen soll, dass es doch noch Höheres und Eminenteres auf der Welt gibt als seine eigenen endlichen und falliblen Weltansichten. Wie eine solche methodologische Grundhaltung zuletzt auch noch auf die Behandlung der Pro-

einem Radiosender und einer einfachen, auf den Träger abgestimmten Pistole. Sie werden schließlich zu Symbolen dafür, dass die Bond-Geschichte heute selbst nur noch im ständigen Übersetzen aus dem einen Medium in das andere funktioniert. Die Hightech-Netzwelt und ihre Virtualität mitsamt den verheerenden Folgen für die analog gebliebene Wirklichkeit und die Lowtech-Welt des Agenten und ihre rettende Wirkung auf die Filmwelt sind so gesehen nur die erzähltechnischen Rahmenbestimmungen, die das filmische Übersetzungsgeschehen in Form eines weiteren Film-Abenteuers einklammern – und eben mit der filmisch geschürten Aufmerksamkeit auf jene Extreme technischmedialer Agentenausstattung – damit auch zusammenhalten.

IV. Akademisches zum Schluss

Zum Schluss bleibt noch eine Frage: diejenige nach dem spezifischen Theoriedesign, das es braucht, um der erzählerischen Emanzipation der Medien und der darin mit ihnen zugleich neu präsentierten Gegenstände gerecht zu werden. Zwei Angebote liegen auf dem Tisch: ein kontinentales und ein anglo-amerikanisches. Das Kontinentale wurde mit Koschorkes Erzähltheorie in seinem hermeneutischen Grundmuster eingangs schon kurz angeschnitten. Entscheidendes Merkmal ist es, dass mit dem neuen medialen ›Nullmedium‹ des Narrativen zuletzt eine horizontale Ordnung der medialen Binnenerzählungen organisiert wird. Es ist zuletzt ein Schema, das aus der Methodologie der modernen Geistesgeschichte geborgt ist. Diese hat lange Zeit damit gerungen, wie die grundsätzlichen und grundlegenden Veränderungen in unserer Sicht auf die klassischen geistigen Produkte zu verstehen sind. Und sie kam gegen Mitte des vergangenen Jahrhunderts zu dem Schluss, dass es gilt, einer so genannten »Horizontverschiebung« der generellen Hinsichten so weit zu folgen, dass man der Verschiedenheit der Hinsichten gerecht wird, dennoch aber nicht den Faden vollkommen verliert, der die vielen Einzelgeschichten auf ein ihnen zugrundeliegendes Thema oder Schema zurückbezieht. Die neue Theorie vom Narrativen versteht es, jenes diachrone horizontale Verlaufsschema nun noch einmal auf die synchrone Ebenenbildung des Erzählens auszuweiten. Zuletzt ist damit der kontinen-

Die Einbettung eben derselben Accessoires in neue mediale Umfelder und vor allem in Konfrontation mit neuen Mitspielern und Mitspielertypen bringt nun zuletzt auch in diesen kulturkritischen Zusammenhängen die gedankliche Wende hervor. Anstatt die menschlichen Charaktere dinghaft festzulegen, werden die Produkte nun selbst zu Agenten möglicher Handlung. Ursache dafür sind ihre neuen medialen Erscheinungsweisen, die sie unterschiedlich handhabbar machen (im Zusammenhang: filmisch, virtuell, reell, comichaft, romanesk etc.), in denen sie zugleich unterschiedlich wirksam werden können (insofern sie mit anderen, neuen Accessoires kombiniert oder mit solchen konfrontiert werden: anderes, überlegenes, unterlegenes Gerät etc.) und somit schließlich auch neue Aussichten darauf geben, wie sich ein Protagonist durch die neuen und veränderten Kontexte hindurchlaviert. Wer die letzte Bond-Verfilmung unter diesem Gesichtspunkt betrachtet, wird nicht verwundert sein, eben jene neue und sehr viel mehr Freiraum gebende Rolle der Gadgets genau unter diesem Gesichtspunkt selbst thematisiert zu finden. So wurde die Präsentation der technischen Bestausstattung des Agenten, die traditionell nicht ohne Erfinderstolz vom jeweiligen Quartiermeister inszeniert wird, diesmal zu einer Demonstration souveränen Verzichts. Die geniale Erfindung und technische Neubestückung bestand in nichts anderem als der Einsicht, dass die Zeit der Festlegung von 007 auf seine Agentenausrüstung nun im Zuge der technisch-erzählerischen Weiterentwicklung endgültig vorbei sein muss: »Did you expect an exploding pen?« ist der kurze Kommentar des neubesetzten Q auf das ersichtliche Fragezeichen in den Augen des Zuschauers wie des Filmhelden, die sonst so opulente Film-Bescherung neuer ›Spielzeuge‹ möge schon zu Ende sein. Im Hintergrund steht die Annahme, das schurkische Geschehen habe sich bereits so weit ins Virtuelle und Hochtechnische der Netzsteuerungen verlagert, dass mit weiterer technischen Hochrüstung diesem Zustand gar nicht mehr beizukommen ist – vielmehr der Ausweg im Film bei den uranalogen Utensilien gesucht werden muss, wie sie in der klassischen Urinszenierung der ersten Agententhriller des 20. Jahrhunderts schon präsent waren, im vorliegenden Falle

als auch dem Handlungsverlauf, in den sie eingebettet ist, neuen Raum zur Entfaltung geben. Ungeahnte fahrerische Risiken lassen sich bspw. eingehen, wo das Game over des Videospiels nochmals das grundsätzliche Reset der Geschichte erlaubt. Und bleiben wir beim Auto, so erscheint es in der Hand des feinsinnigen Romanciers als liebenswerter Oldtimer, mit dem man sich leichter Hand in ein glamouröses Erzählambiente einschreiben kann, unter dem Gasfuß des Actionisten wird es wiederum zum rasanten Fluchtgefährt, um perfider Verfolgung und akuter Gefahr zu entkommen, und so weiter. Der Gesamtzusammenhang der Agentenerzählung ist in solcherlei medialer wie charakterlicher Variation nicht gefährdet; das ist, nochmals betont, das Neue. Es entsteht vielmehr ein beweglicher Kosmos von Geschichten, die zwar immer ein gestalterisches Zentrum haben, aber offene Ränder, was die Dimensionen ihrer Fortentwicklung angeht. Das Forterzählen selbst bildet so und somit zuletzt das eigentliche Zentrum der Geschichten, nicht die dort verhandelten abenteuerlichen Inhalte.

Schließlich und endlich lässt sich im Zuge solcher Überlegungen auch nachvollziehen, wie es zu der anfangs erwähnten Emanzipation der Gegenstände und besonders der Produkte in dem neuen Verständnis vom »Narrativen« in der Geisteswissenschaft kommt. Galt es doch zuvor als ausgemacht und wurde nahezu zum kulturkritischen Credo, dass die Charaktere – dies ganz besonders in unserem Beispielgenre der Agenten- und Abenteuergeschichten – zuletzt auf die ihnen zugeteilten Accessoires reduziert würden. Bond, das war das Auto, Superman der hautenge Anzug, Robin Hood ist Pfeil und Bogen, Ironman ist seine hypersmarte eiserne Rüstung, und wiederum so weiter und so fort. Die Accessoires wirkten erzähltechnisch wie Prothesen, an denen die Charaktere angeflanscht waren, anstatt als frei bewegliche Utensilien von ihnen eigenständig gewählt und bewegt zu werden. Sie bedeuteten zuletzt eine wesenhafte Beschränkung und Einengung der Charaktere, die gedanklich zumindest so weit ging, dass die menschlichen Züge der Protagonisten zuletzt voll und ganz verdinglicht schienen. Wie gesagt, nur anders betont: Bond ›ist‹ das Auto, Robin Hood ›ist‹ Pfeil und Bogen.

sein zu lassen, wie sie sind, oder noch besser, es in seiner medialen Beschränktheit noch zu bestärken. So kann schließlich eben auch noch schwarzweißstumm, filmisch gesehen, heute wieder hochaktuell, weil hochartistisch sein.

III. Die neue Produktsprache im Film

Es ist nun nur noch ein gedanklich kleiner Schritt zu tun, um schließlich auch noch nachzuvollziehen, wie es zur anfangs erwähnten, immer noch erstaunlichen Mitsprache der Produkte bei der Forterzählung unserer lange bekannten Geschichten kommt. Dazu gilt es im Grunde nur noch einmal die »medialen Plattformen« der Erzählung unter die Lupe zu nehmen, genauer noch, sie nun in ihrer spezifisch produkttechnischen Anlage zu verstehen. So finden wir die Erzählfiguren in einem medialen Sinne »codiert«, indem sie mit bestimmten Produkten umgeben sind, die ihr Repertoire charakterlicher Entfaltung und möglicher Handlung ein Stück weit konditionieren. Der Agent, um im Eingangsbeispiel zu bleiben, agiert im Rahmen seiner agentenge-mäßen Ausstattung, die bspw. eben von einem besonderen Auto mit einer besonderen Ausstattung und so weiter ausgeht. Das Accessoire bestimmt dabei mit, wie sich der Charakter gibt und was er prinzipiell zu leisten im Stande ist: ob er mit seinem Fahrzeug nur auf der Straße fahren oder auch fliegen oder unter Wasser tauchen kann etc. pp. und welche Haltung man grund-sätzlich am Steuer eines solchen Gefährtes einnimmt. Die produkttechnische Hardware gibt hier den medialen Rahmen ab für eine darauf zu spielende erzählerische Software.

Mit dem liberaleren Umgang der Erzählmedien unterein-ander und damit dem Ende ihrer darstellerischen Exklusivan-sprüche (»nur in diesem Medium ist die Geschichte die echte Geschichte«) ergibt sich folgerichtig auch eine neue, liberalere Funktion im Umgang mit der in Anspruch genommenen Pro-dukttechnik. Die Übertragung von einer medialen Ebene zu einer anderen (bspw. vom Virtuellen des Videospiels zum Reellen der Freizeitparks) wird nicht mehr einseitig als Gewinn- oder Verlust-geschäft bewertet. Es scheint vielmehr so, als würden, wiederum ausgehend vom Gegenstand, in jeder Übertragung neue Spiel-räume eröffnet – Spielräume, die sowohl dem Charakter der Figur

stumm auftreten kann, insofern dieser Stummfilm selbst als Tonfilm endet und damit als solcher vorführt, was er leistet, wenn er nicht leistet, was er sonst leistet. Inhalt und mediale Anlage gehen hier, wie es der Film an seinem Ende will, in rhythmischer Gegenstellung Hand in Hand. Und der Titel *The Artist* ist selbst wiederum die eine große Stummfilmtafel, die den ganzen Stummfilm in Gegenstellung zum darin ausgeklammerten Ton hochartistisch zum Sprechen bringt. Die Würdigung des Films 2012 durch fünf *Oscars* kann man als das Zeichen der Jury werten, dass sie den Kniff ohne weitere Belehrung seitens des Kulturfeuilletons verstanden hat. Man hat verstanden, dass die Filmerzählung *The Artist* eben gerade kein romantisches Gegenprogramm zum aktuellen Hollywood-Kino ist (auch wenn mancher Kommentator es unbedingt so sehen wollte), sondern vielmehr die eigene und immer aktuelle Geschichte des Film-schaffens als solche uns nahebringt und in längst vergangenem Mediendekor ganz aktuell neuerzählt.

Wenn es so weit kommt, ist in der Tat eine Schwelle in der allgemeinen Wahrnehmung der zeitgenössischen Film- und Medienkunst überschritten. Es gilt nun als ausgemacht, dass sich durch die verschiedenen Erzählebenen wie der damit zu verbindenden Erzählmedien ein (oder besser sehr viele verschie-dene, immer aber tiefrote) Erzählfäden durchwirken lassen derart, dass wir immer schon von einem (nun immerhin mögli-chen) Ganzen einer (durchaus möglichen) Gesamterzählung ausgehen. So wie sich die Form der Medien zusammenführen lässt, so nun auch deren erzählerische Inhalte – und besonders dann, wenn, wie gerade gesehen, diese Art der Zusammenführung selbst formal wie inhaltlich thematisiert wird. Eine langanhal-tende Bewegung der medialen und thematischen Ausdifferenzie-rung wird hierdurch abgeschlossen und durch eine final erscheinende, zumindest als Möglichkeit ›en principe‹ nun mit-bedachte Zusammenführung ersetzt. Anstatt der Maxime gegen-seitiger, medienspezifischer Exklusion gibt es nun die Option einer ebensolchen Inklusion, anstatt eines Anspruches auf darstellerische Alleingeltung gilt das liberale Prinzip des Laissez-faire und der gegenseitigen Zu- und Mitarbeit bei weitestmög-licher Toleranz, das andere Medium und seine Inhalte genau so

als einem medialen Gesamtrahmen möglicher Darstellung zusammen. Denn jener Gesamtrahmen schafft in einer bestimmten Hinsicht Entlastung. Waren nämlich die Binnen-erzählungen zuvor in einer gegenseitigen Konkurrenzsituation befangen, was ihre erzählerischen ›Geltungsansprüche‹ betraf, so finden sie sich jetzt dagegen in einer Konvergenzbewegung wieder. Um auch das zuerst anschaulich zu machen, weil sich die Rede von ›Geltungsansprüchen‹ so abstrakt anhört: Wir alle kennen noch die zum Teil erbittert geführten Diskussionen, die im Filmfach nach der Einführung einer neuen medialen Wiedergabemöglichkeit entbrannt waren. Nach der Erfindung bspw. des Tonfilms beteuerten nicht wenige Intellektuelle, der Stummfilm habe doch bereits die wahre Filmkunst verkör-pert, nach der Einführung des Farbfilms trauerte man dem Schwarzweißfilm hinterher, zuletzt, wenn auch vor allem in den Feuilletons, weniger bei den Zuschauern, wurde bei der Einführung des 3D-Films (so geschehen in einer Kritik zu David Camerons *Avatar*) nochmals bemerkt, über die Poesie des Schwarzweißfilms gehe doch gar nichts.

Nun aber scheint es uns so, als sei das Ausspielen der medialen Ebenen und die Konkurrenz der Plattformen in einem prinzipiellen Sinne zu Ende. Prinzipiell deshalb, weil bereits mit der technischen Überführbarkeit eines medialen Darstellungs-modus in einen anderen eine Souveränität und Gelassenheit im Sinne eines gegenseitigen Geltenlassens einsetzen kann. Bestes Anzeichen dafür: der erstaunliche, jüngste Erfolg eines Schwarz-weißstummfilms wie Michel Hazanavicius' *The Artist*. Erst recht gilt eine solche Feststellung im weiteren Zusammenhang nicht nur für die formale mediale Wiedergabe, sondern auch bei der inhaltlichen Durchdringung der Erzählebenen. Gilt es doch als ausgemacht, wie Jenkins es fordert, dass die Erzählungen nun als aneinander anknüpfend und sogar aushelfend verstanden werden können. Versagt die eine Form der Darstellung, springt die andere episodisch ein. Der eben erwähnte Film *The Artist* ist in Inhalt und Form selbst ja gar nichts anderes als die Illustration eben jener gegenseitigen Aus- und Beihilfe. Dem aus der Mode gekommenen Stummfilmstar gelingt das Comeback im Tonfilm eben dadurch, dass er noch einmal im Stummfilm *The Artist*

Video-Agenten-Spiel einlädt. Im erzählerischen Durchschnitt durch die verschiedenen medialen Plattformen hat man es freilich nicht einfach nur mit einer Transformation der Geschichte zu tun, ausgehend von der immer gleichen Heldenfigur und ihren nun vielsagenden Agentenspielzeugen. Die Geschichte Bond spielt nicht nur auf verschiedenen medialen Klaviaturen. Jede neue mediale Ausformung soll Jenkins zufolge auch zugleich einen unverwechselbaren und eigenständigen Beitrag zur Gesamtgeschichte leisten. Sie ist ausgerichtet »to the hole«. Und nicht nur das, es soll auch noch gelten, dass, zumindest in einer »ideal form of transmedia storytelling, each medium does what it does best«. Kein Medium agiert demnach mehr als eine Second Best Lösung, als ein Notbehelf, weil man anderes und Besseres nicht zur Hand hatte. Sodass bspw. die Bond-Figur im Comic ein Bond für Arme wäre, im Hollywood-Film dagegen für Reiche (oder eben solche, die sich den Gang an die Kinokasse leisten können). Im Gegenteil: Die Medien für die jeweiligen Auftritte ergänzen sich insofern, dass jedes Medium uns genau jene Erfahrung nahebringt, die sich in ihm am besten machen lässt. Nochmals in dem Zusammenhang Jenkins: »its world might be explored through game or experienced as an amusement park attraction«. Was alles im Rahmen derart aufbereiteter Geschichten möglich ist und wie es sich tatsächlich anfühlt, wenn wir in eigenartige Intrigen und gefährliche Umstände verwickelt werden, das erleben wir am besten im Videospiel oder im Abenteuerpark. Wie exzellent und vielschichtig eine solche Geschichte als einmalige Erzählung verfasst sein kann, um das zu erfahren, gehen wir ins Kino. Wie weit man den Kult um den Doppelnull-Agentenstatus und die Teilhabe daran produkttechnisch ausdifferenzieren kann, das führt uns die Werbung vor. Wie der Agent in Diensten ihrer Majestät ihrer Majestät tatsächlich einmal einen Dienst erweist, das erleben wir bei der Eröffnung der Olympiade und so weiter.

Warum das transmediale Erzählen heute ganz offenbar funktioniert, ganz so wie es Jenkins mit seiner Liste der Anforderungen ausformuliert, ist im Lichte der jüngsten Theorieentwicklung nun einigermaßen schlüssig zu reinterpretieren. Das Gelingen hängt ganz offenbar mit der neuen Rolle des Erzählens

beschreibung immer besser bewerkstelligen. Damit wurde der zuvor immer nur gefühlte Abstand zwischen dem, was sich in Codes einfangen ließ, und dem, was sich unserer Welterfahrung sonst noch alles erschließt, immer geringer, und umso geringer dieser Abstand wurde, desto sicherer konnte man dies auch sagen, nicht nur fühlen. Bis zu dem Punkt eben, an dem Koschorke nun feststellt, das Erzählen sei der Code aller Codes, also jene Form der generellen Beschreibung, die alle anderen lokalen Beschreibungen in sich umfasst und diese allererst dynamisch ausdifferenziert. Diese Theoriebewegung, die in der neuen und umfassenden Statuserklärung des Erzählens gipfelt, ist dabei selbst wiederum nur Teil einer weitergehenden Reflexion. Schon bei einer ausreichend gelingenden Abbildung aller analogen Medien in digitale Speicherformen hat man auf die besagte neue Qualität eines medialen Apriori geschlossen[7], ebenso bei der Betrachtung der Folgen, die jene mediale Rahmenbildung um alle Vorgängermedien für unser medientheoretisches Selbstverständnis haben muss[8].

II. b Die spezielle Theorie des *transmedialen Storytelling*

Folgt man einmal der Theorie- und Mediengeschichte der vergangenen 50 Jahre so weit, ergeben sich daraus die Perspektiven, die das Phänomen eines *transmedialen Storytelling* in ebenfalls neuer Weise einsichtig machen. Ganz allgemein wird jetzt zuerst einmal nachvollziehbar, dass es nun zu einer *Convergence Culture* kommen kann, wie sie bspw. Henry Jenkins[9] beschreibt. Es konvergieren in einer *Transmedia Story* demnach »multiple media platforms, with each new text making a distinctive and valuable contribution to the whole«[10]. Die von Jenkins anvisierte Konvergenz geht jedoch theoretisch noch weiter. Nicht nur schneidet die Geschichte in ihrem Verlauf verschiedene mediale ›Plattformen‹ medialer Verwirklichung an, sodass wie im Falle der Bond-Geschichte eine Hollywood-Verfilmung die Geschichte entspinnt, aufwendig gestaltete Commercials im Fernsehen weiter wirken, das olympische Stadionerlebnis mit der englischen Queen die Illusion ins Dreidimensional-Reale überträgt, Pseudo-Bond-Romane daran anschließen (»Bond is back«) und der Held schließlich zum willfährigen Rollentausch im

---

7
Vgl. St. Münker: Emergenz digitaler Öffentlichkeiten. Die sozialen Medien im Web 2.0. Frankfurt am Main 2009.

8
Vgl. B. Stiegler: Etats de choc. Bêtise et savoir au XXIe siècle. Paris, 2012. M. Gessmann: Zur Zukunft der Hermeneutik, München; Paderborn 2012.

9
H. Jenkins: Convergence Culture. Where Old and New Media Collide, New York; London 2006.

10
Ebd., S. 98.

Sinne haltbar ist, was sich in der neuen Computersprache formulieren lässt, also zuletzt in ganz bestimmter Weise binär codieren lässt. Was den Filter des Codes passiert, ist wirklich, was nicht, ist unwirklich, so wirklich uns auch dieses Unwirkliche im alltäglichen Umgang damit erscheinen mag. Hierin war sich die Computerkultur, insofern sie als eine neue Wissenschafts-kultur auftrat, vollkommen sicher. Je nachdem, was nun computer-sprachlich codierbar erschien, erweiterte sich der Kreis dessen, was in binäre Codierung aufgelöst werden konnte. Einfache Handlungsabläufe, die nun als Rückkopplungsschleifen program-miert wurden, lösten die Vorstellung vom Performativen als neuem Apriori aus, die Digitalisierung der analogen Bilder zu Beginn der 1990er Jahre die Ikonische Wende[4].

Das Erstaunliche an Koschorkes neuer Apriori-Behaup-tung ist nun darin zu sehen, dass er in der anskizzierten Über-bietungslinie nicht einfach nur mehr eine weitere Sphäre der Weltcodierung in Anschlag bringt. Er meint nicht, dass nach der Sprache, der Handlung und den Bildern das Erzählen als neueste Errungenschaft unserer Welt-Codierungskünste einfach noch hinzukäme. Er meint vielmehr, dass im Erzählen selbst noch einmal um alle anderen Vorgänger-Aprioris ein medialer Gesamtrahmen aufgespannt werde: »Statt« seinerseits »in binäre Strukturen eingefasst werden zu können, gehen sie [die Erzählungen, M.G.] solchen Strukturverfestigungen vielmehr voraus. Durch ihre Nicht-Festgelegtheit und innere Unruhe stellen sie Zugänge zu einem kulturellen Fluidum her, in dem binäre Codes sich allererst ausbilden, in Konkurrenzen oder Allianzen treten, sich wechselseitig schwächen, stärken, kreuzen, verfestigen und auflösen«[5]. Verständlich wird dieses souverän auftretende Selbstbewusstsein in der Beschreibung des Narrativen vielleicht am besten, indem man folgende einfache Überlegung nachvollzieht. Demnach haben die computerlesbaren Codie-rungen mit zunehmender Mächtigkeit der Programme und ihrer Sprachen das Netz der binären Unterscheidungen im Laufe der Zeit immer enger geknüpft. Konnten am Anfang nur einfache Unterscheidungen codiert werden, so kamen komplexere hinzu. Das, was man in der Ethnologie seit den 1980er Jahren »dichte Beschreibung«[6] nennt, ließ sich auch in der generellen Welt-

4
Um der Einfachheit der Darstel-lung willen folge ich hier Friedrich Kittlers Vorstellung von Medien und Technik als der ›Hardware‹, die unsere kulturelle ›Software‹ der Weltbegriffe maßgeblich vorkonfi-guriert. Eine intensivere Debatte müsste hier vorsichtiger und umsichtiger argumentieren, das sei hier gleich eingestanden.

5
Koschorke (2012), S. 22 (wie Anm. 2).

6
Der Ausdruck stammt von Clifford Geertz: Dichte Beschreibung. Beiträge zum Verstehen kultureller Systeme. Frankfurt am Main 2003.

1
Von »Verdinglichung« ist seit Heideggers technikkritischen Aufsätzen die Rede, der Terminus kommt jedoch über eine Adaption einer marxistischen Kulturkritik ins Spiel, bei G. Lukács: Geschichte und Klassenbewußtsein. Studien über marxistische Dialektik. Berlin 1923.

2
A. Koschorke: Wahrheit und Erfindung. Grundzüge einer Allgemeinen Erzähltheorie. Frankfurt am Main 2012.

3
Vgl. D. Mersch: Medientheorien zur Einführung. Hamburg 2006; Ders.: Was sich zeigt. Materialität, Präsenz, Ereignis. München; Paderborn 2002.

verdinglicht[1], um es mit dem Schlagwort der Kulturkritik des 20. Jahrhunderts zu sagen, sobald sie mit Medien in eine engere Berührung kamen. Nun werden aber in direkter Entgegensetzung zu dieser These die Dinge neuerdings geradezu vermenschlicht. Vermenschlicht zumindest in der Hinsicht, dass die Produkte aktiviert werden im erzählerischen Sinne, vermenschlicht, insofern gerade das kreative Element, das den Menschen von den Medien genommen wurde, nun sogar von den Dingen selbst wieder mit ins Spiel gebracht wird. Dinge und Utensilien werden, wie oben angedeutet, zu aktiven Momenten in einer Handlungsstruktur, insofern sie produktiv und eigenständig zur Fortschreibung der Geschichte beitragen. Wie aber kann das sein? Wie wird aus einer Unterdrückungsgeschichte plötzlich eine Emanzipationsgeschichte? Wie wird aus *den* Medien, bei denen man fraglos davon ausging, dass sie den Menschen entmenschlichen, *ein* Medium, das auch noch die Dinge künstlerisch begabt sein lässt?

II. a Exkurs: Theorie- und Mediengeschichte

Um das zu verstehen, braucht es einen kurzen Exkurs in die jüngste Theorie- und Mediengeschichte. Er beginnt mit dem Stichwort, das auch dem vorliegenden Sammelband zugrunde liegt, dem *Storytelling*, oder dem akademischen Zugang zum Erzählen, der latinisiert mit dem *Narrativen* belegt wird.

Der Konstanzer Literaturwissenschaftler Albrecht Koschorke hat soeben einen Band über die »Grundzüge einer Allgemeinen Erzähltheorie«[2] vorgelegt, der für Aufsehen gesorgt hat. Koschorke stellt darin fest, dass mit dem Narrativen ein neues Apriori gefunden ist. Eine solche Feststellung wäre für sich genommen noch keine echte akademische Sensation – denn wir sind es seit einem halben Jahrhundert gewohnt, dass wir mindestens zu jedem Jahrfünft mit einem neuen Apriori überrascht werden. So folgte nach dem Auftakt des Linguistic Turn bspw. der Performative Turn, später der Iconic Turn mit seinen zahlreichen Ablegern, die den Bilderreichtum unserer Kultur geisteswissenschaftlich ausdifferenzierten.[3] Die Ausgangsevidenz zu solchen Wendebewegungen in der generellen Weltbetrachtung lieferte in den 1960er Jahren die aufkommende Computerkultur. Man ging grosso modo davon aus, dass nur das im wissenschaftlichen

Die geschilderten Vorkommnisse einer Emanzipation von Produkten, die ursprünglich einmal bloße Utensilien (und bestenfalls fassbar gewordene Attribute der Hauptfiguren) waren, zum Kern möglicher Forterzählung, geschehen freilich nicht ganz unvorbereitet. Im Hintergrund steht eine Videospielindustrie, die das geschilderte Prinzip der Fortschreibung der Geschichte zur Serie schon längst erkannt und genutzt hat. Und wenn man der Sache einen theoretischen Moment lang zumindest positiv gegenübersteht, dann hat sie dies in einem durchaus vielfältigen und demokratischen Sinne getan: Denn nicht nur ergeben sich jetzt nahezu unendliche Möglichkeiten der Fortschreibung der Geschichte, ein jedes Mal, wenn das zugehörige Agentenspiel von neuem gestartet wird und der mögliche Ausgang noch offen scheint; auch werden wir alle im Rollenspiel zugleich zum neuen Helden des Dramas. Die einstigen Utensilien werden so zuletzt zu ontologischen Eckpfeilern des Erzählens, insofern sie den Rahmen der Handlung abstecken und erzähltechnisch vorstrukturieren. Sie sind das, was sich in allen Episoden durchhält und die Geschichten zuletzt wiedererkennbar macht.

II. Die Theorie

Eine solche Emanzipation der Gegenstände zu eigenständigen Elementen der Erzählung und autonomen Agenten der Handlung ruft geradezu nach einem theoretischen Kommentar. Denn jene Emanzipationsgeschichte der Dinge gehört thematisch zu einer langanhaltenden Diskussion um die unterdrückende Wirkung der Medien, einer Diskussion, in der sie freilich und ganz offenbar nun eine Gegenstimme bildet. Galt es doch als ausgemacht, dass alle Beteiligten am Medium Film, Fernsehen, Videospiel bis hin zum Freizeitspaß der Technikparks, Disneylands oder Wachsfigurenkabinette nur zu den Verlierern gehören konnten. Verlierer waren sie, insofern sie in den genannten Medien immer mehr entmenschlicht wurden, weil sie passiv und unselbständig agierten, insofern sie in das jeweilige Medium eintauchten und dabei sinnvollerweise nichts anderes tun konnten als den dort gemachten technischen und medialen Vorgaben zu entsprechen. Menschen wurden grundsätzlich

machen durfte. Nun sind es aber eben die Produkte, die selbst in den Darstellerrang aufrücken und damit zum Nukleus einer eigenen Forterzählung werden dürfen. In dieser Gedankenlinie wurden auch schon die Anhänger der Bond-Filme im Sommer 2012 vorgewarnt. Sah man doch zur Eröffnung der Olympiade in London einen Einspieler, in dem wiederum in Bond-Manier Daniel Craig die englische Queen Elizabeth II zum Stadion chauffierte. Nukleus schon dieses royalen Kurz-Serien-Specials waren wiederum die für die Filmfigur typisch attribuierten Transportmittel – konnte doch die Queen wenigstens filmisch den gewagten Sprung aus luftiger Höhe mit dem Fallschirm wagen. Und es ist beinahe unnötig zu sagen, dass die 23. Bond-Verfilmung schließlich das eben skizzierte Prinzip auch noch selbst nach- oder auch vorvollzog, wie man will. Denn – um nur ein Beispiel zu nennen – auch die Rolle des Aston Martin DB 4 von 1964, der den Film transporttechnisch und zugleich symbolisch in das End-Setting des Dramas einführt, ist anders als in früheren Verfilmungen nicht einfach nur ein bloßes Zitat, eine Reminiszenz oder auch ein filmhistorisches Accessoire. Das Utensil weist nicht nur symbolisch auf frühere Episoden, auf frühere Abenteuer und auch nur auf frühere Zeiten zurück. Das Auto agiert vielmehr im Film zuletzt als ein Sinnbild für die ursprüngliche Erzählweise der Bond-Romane und -verfilmungen selbst. Man reist somit im Film nicht nur in eine schottische Feenlandschaft und damit zugleich in das Reich der Kindheits-erinnerungen des Helden, sondern ebensosehr in die Ursitua-tion und dramatische Grundanlage aller Bond-Erzählung selbst. Das Auto, so überladen jener Anspruch in der bloßen Nacher-zählung auch scheinen mag, bildet somit das narrative Moment im Film selbst ab – narrativ deshalb, weil es zum Motiv des Grundmusters allen Erzählens dieser Art wird. Der ganze Film ist so zuletzt nichts anderes als das erzählerische Ausagieren eines Werdeganges, der uns zwar im Laufe der filmischen Fortschrei-bung von den Anfängen weit entfernt hat, zuletzt aber das Dramatische als den Kern der Geschichte wie auch seiner Nacherzählungen wiederentdeckt; dies noch dort, wo die Grundanlage der Bond-Romane durch die Herausforderungen der Gegenwart bereits vollkommen verschüttet scheint.

I. Das Phänomen

Für viele Alltagskonsumenten mag das Phänomen im Herbst 2012 das erste Mal prominent geworden sein. Als James Bond zum 23. Mal auf die Leinwand trat, gab es im TV und in den sonst noch einschlägigen Medien die üblichen Werbetrailer, die den Film *Skyfall* ankündigten. Zugleich sah man aber auch im Fernsehen andere Clips, die mit demselben Darsteller (Daniel Craig) operierten, dasselbe dramatische Setting wie in *Skyfall* benutzten, jedoch Szenen zeigten, die im Film nie vorkamen und auch zur Geschichte des Films keinerlei Beziehung hatten. Es waren Werbefilme, die zu der Hauptfigur noch ein frei gewähltes Hauptprodukt in Szene setzten, jedoch eine fiktive, allerdings durchaus typische Konstellation dazuerfanden, in der sich der Anspruch der personalen wie dinglichen Hauptcharaktere als solche zeigen sollte. Nur mit einem Handy der Marke X konnte der Geheimagent wirklich erfolgreich sein, nur mit einem Rasierwasser der Marke Y und der Uhr der Marke Z. Immer war es »James Bond's choice«. Oberflächlich betrachtet könnte man meinen, es handele sich hier im Grunde nur um eine Variante des klassischen Product Placements in Filmen. Anders jedoch als in der Bond-Verfilmung von 2006 *(Casino Royal)* muss nun nicht mehr die Hauptdarstellerin im ersten Tête-à-Tête mit dem Hauptdarsteller in einer eher peinlich anmutenden, weil ganz offensichtlich extra hinzugeschriebenen Zwischensequenz dessen Luxusuhr rühmen (»beautiful!«). Vielmehr haben es nun die Produkte selbst übernommen, das Zentrum einer fortschreibenden Erzählung zu werden, die in der Art eines Serien-Spin-offs so tut, als entstünde hier ein eigenständiger Ableger der Bond-Geschichte. Solcherlei Ableger waren bisher immer der Emanzipation von Nebenfiguren zu Hauptfiguren vorbehalten, menschlichen Nebenfiguren, die so ins Zentrum einer eigenen, neuen Geschichte rückten. Wer bspw. in den 1980er Jahren regelmäßig die in Boston spielende Serie *Cheers* mitverfolgte, konnte sich in den 1990er Jahren über die Umsiedlung der Nebenfigur *Frasier* nach Seattle freuen, wo die Serie zugleich einen Milieu-Aufstieg vom Souterrain der Bostoner Bar- und Feierabendkultur ins psychoanalytisch-akademische Radiomilieu auf amerikanischem Wolkenkratzerniveau

Transmediales Storytelling und die neue Produktsprache im Film. Oder: Was geschieht, wenn sich auch noch die Dinge zu Wort melden.

Martin

Gessmann

und generellen Vorstellungsbilder vom Kino; anders formuliert, der Common Sense dessen, was wir unter »Film« und »Kino« verstehen, wird neu ausgerichtet. Diese Neuerungen entfalten sich – ähnlich wie von Mulvey/Wollen und Mitchell skizziert – als eine Form der Hypermedialität, in der Film und Kino ein hybrides Diskursfeld ausbilden. Damit werden die ontologischen Bestimmungen des Films, ob er beispielsweise fotografisch sei oder ein narratives Medium, ebenso im Diskursfeld aufgehoben wie die dort stattfindende Begegnung mit anderen Künsten, Medien und die daraus resultierenden Hybridbildungen.

Sabine Nessel
ist zzt. Gastprofessorin für Mediengeschichte an der Universität Wien und war 2010-2012 Vertretungsprofessorin für Filmwissenschaft an der Freien Universität Berlin. Habilitation an der Goethe-Universität Frankfurt/M. zum Thema »Zoo und Kino als Schauanordnungen der Moderne«. Publikationen u.a.: *Kino und Ereignis. Das Kinematografische zwischen Text und Körper* (2008); *Zoo und Kino* (hg. mit Heide Schlüpmann, 2012); *Der Film und das Tier. Klassifizierungen, Cinephilien und Philosophien* (hg. mit Winfried Pauleit et al, 2012).

Winfried Pauleit
Professor an der Universität Bremen mit den Arbeitsschwerpunkten Filmwissenschaft, Medienwissenschaft und Filmvermittlung. Er ist seit 2008 wissenschaftlicher Leiter des Internationalen Bremer Symposiums zum Film und Mitherausgeber der Schriftenreihe/ E-Book-Reihe zu den Symposien. Publikationen: *Filmstandbilder. Passagen zwischen Kunst und Kino* (2004); *Das ABC des Kinos. Foto, Film, Neue Medien* (2009); (www.abc-des-kinos.de) und *Reading Film Stills. Analyzing Film and Media Culture (erscheint 2014).*

Fetischisierung des Fotografischen (Jacksons *King Kong*), in der die Fotografie mit digitalen Mitteln simuliert, aber gleichzeitig das durch sie geknüpfte indexikalische Prinzip entstellt wird.

Diese Konstruktionen zeigen das Digitale als Sensation und damit in der Tradition der technischen Tricks des Kinos, für dessen historischen Beginn in der Filmgeschichte der Name Georges Méliès steht, eine Tradition, die aber auch in die Vorgeschichte der Apparate und Projektionskünste zurückreicht. Gleichzeitig zeigen diese Konstruktionen des Digitalen Momente der Selbstreflexion, Versuche, sich der neuen Technologie als einer neuen Möglichkeit zu versichern. Das Digitale dieses Kinos bildet ein universales Zahlungsmittel, das immer dort eingelöst wurde, wo die ästhetische Strategie auf eine technische Grenze stieß oder wo technischer Eifer ästhetische Strategien nachahmte.

In ähnlichem Sinne hat sich das Digitale auch auf der Ebene des Tons im Kino bemerkbar gemacht. Hierbei ist anzumerken, dass die kreative Arbeit am Ton im Grunde erst in den 1970er Jahren begann: mit dem Kino des New Hollywood und der Entwicklung des Sound Designs.[23] Die kreativen Prozesse im Bereich des Tons haben sich aufgrund der späten Entwicklung viel schneller mit dem Digitalen verbunden. Gleichwohl bildet das (digitale) Sound Design nur eine weitere Facette im Rahmen einer Hybridisierung des Films aus. Der Pragmatismus des Sound Designs bleibt dabei auf ähnliche Weise an den Hörerfahrungen des Alltags orientiert wie die digitale Bildgestaltung am fotografischen Film.

Jenseits des digitalen Sensationskinos gibt es allerdings ein Kino, in dem Ideen des Digitalen historisch vor ihrer technischen Erfindung vorausgedacht sind. Dieses Kino zeigt sich beispielsweise in der Konfrontation von Fotografie und Film sowie in der Kombination mit den literarischen Formen des Romans, und nicht zuletzt in Montagen diverser Ebenen des Tons als hybride Anordnung von Diskursen (*La Jetée*). An dieses Kino knüpft Schanelecs *Orly* an (ohne ganz auf digitale Effekte zu verzichten).

Damit verändert sich nicht nur die Form der Narration, sondern auch das Imaginäre der Zuschauer, unsere konkreten

---

23
Vgl. Barbara Flückiger: Sound Design. Die virtuelle Klangwelt des Films (2001). Marburg 2002. Außerdem vgl. Barbara Flückiger im Gespräch mit Winfried Pauleit: Sound Effects – Zu Theorie und Praxis des Film-Sound Designs (dt./engl.). In: Anne Thurmann-Jajes; Sabine Breitsameter; Winfried Pauleit (Hg.): Sound Art. Zwischen Avantgarde und Popkultur. Köln 2006, S. 219–236.

Von *Orly* aus lässt sich nicht nur ein Bezug zum aktuellen digitalen Film und seinen Effekten auf die Narration herstellen, sondern auch zurückblicken ins prädigitale Kino der 1960er Jahre. In Chris Markers Film *La Jetée* (F 1962), der ebenfalls auf dem Flughafen von Orly spielt, wird – analog zu Mulvey und Wollen – bereits eine Idee des Digitalen vor seiner allgemeinen Verbreitung in den 1990er Jahren entworfen. In den Filmen Markers lassen sich die Spuren des Fotografischen bereits als Diskursfeld lesen, welches die theoretischen Entwürfe von Kracauer, Bazin oder Morin aufgreift und weiterdenkt. Der legendäre Film *La Jetée* ist aus Fotografien montiert. In seiner Anlage stellt er sein Gemachtsein und die Brüche zwischen den Bildern geradezu didaktisch aus; zudem markiert er die in diesem Kontext zentralen Orte als Handlungsorte seines Films: auf der einen Seite das Museum als Archiv und Sammlung der Spuren des Vergangenen (die Sammlungen des Jardin du Plantes), auf der anderen die Startbahn des Flughafens Orly als materialisierten Traum der Moderne. Obwohl der Film sich aus Fotografien zusammensetzt, situiert er seinen Handlungsraum in der Zukunft, der im Bild eines atomaren III. Weltkriegs ein katastrophisches Moment der Moderne thematisiert – der aber schließlich auch in der Zukunft eine mysteriöse Energiezentrale (er)findet, die zumindest aus heutiger Sicht mit dem Bild einer Computerplatine assoziiert ist. Diese von Marker selbst als »roman-photo« bezeichnete Filmform stellt ihren hybriden Charakter auch im Begriffsbild aus.

3. Das Digitale als Erweiterung des Hybridmediums Film

Die zentralen Momente der Konstruktionen des Digitalen sind Teil einer Inszenierung von Differenz. Ob historisch zwischen zwei Versionen eines Filmes oder innerhalb eines Films im Sinne eines medientheoretischen Diskurses, wird das Digitale an der Differenz zum fotografischen Film festgemacht. Umgekehrt erfolgt erst in der Differenz eine Bestimmung des Films als analoges bzw. digitales Werk. Dies geschieht nach demselben Prinzip wie einst die Erfindung des Tonfilms den »Stummfilm« erst hervorbrachte.[22] Ein Effekt aus der Entgegensetzung von fotografischem und digitalem Film ist die vorübergehende

22
Knut Hickethier: Film- und Fernsehanalyse. Stuttgart 2001, S. 95.

unterschiedlicher Filmtraditionen, wie die klassische Studioaufnahme mit Schauspielern samt Regieanweisungen und die ans Dokumentarische anknüpfende Tradition eines Cinéma Vérité oder aber die heimlichen Aufnahmen eines Überwachers oder Peeping Toms.

Daneben ist in *Orly* die Fotografie ein zentrales Thema. Gleich in der zweiten Szene sieht man die Protagonistin des Films, Maren Eggert, auf einem Foto. Es handelt sich um einen Fotoabzug, schwarz-weiß. Die Schauspielerin erscheint darauf viel jünger als im Film. Das Foto verweist auf den länger zurückliegenden Film *Marseille* (D 2004) der Regisseurin, in welchem Maren Eggert eine Fotografin spielt. In *Marseille* war die Fotografie noch allein an die analoge Fotografie gebunden. Dies ändert sich mit *Orly*. Hier wird nicht nur das Fotografieren mit einer digitalen Kamera vorgeführt. Auch der Film selbst ist digital aufgenommen und bearbeitet. Und man stellt fest: Hier wird nicht das neue digitale Kino mit seinen Visual Effects gefeiert (obwohl es offenbar auch solche Effekte zu entdecken gibt), sondern hier wird die Geschichte des Kinos fortgeschrieben, mit digitalen Mitteln – ganz einfach und ohne großes Aufsehen. *Orly* spielt mit den unterschiedlichen Registern, die das Kino konstituieren. Von Anfang an wird der Film von Medien begleitet und gespeist. Dabei ist nicht nur die Fotografie tonangebend, sondern auch die Architektur, die Literatur, die Musik, das Mobiltelefon und das Kino selbst sind bedeutend. Deshalb ist es so schwer zu beschreiben, was der Film eigentlich macht, woraus er besteht, wovon er handelt. In einer spezifischen Narrationsform (episodisches Erzählen) geht er ebenso wenig auf wie in einem spezifischen Genre.

Orly »entwirft« sich wie eine Architektur aus hybriden Elementen, um schließlich auch Architektur zu zeigen. Gezeigt wird der Flughafen Orly – eine Ikone der Moderne – in einer Art Zeitbild; aber auch die Pariser Bibliothèque Nationale im Speicher einer digitalen Fotokamera. Seine Strategie lässt sich vielleicht als strukturelle Verschiebung beschreiben von einer wie auch immer gearteten Anordnung von Geschehnissen im Kontext einer Narration[21] hin zu einer hybriden Anordnung von Diskursfragmenten.

21
Michel Scheffel: Was heißt (Film-) Erzählen? In: Susanne Kaul; Jean-Pierre Palmier; Timo Skrandies (Hg.): Erzählen im Film. Unzuverlässigkeit, Audiovisualität, Musik. Bielefeld 2009, S. 15–31.

2.2. Orly/La Jetée

Im Unterschied zu Filmen wie *The Perfect Storm, Terminator 2* oder *King Kong* von Jackson, welche bezogen auf die Narration das Label »digitales Attraktionskino« verdienen, soll nun anhand des Films *Orly* (D 2010) von Angela Schanelec eine Konstruktion des Digitalen betrachtet werden, welche weniger hemdsärmelig und brachial als Attraktionskino daherkommt. In *Orly* werden Erzählweisen und die Anordnung von Diskursen sichtbar, die in ihrer Spezifik mittels digitaler Aufnahmeverfahren produziert sind. Ein *entspannter* Umgang mit dem digitalen Bild sowie ein Nebeneinander der Aufnahmeverfahren digital/analog im Werk der Regisseurin sind hier kennzeichnend.

Orly spielt auf dem gleichnamigen Flughafen nahe Paris und bringt Mikrogeschichten von Personen, die sich im Flughafen oder auf dem Weg dahin befinden, in einen losen Zusammenhang. Die Episodenstruktur wird mit Ansichten des Flughafens als Ort besonderer Gesetzmäßigkeiten und Abläufe verbunden. Angesichts des Drehortes und der Episodenstruktur des Films mag man entfernt an *Airport* (USA 1970), einen Klassiker des 1970er Jahre Katastrophenfilms mit Burt Lancaster denken, in dem ebenfalls mehrere Geschichten und Schicksale der Protagonisten auf einem Flughafen die Handlung bilden. Im Unterschied allerdings zu *Airport*, der nur vereinzelt dokumentarische Ansichten des Flughafens zu sehen gibt, wurde *Orly* bei laufendem Flughafenbetrieb gedreht. Nacheinander werden Paare in Szene gesetzt, die sich auf dem Flughafen aufhalten, ihr Warten, ihre Geschichten, ihre Gespräche mit dem Mobiltelefon. Die lichtdurchflutete Halle des Flughafens wird zu einem Ort der Begegnung, der Kommunikation, des Geständnisses, kurz, von Mikro-Dramen vor dem Hintergrund des Alltagsgeschehens des Pariser Flughafens. Der Kontakt zu den Schauspielern lief über Funk und Kopfhörer. Die Kamera ist vielfach weit entfernt. Und der Ton hört sich an, als wären akustische Inseln aus dem originalen Soundteppich des Flughafens herausgestellt worden – oder als hätte Gene Hackman in seiner Rolle als Harry Caul (*The Conversation*, USA 1974) diese Tonaufnahmen in ihrer Hybridität (zwischen Kunst und Überwachung) angefertigt. Was das digitale Aufnahmeverfahren in *Orly* ermöglicht, ist die Hybridisierung

Da man es bei den Fotos und Flugbildern aus den 1930er Jahren durchweg mit Schwarz-Weiß-Bildern zu tun hatte, war die Erzeugung des Bildes von der Stadt New York außerdem mit einer kompletten Neuerfindung der Farbigkeit verbunden. Die Doppeldeckerflugzeuge, die nostalgisch für den Traum vom Fliegen stehen – aber auch die digital (oder wie auch immer) erzeugten rauchenden Schornsteine der Fabriken – sprechen für einen historistischen Umgang des Films mit Geschichte, der das Gewesene nicht als Spur im Dokument belässt, sondern im Sinne einer vollständigen Bebilderung des Gewesenen ausmalt. Das im neuen digitalen Kino nicht immer so humorlose Ausmalen von etwas, das zuvor als Realität definiert worden ist, fand in Peter Jacksons *King Kong* mit dem Versuch, sogar auch noch den alten Traum vom Fliegen digital zu restaurieren, einen absurden Höhepunkt. Denn die fotografischen Flugbilder vom New York der 1930er Jahre sind in diesem Fall nicht auf der Leinwand zu sehen. Sie werden vielmehr Teil einer Simulation des Fotografischen, welche die Museen und Archive unserer Gegenwart überformt – seien es fotografische Bilder oder die Knochen eines Mammuts in der paläontologischen Abteilung des Jardin du Plantes. Damit wird das Prinzip von Spur und Indexikalität entwertet. Jacksons Projekt illustriert damit die grundsätzlichen Bedenken der Vertreter einer klassisch materiellen Archivierung gegenüber dem Digitalen.

Der vergangene Traum vom Fliegen, der zeitgleich mit der Erfindung des Kinos in Erfüllung ging,[19] kehrt in Jacksons Remake zwar wieder, er verweist aber nicht mehr auf das Flugzeug als Neuerfindung. Vielmehr wird er zum leeren Zeichen, das im Imaginären des Zuschauers kein Pendant mehr findet, höchstens das der Amnesie. Dem Zuschauer bleibt allein der Effekt und die Ebene des Filmtextes, der, so fotografisch er auch erscheinen mag, nur noch als leere Hülle existiert, abgeschnitten von der Welt und zutiefst nostalgisch. Mit der Simulation von Indexikalität werden die Potentiale des Archivmaterials verschüttet, gerade weil die produktiven Leerstellen zwischen den Dokumenten digital aufgefüllt sind. Eine produktive Neuanordnung des Archivmaterials, die Kracauer bereits 1927 in seinem Aufsatz zur Fotografie als das Vabanquespiel der Geschichte bezeichnete, wird damit unmöglich.[20]

19
Edgar Morin: Der Mensch und das Kino. Eine anthropologische Untersuchung. Stuttgart 1958.

20
Siegfried Kracauer: Die Photographie (1927). In: Ders., Das Ornament der Masse, Frankfurt am Main 1977, S. 21–39.

2.1. *King Kong* (1933/2005)

Um die Konstruktionen des Digitalen zu analysieren, erweist sich der Vergleich von Filmfassungen als ergiebig. Das Bild von King Kong auf dem Empire State Building im Kampf mit den Flugzeugen wurde 1933 von Merian C. Cooper und Ernest B. Schoedsack spektakulär inszeniert und mit Peter Jacksons *King Kong* (USA, NZ, D 2005) zu einer Ikone des digitalen Films. In den beiden Filmversionen wird dieses berühmte Bild, das in die Kulturgeschichte des 20. Jahrhunderts eingegangen ist, mit unterschiedlichem Fokus präsentiert. Bei Cooper und Schoedsack steht 1933 die Rettung durch die Flugzeuge im Zentrum, als zweite Attraktion neben dem Monster King Kong. Im Remake Peter Jacksons wird der Fokus der Attraktion auf die digitale Technik verschoben. Was beide Filme verbindet, ist die Verschränkung des Kampfs zwischen Mensch und Monster mit der Präsentation des Neuen.

In *King Kong* (USA 1933) werden die Flugzeuge als das Neue präsentiert, zusammen mit ihrer neuen Perspektive der Flugbilder. Bevor sie ins Bild kommen, sind sie zunächst Gegenstand des Dialogs. Sie werden als letzte Rettung eingeführt: »There is one thing, we can do: aeroplanes!« In *King Kong* (2005) erscheinen die Flugzeuge ohne vorherige Ankündigung. Die Doppeldecker mit den Piloten im offenen Cockpit treten nun in Farbe in Erscheinung, und die Stadt New York liegt unter ihnen in der Abendsonne. Das Neue sind in diesem Fall nicht die Flugzeuge und die mit ihnen verbundene Perspektive. Es handelt sich bei ihnen vielmehr um Oldtimer im besten Sinne des Wortes. Das Neue ist dagegen ein riesiger Visual Effect, der als Stadtansicht von New York erscheint, produziert mit den Computern Peter Jacksons. »So hat man New York noch nie gesehen.«[18]

War der Visual Effect in *Terminator 2* noch auf eine einzelne Figur beschränkt, sind es hier die Straßenzüge einer Metropole, eine Stadtlandschaft als Gesamtbild, die mit digitaler Technik erschaffen worden ist. Das Stadtbild von New York wurde auf der Grundlage von Flugbildern und Fotos aus den 1930er Jahren zunächst rekonstruiert. Gebäude von heute, die es damals noch nicht gab, wurden entfernt und durch digitale Rekonstruktionen ersetzt.

18
Eileen Moran: Visual Effects-Produzentin von King Kong. Vgl. Eileen Moran zu Visual Effects von King Kong (NZ/USA 2005, Peter Jackson). In: Booklet der DVD, Universal 2006.

Filmkritikern vielleicht einige Gemälde William Turners angeboten, welche als statische Bilder zwar anders angelegt sind, die
aber gleichfalls aus einer existentiellen Erfahrung der Natur-
gewalt des Meeres herrühren.

Solche Rückbesinnungen auf das frühe Kino oder auf
noch ältere Gestaltungsebenen von Bildlichkeit – hier die Malerei
Turners – lassen sich zum einen als Symptom einer gesellschaftlichen Verunsicherung deuten. Zum anderen lassen sie sich aber
auch als eine innere Stärke und als Akt einer Emanzipation
begreifen, in der eine kulturelle Sphäre nicht mehr dem Zwang
zur ewigen Wiederholung narrativer Strukturen samt Happy End
sich verpflichtet sieht, sondern tatsächlich Experimente wagt.

Rezeptionsästhetisch betrachtet lässt sich der Anfang der
Geschichte des digitalen Films recht genau bezeichnen. Sie beginnt
im Jahr 1991 mit dem Film *Terminator 2*. Die digitale Technik
wird in diesem Film erstmals in Form eines Visual Effects[16] ausgestellt. Bis dahin vor allem zur Unterstützung der Filmhandlung
eingesetzt, sind die digitalen Bilder hier Star und Publikumsmagnet.
Der Film präsentiert eine multiple Terminator-Figur, die sichtbar
ohne Schnitt ihre Gestalt wechselt; die sich z.B. zur Überwin-
dung eines Eisengitters verflüssigt, um sich anschließend fließend
in ihr Ursprungsdesign rückzubilden. Der Visual Effect wird in
diesem Fall noch von einem ausgefeilten digitalen Sound Design
flankiert, das dem Bild die überzeugende materielle Ausstrahlung
verleiht. Der halb flüssige, matschige und gleichzeitig metal-
lische Klang ist digital produziert, basiert aber gleichwohl auf
Geräuschen unserer Alltagserfahrung. In diesem Falle wurde er
durch eine Verfremdung des Geräuschs beim Entleeren einer
Dose Hundefutters erzeugt. Dieser bis heute in Bild und Ton faszi-
nierende Effekt ist in die Technikgeschichte des Films eingegangen.[17]
Terminator 2 bildet den Auftakt zu einer Reihe von Katastrophen-
filmen des neuen digitalen Kinos, die um die Jahrtausendwende
Sound Design und Visual Effects als Attraktionen präsentierten.
Die Frage »Was ist Film?« wird in dieser Dekade der Filmgeschichte erneut aufgeworfen. Wie in der Frühzeit des Films, geht
es in diesen Filmen wieder primär um die Zurschaustellung
von Attraktionen und darum, dass sich eine neue Technologie
mit Stolz präsentiert.

16
Im Unterschied zu Special Effects,
die am Set gedreht werden,
entstehen Visual Effects im
Rahmen der Postproduktion am
Computer.

17
Vgl. Bernd Willim: Filme aus dem
Rechner. In: Fernseh- und Kino-
technik 52 (5/1998), S. 255–260.

2. Konstruktionen des Digitalen

Der Filmwissenschaftler David Rodowick hat sich zur Digitalisierung des Kinos wie folgt geäußert: »Auf den ersten Blick ist das nicht die Revolution, von der die Industrie gerne spricht. Die digital produzierten Hollywoodfilme [...] erzählen Geschichten, wie es Filme im Grunde seit 1915 tun. [...] Die Grundform des Erzählens und die räumliche Organisation durch den Schnitt sind unverändert«[15]

Rodowicks Diagnose gilt zwar noch für den Großteil der Hollywood-Produktionen der Gegenwart. Dennoch finden sich seit einigen Jahren auch Verschiebungen in der »Grundform des Erzählens«, insbesondere in Form von Reduktionen und Verkürzungen. In einzelnen Filmproduktionen – auch oder gerade aus Hollywood – gibt es zudem eine Rückbesinnung auf das frühe Kino, das Kino der Attraktionen, mit seiner anderen, direkten Ansprache der Zuschauerschaft. Man denke an das Genre des Katastrophenfilms, dessen Filme im Übergang vom 20. ins 21. Jahrhundert zu einer Art Testfeld für digitale Effekte wurden. Als beispielhaft kann Wolfgang Petersens *The Perfect Storm* (USA 2000) gelten, ein Film, der damals in den Kinos floppte und wahrscheinlich von den meisten bereits vergessen ist. Erst nachträglich werden die Ausmaße der Effekte der Inszenierung des Digitalen auf die Narration sichtbar. Das Digitale trat in diesem Film (wie in vielen anderen dieser Zeit) in Gestalt eines überdimensionalen Visual Effects auf. Für die Präsentation der digitalen Ozeanwellen wurde der gesamte Handlungsrahmen so weit verkürzt, dass es sich bei dem Film im Grunde um die bloße Inszenierung eines einzigen, lang gezogenen Visual Effects handelt. Zumindest aus medientheoretischer Sicht stellt dieser Film ein Experiment dar. Die Filmkritiker allerdings blieben vielfach sprachlos in ihren Kinositzen zurück, weil es kaum narrative Anknüpfungsmöglichkeiten gab. Petersens Film war anders angelegt als z.B. der ebenfalls mit digitalen Innovationen auftrumpfende *The Matrix* der Wachowskis (USA 1999). Der stark verkürzte Plot kommt bei Petersen ohne Heilsgeschichte und ohne Heldenfigur aus. Der einzige wirkliche Held des Films sind die digital konstruierten Ozeanwellen. Als Anknüpfungspunkt an eine solche ästhetische Erfahrung hätten sich den sprachlosen

15
David Rodowick im Gespräch mit Claudia Lenssen: Digitale Fotografie ist paradox. In: Die Tageszeitung, 6.11.2003.

Damit denken Mulvey und Wollen ein Projekt voraus, welches den Film tatsächlich zu einem reflexiven Leitmedium unserer Kultur werden lässt, das nicht mehr an die Materialität des Celluloidfilms gebunden ist, sondern das sich als Hypermedialität ebenso im Videoformat fassen lässt, wie dies zunächst beispielhaft von Jean-Luc Godard in *Histoire(s) du Cinéma* (1988–1998) realisiert wurde. Weitergeführt wurde diese Idee der Hypermedialität des Films von Chris Marker in seinen computergestützten Multimediainstallationen wie *Zapping Zone* (1990) oder seiner CD-Rom *Immemory One* (1997). Gegenwärtig findet diese Idee ihre Fortsetzung in netzbasierten Dokumentarfilmproduktionen (i-Docs).[12]

In eine ähnliche Richtung wie Mulvey und Wollen geht W.J.T. Mitchell (1994), der in seinem Buch *Picture Theory* das Konzept des Einzelmediums hinterfragt.[13] Hierzu führt er den Begriff »Imagetext« ein. Die Basis für diese Operation ist ein (ästhetisches und politisches) Misstrauen in alle Ansätze des Medienvergleichs und auch in alle Ansätze einer generalisierenden Systematisierung bzw. Schematisierung von Medienbeziehungen. Mit dem Begriff »Imagetext« unternimmt Mitchell eine Entgegen-Setzung zu einem traditionellen Verständnis von Intermedialität, und er geht davon aus, dass es nicht ein Verhältnis zwischen den Künsten und den Medien, sondern in allen so genannten Einzel-Künsten (und Einzel-Medien) ein unvermeidbares Verhältnis von Bild und Text gebe. Seine Zusammenfassung dieser Überlegungen lautet: Alle Künste sind Composite Arts (bestehend aus Text und Bild), alle Medien sind Mixed Media, die unterschiedliche Codes, Diskurse, Kanäle sowie unterschiedliche Wahrnehmungs- und Beurteilungsweisen umfassen.[14] Mitchell begreift den Imagetext nicht als ein Konzept, sondern eher als eine theoretische Figur (analog zu Derridas Différance), als einen Ort von dialektischer Spannung und Transformation. Unter dieser Voraussetzung stellt sich eine Filmwissenschaft ohne die Einbeziehung von anderen Künsten, Medien, ihren Hybridbildungen und Diskursproduktionen als das Unternehmen einer kulturellen Purifizierung dar.

12
Vgl. Stefano Odorico (2012) i-Docs: Interactivity, Documentary and Memories. In: Antonio Costa Valente; Rita Capucho (Hg.): Avanca I Cinema, Avanca 2012, S. 1140–1146.

13
W.J.T. Mitchell: Picture Theory. Chicago 1994.

14
Aus heutiger Sicht müsste man wohl die Ton- oder Soundebene ergänzen und von einem »Sound-imagetext« sprechen, wenn man an diese Überlegungen anknüpfen will.

8
Laura Mulvey: Visual pleasure and narrative cinema (1975). In: Philip Rosen (Hg.): Narrative, Apparatus, Ideology. New York 1986, S. 198–209, hier S. 200.

9
Peter Wollen: Godard and Counter cinema: Vent d'est (1972). In: Ders.: Readings and Writings. Semiotic Counter-Strategies. London 1982, S. 79–91, hier S. 87.

10
Peter Wollen: The Two Avant-Gardes (1975). In: Ders.: Readings and Writings. Semiotic Counter-Strategies. London 1982, S. 92–104, hier S. 104.

11
So lautet der Untertitel von Kracauers Theorie des Films. Vgl. Kracauer 1960 (wie Anm. 6).

Begehrens, die allerdings das alte Kino nicht zurückweist: »The alternative is the thrill that comes from leaving the past behind without rejecting it [...] in order to conceive a new language of desire.«[8]

Wollen formuliert modellhaft einen erweiterten Kinobegriff: »The text/film can only be understood as an arena, a meeting-place in which different discourses encounter each other [...]. [These] can be seen more as [...] palimpsests, multiple *niederschriften* (Freud's word) in which meaning can no longer be said to express the intention of the author or to be a representation of the world, but must like the discourse of the unconscious be understood by a different kind of decipherment.«[9]

In einem anderen Aufsatz präzisiert Wollen seine Überlegungen in Richtung eines Verständnisses von Film als Hypermedium: »the cinema offers more opportunities than any other art – the cross-fertilization. [...] the reciprocal interlocking and input between painting, writing, music, theatre, could take place within the field of cinema itself. This is not a plea for a great harmony, a synesthetic *gesamtkunstwerk* in the Wagnerian sense. But cinema, [...] [as] a dialectical montage within and between a complex of codes.«[10]

Bei genauer Lektüre ergibt sich im Vergleich mit den Positionen von Bazin und Kracauer weniger eine Gegenüberstellung zu diesen als eine Radikalisierung der Bestimmung des Films. Auch Mulvey und Wollen charakterisieren die spezifische Eigenheit des Films als Kulturtechnik, die sich in den Facetten bei Bazin und Kracauer bereits andeutet. Mulvey und Wollen formulieren in ihrer Beschreibung jedoch die Grundlagen für ein Verständnis des Films als Hypermedium. Gleichwohl orientieren sie sich an jenem Phänomen des Films, das Kracauer 1960 als »die Errettung der äußeren Wirklichkeit«[11] mit Bezug auf den fotografischen Charakter des Films beschrieben hatte. Allerdings hat sich die »Errettung« Kracauers, die das Verhältnis von äußerer Wirklichkeit und Kino umfasst, gewandelt. Mulveys und Wollens Modell ist komplexer geworden. Neben dem Fotografischen integriert es die unterschiedlichen Facetten des Films ebenso wie andere ästhetische Produktionen, Künste und Medien.

Welt automatisch, ohne schöpferische Vermittlung des Menschen und nach einem strengen Determinismus. Die Persönlichkeit des Photographen spielt nur in der Anordnung des Gegenstands und bei der beabsichtigten Wirkung eine Rolle: So sichtbar seine Persönlichkeit im fertigen Werk sein mag, so ist sie doch weit weniger maßgeblich als die des Malers. [...] Das Bild mag verschwommen sein, verzerrt, farblos, ohne dokumentarischen Wert, es gründet durch die Art und Weise seiner Entstehung im Dasein des Modells; es *ist* das Modell.«[4]

Die Ontologie des fotografischen Bildes bewirkt die »Enthüllung des Wirklichen«[5] im Modell jenseits des bloß dokumentarischen und jenseits des Künstlersubjekts.

Ähnlich argumentiert Siegfried Kracauer in seiner *Theorie des Films* (1960): »Kurz, mein Buch entspringt der Absicht, Einblick in die besondere Natur des photographischen Films zu gewinnen.«[6] Diese Absichtserklärung stammt aus dem Vorwort, und bevor Kracauer sich dem Film zuwendet, vergehen fünfzig Seiten, die von der Fotografie handeln. Kracauer nennt vier Affinitäten des Fotografischen. Die Fotografie besitze erstens »eine ausgesprochene Affinität zur ungestellten Realität«, zweitens zum Zufälligen, drittens tendiere sie dazu, »die Vorstellung von Endlosigkeit zu erwecken« und viertens weise die Fotografie »eine Affinität zum Unbestimmbaren« auf.[7]

In beiden Theoriepositionen bildet die Fotografie jeweils eine zentrale Facette in der medientheoretischen Beschreibung des Films. Während bei Kracauer daneben auch der traumähnliche Zustand des Zuschauers genannt wird, benennt Bazin beispielsweise den Film auch bzw. gleichzeitig als eine Sprache. Gemeinsam ist beiden, dass sie dem Film auf der Basis dieser Facetten eine spezifische Eigenständigkeit als Kunst, als Medium bzw. als Kulturtechnik bescheinigen.

1.2. Der Film als hybrides oder Hypermedium

Laura Mulvey und Peter Wollen skizzieren im Zeitkolorit der 1970er Jahre und unter dem Einfluss poststrukturalistischer Theorien aus Frankreich (Barthes, Derrida, Lacan) ein utopisches, anderes Kino. Mulvey betont die Geste eines feministischen Befreiungskampfs und sucht nach einer neuen Sprache des

---

4
Ebd., S. 38f.

5
Ebd., S. 39.

6
Siegfried Kracauer: Theorie des Films. Die Errettung der äußeren Wirklichkeit (1960). Frankfurt am Main 1996, S. 45–46, S. 9.

7
Ebd., S. 45f.

man zu den Akten legen kann. Zum anderen die Beschreibungen eines »cinema impur«, eines »hybriden Kinos«, von dem bereits Bazin spricht und welches in den Überlegungen von Peter Wollen und Laura Mulvey der 1970er Jahre und W.J.T. Mitchell in den 1990er Jahren im Kontext von Poststrukturalismus und Dekonstruktion die theoretische Form eines Hypermediums bzw. Imagetextes annimmt.

1.1. Der Film als fotografisches Medium

Als fotografisches Medium ist der Film in einer besonderen Weise der physischen Realität verpflichtet. Der Realitätsbezug des fotografischen Films geht in der Idee eines bloßen Abbildrealismus jedoch nicht auf, sondern es kommt durch den Film etwas hinzu, das zuvor nicht sichtbar gewesen ist. André Bazin (1945) spricht in Bezug auf den fotografischen Film von einer »Mumie der Veränderung«, deren ästhetisches Potential in der Enthüllung des Wirklichen liege. Der Film wird als Vollendung der fotografischen Objektivität der Zeit gefasst, der den Gegenstand nicht mehr nur in einem Augenblick festhalte, sondern diesen aus der Erstarrung befreie.

»Die Photographie erschafft nicht, wie die Kunst, Ewigkeit, sondern sie balsamiert die Zeit ein, entzieht sie ihrem Verfall. Aus dieser Perspektive erscheint der Film wie die Vollendung der Photographischen Objektivität der Zeit. Der Film hält den Gegenstand nicht mehr nur in einem Augenblick fest, wie der Bernstein den intakten Körper von Insekten aus einer fernen Zeit; er befreit die Barockkunst von ihrem Starrkrampf. Zum ersten Mal ist das Bild der Dinge auch das ihrer Dauer, es ist gleichsam eine Mumie der Veränderung. Die Kategorien der Ähnlichkeit, die das photographische Bild kennzeichnen, sind also, anders als in der Malerei, auch für seine Ästhetik bestimmend. Das ästhetische Wirkungsvermögen der Photographie liegt in der Enthüllung des Wirklichen.«[3]

Als Argument dafür, dass die Fotografie Wirklichkeit nicht abbildet, sondern enthüllt, werden die durch die technische Apparatur festgelegten kulturellen Handlungsbedingungen angeführt, die das Modell anstelle des Künstlers herausstellen: »Zum ersten Mal entsteht ein Bild von der uns umgebenden

3
André Bazin: Ontologie des photographischen Bildes (1945). In: Robert Fischer (Hg.): André Bazin. Was ist Film? Berlin 2004, S. 33–42, hier S. 39.

die Filmnarration sei durch das Digitale weitgehend unverändert. Drittens schließlich soll die These aufgestellt werden, dass der Film als Hypermedium von Bild, Text und Sound eine Ästhetik des digitalen Kinos bereits vorausdenkt. In dieser Perspektive generiert sich das Neue nicht aus einem technischen Quantensprung ins Digitale, sondern aus einer vielfältigen Entwicklungsgeschichte kulturellen Handelns, die von anscheinend fundamentalen technischen Neuerungen (z.B. zum Tonfilm, zum Farbfilm usw.) begleitet wurde. Das prägende Moment des Neuen lässt sich somit gerade nicht allein in den technischen Innovationen fassen, sondern in der Arbeit an einer Kulturtechnik, die sich als Film/Kino in ihrer spezifischen, hybriden Eigenständigkeit im 20. Jahrhundert herausgebildet hat: konkret gefasst, als kulturelles Handeln in einem Diskursfeld, welches ästhetische und kommerzielle Strategien erprobt und dafür technische Möglichkeiten sondiert. In dieser Perspektive stehen nicht in erster Linie veränderte filmische Narrationen zur Diskussion, sondern jenes kulturelle Geschehen im Diskursfeld, das in den Filmen aufscheint.

1. Medientheoretische Beschreibungen des Films

Was die filmtheoretischen Schriften verbindet und auszeichnet, ist die Vorstellung, dass es neben dem einzelnen Film, den man im Kino oder anderweitig sehen kann, etwas eigens Filmisches gibt, einen genuinen, einheitlich abgrenzbaren Gegenstand, der anhand spezifischer Eigenschaften von anderen Künsten und Medien, wie z.B. dem Theater, der Literatur, dem Fernsehen, unterschieden werden kann. Die für den Film charakteristischen Elemente und Tatbestände sind historisch unterschiedlich gefasst worden: in der Laufbewegung der Bilder, der filmischen Apparatur, der Montage, der Indexikalität des fotografischen Bildes, seiner Materialität, in der Großaufnahme uvm.

Zwei unterschiedliche medientheoretische Perspektiven auf den Film sollen im Folgenden kurz skizziert werden. Zum einen die Beschreibungen des Films von André Bazin und Siegfried Kracauer, die den Film ausgehend vom Fotografischen denken. Beide Positionen erscheinen im Zuge der Digitalisierung auf den ersten Blick als überholt, als historische Kapitel, die

Die allgemeinen Erwartungen über das Neue in Film und Kino haben sich in jüngerer Vergangenheit fast ausschließlich auf die Digitalisierung gerichtet, bevor 2010 anlässlich von Filmen wie *Avatar* (2010) oder *Shrek 4* (2010) die Technologie des 3D als Neuheit präsentiert wurde, die das Kino revolutionieren sollte.[1] Dieser Umstand allein ist bemerkenswert. Historisch betrachtet, wurde das Neue im Kino zumeist viel konkreter, d. h. nicht allein an technischer Neuerung festgemacht. Zwar gab es schon immer den Blick auf die technisch-mediale Weiterentwicklung, doch die allgemeine Erwartung, insbesondere des Publikums, richtete sich z.B. in der Frühzeit auf die sichtbaren Attraktionen, im Starsystem Hollywoods auf den neu entdeckten Star und im modernen Kino auf die Formen einer neuen Ästhetik, die als Differenz hörbar und sichtbar wurde. Das Paradox der mit der Digitalisierung verbundenen Erwartung besteht, kurz gesagt, darin, dass das neue Digitale zwar in Erscheinung tritt, dass diese Erscheinung aber am alten, fotografischen Look gemessen wird: Die Schlagzeilen der digitalen Filmprojektion im Kino zeichneten sich nämlich dadurch aus, dass man die klassische Projektion des Filmstreifens auf Celluloid nicht mehr von der digitalen Projektion unterscheiden könne. Worin besteht bzw. bestand dann aber das neue, digitale Versprechen des Kinos?

Was wir im Folgenden vorhaben, ist, in drei Schritten eine Bestandsaufnahme der Diskurse vorzunehmen, die für das digitale Kino und seine Bildlichkeit bisher relevant erschienen.[2] Der erste Punkt betrifft die Darstellung von medientheoretischen Beschreibungen des Films: einerseits mit einer heute klassisch anmutenden Ableitung des Films vom Fotografischen (Kracauer, Bazin) und andererseits mit einer medientheoretischen Auffassung des Films als hybrides oder Hypermedium (Mulvey/Wollen, Mitchell). Im zweiten Teil soll es darum gehen, anhand von Filmen des digitalen Attraktionskinos (*The Perfect Storm* 2000, *King Kong* 2005) und Produktionen, die sich durch einen *entspannten* Umgang mit dem digitalen Bild auszeichnen (*Orly* 2010), die Ausformungen des Digitalen und des Analogen in ihrer konkreten Konstruktion herauszustellen. Ausgangspunkt dafür bildet das Statement des Filmtheoretikers David Rodowick,

1
Die 3D-Technologie geht auf die Ende des 19. Jahrhunderts entwickelte Stereoskopie zurück und wird im Zuge der Digitalisierung des Films heute ›neu‹ entdeckt. In zahlreichen Artikeln wird auf die Geschichte von 3D, vor allem auf die Weiterentwicklung in den 1970er Jahren Bezug genommen. Zugleich wird 3D aber als ›Revolution‹ gehandelt.

2
Eine erste Version dieses Aufsatzes wurde unter folgendem Titel publiziert: Das Neue in Film und Kino. Filmästhetik und Digitalisierung. In: Wolfgang Sohst (Hg.): Die Figur des Neuen. Berlin 2008, S. 331–356.

Konstruktionen des Digitalen Films. Ästhetik, Narration, Diskurs

Sabine Nessel

Winfried Pauleit

Juliane Rebentisch
ist Professorin für Philosophie und Ästhetik an der
Hochschule für Gestaltung in Offenbach am Main und assoziiertes
Mitglied des Frankfurter Instituts für Sozialforschung. Arbeits-
schwerpunkte: Ästhetik, Ethik, politische Philosophie. Bücher u.a.:
Ästhetik der Installation (2003)/*Aesthetics of Installation Art* (2012);
Kreation und Depression. Freiheit im gegenwärtigen Kapitalismus
(hg. mit Ch. Menke, 2010); *Die Kunst der Freiheit. Zur Dialektik
demokratischer Existenz* (2012). In Vorbereitung: *Theorien der
Gegenwartskunst zur Einführung.*

Letterman: How are you doing? (*Lacht*) You know, I've always liked you, I've been to see your movies, I've always liked you, I recognise you as a powerful talent. The Johnny Cash thing, you were tremendous in that.
(*Applaus*)
Phoenix (*zum Publikum*): Thank you. Thank you.
Letterman: And then, a year and a half ago, you come out, and honestly, it's like you slipped and hit your head in the tub.
(*Gelächter*)
Letterman: And I knew immediatly, when you sat down, something ain't right, because if you're really the way you appeared to be, you don't go out.
(*Gelächter*)
Letterman: You know what I mean? People don't let guys like you out, if you're really like that. You don't go out.
Phoenix (*lakonisch*): Right.
Letterman (*nach einer kurzen Pause, die an seine Ratlosigkeit gegenüber der gespielten Einsilbigkeit seines damaligen Gesprächspartner erinnert*): Yeah.
(*Gelächter*)
Letterman (*setzt nachdrücklich nach*): So what do you have to say for yourself?
(*Gelächter*)

Auch wenn die Rehabilitierung für Phoenix zu dem Preis erfolgte, für alle wieder nichts anderes zu sein als der so überaus talentierte Charakterdarsteller aus *Walk the Line* – mit *I'm Still Here* hat er nicht nur erreicht, dass Lettermans Witz, »Joaquin, I'm sorry you couldn't be here tonight«, eine Bedeutung bekommt, die sein Projekt nicht nur durch die Anspielung im Titel an das von Haynes heranrückt. Der Einsatz ist jedoch bei Phoenix nicht die Öffnung des Biopic auf die Potentialität des Lebens, sondern die der Reality-Formate auf die Dimension der Erzählung. In beiden Projekten geht es nicht zuletzt darum, das existentielle Gewicht der situativen Frage zu verteidigen: *What do you have to say for yourself?*

Letterman (*nach einer sehr langen Pause des Schweigens zu Phoenix,
        dessen Aussehen in der Tat an das von Theodore Kaczynski
        erinnert*): So what can you tell us about your days with
        the unabomber? [...]
Phoenix (*nuschelt durch seinen Kaugummi*): Well, I've been wor-
        king on my music. [...]
Letterman: You're not gonna act anymore?
Phoenix: No. [...]
Letterman (*nach einer erneuten Pause*): Joaquin, I'm sorry you
        couldn't be here tonight.
Phoenix (*grinst, zeigt mit dem Daumen auf Letterman*): He's funny.
        [...]
Letterman: Now – can you set up the clip for us, Joaquin? [...]
Phoenix: I don't know what the clip is.
Letterman: You don't know what the clip is? It's a scene with you
        and Gwyneth Paltrow.
Phoenix (*aufmunternd*): Ah – you're doing fine.
Letterman (*ärgerlich*): Oh, thanks – that's a high praise coming
        from you.
        (*Phoenix beugt sich vor, macht träge Anstalten, auf die
        Beleidigung zu reagieren.*)
Letterman (*einlenkend*): We're having fun.
Phoenix: Is that fun?
Letterman: We're having fun, just relax, seriously.
        (*Phoenix lehnt sich wieder zurück, kaut an seinem Kaugummi.*)
Letterman (*erneut ärgerlich*): I'll come to your house and chew
        gum.
Phoenix: No, I don't have to chew gum. (*Nimmt den Kaugummi
        aus dem Mund und klebt ihn Letterman unter den Tisch.*)
        I won't chew the gum.
Letterman: Wow.

Inzwischen hat sich Phoenix in den Augen der Öffentlichkeit freilich wieder rehabilitiert, und zwar als souveräner
Schauspieler, der noch den eigenen Verfall darzustellen weiß,
ohne je aus der Rolle zu fallen. Aufgeräumt, frisch rasiert und
ohne Kaugummi im Mund kehrte er denn auch in Lettermans
Show zurück (23.09.2010):

Ein kleiner Abspann noch: War es das Problem des konventionellen Biopic, also zum Beispiel von *Walk the Line*, dass es die Differenz zwischen Erzählung und Leben auf der Seite der Erzählung tendenziell zusammenfallen lässt, so ist es das Problem vieler aktueller Reality-Formate, dass sie die Erzählung tendenziell im Leben aufgehen lassen – und auf diese Weise jedes Bewusstsein um die Potentialität der menschlichen Existenz verschwinden lassen, allerdings nicht im schicksalhaften Plot, sondern in der Verdinglichung der menschlichen Potentialität selbst zum Produkt. Die Dokumentation der Lebensvollzüge, ohne den konstruktiven Filter der Erzählung, hat hier, anders als in Warhols formal strengen Anordnungen, nicht den Effekt des Entzugs, sondern der endlosen Verfügbarkeit der Personen, die unter der panoptischen Präsenz der Kameras noch dann zu performen haben, wenn es nichts zu erzählen gibt.

Interessanterweise begegnet uns Joaquin Phoenix auch an diesem Ende einer falschen Identifikation von Erzählung und Leben. Für die in Zusammenarbeit mit Casey Affleck entwickelte Mockumentary *I'm Still Here* (2010) spielte der für seine Rolle in *Walk the Line* allgemein geschätzte Phoenix sehr buchstäblich die Rolle seines Lebens: die des ausgestiegenen Schauspielers Phoenix nämlich, der nunmehr eine Karriere als Hiphop-Musiker plant, daran grandios scheitert und dessen Leben auch sonst moderat entgleist. Während der Zeit der Produktion wurde er, so suggeriert zumindest das zusammengeschnittene Material, permanent von einer Kamera begleitet. Darüber hinaus besuchte er Live-Sendungen, in denen er als er selbst, also als ein veränderter Joaquin Phoenix, auftrat.

In einem Auftritt in der *Late Show* von David Letterman (11.02.2009) beispielsweise gab sich ein bärtiger, sonnenbebrillter Phoenix, der eingeladen war, über seinen neuesten Film mit Gwyneth Paltrow (*Two Lovers*) zu sprechen, sehr einsilbig. Nachdem das Gespräch nicht anlaufen wollte – weder seine neugierigen Fragen zum ungewohnten Aussehen von Phoenix noch die höflichen zum neuen Film fruchteten –, wurde Letterman langsam ungehalten. Hier sind ein paar Auszüge aus der Begegnung:

zukommt, wenn man sie von dem Anspruch entlastet, das Ganze des Lebens rechtfertigen zu sollen. Die Erzählung beschränkt sich dann auf bestimmte Aspekte, die in einem bestimmten praktischen Zusammenhang, einer bestimmten Welt, hervortreten – andere bleiben unberücksichtigt.[23] Genau durch diese Beschränkung wird indes der Unterschied zwischen dem Leben und den jeweils aufgebrachten Erzählungen bekräftigt, ohne diesen dadurch ihre situative Evidenz zu nehmen – und von der Einsicht in die Fallibilität solcher Erzählungen auf ihre situative Bedeutungslosigkeit zu schließen.

Das Problem des Verhältnisses zwischen Bestimmtheit und Unbestimmtheit (im Unterschied zu dem zwischen der bloßen Rolle und der authentischen Person »dahinter«), um das es hier geht, wird von Haynes in *I'm Not There* allerdings, wie wir jetzt sehen können, an einem zu Warhol komplementären Pol aufgenommen. Wo dieser die nach Cavell so spezifisch filmische Betonung des Schauspielers vor der Rolle in der Weise isoliert hatte, dass das Gesicht in seiner singulären Konkretion gleichsam zur Chiffre der Potentialität wird, fasst Haynes das Problem von einer anderen Seite an: Die Potentialität der Person kommt hier nicht durch einen Entzug jeglicher Erzählung, noch nicht einmal jeglicher Legende mit ihren schicksalhaften Anteilen zum Ausdruck, sondern dadurch, dass er der Erzählung einen anderen Status anweist. Den eines situativ beschränkten, an eine je konkrete Welt gebundenen Rechtfertigungsnarrativs, das, wiewohl wir um seine Beschränktheit wissen, für uns jeweils »die Welt« bedeutet. Das spiegelt sich gewissermaßen in der Haltung, die *I'm Not There* einfordert, die Haltung einer, wie Alexander García Düttmann formuliert, »doppelten Teilhabe«[24] am Film, für die das Wissen um den Konstruktionscharakter und die Beschränktheit der Erzählungen kein Grund ist, aus ihnen auszusteigen. Die Ethik, die einer solchen Haltung entspricht, wäre eine, die den anderen weder auf eine Erzählung oder eine Legende festlegen will noch aber sich auf eine Position der Indifferenz der situativ je Geltung beanspruchenden Erzählung zurückzieht. Es ist dies eine Haltung, die die Differenz zwischen Leben und Erzählung austrägt, ohne das eine auf das andere zu reduzieren.

*

23
Vgl. Thomä (2007), S. 271 (wie Anm. 17).

24
Düttmann (2009), S. 163 (wie Anm. 22).

der zwischen ihnen inszenierten Brüche – *jeweils* in ihren Bann ziehen, unterstreicht *I'm Not There* in besonders ausdrücklicher Weise eine Paradoxie, die alle Spielfilmerfahrung mehr oder weniger latent durchzieht: dass der Film ein Moment des unmittelbaren Glaubens an die von ihm eröffnete Welt ebenso fordert wie eine diesen Glauben brechende Aufmerksamkeit für seine Vermitteltheit als filmische Konstruktion.[22] Die Betonung dieser Paradoxie hat hier, im Blick auf *I'm Not There*, aber auch eine gewisse ethische Resonanz: Denn auf diese Weise setzt sich der Film deutlich von der These ab, der zufolge es hinter den vielen Gesichtern von Dylan ein metasouveränes Subjekt gibt, für das all seine Identitäten nichts als äußerliche Masken sind, mit denen es sein Publikum verwirrt. Man kann auch sagen: Sofern der Film eine These über die Ironie Dylans vertritt, wäre es nicht die Ironie des seiner eigenen sozialen Identität gegenüber indifferent-überlegenen Metasubjekts. Hier geht es nicht um ein Subjekt, das der sozialen Praxis *im Ganzen* indifferent-überlegen gegenübersteht, sondern um eines, das sich von je konkreten Bestimmungen absetzt, etwa weil es sich von ihnen entfremdet hat, und das deshalb nach einer neuen Bestimmung sucht, die es wieder mit sich in Einklang bringten möchte. Ein solches Subjekt wäre ironisch nicht im Sinne einer nihilistischen Haltung, der die Welt *im Ganzen* nichts als Schein ist; ironisch ist ein solches Subjekt vielmehr im Sinne eines ausgeprägten Fallibilitätsbewusstseins. Das, was uns heute nach bestem Wissen und Gewissen als das Richtige für uns erscheint, kann sich morgen im Lichte anderer Ereignisse oder auch schleichenderer Entwicklungen als unzureichend, als falsch erweisen. Das relativiert aber nicht die jeweiligen Entscheidungen und auch nicht die mit ihnen einhergehenden situativen existentiellen Rechtfertigungsnarrative. Die haben vielmehr jeweils – situativ – volle Gültigkeit und existentielles Gewicht.

Dennoch verbindet sich ein solches Fallibilitätsbewusstsein mit einem Bewusstsein um die Differenz, die stets zwischen Erzählung und Leben besteht. Dabei weiß es aber nicht nur um das Unerzählte und Unerfasste des Lebens und um seine Potentialität gegenüber identitären Bestimmungen, sondern ebenso um die konstruktive Funktion, die den Erzählungen gerade dann

22
Vgl. hierzu Alexander García Düttmann: QUASI. Antonioni und die Teilhabe an der Kunst. In: Neue Rundschau 4 (2009), 151–165.

Doch die Ausstellung der filmischen Hilfsgenres, die die jeweilige Welt konturieren, die Markierung der entsprechenden Genres durch die harten Schnitte, das Hin- und Herschalten zwischen inhaltlich und formal sehr unterschiedlichen Welten, schmälert interessanterweise nicht ihre *jeweilige* illusionistische Wirkung. Man ist jeweils in der Welt, die man sieht, glaubt ihr unmittelbar, obwohl man zugleich aufgefordert ist, sie als vermittelte, als Konstruktion wahrzunehmen. Diese doppelte Einstellung ist für jedes Sehen von Film konstitutiv, aber sie wird auf unterschiedliche Weise wirksam. So verweist das klassische Biopic auf seine Weise auf die Konstruktion. Das gilt nicht nur hinsichtlich der Lebensgeschichte, die zum Drehbuch wird, oder hinsichtlich der schauspielerischen Leistung, die sich dem öffentlich bekannten Vorbild möglichst getreu anzuverwandeln hat und es doch nie ganz kann. Es gilt auch hinsichtlich der Rekonstruktion von Welt, und zwar zum Teil durchaus im direkten Zitat bereits durch Bilder erschlossener, also ikonisch gewordener historischer Ereignisse. Dass auch dieser letzte Aspekt für das traditionelle Biopic charakteristisch ist, kann man sich an vielen Beispielen klarmachen, so etwa an der Nachstellung bekannter Bilder von Arthur Miller und Marilyn Monroe in *My Week with Marilyn* (2011) mit Michelle Williams als Marilyn Monroe oder auch an den berühmten Cash-Auftritten im Gefängnis von San Quentin, die in *Walk The Line* zitiert werden.

Obwohl uns auch in den detailgetreuesten Rekonstruktionen bewusst bleibt, dass Joaquin Phoenix nicht Johnny Cash und Michelle Williams sehr deutlich nicht Marilyn ist, und obwohl selbst noch Cate Blanchetts schauspielerischer Triumph in *I'm Not There* sich natürlich gerade aus der stets präsent bleibenden (Geschlechter)Differenz zum Vorbild ergibt, bleibt es keineswegs allein beim formalistischen Bewusstsein um die Konstruktion. Die ganze filmische Welt mag zitiert sein, aber für uns gilt sie trotzdem *auch* unmittelbar. Wir denken selbst bei *Walk the Line* nicht permanent »Joaquin Phoenix«, sondern folgen seiner Figur, seinem Johnny Cash.

Durch die Pluralisierung, die Konstellation der unterschiedlichen mit Dylan assoziierten Welten, die uns – ungeachtet

rechtfertigt, wenn man so sprechen will, filmisch die Welt jeder einzelnen Figur. Denn vervielfältigt werden nicht nur die Charaktere, sondern auch die Erzählstile. Jeder Figur entspricht eine eigene filmische Welt. So könnte es keinen größeren Kontrast geben als den zwischen der 1960er-Jahre-Welt aus Schwarz und Weiß, durch die sich Jude Quinn (Cate Blanchett) bewegt, und der stets in ein sehr spezfisches, weiches Licht getauchten Welt des 1970er-Jahre-Westerns, durch die Billy McCarty (Richard Gere) reitet.

Damit legt Haynes auch ein wichtiges Strukturmerkmal des Biopic offen. Das Biopic sei nämlich, schreibt Henry Taylor in seinem Buch über die *Filmbiographie als narratives System*, selbst ein Chamäleon-Genre, das keine eigene Stilrichtung etabliert, also keinen distinktiven »Look« ausgebildet habe.[21] Vielmehr präge jeweils ein so genanntes Hilfsgenre die stilistische Gestaltung des Biopic. In unserem Beispiel eben wären solche Hilfsgenres etwa der 1970er-Jahre-Western oder die 1960er-Jahre-Schwarz/Weiß-Ästhetik, die natürlich von *Don't Look Back* beeinflusst ist, D.A. Pennebakers berühmtem Dokumentarfilm über Dylans 1965er Tour durch England, aus dem auch der berühmte Clip zu *Subterranean Homesick Blues* hervorging. Weitere, ziemlich offensichtliche Quellen für die Blanchett-Szenen sind Murray Lerners Dokumentation *The Other Side of the Mirror: Bob Dylan at the Newport Folk Festival*, die zeigt, »how Bob Dylan plugged in a whole generation«, sowie eine Serie von Fotos, die Berry Feinstein 1966 auf einer weiteren England-Tour von Dylan gemacht hat. All diese Referenzen sind recht bekannt, werden bis ins Detail rekonstruiert; es handelt sich um eine Art Spielfilm-Remake solcher dokumentarischer Materialien. In Klammern sei bemerkt, dass Haynes natürlich auch für jede Theorie des Remake einschlägig ist: 2011 ist er mit einem sehr empfehlenswerten Remake von *Mildred Pierce* hervorgetreten, ursprünglich ein Melodrama von Michael Curtiz aus dem Jahr 1945 mit Joan Crawford in der Hauptrolle; bei Haynes wird daraus eine HBO-Miniserie, in der Kate Winslet der Hauptfigur eine ganz andere Note gibt.

*

21
Henry M. Taylor: Rolle des Lebens. Die Filmbiographie als narratives System. Marburg 2002, S. 21.

Billy McCarty, der sich – wie die Woody-Figur – weitgehend aus dem *Werk* Dylans speist. Der Name Billy erinnert an Billy the Kid; die Charaktere, auf die Billy in der Stadt mit dem bezeichnenden Namen Riddle trifft, tragen Namen, die in Songs von den so genannten *Basement Tapes* vorkommen, die Dylan bereits 1967 mit *The Band* aufgenommen hatte, die aber erst 1975 offiziell veröffentlicht wurden und von denen auch der Titelsong *I'm Not There* stammt. Wie in *Velvet Goldmine* also haben wir es hier mit einem Ineinander von Referenzen auf Werk und Leben zu tun, dessen Ergebnis lauter auf mehreren Ebenen von Dylan inspirierte Figuren sind, die zugleich bereits auf der Plot-Ebene als Fiktionen markiert sind. Im Abspann des Films steht dann auch – wahrheitsgemäß – folgender Satz: »This motion picture is fictional but some elements have been inspired by real people and real events.«

Ein weiterer Effekt dieses Vorgehens ist, dass der Versuch, die Figuren in eine klare Chronologie zu bringen, sie klar bestimmten Lebensabschnitten von Dylan zuzuordnen, in gewisse Schwierigkeiten gerät. Das gilt natürlich insbesondere für die erste und die letzte Figur, also für Woody und für Billy, die weniger aus dem Material des Lebens denn des Werks von Dylan hervorgehen, wobei beide Figuren jeweils Elemente aus sehr unterschiedlichen Werkphasen aufnehmen. Aber auch die anderen Figuren greifen zuweilen, in kleinen Details, auf die jeweils anderen so aus oder zurück, dass sie der Tendenz nach eher in eine spannungsvolle Konstellation treten denn in ein selbst wiederum erzählbares Nacheinander. Hier geht es also offenkundig nicht darum, die Veränderung auszuerzählen. Davon, wie die Figuren zusammenhängen, erfahren wir kaum etwas. Selbst Jack Rollins taucht im letzten Drittel des Films einfach, zu Pastor John geworden, als ein anderer auf.

Der Film, könnte man vorderhand meinen, rechtfertigt nichts. Jedenfalls erklärt er keinen Identitätswechsel, um so die Abfolge in die Kohärenz einer abgeschlossenen Lebensgeschichte zu bringen, wie das klassische Biopic, das ja aus der Dramaturgie auserzählter Identitätskrisen und -wendungen lebt, siehe *Walk the Line*. *I'm Not There* macht aber etwas anderes: Er verleiht jedem einzelnen Charakter filmische Evidenz;

schauspielerischer Leistungen überhaupt ab, auch geht es nicht
darum, das immersiv-illusionistische Potential des Films zu
negieren. Der offensichtlichste und zugleich sehr weitreichende
Eingriff, den Haynes am Biopic vornimmt, ist vielmehr ein
anderer: die Vervielfältigung der Figur in sieben sehr unterschiedliche Charaktere, die von sechs Schauspielern gespielt werden –
darunter eine Frau (Cate Blanchett) und ein schwarzer Junge
(Marcus Carl Franklin). Keiner dieser Charaktere erhält den
Namen Bob Dylan – auch das ein Bruch mit dem traditionellen
Biopic. Der Junge heißt im Film Woody Guthrie, wie der von
Dylan verehrte Protestsänger, und es ist auch dessen, nicht
Dylans Spruch, der auf dem Gitarrenkasten steht, den der Junge
auf seinen Güterzugreisen durch die USA mitnimmt: »This
machine kills fascists.« Zugleich wird der Junge gleich zu Beginn
des Films als »fake« bezeichnet; er steht nämlich auch für die von
Dylan selbst gestreuten Geschichten über eine Jugend als Ausrei-
ßer, die eine Zeitlang in den offiziellen Dylan-Biographien
auftauchten, bis herauskam, dass sie nicht stimmen. Ben Winshaw
spielt den scharfzüngigen Poeten, der sich im Film selbst
Arthur Rimbaud nennt. Der Folk- und Protestsong-Dylan aus der
Phase mit Joan Baez (die im Film Alice Fabian heißt und von
Julianne Moore gespielt wird) heißt im Film Jack Rollins. Er wird
von Christian Bale gespielt und hat als einzige Figur eine Entwicklung: Es ist dieser Jack Rollins, der in einer späteren Phase
zum Pastor John wird, also zu einer Cover-Figur für Dylans
religiöse Phase. Cate Blanchetts Figur heißt im Film Jude Quinn.
Sie bezieht sich auf den Dylan, der seine Folkfans mit E-Gitarren-
Sound und Rock'n'Roll vor den Kopf stößt. An einer Stelle
wird Jude Quinn von der Presse mit der Veröffentlichung seines
richtigen Namens konfrontiert; der sei nämlich gar nicht Jude
Quinn, sondern Aron Jacob Edelstein – in Analogie zu Dylans
ursprünglichem Namen Robert Zimmerman. Heath Ledger spielt
(in seiner letzten Rolle übrigens) eine Figur namens Robbie Clark,
einen Schauspieler, der einmal in einem Biopic über Jack Rollins
die Hauptrolle spielt, ein andermal sich erfolglos als Filmemacher versucht und ansonsten in seiner Ehe mit Claire, gespielt
von Charlotte Gainsbourgh, scheitert. Bleibt noch Richard Gere;
seine Figur ist ein in die Jahre gekommener Outlaw namens

nalen Welten überblendet, die von diesen geschaffen wurden: Bowie vermischt sich ununterscheidbar mit Ziggy. Nun ist *Velvet Goldmine* kein Biopic; aber er enthält gleichwohl eine filmische Annäherung an einen Star, der, wie Dylan, als ein chamäleonhafter Charakter bekannt ist, der sich durch seine wechselnden personae entzieht: Bowie. Nicht zufällig finden sich auf der meiner Meinung nach besten Bowie-Platte *Hunky Dory* nicht nur Bowies berühmte *Changes*, sondern auch ein Song mit dem Titel *Andy Warhol* sowie schließlich auch ein *Song for Bob Dylan*.

*

I'm Not There (2007) nun *ist* ein vom Regisseur so bezeichnetes Biopic, das aber gerade das Anti-Legendäre, den Entzug Dylans, zum titelgebenden Thema macht. Ursprünglich sollte der Film übrigens *Alias* heißen, nach Dylans Charakter in *Pat Garret jagt Billy the Kid*; dann aber kam eine amerikanische Action-Fernsehserie mit diesem Titel dazwischen.[20] »*I'm Not There*« trifft den Punkt aber ebenfalls: Es geht hier um die Unergründlichkeit des Selbst gegenüber allen Rechtfertigungsnarrativen, die man sich, ja, die Dylan sich selbst zu einem bestimmten Zeitpunkt über Dylan erzählt haben mag. Es geht um eine Potentialität des Selbst gegenüber je konkreten Bestimmungen, um das Moment einer Freiheit *von*, die es auf der Reise hält. »People are always talkin' about Freedom«, sagt eine Stimme im Trailer von *I'm Not There*, »Freedom to live a certain way. Of course the more you live a certain way, the less it feels like freedom. Me, I can change during the course of a day. By waking I'm one person, and when I go to sleep, I know for certain I'm somebody else.«

Sich filmisch dem Thema der Freiheit von identitären Festlegungen zuzuwenden, heißt, die Differenz von Erzählung und Leben mit zu behandeln und für diese Differenz eine Form zu finden. Das zu unternehmen, heißt natürlich sogleich, sich gegen die, sagen wir ruhig, Ideologie des Biopic zu wenden, die diese Differenz in Authentizitätsbehauptungen verdeckt – der authentischen Geschichte wie des freilich nur durch höchste schauspielerische Disziplin zu erreichenden Ausdrucks von Authentizität auf der Ebene der Darstellung. Indes wendet sich Haynes keineswegs, wie in *Superstar*, von der Verwendung solch

---

20
So Todd Haynes in einem Gespräch mit Jim Hoberman anlässlich einer Haynes-Retrospektive an der Cornell University. URL: http://www.youtube.com/watch?v=eMfr_pzBU18 (Stand: 12.08.2013).

19
Vgl. Christina von Braun: Nichtich.
Logik, Lüge, Libido. Frankfurt am
Main 1990, S. 460.

Allgemeine der Magersucht als einer Frauenkrankheit nämlich, die nicht zuletzt als eine Art »Desinkarnation«[19] des idealen Bilds der Frau (Barbie) gedeutet werden kann. Es handelt sich bei *Superstar* also gewissermaßen um ein Lehrstück. Die Familie von Karen Carpenter, die in diesem Lehrstück nicht besonders gut wegkommt, war natürlich nicht begeistert. Richard Carpenter klagte gegen den Film und bekam vor allem wegen der ungeklärten Musiklizenzen Recht; der Film wurde tatsächlich vom Markt genommen und war lange Zeit nicht verfügbar. Mittlerweile kann man ihn sich in voller Länge auf *YouTube* ansehen. Der Titel des Films, *Superstar*, verweist hier freilich weniger auf Warhol denn auf den berühmten Song der Carpenters, in dem es um die Sehnsucht einer Frau nach der Person hinter dem Star geht, doch der bleibt in der falschen Nähe, die sein Image vermittelt, abwesend: »Your guitar, it sounds so sweet and clear. But you're not really here. It's just the radio.« In unserem Zusammenhang entscheidend ist jedoch weniger die Thematisierung der Mensch-Star-Differenz, von der das Biopic generell lebt, denn die Radikalisierung der Legende zum Lehrstück, durch die bereits die Erzählung als eine Konstruktion markiert wird, die in einer Differenz zum Leben steht, das ihr das Material liefert.

Als ein weiterer Vorläufer von *I'm Not There* ist darüber hinaus natürlich Haynes Spielfilm *Velvet Goldmine* von 1998 zu nennen. Der Plot ist orientiert an *Citizen Kane*: Ein Reporter, gespielt von Christian Bale, versucht, Jahre später, das mysteriöse Verschwinden eines Glam Rock Stars aufzuklären, reist dafür herum, um mit Leuten zu sprechen, die den Star gekannt haben und die sich dann in Rückblenden erinnern. Die Figur des von Jonathan Rhys Meyers gespielten Stars ist offensichtlich inspiriert von David Bowie und, etwas weniger deutlich, Marc Bolan; Ewan McGregor spielt eine an Iggy Pop und Lou Reed angelehnte Figur. Darüber hinaus aber basiert der Plot auch auf Elementen aus der Geschichte, die Bowies *Ziggy Stardust*-Album erzählt, das bekanntermaßen mit dem ambivalenten *Rock'n'Roll Suicide* der Figur endet. Die Annäherung an die Stars der Glam Rock-Ära erfolgt hier also durch strikte Fiktionalisierung. Die Figuren haben alle andere Namen, die Anspielungen auf Ereignisse im Leben historischer Personen werden mit Bezügen auf die fiktio-

nicht auf der Seite des Schauspielers, der einen Typen hervorbringt, der für immer mit ihm verbunden sein wird. Die Betonung der Einzigartigkeit liegt im Biopic vielmehr auf der Seite des
Charakters, der mit dem Schauspieler besetzt wird: Johnny Cash.
Man könnte in dieser für das Biopic so charakteristischen Änderung der Relation von Schauspieler und Rolle freilich auch
umgekehrt den Grund dafür sehen, dass die *Oscars* für die besten
schauspielerischen Leistungen auffallend häufig an die Hauptdarsteller von Biopics gehen. Gerade weil jeder das Original
kennt, demonstriert sich hier sehr deutlich, was es heißt, sich
einem Anderen anzuverwandeln. Im Fall von *Walk the Line* ging
er allerdings nicht an Phoenix, sondern an Reese Witherspoon
für ihre Darstellung von June Carter.

Die Herausforderung, die sich im Blick auf die Anti-
Legende Dylan für das Biopic ergibt, ist also immens. Todd
Haynes ist sie angegangen. *I'm Not There* war jedoch keineswegs
sein erstes Biopic-Projekt. Bekannt wurde er mit dem kurzen
43-Minuten-Film *Superstar: The Karen Carpenter Story* von 1987,
der Karen Carpenters Leben von ihrer Entdeckung 1966 bis zu
ihrem Tod an den Folgen einer Magersucht im Jahre 1983 mit Bar-
biepuppen erzählt. Alle Sets wurden dafür in Miniaturgröße
angefertigt, die Magersucht von Karen Carpenter wurde durch
das von Szene zu Szene weggeschnittte Volumen im Gesicht und
an den Armen der Karen-Puppe veranschaulicht. Der Plot folgt
dem üblichen Biopic-Interesse an dem Menschen hinter den
Rollen, hier: dem Scheitern der Person am öffentlichen Image
beziehungsweise an dem Druck, diesem entsprechen zu müssen.
Dennoch unterscheidet sich *Superstar* signifikant von anderen
Spielfilmen über weibliche Stars – denkt man zum Beispiel an den
an das Leben von Janis Joplin angelehnten *The Rose* (1969) mit
Bette Midler in der Hauptrolle oder auch an das Biopic *What's
Love Got to Do with It* (1993) mit Angela Bassett, in dem es um
Tina Turners Befreiung von Ike und zur Solokarriere geht.
Während diese beiden Filme von den Blut, Schweiß und Tränen-
Performances ihrer Hauptdarstellerinnen Bette Midler und
Angela Bassett leben, wird der Authentizismus solcher Darstel-
lungsformen bei Haynes geradezu brechtianisch negiert, um
durch die Konstruktion ein Allgemeines zu sehen zu geben: das

im Lichte einer anderen Erfahrung neu beleuchtet. Ein zuvor übersehenes Detail kann nun plötzlich als »Menetekel der kommenden Krise«[18] erscheinen. Die Fäden der Erzählung spannen sich also unter Umständen nach vorne wie nach hinten neu. Freilich kann auch die neue Erzählung kein abschließendes, deckendes Bild des eigenen Lebens liefern. Vielmehr machen solche Krisen und Wendungen im Leben deutlich, dass es am menschlichen Leben immer etwas Unerzähltes und Unerfasstes gibt. Es tritt dadurch ein Unterschied zwischen Erzählung und Leben hervor, der allerdings nicht die konstruktive Funktion der Erzählung für das Leben schmälert. Vielmehr lässt sich gerade aus dieser Differenz heraus, so Thomäs These, die konstruktive Funktion der Erzählung für das Leben genauer bestimmen. Sie sei dann nämlich aus ihrem Situationsbezug heraus zu verstehen, das heißt im Blick auf die Gegenwart des jeweiligen Lebensvollzugs. Sie erscheint dann als das Medium, in dem ein Subjekt jeweils versucht, sich selbst und anderen – erneut – intelligibel zu werden; sie erscheint dann, könnte man auch sagen, als Medium einer Rechtfertigung. Dem Bewusstsein um die situative Rolle solcher Narrative – und das heißt: dem Bewusstsein um die Differenz zwischen Erzählung und Leben – entspricht aber auf der anderen Seite auch der Respekt vor der Potentialität, der Unausschöpflichkeit der menschlichen Existenz.

*

Die Verbindung Dylan-Warhol hat auf freiheitstheoretische und narratologische Motive geführt, die – im Hinweis auf die Potentialität des Filmschauspielers – eine gewisse Korrespondenz zur Ontologie des Films unterhalten, aber sie hat denkbar weit weg geführt vom Biopic, könnte man meinen. Zumindest vom traditionellen. Nicht nur widerspricht der narrative Schematismus des gewöhnlichen Biopic jedem Potentialitätsbewusstsein, auch nähert das konventionelle Biopic den Film hinsichtlich der von Cavell angesprochenen Relation von Schauspieler und Rolle wieder dem Theater an. Dies mag sogar nicht der geringste Grund dafür sein, dass das Biopic ein filmisch so unüberzeugendes Genre ist. Joaquin Phoenix ist nicht Johnny Cash – jeder weiß das; die entfernte Ähnlichkeit unterstreicht bloß die Differenz. Die Betonung der Einzigartigkeit liegt hier

18
Ebd., S. 259.

Juliane Rebentisch
Erzählung des Lebens

dern eher wie der Prototyp einer Subjektivität, die ihre Freiheit nur in einem Prozess realisieren kann, in dem sie das Spannungsverhältnis zwischen einer Freiheit vom Sozialen, einer Freiheit von identitären Zuschreibungen, und einer Freiheit zum Sozialen, einer Freiheit zur identitären (Neu-)Bestimmung dialektisch austrägt.[15] Ein solcher Prozess lässt sich denn auch gerade nicht so beschreiben, dass es ein souveränes Metasubjekt gibt, das all seinen sozialen Rollen gegenüber ebenso indifferent wie überlegen ist. Vielmehr stehen in den Veränderungen von einer Identität zur anderen das Subjekt und seine Souveränität mit zur Disposition: Aus den zuvor gültigen identitären Selbstverständnissen befreit sich das Subjekt nicht aus der imaginären Position eines sich selbst überlegenen Souveräns, sondern durch die im Austausch mit einer ihrerseits veränderlichen Welt sich einstellende Erfahrung von Strebungen, die den zuvor affirmierten Selbstbildern zuwiderlaufen. Die Veränderungen werden hier nicht von einem Metasubjekt voluntaristisch verfügt, sondern wurzeln im Gegenteil in Erfahrungen einer Selbstdifferenz, die das Subjekt dazu anhalten, sich selbst und sein Selbstverständnis, den Sinn seiner Subjektivität aus einer Distanz zu sich neu zu ergreifen.[16]

Das Verhältnis, das ein solches Bild eines sich verändernden, wechselnde soziale Identitäten annehmenden Lebens zur Erzählung unterhält, ist freilich kompliziert oder besser: exzentrisch. In seinem irreführenderweise *Erzähle Dich selbst* betitelten Buch vertritt Dieter Thomä die These, dass dies – sich selbst zu erzählen – unmöglich ist; jedenfalls dann, wenn man damit den Anspruch verbindet, eine biographische Ganzheit zu erfassen, das Leben in einer Erzählung aufgehen zu lassen.[17] In dem Moment nämlich, in dem ich mit mir selbst in Konflikt gerate, mich sozusagen an mir selbst stoße, mit meinem bisherigen Selbstverständnis hadere, wird auch jene Erzählung in eine Krise geraten, die ich von mir selbst bislang gegeben habe. Und zwar kann dies sowohl die prospektive Dimension meines Selbstverhältnisses betreffen, meinen Selbstentwurf, als auch die retrospektive Dimension meines Selbstverhältnisses, das Verständnis meiner Vorgeschichte. Auch das Material des eigenen Lebens, auf das sich die Erzählung der eigenen Vorgeschichte bezieht, wird

15
Vgl. hierzu Axel Honneths These, dass Dylan für die Spannungsverhältnisse stehe, die den Begriff der Freiheit selbst durchziehen: Honneth (2007) (wie Anm. 7).

16
Vgl. zu dieser Dialektik ausführlich Juliane Rebentisch: Die Kunst der Freiheit. Zur Dialektik demokratischer Existenz. Berlin 2012.

17
Dieter Thomä: Erzähle dich selbst. Lebensgeschichte als philosophisches Problem. Frankfurt am Main 2007.

14
Stanley Cavell: Die andere Stimme.
Philosophie und Autobiographie.
Berlin 2002, S. 201.

zulassen könnte (und es auch tun wird) (das heißt, dort wird die Schicksalhaftigkeit der menschlichen Existenz betont, das Endgültige und das Typische des Selbst bei jedem Schritt auf seiner Reise).«[14]

Das freiheitstheoretische Motiv, das Cavell hier anspricht, das der Potentialität der menschlichen Existenz und der Reise des Selbst, auf der dieses verschiedene Rollen übernehmen mag, nun ist *nicht* identisch mit einem anderen freiheitstheoretischen Ansatz, der im Blick auf den Schauspieler ebenso naheliegen könnte wie im Blick auf Dylan: dass es nämlich hinter den jeweiligen sozialen Rollen etwas wie ein wirkliches Selbst gibt, das diese souverän an- und ablegt. Aus dieser Perspektive könnte der Theaterschauspieler sogar freier erscheinen als der Filmschauspieler. Während der Theaterschauspieler nämlich immer eine gewisse Distanz zur Rolle mit exponiert, die er auf seine Weise zeigt, scheint der Filmschauspieler mit seinen Rollen weitgehend zu verschmelzen. Tatsächlich existiert die Rolle im Film in der Regel nicht unabhängig vom Schauspieler; es gibt keine Charaktere im theatralen Sinne, sondern nur Typen, die allererst von den Stars definiert werden, die sie einmalig besetzen (man denke an De Niros *Taxi Driver* beispielsweise). Filmstars sind daher auch, im Gegensatz zu Theaterschauspielern, wesentlich unaustauschbar. Cavell zielt aber auf einen anderen Punkt: dass nämlich der Filmstar sein Potential bewusst hält, im nächsten Film ein ganz anderer zu sein (man denke weiterhin an De Niro, an die erstaunliche Wandlungsfähigkeit, die sich in seiner Filmographie dokumentiert). Das Modell von Freiheit, um das es hier geht, ist nicht das einer inneren Distanz des Selbst gegenüber vorgegebenen Rollen (nach dem Modell des Theaterschauspielers), sondern das der Veränderbarkeit des Selbst. Die Spaltung, um die es geht, ist dann nicht die zwischen eigentlicher und uneigentlicher Identität, sondern, noch einmal, die zwischen Identität und Potentialität, zwischen der Bestimmtheit der jetzt gerade verkörperten Identität und der Möglichkeit noch unbestimmter zukünftiger Identifikationen.

Blickt man auf Bob Dylans Identitätswechsel aus dieser Perspektive, so erscheint er nicht mehr als das Ausnahmesubjekt, das mit allen anderen sein ausgebufftes Spiel treibt, son-

zubringen antritt. Denn sie ereignen sich im Modus einer Äußerlichkeit, die unzugänglicher und rätselhafter ist als die psychologische Innerlichkeit, die wir im so genannten Charakterschauspiel entziffern sollen. Das ist natürlich an nahezu allen *Screen Tests* zu studieren, nicht zuletzt aber auch an den *Screen Tests* # 82 und # 83 von 1966, deren *Subject* im doppelten Sinne Bob Dylan ist.

Der Effekt der *Screen Tests* jedenfalls ist offenkundig nicht Authentizität, sondern eine spezifische Opazität, die sich gerade durch das ergibt, was in keiner Darstellungsleistung aufgeht. Das indexikal erzeugte »Optisch-Unbewusste«[13] des Films, das uns auf Dinge aufmerksam macht, die sich unserer an Praxis und Sinn ausgerichteten Weltwahrnehmung normalerweise entziehen, zeigt nicht etwa auf eine wahre Identität der Person hinter allen Rollen oder Posen, sondern auf eine Potentialität, die sich jeder Bestimmung in terms einer bestimmten Identität (sei es der selbst gewählten oder einer von der Regie fremdbestimmten) entzieht. Die Differenz, um die es hier geht, ist, mit anderen Worten, nicht die von authentischer Person und Rolle, sondern die von Bestimmtheit und Unbestimmtheit.

*

Eben darin ist Warhol relevant für den Zusammenhang, in dem die Diskussion um die Figur des Schauspielers immer schon zum Problem der Freiheit steht. Und sein »Genie für Abstraktion« hat ihn ein Spezifikum des Films in dieser Hinsicht erkennen und zur Kenntlichkeit hervortreiben lassen. Warhols Abstraktionsleistung, könnte man auch sagen, verdankt sich einer tiefen Einsicht in die spezifische Ontologie des Films. So schreibt Stanley Cavell in seinem Autobiographiebuch *Die andere Stimme*, ein Argument aus seinem Filmbuch *The World Viewed* wieder aufnehmend, dass es für die Ontologie des Films von Bedeutung sei, »daß das Medium des bewegten Bildes die im Theater stattfindende größere Gewichtung der Rolle gegenüber dem Schauspieler umkehrt; auf der Leinwand ist der Schauspieler das Motiv (subject) für die Kamera, und es wird betont, daß dieser Schauspieler andere Rollen spielen könnte (oder gekonnt hätte) (das heißt, es wird die Potentialität der menschlichen Existenz und die Reise des Selbst betont). Dies steht im Gegensatz zu der Betonung im Theater, daß diese Rolle andere Schauspieler

13
Ebd.

Chronisten der New Yorker Theater- und Performanceszene der 1960er und 1970er Jahre, in seinem legendären Buch *Queer Theatre* – Warhols »Genie für Abstraktion« also ließ ihn überdies erkennen, dass es nicht so sehr der je konkrete Star, sondern die Qualität des Startums selbst ist, die den Konsumenten nach der Ware Film süchtig macht. Warhol vermochte es, so Brecht weiter, »diese Qualität zu isolieren und erfolgreich unter dem Namen ›Superstar‹ zu vermarkten.«[11] Was Warhols Filme angeht, so entsprach dieser Abstraktionsleistung allerdings nun gerade nicht, wie man vielleicht annehmen könnte, der Wunsch, aus dem visuellen Potential seiner Laiendarsteller/innen ein ideales Image zu destillieren. Im Gegenteil ist es der Witz der meisten seiner *Screen Tests*, dass die neutrale Anordnung – die Konfrontation einer Person mit einer laufenden Kamera ohne Drehbuch, ohne Regieanweisung – früher oder später auch das einfangen wird, was aus dem kontrollierten Image herausfällt, was nicht in ihm aufgeht. In einer Perversion dessen, was Walter Benjamin in seinem berühmten Kunstwerk-Aufsatz die für die Produktion von Filmen charakteristische, weil auf den idealen Take ausgerichtete »Testleistung«[12] des Filmschauspielers nennt, erklärte Warhol die Situation der Screen Tests selbst zum entscheidenden Ereignis. Nur sehr vordergründig geht es in Warhols fingierten *Screen Tests* denn auch darum, das Bildwerdungspotential von Darstellern oder deren Leistungsbereitschaft festzustellen. Tatsächlich zielen sie nicht darauf, bestimmte darstellerische Leistungen oder Talente zu identifizieren, sondern darauf, Momente einzufangen, in denen wir im Gesicht des Stars keine Rolle, keine Pose, keine Legende mehr lesen, weil sich das Gesicht selbst zu lesen gibt. Solche Momente passieren dem Film gewöhnlich, sie unterlaufen ihm. Die fotografische Technik der Kamera registriert Bewegungen, die keiner Darstellungsfunktion mehr unterstehen oder doch zumindest nicht in ihr aufgehen; sie produziert auf beiläufige und zufällige Weise Momente unbedarfter Kontingenz, in denen das Allgemeine einer Rolle, aber auch das Allgemeine dessen, was sich als Image des Stars ansprechen lässt, vor dem Ausdruck der Singularität dieses Gesichts in diesem kurzen Augenblick zurückweicht. Solche Momente sind gerade nicht mit dem Ausdruck des Authentischen zu verwechseln, den das ›gute Schauspiel‹ hervor-

11
Stefan Brecht: Queer Theatre. The original theatre of the City of New York: From the mid 60s to the mid 70s, Bd. 2. Frankfurt am Main 1978, S. 113f.

12
Vgl. Walter Benjamin: Das Kunstwerk im Zeitalter seiner technischen Reproduzierbarkeit (1). In: Ders.: Gesammelte Schriften, Bd. I.2. Frankfurt am Main 1974, S. 435–469, S. 448f.

Dylan als Regisseur selbst einen Film, *Renaldo & Clara*, der 1977 in einer viereinhalbstündigen Fassung in die Kinos kam, wo er im großen Stil floppte, und zwar sowohl beim Publikum als auch bei der Kritik. In diesem tatsächlich ziemlich desaströs unorganisierten Film tauchen Bob und Sara Dylan scheinbar als sie selbst auf, spielen aber die beiden Figuren Renaldo und Clara. Ronnie Hawkins, der frühere Sänger von Dylans Begleitband, *The Band*, spielt Bob Dylan. Allen Ginsberg spielt einen Charakter namens Vater, Joan Baez ist eine so genannte Frau in Weiß, andere bekannte Größen der damaligen Kulturszene spielen sich selbst oder Kollegen. Dokumentarische und inszenierte Sequenzen wechseln einander ab. Der historische Index der 1970er Jahre haftet dem Film vor allem hinsichtlich des zeitgenössischen Geschmacks für *Die Kinder des Olymp* und die entsprechenden Gauklerwelten an, auch die Begeisterung für das Spiel mit den Geschlechterrollen und der rocktheatralen Maske steht in diesem Zusammenhang. Interessanter als diese Begeisterung für die Maske und das Rollen-Verwirrspiel, durch dessen Regie sich der Star souverän zu entziehen versucht, ist jedoch, dass der Film *als Film* diesen Entzug noch auf eine ganz andere, spezifisch filmische Weise herstellt.

So schrieb die Kritikerin Pauline Kael im *New Yorker*: »More tight close-ups than any actor can have had in the whole history of movies. He's overpoweringly present, yet he's never in direct contact with us... We are invited to stare... to perceive the mystery of his elusiveness – his distance.«[9] In seiner Vorliebe für Close Ups ist Dylan offenkundig von Andy Warhol beeinflusst. In einem Interview mit Jonathan Cott über Fragen seiner Filmästhetik sagte Dylan jedenfalls, dass es darauf ankomme, Vertrauen in den Film zu haben. Und dann: »You know who understood this? Andy Warhol. Andy Warhol did a lot for American cinema.«[10] Es ist freilich kein Zufall, dass Warhols Filme in einem direkten Zusammenhang mit einer Reflexion auf das Phänomen des Stars stehen. So hatte Warhol um 1965 herum nicht nur entdeckt, dass die Stars in Hollywoods Filmindustrie regelrecht *gemacht*, produziert werden. Warhols »Genie für Abstraktion«, so formulierte es Bert Brechts Sohn Stefan Brecht, seines Zeichens Theaterkritiker und einer der wichtigsten

9
Zit. nach Diedrich Diederichsen: Eigenblutdoping. Selbstverwertung, Künstlerromantik, Partizipation. Köln 2008, S. 103.

10
Jonathan Cott: Bob Dylan Interview #1 (1977). In: Ders.: Back to a Shadow in the Night. Music, Writings, and Interviews 1961–2001. Milwaukee 2002, S. 47–73, hier S. 69.

Skyline-Dylan, den Gospel Dylan, den kaputten Dylan der achtziger Jahre, den Dylan der *Never Ending Tour* usw. kennengelernt haben, wissen wir inzwischen: Den einen, eindimensionalen echten Dylan gibt es nicht. Es gibt lediglich den denkenden und spielenden Künstler, der sein Kunstwerk Dylan stets neu definiert und interpretiert, der davon lebt, die von ihm geschaffenen Images immer wieder zu destruieren.«[6]

»Es ist [das] existentialistische Motiv der Selbstwahl, das Sartre nachempfundene Pathos eines permanenten Sich-Neuentwerfens«, ergänzte Axel Honneth, »welches Dylan in der musikalischen Artikulation von Freiheit und Distanznahme vergegenwärtigt; inmitten von Protestbewegung und Hippiekultur, zwei sozialen Strömungen, die einen starken Erwartungsdruck entweder in Richtung des politischen Wohlverhaltens oder der Authentizität ausübten, verteidigte er mit der ständigen Erprobung neuer Arrangements, mit der exzentrischen Phrasierung seiner Lieder, mit der Blasiertheit seiner Stimme, das Recht des Einzelnen, sich stets radikal neu zu entwerfen.«[7]

Ich möchte die freiheitstheoretischen Motive, die Dylan hier zugeschrieben werden, zunächst unkommentiert lassen und lediglich zusammenfassen: Bob Dylan ist eine Herausforderung für das Genre des traditionellen Biopic. Sein Charakter entzieht sich immer wieder in andere Identitäten, zwischen denen Sprünge bestehen, die sich nicht nur der Kontinuität des üblichen Aufstieg-Fall-Aufstieg-Plots entziehen, sondern überhaupt jede biographische Erzählung in Verlegenheit bringen, die all diese Identitäten in den entwicklungslogischen Zusammenhang *eines* Lebens bringen will. Wer die Herausforderung dennoch annehmen will, hätte vermutlich als Erstes zu berücksichtigen, dass Dylan selbst einige Begegnungen mit dem Film hatte, in denen sich die Problematik seiner Unfasslichkeit ebenfalls auf spezifische Weise reflektiert.

Die erste Rolle, die Dylan in einem Spielfilm übernahm, nämlich in Sam Peckinpahs *Pat Garret jagt Billy the Kid* (1973), lautete bezeichnenderweise Alias. Das ist der perfekte Name für das performative Prinzip, für das Bob Dylan bei einem Großteil seiner Kritiker steht. Er ist immer er selbst, immer Bob Dylan, aber immer, so scheint es, als jemand anderer.[8] 1975/76 drehte

6
Rüdiger Dannemann: Maskenspiele der Freiheit. Songwriting zwischen Folk, Rockavantgarde, Literatur und Philosophie. In: Axel Honneth; Peter Kemper; Richard Klein (Hg.): Bob Dylan. Ein Kongreß. Frankfurt am Main 2007, S. 50–69, hier S. 62f.

7
Axel Honneth: Verwicklungen von Freiheit. Bob Dylan und seine Zeit. In: Honneth; Kemper; Klein (2007), S. 15–28, hier S. 20f. (wie Anm. 6).

8
Stephen Scobie; Alias Bob Dylan: Revisited. Calgary 2004.

Juliane Rebentisch
Erzählung des Lebens

pero weiter, pressten das widerspenstige Leben ihrer Charaktere in ein rigides Aufstieg-Fall-Aufstieg-Schema. Sie seien immer mehr an den Höllen aus Alkohol und Drogen interessiert als an den künstlerischen Leistungen. Angesichts der Schematismen aus Populärpsychologie und alterndem Make up, die zumeist von einer Sequenz unterbrochen würden, in denen die Hauptperson in einem Moment der Inspiration ihren bekanntesten Hit komponiert, müsse man schon die Zähne zusammenbeißen.[4]

Ein Beispiel für ein konventionelles Biopic über einen Musiker, der übrigens auch mit Bob Dylan kooperiert hat[5], ist *Walk the Line* (2005). Der Film erzählt eine Episode aus dem Leben von Johnny Cash. Abgesehen von der bemerkenswerten musikalischen Leistung von Joaquin Phoenix und Reese Wither-spoon, die als Johnny Cash und June Carter auch alle Gesangs-einlagen selbst übernommen haben, handelt es sich hier doch um ein Biopic des beschriebenen Typs. Im Zentrum des Plots steht die Tablettensucht Cashs, die mehr oder weniger küchen-psychologisch auf einen Konflikt in der Kindheit zurückgeführt wird, um am Ende durch die Liebe zu June Carter geheilt zu werden. Dazwischen sind Szenen eingestreut, die zeigen, wie Cash musikalisch seinen Stil findet oder June Carter am Küchen-tisch *Ring of Fire* komponiert.

*

Nun, anders als Johnny Cash eignet sich Bob Dylan von vornherein offensichtlich nicht als Gegenstand für ein derartiges Unterfangen. Wenn Dylan eine Legende ist, dann die einer sich in sehr unterschiedlichen, teilweise miteinander inkompatiblen Identitäten vervielfältigenden und dadurch entziehenden Anti-Legende. Anlässlich eines Bob-Dylan-Kongresses, der vor ein paar Jahren in Frankfurt stattfand – einer Art Gipfeltreffen der deutschen Dylanologie –, fragte zum Beispiel Rüdiger Danne-mann rhetorisch: »[W]er ist nun der echte Dylan? Der Hobo oder der Dandy, dem die Attitude des L'art pour l'art auf den Leib geschneidert scheint? Der Nachfahre Rimbauds, Baudelaires und Wildes oder der Verehrer Woody Guthries? Der Protagonist des Videos zu *Subterranean Homesick Blues*, diesem ersten bedeuten-den Beispiel dieses Genres, in dem die Grundregeln der Semiolo-gie demonstriert werden? Nachdem wir bereits den Nashville

---

4
Vgl. Prospero, How to make a good biopic (2011). URL: http://www.economist.com/blogs/prospero/2011/11/new-film-my-week-marilyn (Stand: 12.08.2013, Übers. J.R).

5
So nahmen Dylan und Cash am 17. und 18. Februar 1969 eine Session auf, aus der unter anderem eine großartige, im Duett gesungene Fassung von *Girl from the North Country* hervorgegangen ist.

Bevor wir uns Todd Haynes' Hommage an Bob Dylan zuwenden können, die zugleich eine Auseinandersetzung mit dem Genre des Biopic ist, seinem Spielfilm *I'm not There* (2007), muss man fragen: Was ist überhaupt ein Biopic? *Wikipedia* gibt folgende Definition: »Eine Filmbiografie, auch *Biopic* (von engl. *biographical* und engl. *motion picture*), bezeichnet einen Film, der in fiktionalisierter Form das Leben einer geschichtlich belegbaren Figur erzählt. Das Biopic ist eines der ältesten Filmgenres. [...] In einem Biopic muss nicht die Lebensgeschichte einer realen Person von der Geburt bis zum Tod erzählt werden, es genügt vielmehr, dass ein oder mehrere Lebensabschnitte zu einem filmischen Ganzen dramaturgisch verknüpft werden. Ein zentrales Kriterium des Biopics ist die Nennung des Namens der realen Person. Meistens wird im Biopic vorausgesetzt, dass die dargestellte Person gesellschaftliche Relevanz besitzt.«[1]

Die Geschichten, die in Biopics erzählt werden, sind so unterschiedlich wie das Leben selbst. Dennoch, so weiß *Wikipedia*, »hat sich gezeigt, dass vor allem Figuren der Devianz spannend für Drehbuchautoren und Produzenten sind. Das sind Figuren, deren Leben aus den konventionellen Bahnen gerät und sich meist nicht mehr im moralischen Normbereich befindet.«[2] Nicht zufällig handelten Biopics denn auch besonders häufig von Künstlern. Der »Legendencharakter« der Figur werde durch die Verfilmung »aktualisiert und verstärkt«.[3] Das heißt auch, dass das Biopic weniger an der detailgetreuen Darstellung des Lebenslaufs interessiert ist denn an dem, was sich an diesem Leben den Stereotypen über die Nähe von Genie und Wahnsinn fügt.

Das Problem mit konventionellen Biopics sei, schreibt ein Blogger namens Prospero dazu treffend, dass sie weder der »Bio«- noch der »Pic«-Abteilung gerecht würden. Sie hätten nicht genug narrativen Schwung, um als dramatischer Spielfilm zu funktionieren, zugleich frisierten und verfälschten sie aber ihre Stoffe zu sehr, um noch als seriöse Biographien durchgehen zu können. Wenn man bereits über die Person informiert ist, die porträtiert wird, sei man gemeinhin enttäuscht, wie viel verzerrt und weggelassen wurde. Wenn man hingegen nicht als Experte ins Kino geht, könne man nie sicher sein, wie viel von dem, was man sieht, tatsächlich den Fakten entspricht. Biopics, so Pros-

1
Vgl. den *Wikipedia*-Eintrag zur Filmbiographie. URL: http://de.wikipedia.org/wiki/Filmbiografie (Stand: 12.08.2013).

2
Ebd.

3
Ebd.

Erzählung des Lebens.
Die Filmbiographie und ihre Dekonstruktion in Todd Haynes' *I'm Not There*

Juliane
Rebentisch

Formen der Verschwendung von Zeit und der Aufhebung der Zeitökonomie. Und in der Verschwendung, daran sein mit Bataille noch einmal erinnert, liegt der eigentliche Sinn der Ökonomie.

32 Minuten dauert im Übrigen *Nuit et Brouillard* von Alain Resnais aus dem Jahr 1956, neun Stunden dauert Claude Lanzmanns *Shoah* von 1986. *Nuit et Brouillard* besteht aus Filmaufnahmen aus Ausschwitz und fotografischem Archivmaterial, begleitet von einem Kommentar von André Cayrol und Musik von Hanns Eisler, und erklärt die Funktionsweise der Konzentrationslager. Der Film, gegen dessen Uraufführung auf dem Festival von Cannes die damalige Bundesregierung einen diplomatischen Protest einlegte (man fühlte sich noch nicht in dem heute gängigen Maße verantwortlich für die Verbrechen der voraufgegangenen deutschen Regierung), hatte unter anderem die richtige Länge, um im Fernsehen immer dann im Hauptabendprogramm nach den Nachrichten ausgestrahlt zu werden, wenn sich in der französischen Öffentlichkeit wieder einmal ein Holocaust-Leugner zu Wort gemeldet hatte. *Shoah* wiederum, der nur aus Interviews mit Überlebenden an den Schauplätzen des Verbrechens und den Orten ihres Lebens nach dem KZ besteht, hat die Ausmaße eines Monuments in der Zeit. Über die Darstellung und die Darstellbarkeit des Holocaust ist viel gestritten worden, so aus Anlass der US-Serie *Holocaust* und vor allem aus Anlass von Spielbergs *Schindler's List* von 1994, den von Lanzmann bis Godard die versammelte europäische Kinointelligenz als unentschuldbare Transgression verdammte. Lanzmanns eigener Film und Resnais' Film sind, von der Anfangskontroverse um Resnais' Film einmal abgesehen, von diesen Streitigkeiten ausgenommen geblieben. Sie gelten vielmehr als die beiden Referenzpunkte in dieser Debatte. Möglicherweise ist das richtige Verhältnis von Film und Geschichte auch eine Frage der richtigen Länge des Films.

Vinzenz Hediger
ist seit 2011 Professor für Filmwissenschaft an der Goethe-Universität Frankfurt am Main. 1999 wurde er an der Universität Zürich mit einer Arbeit zum amerikanischen Kinotrailer promoviert und war bis 2004 Postdoktorand am dortigen Seminar für Filmwissenschaft. 2004 erfolgte die Berufung auf den neu geschaffenen Krupp-Stiftungslehrstuhl für Theorie und Geschichte bilddokumentarischer Formen an der Ruhr-Universität Bochum. Er ist Mitbegründer des europäischen Forschungsnetzwerks NECS (www.necs.org) und Gründungsherausgeber der *Zeitschrift für Medienwissenschaft* (www.zfmedienwissenschaft.de).

Dauer, hat also eine Laufzeit von über 7300 Minuten bzw.
121 Stunden, aber Reitz war immerhin früher am Start. Gleichsam
im gesicherten Mittelfeld bewegt sich da mit einer Gesamtlänge
von 2535 Minuten im Übrigen eine andere deutsche Produktion,
die Langzeitdokumentation *Wir Kinder von Golzow* von Wilfried
und Bärbel Junge, welche in zwanzig einzelnen Filmen die
Geschicke eines Dorfes im Oderbruch von der Zeit des Mauer-
baus bis 2006 verfolgt.

Zum Phänomen der »Qualitäts«-Serien gehört indes nicht
nur deren Länge. Der exzessiven Länge entspricht mittlerweile
auch ein exzessives Sehverhalten, auf amerikanisch »binge
viewing« genannt, in Anlehnung an den Ausdruck »binge drinking«, zu Deutsch »Komasaufen«. »Komakucken«, wenn man den
Begriff so eindeutschen mag, meint das Ansehen einer großen
Anzahl von Episoden einer Serie hintereinander, mitunter einen
ganzen Tag und eine ganze Nacht durch, als ein Filmsehen in
einem Zeithorizont, der selbst den Tageszyklus von *24 Hour Psycho*
und *The Wire* noch sprengt. Die Langform ermöglicht, wenn sie
erst einmal vom ökonomischen Raster der Programmstruktur des
Fernsehens abgekoppelt ist und die Teile der Serie auf DVD, über
Streaming- und File Sharing-Plattformen verfügbar werden,
Episoden und Exzesse der Verschwendung von Zeit in bislang
ungekannten Ausmaßen. Dem Trend zum »Komakucken« trägt die
Industrie auch schon Rechnung. Der Videovertrieb *Netflix*, der
DVD per Post verleiht und eine große Streaming-Plattform betreibt,
ist mit *House of Cards*, einer Serie über das politische Geschehen in
Washington unter der Regie von Hollywood-Regisseuren wie David
Fincher und Joel Schumacher, mittlerweile auch ins Produktions-
geschäft eingestiegen, um nicht von den Inhalten der Hollywood-
Studios und Kabelfernsehgesellschaften abhängig zu sein. Am
1. Februar 2013 veröffentlichte *Netflix* gleichzeitig alle dreizehn
Episoden der ersten Saison von *House of Cards* auf seiner Website,
ausdrücklich auch in der Absicht, den Bedürfnissen der »Koma-
kucker« zu entsprechen.

Die digitale Verfügbarkeit filmischer Formate, des Fragments und der kurzen Clips ebenso wie der langen Serie, unterläuft die Balance von Lebenszeit und Filmzeit, die sich mit
der Standardlänge des Kinofilms etabliert hatte, und schafft neue

bestehen denn auch aus solchen Szenen: Sie zeigen den Film im Futurum Exactum, also aus der Sicht der vorweggenommenen Erinnerung an den kommenden Film. Man könnte in der Kürze der *YouTube-* und *Vimeo-*Videos eine Steigerung des Prinzips der Zeitökonomie sehen. Das Gegenteil ist der Fall: Sich gegenseitig Links zu Clips zuzuspielen, über E-Mail oder Posts auf Social Network-Seiten wie *Facebook*, ist für Menschen mit Internet zu einem priviliegierten Modus der Zeitverschwendung geworden.

Die Langform wiederum hat sich ebenfalls als Standard neben der Norm verfestigt, und zwar über die gelegentlichen – und kommerziell nicht relevanten – Längenexzesse von Autorenfilmern wie Béla Tarr und Dokumentaristen wie Wang Bing hinaus. »Mit den neuen Serien können wir endlich das machen, was wir in den 1970er Jahren im Kino machen wollten«, begründete jüngst Martin Scorsese seine Beteiligung an der HBO-Serie *The Boardwalk Empire*, einer Art *Sopranos* der Prohibitionszeit, die gerade in die vierte Saison geht und den Gangsterkönig der Spielerstadt Atlantic City in New Jersey zur Hauptfigur hat. Die aktuellen so genannten »Qualitäts«-Serien – wie *Mad Men, Breaking Bad* und *The Wire*, denen *The Sopranos* in den späten 1990er Jahren das Terrain bereitet hat und die vorzugsweise für Kabelsender produziert werden, die ihrer zahlenden Kundschaft mehr Sex und Gewalt zeigen dürfen als das Gratisfernsehen (und mindestens so viel wie ein Kinofilm) – seien das neue, bessere Kino und natürlich auch besser als Romane, so die Kritiker in durchaus schon verdächtiger Einhelligkeit. Ob dem so sei, lassen wir fürs Erste dahingestellt. Kaum erwähnt wird in diesen Diskussionen, dass das Format der Langform des Films auf Kinoniveau, der zunächst fürs Fernsehen produziert wurde, seinen Ursprung in Deutschland hat: bei Fassbinders *Berlin Alexanderplatz* von 1980 (13 Folgen plus Epilog, 894 Minuten) und natürlich bei *Heimat*, der Chronik eines Dorfes im Hunsrück, die Edgard Reitz als Antwort auf die amerikanische TV-Serie *Holocaust* zu Beginn der 1980er Jahre in Angriff nahm und mittlerweile bei drei langen Staffeln und einer Laufzeit von 3131 Minuten oder etwas mehr als 52 Stunden angelangt ist. *The Sopranos*, die Mutterfolie aller amerikanischen »Qualitäts«-Serien, besteht zwar aus sechs Spielzeiten und 86 Episoden von jeweils 55 Minuten

Überwältigen und die Erfahrung des Erhabenen herbeiführen können auch Filme, die mehr oder weniger der Standardlänge entsprechen. Stanley Kubrick etwa, nach meiner bisherigen Erfahrung der Lieblingsregisseur aller Deutschen, die sonst
vom Kino nichts verstehen, verstand sich auf solche Momente –
man denke an die Raumschiffsequenz zu Strauß-Klängen am
Anfang von *2001 – A Space Odyssey* –, oder auch David Lean, der
sich in *Lawrence of Arabia* mit der Inkommensurabilität von
Mensch und Wüste auseinandersetzte.

Die Erfahrung des Erhabenen, die sich bei Werken wie
24 Hour Psycho und *The Clock* an die Zeitangabe knüpft, bildet
aber nur eine Vor- oder Zwischenstufe. Jenseits davon lauert
noch etwas anderes.

Auf meine Frage, ob er sich *24 Hour Psycho* je ganz angeschaut habe, antwortete ein Pariser Kollege vor einigen Jahren
mit dem empörten Ausruf »Ich bin doch nicht verrückt!«. In
seiner Novelle *Point Omega* von 2010 geht Don DeLillo genau der
Frage nach, was passiert, wenn sich jemand Douglas Gordons
Arbeit in dieser Weise aussetzt. DeLillos Antwort lautet: Er
verwandelt sich in Norman Bates. Jenseits der Normlänge des
Films lauert der Wahnsinn.

Weshalb also dauert ein Film in der Regel anderthalb bis
zwei Stunden und nicht zwanzig Minuten oder neun Stunden?

Weil die Standardlänge die richtige Balance zwischen
Zeit des Erzählens und Lebenszeit, zwischen Zeitökonomie und
Zeitverschwendung trifft, könnte eine Antwort lauten.

Allerdings ist es keineswegs nur die Bildende Kunst, der
ja eine privilegierte Rolle bei der Stiftung kulturellen Sinns
immer zuzutrauen ist (und zumeist zugeschrieben wird), welche
derzeit daran arbeitet, den etablierten Rahmen der Standardlänge
des Films zu sprengen.

Die Kurzform, der Splitter und das Fragment sind mit der
digitalen Netzwerkkommunikation und der Etablierung von
Videoplattformen wie *YouTube* und *Vimeo* zu einem Standard
neben der Norm geworden. Man kann das Einstellen von Filmclips auf *YouTube* als eine Form des veräußerlichten Filmerinnerns
beschreiben. Von Filmen bleiben in der Regel nicht die ganzen
Plots in Erinnerung, sondern besonders dichte Szenen. Trailer

24 Hour Psycho oder *The Clock* dauert, nicht die Zeit, die ein kunstsinniges Publikum mit und vor diesen Werken verbringen soll. Die durchschnittliche Verweildauer des Museumspublikums vor einer Bewegtbildinstallation beträgt, wie entsprechende Studien zeigen, wenige Minuten; auch *24 Hour Psycho* und *The Clock* ziehen in der Regel kaum länger die Aufmerksamkeit eines Publikums auf sich. Kaum jemand hat je verifiziert, ob die beiden Arbeiten wirklich 24 Stunden dauern. Man glaubt den Künstlern und Kuratoren, die eine solche Angabe machen, so wie man den Angaben zur künstlerischen Technik und zum Format glaubt, die auf einem Schildchen neben einem Gemälde im Museum gemacht werden, ohne dass man die Technik selbst überprüft oder die Maße des Gemäldes selbst nachmisst. Auch wenn begeisterte Rezensenten von Marclays *The Clock* – wie etwa die britische Schriftstellerin Zadie Smith in einer Besprechung in der *New York Review of Books* – ihren Lesern raten, mit Schlafsack und Proviant im Ausstellungsraum Quartier aufzuschlagen, geht es weder bei *24 Hour Psycho* noch bei *The Clock* darum, das Werk in seinem ganzen Umfang und seiner ganzen Länge zu absorbieren, sondern darum, sein Prinzip zu erkennen und zu verstehen.

Die Zeitangabe – 24 Stunden, ein ganzer Tag! – ist allerdings ein wesentlicher Teil des Werks. Sie zeigt an, dass die Arbeiten wohl eine begrenzte Dauer haben, diese Dauer sich aber zugleich ins Unendliche erstreckt. »If time is passed, please wait for tomorrow or another day«: Der Tag der Aufführung entspricht jedem möglichen folgenden Tag, der Tag wiederholt sich und mit ihm – potentiell – das Werk in der Aufführung, oder in der Aufführung des Werks der Tag. Ans Unendliche rühren diese Arbeiten auch noch in einem anderen Sinn. Eine extrem langsame Projektion von *Psycho* hat ihren Reiz, eine extrem langsame Projektion von *Psycho*, die einen ganzen Tag dauert, hat etwas Überwältigendes: Die Zeitangabe lässt diese zeitbasierten Werke als Gegenstände erscheinen, die den Horizont der subjektiven Zeiterfahrung übersteigen, ja zu sprengen drohen. Die Arbeiten von Gordon und Marclay bilden eine zweite Natur, die »über alle Vergleichungen groß ist«, wie Kant sagt: Die Zeitangabe verleiht ihnen die Dimension des Erhabenen.

meiner beruflichen Tätigkeit, lässt sie andererseits aber auch leer schlucken. Die Gedanken, sich diesen Film – oder Béla Tarrs *Sátántángó* (1994, ebenfalls neun Stunden) oder Andy Warhols *Empire* (1964, acht Stunden) – in voller Länge anzuschauen, scheint etwas Schwindelerregendes zu haben. Interessant zu wissen, aber antun möchte man sich selbst das nicht.

Die bildende Kunst hat den Schwindel der Überlänge mittlerweile zum Element der ästhetischen Erfahrung erhoben. Zwei der am meisten diskutierten Werke der bildenden Kunst der letzten Jahrzehnte sind Douglas Gordons Installation *24 Hour Psycho* von 1993 und Christian Marclays Filmarbeit *The Clock*, die auf der Biennale von Venedig 2011 den großen Preis gewann und seither auf Tournee durch die großen Museen der Welt ist. Gordons *24 Hour Psycho* ist eine auf die Länge eines ganzen Tages ausgedehnte, verlangsamte Projektion von Hitchcocks Film *Psycho*. *The Clock* wiederum ist ein Zusammenschnitt von Ausschnitten aus Kinofilmen, in denen eine Uhr vorkommt. Die Ausschnitte sind so ausgewählt, dass sich eine zeitliche Abfolge ergibt. Aufgeführt wird die Arbeit üblicherweise in Synchronisation mit der Ortszeit. Der jeweiligen Ortszeit entspricht die Zeit, die gerade von den Uhren in den Filmausschnitten angezeigt wird. Diesem Prinzip versuchen auch noch die Autoren eines *YouTube*-Clips Nachachtung zu verschaffen, der offensichtlich mit einer Handy-Kamera gedreht wurde. »In order to respect the concept of Christian Marclay's work«, so schreiben die Urheber dieses Videos, das streng genommen eine Verletzung von Marclays Urheberrecht darstellt, »spectators are kindly requested to play this video at 0.04 pm, local time.« In ihrem gesamten Ablauf dauert die Arbeit ebenfalls 24 Stunden, also einen ganzen Tag. »If time is passed«, so der Kommentar zu dem *YouTube*-Ausschnitt weiter, »please wait for tomorrow or another day.«

Gleichwohl erwartet niemand, und wohl noch nicht einmal die Künstler selbst, dass man sich vor *24 Hour Psycho* und *The Clock* einen ganzen Tag lang aufhält. Während man eine Symphonie im Konzerthaus bis zum Verklingen des letzte Akkords anhört – es sei denn, sie sei so schlecht gespielt, dass man den Saal aus Protest verlässt, oder so unerhört neu, dass man sie nicht erträgt –, sind die 24 Stunden, die eine Darbietung von

Rechtfertigung seines erratischen Erzählstils behauptete: Sie haben einen Anfang, eine Mitte und ein Ende, aber nicht notwendigerweise in dieser Reihenfolge. Beim Hollywood-Film geht es allerdings darum, dass man am Ende – das heißt mitunter, wenn man wieder in der Mitte angelangt ist – den ganzen Film gesehen hat. Genau gegen diesen Zwang des Formganzen setzte sich im Übrigen Andy Warhol mit *Empire* zur Wehr: Seinen Acht-Stunden-Film rechtfertigte er damit, dass man in herkömmlichen Filmen nicht zwischendurch das Kino verlassen und einkaufen gehen kann, ohne etwas zu verpassen, und dass er es für geboten hielt, einen Film zu drehen, der dies zuließe. Sein Film war eine achtstündige Rebellion gegen die Disziplin des Ruhigsitzens und des Sitzenbleibens im Film. Godards Erzählstil wiederum kann man als Ausdruck eines Bemühens lesen, den Rätsel- und Puzzlecharakter des Filmsehens in der klassischen Ära des Hollywood-Kinos in die nachklassische hinüber zu retten. Auch in diesem Sinne ist Godard ein Historiker des Kinos, ist sein Kino erlebte Kinogeschichte. Filme neueren Datums – wie etwa *Inception* oder *The Sixth Sense* wiederum, die ihre Geschichte in Splittern und Fragmenten erzählen und uns mitunter zwingen, die ganze erzählte Welt, die sich sonst im Zug des Films recht linear und in zuverlässiger Weise aufbaut, am Ende ganz neu zusammenzusetzen – lassen sich so gesehen auch als zeitgenössische Versuche lesen, jene narrative Konfusion wiederherzustellen, die einst elementarer Bestandteil der Kinoerfahrung war.

Aufhebung der Zeitökonomie meint aber nicht nur die Wiederherstellung der Komplikationen des Filmverstehens. Aufhebung der Zeitökonomie meint auch, den äußeren Rahmen des Standardformats des Films zu sprengen.

Wenn man von Berufs wegen etwas mit Film zu tun hat, wird einem unvermeidlicherweise die Frage gestellt, von welchem Film man denn in jüngster Zeit besonders beeindruckt gewesen sei. Darauf antworte ich seit einiger Zeit mit dem Hinweis auf Wang Bings Dokumentarfilm *West of the Tracks* (2003), der von der De-Industrialisierung der nordostchinesischen Stadt Shenyang handelt. Die Information, dass der Film nahezu neun Stunden dauert (wenn auch aufgeteilt auf drei Teile), stärkt einerseits das Vertrauen der Fragenden in den Ernst

jener Konfusion fortleben, die er bemeistert, indem er der Zeiterfahrung die Ordnung der narrativen Form verleiht.

Einen Film anzuschauen heißt heute in der Regel, ihn von Anfang bis Ende zu sehen. Im Kino ist eine solche Praxis allerdings relativ neu. Hitchcock brachte *Psycho* 1960 mit einer Werbekampagne ins Kino, deren Slogan lautet: »The Film you must see from the beginning – or not at all.« Wer den Film kennt, wird verstehen, worum es Hitchcock zu tun war: Wer bei *Psycho* eine halbe Stunde zu spät kommt, wird vergeblich auf den Auftritt von Janet Leigh warten, den Star des Films. Die berühmte Duschsequenz kommt schon nach 25 Minuten; danach ist die von Janet Leigh gespielte Figur tot und aus dem Film verschwunden. Der Slogan war aber nur deshalb notwendig, weil Filme in den 1960er Jahren noch im Séance Continue-Verfahren gezeigt wurden. Das Kino öffnete um 11 Uhr, und der Film lief danach ohne Unterbrechung als Loop bis nach Mitternacht. Die Kinos in New York begannen erst in den 1950er Jahren, Anfangszeiten in der Werbung zu veröffentlichen. Diesem laschen Regime des durchgehenden Einlasses wollte Hitchcock zumindest für *Psycho* ein Ende setzen. Seinem Vorbild folgten im Laufe der 1960er Jahre schließlich alle Kinos, bis auf die Bahnhofkinos, die noch bis in die 1980er Jahre durchgängig Einlass boten.

Vor 1960 und vor Hitchcock aber war es durchaus üblich, sich Filme von der Mitte bis zur Mitte anzuschauen. »This is where we came in« lautete eine Formulierung der amerikanischen Umgangssprache, mit der Kinobesucher sich einst gegenseitig zu verstehen gaben, dass sie nunmehr den ganzen Film gesehen hatten. Das setzt voraus, dass man sitzen bleibt, bis man wieder am Ausgangspunkt angelangt ist. Der Loop ist keine Erfindung aus dem Zeitalter der Videoinstallation, sondern der Default-Modus der Filmsichtung vor 1960. Aus diesem Grund arbeiten klassische Hollywood-Filme auch mit vielen Redundanzen und erzählen alles immer zwei Mal: Nicht, weil die Regisseure und Drehbuchautoren davon ausgehen, dass ihr Publikum nicht sehr klug sei, sondern weil sie damit rechnen, dass das Publikum irgendwann mitten in der Geschichte in den Film hineinplatzt und sich rasch in der erzählten Welt zurechtfinden muss. Schon für klassische Hollywood-Filme galt demnach, was Godard zur

Es fällt also nicht schwer, die Standardfilmlänge auf kaufmännische Gründe zurückzuführen. Dem Zwang der Buchhalter allein ist aber noch keine prägende kulturelle Form entsprungen. Man muss zu den kaufmännischen Gründen mindestens auch noch solche der Zeitökonomie hinzurechnen.

Ins Kino geht man, wie Fassbinder sagte, um etwas zu erleben: in eine narrative Welt eingebunden zu werden oder »einzutauchen«, um eine beliebte Metapher der neueren Medien- und Erzähltheorie aufzugreifen, die Metapher der Immersion, und dass es für diese Erfahrung ein passendes Maß gibt. Der Film ist nicht das Leben, aber er wird, wenn er reüssiert, zu einem wichtigen Teil des Lebens seiner Zuschauer. Dafür braucht es offenbar Zeit. Man muss mit den Figuren Zeit verbringen können, damit sie sich in den eigenen Lebenszusammenhang eingliedern. Allerdings darf der Film nicht überhandnehmen. Es kommt zumindest dem klassischen Kino darauf an, dass man den ganzen Film sieht, aber der Film darf nicht zum Lebensinhalt werden. Ein Zwei-Stunden-Film passt sich gut einer Tagesplanung ein, in der andere Dinge Priorität haben. Die Standardlänge eines Films bemisst sich danach, wie viel Zeit einem noch bleibt, wenn man die grundlegenden Dinge erledigt hat. Nicht von ungefähr dauert ein Fußballspiel mit Pause genau gleich lang wie ein durchschnittlicher Spielfilm. Cricket hingegen ist offensichtlich eine Sportart für Leute, die wohl Schlaf brauchen, aber nicht so viel arbeiten; wie sonst könnten Cricketspiele mehrere Tage dauern? Baseball wiederum scheint eine Sportart zu sein für Leute, die arbeiten, aber nicht unbedingt viel Schlaf brauchen. Die Spiele beginnen zumeist am Abend und können bis zu vier Stunden dauern. Fußball und Kinofilme sind für Leute gedacht, die viel arbeiten und viel schlafen.

Die Ökonomie, sagt der französische Philosoph Georges Bataille, impliziert aber immer auch die Verausgabung, die Verschwendung. So, wie das Gesetz seine Übertretung impliziert – denn erst in ihrer Verletzung wird die Norm wirksam –, so bedingen sich auch Zeitökonomie und Zeitverschwendung gegenseitig. In der strikten Ökonomie der Standardlänge des Films müsste demnach auch – gut dialektisch – ihre Aufhebung enthalten sein und in der starren Form des Films eine Ahnung

Erfolg »Artikel und Buchauszüge von bleibendem Wert« veröffentlicht, wie es im Slogan für die deutschsprachige Ausgabe heißt. Im Unterschied zu *Reader's Digest,* die 16 Millionen Abonnenten hat, blieb die Reichweite des 9.5 mm-Systems von *Pathé* auf einen relativ kleinen Kreis kaufkräftiger Kunden beschränkt. Erst mit dem VHS-Videorekorder wurde das Heimkino zum Breitenphänomen. Die Pointe des VHS-Rekorders bestand aber eben gerade darin, dass er die Aufzeichnung und Wiedergabe von Spielfilmen in voller Länge erlaubte.

Dafür, dass die Standardlänge in der Praxis des Kinos weiterhin die Norm bleibt, sind aber auch die Verleiher und Kinobetreiber verantwortlich. Die Idee, dass der Regisseur der Autor seines Films sei – eine Idee, die französischen Ursprungs ist und in Frankreich schon in den 1920er Jahren dazu diente, die künstlerisch wertvollen französischen von den industriell produzierten amerikanischen Filmen abzugrenzen –, hat längst auch Hollywood erreicht. Die Regisseurengewerkschaft, die Director's Guild of America (DGA), hat mittlerweile durchgesetzt, dass in den Credits eines Films mit der Formulierung »a [Name des Regisseurs] film« dem Regisseur die Autorschaft zugeschrieben wird. Teil dieses Rollenwandels ist der Anspruch vieler Regisseure, sich nicht an die Normvorgaben der Filmvermarktung zu halten und ihre Filme nicht auf die Standardlänge von zwei Stunden zu kürzen. Letztlich aber setzten sich doch immer die Marketingleute durch, aus dem einfachen Grund, dass ein Film, der zwei Stunden dauert, pro Tag mindestens einmal mehr gezeigt werden kann als einer, der drei Stunden dauert. In einem Vermarktungsregime, bei dem die Zuschauer die Filme von Anfang bis Ende schauen und am Anfang der Vorstellung im Kino sind, also für jede Vorführung des Films gesondert bezahlen, ergibt sich daraus eine wichtige Mehreinnahme. Um die Vision des Regisseurs ist es deswegen nicht gleich geschehen. Zu ihrem Recht kommt sie mit dem so genannten Director's Cut, der auf DVD veröffentlicht werden kann. Der Director's Cut bringt auch der Marketingabteilung Vorteile. Am besten veröffentlicht man diese Fassung des Films mit etwas Abstand nach der DVD-Veröffentlichung der Kinofassung. So kann man einen Film seinen Liebhabern noch ein weiteres Mal verkaufen.

Solange Filme nur im Kino zu sehen waren, gab es für die Zuschauer zur Standardlänge kaum eine Alternative. Bis in die 1960er Jahre gehörten zum Filmprogramm immer auch Kurzfilme: Cartoons oder Zeichentrickfilme und Kurzspielfilme in den USA; in Deutschland etwa mussten Kulturfilme von Gesetzes wegen gezeigt werden und damit einen Bildungsauftrag erfüllen, von dem das Kino erst durch die Einrichtung der öffentlich-rechtlichen Fernsehanstalten entlastet wurde. Kernstück des Programms war aber der Spielfilm, in Deutschland zumal, wo die Kulturfilme oft als Strafaufgabe wahrgenommen und als Gelegenheit zur Konversation genutzt wurden. Auch die Einführung von Heimvideo änderte an der Vorherrschaft dieser Standardlänge nichts. Im Gegenteil. Das erste marktfähige Videosystem, *Betamax* von *Sony*, das 1975 in Japan und den USA herauskam, war gedacht als »time-shifting device«, als Gerät zur Aufzeichnung von Fernsehprogrammen, die man sonst verpasst hätte. Die Aufzeichnungsdauer betrug sechzig Minuten, abgestimmt auf den Programmraster des amerikanischen Fernsehens, der aus einstündigen »windows« besteht. *Sony* verlor den Kampf gegen das Konkurrenzsystem VHS (Video Home System), das von *Matsushita/ Panasonic* und JVC gemeinsam entwickelt und 1976 auf den Markt gebracht wurde, vor allem deshalb, weil VHS-Kassetten über eine Speicherkapazität von zwei Stunden verfügten und damit für die Aufzeichnung und Wiedergabe von Spielfilmen ausgelegt waren. Kinofilme für die Vorführung im Heimkino gibt es zwar schon seit den 1920er Jahren, als *Pathé* eine Vielzahl von Filmen auf das im Dezember 1921 lancierte 9.5 mm-Pathé-Baby-Format reduzierte und für den Heimmarkt verfügbar machte. Diese Filme waren indes im doppelten Sinne reduziert: Nicht nur betrug die Breite des Filmstreifens 9.5 mm statt der seit 1905 im Rahmen einer internationalen Konvention in Paris als Weltstandard eingesetzten 35 mm, die Filme wurden auch stark gekürzt und bestanden nunmehr aus einem in der Regel rund halbstündigen Zusammenschnitt von Höhepunkten, verbunden durch Zwischentitel. Es handelte sich um eine inhaltliche Reduktion, wie sie auch die Zeitschrift *Reader's Digest* praktiziert, die am 5. Februar 1922 erstmals erschien, also nur zwei Monate nach der Einführung von *Pathé Baby*, und die nach wie vor mit immer großem

Warum dauert ein Kinofilm in der Regel anderthalb bis zwei Stunden? Warum nicht zweiundreißig Minuten und warum nicht neun Stunden?

Die Normlänge von anderthalb bis zwei Stunden ist beinahe so alt wie das Kino selbst. Sie etablierte sich in den frühen 1910er Jahren, als der Spielfilm den Kurzfilm des Attraktionskinos als Standardformat des Filmverleihs ablöste. Langspielfilme hatten zunächst entscheidende geschäftliche Vorteile. Sie konnten in größeren Häusern zu höheren Eintrittspreisen gezeigt werden als die zuvor üblichen Zehn-Minuten-Filme. Sie sprachen damit ein größeres Publikum an, dem auch die kaufkräftige bürgerliche Mittelschicht angehörte, das die Standards des Konsums setzte. Mit der Einführung des Langspielfilms und dem Umzug des Kinos in große Häuser, die dem Vorbild der Oper nachempfunden waren, erlangte die Filmindustrie Glaubwürdigkeit in den Augen der Banken. Erst mit den großen Kinos, die zugleich als Investitionsobjekt und als Bankgarantie dienten, kamen die Filmproduzenten zu den Bankkrediten, die sie für die Produktion von aufwendigen Langspielfilmen brauchten. Der Langspielfilm in der Länge von anderthalb bis zwei Stunden war für die Filmindustrie die Eintrittskarte zum Big Business.

Die Spielfilmlänge blieb allerdings durchaus variabel. In den 1920er Jahren dauerten aufwendige Filme manchmal vier oder sechs Stunden, zumal solche aus deutscher Produktion. Die erste Fassung von *Das indische Grabmal*, realisiert 1921 von Joe May nach einem Drehbuch von Fritz Lang und Thea von Harbou, dauerte über vier Stunden, Langs *Nibelungen* von 1924 über fünf Stunden. Diese Filme wurden aber mit einer Pause nach zwei Stunden gezeigt oder über zwei oder drei Abende verteilt, die *Nibelungen* etwa in den zwei Teilen *Siegfried* und *Kriemhilds Rache*. In den 1950er und 1960er Jahren tauchte der Vier-Stunden-Film in Form von Großproduktionen wie *Lawrence of Arabia*, *Dr. Zhivago* oder *The Sound of Music* wieder auf. Fritz Lang legte bei der Gelegenheit die letzte der drei Versionen von *Das indische Grabmal* vor, die 1958 in Deutschland produziert wurde. Das Format mit den zweiten Teilen und der Pause wurde aber beibehalten, und den Grundbaustein des Programms bildete eine Einheit mit einer Richtlänge von zwei Stunden. Also der Normlänge des Spielfilms.

Keine Eile, keine Zeit. Zur Frage der richtigen Dauer eines Films

Vinzenz Hediger

(AMC, seit 2007) inszeniert im Rückblick auf die 1960er Jahre ein von Sexismus und Machismus beherrschtes Karrieremuster, das an das Publikum stets die Frage richtet, ob und inwieweit dieses denn überwunden ist; *Homeland* (Fox 21, seit 2010) führt in eine Atmosphäre des permanenten Verdachts, mit der der »Krieg gegen den Terror« den Lebensalltag in den Vereinigten Staaten infiziert.

Das Neue dieser und anderer Serien liegt nicht allein (und oft gar nicht besonders) in einer mehrdimensionalen Erzählweise. Es besteht auch nicht allein darin, dass hier allgemeine soziale, politische und existentielle Themen anhand komplex konzipierter Figuren präsentiert werden, die im Verlauf der Serien einer deutlichen Entwicklung unterliegen. Es zeigt sich vor allem in der offenen Form ihres Episodencharakters, die erhebliche Variationen, Digressionen und Umbrüche der Handlungslinien zulässt und somit Transformationen des anfänglichen Grundschemas der jeweiligen Serien erlaubt. In der Komposition ihrer Geschichten brechen sie die Geschlossenheit ihrer Episoden auf und gewinnen dadurch eine epische Qualität, durch die sie zugleich eine veränderte, für den Großrhythmus ihrer Staffeln aufmerksame Rezeption anbieten. Diese Serien eröffnen sich nicht allein neue Möglichkeiten des Erzählens vergleichsweise unendlicher Geschichten, sie sind zugleich ein Beleg für die unendliche Geschichte filmischer Geschichten selbst – und damit ein weiteres Zeugnis der Unverwüstlichkeit der kulturellen Praxis des Erzählens innerhalb wie außerhalb der Künste.

Martin Seel
ist Professor für Philosophie an der Johann Wolfgang Goethe-Universität Frankfurt/M. Zu seinen Buchpublikationen zählen: *Eine Ästhetik der Natur* (1991); *Versuch über die Form des Glücks* (1995); *Ästhetik des Erscheinens* (2000); *Sich bestimmen lassen. Studien zur theoretischen und praktischen Philosophie* (2002); *Die Macht des Erscheinens. Texte zur Ästhetik* (2007); *Theorien* (2009); *111 Tugenden, 111 Laster. Eine philosophische Revue* (2011); *Die Künste des Kinos* (2013).

Nach dem Kino

Freilich hat sich das filmische Erzählen mittlerweile längst von seiner Gebundenheit an das Kino als dem primären Schauplatz seiner Darbietung emanzipiert. Das Kino ist nur noch einer unter vielen anderen Schauplätzen des Erscheinens von Filmen. Außerhalb des Kinos aber verändern sich die Bedingungen der Rezeption von Filmen. Das zeitliche Diktat des Kinofilms kann im Fernsehen, am Computer und auf mobilen Geräten jederzeit suspendiert werden. Die Irreversibilität des Verlaufs kann durch Zappen, Anhalten, Vorlauf, Rücklauf und andere Eingriffsmöglichkeiten jederzeit aufgebrochen werden. Der Film springt hier nicht länger in der althergebrachten Weise mit seinem Publikum um, dieses kann nun mit ihm auf eine Weise umspringen, wie es im Kino nicht möglich ist. Damit aber verändert sich auch die zeitliche Form der Wahrnehmung von Filmen. Die Zuschauer können nun die Eigenzeit eines Films mit ihrer eigenen zeitlichen Disposition kombinieren. Sie können *ihren* Rhythmus mit *seinem* Rhythmus interferieren lassen. Sie können die Zumutungen seiner Gegenwart nach Lust und Laune ganz unterschiedlich dosieren. Sie können den Filmen ihrer Wahl eine – je nach Situation – starke oder schwache, beiläufige oder beherrschende Präsenz innerhalb der Gegenwart des eigenen Lebens verleihen.

Diese neuen Formen der Aneignung filmischer Geschichten färben zugleich auf die Modi ihrer Darbietung ab. Mit den veränderten Bedingungen der filmischen Rezeption entstehen veränderte Formen der Produktion. Das Erscheinen *von* Filmen auf Bildschirmen aller Art hat eine gesteigerte Produktion *für* ihre Wahrnehmung in neuen technischen Medien zur Folge. Ein Beispiel hierfür sind die so genannten, vor allem – aber keineswegs allein – in den USA entstandenen Neuen Serien. *The Sopranos* (HBO, 1999–2007) behandelt den unauflöslichen Konflikt zwischen Familie und Clan; *The Wire* (HBO, 2002–2008) entfaltet im allegorischen Kosmos der Großstadt den Widerstreit zwischen Individuen und Institutionen; *In Treatment* (HBO, 2007–2010) dramatisiert das fragile Verhältnis von menschlicher *Nähe und Distanz* am Beispiel der Psychotherapie; *Mad Men*

Präsens – auch und gerade dort, wo das, wovon erzählt wird, weit in Vergangenheit oder Zukunft liegt.

In den meisten Modi des Erzählens hingegen ist das, was erzählt wird, zum Zeitpunkt der Erzählung unwiderruflich vorbei. Dies hat seinen Grund darin, dass sich handelnde Lebewesen als Angehörige historischer Lebensformen in einem über ihre Gegenwart hinaus gespannten zeitlichen Horizont bewegen. »To exist historically is to perceive the events one lives through as part of a story later to be told«, notiert Arthur Danto in seiner Analyse der Grammatik historischer Erzählungen lakonisch.[3] »The cognitive openness of the future is required if we are to believe that the shape of the future is in any way a matter of what we choose to do.«[4] Menschliche Handlungsfähigkeit ist nur in einer Konstellation von unübersehbaren Möglichkeiten gegeben, deren Bedeutsamkeit für das eigene Tun und Ergehen nicht von vornherein feststeht. Allein ex post können die Vollzüge und Prozesse individuellen oder kollektiven Verhaltens in Form einer erzählenden Erklärung und Deutung gegossen werden. Auch das filmische Erzählen kann diese Bedingungen nicht grundsätzlich außer Kraft setzen. Auch seine Geschichten sind von den temporalen und kognitiven Asymmetrien der erzählenden Kommunikation geprägt. Nicht anders als die meisten künstlerischen Fiktionen (soweit sie auf der Bühne nicht für eine improvisierende Darbietung offen sind) sind auch seine Geschichten abgeschlossen, wie offen ihr Ende auch immer sein mag. Auch sie nehmen einen Gang, indem sich die Optionen ihrer Figuren nach und nach schließen. Auch sie bewegen sich in der Darstellung der Widerfahrnisse ihrer Charaktere fortwährend auf eine vergangene Zukunft zu. Aber durch die Art seines Erzählens verhält sich das Kino anders zu der vergehenden Zeit, als die übrigen narrativen Künste es vermögen. Alles, was sich hier abspielt, spielt sich in einem Modus vergegenwärtigter Gegenwart ab. Ein geschehender Raum ereignet sich, während der Film sich ereignet. In diesen seinen eigenen Raum und diese seine eigene Zeit nimmt der Film sein Publikum mit. In dieser irreversiblen Raumzeit vollziehen sich die von ihm erzählten Geschichten.

3
Arthur C. Danto: Narration and Knowledge. New York 2007, S. 342–383, hier S. 343.

4
Ebd., vgl. S. 353, vgl. S. 363.

Figuren selbst als auch für die Zuschauer unüberschaubaren Raum des filmischen Geschehens geführt – so, dass nicht nur ihr Horizont, sondern auch der des Publikums fortwährend überschritten wird.

Jeder der gerade genannten Filme entwarf zu seiner Zeit ein verändertes Erzählen. John Ford hat zusammen mit anderen die Phase des Spätwesterns eingeläutet, Abbas Kiarostami hat eine neue Ästhetik der Langsamkeit entwickelt, Paul Greengrass dagegen die Bildbewegungen des Actionfilms nochmals beschleunigt. Jeder intensive Film variiert die Möglichkeiten filmischen Erzählens, wie es ebenso in den anderen narrativen Künsten der Fall ist. Dies gilt nicht allein für Epochen und Stile des Filmemachens, wie den amerikanischen Film Noir, die Nouvelle Vague, das Neue Deutsche Kino, New Hollywood usw., sondern für einzelne Filme, die mit ihrer Erzählweise stets zugleich die Genres modifizieren, denen sie angehören oder die sie berühren – man denke nur an Filme wie *Dancer in the Dark* (Lars von Trier, Dänemark et al. 2000), *Memento* (Christopher Nolan, USA 2000), *Code inconnu* (Michael Haneke, Deutschland/ Frankreich/Rumänien 2000) oder *Kill Bill* (Quentin Tarantino, USA 2003/2004).

Trotz der Heterogenität und Varietät allein der wenigen hier genannten Filme aber gibt es eine formale Grundeigenschaft, die Spielfilme im Kino miteinander teilen. Denn der besonderen Verlaufsform des filmischen Erzählens entspringt die besondere Zeitform seiner Erzählungen. Dadurch nämlich, dass die Zuschauer im Dunkel des Kinos dem Geschehen der Filme unvermeidlich unterliegen, bleibt alles, was sich dort abspielt, von dem Hier und Jetzt ihres audiovisuellen Erscheinens abhängig, einschließlich des Unsichtbaren und Unhörbaren, von dem es fortwährend umgeben ist. Im Kino sind die Zuschauer auf eine ausgezeichnete Weise bei dem *Erzählten* dabei, weil sie in besonderer Weise bei der *Erzählung* dabei (nämlich von ihr umfangen und an ihren Verlauf gefesselt) sind. Sie befinden sich in der Gegenwart eines audiovisuellen Erscheinens, das auf alles abfärbt, was dort in narrativen Ordnungen eines temporalen und kausalen Nacheinanders dargeboten wird. Für den Spielfilm gilt: Das Tempus des filmischen Erzählens ist das

Zeiten vollzieht, der dem Geschehen auf Leinwand oder Bildschirm entzogen bleibt. Auf diese Weise vermag er die Wahrnehmung seiner Betrachter in und durch eine virtuelle, allein sehend und hörend erfahrbare Welt zu führen – in eine Welt freilich, die mit der realen in sehr unterschiedlichen Graden verschwistert und in ebenso unterschiedlichen Maßen auf sie bezogen sein kann. Diese Disposition befähigt das narrative Kino zugleich, Situationen in besonderer Intensität aus der Warte der an ihnen Beteiligten zu präsentieren und zugleich auf Situationen geschilderten Handelns und Widerfahrens eine Sicht zu eröffnen und damit dem Publikum nahezubringen, die von denjenigen der handelnden Figuren oder Charaktere mehr oder weniger stark differiert. Dies ist einer der Gründe dafür, warum zumal in bedeutenden Spielfilmen das in ihnen dramatisierte Geschehen zwar einerseits verständlich gemacht, andererseits aber auch wieder verrätselt wird, wie es in den großen künstlerischen Erzählungen eigentlich immer geschieht.

Bis zum Ende von John Fords *The Searchers* (USA 1956) bleibt es undurchsichtig, was Ethan Edwards – ein Mann, dessen Vorleben seit seinem Engagement auf Seiten der Südstaaten im amerikanischen Bürgerkrieg weitgehend im Dunkeln bleibt – bei seiner langjährigen Suche nach seiner entführten Nichte Debbie eigentlich bewegt, und erst recht, was ihn dazu bringt, die junge Frau, deren Leben er mehrfach für nicht länger lebenswert erklärt hat, dann doch in die Arme zu schließen und »nach Hause« zu bringen. *Der Geschmack der Kirsche* von Abbas Kiarostami (Irland/Frankreich 1997) verfolgt den möglicherweise letzten Lebenstag eines Mannes, der vorhat, sich das Leben zu nehmen, ohne die geringste Andeutung darüber, was der Grund für diesen Vorsatz ist. Der Held in *The Bourne Supremacy* von Paul Greengrass (USA 2004) weiß so wenig wie die Zuschauer, die ihm auf seinen gewaltsamen Suchbewegungen folgen, wie er zu dem geworden ist, der er ist; allein Bruchstücke seiner Vergangenheit werden für ihn und das Publikum nach und nach erkennbar (die in *The Bourne Ultimatum* [Paul Greengrass, USA 2007] teilweise zusammengesetzt werden). Jeder dieser Filme ist in hohem Maß um seine Hauptfiguren zentriert; über weite Strecken sind sie auf der Leinwand präsent. Aber sie werden durch einen sowohl für diese

Von exemplarischer Bedeutung können dabei auch die Einstellungen sein, aus denen von den jeweiligen Vorkommnissen berichtet wird. Durch die Art ihrer Gestaltung präsentiert jede Erzählung eine Sichtweise dessen, was immer sie präsentiert. Diese manifestiert sich weniger durch explizite Bewertungen, sondern vor allem im Stil des jeweiligen Erzählens. Erzählungen, die so verfahren, geben nicht nur dem Erzählten, sondern auch der Erzählung eine besondere Zuspitzung. Sie machen verständlich oder stellen infrage, wie angemessen oder unangemessen, recht oder gerecht, besonnen oder verrückt in gegebenen Situationen gehandelt wurde, und auch, wie viel Recht oder Unrecht, Zumutbares oder Unzumutbares, Wahrscheinliches oder Unwahrscheinliches, Erstaunliches oder Banales den aktiv wie passiv Beteiligten dabei widerfahren ist. Durch das Wie der Erzählung lassen sie dabei – mit der Wahl ihrer Worte, mit der Auswahl von Szenen, in der Komposition von Anfang und Ende, im Verweilen bei bestimmten Ereignissen und im Übergehen anderer, in der Verzögerung und Beschleunigung des Handlungsverlaufs und durch viele andere stilistische Mittel – ein spezifisches, auf die eine oder andere Weise wertend gefärbtes Licht auf das Was des dargebotenen Geschehens fallen. Jede Erzählung gibt unausweichlich eine Deutung dessen, wovon sie erzählt.

Mit dieser Perspektivität des Erzählens hat es eine besondere Bewandtnis. Denn die Sichtweisen, die Erzählungen auf das Tun und Erleiden, Befinden und Bestreben ihres Personals eröffnen, sind niemals völlig kongruent mit derjenigen ihrer Akteure. In mehr oder weniger hohem Maß differieren sie von deren Perspektive. Kontraste dieser Art kommen bereits in alltäglichen Erzählungen vor – umso mehr aber in der Form religiöser, historischer und politischer Großerzählungen bis hin zu denen des Mythos und der Kunst.

Filmisches Erzählen

In all den genannten Hinsichten bringt der Film seine eigenen Möglichkeiten ins Spiel.[2] Mehr noch als andere Erzählformen kann der Film die Situationen, durch die er führt, von innen heraus entfalten, weil sich alles, was in seinem Verlauf sichtbar und hörbar wird, in einem Horizont von Räumen und

2
Zum Folgenden ausführlich: Martin Seel: Die Künste des Kinos. Frankfurt am Main 2013, Kap. 3 u. 5.

Soweit menschliche oder menschenähnliche Akteure im Spiel sind, wird dabei fast immer mit erzählt, wie es ist, war, gewesen wäre oder sein würde, in den betreffenden Situationen zu sein oder das betreffende Schicksal zu erleiden. Insbesondere dann, wenn Unerwartetes und Unerwartbares bis hin zum schieren Zufall ihre Hand im Spiel haben, zumal in der Form, in der Individuen oder Kollektiven etwas zum Ereignis wird, das die Koordinaten ihres bisherigen Begreifens und Handelns sprengt, können Erzählungen verständlich machen, oder es versuchen, wie eine Anzahl von Vorkommnissen kausal und motivational miteinander verknüpft war. Sie bieten damit zugleich Erklärungen dafür an, wie das, was *auf*einander folgte, *aus*einander folgen konnte oder musste.

Das Erzählen gibt einen durchaus anderen Aufschluss als ein nomologisches Erklären, mit dem das kontingent Erscheinende auf gesetzmäßige Verläufe zurückgeführt wird.[1] Denn Erzählungen sind auf eine Darstellung der Individualität faktiver oder fiktiver biographischer und historischer Prozesse spezialisiert, die sich einer gesetzmäßigen Rekonstruktion entziehen. Dabei wird die tatsächliche oder scheinbare Kontingenz von Geschehendem im Format des Erzählens nicht immer und oft nicht in jeder Hinsicht beseitigt. Zufälligkeit und Chaos müssen im Gang einer Erzählung nicht ausgeräumt, überwunden und beseitigt, sie können auch ausgestaltet und ausgestellt werden. Vor allem in künstlerischen Erzählungen werden Entwicklungen nicht selten gerade in ihrer Kontingenz vergegenwärtigt, wie etwa in Heinrich von Kleists Erzählungen *Das Erdbeben in Chili* und *Michael Kohlhaas*, bei den Schilderungen von Kriegsszenen in Claude Simons Roman *La Route des Flandres* oder auch in Filmen wie Robert Altmans *Short Cuts* (USA 1993) und *Amores Perros* von Alejandro González Iñárritu (Mexiko 2000).

Außerdem steht der Fokus von Erzählungen auf der Besonderheit von Ereigniszusammenhängen nicht in einem Gegensatz zu einer möglichen Allgemeinheit ihres Gehalts. In Form einer exemplarischen Darstellung können sie an einem individuellen Geschehen generelle Konturen einer Situation, eines Konflikts oder Schicksals hervortreten lassen.

1
Vgl. hierzu Michael Hampe: Kleine Geschichte des Naturgesetzbegriffs. Frankfurt am Main 2007, bes. S. 22–28.

Erzählen

Durch Erzählungen machen Menschen sich selbst und anderen verständlich, was in Geschichte und näherer Gegenwart geschehen ist oder in Zukunft geschehen könnte. Sie stellen Beziehungen zwischen Zuständen und Ereignissen her, die verdeutlichen, wie und warum es zu Vorkommnissen und Veränderungen einer bestimmten Art kam – oder hätte kommen können. Erzählungen handeln davon, wie es Individuen oder Kollektiven ergangen ist oder wie es sich mit etwas zugetragen hat – seien es alltägliche Handlungen, politische Umwälzungen, wissenschaftliche Entdeckungen oder Prozesse der natürlichen Evolution. Sie bringen faktische oder fiktive Verläufe auf unterschiedlich komplexe Weise in einen mehr oder weniger durchsichtig gegliederten Zusammenhang. Kausale Verbindungen spielen dabei immer eine entscheidende Rolle; rekonstruiert oder imaginiert wird, welche Zustände und Vorkommisse für welche anderen Begebenheiten ursächlich waren. Zu diesen Faktoren gehören wesentlich auch die affektiven und rationalen Einstellungen derer, die von den jeweiligen Ereignissen betroffen waren oder sind. Schließlich steht in den meisten alltäglichen wie künstlerischen Erzählungen das menschliche Tun und Widerfahren im Vordergrund (oder solches von Fabelgestalten aller Art, in dem sich das menschliche spiegelt). Im Kontext äußerer Wirkkräfte werden Empfindungen, Stimmungen, Gefühle, Überzeugungen und Absichten in ihrem Einfluss auf das Verhalten der jeweiligen Protagonisten vorgestellt. Aus diesen Verstrickungen ergibt sich der Gang der erzählten Geschichte, die sich häufig von einem signifikanten Einsatzpunkt zu einem markanten Schlusspunkt hinbewegt: zu der Auflösung eines Konflikts, einem verhängnisvollen Ausgang oder dem Helldunkel eines offenen Endes. Ob eine Erzählung vom Gelingen oder Scheitern – oder Gelingen *und* Scheitern – von Handlungen, Tätigkeiten, Projekten, Ambitionen und Hoffnungen handelt, ihre Pointe liegt stets in der Vergegenwärtigung der besonderen Bedeutsamkeit, die die erzählten Verläufe für die Beteiligten hatten, haben oder hätten haben können.

Mit vielen Abstufungen können sich Erzählungen in dem Modus eher eines Realis oder eines Irrealis vollziehen.

Eine besondere narrative Befähigung ist kein Privileg der Literatur und des Films allein. Fast alle Künste haben eine Affinität zu erzählender Gestaltung. Narrativ verfährt nicht nur das herkömmliche Theater, auch die Bildenden Künste kennen eigene Formen der Narration. Spurenelemente narrativer Gestaltung finden sich gelegentlich sogar in der instrumentalen Musik. Wo die Musik sich – in Liedern und Songs, vor allem aber in den Dramen der Oper – mit Texten und szenischer Darbietung verbindet, wird auch sie zu einem genuinen Medium des Erzählens. Selbst die Architektur, die für sich genommen – anders als die Plastik – über kein narratives Potential verfügt, kann durch die Ausgestaltung von Fresken, durch Wandmalerei und die Aufnahme anderer Bildformen eine Liaison mit den erzählenden Künsten eingehen.

Die narrative Affinität so vieler Künste kommt nicht von ungefähr. Sie hat ihren Ursprung in der narrativen Disposition des Menschen. Handelnde sind von Natur aus Erzählende. Sie sind auf Kulturen des Erzählens angewiesen. In fast allen Lebensbereichen bedürfen sie einer Verständigung durch eigene und fremde Erzählungen. Die Kunst des Erzählens reicht weit über die Sphäre der ästhetischen Künste hinaus. Denn das Erzählen ist eine universelle, anthropologisch fundierte Praxis, die in der Herstellung und Aufnahme künstlerischer Erzählungen sowohl eine Fortführung als auch eine Brechung erfährt.

Diese Brechungen rufen ein ums andere Mal neue Brechungen hervor, angestoßen nicht zuletzt durch die fortlaufende Evolution diverser Medien und Schauplätze der Konstruktion, Darbietung sowie der Rezeption von Geschichten. Sowenig es je ein Ende der Kunst, sondern nur immer neue Transformationen der künstlerischen Gestaltung gegeben hat, sowenig kann es innerhalb menschlicher Kulturen ein Ende des Erzählens geben. Mit Verschiebungen der narrativen Verständigungsverhältnisse aber ist jederzeit zu rechnen. Von Anfang an gilt dies auch für den Film, und hier vor allem für die Entwicklungen des Spielfilms und seiner komplexen Interaktion mit den anderen narrativen Künsten. Zwar liegen dessen Attraktionen keineswegs in der Erfindung fesselnder Geschichten allein. Aber soweit Spielfilme narrativ verfahren, machen Varianten und Variationen auch hier das Lebenselixier des Erzählens aus.

Varianten filmischen Erzählens

Martin Seel

Expanded Narration.
Das neue Erzählen.

B III Biennale des
bewegten Bildes 2013

Danksagung

B3 Biennale des bewegten Bildes 2013
Expanded Narration. Das neue Erzählen.
30.10.–03.11.2013
Frankfurt Rhein Main
b3biennale.com

Veranstalter

in Kooperation mit

Träger

Förderer   Hessisches Ministerium für Wirtschaft, Verkehr und Landesentwicklung   Europäische Union

Förderer B3 Parcours   kulturfonds frankfurtrheinmain

Parcourspartner/Veranstaltungsorte   ALTANA Kulturstiftung   Astor Film Lounge   Atelierfrankfurt   Basis e.V.   Deutsches Filmmuseum   E-Kinos   Exzellenzcluster Normative Orders   Frankfurter Kunstverein   Galerie Anita Beckers   Galerie Heike Strelow   Gibson Club   Haus am Dom   Hochschule für Musik und Darstellende Kunst   Kai Middendorff Galerie   Kinothek Asta Nielsen e.V.   MMK Museum für Moderne Kunst   Museum Angewandte Kunst   Museum für Kommunikation Frankfurt   Museum Wiesbaden   Nassauischer Kunstverein Wiesbaden   Portikus   Robert Johnson   Römerhallen   Schirn Kunsthalle Frankfurt   Städelschule   Weißfrauen Diakoniekirche   Weltkulturen Museum

Partner   Aventis Foundation   Brehm & v. Moers   Dr. Hauschka Kosmetik   FunDeMental Studios   Leo Burnett   Satis&fy   Sky Deutschland   Von Kelterborn/OSMO Collection   Wirtschaftsförderung Frankfurt GmbH   **Hotelpartner**   Lindenberg   Nizza Hotel   Westin Hotels & Resorts   **Medienpartner**   BlickpunktFilm   De:Bug   Frankfurter Allgemeine Zeitung   GamesMarkt   HORIZONT   Journal Frankfurt   Medien Bulletin   Ströer Media AG   taz.die tageszeitung
Versicherungspartner   ARTIMA

Impressum

Bibliografische Information der Deutschen Nationalbibliothek
Die Deutsche Nationalbibliothek verzeichnet diese Publikation in der Deutschen Nationalbibliografie; detaillierte bibliografische Daten sind im Internet über http://dnb.d-nb.de abrufbar.

© 2013 transcript Verlag, Bielefeld
Die Verwertung der Texte und Bilder ist ohne Zustimmung des Verlages urheberrechtswidrig und strafbar. Das gilt auch für Vervielfältigungen, Übersetzungen, Mikroverfilmungen und für die Verarbeitung mit elektronischen Systemen.

Herausgeber
Bernd Kracke, Marc Ries
Hochschule für Gestaltung Offenbach
Schlossstr. 31, 63065 Offenbach am Main

Gestaltung
Karin Rekowski
Supervision: Klaus Hesse, Nikolas Brückmann, Yuriy Matveev (B3 Designstudio)

Redaktion
Marc Ries, Norman Hildebrandt

Lektorat
Christine Taxer, Isa Bickmann, Keonaona Peterson

Übersetzungen
Geraldine Bleck, Jim Gussen, Steven Lindberg, Marcel René Marburger, Robert Nusbaum, Übersetzungsbüro Oskana Peters, Alan Shapiro, Alexander Schneider, Mark Schreiber, Anja Wiesinger

Papier
90g/m^2 Fly Design, weiß

Schriften
Akkurat, Stone Serif

Produktion
brandbook, Frankfurt am Main

ISBN: 978-3-8376-2652-0

Inhalt

9   Bernd Kracke, Marc Ries
Vorwort

13   Bernd Kracke
Wohin mit der Kamera? *B3*, die 1.

21   Marcel Schwierin
Das Neue Erzählen

29   Marc Ries
Erzählen im Netz

45   Hans Ulrich Reck
Jenseits des Strukturalismus. Erweiterndes Erzählen zwischen Texten und Bildern

57   Ferdinand Schmatz
Die Sprache drängt

61   Usha Reber
Es wird Wirklichkeit gewesen sein. Alban Nicolai Herbsts erweiterte Schreibstätten

81   Holger Kube-Ventura
Dinge im Rückspiegel sind näher als sie erscheinen. Zum Selbstporträt in der zeitgenössischen Videokunst

99   Rotraut Pape
Befreite Bilder und Töne. Eintauchen in den 360° Full-Dome-Kosmos

115 Christian Janecke
Narrativer Grenznutzen. Format und Immersion beim 360°-Dome-Film

129	**Erkki Huhtamo** Illusion und ihre Umkehrung. Über die künstlerische Erforschung des stereoskopischen 3D
143	**Bjørn Melhus, Yves Netzhammer** Zeitsuchende Verbindungen. Zwei Interviews
159	**Eva Paulitsch, Uta Weyrich** Loop Narration und hyper-überlagerte Narrative
171	**Sabine Breitsameter** Hören gehen. Eine kleine Geschichte der Hörspaziergänge

---

187	**Martin Seel** Varianten filmischen Erzählens
197	**Vinzenz Hediger** Keine Eile, keine Zeit. Zur Frage der richtigen Dauer eines Films
211	**Juliane Rebentisch** Erzählung des Lebens. Die Filmbiographie und ihre Dekonstruktion in Todd Hayne's *I'm Not There*
235	**Sabine Nessel, Winfried Pauleit** Konstruktionen des Digitalen Films. Ästhetik, Narration, Diskurs
251	**Martin Gessmann** Transmediales Storytelling und die neue Produktsprache im Film. Oder: Was geschieht, wenn sich auch noch die Dinge zu Wort melden.
269	**Jos Diegel** Spoileralarm!: Immer mußt du etwas machen, was keinen Anfang und kein Ende hat, und irgendwelchen Kleinkram in großen Bildern zeigen

275 Steffen Huck, Diana Iljine, Sir Peter Jonas
Eine narrative Revolution

285 Christine Lang
»Gonna Break Bad?«
Über *Implizite Dramaturgie* in *Breaking Bad*

299 Alain Bieber
Tausendundein #Neuland

305 Markus Kuhn
Von einsamen Mädchen, Prom-Queens und ›coolen Säuen‹. Die Webserie als neue audiovisuelle Erzählform im Internet

325 Michel Reilhac
Einen Gang hochschalten. Wo stehen wir hinsichtlich des aktuellen Aufkommens des interaktiven Geschichtenerzählens?

341 Claudia Söller-Eckert
Transmedia Storytelling und Participation Experience

361 Ramón Reichert
Social Media Storytelling

381 Stephan Günzel
Bild und Erzählung im Computerspiel

391 Alan N. Shapiro
Software Code als Expanded Narration

409 Jonas Englert, Norman Hildebrandt
Mütter, lasst uns wieder nach Hause kommen! Diese Freiheit macht uns Angst.

»... ungefähr einmal alle hundert Jahre wurde sich jeder der Sache bewußt daß jeder dahin gelangt war andere Dinge zu tun das heißt dahin gelangt war die gleichen Dinge auf eine andere Art zu tun auf eine Art die so anders war daß ein jeder dahin gelangen konnte diese Sache zu wissen wissen daß es eine wirklich andere Art war und daher natürlich eine andere Art die gekommen war um zu bleiben.«
Gertrude Stein

Vorwort

Bernd Kracke

Marc Ries

Im Zusammenhang mit der Ausarbeitung einer Programmatik für die erste *B3 Biennale des Bewegten Bildes* in Frankfurt am Main (30.10.–3.11.2013), die als ihr Referenzthema *Expanded Narration. Das Neue Erzählen* auswies und der Ahnung folgte, »daß es eine wirklich andere Art« ist, mit der mediale Techniken heute zu erzählen ermöglichen, ist auch die Idee zu dieser Publikation ›aufgeblitzt‹. In Umkehrung des Benjamin'schen Bildes einer Vergangenheit, »das vorbeihuscht«, sollten mit einer Sammlung unterschiedlich motivierter Texte die Bilder jener zukünftigen Erzählwelten bedacht werden, die bereits in der Gegenwart an vielen Orten »vorbeihuschen«, die wir miterleben und vor allem auch mitgestalten, deren Feinstruktur und Einwirkungen auf das gesellschaftliche und individuelle Gewebe zurzeit jedoch nur unmerklich und unscharf in ihrem Gebrauch sichtbar sind.

Auf zwei Ebenen ist das Expandieren neuer Erzählformate im Zusammenhang mit dem Bewegtbild heute zu beobachten. Da sind zum einen die Serienformate im Fernsehen (und im Netz), mit denen über viele Folgen hinweg ein Erzählraum exploriert wird, dem ungewöhnliche, dramaturgische Potentiale zukommen. Hinzu kommen die über ein *transmediales Erzählen* provozierten Überschreitungen der Werk- und Mediengrenzen, deren Einbinden der Zuschauer in die Dramaturgie irritierende Hybride aus Autorenschaft und kollektiver Partizipation anbietet. Und die in der Bildenden Kunst zu beobachtenden neuen Erzählweisen, die, gerade im Zusammenhang mit der schnellen Verfügbarkeit von Videotechniken, eine andere Politik der Bilder vorstellen. Zum anderen sind es aber auch die im Internet über (Video)Blogs und vor allem Plattformen wie *Facebook*, *Twitter*, *YouTube* evozierten Mikroerzählungen, die ihre User und deren Lebensformen mit den visuellen und auditiven Formen der alltäglich benutzten Medien untrennbar verbinden und die als *Social Media Storytelling* dem früher intimen Akt der Selbsterzählung eine bemerkenswerte, wenngleich auch widersprüchliche Öffentlichkeit ermöglichen.

Dieses Buch versteht sich selbst als *Erzählung*, eine polychrome Erzählung aus verschiedenen Textgenres, die gegenstands- und disziplinenübergreifend auf die neuen

Phänomene reagieren. Es sind Notizen, Beobachtungen und emphatische Besprechungen derjenigen, die unmittelbar an der Hervorbringung oder Ausstellung der neuen Narrative beteiligt sind; es sind essayistische Spekulationen, präzise Analysen und theoretische Modelle, die aus Literatur- und Medienwissenschaft, Philosophie und Kunstwissenschaft jene Werke und Prozesse befragen, die diese Narrative auszeichnen und zu einem Brennpunkt vieler kultureller und sozialer Bewegungen machen. Dabei changiert die Perspektive unentwegt, sei diese nun eine der Autorenschaft, der »Dividuen« oder des jeweiligen Gegenstands; also finden sich in dieser Kompilation Darstellungen medien-affinen, literarischen Schreibens, neuer Filmnarrative und videokünstlerischer Erzählweisen, von Fernsehserien, Computerspielen, transmedialen Produktionen, Mikronarrativen im Sozialen Netz oder »expressiven« Codes. Zudem sind drei literarische Texte eingestreut, die innerhalb ihrer je singulären Schreibformen über diese im Gesamt des Aufbruchs zu neuen Erzählwelten Auskunft geben.

Wir freuen uns sehr, dass sich 30 Autoren(gruppen) bereit erklärt haben, Gertrude Steins Verweis auf die kulturelle Zeit, die sich alle hundert Jahre erneuere, im Zusammenhang mit dem *Neuen Erzählen* aufzugreifen und diese Publikation im Einklang mit den Erkundungen der *B3 Biennale des Bewegten Bildes* zu ermöglichen. Den Autoren und Autorinnen dieser ersten Allianz gebührt unser großer Dank, ebenso wie den Trägern, Förderern und Partnern.

Wohin mit der Kamera?
B3, die 1.

Bernd Kracke

Es war ein stummer Urknall, der fast zeitgleich in Chicago und Paris, in New York und Berlin ein neues Universum begründete. Das Publikum in den Cafés und Varietés kam aus dem Staunen nicht heraus, manche waren schockiert. Berichtet wird von Zuschauern, die in Panik aus dem Raum rannten, die unter den Tisch krochen und hinter Stühlen Schutz suchten, als sie in dem Film *Ankunft des Zuges* eine Lokomotive auf sich zukommen sahen. Sofern man von einem Film überhaupt sprechen kann.

Südfrankreich. Ein kleiner Bahnsteig in der Sommersonne. Aus der Entfernung nähert sich in rasantem Tempo eine Dampflok, wird ununterbrochen größer und größer, ein schwarzes Ungeheuer, Katastrophe droht. Beängstigend nah fährt der Zug vorbei und kommt zum Stehen. Aufatmen. In schöner Gelassenheit steigen die Reisenden aus und ein. Das war's. Nur eine einzige Einstellung, nur 47 Sekunden und trotzdem ein in der Tat bahnbrechendes Ereignis. Seitdem hat sich unser Horizont um ein Vielfaches erweitert. Die Linse der Kamera ist unser drittes Auge geworden.

Expansion eines jungen Universums

Die legendäre Zugszene der Gebrüder Lumière, nur eine kleine Impression mit Happy End, besitzt bis heute ihre ganz spezielle Magie. Dagegen war die Mehrzahl der Filmchen schlichtweg Schaubudenspektakel, allerdings mit einer sensationellen Wirkung. Die Leute lachten, jubelten, johlten, applaudierten. Die Sache war ihr Geld wert.

Von der wachsenden Begeisterung bis zur Wachstumsbranche war es denn auch nicht allzu weit. Der Kreislauf von Investieren, Kasse machen, erneut Investieren kam in Schwung. Die unaufhaltsame Expansion eines jungen Universums konnte beginnen.

Tatsächlich gab es bald in jeder Stadt ein Kinohaus, das sich *Universum* nannte. Premieren wurden gefeiert und kritisiert, Schauspieler avancierten zu Stars. Ständig gab es neuen Gesprächsstoff: »Schon gesehen?« Das Bewegtbild wurde

– mit allem, was dazu gehörte – zu einem Thema, das die Gesellschaft bewegte. Das einstige Schaubudenspektakel entwickelte sich zu einer neuen, unwiderstehlichen Kunstform, die weit über ihre alten Grenzen hinaus expandierte.

Das Bewegtbild befreite sich aus den Kinos und expandierte via TV in die Wohnzimmer. Es befreite sich aus den Wohnzimmern, Büros und Museen und expandiert jetzt via Internet, Mobile, Immersion in die Allgegenwärtigkeit. Es bedient jedes Anspruchsniveau. Es ist eine entscheidende Schnittstelle zwischen Technologie und Kultur geworden – und baut seinen Einfluss immer weiter aus. Es beeinflusst und erweitert die Möglichkeiten der Musik und Bildenden Kunst, der Forschung und Lehre, der Medien, kurz der Kommunikation insgesamt. Jeder, der will, kann sich jederzeit einbringen.

Powerplayer Publikum

»Jeder hat eine Geschichte zu erzählen«, sagte Woody Allen, »eine mindestens.« Ist zwar schon ein paar Tage her, lieber Woody, aber wer hätte damals gedacht, dass Du ausnahmsweise keinen Witz machst, sondern die Zukunft voraussagst? Vermutlich geht es den Leuten heute ähnlich wie Dir, als Du sechzehn warst. Gags schreiben, Drehbücher schreiben und dann die Leidenschaft für Stand-up Comedians. Aber immer nur zugucken, immer nur Publikum sein? Schwierig für das hellwache Gehirn, schließlich haben auch Bewegtbilder ihre Nebenwirkungen. Erstens: das Lernen durch Beobachten. Zweitens: die Motivation zur Nachahmung.

Mittlerweile hat sich das lernende und motivierte Publikum zum größten Produzenten der Welt gemausert. Millionen von Bewegtbildbeiträgen gehen jeden Tag auf Sendung. Manche sind sogar lustig. Dahinter steckt nicht immer ein explizites Geschäftsmodell, vielmehr zeichnet sich ein neues Sozialverhalten ab. Aber vielleicht ist es gar nicht so neu. Vielleicht zeigt sich das gute, alte Mitteilungsbedürfnis lediglich in einer neuen Form. Smartphones und Apps ermöglichen kurze, mitunter erstaunliche Einblicke ins Leben. Unsere Welt scheint phantastischer zu sein als gedacht. Umgekehrt entdecken arrivierte Regisseure

Streaming als zukunftsfähige Vertriebsform und drehen Filme für Smartphones.

Jeder kann eine Kamera in die Hand nehmen. Und dann?

Dann wird es unendlich überraschend und faszinierend. Mit der Kamera zu erzählen, ist eine Sache der Einstellung. Der eine hält drauf und überlässt es dem Zufall. Zufall? Was aussieht wie Zufall, kann auch etwas anderes sein. Instinkt. Eingebung. Ein Gefühl für die Situation, für den entscheidenden Moment, für das Ereignis, das sich anbahnt, für den bezeichnenden Augenblick. Ein Talent, wie Künstler es haben. Eine Gelinggarantie allerdings gibt es nicht.

Deshalb gibt es die anderen, die am liebsten nichts dem Zufall überlassen möchten. Sie stellen sich die schlichte Handwerkerfrage: Wohin mit der Kamera? Von welchem Standpunkt aus sollen die Handlungsschritte, die Szenen, die Sequenzen erzählt werden? Aus welchen Blickwinkeln setzt sich die Geschichte zusammen? Und überhaupt: Was ist eine gute Geschichte, und wie erzählt man sie am besten?

Gerade, wenn es um die Erzählkunst in bewegten Bildern geht, sind Handwerk und Philosophie kaum voneinander zu trennen. Im Kleinen zeigt sich das Große, im Großen das Ganze. Es ist nicht kompliziert, nur ein wenig komplexer als es aussieht, vor allem, wenn man dem Publikum serienmäßig ein befriedigendes Erlebnis verschaffen will.

Zwischen alter und neuer Geschichte: *B3*

Viele der Fragen, die wir uns immer wieder stellen, sind bereits beantwortet, nicht endgültig, aber ansatzweise. Die letzten zehn Jahrzehnte haben uns eine ungemein facettenreiche Erzähltradition hinterlassen: experimentierfreudig und ausdifferenziert. Wir können zu den Vorläufern stehen, wie wir wollen. Aber ignorieren können wir sie nicht. Wie jede Geschichte hat auch das aktuelle Bewegtbild-Geschehen eine

Vorgeschichte, die eine Weiterentwicklung geradezu herausfordert.

Hier, an dieser Grenze zwischen alter Geschichte und neuer Geschichte, ist die *Biennale des bewegten Bildes* 2013 verortet. Hier stellt sie ihre Kamera auf. Insbesondere das *B3-Festival,* der *B3-Parcours* und der *B3-Campus,* aber auch dieses Buch werden versuchen, durch die kritische Auseinandersetzung mit Vergangenheit und Gegenwart die neuen Bedürfnisse, neuen Sehnsüchte, neuen Träume und neuen Themen aufzuspüren. Neu von Grund auf? Nun, es ist wie mit den alten und neuen Medien; die alten sind nicht totzukriegen. Die Kinoleinwand, bildgewaltig und soundverwöhnt, bleibt das Größte. Zudem gibt es andere Gründe, Neu und Alt nicht als ein Entweder-oder zu sehen, sondern als einen Prozess der Erneuerung.

Eine Erzählkunst, die nicht erzählt

Schauen wir uns die Sprache des bewegten Bildes an. Bis heute kennt sie keine Grammatik und kein festgeschriebenes Vokabular im herkömmlichen Sinn. Wozu auch? Die Welt steht ihr auch so offen. Worte müssen synchronisiert werden, Bilder nicht. Sie werden intuitiv wahrgenommen, müheloser und schneller als der Verstand denken kann. Bewegtbilder erzählen deshalb nicht im klassischen Sinne, erst recht nicht abstrakt. Stattdessen inszenieren sie konkret und anschaulich, von Einstellung zu Einstellung; und zwar alles, einschließlich der Poesie des Unsichtbaren, wie Gefühle, Motivationen, innere Haltungen. Alles äußert sich in Farbtönen und Klangfarben, im Spiel mit dem Licht, im Dialog, in der Stimmung, die in den Stimmen mitschwingt, in Mimik und Gestik, im Verhalten und in der Ereignisfolge. Das Publikum will sich selbst ein Bild machen und sich selbst überzeugen. »Erzähl mir nichts, sondern zeig es mir.« Es will sich spiegeln können.

Dabei ist das Publikum auf eine passive Art durchaus aktiv. Es fühlt mit, antizipiert, gestaltet mit, die ganze Zeit über. Als Leser malen wir uns die Geschichte aus, als Zuschauer erzählen wir uns die Geschichte aufgrund der Bild- und Ereignisfolge selber. Mitfühlen, Miterleben, Mitteilen: Auf dieser Grundlinie basiert vieles, so auch die Erzählkunst in bewegten Bildern, und daran dürfte sich in absehbarer Zukunft nicht viel ändern. Alles andere dagegen stößt immer wieder an seine Grenzen.

Die Standards von heute: Was sind sie morgen wert?

Das Neue Erzählen ist die Folge eines permanenten Veränderungsdruckes. Dieser Druck resultiert aus der Gleichzeitigkeit der Gegensätze auf allen Kanälen in allen Medien. Qualität und Quote konkurrieren gnadenlos. Diese Vielfalt und Reizfülle sorgen inzwischen für einen geradezu irren Wahrnehmungswettbewerb. *Transmedia* ist das neue Zauberwort. Aber das Publikum kann seine Zeit und Aufmerksamkeit nur jeweils einem Ereignis schenken. Doch welchem? Gäbe es hier nur die eine Antwort, bräuchte es weder dieses Buch noch die *B3*. Wir leben in Zeiten der Differenzierung und Individualisierung. Versuch und Irrtum beherrschen die Entwicklung auch weiterhin.

Etablierte Akteure haben zwar ihre Erfolgsrezepte, teilweise bis auf die Minute durchgetaktet, nicht selten in dogmatischen Formaten. Doch gerade die erfolgreichen Standards werden sofort und so oft kopiert, bis nichts mehr geht. Auserzählt und sattgesehen. Etwas anderes muss her. Das kreative Denken vernetzt sich neu.

Vor diesem komplexen und dynamischen Hintergrund ist die *Biennale des bewegten Bildes* 2013 ein erster Versuch, die Vielfalt und erweiterten Möglichkeiten des Neuen Erzählens aus den unterschiedlichsten Perspektiven einzufangen und zu präsentieren. Vielleicht gelingt es, die Kamera neu zu positionieren und auf eine neue Art durch den Sucher zu blicken. Denn das gehört zu den Voraussetzungen für ein Neues Erzählen: ein neues Sehen, eine neue Perspektive, ein anderes Denken.

Bernd Kracke
lehrt als Professor für Elektronische Medien seit 1999 an der Hochschule für Gestaltung (HfG) Offenbach und ist seit 2006 deren Präsident. Von 2001 bis 2006 leitete er den Fachbereich Visuelle Kommunikation. Er gründete 2000 das *CrossMediaLab* als Forschungs- und Experimentalplattform zur Vernetzung analoger und digitaler Technologien sowie deren innovativen Einsatz im Kontext von Kunst und Gestaltung. Dabei stützte er sich auf Erfahrungen aus seinen Tätigkeiten am M.I.T. Cambridge/USA (1979–1985) und der Kunsthochschule für Medien Köln (1990–1999) sowie aus seiner Praxis als selbständiger Mediengestalter und Medienkünstler. Seit 2008 ist er Präsidiumssprecher der Hessischen Film- und Medienakademie (hFMA), dem Netzwerk der 13 hessischen Hochschulen. 2012 übernahm Bernd Kracke die Gesamtleitung der von ihm mitinitiierten *B3 Biennale des bewegten Bildes* Frankfurt RheinMain.

Das Neue Erzählen

Marcel Schwierin

In der Bewegtbildkunst deutet sich ein grundlegender Wechsel an. Diese Beobachtung war auch ein wesentlicher Impuls für das Thema der *B3 Biennale des bewegten Bildes* 2013.

Seit der Jahrhundertwende war Videokunst durch ein Genre geprägt, das vor allem aus dem Film bekannt ist, dem Dokumentarischen. Nicht nur haben viele Künstler dokumentarische Formate und Methoden verwendet, auch klassische Dokumentarfilmer wie zum Beispiel Harun Farocki tauchten im Ausstellungs- und Biennalenkontext auf. Schaut man sich jedoch die neuesten Einreichungen gerade auch junger Künstler zu aktuellen Festivals an, so scheint es, als ob die Dominanz des beobachtenden Blickes durch eine neue Lust am Erzählen abgelöst werde. Die Spanne ist dabei weit gestreut, sie beginnt bei der subtilen Fiktionalisierung des Dokumentarischen und endet bei dem fiktivsten aller filmischen Genres, der Science Fiction, die eigentlich großen Hollywood-Studios und der Spieleindustrie vorbehalten war. Sollte diese noch sehr vorläufige Beobachtung – es geht hier vor allem um die letzten zwei bis drei Jahre – zutreffen, gäbe es also tatsächlich mehr narrative Arbeiten in der Bewegtbildkunst, so stellte sich die Frage nach dem Warum. Woher kommt das neue Interesse der Kunst am fiktionalen, ja am phantastischen Format?

Die dokumentarische Kunst

Wie so oft in der Geschichte der Medien, entstand die Dominanz der dokumentarischen Videokunst durch einen technischen Impuls. Dokumentarfilm war früher eine aufwendige Angelegenheit, das Team bestand normalerweise aus Regisseur, Kameramann und Tonmann. Teuer wurde das Format auch durch das berüchtigte Drehverhältnis, auf eine Minute im fertigen Film kamen oft 10, 20 oder mehr Minuten Filmmaterial. Damit war der Dokumentarfilm weitgehend dem professionellen Filmbetrieb vorbehalten. Das änderte sich grundlegend mit der Einführung der digitalen Filmtechnik. Die halbautomatischen Videokameras machten ein Team (fast) überflüssig, das Material war praktisch gratis, und der heimische Rechner ersetzte das Studio. Damit wurden die klassischen Dokumentarfilmformate auch für Künstler erschwinglich, und die dokumentarische Videokunst wurde zum zentralen Medium der Biennalen.

Die reale und die virtuelle Welt

Gleichzeitig entstand im Internet das, was man als die »virtuelle Welt« verhandelte. Auch wenn es sich dabei am Anfang vielleicht mehr um eine Mischung aus Hype und Marketing als um ein reales Phänomen handelte, so war doch unverkennbar, dass sich hier eine völlig neue Form der Informations- und Wirklichkeitsvermittlung auftat, die sich ästhetisch in einer übersteigerten Künstlichkeit äußerte. Das Dokumentarische in der Kunst war daher auch eine Reaktion auf diese virtuelle Welt und ihre phantastischen Versprechungen einer Loslösung von irdischen Mühen – man denke nur an den Hype um den sogenannten Cybersex. Je abgehobener sich das neue Leitmedium gab, desto mehr erdete sich die dokumentarische Kunst. Sie verweigerte sich dem Internet aber nicht nur ästhetisch, sondern auch medial: Alles Mögliche findet man im Netz, nur nicht die Produkte des limitierten Kunstbetriebes. Darin liegt aber auch der Grundwiderspruch der dokumentarischen Kunst – die Limitierungen des Marktes konterkarieren die aufklärerische Absicht. Sozialkritik wird Business, Massenmedium wird Edition.

Die Professionalisierung des Kollektivs

War die digitale Videokamera verantwortlich für die Entwicklung des künstlerischen Dokumentarfilms, so markiert ein weiterer technologischer Schritt den Übergang zum Dokumentarfilm des Kollektivs: das Handy. Seit die Bildqualität der kleinen Geräte sogar für große Leinwände ausreicht und allemal gut genug ist für Monitore, wird fast jeder Zeitzeuge zu einem potentiellen Dokumentarfilmer. Über Portale wie *Mosireen*, die wiederum auf Plattformen wie *YouTube* und *Vimeo* basieren, werden diese Handyfilme editiert, teilweise sogar öffentlich – *Mosireen* stellt zunächst das Rohmaterial online und erst in der Folge die geschnittene Fassung. Damit bekommt der Dokumentarfilm eine direkte Qualität von der Straße, die weder von klassischen Fernsehsendern und Dokumentarfilmteams noch von einzelnen Künstlern gewährleistet werden kann. Die Verbreitung dieser Filme richtet sich wiederum direkt nach dem Interesse des Publikums, da kein kommerzieller Filter – sei es Sendeplatz oder Galerie-Edition – zwischen den Produzenten und den Zuschauer geschaltet ist. Angesichts dieser Entwicklung verliert der künstlerische Dokumentarfilm, der seine besondere Qualität auch daraus bezog, dass er von Produzenten, Redaktionen und Förderern relativ unabhängig war, durchaus an Bedeutung.

Geschichten ohne Ende

Parallel zu dieser Entwicklung des Dokumentarischen vollzieht sich ein Wandel in der filmischen Erzählung. Lange war diese vom Kinofilm als Leitmedium dominiert, dem das Fernsehen als Drittverwertung (dazwischen lag noch die DVD) und Hersteller zweitklassiger Bewegtbilder hinterherhinkte. Das hat sich mit den neuen Serienformaten, wie *The Wire*, *Mad Men* oder *Breaking Bad* geändert. Zumindest temporär lösen sie den Spielfilm als diskursbestimmendes Medium ab. Ihre besondere Qualität liegt darin, dass sie in der Entwicklung der Erzählung und ihrer Charaktere auf die Reaktionen der Zuschauer reagieren können, somit ein gewisses Maß an Interaktivität gewährleisten. Darüber hinaus sind sie, anders als das Kino, kein Raum außerhalb des eigenen Lebens, in dem der Zuschauer die Phantastik erlebt, die er im realen Leben vermisst, sondern sie treten in das Leben der Menschen hinein, sowohl durch die Apparatur des wohnzimmerlichen Fernsehers als auch durch die Begleitung der Charaktere über viele Staffeln hinweg. Serienhelden sind weniger ferne Abenteurer, sondern eher Freunde oder Verwandte, deren Lebensweg man aus Neugier und persönlicher Anteilnahme verfolgt. Entsprechend intensiv werden Serien und ihre Charaktere auch in den Social Media diskutiert, und wie Politiker müssen sich ihre Autoren inzwischen für ihre dramaturgischen Entscheidungen öffentlich rechtfertigen.

Die millionenfache Erzählung des Selbst

Doch auch diese epischen und weltweit vertriebenen Formate sind klein, verglichen mit dem Netzwerk an Erzählungen, die im Rahmen der Social Networks entstehen: »*Facebook* is all about the individual and collective experiences of you and your friends. It's filled with hundreds of millions of stories.« (Selbstbeschreibung) Mit der 2011 eingeführten Timeline-Funktion, die inzwischen in der Nutzung sogar obligatorisch ist, werden die Einträge der Nutzer automatisch in eine chronologische Erzählung ihres (medialen) Lebens verwandelt. Da die Nutzer wissen, dass das von ihnen Eingestellte bis zu einem gewissen Grade öffentlich ist, kann man es mit den traditionellen autobiographischen Formaten wie Tagebuch oder Fotoalbum nicht mehr vergleichen. Die Menschen dokumentieren in *Facebook* nicht einfach ihr Leben, sie schaffen idealisierte Abbilder ihrer selbst, eine weit subtilere Form des Avatars als etwa die plumpen Animationen aus *Second Life*. In diese neuen Erzählungen des Selbst mischen sich dokumentarische und fiktionale Elemente zu einem ununterscheidbaren Dritten.

Das Neue Erzählen in der Bewegtbildkunst

Künstler nehmen diese verwobenen Formen auf und erzählen ihre Geschichten mit einer Vielzahl inszenierter und dokumentarischer Methoden. Drei Werke mögen dafür als Beispiele dienen.

Hassan Khan inszenierte in *Blind Ambition* (*documenta 13*) 27 Schauspieler an öffentlichen Plätzen in Kairo. Sie besprechen alles Mögliche, mal im Café, mal in einer Shopping Mall, mal auf der Straße. Der Betrachter erfährt über die ständig wechselnden Protagonisten und Orte nicht mehr, als ein zufällig mithörender Passant mitbekommen würde. Gefilmt wurde mit einem Smartphone, was den Bildern zum einen trotz ihrer sorgfältigen Komposition eine Aura des Zufälligen gibt und es dem Künstler zum anderen ermöglichte, seine Inszenierungen inmitten der dichten Öffentlichkeit Kairos und dennoch unbemerkt zu machen: Fragmente alltäglichen Lebens.

Ho Tzu Nyens komplexe Installation *The Cloud of Unknowing* (54. Biennale von Venedig) basiert auf einem Buch des französischen Philosophen Hubert Damisch über die Funktion der Wolke in Gemälden in der europäischen und chinesischen Kunst. Der Film erzählt die Begegnung von acht Charakteren mit wolkenartigen Erscheinungen in ihren Wohnungen. Auch hier bleibt die Narration extrem fragmentarisch, die einzelnen tableauxartigen Episoden ähneln eher den – ebenfalls sehr narrativen – Fotografien eines Jeff Wall als den normierten Erzählstrategien des Spielfilms. Der Soundtrack besteht aus 200 miteinander verflochtenen Popsongs zum Thema, wie eine remixte Playlist der globalen Cloud.

Laura Horellis Vater war Diplomat, so reiste die Familie viel. Über mehrere Arbeiten spürt sie den Fragmenten ihrer Kindheit nach, manchmal durch die Orte, an denen sie gelebt hat, manchmal durch Film- und Fotodokumente. In ihrem Voice-over adressiert sie direkt die Protagonisten ihrer Filme. In *Haukka-Pala* (2009) versucht sie, über TV-Aufzeichnungen einer finnischen Ernährungsshow, deren Hauptdarstellerin ihre früh verstorbene Mutter war, Kontakt zu ihr aufzunehmen. Zwei Jahre später dreht sie in *The Terrace* an dem ehemaligen Haus ihrer Familie in Nairobi, sie sucht die damaligen Kontakte der Familie vor Ort, das Kindermädchen, die Nachbarn. Ihre Mutter taucht in diesem Film nur am Rande in einigen Fotografien auf, während sie in ihrer neuesten Arbeit *A Letter to Mother* (2013) wieder die Hauptfigur wird. So fragmentarisch die einzelnen Filme in ihren Erinnerungen sind, so episch werden sie in ihrer Gesamtheit – wie in einem Familienroman oder eben einer Serie wechselt die Stellung der Protagonisten in den verschiedenen Teilen des Werkes.

All diesen Arbeiten gemeinsam ist der Wechsel zwischen den verschiedenen künstlerischen Strategien. Das Dokumentarische verschwindet nicht, es wird eines von vielen Momenten der Erzählung. Orte, Personen und Handlungen werden in ihrer medialen Bedingtheit reflektiert, ohne dass das Medium jemals die McLuhan'sche Zentralbedeutung wie in früheren Epochen der Videokunst bekäme. Diese Reflexionen wiederum werden die fragmentarischen Elemente der neuen Narration, die sich, gerade weil sie nichts wirklich auserzählt, jederzeit in alle Richtungen entwickeln kann. Darin liegt ihre erzählerische Freiheit und ihre besondere Faszination.

Marcel Schwierin
ist Kurator, Filmemacher und Co-Gründer der Werkleitz Biennale, der Experimentalfilmdatenbank *cinovid* und des Arab Shorts Festivals in Kairo. Filme u.a.: *Die Bilder* (Experimentalfilm, 1994), *Ewige Schönheit* (Dokumentarfilm, 2003). Er kuratiert regelmäßig Filmprogramme für Goethe-Institute, Werkleitz Biennalen, die Internationalen Kurzfilmtage Oberhausen und andere. Seit 2010 ist er der Film- und Video-Kurator der *transmediale*.

Erzählen im Netz

Marc Ries

1

Viele Kinderbücher sind, wie die meiste andere Literatur, im Modus der Vergangenheit geschrieben. Ich meine nicht das Märchen, das ja seine fiktionale Unangreifbarkeit über einen starken Zeitsprung, »Vor langer Zeit...«, gewährleisten muss. Sondern die vielen Geschichten, die von ihrem Sujet aus eine Parallelgegenwart entwerfen, also eine Komplizenschaft mit dem Leben der Kinder andeuten und dennoch im Präteritum ihren Fortgang erzählen. Die Geschichten sind ja im Moment des Lesens auch bereits abgeschlossen, sie befinden sich »in« einem Buch zwischen zwei Deckeln. Beim Vorlesen der Geschichten bin ich von dieser Setzung des »Vorhergegangenen« immer wieder von Neuem irritiert. Ich forme dann Sätze in die Gegenwart um, doch nach einer Weile, da diese Korrektur ja eine zusätzliche Aufmerksamkeit voraussetzt und vom eigentlichen Lesefluss abhält, falle ich wieder in die vorgegebene Vergangenheit der Geschichte zurück. Ich habe den Eindruck und Verdacht, dass das Zurückversetzen der Geschichte in eine frühere Zeit es dem Kind erschwert, in die Geschichte einzutauchen, Teil der Geschichte selber zu werden. Die erzählte Zeit verweist auf einen auktorialen Erzähler, der es verbietet, dass seine Leser oder Zuhörer quasi gleichberechtigt zu ihm den Erzählfaden aufnehmen und ihm folgen. Die Vermutung, ein Kind – oder doch nur ich selbst? – liebe es, an der unmittelbaren Gegenwart eines Geschehnisses teilzunehmen und sich als ein Mitspieler der erzählten Handlung zu erfahren, kann ich natürlich nicht überprüfen, nehme aber wahr, dass es den Kindern in ihren eigenen Erzählungen, ihren kleinen Alltagserfindungen, sehr wohl darauf ankommt, sich in ihrer Gegenwart mit fiktiven Geschwistern und handelnden Tieren und Puppen zu umgeben, die als Erzählte – im Präsens – Anteil an ihrem Leben nehmen. Auch gibt es in ihren jeweiligen kleinen Geschichten keine Probleme, Tag und Nacht in ganz kurzer Zeit aufeinanderfolgen zu lassen – dies ja womöglich ein wesentlicher Grund für die Unterscheidung einer erzählten Zeit, die vergangen ist, und einer gestaltenden Erzählzeit in der Literatur. Mit Beginn einer medialen Erziehung treffen die Kinder jedoch auf zwei unterschiedliche Zeittechniken in

Erzählungen. Da sind zum einen die Filme, die ihre erzählte Zeit gleichfalls gerne von der Jetztzeit absetzen – Michel von Lönneberga lebte auch »vor langer Zeit«, obwohl die Figur als zeitlose auftritt. Dann aber sind es Serien, die Ziel medialen Begehrens werden, zunächst vor allem Animationen oder animationsähnliche Filme, deren erzählte Handlungen genau dann passieren, wenn die Kinder zuschauen, etwa die *Teletubbies* oder die *Simpsons*. Zwischen den jungen Zuschauern und ihren Lieblingsfiguren wirken Bindungskräfte, die wesentlich über eine geteilte Gegenwart, eine Unmittelbarkeit und Gleichzeitigkeit im Erfahren von Wirklichkeit hier und dort, sich voranentwickeln.

Jeden Tag um die gleiche Zeit treffen viele Heranwachsende in Springfield ein, im Hause von Homer Simpson und seiner Familie. Sie alle tun das Gleiche wie die Simpsons, nämlich fernsehen. Sie verbringen den Alltag mit Homer, Marge, Bart, Lisa und Maggie, den westlichen Alltag einer für heroische oder glamouröse Identifikationen kaum geeigneten Durchschnittsfamilie mit großen und kleinen Freuden, Problemen, Absurditäten. Sie begegnen einer Vielzahl von aktuellen Konflikten und kulturellen Referenzen, die in die Serie eingebaut sind, vermutlich haben viele zu Hause in ihrem Zimmer Poster der Simpsons hängen, Kakaobecher und T-Shirts mit Bart, gar eine Karte von Springfield. Denn dieses Leben, das Kollektiv der Simpsons, ist Teil ihrer eigenen Kartographie, ihres eigenen Lebens geworden, mediale Beziehungen (keine »Kopien«), die die Heranwachsenden mit ihrer eigenen Gegenwart verknüpfen und also im gestimmten Zwischenraum der Medien auch das Selbsterzählen stimulieren.[1]

Ab einer weiteren Verdichtung medialer Umgebungen – Rechner(Spiele), Mobiltelefon, Internet – werden die (Selbst)Erzählungen befreit von ihrer Gefolgschaft den Systemmedien und deren Vorbildern gegenüber. Mit *Facebook*, *YouTube*, SMS und *Twitter* und einigem mehr kann der Heranwachsende seinen Mediengebrauch individuieren und teilnehmen an Sozialen Netzen, in welchen er auf unendlich viele andere Erzähler trifft und sich mit diesen in einer geteilten Gegenwart »alles Mögliche« teilt. Zum anderen wird er als Zeuge, als Mithervorbringender

[1] Siehe hierzu auch meinen Text: Homers Home. Einige Nachüberlegungen zum Verständnis von Heimat. In: Oliver Decker; Tobias Grave (Hg.): Kritische Theorie zur Zeit. Festschrift für Christoph Türcke. Springe 2008, S. 309–315.

und Mittragender der Zeitgeschichte Informant und Erzählender politischer ›Bewegungen‹, Erzählungen, die als direkte Abbildung von Krisen in Nachrichtenkanälen oder als ihre Nacherzählung und Kommentierung in Blogs Ereignisse vergegenwärtigen. Frage ist, wie denn das Neue Erzählen, das hier öffentlich wird, mit einem kulturellen Verständnis und einem kulturtheoretischen Begriff von Erzählung darstellbar ist und *wie* denn erzählt wird – was dieses von den Autoritäten der alten Erzählinstanzen, den Literaten wie den Journalisten, unterscheidet?

2

Erzählung ist was jeder über irgend etwas das auf irgendeine Weise geschehen kann geschehen ist geschehen wird auf irgendeine Weise zu sagen hat. (Gertrude Stein)

Voraussetzen möchte ich, dass (Selbst)Erzählen und Lebensgeschichte in einem notwendigen Verhältnis zueinander stehen, »dass narrative Strukturen aus der Art, wie Menschen ihr Leben leben, nicht wegzudenken sind«[2]. In vortechnischer Medienzeit gab es Autoritäten des Erzählens, die teils Master Narratives erzeugten, sich jedenfalls als eine öffentliche Instanz verstanden, und es gab die vielen einzelnen, kleinen Geschichten, die stets nur innerhalb der Kreise der Lebenswelten wanderten und oftmals nur an wenige Generationen geknüpft waren. Medientechniken wie Blogs, SMS, *Twitter*, die Aktivitäten auf *Facebook*, *YouTube*, *Flickr* folgen – auch – einem Erzählbegehren, bringen *liquide*, *versatile Erzählungen* hervor, gestalten narrative Aussagen, die einer anderen Diegese zusprechen, eine andere erzählte Welt beschwören, denn die aus literarischem Erzählen bekannten. Heute konkurrieren in gewisser Weise Systemerzählungen, die kulturindustriell – Kino, TV, Games – geformt sind, mit Erzählungen von Individuen, die in offenen, sozialen Mediensystemen nicht regulierbar fließen. Das Internet hat den traditionellen, zentralisierten Erzählungen die Alleinherrschaft genommen und bietet dem Strom der Alltagserzählungen und Lebensgeschichten die Möglichkeit, von Vielen medial produziert, gehört, gesehen zu werden. Doch greifen

[2] Dieter Thomä: Erzähle dich selbst. Lebensgeschichte als philosophisches Problem. Frankfurt am Main 2007, S. 23.

mittlerweile auch Systemerzählungen[3], das Transmedia Storytelling etwa, auf die angeschlossenen User für ihre Zwecke zu, binden sie in eine kooperative Struktur ein, die zumindest eine Ahnung von Mitautorenschaft und Eigensinn aufkommen lassen soll. Jedenfalls kann die erstaunliche Entwicklung von individuellen Narrativen im Netz als eine Bestätigung für »das narrative A priori des Sich-Einrichtens in der Welt« verstanden werden.[4]

Was ist ein Soziales Medium? Ein solches Medium ist ein Tausch und (selbst)reflexiven Austausch ermöglichendes und gestaltendes technisches Gefüge, ist also ein relationaler, uneigentlicher Raum, dessen Gebrauch vielen möglich ist. Soziale Medien erwarten, provozieren geradezu ihren permanenten Gebrauch. Die von den Techniken kontinuierlich emittierte Aufforderung, an andere zu schreiben, Bilder und Sounds zu verschicken und die der anderen wahrzunehmen, bewirkt eine Singularisierung der Botschaften, der Text- und Bildformen, erweitert, überhöht sie in eine erzählerische Materie, die aus den Berichten, was man gerade tut, den Kommentaren zum Zeitgeschehen, den Einblicken in intime Geschehen eine Erzählform des eigenen Lebens emergieren lässt, die sich anderen zuwendet, die Gleiches mit ihrem Leben tun. Vermutlich ist die Überraschung darüber, dass in den unendlich vielen Kommunikationen so wenig »faktuale« Informationen oder so viele redundante Inhalte zirkulieren, nur so lange eine solche, als die gewaltige Fabrikation von erzählten Welten voller Bruchstücke, Kontingenzen in diesen Kommunikationen nicht auf ihre eigentlich expressive oder auch existentielle Kraft hin erkannt worden ist.

Im Storyversum des Internet ist eine Umgewichtung zu beobachten von der die Geschichte formenden Diegese zum *Diskurs des Erzählens* und zum *narrativen Akt* selbst. Die Erzähltheorie von Gérard Genette hatte diese Dreiteilung eingeführt und als ihren eigenen Gegenstand den Diskurs, die Modalitäten des Erzählens, die narrative Aussage benannt; dem Erzählen in Sozialen Medien ist nun der narrative Akt selber auf eigentümliche Weise ins Zentrum der Handlung eingerückt. Bei Genette verbleibt der narrative Akt in einer gewissen Uneindeutigkeit; er meint zum einen die reale oder fiktive Situation, in der er erfolgt, zum anderen den Akt des Erzählens inmitten der eigenen

---

[3] Ich unterscheide zwischen »Systemerzählungen«, solchen, die in medien-industriellen Gefügen arbeitsteilig produziert werden, und »Individualerzählungen«, solchen, die – mittels Medientechniken – von Individuen eigenmächtig hervorgebracht werden.

[4] Siehe Albrecht Koschorke, Wahrheit und Erfindung. Grundzüge einer Allgemeinen Erzähltheorie. Frankfurt am Main 2012, S. 16.

Lebensgeschichte des Autors – die selber stets unbefragt bleiben muss, da sie von außerhalb nur triviale Einsichten in den Zusammenhang von Werk und Biographie zulässt.[5] Nun aber wird mit der narrativen Tätigkeit im Netz zugleich eine Umwertung dieser Instanzen und auch eine solche von Öffentlichkeit vorgeführt. Jedermann steht im Web 2.0 im Vollzug einer Öffentlichkeit, die ihm Autorenschaft zuspricht, da sie selber nur aus *Autoren* sich zusammensetzt. Während sich das Erzählen in den viel besprochenen neuen TV-Serien auf subtile Expansionen der Erzählmodalitäten einspielt, die Rollenverteilungen und das Werkverständnis aber annähernd gleich bleiben, wird sowohl in Sozialen Medien als auch mit transmedialen Erzählweisen die narrative Eigenlogik in ungewöhnlicher Weise mit dem narrativen Akt wirkmächtig erweitert.

Thesenhaft formuliert, sind die Erzählungen im Web 2.0 weniger bedeutsam im Zusammenhang mit einer kohärenten Geschichte, einer einfallsreichen *fabula* – hierin sind sie zumeist eher redundant, an Schemata orientiert, oder aber sie verlieren sich in Alltagschimären –, als mit der *Selbstermächtigung* eines Erzählers, einer Erzählerin in und mit einer Öffentlichkeit, die so noch nie zur Verfügung stand. Eine Öffentlichkeit, die immer und überall mit Individualmedien nutz- und darstellbar ist. Gleichermaßen wichtig ist, dass die Veröffentlichung der Mikronarrative im Wissen darüber passiert, dass die Adressaten nicht nur lesen, betrachten und hören, sondern selber schreiben, filmen und Musik losschicken. Ein jeder Erzähler im Universum des Social Media Storytelling produziert seine Erzählung jeweils für andere Erzähler, erwartet deren narrative Fragmente und erzeugt selbst wiederum neue. Damit ist das von wenigen für viele geschaffene Erzählen von Geschichten gekippt, relativiert zugunsten extrem produktiver, horizontaler Fabrikationen von Narrativen, die mediale Ereignisse ausformen, ohne die realen Ereignisse, auf die sie sich beziehen, exklusiv zu fokussieren. Das Erzählen und die Erzählung als mediales Ereignis werden bedeutsamer als die Geschichte und die sie motivierende Handlung. Von daher ist die Frage nach dem Begehren, das all die unzähligen narrativen Akte tagtäglich antreibt, wichtig, denn »Namen« haben die vielen Autoren und Autorinnen ja keine, das wissen sie und das ist auch

---

5 Siehe Gérard Genette: Die Erzählung. Paderborn 1998, S. 12.

nicht ihr Wunsch. Ebenso wenig, wie ihre Inhalte den Anspruch haben, Kunst oder Analyse zu sein. Insofern sind die Autobiographismen im Netz weniger von kulturellem Wert als für die Selbstwahrnehmung der Individuen in uneindeutigen Lebenszusammenhängen bestimmend. Wie gelingt nun die erwünschte Selbstermächtigung?

3

Erzählen [ist] ein in hohem Ausmaß unspezifisches Medium [...]; seine kulturelle Leistung liegt weniger im Trennen als im Verbinden. (Albrecht Koschorke)

Gerade die vielfältigen Erzählweisen im Netz bestätigen eine wesentliche Eigenheit aller medialen Kommunikation. Um sich mitzuteilen, bedarf es einer *Teilung* als Division und Segmentierung dessen, was gesagt und erzählt werden will. Das stark referentielle, also auf unmittelbares Geschehen bezogene Erzählen in Sozialen Netzen muss medientechnische Prozesse zulassen, die sich durch Partialisierung, Reduktion und Selektion definieren (dies trifft auf Affekte, die erzählt werden wollen, etwa auf die Innen-Referenzen von Dating-Foren, ebenso zu). Eine Handlung, ein Geschehen, das eine bestimmte Auswirkung hat, wird gemäß dem verwendeten Medium sowohl teilsinnlich (Sprache, Bild, Klang) reduziert als auch in Teile, Zeichen zerlegt werden müssen, die das Geschehen in dafür vorgesehene Formen übersetzen. Für die Sprache meint dies etwa die Sequentialisierung des Geschehens in Satzkonstruktionen mit definierten Teileelementen, für die Bildproduktion das Auswählen von Ausschnitten und Perspektiven, für den Ton das Selektieren der Klangquellen. Übertragen auf Online-Techniken ist dieser Prozess beispielsweise für Tweets oder Blog-Einträge so nachzuvollziehen, dass Informationen grundsätzlich in einer Tabellenstruktur segmentiert und in einer relationalen Datenbank gespeichert werden müssen. Erst über diese umfassenden Prozesse des *dividere*, des Unterteilens und Segmentierens, kann ein Mitteilen, eine Kommunikation erfolgen und ein Teilnehmen, ein *participere*, in Aussicht gestellt werden. Das Teilen ist jedoch auch auf der

Ebene des Informationsaustauschs wirksam. *Sharing* wird zu einer (über)lebensnotwendigen Aufgabe aller aktiven Social Web User. Vom *Like* auf *Facebook* über das Teilen von visuellen und auditiven Files und das Weitergeben von URLs lebt das Netz von einem aktiven Modus des Teilens. Dieses bewirkt ein von Medientechniken implizit formuliertes Angebot, das Kapital zu umgehen (P2P), die Identität zu relativieren (Nicknames, Avatare), die Gemeinschaft (*Second Life*) zu paraphrasieren.[6]

Die Frage, wie heute mit Neuen Medien erzählt wird, betrifft nicht mehr alleine den Modus des Erzählens, das *sjuzet* und den narrativen Akt, sondern die medialen Konditionen, die Handlungen im Netz rahmen, ermöglichen, ja evozieren, Protokolle also, Software-Programme und Share-Schnittstellen. Zu beobachten ist, dass Eigenschaften und Inhalte von Online-Erzählmedien, ihre Schreib- und Zeigetechniken wie ihre Veröffentlichungsangebote, über APIs (*Application Programming Interfaces*) zunehmend deterritorialisieren, zirkulieren zwischen unterschiedlichen Plattformen, aufgenommen werden von den imperialen Netzwerken wie *Facebook* oder *YouTube*, mit einem einfachen IFTTT-Code, *If This is Then That,* ausgestattet, das Teilen der Daten und Erzählungen gemäß den Verteilungswünschen der Akteure (Produzenten wie Leser, Schauende und Hörende) ermöglichen. Dies führt zu Wanderbewegungen der Botschaften, der Texte, Videos und Sounds, zwischen den Netzorten, es wird offensichtlich, dass es keinen eindeutigen Ursprung der Hervorbringung von Erzählungen mehr gibt, sondern dass diese an verschiedenen Orten gleichzeitig auftauchen, mitgeteilt und geteilt werden.

Das Erzählen im Netz übernimmt und verstärkt zudem die »ontologische Indifferenz« von Erzählungen.[7] Erzählen überspielt, ignoriert die für Funktionssysteme unerlässliche Grenze zwischen dem, was wahr, verbindlich, real ist, und dem, was fiktional, uneigentlich, Spiel, Täuschung ist. »Das Erzählen kann als Technik der Wissensübermittlung anerkannt oder verworfen werden, mit tieferen Wahrheiten im Bunde stehen oder den Makel der Betrügerei an sich tragen. Uneindeutigkeit hinsichtlich der Alternative wahr/unwahr betrifft also nicht nur den Inhalt der jeweiligen Einzelgeschichte, sondern ganz

---

6
Siehe zum Doppelsinn von Teilen in Netzdramaturgien meinen Text: »Zeigt mir, wen ich begehren soll«. Begegnung und Internet. In: Marc Ries, Hidegard Fraueneder, Karin Mairitsch (Hg.), dating. 21. Liebesorganisation und Verabredungskultur. Bielefeld 2007, S. 11–24.

7
Zur »ontologischen Indifferenz« siehe Koschorke (2012), S. 16 (wie Anm. 2).

allgemein die kulturelle Gültigkeit der symbolischen Transaktionen, bei denen von der Technik der Erzählens Gebrauch gemacht wird.«[8] Die ontologische Indifferenz medialen Erzählens ist Teil des Paktes zwischen den Erzählern im Netz auf den unterschiedlichsten hierfür vorgesehenen Ebenen. Sie berührt zum einen die »Ekstasen des Gewöhnlichen« in den vielen sozialen Räumen im Netz.[9] Allein, dass jemand eine Kamera in seinem Jugendzimmer aufstellt und sein Leben in kurzen Clips nacherzählt, seine oftmals unspektakuläre, durchschnittliche Existenz *als diese* kommentiert, bewirkt ein Heraustreten, ein Herauskippen aus ihr, also aus der Stasis, ohne dass nun diese Existenz eine außergewöhnliche würde. Man hat eher den Eindruck, als ob ihr Etwas-sein erst durch ihre Veröffentlichung auch eine *Etwas-Kontur* gewinnt. Da ändert es auch wenig, wenn diese Existenz als »inszenierte« entlarvt wird. *lonelygirl 15*, jene frühe Webserie der 16-jährigen Bree, die 2006 auf *YouTube* von ihrem zunächst normalen Alltag berichtete, zeigt den tatsächlichen Antrieb hinter der Ekstase: Auch nach der Enttarnung als Fiktion wurde die Serie fortgesetzt und blieb, obwohl es sich um ›Schauspiel‹ handelte, gerne gesehen. Es war die Geste der Extension, der Ekstase, die zählte, nicht ihr Wahrheitsgehalt.[10] »Als funktionsentlastete Sphäre gesellschaftlicher Produktion haben die Künste [und die Kulturindustrie; M.R.] fiktionale Darstellungsformen entwickelt, die ihnen deshalb einen freien Umgang mit Stoffen von zweifelhaftem Wahrheitswert erlauben, weil sie ihre ontologische Indifferenz, so scheint es, sozial folgenlos und damit unschädlich machen.«[11] Die Indifferenz hat, abseits von Wahrheits- oder deontologischen Fragen, im Territorium des Internet noch eine weitere Ausdehnung. Diese betrifft die Wahllosigkeit oder die Expansion der Motive und Themen, die *erzählbar* werden; die Erfahrbarkeit trifft hier auf die Erzählbarkeit einer Lebensform, die sich weniger an großen Fragen abmüht als an minoritären Suchbewegungen orientiert, ein Tasten im kleinen, jedoch allanwesenden Gestrüpp der näheren Umgebungen, in den Verstrickungen des Alltags, die von den Systemen kaum beachtet werden. Mit Vielen und über unendlich Vieles wird erzählt, das, als ›Information‹ verdichtet, zur Anreicherung und Fülle der Mikronarrative beiträgt, die im Sozialen

---

[8] Ebd., S. 17.

[9] Zu diesen »Ekstasen« siehe auch: Birgit Richard, Alexander Ruhl: Der »Tag« ist das Bild. »Ich«-Sharing im kollektiven Universum der visualisierten Schlagworte. In: Marc Ries et al. (Hg.) (2007), S. 173–192 (wie Anm. 6).

[10] Die Extension findet in der Formel »The extent to wich users…« ihre soziologische Übersetzung; vgl. hierzu die »honeycomb of social media« in: J.H. Kietzmann; K. Hermkens; I.P. McCarthy; B.S. Silvestre: Social media? Get serious! Understanding the functional building blocks of social media. In: Business Horizons 54, Nr. 3, 2011, S. 241–251.

[11] Koschorke (2012), S. 18 (wie Anm. 2).

Netz zu beobachten sind. Die Gleichgültigkeit oder auch Souveränität, mit der das Medium allem Zugang und Distribution ermöglicht, irritiert die alten Zentren der literarischen Sinnverwaltung, doch dessen Nutzen ist kaum abzuweisen. Hier mag die Media Richness Theory richtig liegen, die auf der Vermutung aufbaut, »that the goal of any communication ist the resolution of ambiguity and the reduction of uncertainty«, ein Ziel, das gerade von einer exzessiven Vervielfältigung von Narrativen motiviert ist.[12]

12
Siehe Andreas M. Kaplan; Michael Haenlein: Users of the world, unite! The challenges and opportunities of Social Media. In: Business Horizons 53, Nr. 1, 2010, S. 59–68.

4

Geschichten werden erzählt, um etwas zu vertreiben. Im harmlosesten, aber nicht unwichtigsten Falle: die Zeit. Sonst und schwererwiegend: die Furcht. In ihr steckt sowohl Unwissenheit als auch, elementarer, Unvertrautheit. (Hans Blumenberg)

In seinen ethnologischen Studien zur Sprache hat Bronislaw Malinowski einen fundamentalen Befund an den Anfang seiner Überlegungen zu einem »new type of linguistic use – phatic communion« gestellt:

»[...] to a natural man another man's silence is not a reassuring factor, but on the contrary, something alarming and dangerous [...]. The breaking of silence, the communion of words is the first act to establish links of fellowship, which is consummated only by the breaking of bread and the communion of food. The modern English expression, ›Nice day to-day‹ or the Melanesian phrase ›Whence comest thou?‹ are needed to get over the strange unpleasant tension which men feel when facing each other in silence. After the first formula, there comes a flow of language, purposeless expressions of preference or aversion, accounts of irrelevant happenings, comments on what is perfectly obvious [...] There can be no doubt that we have a new type of linguistic use – phatic communion. [...] Each utterance is an act serving the direct aim of binding hearer to speaker by a tie of some social sentiment or other. [...] ›phatic communion‹ serves to establish bonds of personal union between people brought together by the mere need of companionship and does not serve any purpose of communicating ideas.«[13]

Ich möchte Malinowskis Analyse und seine Begrifflichkeit des Phatischen in den Kontext Neuen Erzählens setzen und davon ausgehen, dass die essentielle Verunsicherung, die Malinowski ursprungserklärend an die Erfindung der neuen Begriffsformel setzt – »the strange unpleasant tension which men feel when facing each other in silence« –, nicht nur als Auslöser für eine anthropologische Beziehungsfigur gesehen, sondern auch als eine gesellschaftliche Symptomatik in Augenschein genommen werden kann, die uns heute allgegenwärtig ist. *Die Welt schweigt*, eine *Weltenstille* wird für den Zivilisationsprozess als eine konstitutive Bedrohung und ein Ausgangspunkt von Sprache, Musik und Lärm angenommen. Das Schweigen der Welt, das meint zum einen die prinzipielle Uneinnehmbarkeit von Natur, das Scheitern hermeneutischer Zudringlichkeit auf die Darstellbarkeit von Welt, die Grenzen hörenden und erklärenden Zugreifens auf Naturprozesse, das meint ein in Schweigen gewandter »Absolutismus der Wirklichkeit«, demgegenüber »der Mensch die Bedingungen seiner Existenz annähernd nicht in der Hand« hat.[14] Zum anderen ist die Stille – als semantische Leere – ein Effekt selbstproduzierter Abstraktion als Entsinnlichung von Daseiendem. Hierin muss das Schweigen in Analogie zu einem allgegenwärtigen *Rauschen* gesetzt werden, wovon das allerorten beklagte sinnexzedierende wie -ferne Rauschen der Bilder, Texte und Sounds berichtet. Im selbst hervorgerufenen, ubiquitären Lärm der hoch ökonomisierten Welt stellt sich die Grenzerfahrung einer überfordernden, alarmierenden, gefährlichen Unverständlichkeit, Hilflosigkeit, einer dissemantischen Stille, eines negativ besetzten Schweigens ein. Die Versuche, dieser Bedrohung entgegenzutreten, sind allemal assoziierbar mit dem fundamentalen Eingeständnis: *narrare necesse est*.

Malinowski spricht von einer phatischen Kommunion, die dem Schweigen antwortet. Wichtig ist, dass es nicht eine gerichtete Kommunikation ist, die hier vorgestellt wird, sondern eben eine »Kommunion«, als das jedem Zusammenkommen von

---

13
Bronislaw Malinowski: The problem of meaning in primitive languages. In: CK. Ogden; I.A. Richards: The meaning of meaning [1923]. Supplement I, S. 296–336. URL: http://faculty.washington.edu/cbehler/glossary/malinowsPM.html (Stand: 23.09.2013).

14
Hans Blumenberg: Arbeit am Mythos. Frankfurt am Main 1979, S. 9.

Menschen grundgelegte Begehren, die eigene *Anwesenheit* über eine Teilnahme an der Anwesenheit eines oder von anderen – sei diese Teilnahme nun symbolisch, nur bildlich oder rein auditiv artikuliert – mitzuteilen, sich dabei ein Stück weit von der eigenen Identität abzuteilen und eine Gemeinschaft auszubilden.

Dennoch ist die soziale Bindungskraft der Sprache gleichermaßen gekoppelt an eine Beziehung mit der (arte-)faktischen Welt, also nicht nur an eine Art medienkollektive Eucharistiefeier mit dem Anderen, sondern auch an eine Beschwörung der *Deixis*, indexikalischer Verweisakte also, die eine existentielle Situierung der – wie entfernt auch immer – Anwesenden ermöglichen, über das *ich, du, dort, hier...* diese und sich selber stets von Neuem mit der Welt verklammern.

Twitter ist wohl ein prägnantes Beispiel für diese Art von selbstreferentiellem Schreiben. Offenbar dient das Medium einer schnellen Weitergabe von Nachrichten als Tweets, also von 140 Zeichen-Nachrichten. Nun demonstriert aber alleine schon die Menge der von 300 Millionen aktiven Usern tagtäglich versandten Tweets, dass hier von ihren Urhebern weniger an eine konventionelle Kommunikation gedacht ist als an eine stenographische Weitergabe ihrer unmittelbaren Lebens- und Arbeitssituation, es sind minimale Sprechakte, die die Handlungen, als verursachte oder erlebte oder erlittene (man denke an die bürgerkriegsähnlichen Situationen weltweit), im jeweiligen Alltag spiegeln, Akte, die ihnen ermöglichen, sich ihrer territorialen Anbindung ebenso zu versichern wie sie ihrem Wunsch Ausdruck verleihen, nicht alleine zu sein, gegen das Schweigen – der Systeme, der Institutionen – die je singuläre Anwesenheit ihrer selbst und der Anderen zu behaupten.

Allgemein zu den medialen Erzählformen in Netzräumen ist zu sagen, dass es nicht das Handwerk und die formale Qualität sind, die diese Texte und Bilder antreiben, sondern jene früheste Begehrenspolitik des Individuums, (s)ein ephemeres, vereinzeltes, entschwindendes Geschehen mit der Aufzeichnung, mit der Kamera zu bezeugen, die Furcht zu vertreiben, das Schweigen zu bannen. Waren diese Bewegungen in der ersten Phase technischer Medien dem privaten Gebrauch vorbehalten oder der journalistischen Verwertung, so heute dem wuchernden

Kollektivraum eines allumfassenden und allgegenwärtigen Netzes. Und beide bedingen sich wechselseitig. Ein Medium treibt ein anderes an, in ihm sich gegenwärtig zu halten. Das Netz evoziert und provoziert eine ungehemmte textuelle und fotografisch-filmische Produktion als Rohstoff für seine Austauschszenarien. Der Online-Text und die digitale Fotografie wiederum kennen nicht das Paradigma des guten oder gelungenen Werkes, sie wollen einfach nur mitteilen, das aufzeichnen, was der Einzelne gerade sieht, erlebt und es dann schnellstmöglich publiziert und verbreitet sehen im globalen Netz. Auf diese Weise gelangen alle, beinahe alle Geschehnisse, die belanglosen wie die besonderen, als ihre Online-Existenz ein zweites Mal in die Welt.

Man kann diese technischen Errettungsphantasien mit einer Überlegung von Michel Foucault zur »photogenen Malerei« im 19. Jahrhundert erweitern: Mit dem Aufkommen der Fotografie hatten auch die anderen bildenden Künste den Auftrag, *hinter* oder *neben* ihrer Malerei, ihrer Zeichnung »das Bild selbst« zu suchen, ein Bild, das unabhängig von einem Träger, von Sprache und Syntax beständig zirkuliert, gleitet, auf Wanderung ist. In der Gegenwart ist es das Internet, das dazu drängt, alle möglichen »Bilder in Umlauf zu bringen, sie übergehen zu lassen, sie zu verkleiden, sie zu verformen, sie bis zur Rotglut zu erhitzen, sie einzufrieren, sie vielfältig zu übersetzen«[15]. Mit diesen Bildern erlebt auch der in mediale Formen übersetzte Körper, der handelnde, sich darstellende, verkleidende, verformende, also spielende Körper eine neue Attraktion in seinem Gebrauch *als Bild*.

[15] Michel Foucault: Die photogene Malerei (Präsentation). In: Ders.: Dits et Écrits. Schriften. Bd. 2: 1970–1975. Frankfurt am Main 2002, S. 872.

5

... glücklicherweise unterhaltsam. (Marcel Reich-Ranicki)

Es bleibt noch eine wichtige Frage: »Wie findet man sich mit sich selber zurecht, wenn man auf drei Instanzen ›verteilt‹ ist und dort jeweils als *alter ego* gefragt ist?« Die drei Instanzen, das ist der *Erzähler* der Geschichte (ob schreibend, filmend...), das ist der *Protagonist*, also derjenige, von dem erzählt wird, und es ist die *Person*, jene Instanz, mit der »die Erzählung über ihre eigenen Grenzen hinaus gerät«. Wenn auch »die drei Instanzen, die bei dieser Anwendung der Erzählung zusammenspielen, letztlich *einen* Menschen meinen, so ist die Identität, die hier angezielt wird, prekär«[16]. Die von Dieter Thomä entwickelten Modelle lassen zwei Variationen erkennen, die für die narrative Existenzweisen im Netz gleichfalls anwendbar sind. Ich will hier kurz auf sie eingehen.

Da ist jener Prozess der Selbsterzählung, der sich in Blogs oder auch auf *Facebook* aus dem Motiv der *Selbstfindung* und der *Selbsterfindung* heraus manifestiert. Dieserart nimmt sich der/die Erzählende als ein »Gegenstand« wahr, denn »das gegenständliche Selbst ist wohl Voraussetzung dafür, dass von ihm erzählt werden kann, zum anderen bleibt das, was man sich zugeschrieben hat und zuschreibt, in der textuellen Struktur gefangen, rückt von der handelnden Instanz ab. Auf dem Umweg über jene Vergegenständlichung kommt jemand zu der emphatischen Bekundung, wer ›er selbst‹ sei; genau darin bleibt er jedoch getrennt von dem, was sich bei ihm gerade tut oder was er tut«[17].

Demgegenüber kann »die Art, wie ein Mensch sein Leben führt, sich der Art, wie er es erzählt«, annähern. »Diese Annäherung findet insbesondere dann statt, wenn er etwas tut. Was eine Person erleidet, wahrnimmt, erfährt, fühlt – all das geht nicht so leicht in ihre narrative Selbstzuschreibung ein wie das, was sie tut (nachdem sie etwas getan hat und bevor sie etwas tun wird). Hier ist eine pragmatische Übersichtlichkeit, ein vorweg beschränkter Bedeutungszusammenhang gegeben, der in einer Erzählung ziemlich verlustfrei zu fassen ist. [...] So wird der Erzähler zum Pendant der Person, die etwas tut, ohne von diffusen Gefühlen abgelenkt oder von überwältigenden Erfahrungen hingerissen zu werden.«[18] Das »Tun« scheint denn auch direkt in das oftmals spontane, unruhige und undifferenzierte Schreiben und Filmen, mit Mobiltelefonen etwa, einzuwirken, die phatische Uneigentlichkeit, die diese Bruchstücke erfahrenen Lebens kennzeichnet, steht der Eigentlichkeit früherer identitätslastigen Erzählens mehr oder wenig schroff entgegen.

---

16 Siehe Thomä (2007), S. 27 (wie Anm. 3).

17 Ebd., S. 171.

18 Ebd., S. 274.

Vielleicht hat sich für viele mit der Teilnahme an den neuen Erzählformen im Netz eine Art existentielle Spannung eröffnet. Ihnen allen ist das »primitiv Epische« des privaten Lebens zwar nicht »abhanden gekommen«, wie Robert Musil seine Figur Ulrich berichten lässt. Aber sie koppeln die »perspektivische Verkürzung des Verstandes«, mit der einst der »Faden der Erzählung« als schönes Kontinuum den »Lebensfaden« lenkte, an eine polyperspektivische Verstrickung in der »unendlich verwobenen Fläche« der neuen medialen Öffentlichkeiten.[19] Und was die Hauptsache ist, ihre Unterhaltungen sind, in ihrem Unterhalt gewähren, oftmals ziemlich unterhaltsam.

19
Siehe Robert Musil: Der Mann ohne Eigenschaften. Reinbek bei Hamburg 1978, S. 648f.

Marc Ries
Promotion 1995 am Institut für Philosophie der Universität Wien. Ausgehend von kulturtheoretischen und ästhetischen Fragekomplexen entstehen Studien zu Massenmedien, Gesellschaft und Kunst. Vertretungsprofessuren an der F.-Schiller-Universität Jena und an der Hochschule für Graphik und Buchkunst Leipzig. Seit 2010 Professor für Soziologie und Theorie der Medien an der Hochschule für Gestaltung in Offenbach. 2009 Konzept und Co-Kurator der Ausstellung *talk.talk Das Interview als ästhetische Praxis*, Leipzig/Graz/Salzburg. Ausgewählte Publikationen: *Medienkulturen* (2002); Mithg.: *DATING.21 Liebesorganisation und Verabredungskulturen* (2007).

Jenseits des Strukturalismus. Erweiterndes Erzählen zwischen Texten und Bildern

Hans Ulrich Reck

1. Mit Abraham A. Moles

»Grundlegend für die neue Entwicklung der Bilder ist die strukturale Idee der Quantifizierung der Bilder in ausgewählten Punkten, die von einem anfänglichen Realen (Ikone) aus gewonnen werden. Die einfachste und naheliegendste Möglichkeit wäre die, dass man alle existierenden Punkte der Wirklichkeit aufnimmt und vollständig wiedergibt. Aber das statistische Denken, das von der Stetigkeit des physischen Universums ausgeht, legt uns nahe, dass die Wiedergabe der Wirklichkeit sich auch mit einer Stichprobenauswahl begnügen könnte: mit der Aufnahme von weniger Elementen als dann wiedergegeben werden. Im endgültigen Bild wird die Wirklichkeit mittels einer begrenzten Zahl von Daten rekonstruiert, sofern man die fehlenden Elemente aufgrund der bereits bekannten interpolieren kann. Das ist die Idee der Stichprobenrekonstruktion einer Kurve oder einer Oberfläche: die Rekonstruktion ihrer Grundgesamtheit mittels einiger bekannter Teile. Diese Idee, die der Gipfel des strukturalen Denkens ist, wird die Entwicklung der Bilder im 21. Jahrhundert bestimmen. Es wird nicht mehr die ›Lichtschrift‹ im Sinne der klassischen Fotografie geben. Sondern die systematische Zerlegung der Welt und die Rekonstruktion eines Punkt für Punkt stetigen Simulakrums, das nur mehr eine Stichprobenauswahl des zugrunde liegenden Wirklichen ist. [...] Das klare Denken wird von der Schematisierung des Realen vorangetrieben, denn diese reduziert den überflüssigen Reichtum der ›thematischen Welt‹ auf die begrenzte Informationsverarbeitungsfähigkeit. Die Schematisierung steigert die Lesbarkeit der Welt. [...] Der Schlüsselbegriff ›Bild‹ hat zwei Aspekte. Zum einen sind die sichtbaren Bilder Rohstoff für die ›wissenschaftliche Theorie‹, die die Erscheinungen erklären will, die unter dem Mikroskop oder in der Kamera gesehen werden. [...] Zum anderen sind die Bilder Ergebnis eines Verfahrens zur Steigerung der Lesbarkeit der Welt. Das impliziert eine Neudefinition des ›Sichtbaren‹: es ist alles, was man von der Welt sehen könnte und was verborgen ist, was uns aber von einer geeigneten Technik enthüllt werden könnte. ›Sichtbar‹ heißt hier soviel wie ›objektivierbar‹, ›aufdeckbar‹. Die Techniken der Aufdeckung sind solche der ›Entwicklung‹: analog zur Fotografie. Das ›latente‹ Bild ist da. Die Operation unseres Geistes und unserer Techniken macht die unsichtbaren Größen sichtbar, indem sie die latenten Formen aufdeckt, die unseren beschränkten Sinnen nicht erscheinen.«[1]

Was der Ästhetik- und Informationstheoretiker Abraham A. Moles so prägnant skizziert, dient hier als Kontrastfolie für eine poetische verallgemeinerbare, jenseits der medialen Differenzen von Bild, Bewegtbild, Poetik und Text liegende Theorie des Erzählens. In diesem nämlich kommt es nicht auf strukturale Datenkomprimierung an. Sondern ganz im Gegenteil auf seine poetische De-Komprimierung, also auf seine Ausweitung. Neues Erzählen besteht in der Steigerung der Komplexität und der poetischen Verflechtungen. Es bedarf der Ausbrüche und Weiterungen. Das gilt sowohl für Texte wie für Bilder, erst recht für Bewegtbildmedien. Kann man Daten und Klänge im Samplingverfahren komprimieren, so gelingt das bei narrativen Texten und Bildern ohne merkliche Verluste nicht, oder wenn, dann nur in unwesentlichen Dimensionen. Es ist also die poetische Gestalt, nicht das oft in Diagramme einmündende technische Verfahren der strukturellen Thematisierung, das über die Poetologie der Narration entscheidet. Es geht nicht um Lesbarkeit der Welt, sondern ihre Verrätselung. Sonst ergibt der Begriff »Erzählung« keinen Sinn. Auch »wissenschaftliche Erzählungen« sind solche, die sich im undurchschaubaren Bereich des Hermetischen bewegen. Denn klar sagen, im Sinne der Informationen, lassen sich nur Erkenntnisse, die in Protokollsätzen gefasst werden können. »Erzählen« ist a priori ein Prinzip jenseits der Komprimierungen und der Protokolle. Abschweifung, nicht Verkürzung ist das Prinzip. Davon gibt Jorge Luis Borges ein meisterlich ausgetüfteltes Bild und Beispiel.

2. Mit Jorge Luis Borges

»Vor fünfhundert Jahren stieß der Chef eines höheren Sechsecks auf ein Buch, das so verworren war wie die anderen, das jedoch fast zwei Bogen gleichartiger Zeilen aufwies. Er zeigte

---

[1] Abraham A. Moles: Die thematische Visualisierung der Welt. In: Tumult. Zeitschrift für Verkehrswissenschaft, Nr. 14: Das Sichtbare (1990), S. 111ff.

seinen Fund einem wandernden Entzifferer, der ihm sagte, sie seien in Portugiesisch abgefasst: andere sagten dagegen, in Jiddisch. In weniger als einem Jahrhundert konnte die Sprachform bestimmt werden: Es handelte sich um eine samojedisch-litauische Dialektform des Guarani mit einem Einschlag von klassischem Arabisch. Auch der Inhalt wurde entschlüsselt: Begriffe der kombinatorischen Analysis, dargestellt an Beispielen sich unbegrenzt wiederholender Variationen. Diese Beispiele erlaubten es einem genialen Bibliothekar, das grundlegende Gesetz der Bibliothek zu entdecken. Dieser Denker stellte fest, dass sämtliche Bücher, wie verschieden sie auch seien, aus den gleichen Elementen bestehen: dem Raum, dem Punkt, dem Komma, den zweiundzwanzig Lettern des Alphabets. Auch führte er einen Umstand an, den alle Reisenden bestätigt haben: In der ungeheuren Bibliothek gibt es nicht zwei identische Bücher. Aus diesen unwiderleglichen Prämissen folgerte er, dass die Bibliothek total ist und dass ihre Regale alle irgend möglichen Kombinationen der zwanzig und soviel orthographischen Zeichen, deren Zahl, wenn auch außerordentlich groß, nicht unendlich ist, verzeichnen, mithin alles, was sich irgend ausdrücken lässt: in sämtlichen Sprachen. Alles: die minutiöse Geschichte der Zukunft, die Autobiographien der Erzengel, den getreuen Katalog der Bibliothek. Tausende und Abertausende falscher Kataloge, den Nachweis ihrer Falschheit, den Nachweis der Falschheit des echten Kataloges, das gnostische Evangelium des Basilides, den Kommentar zu diesem Evangelium, den Kommentar des Kommentars dieses Evangeliums, die wahrheitsgetreue Darstellung deines Todes, die Übertragung jeden Buches in sämtliche Sprachen, die Interpolation jeden Buches in allen Büchern. [...] Die Gewissheit, dass irgendein Regal in irgendeinem Sechseck kostbare Bücher barg und dass diese Bücher unzugänglich waren, schien nahezu unerträglich. Eine Lästersekte schlug vor, man solle die Suche einstellen, alle Menschen sollten Buchstaben und Zeichen so lange durcheinanderwürfeln, bis sie auf Grund eines unwahrscheinlichen Zufalls diese kanonischen Bücher zusammenbrächten. [...] Die Bibliothek ist so gewaltig, dass jede Schmälerung durch Menschenhand verschwindend gering ist. Jedes Exemplar ist einzig, aber da die Bibliothek total ist, gibt es immer einige Hunderttausende unvollkommener Faksimiles: Werke, die nur in einem Buchstaben oder Komma voneinander abweichen. [...] In der Tat birgt die Bibliothek alle Wortstrukturen, alle im Rahmen der fünfundzwanzig orthographischen Symbole möglichen Variationen, aber nicht einen absoluten Unsinn. [...] Ich kann nicht etliche Schriftzeichen kombinieren

    d h c m r l c h t d j

die nicht die göttliche Bibliothek bereits vorausgesehen hat und die in irgendeiner ihrer Geheimsprachen einen furchtbaren Sinn bergen. Niemand vermag eine Silbe zu artikulieren, die nicht voller Zärtlichkeiten und Schauer ist, die nicht in irgendeiner dieser Sprachen der gewaltige Name eines Gottes ist. Sprechen heißt in Tautologien verfallen. Diese überflüssige und wortreiche Epistel existiert bereits in einem der dreißig Bände der fünf Regale eines der unzähligen Sechsecke – und auch ihre Widerlegung. [...] Die Gewissheit, dass alles geschrieben ist, macht uns zunichte oder zu Phantasmen. Ich kenne Bezirke, in denen die Jungen sich vor den Büchern niederwerfen und mit ungezügelter Wildheit die Seiten küssen, aber nicht einen Buchstaben verstehen. [...] Die Bibliothek ist schrankenlos und periodisch. Wenn ein ewiger Wanderer sie in irgendeiner beliebigen Richtung durchmessen würde, so würde er nach Ablauf einiger Jahrhunderte feststellen, dass dieselben Bände in derselben Unordnung wiederkehren (die, wiederholt, eine Ordnung wäre, der Ordo). Meine Einsamkeit gefällt sich in dieser eleganten Hoffnung«.[2]

Das besondere Alphabet, das die Ordnung und die Spuren des Heiligen in diesem Text bestimmt, markiert einen wesentlichen Unterschied zur mediosphärischen Technisierung der in der Erzählung versammelten zeichentheoretischen Aspekte wie Aleatorik, Reproduzierbarkeit, Variation, Replikation, Generierung. In der entfalteten Technisierung der medialen Arrangements dagegen, der Verschaltung der Sinne und Kognitionen mit den Apparaten, sowie im umfassenden Medienverbund schwinden solche Zeit-Räume drastisch.

---

[2] Jorge Luis Borges: Die Bibliothek von Babel. In: Ders.: Gesammelte Werke Bd. 3. Erzählungen 1. München; Wien 1981, S. 148–154 (Auszüge).

3. Mit Kasimir Malewitsch

Moderne Kunst gipfelt in der oder kapriziert sich auf die Darstellung des Nicht-Darstellbaren, auf ein Sichtbarmachen des Nicht-Sichtbaren. Das Kunstwerk wird zu einem Moment im Erfahrungsprozess der Kunst, welche die »Bildlosigkeit des Absoluten«[3] erfährt. Das Werk kann hier nicht länger als Anschauungsgegenstand oder Medium von Repräsentation gelten. Es wird zu einem Ausdruck problematisierender Erfahrungen, die im Hin und Her zwischen Betrachter und Werk sich abspielen und nicht mit dessen stofflichen Äquivalent, dem Kunstwerk als Text oder Bild, zusammenfallen. In dieser Bewegung entwickelt sich das, was Aussage ist oder als solche anerkannt werden kann, erst durch einen Abzug der Bedeutungen (Signifikate) aus den Zeichen (Signifikanten). Das Scheitern der Darstellung des Absoluten wird nicht allein zur anstoßenden Bewegung des Betrachters im Hinblick auf das Werk, sondern zu dessen immanenter Dynamik, die dem Werk einen Betrachter sucht, der seine Aussage vollendet.[4] Diese Erzeugung der Aussage aus dem Blick des Betrachters ist das Organisationsprinzip der modernen Erzählung. Textorganisation wie bildnerische Syntax haben dem zu dienen.

Die den Bildern wie den textlichen Erzählungen, kurzum: aller Bildsprachlichkeit zugeschriebene rhythmische Qualität, also das Musikalische als neues Leitbild eines in allen Techniken, Gattungen, Genres, Sparten und Medien stetig erweiterten Erzählens, wird zum prototypischen Verfahren der modernen Kunst: Zeit-, nicht mehr Raumkünste bilden das Experimentierfeld. In direkter Zeitgenossenschaft zur konzeptuellen Erneuerung des expressionistischen Formimpulses, der vehement auf diese Aufspaltung hingearbeitet hatte, notierte Ernst Bloch um 1920: »das rein Malerische, das wiedergefunden zu haben den unklaren Stolz vieler Impressionisten bildete, tritt vor dem Zwang zur Aussage notwendig zurück«[5]. Die Bedeutungen entspringen von nun an dem Prozess des Sich-Einlassens auf die Gehalte des Kunstwerks, nicht mehr der bloßen Topographie der Motive, Ikonographien und Symbole. Der Ton werde innerlich, der Klang der Bilder entspreche der Gespanntheit

---

3
Georg Picht: Kunst und Mythos. Stuttgart 1987 (2. Aufl.), S. 74.

4
Umberto Eco: Das offene Kunstwerk. Frankfurt am Main 1973.

5
Ernst Bloch: Geist der Utopie. Frankfurt am Main 1964, S. 41. (unveränderter Nachdruck der bearbeiteten Neuauflage der zweiten Fassung von 1923).

einer aufbrechen wollenden Seele. Kontemplation sei den Werken nicht mehr angemessen. Die Erzählung als lebendige müsse real erlebt werden und setze, was sie erfordere, immer auch frei: Erweiterungen, Expansionen. In seiner zu Beginn der 1920er Jahre besonders markanten, expressionistisch emphatisierten Sprache fährt der Philosoph fort: »Wenn aber das, was der Ton sagt, von uns stammt, sofern wir uns hineinlegen und mit diesem großen, makanthropischen Kehlkopf sprechen, so ist das nicht ein Traum, sondern ein fester Seelenring, dem nur deshalb nichts entspricht, weil ihm draußen nichts mehr entsprechen kann, und weil die Musik als innerlich utopische Kunst über alles empirisch zu Belegende im ganzen Umfang hinausliegt. [...] Die Domestikentür bloßer Kontemplation ist gesprengt, und ein anderes als das allegorische Symbol erscheint, wie es menschenfremd, zum mindesten halb außermenschlich war, das uns, wenn es gänzlich sichtbar geworden wäre, gleich dem ungemilderten Zeus erdrückt, verbrannt hätte und dessen im Sichtbaren, uns Zugeneigten immer noch ungelöste transzendente Unfassbarkeit gerade seinen Symbolcharakter konstituiert hatte.«[6]

6 Ebd., S. 206.

4. Mit Witold Gombrowicz

Witold Gombrowicz pointiert in einem scharfen Szenario oder Gedankenbild – dramaturgisch wählt er ein Streitgespräch – das Prinzip der Iteration des Erzählens, also den Fortgang seiner notwendigen Expansion, wie folgt: »Sie: Mensch! Du hast kein Gespür für die Malerei! Keine Ahnung! Kein Verständnis! Du begreifst das nicht! Ich: Seht mal diese drei Streichhölzer, die ich auf den Sand lege. Stellt euch vor, in einer Gruppe von Menschen entsteht ein erbitterter Wettstreit darum, wie man diese drei Streichhölzer so anordnen kann, dass sie in künstlerischer Hinsicht zu einer möglichst großen Offenbarung werden, [...] stellen wir uns vor, die ungeheure Anstrengung vieler erfahrener ›Streichholzkünstler‹ geht darin ein; manche sind mehr, andere weniger einfallsreich; es entstehen Hierarchien; Schulen und Stile bilden sich heraus; Kennertum entwickelt sich... Warum sollte das absurd sein, frage ich? Schließlich bringt der Mensch sogar mit diesen drei Streichhölzern etwas zum Ausdruck – von sich, von der Welt. Schließlich können wir, wenn wir unsere ganze Aufmerksamkeit auf diese drei Streichhölzer konzentrieren, das Mysterium des Kosmos in ihnen entdecken. [...] Das alles unter der Voraussetzung, dass wir sie nur innig genug betrachten. Die Frage aber ist – lohnt es, lohnt es, lohnt es? [...] Und ich leugne es nicht: Wenn wir einen Cézanne mit dieser Intensität betrachten, dann wird Cézanne zu einer Offenbarung. Die Frage ist nur – lohnt es, lohnt es, lohnt es? Warum solche Offenbarungen nicht woanders suchen?«[7] Und so wäre weiter zu fragen: Wieso überhaupt Offenbarungen in der Kunst suchen? Statt einfach den Erzählungen zu folgen und sie weiterzutreiben?

[7] Witold Gombrowicz: Sakrilegien. Aus den Tagebüchern 1953 bis 1967. Frankfurt am Main 2002, S. 140f.

5. Weniges zu Schleier, Fiktion, Abstraktion

Ernst Mach exponiert 1905 in seinem Buch *Erkenntnis und Irrtum* eine ganze Reihe von Beispielen aus den ›harten‹ Naturwissenschaften, in denen der Zufall die entscheidende Rolle spielt.[8] Wissenschaftliches Tun sei, so Mach im Vorwort zu diesem Buch, grundiert in den Tiefen der Instinkte, verliere sich in undurchschauten Dispositionen und entwerfe im Prospekt seiner rationalen Ziele mitnichten eine ›ganze Vernunft‹.

1954 schrieb Max Ernst – von ganz anderer Seite her, aber im selben Geiste und mit derselben Inspiriertheit – unter dem Titel *Was ist Surrealismus* zur Ausstellung im Zürcher Kunsthaus über seinen Frottagen-Zyklus *Histoire naturelle* (1926): »Die revolutionäre Bedeutung dieser ersten vielleicht absurd anmutenden Naturbeschreibung wird vielleicht deutlicher dadurch, dass analoge Resultate aus der modernen Mikrophysik vorliegen. P. Jordan stellt als Resultat einer Messung an einem kraftfrei bewegten Elektron und nachherigen Messung des Ortes fest: ›Aber dieser Unterscheidung von Außen- und Innenwelt wird eine Hauptstütze entzogen mit der experimentellen Widerlegung der Vorstellung, dass in der Außenwelt Tatbestände vorliegen, welche unabhängig vom Beobachtungsprozess ein objektives Dasein besitzen.‹ [...] Der Naturwissenschaft substituiert sich so die Wissenschaft von den Reaktionen, die durch die Beobachtungsmethoden

[8] Ernst Mach: Erkenntnis und Irrtum. Skizzen zur Psychologie der Forschung. Darmstadt 1991 (unveränderter reprographischer Nachdruck der 5., mit der vierten übereinstimmenden Auflage, Leipzig 1926).

hervorgerufen werden.«[9] Solche Weigerung, die Trennung von Dokumenten, Imagination und Fiktion zu akzeptieren, ja: sie überhaupt schon nur für möglich zu halten, bildete wenig später den revolutionären Ausgangspunkt der dispositionalen Wissenschaftsgeschichte von Michel Foucaults *Les Mots et les Choses* (1966).

Nicht nur die poetische Inspiration der Künstler, sondern auch eine paradigmatisch veränderte erkenntnistheoretische Methodeneinschätzung seitens der Naturwissenschaft im Gefolge eher erlittener als erwünschter Revolutionierungen spricht von solchem Entzug einer tatsachenkonsistenten, beobachterunabhängigen, klar in innen und außen geschiedenen »objektiven Wirklichkeit«[10]. »Heute sind wir so weit, dass sich die gesamte wahrgenommene Welt in ein Meer von Täuschung verwandelt hat; Vorhang auf Vorhang wurde beiseitegezogen, bis wir endlich vor einem letzten Vorhang der Wirklichkeit zu stehen glauben, auf dem nur noch Elektronenschatten vorüberhuschen, gespenstisch und kaum zu fassen. Der rechnende Verstand hat hier das letzte Wort; aus dem Vordergrund der Wahrnehmung rückt die Welt in den Hintergrund des Gedankens.«[11] Was Ernesto Grassi für das Stichwort »Natur« zu Werner Heisenbergs *Das Naturbild der heutigen Physik* so deutlich formuliert, datiert von 1955. Erschien damals das Wissen von der Welt wie diese selbst endgültig als nicht mehr symbolfähig? Wurde solches Ende der Symbolisierbarkeit der Welt tief empfunden oder nur oberflächlich dekretiert? Drücken sich darin weitere, nur noch nicht gut bemerkte Zwischenstadien in der Geschichte menschlicher Erkenntnisirrtümer aus, diesmal in Gestalt der Mathematisierbarkeit einer unvorstellbar gewordenen, aber gleichwohl berechenbar gebliebenen Welt?

6. Metapher, ›Polysemie‹ und die Kunst der Fiktionen als Fortgang des Erzählens

In *Le musée imaginaire* diagnostiziert André Malraux im Jahre 1949 für das Zeitalter der Reproduktionstechniken, dass, unwiderruflich, die Fiktion den Stil abgelöst habe.[12] Es ergebe

---

[9] Max Ernst: Was ist Surrealismus. In: Karlheinz Barck (Hg.): Surrealismus in Paris 1919–1939. Ein Lesebuch. Leipzig 1990.

[10] Werner Heisenberg: Das Naturbild der heutigen Physik. Hamburg 1955.

[11] Ernesto Grassi: Die Macht der Phantasie. Zur Geschichte des abendländischen Denkens. Königstein 1979.

[12] André Malraux: Das imaginäre Museum. Frankfurt am Main; New York 1987.

sich zwangsläufig ein spielerisches Training in der alltäglichen Ausbildung von Artefakten und Manierismen, weshalb die Mediatisierung der Alltagswelt durch ein wachsendes Expertenwissen der Rezipienten und, in umgekehrter Richtung, die bisherige unberührbare Welt der Experten zugleich durch eine Mediatisierung der Informationsbehauptungen, eine starke aufmerksamkeitsschürende Ritualisierung, ausgezeichnet sei.

Die Fiktion der Kunst weicht der Kunst der Fiktion. Und immer und immer weiter muss erzählt werden. Und zwar auf allen Seiten: der der Produzenten wie der der Rezipienten. Alles erweist sich vorrangig als Mittel zur Fortsetzung und Ausweitung des Erzählens. Es ist unser Zeitalter nicht nur durch telekommunikative Apparateverbände, Bewusstseinsindustrie und als Information getarnte Wissensenteignung/Desinformation gekennzeichnet, sondern auch durch eine allgemeine Poetologie des unentwegten und stetig ausgedehnten und erweiterten Erzählens. Und dies auch in den Wissenschaften, in denen das Rationale nicht die herausragende Rolle spielt, die man eigentlich zu Recht annehmen könnte.

Die Wirklichkeit wird zunehmend von Phantasie und Imagination bestimmt, ja von diesen abhängig. Es gibt keinerlei Norm, welche technische Manipulationen qualitativ ausschließen oder begrenzen könnte. Die eigentliche orientierende Größe innerhalb der Kunst der Fiktionen, welche die Willkürlichkeit jedes imaginären Museums und Archivs auszeichnet, sei es in der Sphäre der Künste oder der Wissenschaften, ist das Fragment. Dass die ganze Welt darin – stellvertretend, beispielgebend oder auch ruinös – zum Bild werden kann, ist nur die eine Seite des Vorgangs. Erst in dieser Re-Organisation der technischen Bilder als Bildmontage wird die naive Objektreferenz überwunden. An die Stelle der gegenständlichen Eigenschaft tritt die komparatistische Einsicht in die Funktionslogik der künstlerischen wie der wissenschaftlichen »Stile« oder nun eben: »Fiktionen«. Und diese müssen erzählt werden, damit sie wirklich werden können.

Fiktion ist der wesentliche Schlüssel zur Erzeugung jedes Modells, das Realität verstehbar macht und deshalb »ontologisch« real ist. Im Hinblick auf Andrej Andrejewitsch Markov formuliert: Wenn die Reduktion einer komplexen Datenmenge auf ein weniger komplexes Programm den Effekt hat, dass dieses Programm die Ausgangsmenge reproduzieren kann, dann *versteht* dieses Programm diese Datenmenge. Eine Theorie ist ein Programm, das Beobachtungen berechenbar macht. Ein Programm, das eine Theorie zu simulieren vermag, die komplizierter ist als die dem Programm zugrundeliegende Ausgangstheorie, liefert diese avanciertere Theorie durch Selbstentwicklung eines verbesserten »Verstehens«. »Intelligenz« ist dafür mehr als eine Metapher. Aber sie reicht nicht. Immer nämlich bleibt eine Differenz bestehen. Exaktes Sprechen ist nicht möglich. Jede exakte Sprache erweist sich als abhängig von narrativen Elementen, insbesondere von Metaphern. Die Metapher selber mäandert, bewegt sich, ist dynamisch. Sie »lebt«, wie Paul Ricœur eindringlich nachgewiesen hat.[13] Was aus der erweiterten Erzählung und der allgemeinen Poetologie erfolgt, ist also eine Vieldeutigkeit oder, mit einem Fremdwort oder Fachausdruck, »Polysemie«. Diese bedeutet: Ein Bild, aber auch ein Text, kann je nach Kontext verschiedene Bedeutungen haben. Dinge, Bilder, Zeichen, Worte ›gehen fremd‹. Die Identität eines Bildes bedingt eine interne Doppelcodierung: Sich-Selbst-Gleichheit und Heterogenität, welche Pluralität und damit Kontextoffenheit zulässt. Ein Zeichensystem muss eine bestimmte Beschaffenheit haben, damit es kontextoffen ist – diese Qualität entspringt nicht den Kontexten selbst. Die typische Ambivalenz moderner Kunstwerke (Texte, Bilder, Medien) gründet darin, dass nur Polysemie und nicht eine mono-semische Identität die Übertragbarkeit von Erkenntnissen ermöglicht. Eine Bilderwelt ohne Polysemie würde das Prinzip der Signalökonomie verletzen, würde doch das Vokabular ins Unendliche ausgedehnt. Bilder werden wirksam als typologische Konstrukte, als paradigmatische Modelle – das können sie, scheinbar paradox, nur in singulärer Gestalt erreichen. Medien der Kunst wie Kunst als Medium sind, so zeigt sich nachhaltig, prozessuale und dynamische Größen, spezifische Weisen des Herausbildens und Verknüpfens von partikularen Zusammenhängen. Und eben dies vereint im Gedanken des Erweiterten Erzählens die Gattungen und Medien von Texten, Bildern, Sprachen, Sprechweisen.

13
Paul Ricœur: Die Lebendige Metapher. München 1986.

Der Traum von der exakten, idealen, metaphernfreien Sprache ist ein Traum, der im 20. Jahrhundert – auf höchstem Niveau mit Rudolf Carnap – gescheitert ist. Lange schien dieser Traum eine Option, an der bedingungslos zu arbeiten sei. Das rührte jedoch einzig von der dogmatisierten Auffassung her, dass es in einer rationalen Theorie – wie etwa beim frühen Wittgenstein – immer um eine exakt abbildende Sprache gehe. Dieser entsprechend, wurde alle Metaphorik bereits als Metaphysik oder ›ins Unreine verführende‹ Rhetorik betrachtet und abgelehnt. Heute bietet sich jedoch an, von der Modellkonstruktion, nicht vom Abbildtheorem auszugehen. Nicht Abbildung wäre das Ziel, sondern die Selbstwahrnehmung des Prozesses des Abstrahierens einerseits, des Erzählens andererseits. Um Erweiterungen und neue Unterscheidung ist es dann zu tun. Die Metaphern laufen derweil fröhlich mit – »irgendwohin«. Und stören nicht länger, mögen sich zuweilen gar entschieden nützlich machen. Abstraktionen sind nach Akzentuierungen spezifisch gegliederte Prozesse der Herausbildung einer Form resp. die eine Hierarchisierung der bestimmenden Aspekte steuernde Auswahl/Anordnung. Sie ermöglichen ein Weglassen der unwichtigen Aspekte zugunsten der Unterordnung des Ausgewählten unter den Gesichtspunkt des je gewählten Wichtigen. Das ist, offenkundig, immer schon der – literarische, dramaturgische, gattungstypische – Kern eines novellistischen Erzählens, genereller: des künstlerischen Darstellens gewesen. Das *Neue* oder *Expandierende Erzählen* kommt jenseits der Genres und Gattungen erst heute zu seinem vollen Recht. Es trainiert Skepsis, Agilität, Geschmeidigkeit in allen Fragen, testet Philosophie als Rhetorik.

Hans Ulrich Reck
ist Philosoph, Kunstwissenschaftler, Publizist, Kurator. Seit 1995 Professor für Kunstgeschichte im medialen Kontext an der Kunsthochschule für Medien in Köln, davor Professor und Vorsteher der Lehrkanzel für Kommunikationstheorie an der Hochschule für angewandte Kunst in Wien (1992–1995), Dozenturen in Basel und Zürich (1982–1995), Publikationen zuletzt: *Pier Paolo Pasolini – Poetisch Philosophisches Porträt* (Berlin 2012); *Spiel Form Künste. Zu einer Kunstgeschichte des Improvisierens*, hg. v. Bernd Ternes (Hamburg 2010); *Traum. Enzyklopädie* (München, 2010); *Index Kreativität* (Köln 2007); *EIGENSINN DER BILDER. Bildtheorie oder Kunstphilosophie?* (München 2007); *Das Bild zeigt das Bild selber als Abwesendes* (Wien/New York 2007).

Ferdinand Schmatz
Das Drängen der Sprache

1

Die Sprache drängt. Sie drängt in uns, zu benennen, das, was wir wahrnehmen. Auch, um es uns zu- und einzuordnen und dadurch kommunizieren zu können.

Aber diese Ordnung, der fremdbestimmte Diskurs, wird nicht selten als ein Zwang erfahren, der von außen kommt: von den Systemen, die das innersprachliche Drängen kanalisieren durch ihre Kontexte, die diese Sprache umgeben. Und, die nicht nur sprachliche Darstellungsformen einsetzen, um ihre Ziele zu verwirklichen.

Diese Ziele liegen auf der Hand, die übrigens längst nichts mehr mit dem Gegenstand der Erzeugung zu tun hat. Öffnen wir nur das Auge, dass es uns den Verstand erhellt: dann heißt Verwirklichen nichts anderes als Grenzen zu setzen, in denen die Eingeschulten jene Felder zu bestellen lernen, damit deren Erträge von den Systemen geerntet werden können.

Die Einschulung erfolgt dabei medial umfassend. Sie bedient sich der Worte, aber noch mehr der Bilder und anderer Repräsentationsformen, um daraus jene Wirklichkeit zu bauen, die eine Transparenz des Alles-ist-Machbaren vorgibt, in der dadurch nichts mehr machbar wird. In der abstrakte Werte zu realen werden und die realen, auch körperlichen, zu abstrakten, abgesetzten, weit weg von jeder individuellen Erfahrung.

Es geht also um mehr als Sprache, es geht um die Systeme der Zeichen, die von den medialen Maschinen gesetzt werden, um Ordnungen zu schaffen, in denen Ich, Du, Wir zu Trägern gestanzter Zeichen werden. Ordnungen, die ihre Inhalte nicht aus dem individuellen Bedürfnis des Ichs oder der sozialen Gruppe schöpfen, sondern ihre marktkonformen Oberflächenwerte den Individuen als tiefe eigene suggerieren.

Das bedeutet die Einbindung und das Abverlangen von Sprach- und Darstellungsformen des Gegebenen als Verhaltensformen im individuellen wie sozialen Raum. Was nichts anderes darstellt als Normerfüllung, Entfremdung, die nicht nur den von abstrakten Strukturen in ferngesteuerten Maschinen hergestellten Gegenstand, sondern das ganze Lebensgefühl betrifft.

2

Das Werk drängt. Es drängt in andere Werke, die es aufsucht, mit deren medialen Mitteln es spielt und experimentiert, um zur eigenen Intention zurückzukehren, dem Werk als Einheit von Inhalt und Form. Als Kunst, in der nicht über Form kommuniziert wird, sondern durch und als Form – die in sich und aus sich und über sich hinaus jene politisch und theoretisch gewichteten Inhalte der nominalisierten und begrenzten Wirklichkeit thematisiert, anspricht, aufzeigt, und durch Entgrenzungstendenzen versucht, zu verwandeln.

Dazu kann das Werk kurzweilig die Gestalt anderer Medienformen der Kunst annehmen, die auch durch den Einbruch empirischer Realitäten begründbar ist. Die eigentlich bestimmende Intention des Werkes, eben dieses Werk zu sein, wird dadurch nicht beschnitten. Im Gegenteil kann es seine Möglichkeiten, die damit verbundene Botschaft zu vermitteln, erweitern.

3

Diese Form ist die Intervention in einem Raum, der den Schreibtisch, das Buch, das Blatt verlässt und sich in den Raum des Sozialen, des Marktes an sich begibt – und beim Begriff, beim Wort und beim Ort nimmt.

Das Wort –

ein Text aus Texten, eine Flut von Zeichen, ein scheinbares Chaos, das aber Ordnungsmuster hat, die einwirken und einwirken und einwirken. Die Schule des Marktes! Diese Ein-Wirkung ins Bewusste zu heben, um sie derart zum realen Raum zu gestalten, in den eingegriffen werden kann, ja, das gilt der Kunst:

am konkreten Ort –

mit Medien aus anderen Bereichen der Kunst – Objekte, Fotos, Video – eine künstlerische Erweiterung des »ureigenen«, sprachlichen Mediums, das letztlich wieder in sich als Text zurückfließt.

Ein Werk aus Werken, einer pluralen Autorenschaft, die diesen Raum spezifisch wählt, um ihn zu erforschen und in ihm zu forschen, zu analysieren. Die auf die Bedingungen im Speziellen aufmerksam macht, um auf mögliche allgemeine, die für den Zustand einer sozialökonomischen Zeichen-Bindung stellvertretend sind, aufmerksam zu machen:

Auf das, was Normierung und Automatismus sind, Einwirkungen und Manipulationen auf das Unbewusste und welche Rolle der dort Eingebundene zu spielen hat.

Das künstlerische Spiel wird dem ernsten des Eingeschlossenseins entgegengesetzt, eine Art Revolte der Eigenermächtigung durch sprachlich bildlich aktionistische Darstellungs- und Handlungsformen.

In diesen und immer wieder auf sich zurückweisend, steht die Sprache als Bearbeitungsmaterial im Zentrum, das, wie gesagt, angeknabbert wird von anderen künstlerischen Darstellungsweisen, wie dem körperlichen Agieren, den eingebrachten Objekten in eine Ding- und Wesenwelt des Gegebenen, die kapitalistischen Gesetzen unterliegt, die aber als frei suggeriert werden: als Versuch, sich davon frei zu spielen, und andere daran partizipieren zu lassen.

Die Intervention im Raum ist eine kurzweilige, aber nachhaltig wirkende Störung des Gegebenen und seiner Automatismen, mit anderen Mitteln als mit jenen der Sprache allein, auch wenn es um Dichtung und Literatur geht!

In etwa als
SPRACH RAUM
aus
Klang Bild Wort –
ein tatsächlicher als fragmentarisch gestalteter Raum aus Texten, Textbildern, Text-Fahnen, Text-Objekten und diversen Bildstrecken in geschriebener, abgebildeter, gesprochener wie gesungener und gespielter Form.

Die Basis für diesen beweglichen Raum als Modul für Präsentationen vorrangig aus den Gebieten der Poesie und Musik bildet ein Grundriss von drei mal zwei Metern, der von einer Wand ausgeht und mit Kreidelinien markiert ist.

Diese grenzen den Raum ab, laden aber genauso zur Überschreitung ein, real verweisend auf die anderen Darstellungsformen der Essence, wie auch sinnbildlich auf die Grenzüberschreitungen innerhalb der Sprachkunst, die sich mit Musik, Bild und dem öffentlichen Raum verzahnt.

Der Raum, unser Raum, jener der Sprache, jener des Sozialen, des Individuellen und des Kollektiven –

bildet die Grundlage des Hereinholens und Ausschweifens verschiedenster Darstellungsformen innerhalb und außerhalb des eigenen Arbeitsgebietes, der Literatur, der Kunst, der Universität, der Institute, der Klassen.

Am Rande der Zentren steht, liegt, schwebt, also bewegt sich das Unterfangen:

REINHEIT UND RAUSCHEN, eine künstlerische Zusammenarbeit im Spannungsfeld von Poesie und Musik :

Wort, Satz, Ton und Klang werden von einer gemeinsamen Ausgangsbasis aus thematisch wie materiell verflochten, Kompositionen aus Stimme, Instrument, getragen vom Geist der Erweiterung nicht nur von Dichtung und Musik, sondern von Dialogformen, die Botschaften als rein und verrauscht zugleich entwickeln, hervorbringen und kommunizieren.

Der SPRACH RAUM dient als Aufführungsort für die Wort-Klang-Kompositionen genauso wie als Grundriss, auf dem tatsächliche und imaginäre Wände wachsen – in Form einer offenen, durchlässigen Fläche, auf die Text- und Bildarbeiten wie Objekte aus Sprache und anderen Materialien projiziert und eingebracht werden können: und dessen Eckpunkte durch eine Art Säule gesetzt werden, die aus einem Wort-Bild-Projekt besteht – in Form einer Zeitung, die sich der kontextuellen Darstellungsweise Aby Warburgs annäherte und sie erweiterte, der Atlas und sein Blatt im Medium der Zeitung und deren Blattsalat:

Das Blatt. Der Salat.

…

Ferdinand Schmatz
schreibt Gedichte, Prosa und Essays. Er ist Träger zahlreicher Preise (u.a. Trakl-, Artmann- und Jandl-Preis). Er lehrt an der Universität für Angewandte Kunst in Wien und ist dort Leiter des Instituts für Sprachkunst. Schmatz lebt in Wien. Veröffentlichungen (Auswahl): *Maler als Stifter. Poetische Texte zur bildenden Kunst* (1997), *Farbenlehre* (mit Heimo Zobernig, 1995), zuletzt: *Durchleuchtung. Ein wilder Roman aus Danja und Franz* (2007), *Quellen. Gedichte* (2010).

Es wird Wirklichkeit gewesen sein. Alban Nikolai Herbsts erweiterte Schreibstätte

Usha Reber

Das Unternehmen *Expanded Narration* bietet einen unscharfen Begriff an, der von Neuerungen, Vernetzungen, Entgrenzungen, aber auch schäumenden und weitschweifigen Erzählungen spricht. Mithin wird ein weites und vieldeutiges Feld vorgelegt, dessen einige wenige Seiten ich mithilfe des Schreibens und Erzählens von Alban Nikolai Herbst, einem in Berlin lebenden Autoren, erhellen möchte. Herbst hat sich selbst die Marke *Kyberrealismus* geschaffen, auch gehört er zu jenen AutorInnen, die ihr eigenes Schreiben, ihre Methode des Erzählens und Fingierens genauestens reflektieren. Er gibt also durchaus Einordnungs- und Interpretationsrichtungsanweisungen. Solchen Spuren, die Herbst in seinem literarischen Weblog, seinem »Fiktionsraum« auf *twoday.net* legt, soll im Folgenden nachgegangen und dabei der Versuch unternommen werden, die Entgrenzungen der kyberrealistischen Erzählmethode aufzuspüren und zu analysieren.

In einem früheren, umfassenden Werk habe ich mich bereits ausführlich der Herbst'schen Poetologie unter dem Aspekt des metamorphotischen Schreibens gewidmet.[1] Einiges wird hier wieder aufgenommen und unter einem verschobenen Blickwinkel neu betrachtet werden. Die Leitfrage für diesen Beitrag lautet, wie literarisch und als Kunst neu und erweitert erzählt werden kann. Diese Frage stellt sich Alban Nikolai Herbst selbst immer wieder und beantwortet sie mit einer Möglichkeitenästhetik »alter Formen in der Gegenwart der Zukunft«. Damit sind die Schwerpunkte der Analyse vorgegeben, indem dem Verhältnis von Zeit und Erzählen, der Form und des Stils sowie dem Denken in/von Möglichkeiten nachgegangen wird.

Kontinuum/Kompossibilität

Alban Nikolai Herbst unterstellt sein Schreiben in dem Roman *Wolpertinger oder das Blau*, 1993 bei *Dielmann* erschienen, dem Lacan'schen Motto[2]: »Was sich in meiner Geschichte verwirklicht, ist die Zweite Zukunft dessen, was ich gewesen sein werde, für das, (...) was ich dabeibin zu werden. *Lacan*«. Tatsächlich lässt sich das leicht paradoxe Verfahren, über einen Zustand in der Vergangenheit zu erzählen, der in der Gegenwart noch im Vollzug ist, was ein philosophisches Paradox der Vorhersagbar-

[1] Ursula Reber: Formenverschleifung. Zu einer Theorie der Metamorphose. Paderborn 2009.

[2] »Ce qui se réalise dans mon histoire, n'est pas le passé défini de ce qui fut puisqu'il n'est plus, ni même le parfait de ce qui a été dans ce que je suis, mais le futur antérieur de ce que j'aurai été pour ce que je suis en train de devenir.« Jacques Lacan: Fonction et champs de la parole et du langage. In: Écrits. Paris 1996, S. 300. Zuerst veröffentlicht in: Sur la parole et le langage. In: La psychanalyse, Nr. 1 (1956), S. 81–166; www.ecole-lacanienne.net/documents/1953-09-26b.doc (Stand: 20.09.2013).

keit dessen bildet, was gewesen sein wird, auf sein gesamtes Schreiben und Erzählen übertragen. Ein Paradox der In/Kompossibilität wird dargeboten, das sowohl die Zeitebene/n als auch die erzählerische Kohärenz betrifft.

Alban Nikolai Herbst benutzt das Begriffspaar in seinen poetologischen und kyberrealistischen Reflexionen nicht, das Prinzip der »Pyramide ohne Basis«[3] ist ihm jedoch wohlbekannt. Unter verschiedenen Begriffen und im Kontext mehrerer Erzählverfahren taucht es auf. Prominent steuert es die Ausdifferenzierungen der Ereignisse im jüngsten Roman *Argo. Anderswelt* (im September 2013 bei *Elfenbein* erschienen) als »Nebelkammer«, in der »wirkende Unendlichkeit« sichtbar wird als »Kondensstreifen, kurze dünne Fäden und sich aufblähende Körper wie von Gespenster-Raupen«[4]. Deutlicher formuliert findet sich das Prinzip in einem Notat vom 29. Dezember 2007:

»In der Matrix des Kybernetischen Realismus stehen nicht nur faktische Er/Kenntnisse als Komponenten, sondern auch Möglichkeiten; das ist der entscheidende ästhetische Ansatz, daß er *kein ausschließendes* poetisches Verfahren ist, *sondern ein integratives,* das kausale Zusammenhänge eben n i c h t festfährt. Für einen Roman bedeutet das, daß dieselben Erzählstränge sich ebenso spalten können wie die erzählten Subjekte und daß diese gespaltenen Erzählstränge jeder zu anderen Weiterhandlungen führen, die parallel miterzählt werden, ohne daß es einen Akzent auf eine bestimmte Weiterhandlung gäbe.«[5]

Die bereits oben nach Vogl angeführte »Pyramide ohne Basis«, die der *Theodizee* Leibnizens (416) entnommen ist, gibt die Grundfigur für Herbsts Kyberrealismus ab; die Passage enthält überdies eine ähnliche Formulierung wie das ebenfalls oben geführte Lacan-Zitat, wenn konstatiert wird, dass jeder möglichen Welt ein römischer Prinz Sextus Tarquinius entspricht, wenn auch nicht derselbe, dem immer bereits implizit ist, was er werden wird (414). Herbsts poetisches Verfahren enthebt jedoch die Bedingung der Kompossibilität bzw. stellt er sie infrage oder möglicherweise, das wird zu sehen sein, auf ein neues Fundament. »Gemeinsam möglich« werden im Grunde alle zeitlich und immanent getrennten Kompossibilitäten, die bei Leibniz

[3] Siehe Joseph Vogl: Was ist ein Ereignis. Vortrag vom 26.10.2003. In: ZKM Symposion: Deleuze und die Künste. Wiederholung und Differenz. http://on1.zkm.de/zkm/stories/storyReader$4048 (Stand: 31.07.2013).

[4] Alban Nikolai Herbst: Eintrag Nebelkammer (1). Argo. Anderswelt (64), vom 06.12.2004. http://albannikolaiherbst.twoday.net/stories/428868/ (Stand: 31.07.2013).

[5] Alban Nikolai Herbst: Desideria: Markus A. Hediger und Die Möglichkeitenpoetik. In: Kyberrealism. http://albannikolaiherbst.twoday.net/topics/KYBERREALISM/?start=40 (Stand: 31.07.2013).

über die Gemächer in der Pyramide geschieden sind. In diesem Sinne behauptet Herbst ein »integratives« Verfahren, das auf der Spaltung beruht. Im Gegensatz zum obigen Zitat, das durchaus die Regeln der Kompossibilität, der Einheit von Subjekt und Prädikat(ion) beachtet, verlaufen seine Erzählungen über nicht integrative oder zu integrierende Schnittmengen.

Entfaltungen/Spaltungen

Gilles Deleuze erklärte die Falte, Faltungen in ihren Variationen zu einem Prinzip der Welterschließung des Barock, insbesondere bei Leibniz, dem in der Seele die Welt eingefaltet, die Welt aber die Ausfaltung der Seele wiederum sei. Seele und Welt kleiden einander in diesem Sinne ein bzw. aus, wobei das dauernde Spiel von Développement und Enveloppement[6] der beständigen wechselseitigen Übersetzung unterliegt. Die Faltungen korrespondieren einander, jedoch können sie immer wieder neu gelegt werden, Falten sind keine statischen Gebilde, sondern offene, die nachgerade nach Bewegung drängen. Eigentlich verwundert wenig, dass auch Alban Nikolai Herbst die Faltung für seine Poetologie beansprucht, wenn er in einem *Arbeitsnotat 11.11.2004. Zur praktischen Romantheorie. Argo. Anderswelt (46)* feststellt:

»Interessant, daß ARGO wie ein sich selbst generierender Text funktioniert: aus- und ineinander gefaltete, sich faltende Welten, die sich gegenseitig kommentieren.«[7]

Die Autopoiesis der Textwelten in Form einer Versuchsanordnung, eines Spiels mit medialen Möglichkeiten, Störfaktoren von korruptem Quellcode inklusive, muten in den Romanen als Analogie, manchmal auch nur als bloße Behauptung an. Während im *Wolpertinger* voll des Spielcharakters und der mehrfach gebrochenen Analogie zu einander überlagernden und überschreibenden Kulturen die Feenwelt per Diskette ins Netzwerk der Computer geladen wird und von dort aus im pixelig-grobstrukturierten Stil früher Computerspiele und des Comics in das biologische Leben übergreift, verwendet Herbst in *Thetis. Anderswelt*, *Buenos Aires. Anderswelt* und *Argo. Anderswelt* eine kybernetische Versuchsanordnung von »Welt«, »Anderswelt«

---

[6] Gilles Deleuze: Differenz und Wiederholung. Aus dem Frz. von Joseph Vogl. 3. korr. Aufl. München 1997.

[7] Alban Nikolai Herbst: Arbeitsnotat 11.11.2004: Zur praktischen Romantheorie. Argo. Anderswelt (46). In: Panoramen der Anderswelt/Expeditionen ins Werk von Alban Nikolai Herbst. Ausgewählt und zusammengestellt von Ralf Schnell. Redaktion: Johann P. Tammen. In: die horen, Bd. 231 (2008), S. 134.

und »Garraff« derart, dass sich programmierte Welten selbsttätig entwickeln. Die Versuchsanordnung blendet eine konformistische Realwelt dadurch, dass auch »Welt« als Programm zu verstehen ist, aus. Was in der Versuchsanordnung nicht vorgesehen war/ist, ist die gegenseitige Interaktion der ursprünglich getrennt existierenden, inkompossiblen Welten. Diese kommt aber zustande, zunächst tauschen verschiedene Deters-Figuren die Welten, dann überschreitet die Figur Broglier die Systemgrenzen, und die Welten beginnen ihre »Kommentartätigkeit« durch Austausch und Reaktion.

»War ich deshalb aus Garraff verschwunden? Das hat mich lange beschäftigt und geht mir bisweilen immer noch nach. Oder kann man sich innerhalb desselben Bezugssystems sozusagen verdoppeln? Werden die Welten auf diese Weise ineinander verschränkt? Das könnte die Irregularitäten erklären, welche die Anderswelten offenbar voneinander nicht mehr trennen ließen. Nach dem ersten Hauptsatz der Themodynamik [sic] hätte ich im selben Moment, da ich in Buenos Aires *hinzukam*, aus Beelitz und überhaupt der Welt gelöscht sein müssen. Es sei eben denn, Broglier sowie die anderen Cyborgs, die ihre Welt verlassen hatten, und dann eben auch ich (k e i n Cyborg!), hätten durch unsere jeweilige sagen wir ›Wanderung‹ die geschlossenen Systeme tatsächlich um das je andere erweitert. Das ist nicht ganz von der Hand zu weisen. […] Meiner Rechnung zufolge bin ich unterdessen schon ein ziemlich genaues Jahr hier, da läßt sich von *Schwankung* allenfalls dann sprechen, wenn die Systemzeiten nicht konvergieren sollten. Dafür finde ich bislang kein Indiz. […] Transsystemisch wandernde Einheiten – zu denen auch ich jetzt gehöre – sind gewissermaßen Bühne und Lähnung [sic] sich komplex ineinander erweiternder datischer und physischer Welten. ([…]) Indem man Welt transponiert, wird das Transponierte zu ihr hinzugetan. Sie wächst also an. Infinit, fürchte ich.«[8]

Das infinite Anwachsen wird von den Weltenwanderern bedingt, die gemäß ihren seelischen Einfaltungen mit hineintragen, was aus der jeweils anderen Welt stammt. Eindrucksvoll

---

8
Alban Nikolai Herbst: ARGO-ÜA (16). Gestrichenes. »Transsystemisch«. http://albannikolaiherbst.twoday.net/stories/3140626/ (Stand: 03.08.2013).

führt Herbst dies anhand einer Deters-Figur vor, die aus der Welt auch in die Anderswelt eine Dunckerstraße nach Buenos Aires mitbringt.⁹ Bei der beständigen Verschränkung der inneren und äußeren Weltbegriffe, der jeweiligen Kompossibilitäten, die miteinander doch inkompossibel sind, scheint es tatsächlich nur zwei Möglichkeiten zu geben: entweder die Implosion des Gesamtkonstrukts oder die infinite Erweiterung der inkompossiblen Elemente zu neuen Kompossibilitäten.¹⁰

Der Begriff der Autopoiesis wurde bereits einige Male auf Herbsts Romanwelten angewendet,¹¹ nicht zuletzt, weil Herbst selbst nicht müde wird, ihn für sein Verfahren, oder das Verfahrende der Texte selbst, nahezulegen. Er funktioniert auf diegetischer und semiotischer Ebene hervorragend, als Beschreibung des Erzählverfahrens und damit der Herstellung der Texte ist er allerdings nur unter Anführungszeichen brauchbar und nur im Bewusstsein der Verführung durch Herbsts *Sujet* und begleitende Reflexion anzuwenden. Denn auch für die Mannigfaltigkeit der Herbst'schen Welten gilt letztlich bei aller erzählten Inkompossibilität deren letztliche Kompossibilität, die sehr konservativ über den Schreibenden, den leibhaften Autor akribisch hergestellt wird. Die Harmonie, der wählende Intellekt, der ermöglicht, dass sich in den vielfältigen und scheinbar unendlich gefalteten Welten »expressive Zentren« herausbilden können, »in denen sich immer jeweils die gesamte Welt unter einem gewissen Gesichtspunkt einhüllt«,¹² trägt den Künstlernamen Alban Nikolai Herbst,¹³ der sein erzählerisches »Handwerk« beherrscht. Die Sorge darum verbalisiert Herbst an mehreren Stellen, so besonders eindrücklich in einem Notat zu *Hängenden und abgeschlossenen Motiven*. Dem »hängenden Motiv« bescheinigt er einerseits »etwas Schmarotzendes« und das Bezeugen »erzählerischer Schwäche«, wenn es als unabgeschlossenes, »neue Erzählcluster« einfügendes Motiv laut auf sich aufmerksam macht, andererseits betont Herbst seine Funktionalität, insofern es notwendige, verknüpfende Elemente für verschiedene Erzählstränge unterschwellig anbietet, zur Wahrung dieser Unterschwelligkeit jedoch auf die genaueste Gestaltung durch den Autor angewiesen ist.¹⁴ Das »hängende Motiv« verrät also die sozusagen systeminterne Funktion des Autors als Ratio

---

9 Alban Nikolai Herbst: Buenos Aires. Anderswelt. Kybernetischer Roman. Berlin 2001, S. 97.

10 Vgl. dazu Ursula Reber: Formenverschleifung. Zu einer Theorie der Metamorphose. Kap. 5.6.2: Bauprinzipien des Ortswechsels. München 2009, S. 376–387.

11 So bspw. die Beiträge von Hans Richard Brittnacher, Christoph Jürgensen, Renate Giacomuzzi In: die horen, Bd. 231 (2008).

12 Deleuze (1997), S. 48 (wie Anm. 6).

13 Getauft wurde Alban Nikolai Herbst auf den Namen Alexander Michael von Ribbentrop; 1981 legte er sich den Namen Alban Nikolai Herbst zu, mit dem er seitdem als Schriftsteller auftritt.

14 Alban Nikolai Herbst: Das hängende Motiv. Argo. Anderswelt (204). http://albannikolaiherbst.twoday.net/stories/1540945/ (Stand: 02.08.2013).

sufficiens, als jene Instanz, welche für die Kompossibilität der erzählten Welten sorgt.

Autorfiguren bilden weiterhin ein wichtiges, wenn nicht das wichtigste Figureninventar der Romane. Besonders in *Wolpertinger oder das Blau* überstrahlt der Diskurs des Erzählens, Gegenerzählens, der Autorschaft vs. Autopoiesis den Plot. Insgesamt treten vier Autorfiguren auf (die freilich durch weitere, v.a. durch weibliche Gegenparts weiter ergänzt werden), von denen einer namenlos bleibt, zwei sich denselben Namen, Hans Deters, teilen, außerdem ein Autor, der sich mit den Detersen große Teile der Biographie teilt, aber einen anderen Namen, nämlich Eckehard Cordes, trägt. Das Verfahren, die Autorfiguren in die erzählte und erzählende Realität zu überführen, ist zweifach. Herbst benutzt dabei sowohl das Prinzip der Spaltung, das aus dem einen Autor einen weiteren hervortreibt usf., als auch jenes der Faltung, da jeder Autor aus sich eine kompossible Welt entfaltet, die dadurch, dass die Autoren großteils miteinander deckungsgleich sind, zugleich aber einander gegensätzliche, teils sogar feindliche Ziele in ihrem Schreiben/Schaffen verfolgen, Überschneidungsflächen haben (»Obwohl aber, wenn überhaupt, er es war, der dies durchlebte, hat er nichts mehr damit zu tun. Ich habe lange gebraucht, das zu kapieren. Unversehens ist es meine Geschichte geworden und wird es immer mehr.«[15]). So kommt es bei den Einfaltungen der jeweiligen Welten durch diese auch personalen Überschneidungen zur akuten Existenz von Inkompossibilitäten, die zunehmend auf eine Implosion aller Wirklichkeit/en zusteuern.

»Die Geschichte des Autors ist ergo eine andere als die, die ich ihm schreibe. Aber meine kommt den Sachverhalten näher. Wenn der Autor außerdem unter Aldas Protektorat den Roman im Prozeß seines Entstehens schreibt, braucht er eine Hilfskonstruktion, die ihm erlaubt, sich zu sehen. Das bin in diesem Fall ich. Daraus erhellt ebenfalls unschwer, daß wir nicht identisch sein können, und zwar so wenig, wie Hans Deters noch Ähnlichkeit mit Ulf Laupeyßer oder Claus Falbin hat. Problematisch ist freilich, daß es Hans Deters – nehme ich an – nicht gibt,

---

15
Alban Nikolai Herbst: Wolpertinger oder das Blau. München 2000, Erstausgabe: Frankfurt am Main 1993, S. 561.

wohl aber den Autor und mich. Andererseits sind die beiden Deters' Hilfskonstruktionen, und der Autor meine.«[16]

[16] Alban Nikolai Herbst: Wolpertinger oder das Blau, S. 563 (wie Anm. 15).

Ulf Laupeyßer und Claus Falbin sind frühere Identitäten/Persönlichkeiten von Deters I, die aus dem Vorgängerroman *Die Verwirrung des Gemüts* (1983 bei List erschienen) stammen. Der Auf- und Abspaltungen, der Produktion von Doppelgängern ist kein und war niemals ein Ende; die Existenz von Mehrfachidentitäten und gespaltenen Persönlichkeiten reicht bis in die Voranfänge jeder Erzählung oder Lebensgeschichte zurück. So steigt im Identitätskampf zwischen Laupeyßer und Falbin eine dritte und neue Figur in den Zug ein und als Hans Deters im *Wolpertinger* wieder aus.

Angesichts dessen, dass Hilfskonstruktionen ihrerseits Hilfskonstruktionen ersinnen und ausformen, hat man es mit Mehrfachidentitäten, mit »Dividuen«, Teilbaren, statt »In-Dividuen«, Un-Teilbaren, zu tun. Auf der Text- und der Satzebene zeichnet sich die zerteilte Einheit als ein ständiger Wechsel von erzählendem »ich« und »er«, als sich gegenseitig das Wort aus dem Mund nehmende Erzähler-Autoren ab:

»Cordes reagierte auf sowas, sah schon die Szene leibhaftig vor mir, da kann man dann immer nur abhaun.«[17]

[17] Alban Nikolai Herbst: Argo. Anderswelt (2008), II, 7 auf 8. In: die horen, Bd. 231 (2008), S. 27f., hier S. 28.

»In ein- und demselben Satz sprechen bisweilen zwei verschiedene Subjekte als ›Ichs‹, und indem das eine ins andere Subjekt (Substantiv) wechselt, changieren sofort auch die Räume. Also ein Satz beginnt in Hamburg und endet in Frankfurtmain, ohne das selbstverständlich von einer Reise erzählt würde.«[18]

[18] Alban Nikolai Herbst: Arbeitsnotat 11.11.2004.

In diesem Zusammenhang ist der Versuch lohnend, mit Deleuze/Guattari Hans und Deters und Eckhard und Cordes und Ich und Er als Gefüge anzusehen, d. i. als eine Mannigfaltigkeit, die beständigen Transformationen unterliegt bzw. sich »deterritorialisiert« und »reterritorialisiert«. Wenn all die verschiedenen Erzähler eine »Population« bilden, ist nach den Gesetzen des Gefüges fast schon erforderlich, dass sie sowohl ein Ich als auch ein Ich und Er, dass sie Hans Deters und Nicht-Hans Deters etc. sind. Das Erzählerterritorium wäre, so gesehen, gewissermaßen Hans Deters und Ich; über Deterritorialisierungen transformiert sich dies in ein Er, in einen anderen Hans Deters, in den Autoren, in Eckehard Cordes, in Herbst und reterritorialisiert sich wieder, sodass erneut ein Ich, ein Hans und ein Deters vorhanden sind. So erlaubt der Begriff der Mannigfaltigkeit oder der Population die Vorstellung eines variablen Erzählergefüges, in dem die Erzählrichtungen und -intentionen, die Versprechungen und Verwünschungen, die Subjektivierungen und Objektivierungen wechseln. In einem solchen Erzählterritorium, welches den gewöhnlichen Pakt zwischen LeserIn, ErzählerIn, Figur und AutorIn darüber, was als tatsächlich und was als fiktiv zu verstehen sei, an gleich mehreren Stellen bricht, sind alle Personen sowohl real als auch fiktiv; sie deterritorialisieren sich in Geschichten, die übereinander erzählt werden, wo sie sich reterritorialisieren und Fiktion werden.[19] Dabei handelt es sich nicht um einen Gegensatz zwischen real und fiktiv, sondern Realität ist der Ausdruck des Fiktiven als Inhalt und umgekehrt das Fiktive die Ausdrucksform der Realität als Inhalt im bereits angesprochenen Wechselspiel von Einfaltungen und Ausfaltungen.

Dividualität / Möglichkeitenpoetik

Dividualität bildet ein Prinzip des Herbst'schen kyberrealistischen Programms. Christoph Jürgensen weist darauf hin, dass Herbst im Rahmen seiner Technikbejahung das Prinzip der Aufteilung des Subjekts auf eine Population bereits zu Beginn seiner schriftstellerischen Karriere, 1985, in der Literaturzeitschrift *Dschungelblätter* formulierte[20] und von da an konsequent literarisch umsetzte. Tatsächlich leitet die Dividualität nicht nur das Geschehen in den Romanen, sondern Alban Nikolai Herbst besteht für seine gesamte schriftstellerische Existenz darauf: Er »bekennt« am 8. Mai 1999 in *Die Welt*, dass nicht er, sondern Hans Deters der Verfasser seiner Werke sei.[21] Der Text führt in Kürze das Überschreiben, Gegeneinanderschreiben, Nichtschreiben, wie es aus den Romanen bekannt ist, vor. Mit diesem sorgfältig gestalteten Verwirrspiel von Autorschaft, Erzählerstimme und Realität(sbezug) liefert er das ›reale‹ Gegenstück dazu, dass er sich als leibhaftige Autorfigur Herbst auch in seine Romane hineinschreibt, denn eines Tages findet sich Hans Deters in *Buenos Aires. Anderswelt* mit einem Firmenschild an seiner Haustür

---

19 Anton Moosbach liefert eine klare und sehr überzeugende Analyse der Deters-Figur als »Begriffsperson für das Konzept der Deterritorialisierung«. Vgl. Anton Moosbach: Das Ribbentrop-Rhizom. Ein Experiment mit den Werken von Alban Nikolai Herbst und Gilles Deleuze/Félix Guattari. Lizenziatsarbeit Zürich 2005, verfügbar als PDF auf http://www.die-dschungel.de/ANH/main.html unter »Sekundäres« (Stand: 02.08.2013).

20 Christoph Jürgensen: Unwirkliche Städte, unwirkliches Ich. Zum Verhältnis von Stadt und Individuum in Herbsts Buenos Aires. Anderswelt. In: die horen, Bd. 231 (2008), S. 99–111, hier S. 101.

21 Hans Erich Deters: Eine Beichte. Wie ich zum Schreiben kam. (Gar nicht, ich kam zum Veröffentlichen). In: Die Welt, 08.05.1999, sowie http://www.die-dschungel.de/ANH/txt/pdf/schreiben.pdf (Stand: 03.08.2013).

konfrontiert: »Herbst & Deters. Fiktionäre«. Ebendieses Schild sorgt für weitere Verflechtung auf Herbsts Weblogaccount, wo er zudem unter der Rubrik »Biografie« sich als Dividualität vorstellt, als Justitiar Gregor Lethen, Menschenspekulant und Esoteriker Dietrich Daniello, Unternehmensberater, Vortragsreisender und Mädchenhändler Alexander v. Ribbentrop, als Desinformatiker Hans Erich Deters, Ghostwriter Alban Nikolai Herbst sowie als Cyberfigur Titania Carthaga.

Herbst geht noch über die eigene Dividualisierung hinaus und bezieht seine LeserInnen mit ein. Das Weblog, das er seit 2003 betreibt, erlaubt in seiner Struktur die fortlaufende Kommentartätigkeit von LeserInnen, die streckenweise recht aktiv genutzt wird, sodass sich Diskussionen um einzelne Themen entspinnen. Allerdings ist hinsichtlich der Möglichkeit, die einzelnen Kommentare Personen zuschreiben zu können, Vorsicht geboten, da Herbst nicht nur die »biographisch« erwähnten, sondern weit mehr Personae bzw. Avatare benutzt, mit deren Hilfe er sich selbst beständig kommentiert oder zumindest entstehende Diskussionen in von ihm erwünschte Richtungen lenkt. Als gesichert darf nach Renate Giacomuzzi gelten, dass Paul Reichenbach zu Herbsts Dividualität gehört.[22] Selbstverständlich spielt die Unentscheidbarkeit der Autorschaft dem Herbst'schen Konzept zu.

»Ich habe, während ich das Verfahren entwickelte – besser: während e s sich entwickelte – auch Leser meiner Arbeiten darin hineingenommen, die auf meine Arbeit reagiert haben; in *Der Dschungel* ist das ja sehr gut möglich. So schrieb mir am 29. November 2005 ein Kommentator, der sich *mimikry* nannte, das Folgende in das Literarische Weblog [...]. Hier also *mimikry*s Kommentar*.«[23]

Nach Anklicken des angebotenen Links zu besagtem Kommentar findet sich allerdings überraschenderweise ein Romanauszug aus *Argo*, sodass wohl auch bei »mimikry« mit dem programmatischen Namen die Herbst-Dividualität zu veranschlagen ist. Die mit * gekennzeichnete Fußnote besagt das Folgende:

»[*: Der durchaus reale Schweizer Schriftsteller Markus A. Hediger schrieb daraufhin drei Tage später in *Der Dschungel*:

---

22 Renate Giacomuzzi: Die ›Dschungel.Anderswelt‹ und A. N. Herbsts ›Poetologie des literarischen Bloggens‹. In: die horen, Bd. 231 (2008), S. 137–150, hier S. 143.

23 Alban Nikolai Herbst: http://albannikolaiherbst.twoday.net/topics/KYBERREALISM/?start=40 (Stand: 04.08.2013) (wie Anm. 5).

›Romanfigur Hediger (3). Als diese sehe ich mich selbst spätestens seit ich der Romanfigur Herbst in Berlin begegnete. Und bin ausserordentlich verwirrt deshalb, weil ich nun den Verdacht nicht loswerde, Herbst habe mich tatsächlich erfunden. Nun bin ich Romanfigur, die sich in Variationen selber liest.‹]«

Im Fortgang der Kommentare und Gegenkommentare treibt die Herbstdividualität erwartungsgemäß ihr Spiel mit der Autorschaft und der Fiktionalität der Figuren, indem Herbst unter verschiedenen Beiträgernamen scheinbar enthüllt, welche Figur er erfunden habe und welche nicht. Dabei kommen auch die Figuren zu Wort, um ihn in bekannter Manier zu korrigieren, was bspw. das Datum ihrer Erschaffung betrifft. Sicher ist jedoch, dass eine Figur über eine *eBay*-Auktion entstand, in der entweder die Rolle als Neben- oder als Hauptfigur ersteigert werden konnte.[24]

Bezüglich des Kommentars bzw. des Fortschreibens des Romantextes durch mimikry merkt Herbst an, er sei den »gelegten Spuren weitergefolgt, das heißt, [er habe] [...] das, was als mögliche Folge einer Romanhandlung [...] fantasiert worden ist, wie eine Tatsache behandelt – als eine matrische Komponente eben, mit der [...] die poetischen Rechenvorgänge als Möglichkeit durchgearbeitet [...], die, und das ist jetzt wichtig, anderen Möglichkeiten durchaus widersprach«.[25] Damit lange ich wieder beim In/Kompossibilitätsprinzip und seiner Ordnung an, das in Herbsts Poetologie als eine der Möglichkeiten, die unbedingt ihre Verwirklichung anstreben, entwickelt wird. Dieser Möglichkeitenpoetik kommt im Roman eine »Verfügungs- und Verknüpfungsschönheit«[26] zu. In der Wahl und Ausführung der Motive wird dabei eine Form der Abgeschlossenheit im Motivischen, der zugleich der kunstvolle »Eindruck einer *möglichen Beliebigkeit*« entspricht, suggeriert. Diese Möglichkeitenpoetik wird im Weblog zu einer Modalitätenästhetik der kybernetischen Totalität erweitert, die qua ihrer Unüberschaubarkeit für Individuen eine »mythische« Ästhetik genannt wird.[27] Sowohl die kybernetische als auch die mythische Totalität sind dabei als Projekte zu verstehen: Ihre Unüberschaubarkeit verhindert auf der einen Seite die Abschließbarkeit von Erklärungen für einzelne Phänomene. So werden immer weitere In/Kompossibilia hinzugefügt

24
Vgl. Giacomuzzi (2008), FN 22 (wie Anm. 22).

25
Alban Nikolai Herbst: http://albannikolaiherbst.twoday.net/topics/KYBERREALISM/?start=40 (Stand: 04.08.2013) (wie Anm. 5).

26
Alban Nikolai Herbst: Romantheorie. Argo. Anderswelt (152). Kleine Theorie des Literarischen Bloggens (52). Eintrag vom 30.09.2005. http://albannikolaiherbst.twoday.net/stories/1018688/ (Stand: 04.08.2013).

27
Alban Nikolai Herbst: Romantheorie. Argo. Anderswelt. Eintrag vom 30.09.2005 (wie Anm. 26).

und verknüpft (›verlinkt‹), die aber stets neuen Erklärungsbedarf produzieren. Auf der anderen Seite stellen beide Systeme das Individuum, die Unteilbarkeit selbst, infrage, aus dessen/deren Perspektive lediglich Zusammenhanglosigkeit sichtbar wird.

Erneut darf jedoch Herbst, der Autor, nicht beim Wort genommen, sondern es muss bedacht werden, dass auch dieses poetologische Programm Teil ebendieser Ästhetik ist. Die behauptete Wiedergeburt des Mythos aus dem Computer entspricht dem Herbst'schen *Stil* der literarischen Umsetzung der Modalitätenästhetik. Wie bereits oben ausgeführt, ist diese jedoch ein schriftstellerisches Produkt, ohne dass tatsächlich ›der Computer‹ oder ein Softwareprogramm an seiner Entwicklung mitschriebe. Treffender charakterisiert ist das wahrnehmungs- und kommunikationsbezogene Problem der Modalitäten im Abschnitt »ARGO-ÜA (23). Gestrichenes (ff.). Wirklichkeit & Gegenwart«[28] im Reflex über die fiktionäre Durchdringung von medialer und realer Gegenwart als Gegenwartsroman in doppeltem Sinne:

»Der klirrenden Kälte wegen kann es kaum der späte Oktober, frühe November s e i n, an dem dieser Roman eigentlich spielt; seine Entstehung braucht mehr Zeit als die Handlung [...]. Will er also Gegenwartsroman bleiben, dann müssen die Geschehen die Gegenwart vor sich herschieben oder wenigstens mit sich ziehen, und zwar jeweils in eine neue Gegenwart hinein; dem entspricht die Vorstellung von Gleichzeitigkeit (geschichtsmoralisch ausgedrückt: der Anwesenheit des Vergangenen im Jetzt, seine Metamorphose). Das fiel Eckhard Cordes soeben zur Erklärung ein, und er dachte, es müsse dieses sich-ineinander-Verhaken [sic] dazu führen, daß die einzelnen Erzählfragmente selbst immer kleiner würden, es seien schließlich narrative Punkte, *entities*, hätte Whitehead gesagt, die insgesamt wie Tausende Pixel das flächige Bild, das Tableau, über die Entfernung bewirkten, die jemand dazu einnimmt. Stehe er zu nahe daran, dann zerfalle das Bild. Das ist eine Beobachtung Vilém Flussers. Unsere Wirklichkeit sei nämlich schon deshalb nicht stetig, w e i l sie pointilliert sei. Die Wahrnehmung eines Geschlossenen und Stetigen stelle sich rein deshalb her, weil das Gehirn die Wirklichkeit so interpretiere [...].«

28
Alban Nikolai Herbst: ARGO-ÜA (23). Gestrichenes (ff.). Wirklichkeit & Gegenwart. http://albannikolai-herbst.twoday.net/topics/ARGO-ANDERSWELT/?start=40 (Stand: 04.08.2013).

Nun *wirkten* die Wirklichkeitspunkte selbstverständlich gegenseitig aufeinander, das halte die Wirklichkeit überhaupt zusammen wie die Anziehungs- und Fliehkräfte die Körperchen des Moleküls und wiederum diese die Zelle und die den Körper insgesamt, welcher wiederum auf eine ganz analoge Art mit anderen Körpern, schließlich der Welt und dem Kosmos interagiere; indes sei die Art dieser Kräfte völlig verschieden: in der Poesie nennt man sie Inspiration.«

Dass auch die globalisierte Gegenwart in ihren mehrfach gedoppelten, gespiegelten und medialisierten gleichzeitigen Ungleichzeitigkeiten unüberschaubar geworden ist, ist spätestens seit Baudrillard zum Schlagwort verkommen. Worin Herbsts Modalitätenstil als ein produktiver Spiegel funktioniert, ist, den »Strom der Erzählungen von Gleichzeitigkeiten« in einer poetologischen Zeitlichkeit umzusetzen, welche den üblichen Chronotopos der Erzählung in eine Konsistenzebene versetzt, in welcher erzählte Zeit, Erzählzeit und Lebenszeit zum Begriff von Zeit werden, zu den angesprochenen »narrativen Punkten«, die aufeinander wirken in der Art des schon zu Beginn bemühten Zitat Lacans, das die vollzogene Zukunft der Vergangenheit als Gegenwart/*Präsenz* hervorbringt.[29]

Herbst arbeitet mit der ›Zeitigung‹ sorgfältig und höchst bewusst, ist doch Ziel, seinem Werk, inklusive des Weblogs, den Mythos einzuschreiben. Als Bild benutzt der ›Kybernetiker‹ den Regelkreis:

»[Z]wischen dem scheinbaren Wiederanfang und dem tatsächlichen Neuanfang [einer veranschlagten Linie; U.R.] klafft eine Lücke. Denn eben gerade nicht findet eine Ewige Wiederkehr des Gleichen statt, sondern die Erzählung bildet geschichtliche Strukturen ab, die nach Mustern organisiert sind, welche sich zugleich irreversibel über fortlaufende Metaebenen auf dem Zeitstrahl voranbewegen. Hat man den Eindruck, ein Erzählzyklus komme wieder an seinem Anfang an, so haben sich doch sämtliche Beteiligten und hat sich auch das grundlegende Setting verändert. [...]

Man kann sich das durch ein Gedankenspiel, also ein Modell, klarmachen, dass die Spirale selbst sich in einer Vierten Dimension, nämlich der Zeit, auffalten läßt.«[30]

[29] Ausgeführt habe ich die Zeitort- und Medienstrukturen unter verschiedenen Aspekten in: Reber (2009), Kap. 5.4 u. 5.6 (wie Anm. 1).

[30] Alban Nikolai Herbst: Graphen der Erzählbewegung. Dritte Heidelberger Vorlesung (5). Aus der Erweiterung des Anfangs. Eintrag vom 07.01.2008. http://albannikolaiherbst.twoday.net/stories/4590233/ (Stand: 04.08.2013).

Wieder begleitet das Herbst'sche theoretische Denken die Falte, hier die Auffaltung einer um sich und in sich gedrehten – bzw. gefalteten – Linie zu einer Spirale, durch die als Ganzes, so Herbst weiter, der gesamte Strom an Erzählungen fließt.

»Nun setzt sich die scheinbare Stetigkeit dieses Stromes der Erzählungen (in Somadevas um das Jahr 1000 herum entstandenen Kathasaritsagara war noch ein Ozean, also Stetigkeit der Ströme der Erzählungen vorgestellt) aus zahllosen, letztlich unendlich vielen Erzählungen zusammen; das, addiert, ergibt dieses stetig [sic] Bild (es heißt aber wohl nur, daß die Sprünge verschwindend kleine Dimensionen annehmen). Nehmen wir indes eine einzige Erzählung aus dem Strom heraus, läßt sich die Spirale und lassen sich deshalb die Sprünge erkennen, die die ›Anfänge‹ und ›Enden=Wiederanfänge‹ der Regelspiralen, bezogen auf diese einzige Erzählung, vollziehen; man sieht jetzt deutlich, daß es sich eben nicht um Redundanzen handelt.

Diese Kippleistung vollbringt die poetische Inspiration. Letztlich ist ein Roman der Schatten, den ein vier- bzw. mehrdimensionaler Erzählkörper, also die ihm zugrundeliegende, aus seinen Gründen herauswirkende Wirklichkeit, auf die Buchseite in die Schriftform wirft.«

So, wie Deleuze die aktive Faltung der Seele, ihre Neigung, einen Ausdruck der Gegenwart nennt,[31] »wenn sich der Einschluß in die Vergangenheit und in die Zukunft ins Unendliche erstreckt, dann weil er zunächst die lebendige Gegenwart betrifft, die deren Verteilung jedesmal vorsitzt«,[32] so spielen sich in einem Bündel an Erzählungen, das stets von der vollzogenen Zukunft spricht, die Geschichten der Herbst'schen Figuren und Avatare in einem dauernd verschwimmenden, transitorischen Jetzt ab, das je nach Roman nie den Nachmittag eines Donnerstags (oder Mittwochs), den 1. November, einen Mittag, den Moment der Empfindung verlässt.

Dieses transitorische Präsens, die stetige Präsenz wird sichtbar in rekurrenten Wahrnehmungströmungen sowie über jene oben genannte Technik, eine Erzählung nur aus dem Strom herauszunehmen, um die Sprünge, die Lücken innerhalb aller

---

31 Gilles Deleuze: Inkompossibilität, Individualität, Freiheit. In: Die Falte. Leibniz und der Barock. Aus dem Frz. v. Ulrich Johannes Schneider. Frankfurt am Main 2000, S. 113–119, hier S. 117.

32 Deleuze (2000), S. 117 (wie Anm. 31).

Erzählungen und auch zwischen ihnen sichtbar zu machen. Eines der wichtigsten Mittel ist, Asyndeta, Ellipsen, also unverbundene und subjektlose Sätze einzusetzen. Die erzählenden Figuren kommen dabei nicht zur Handlung, Sinneseindrücke werden im Stil von Kamerafahrten und Close-ups wiedergegeben. Das Filmbild literarisch umzusetzen, erlaubt, einen reinen Wahrnehmungs- und Sensationsraum zu präsentieren: »Hence the observer and the observed fuse or interchange so rapidly that fusion is apparent. Instead of discourse – a running between or running back and forth – there is intercourse, a running together.«[33]

33
Mark Slade: Language of Change. Moving Images of Man. Toronto, Montreal 1970, S. 96.

Das Filmbild objektiviert durch die Vorrangstellung der Wahrnehmung und des Beobachtens das klassische (autonome) Subjekt, das nicht mehr mit seinem Blick auf die Welt alleine ist und die Interpretationshoheit über diesen Blick und das Wahrgenommene innehat, sondern die Beobachter-Prämisse bedingt, dass auch er bzw. sie ständig angeblickt wird. Auch dies nimmt mit anderen Mitteln eine bekannte Struktur wieder auf: Die Erzählbarkeit des Mythos, des mythischen Raums, verlangt Beobachter. Die Blicke von Sich-Verwandelndem/Verwandelnder, verwandelnder Kraft und Zuschauer/in überkreuzen sich auf der veränderbaren Körperoberfläche des/der Sich-Verwandelnden. Der Körper wird so zur Leinwand des Netzes der Blicke. Herbsts postapokalyptische Großstadtträume, deren Plätze, Straßen und Gebäude in beständigem Umbau und Verwandlung sind, erfüllen in diesem Zusammenhang eine doppelte Funktion: Einerseits fungieren auch sie als Leinwand für die Blicke der Zuseher, ohne die nicht möglich wäre, die Namensänderungen, die Verschiebungen der Architekturen sichtbar zu machen. Andererseits wird das Rauschen selbst auf ihnen sichtbar, wenn das Flimmern signalschwacher elektronischer Bilder auf und an ihnen sichtbar wird oder Szenerien wie bei schlechtem WLAN-Empfang einfrieren. Der Sensationsraum wird mehr durch die Grenzen zwischen den einzelnen Bildern, durch die Lücke zwischen den Einstellungen bestimmt.

Die Erzählzeit der Romane, auch wenn, wie in der erzählenden Literatur üblich, über weite Strecken hinweg das

Präteritum gewählt wird, ist, passend zur zeitlichen Entrücktheit mythischer und halbmythischer Figuren wie Chill Borkenbord, Odysseus, Deidamia usw., das Präsens. Die Augen der nicht einmal beobachtenden, sondern zumeist wie reizüberfluteten zufälligen Zuschauer übernehmen die Rolle der Videokamera, sie nehmen wahr, verzeichnen, speichern ab, wobei der Strom des Wahrgenommenen unentwegt über sie hinweggleitet wie über eine Bildschirmoberfläche.[34]

Pathos/Rhythmus

Die Konsistenzebene der Zeit interagiert mit einer weiteren der Empfindung, welche den Begriff des Pathos über die Sprache hervorbringt. Empfindungen, Leidenschaften und Pathos werden von Herbst nicht erzählt, sondern tatsächlich über seinen Stil, seine Haltung hervorgebracht. Herbsts Schreiben nutzt alle Stilebenen, vom Derben über die Versprachlichung von Comic und Computerspiel bis zum Elegischen. Auf allen Ebenen herrscht eine bilderreiche und ausdrucksstarke Sprache, deren größte Eigenheit die Inversion ist, die der Alltagssprache gegenläufige Wortstellung. Zwar kann das Vorziehen des postpositionalen Konjunktionaladverbs »nämlich« an den Satzanfang, an dem Herbst eindeutig zu erkennen ist, und zwar sowohl in den Romanen als auch im Weblog, eher als Marotte gewertet werden. Die Kombinatorik der Stilebenen und die nachgerade obsessive Nutzung ausgefallener und altertümlicher rhetorischer Figuren jedoch als Stil und Stilisierung reiht Alban Nikolai Herbst unzweideutig unter die asiatischen Schriftsteller, denen das Ornament, die Beigabe zur eigentlichen Botschaft wird.[35]

In *Wolpertinger oder das Blau* tritt die Leidenschaft, das Pathos, die zur mythischen Landschaft und zum mythischen Narrativ als deren Motivation dazugehören,[36] einesteils unverdeckter, andernteils im Stil der Ironie auf. Im Fall der Figurenzeichnung von Lipom, eines Oberon-Avatars, und seiner umständlichen, weitschweifigen, von Gottfried Benn-Zitaten sowie von Ächzern und Stöhnen durchsetzten Sprache erschließt sich das Herbst'sche Dilemma, wie sich mithilfe des Pathetischen nichtironisch und zugleich ironisch erzählen ließe.[37] Das Pathos unterläuft in der unbedingten Grausamkeit

[34] Dass nicht nur die Augen, sondern überhaupt die Körper der Akteur/innen als Interface für die nicht nur optischen Wahrnehmungsbilder ihrer Umgebung funktionieren, wird spätestens in Buenos Aires offenbar, wenn sie wörtlich als Screen benutzt werden, über die ID-Cards gescannt werden und Chat-Nachrichten hinweglaufen.

[35] Vgl. dazu Hans Richard Brittnacher: Der verspielte Untergang/Apokalypsen bei Alban Nikolai Herbst. In: die horen, Bd. 231 (2008), S. 29–42, insbes. S. 39–40.

[36] Vgl. zum Komplex der Leidenschaften im Mythos Heinz-Peter Preußer: Achilleus als Barde/Kybernetische Mythenkorrektur bei Alban Nikolai Herbst. In: die horen, Bd. 231 (2008), S. 73–89.

[37] Vgl. Das Innen ein Hotel (2). Korrespondenzen: An Albert Meier, Uni Kiel. Eintrag v. 29.05.2011.

die Distanz der Ironie, in welcher »der Pathetiker« und wortreiche sowie -gewandte Elfenfürst an der Aufhebung des ausgeschlossenen Dritten arbeitet, es zelebriert Leidenschaft und Affekt, es ist in dieser Hinsicht und jeder Form distanzlos grausam. So grausam wie Lipom, der schrittweise sein lügenhaft-fiktionäres Verwirrspiel mit den Detersen zugunsten der ihm eigenen Bösartigkeit und Magie ablegt und sich als rasender Dionysos des Untergangs zeigt.[38]

Alban Nikolai Herbst erhebt das Pathos zum ästhetischen Programm,[39] das jedoch über bloße Rhetorik hinausgeht. Das Pathos wird dem Literaturmarkt und dem Entertainment als literarische Strategie entgegengesetzt, geht in Form einer sprachlich und über die Weblogeinträge/Logbucheinträge medial stilisierten Authentizität, für eine Modalitätenpoetik der Dividualität folgerichtig, in das gelebte Leben über, begründet demnach einen holistischen Stil. Renate Giacomuzzi zeichnet diesen Stil in seiner Ungewöhnlichkeit und Anstößigkeit knapp in einigen Stationen von der radikalen Offenlegung des Privaten im ersten Web-Tagebuch über die Programmatik des Märtyrers in der Weblog-Ästhetik und das Involviertsein in gesellschaftlich tabuisierte Leidenschaftspraktiken des SM.[40] In dieser Form eines Stils im Sinne des Habitus ist Giacomuzzi unbedingt recht zu geben, dass der Computer und das Netz sich als »kongeniale ›Partner‹ des Autors«[41] erweisen. Bei dieser nietzscheanisch geprägten Experimentalanordnung der Formgebung des eigenen Lebens arbeiten die Möglichkeiten des Weblogs und des Arbeitsjournals der Herbst'schen Fiktionäre der Entfaltung eines solchen Stils der Leidenschaften zu. Dabei sind Pathos und Leidenschaften nicht (nur) als Themen zu verstehen, das Experiment selbst des fiktionären Stils zwischen Mensch und Maschine, Autor und Netz, privat und öffentlich, fungiert gewissermaßen als jene Affizierung, welche die Entfaltung des Pathos gewährleistet.

Der Affekt als körperlicher Zustand, als Affiziert-Sein durch einen anderen Körper und als Zwischenbereich zur Handlung gibt auch das eigentliche Sujet der *Anderswelt*-Romane ab. Alban Nikolai Herbst unterliegt, wie einigen poetologischen Unterhaltungen auf seinem Weblog zu entnehmen ist, der

---

[38] Eine vollständige Analyse des Dionysischen und der Lipom-Figur in Reber (2009), Kap. 5.4 (wie Anm. 1).

[39] Zum Pathos als literarisches Programm vgl. Uwe Schütte: Erzählen für morgen/Zur poetologischen Genealogie des Kybernetischen Realismus bei Alban Nikolai Herbst.In: die horen, Bd. 231 (2008), S. 121–130, hier S. 126f.

[40] Giacomuzzi 2008, S. 142f. (wie Anm. 22).

[41] Ebd., S. 145.

Faszination der Neurowissenschaften, die sich mit den materiellen Bedingungen der Affizierung beschäftigen. In seinen künstlerischen Produkten, den auf dem Buchmarkt erscheinenden und vertriebenen Romanen in Buchform wird diese Basis einer affektiven Poetologie zum Verschwinden gebracht. Die Form, in der hier Affekte zum Anschein gebracht werden und die Affizierung auch der LeserInnen vorgenommen wird, ist die sprachbildliche Darstellung, teils Evokation von Emotion und Leidenschaft, weit wirksamer aber die rhythmische Gestaltung der sprachlichen Form.

Bereits die Sprache an sich versteht Herbst in Absetzung zu ihrer grammatischen, subjekt- und bewusstseinskonstituierenden Form als ein »Mitteilungssystem außerhalb des Empfindens«.[42] Mit dem »außersprachlichen Empfinden« arbeitet Herbst, um den Affekt fließen zu lassen und dem Pathos eine Ausdrucksebene zu verleihen, über Rhythmisierung. Rhythmisierende Elemente lassen sich auf allen Ebenen der Dichtung ausmachen. Bereits der einfachen Lektüre erschließt sich die sonatenförmige Anordnung der In/Kompossibilitätsstränge, die in jedem Buch in ein durchvariiertes »Finale furioso« münden. Den In/Kompossibilitätssträngen sind Motive zugeordnet. Gemeinsam zugleich mit den Weltenwechseln und -überschneidungen werden solche Motive einander anverwandelt und ineinander überführt, synkopisch zunächst, Satz-, Absatz-, Kapitelgrenzen überschreitend, sodass verschiedenen Subjekten dieselbe Empfindung oder Sensation zugeschrieben wird.[43] Leitmotive im Versmaß bilden eine Art des innerpoetischen Gedächtnisses, sie tönen abgelöst von aktual erzählenden Stimmen wie eine Mahnung immer wieder auf: »Blut und Hirn verspritzten sich rings um die Wände« in *Wolpertinger*, »Three things that enrich the poet:/myths, poetic power and a store of ancient verse« sowie »die Rinder des Thetra« in *Thetis*. In *Argo* tritt die leitmotivische Strukturierung zugunsten einer Gesamtversifizierung in den Hintergrund. Grund und Methode legt Alban Nikolai Herbst offen, macht er sich doch konkret an eine Neudichtung von Goethes *Achilleis* in einer vers- und metrikgenauen Umwandlung.[44] Unterlegt und durchmischt mit Zitaten aus weiteren epischen Werken wie der *Ilias* durchziehen diese

---

42 Vgl. dazu den Kommentar v. 13.03.2013.

43 Beispiele dazu siehe Ursula Reber: Avatarische Intensitäten. Affektive Landschaften in Alban Nikolai Herbsts Anderswelt-Romanen. In: die horen, Bd. 231 (2008), S. 49–65, hier S. 61.

44 Textbeispiele In: die horen, Bd. 231 (2008), S. 97f.

neuen Verse den Roman, einen rhythmischen und motivischen neuen Grund für die Exaltationen der Sprache und die Affizierungen der geschilderten Körper zu geben.

Schöne Literatur muss grausam sein! lautet der Titel einer poetologischen Rede, die Alban Nikolai Herbst am 23.03.2002 in Leipzig vor der Deutschen Literaturkonferenz hielt.⁴⁵ In ihr bekennt Herbst sich zur Grenzüberschreitung, zum Ausnahmezustand, kurz gefasst zu einem literarischen Verständnis von Intensitäten. Aus ihr leitet er das Programm der Literatur her, dem Pathos v. a. als dem Leiden Raum zu geben, dem empfundenen Affekt vor der Moral oder ohne Moral eine Stimme zu verleihen und sie dabei auf Mannigfaltigkeiten zu verteilen, die auch die sprachliche, damit die (onto)logische Struktur von Subjekt und Objekt durchbricht, einfach darüber hinwegfegt. Mit andern Worten fordert er eine ekstatische, eine kathartische Literatur.

Wer dabei Modelle antiker Literaturtheorie aus Tragödie und Epos, vermittelt über Nietzsche und die Romantik, weiterentwickelt in der Postmoderne wiedererkennt, geht darin nicht in die Irre.⁴⁶ Worauf die Modalitätenästhetik in einer globalen Welt, die von der Gleichzeitigkeit der ungleichzeitigen Erzählungen gekennzeichnet ist, abstellt,»sind *alte Formen in der Gegenwart der Zukunft* (›in der Gegenwart a l s Zukunft‹)«⁴⁷ gemäß des Verständnisses der fortschreitenden Faltungen aller Empfindungen. Folgerichtig setzt Herbst die Körper seiner Figuren Exzessen an Gewalt aus,⁴⁸ unterstellt den verbalisierten und ›avatarisierten‹ eigenen Körper und seine Empfindungen im Weblog zur Schau und Überschreibung, unterzieht seine Textkörper nachvollziehbar und offen dem endlosen Streichen, Korrigieren, Über- und Neuschreiben und zielt letztlich auch auf die Körper und Gedächtnisse der LeserInnen in seinem Wunsch, den Gesamteindruck eines Verhängnisses einzupflanzen und Stabilität in Instabilität zu überführen.

45
Verfügbar auf: http://www.diedschungel.de/ANH/txt/pdf/schoene_literatur.pdf (Stand: 05.08.2013).

46
Die poetologische Genealogie Alban Nikolai Herbsts Kyberrealismus hat Schütte 2008 (wie Anm. 39) zusammengetragen.

47
Alban Nikolai Herbst: Weshalb Hexameter? The Archaic Revival, vampyroteuthisch. Zum Epilog. Argo. Anderswelt (267), http://albannikolaiherbst.twoday.net/stories/5145659/ (Stand: 05.08.2013).

48
Zu diesem Aspekt vgl. Brittnacher (2008), (wie Anm. 35), sowie Reber (2009), Kap. 5.4. u. 5.5, (wie Anm.1).

Usha Reber
Studium der Klassischen Philologie, Germanistik, Philosophie an der Philipps-Universität-Marburg; 2006 Dissertation *Formenverschleifung. Zu einer Theorie der Metamorphose* an der Universität Wien (Publikation 2008). Seit 2007 Projektleitung der Internet-Plattform *Kakanien revisited* (www.kakanien.ac.at) für SEE/CE Studies. 2006/07 Koordination des Initiativkollegs *Kulturen der Differenz. Transformationen in Zentraleuropa*. Forschungsschwerpunkte und Veröffentlichungen: Literaturtheorie, Intertextualität, Postcolonial Studies, Phantastik.

Dinge im Rückspiegel sind näher als sie erscheinen. Zum Selbstporträt in der zeitgenössischen Videokunst

Holger Kube Ventura

»Die Bilder, die vor mehr als hundert Jahren laufen lernten, haben uns längst überholt. Sie führen ihr dynamisches Eigenleben, sind immer und überall verfügbar und können in unendlich viele Kategorien unterteilt werden. Endlich kann jeder Filme machen – mit minimalem Einsatz von Zeit, Geld und technischem Know-how. Bilderströme rauschen durchs Netz, finden Millionen von Fans und können jederzeit mit einem weltweiten Publikum geteilt werden.«[1] Das gilt insbesondere für Bilder von sich selbst. Und gerade in der zeitgenössischen Videokunst sind die Auswirkungen dieser Entwicklung sichtbar.

In der bereits 50-jährigen Geschichte der Videokunst[2] spielten Selbstporträts und Closed Circuit-Installationen schon immer eine besondere Rolle: als Positionsbestimmung des Künstlers, zur Reflexion des Betrachterstandpunktes, als erkenntnistheoretische Identitätsfrage oder als Narrative des Selbst. Aber seit die tägliche Herstellung und Distribution bewegter Bilder von sich selbst und von probeweise eingenommenen Rollen zur Normalität in Sozialen Netzwerken geworden sind, haben sich für viele Videokünstler neue Fragestellungen ergeben. Was behauptet das Abbild einer Person noch, und was unterscheidet das Abbild vom Spiegelbild? Das ehemals verstörende Vorzeigen des technischen Rahmens eines Bildes ist längst zum Normalfall der Clipkultur geworden. Selbst einfache Videoschnittprogramme in Mobiltelefonen bieten eine Fülle von Gestaltungseffekten, und der Closed Circuit – jenes ehemals aufregende Erlebnis, ein bewegtes Spiegelbild von sich selbst in Echtzeit zu sehen – findet heute bei jedem Skype-Gespräch statt. Mediatisierung ist allgegenwärtig. Wenn die audiovisuelle Apparatur im Bilderkonsum längst permanent präsent ist, wenn also jedes Bild und jedes Selbstbild einerseits stets verfügbar ist und andererseits seine eigene technische Relativierung und Bezweiflung immer schon bereit hält, welchen Status hat dann noch das Bild einer Person und welche Identifizierungen können seine Betrachter noch wagen?

In der gegenwärtigen Videokunst ist dies zu einem wichtigen Thema geworden. Zahlreiche Künstler beschäftigen sich in ihren Arbeiten mit Fragen nach der visuellen Konstituierung eines Subjekts: Wie manifestieren sich Identitäten in Abbildern, was ist ein Sprechender, was ein Sich-Abbildender,

---

1
Zitiert aus einem unveröffentlichten Konzeptpapier (Oktober 2012) der B3 Biennale des Bewegten Bildes.

2
Als Geburtsstunde wird immer wieder Nam June Paiks Einzelausstellung *Exposition of Music – Electronic Vision* im März 1963 in der Wuppertaler Galerie Parnass genannt.

wodurch entsteht ein Gegenüber und kann ich in einer Spiegelung mich selbst sehen? Künstler nehmen verständlicherweise meist eine eher kritische Haltung ein zu den Möglichkeiten der Identifizierung via Abbild und interessieren sich stattdessen für deren Bedingungen. Darüber hinaus stellen sie die Befragung von Rollenvorstellungen ins Zentrum ihrer Arbeit (z. B. durch Reenactments) und loten Eigenarten von Bildern, Spiegelbildern und Gegenbildern aus. Nicht zuletzt geht es dabei um verschiedene Ästhetiken, die in den Dekonstruktionen des Bildes von sich selbst zu finden sind, wenn das Begehren danach durchkreuzt oder aufgefächert wird und die Differenz zwischen Fassung und Person hervortritt. Solche Strategien können als Reaktion auf die Allgegenwart von Selbstdarstellungen (z. B. auf *Facebook*) gelesen werden – und als ihr künstlerisches Korrektiv.

Anlässlich der ersten Ausgabe der *B3 Biennale des bewegten Bildes* im Herbst 2013 präsentierte der Frankfurter Kunstverein eine große Gruppenausstellung unter dem Titel *Per Speculum Me Video* (31.10.2013–05.01.2014). Der Titel behauptete in der toten lateinischen Sprache, dass ein Ich sich mit dem Spiegel sehen könnte oder sehen würde. Durch seine Diktion wirkte der Titel wie ein in Vergessenheit geratener Zauberspruch, der die Theorie des französischen Psychoanalytikers Jacques Lacan über die Koppelung der Selbstwahrnehmung und Ich-Entwicklung an das Erkennen des eigenen Spiegelbildes beschwört. Der Schwerpunkt der Ausstellung lag auf Videoinstallationen, ferner wurden fotografische und akustische Arbeiten gezeigt. Im Folgenden soll anhand einiger ausgewählter Werke nach der Bedeutung von Selbstporträt und Selbstbeobachtung in der gegenwärtigen Videokunst gefragt werden: Was ist aus ehemaligen Potentialen von Closed Circuit-Konzepten geworden und welche Formen können Rollenspiele in Spiegelbildern heute annehmen?

Das charakteristischste Merkmal der Videotechnik gegenüber der des Films ist die Möglichkeit zu simultaner Aufzeichnung und Wiedergabe. Bereits 1936 war in öffentlichen Fernsehstuben die erste Live-Übertragung der Olympischen Spiele zu sehen gewesen, aber erst 30 Jahre später – als die Firma *Sony* mit dem *Portapak* das erste erschwingliche, tragbare Video-Aufnahmesystem auf den Markt brachte – bekamen Künstler die

Möglichkeit zur elektronischen Spiegelung. Schon bald darauf war die oft intime Selbstreflexion in geschlossenen Kreisläufen aus Überwachung und Darstellung zur Basis vieler Videoarbeiten der 1970er Jahre geworden. Es entstand ein interdisziplinärer Bereich aus Performance, Theater, Körperexperiment und Videofilm. Das im Closed Circuit aus Videokamera und Monitor herstellbare und konservierbare Spiegelbild ermöglichte es Künstlern wie etwa Bruce Nauman oder Peter Campus, das eigene Selbst anhand bewegter Selbstbildnisse zu erforschen. Während im traditionellen Theater stets eine inszenierte Realität (vor)gespielt wird, untersuchten die neuen Videoperformances das Sich-in-Szene-Setzen im wahrsten Sinne des Wortes. Die Länge der produzierten Bänder korrespondierte dabei konsequenterweise häufig mit der Dauer des Geschehens.[3]

Im Gegensatz zum Film war bei der per Live-Monitor kontrollierten Videokamera auf Stativ keine Kameraführung mehr nötig, bewegte Selbstporträts und Selbstbilder ließen sich ohne fremde Hilfe und Verzögerung aufnehmen, beobachten und korrigieren. So konnten in der Privatheit des Studio-Experiments der eigene Körper und das Spiel mit dem eigenen Abbild zu Inhalt und Form der künstlerischen Arbeit werden. Friederike Pezold schrieb dazu einmal: »Mit Video konnte ich das Unmögliche möglich machen, gleichzeitig vor und hinter der Kamera zu stehen. Mit Video konnte ich auch das Unmögliche möglich machen: Gleichzeitig Maler und Modell sein! Gleichzeitig Subjekt und Objekt sein! Gleichzeitig Bild und Abbild sein.«[4] Video war das Versprechen von Autonomie und Selbstermächtigung – und das Versprechen auf eine verstärkte Präsenz von Künstlerinnen in der Öffentlichkeit. Valie Export, Ulrike Rosenbach, Rebecca Horn, Joan Jonas, Annegret Soltau und Barbara Hamman beschäftigten sich mit gesellschaftlichen Frauenbildern und konnten sich in dem neuen Medium nicht zuletzt deshalb entfalten und etablieren, weil Video eben noch nicht Teil einer männlich geprägten Kunstgeschichte war. Auch heute noch scheint im Medium Video die künstlerische Infragestellung von Geschlechterrollen eine Domäne von Künstlerinnen zu sein, und es ist vielleicht kein Zufall, dass die große Mehrheit der an der Ausstellung *Per Speculum Me Video* Beteiligten dann Frauen waren. Neben Martin Brand

---

3
Die Dauer und Ereignislosigkeit vieler Videoperformances der 1970er Jahre konnte durchaus herausfordernd sein. So schrieb der Regisseur und damalige Performancekünstler Oliver Hirschbiegel:»Diese ›Video-Kunst‹ war zu 98 Prozent einfach dämlich, oft viel zu lang, eindimensional und uninteressant.« Aus: No Video-Kunst. In: Verena u. Gábor Bódy (Hg.): Video in Kunst und Alltag. Vom kommerziellen zum kulturellen Videoclip. Köln 1986. Und der Kunstkritiker Alfred Nemeczek gab seinem im März 1983 in der Zeitschrift *Art* erschienenen Überblick den polemischen Titel *Zur Hölle mit der Videokunst!*

4
Friederike Pezold: Die Geschichte der Videopionierin P. und ein Plädoyer für Video. In: Hochschülerschaft an der TU Graz (Hg.): Schrägspur Videofestival. Graz 1985.

(geb. 1975, DE, lebt in Köln) und Benny Nemerofsky Ramsay (geb. 1973, CA, lebt in Berlin) nahmen daran teil: Pauline Boudry & Renate Lorenz (geb. 1972/1963, CH/DE, leben in Berlin), Manuela Kasemir (geb. 1981, DE, lebt in Leipzig), Sabine Marte (geb. 1967, AT, lebt in Wien), Barbara Probst (geb. 1964, DE, lebt in New York), Johanna Reich (geb. 1977, DE, lebt in Köln), Eva Weingärtner (1978, DE, lebt in Offenbach) und Gilda Weller (geb. 1989, DE, lebt in Frankfurt).

In fast allen Videoarbeiten von Eva Weingärtner tritt ausschließlich sie selbst auf. Manchmal scheint die Künstlerin im Closed Circuit aus Kamera, Akteurin und Kontrollmonitor eine Performance oder ein kleines Kammerspiel aufzuführen – ohne Publikum und nur für sich selbst. In anderen Fällen wirken die Aufnahmen wie Übungen oder Experimente, bei denen man eine bestimmte Abfolge oder einen bestimmten Zustand zu sehen bekommen soll. Für alle Videoarbeiten gilt, dass sie eher kurz und enorm spannend sind, weil sie sich trotz ihrer konzeptuellen Vorausplanung unerwartet, aber nicht schockhaft entwickeln. Immer wieder geht es um die Problematik von Fremd- und Eigenwahrnehmung, um das Zeigen oder Verbergen von Stärken und Schwächen. Aber wer sieht dabei wen?

In Weingärtners Videos ist das Setting des jeweiligen Selbstversuchs meist schnell zur Gänze durchschaubar: Es wird mit einfachen Mitteln gearbeitet; Licht, Ton, Ausstattung und Kameraeinstellung sind manchmal im wahrsten Sinne des Wortes ›homemade‹. Alles ist echt, eins zu eins und unprätentiös, mit Atmo-Ton und ohne Nachbearbeitung. Gerade weil die Herstellungsweise der Videos so entwaffnend schlicht ist, kann ihre Dramaturgie eine solche Wucht entfalten. Denn die minimalen Gesten und Handlungsabläufe wandeln sich durch kalkulierte Variation in emotionale Achterbahnfahrten. Keine einzige Sekunde dieser Videos ist unbedacht, bedeutungslos oder überflüssig, jeder Moment des Gesehenen und Gezeigten hat seinen Anteil am Zyklus. Es passiert sehr viel im Wenigen, die Konzentration ist maximal, sowohl für die Künstlerin als auch für die Betrachter ihrer Werke.

In dem vierminütigen Video *2me* (2010) ist eine junge Frau zu sehen, die sich selbst sieht oder mit sich selbst umgeht – oder eben dies nicht hinbekommt? Jedenfalls betrachtet diese

Eva Weingärtner
2me, 2010
Videostill
© Eva Weingärtner

Eva Weingärtner
one me, 2013
Videostill
© Eva Weingärtner

Person still und konzentriert und vor allen Dingen aus allernächster Nähe ihr Spiegelbild, mal kritisch, mal zufrieden, mal sehnsüchtig, mal gelangweilt. Sie drückt es, liebkost es, küsst es, kommt aber weder wirklich an es heran noch davon los: Sie ist geradezu gekettet an dieses Spiegelbild und damit auch an sich selbst. Jede Handlung dieser Akteurin löst andere Mutmaßungen über ihren Zustand aus: Die Bandbreite reicht von Narzissmus und Autoerotik bis hin zu Selbsthass. Das frappierend einfache Bild dieses autonomen, körperlichen Umgangs konfrontiert den Betrachter mit der ganzen Bandbreite möglicher Verhältnisse zu sich selbst.

Das zweieinhalbminütige Gegenstück zu *2me* trägt den Titel *one me* und ist 2013 entstanden. Dieses Mal blickt die junge Frau direkt in die Kamera, fixiert also ihre Betrachter. Dieses Mal scheinen ihre geschürzten Lippen das Küssen, die Zuneigung, die Lust an andere richten zu wollen. Wenn da nicht der harte Schlagschatten auf der einen Gesichtshälfte wäre: Er zeigt an, dass es bei der Suche nach dem richtigen Abstand zum Gegenüber der Kamera wiederum nur um das Aufeinandertreffen der eigenen Lippen mit dem eigenen Abbild geht (das dieses Mal ein Schattenriss ist). Und wiederum ist man fasziniert von dem Kontrast aus einerseits der Durchschaubarkeit des Versuchsaufbaus und andererseits der enorm präzisen Adressierung des Betrachters.

Die Künstlerin Eva Weingärtner wagt viel in ihren Videos. Sie setzt sich aus und gibt sich Blößen. Sie steuert auf emotionale Höhen und Tiefen zu und scheut es nicht, diese erstens zu zeigen, zweitens mit künstlerischen Mittel zu transzendieren und drittens ihren Betrachtern als Spiegelbild anzubieten: Man kann sich in ihr oder durch sie erkennen. Die Protagonistin macht sich zur Mittlerin von existentiellen Fragen. In welchem Maße die intimen Experimente und Versuche der Künstlerin auch Selbstversuche sind und was sie mit der Person Eva Weingärtner zu tun haben könnten, das bleibt – wie bei allen herausragenden Performancekünstlern – unbestimmt. Sie selbst sagt dazu: »Meine Arbeit ist ein großer Teil meiner Identität. Und das ist eine Art von Sich-Aussetzen, die ich praktiziere, seit ich Videos mache. Ich hoffe, damit an Themen und Zustände ranzukommen, die viele Menschen spiegeln.«[5] Genau dies gelingt ihr.

5 Zitiert aus einer E-Mail der Künstlerin vom 08.11.2012 an den Autor.

Johanna Reich
Kassandra, 2008
DV, PAL, 6'00
Still
© VG Bild-Kunst, Bonn 2013
Courtesy Galerie Anita Beckers,
Frankfurt am Main

Bei vielen Videoarbeiten von Johanna Reich kann man sich unmittelbar an die Bildraum-Experimente von Peter Campus (geb. 1937) erinnert fühlen; insbesondere mit ihrem Werkblock *The Presence of Absence* erscheint Reich als Nachfolgerin des US-amerikanischen Videopioniers. Aber auch in Videos wie dem sechsminütigen *Kassandra (Teil 1 Transformationen)* (2008) geht es der Künstlerin um das Aufeinanderführen von Projektionsfläche und realer Oberfläche, um Transformationen zwischen Filmraum und Handlungsraum im Selbstexperiment. Zu sehen ist hier anfangs der mit einer Feinstrumpfhose verhüllte Kopf einer Person, auf den ein filmisches Porträt einer Frau projiziert ist. Die Bewegungen dieses projizierten Kopfes stimmen nicht ganz mit der Haltung der Person überein, das Gesicht passt nicht ganz zum Körper, das Filmporträt blickt ins Leere, während die Protagonistin – es handelt sich um die Künstlerin selbst – gar nichts sieht. Doch dann beginnt sie, mit einer großen Schere Teile des Stoffes herauszuschneiden: Die Projektionsfläche – und damit das Filmporträt – wird durchlöchert, zum Vorschein kommt die Akteurin. Die beiden Gesichter bzw. ihre filmischen Abbilder vermischen sich Schnitt für Schnitt. Je weiter der Prozess fortschreitet, desto besser kann die Protagonistin/Künstlerin sehen, und zwar in die Kamera, und uns somit in die Augen blicken. Gleichzeitig werden die Reste des Filmporträts – insbesondere, wenn dessen Augen sich seitwärts richten – zunehmend zur Fratze. Es ist schon sehr spannend, die kontinuierliche Entwicklung der Situation und der entstehenden Porträtbilder zu verfolgen. Weitere Dimensionen ergeben sich, wenn man die in dieser Arbeit von Johanna Reich zitierten Quellen und Bezüge kennt. Bei dem projizierten Porträt handelt es sich um einen Ausschnitt aus Fritz Langs zweiteiligem Stummfilm *Dr. Mabuse, der Spieler* (1920/21), der als ein abgründiges Spiegelbild der Weimarer Republik gedacht war. Das Selbstporträt beim Zerschneiden eines Nylonstoffes (der an eine Gangstermaske erinnert) ist ein direktes Zitat bzw. ein Reenactment des Videos *Personal Cuts* (1982) von Sanja Iveković. In dieser ebenfalls fast ikonisch gewordenen Arbeit hatte die Künstlerin damals zwischen jeden Schnitt propagandistische Fernsehbilder zur Geschichte Jugoslawiens eingefügt und auf diese Weise einen kritischen Kommentar zum

Sabine Marte
b-star, untötbar, 2009
Videostill
Kamera: Oliver Stotz
Drehort: Kleylehof im
Burgenland, Österreich
© the artist

Sabine Marte
Finale, 2007
Videostill
Kamera: Markus Marte
Drehort: Ringerhalle Götzis,
Österreich
© the artist

Nationalismus nach dem Tod von Staatspräsident Tito formuliert. Auch der Titel von Johanna Reichs Video fügt ihrer Arbeit weitere Bedeutungen hinzu, sobald man sich erinnert, dass *Kassandra* in der griechischen Mythologie die tragische Figur der Seherin ist, deren Weissagungen kein Glaube geschenkt wird.

Auch bei einigen Videoarbeiten der österreichischen Künstlerin Sabine Marte geht es um die Integration bzw. Befragung von einerseits realem und andererseits filmischem Raum – und immer dient dies der zumindest impliziten Thematisierung von Verhältnissen, in denen das sich selbst beobachtende Subjekt zu seiner unmittelbaren Umwelt steht. Auch Sabine Marte nimmt sich in ihren Videoarbeiten selbst auf (in Closed Circuits) oder fokussiert mit der Kamera ihre allernächste Umgebung.

Das Video *b-star, untötbar!* (2009) entwickelt sich in seiner siebenminütigen Laufzeit stark und unerwartet, obwohl das Setting dabei doch eigentlich fast gleich bleibt. Zu Beginn ist nur das in gleißendem Weiß überbelichtete, schemenhafte Halbporträt einer auf einem Sofa sitzenden, gesichtslosen Figur zu sehen (es ist die Künstlerin selbst). Fast nichts passiert in dieser unregelmäßig ruckelnden Superzeitlupe, nur auf der Tonebene schält sich langsam ein Rauschen und Krachen heraus, und plötzlich ist auch eine Frauenstimme zu hören. Diese erzählt fragmentarisch – und dadurch sehr poetisch – von einer Frau (sie selbst?), die das Sprechen mit jemandem suchte und dabei »durch den ganzen Film ging und vergaß, dass es nur Fiktion war; sie brach durch den Screen bis zum vollständigen Zusammenbruch«. Währenddessen hat sich das Bild stabilisiert, die sitzende Frau ist nun klar zu erkennen, sie fixiert die Kamera und somit die Zuschauer des Videos, die aber scheinbar auf genau diesen Abstand zum Sofa gezwungen sind. Denn der Hintergrund des Bildes ist nun in geradezu hektischer Bewegung: Das Sofa und damit auch das feste Band zwischen der Protagonistin und ihrer Kamera scheint sich – wie von Geisterhand animiert – durch den Dachstuhl eines Hauses zu bewegen, scheint aus diesem herausfahren zu müssen. Der ganze Raum ist in Aufruhr, aber die auf dem Sofa Sitzende nimmt keine Notiz davon und konzentriert sich allein auf den Blick in die Kamera. Dann wandeln sich die Bewegungsgeräusche plötzlich auch noch in Musik: Ein

Beat taucht auf, die Stimme wird erst zu einem Sprechgesang (der an Performances von Laurie Anderson erinnert) und gleitet schließlich über in minimal-elektronische Popmusik mit dem zweistimmig kontrapunktischen Refrain: »I'm strong enough – to throw you up – into the sky – you learn to fly. – And you fall back – into my arms – I hold you tight – and then we dance.« Damit hat sich alles in Wohlgefallen und Glück aufgelöst: Die gesichts- und sprachlose Figur vom Anfang, die dann zu einem Subjekt wurde, das dem Chaos seiner Umgebung durch Konzentration auf ein Gegenüber (bzw. durch Konzentration auf sich selbst) widerstehen musste, ist zum Schluss in einen zärtlichen Plural mit sich selbst übergegangen. Innen und außen (Vergangenheit und Gegenwart?) sind überwunden, Happy End. Das Experimentalvideo *b-star, untötbar* ist die Erzählung einer existentiellen Auseinandersetzung mit sich selbst, die berührend und ermutigend für andere sein kann. In der Ausstellung *Per Speculum Me Video* wurde es als sehr überlebensgroße Projektion in einem hohen, 220 Quadratmeter großen Saal präsentiert, der jeden Besucher dazu aufforderte, seinen individuell passenden und aushaltbaren Beobachtungsabstand zu Sabine Martes Position einzunehmen.

    Martes künstlerische Arbeit umfasst auch Performances und darüber hinaus ist sie Mitglied der Musikformationen *SV Damenkraft* und *Pendler*. Wie in vielen ihrer Videoarbeiten spielt auch in *Finale* (2007) die Musik von *Pendler* eine tragende Rolle. Zu sehen ist eine Sportlerin – die Künstlerin selbst – beim Training mit einer Ringerpuppe. Es ist nicht gleich erkennbar, warum der gezeigte Zweikampf so aggressiv und bedrohlich wirkt – bis sich herausstellt, dass das Video zeitlich rückwärts läuft. In Verbindung mit der dunklen Musik von *Pendler* ergibt sich ein höchst verstörender Eindruck dieser doch eigentlich so einfachen Übungssituation zwischen Subjekt und Dummy. Ob dieses Video ursprünglich vielleicht bloß entstanden ist, damit Sabine Marte daran ihre Ringkunst optimieren kann, gefilmt von einer Trainerin, die an dem Video später Schwachstellen erläutert? Die Verfremdung durch die zeitliche Umkehrung der Abläufe und durch die an Lydia Lunch erinnernde Musikunterlegung jedenfalls macht ein wirkmächtiges Kunstwerk daraus.

[6] Bruce Nauman, zitiert aus: Ingo F. Walther (Hg.): Kunst des 20. Jahrhunderts. Köln 2005, S. 598.

»Ein Bewußtsein der eigenen Person entsteht aus einer gewissen Menge an Aktivitäten und nicht nur durch bloßes Nachdenken über sich selbst. Man muß es üben.«[6] Dieses Zitat von Bruce Nauman könnte im Gedenken an seine existentiellen, auf radikale Weise Subjektivität befragenden Arbeiten ein Schlüssel zu einem unbetitelten Video (2011) von Gilda Weller sein, das ebenfalls in der Ausstellung *Per Speculum Me Video* gezeigt wurde. Dabei handelt es sich um eine präzise, kompromisslose filmische Komposition: Drei junge Frauen und ihre Stimmen bilden einen Sinnkomplex zu Fragen der Identität, der Selbstwahrnehmung und der Geschlechterbeziehungen. Offenbar denken die drei jungen Protagonistinnen laut und voller Verve über die ihnen gestellten Fragen nach »Glück«, »Sicherheit« und »Frau-Sein« nach. Unklar ist dabei aber von Anfang an die Situation: Handelt es sich um Schauspielerinnen beim Einstudieren eines Textes oder wurde hier eine ernst gemeinte Befragung durchgeführt? Und wenn ja, dient sie zur therapeutischen Spiegelung per Videobild, um zu überprüfen, wie man wirken würde, wenn man tatsächlich etwas ausspricht, oder war die Aufnahme von Anfang an dazu gedacht, als Film veröffentlicht zu werden? Der raffinierte Bild- und Tonschnitt und das Wechseln zwischen Kopfporträt und starker Makroeinstellung führt zu der spannenden Frage, ab wann – und durch was eigentlich – eine Person, ein realer Mensch durch das Abbild hindurchzudringen scheint. Nach sechs Minuten beginnt der Video-Loop von vorne, sein Ende und Anfang bleiben dabei fast unbemerkt.

Seit es die Fotografie gibt, werden Lichtbilder – denen man im Vergleich zu handgeschaffenen Malereien oder Zeichnungen stets größere Realitätsnähe zuspricht – bearbeitet, manipuliert und gefälscht. Gleiches gilt für die Bewegtbilder in Film und Video, insbesondere seit die Digitalisierung den uneingeschränkten gestalterischen Eingriff auf jeden einzelnen Bildpunkt erlaubt. So konnte der Experimentalfilmer Zbigniew Rybcynski bei seinem mit bahnbrechender HDTV-Technik produzierten Video *Steps* (1987) Bilder einer mit Kameras bewaffneten Touristengruppe in die berühmte Treppenszene von Sergej Eisensteins Film-Ikone *Panzerkreuzer Potemkin* (1925) einfügen. Und Steven Spielberg konnte bei *Jurassic Park* (1992) Bewegtbilder von Sauriern

Gilda Weller
o.T., 2011
Videostill
Kamera: Jonas Englert
© the artist

Manuela Kasemir
afraid of death, 2013
Fotografie
75 cm x 60 cm
© Manuela Kasemir
Courtesy the artist

präsentieren, die trotz ihrer überwältigenden fotorealistischen Qualität ganz ohne Kamera entstanden waren. Obschon wir seit Langem an solche Möglichkeiten der Bildbearbeitung gewöhnt sind und wissen, dass auch die Lichtbilder nicht zwangsläufig irgendetwas mit Wirklichkeit zu tun haben müssen, gilt nach wie vor: Wer fotografiert oder Bewegtbilder herstellt, ist unter den Konstrukteuren der Realität. Eventuell an Bedeutung verloren haben da nur die ehemals strikten Grenzziehungen zu Fiktion und Wunschwelt.

Wie die anderen genannten Künstlerinnen, deren Werke bei *Per Speculum Me Video* präsentiert wurden, so kreisen auch die Arbeiten von Manuela Kasemir um existentialistische Profile, die aus der inszenierten Selbstbeobachtung entstehen können. Allerdings ist ihr Medium dabei nicht das Video, sondern die Fotografie, und ihre Selbst-Aufnahmen geschehen nicht in Closed Circuits, sondern zum Teil a posteriori in der Bildbearbeitung am Rechner.

Die Serie *Urd* (altgermanisch: »Schicksal«, »Vergangenheit«) zeigt auf sieben kleinformatigen Schwarz-Weiß-Fotografien eine junge Person (es ist die Künstlerin selbst) bei der Verrichtung alltäglicher Häuslichkeiten in einem alten, offensichtlich schon seit Langem nicht mehr bewohnten Haus: Sie hängt Wäsche auf dem Dachboden auf, bereitet ein Wannenbad für sich vor, fegt die Stube aus, lüftet das Schlafzimmer, schaut nach dem Briefkasten. Es sind sehr poetische Bilder, die einerseits die verwaisten Interieurs vom ehemaligen Zuhause-Sein früherer Bewohner erzählen lassen und Spuren vergangener Lebenszeiten zeigen. Andererseits fokussieren sie auf diese junge Person, die das ganze Leben noch vor sich hat und aber per unsichtbarem Band mit diesem Haus und mit dieser Vergangenheit verbunden zu sein scheint. Nach einer Weile des Betrachtens ergeben sich Unerklärlichkeiten in diesen präzise komponierten und formal exzellent gesteuerten Bildern. Es sind kleine Details, anhand derer zu erkennen ist, dass die Künstlerin jede Aufnahme mittels digitaler Montage bearbeitet hat: Da steigt Wasserdampf aus einem Kessel, der auf einem doch offenkundig dysfunktionalen Herd steht; da sind plötzlich Familienstammbäume in der Wandtapete zu erkennen; da erweisen sich aufgehängte Wäschestücke als vervielfältigte

Manuela Kasemir
Urd, 2008
Serie bestehend aus 7 Fotografien, 33 x 46 cm (je Foto)
© Manuela Kasemir | Courtesy the artist

Figuren; da scheint plötzlich unklar, ob diese junge Person Mann oder Frau ist. Die Details entfalten einen Sog, durch den schließlich die gesamte Inszenierung der Serie – und damit das Verhältnis der abgebildeten Person zu Vergangenheit und Gegenwart – in Frage steht. Manuela Kasemir hat diese Fotos in jener Wohnung aufgenommen, die in ihren ersten knapp 20 Lebenjahren ihr Zuhause war und schrieb dazu: »Oft träume ich von diesem Ort, von diesem Haus. [...] Eine modrige Kulisse, die ich mit meinen Erinnerungen zu beleben versuche. Die Gegenwart hier ist nur noch Vergangenheit. Das Gewesene zieht durch jeden Türschlitz und klebt an der Tapete.«[7] Und es ist wieder das Selbstporträt, mit dem Kasemir hier sich und ihr Gewordensein befragt, die Umstände und Zuschreibungen, die diese Person und ihre sozialen Beziehungen beeinflussten. Die Künstlerin erscheint als Erforscherin der eigenen Existenz und verweist damit exemplarisch auf Seinsfragen, die sich jedem Betrachter dieser Bilder stellen könnten. Kasemirs Fotografien sind zeitgenössische Formen von Vanitas-Bildern. Sie zeigen, wie die ästhetischen Mittel der Kunst zur Auseinandersetzung mit menschlicher Existenz führen, mit ihrem Werden, ihrem Sein und ihrem Vergehen.

Besonders deutlich war das in jener monumentalen Fotoarbeit (6,25 x 6,25 Meter) von Manuela Kasemir, die an der Fassade des Frankfurter Kunstvereins zum Auftaktwerk der Ausstellung *Per Speculum Me Video* wurde. Das Bild zeigte eine Person vor einem Wandspiegel stehend, der diese allerdings nicht reflektiert, sondern schwarz bleibt. Stattdessen scheint der Spiegel eine Schrift lesbar zu machen, die von einem Faden geschrieben wird, den diese Person offenbar in ihren Händen bewegt. Mit dem Spiegel ist zu entziffern: »I am afraid of death«. Die Spiegelung bringt das Unaussprechliche hervor. Mit dem Spiegel sehe ich mich.

[7] Aus einer Rede der Künstlerin zu ihrer Arbeit *Urd* am 03.07.2008 in der Hochschule für Grafik und Buchkunst, Leipzig.

Holger Kube Ventura
ist seit 2009 Direktor des Frankfurter Kunstvereins und hat dort u.a. die Ausstellungen *Ohnmacht als Situation* (2013), *Malerei der ungewissen Gegenden* (2012), *Über die Metapher des Wachstums* (2011), *Das Wesen im Ding* (2010), *Bilder vom Künstler* (2009) und *Gemeinsam in die Zukunft* (2009) kuratiert. 2001 wurde er mit der Studie *Politische Kunst Begriffe – in den 1990er Jahren im deutschsprachigen Raum* promoviert, (Publikation 2008). 1996–2000 war er Kurator im Vorstand des Kasseler Kunstvereins, 2001–03 Direktor der Werkleitz Gesellschaft e.V. und 2004–09 Programmkoordinator bei der Kulturstiftung des Bundes in Halle/Saale. Kube Ventura ist Autor von über 100 kunstwissenschaftlichen Beiträgen.

Befreite Bilder und Töne. Eintauchen in den 360° Full-Dome-Kosmos

Rotraut Pape

Alien Action,
Ralph Heinsohn,
45:00 Min., 2004

Als Künstler/in lernt man das und übt es jeden Tag: die eigenen virtuellen Realitäten, also das, was man im Kopf hat – innere Bilder, Gedanken, Gefühle, Vorstellungen, eben Virtuelles –, *real* werden zu lassen. Auf Film und Video zum Beispiel. Allerdings ist das freie künstlerische Denken mit technischen Bildmedien immer eng an die technologischen Entwicklungen der jeweiligen Epoche gebunden. Waren zu Beginn der Filmgeschichte die Gerätschaften zu schwer, um sie zu bewegen, bewegte sich natürlich auch das Filmbild nicht, und der Blick blieb statisch nach vorn ausgerichtet. Die Kinoleinwand wurde zu einem Fenster, durch das man aus dem Dunkel des Vorführsaales heraus gemeinsam in eine ferne Welt hineinsehen konnte, in der Arbeiter Fabriken verließen[1] oder rasiert wurden[2]. Fotografie plus Bewegung sozusagen. Oder die Leinwand wurde zu einer Bühne für in Zeit und Raum transportabel gemachte Kulissen mit lebensgroßen Schauspielern, die man bei ihren zauberhaften Reisen bis zum Mond begleiten konnte[3]. Theater quasi, aber noch stumm. Als die Kamera kompakter, leiser, mit Ton versehen und beweglich wurde, rückte man näher ans Geschehen heran, stand bald mitten unter den Akteuren und konnte ihnen zudem beim Flüstern zuhören. Die Leinwand wurde zu einem Loch in der Wand und das Publikum zu Voyeuren und Mitwissern – mit der Entwicklung des Fernsehens noch dazu in Real Time. Video ermöglichte den gleichzeitigen Zugriff auf Bild und Ton, gewährte Künstler/innen ohne nennenswerte Budgets den Zugang auch zum neuen Massenmedium TV und bescherte dem eigentlich durch Einschaltquotenterror gefesselten Bildschirm ganz neue Inhalte – wie es schon einmal Jahre zuvor durch das handliche, userfreundliche 16 mm-Film- und Tonformat gelungen war, als eine unabhängige Filmszene entstehen konnte, deren technisch kompatible Kunstwerke fast in jedem Kino gezeigt werden konnten. Aber einerlei, in welcher Gattung, welchem Genre oder mit welcher Technik wir seit nunmehr fast 120 Jahren unterwegs sind, das Filmbildformat selbst hat sich kaum verändert. Ob Fenster, Bühne oder Schlüsselloch, unser medialer Blick auf die Welt ist auch heute weiterhin in einen rechteckigen Ausschnitt hineingezwungen: Dieses globale Diktat der marktbestimmenden Konzerne konnte man als Künstler/in bislang nur

1
La Sortie de l'usine Lumière à Lyon. (Am 19. März 1895 von Louis Lumière mit dem Kinematographen gedreht. Arbeiter verlassen die Fabrik seines Vaters. Er benutzte den bis heute üblichen perforierten Filmstreifen, noch nicht aus Zelluloid, sondern aus beschichtetem Spezialpapier.)

2
The Barber Shop, Thomas Alva Edison, Black Marie Studio 1894. (Die Filmvorführung kostete 10 Cent, wie eine Rasur.)

3
Le Voyage dans la Lune von Georges Méliès, 1902.

durch ein Expanded Cinema konterkarieren oder mittels des Arrangements raumgreifender Multichannelworks mit Projektionen auf mehrere Leinwände oder in immer neuen installativen Konstellationen in Reaktion auf die örtliche Vorgabe eines Museums oder alternativer Räume. Mit dem Übergang ins dritte Jahrtausend trafen sich nun sämtliche, unsere Sinne verlängernden Medien in einem Gerät, das bald alle anderen ersetzt bzw. in sich aufgehoben haben wird, dem Computer. Alles läuft heute hier zusammen: Die klassisch analogen, audiovisuellen Formate sind endlich untereinander und mit den zeitgenössischen kompatibel. Konzeptuelle und ästhetische Merkmale durchdringen einander und generieren im Zusammenspiel mit der bewussten und unbewussten Wahrnehmung des Zuschauers neue kreative Potentiale. Auch die Formate und die Kantenlängen sind nun nicht mehr starr und unantastbar, vielmehr lassen sie sich digital in alle Proportionen und Dimensionen strecken und biegen. So entstehen gattungsübergreifende, das Genre sprengende Formate, die derzeit – aber in Überschreibung älterer Techniken gleichsam auch rückwirkend – innovativ im Audiovisuellen formulierbar machen, was bislang so nicht formulierbar war.

Die Kuppel, der Dome, zieht sich als besonderer Ort quer durch unsere Kulturgeschichte, als Schutzraum und Kultstätte (Höhle), als Schnittstelle (Kirche), als Manifestation von Macht (Architektur) und Spiritualität (Firmament). Wer hat noch nie unter freiem Himmel – am besten auf einem Hügel oder Berg mit wenig Lichtverschmutzung – in die Sterne geschaut und eine Verbindung zum Jenseits oder zur Unendlichkeit empfunden? Nun bietet sich diese ›Urmutter‹ aller Kuppeln in der domestizierten Form von Planetarien als Ort für Projektionen mit neuen bildgebenden Verfahren an. Das optomechanische Gerät, das diese Kuppeln bislang mit Lichtpunkten bespielte, hält nach nunmehr fast 90 Jahren den gestalterischen Ansprüchen nicht mehr stand, speziell seitdem Teleskope immer detailliertere Bilder aus dem Weltraum funken und uns den bewegten Kosmos visualisieren. Das Angebot[4], Kurzfilme eigens für die im Oktober 2006 eingeweihte erste Laser-Ganzkuppel-Projektion Europas im Zeiss Planetarium Jena zu entwickeln, bot für die Film/Video-Studierenden der HfG Offenbach eine inspirierende Möglichkeit

[4] Von Micky Remann, Dozent im Lehrgebiet Medienereignisse an der Bauhaus Universität Weimar via Birgit Lehmann, Dozentin für Drehbuch, HfG Offenbach, an Rotraut Pape, Lehrstuhl Film/Video, HfG Offenbach 2006.

zur Befreiung ihrer Bilder. Allerdings war es schwierig, sich die Dimensionen, technischen Bedingungen und Voraussetzungen zum Bespielen dieser neuen Leinwand überhaupt vorzustellen. Die Kuppel maß 25 Meter im Durchmesser, die halbkugelförmige 360°-Leinwand umschloss die Zuschauer und bot ca. 800 Quadratmeter Projektionsfläche für die eigenen Gedanken. Jedes einzelne Bild der entstehenden Filmsequenzen musste quadratisch angelegt werden, mit einer Kantenlänge von bis zu gigantischen 4.000 Pixeln. Die Gesetze der Schwerkraft und der klassischen zentralperspektivischen Gestaltung schienen aufgehoben: »Oben« befand sich nicht mehr an der Oberkante eines rechteckigen Bildes, sondern in dessen runder Mitte. Erst Gehirnakrobatik – um sich das alles überhaupt vorzustellen, denn in Ermangelung einer Medienkuppel in der Region konnten wir nicht testen –, dann ›Renderwahn‹, eine neue Mode-Krankheit, die auftritt, wenn Mensch und Maschine überfordert an ihre Grenzen stoßen beim wiederholten Versuch, die meist aus mehreren Bildern zusammengestückelten, großformatigen Einzelbilder für die Krümmung der Kuppel mit dem entsprechenden Plug-in[5] (aus Portugal!) rundzurechnen und ordentlich durchnummeriert aus dem Computer wieder herauszurendern und transportabel zu machen. In Kooperation mit der Bauhaus Universität Weimar[6], der Muthesius Kunsthochschule Kiel[7], der Fachhochschule Kiel[8] und der HfG Offenbach[9] fand am 16.03.2007 im Zeiss Planetarium Jena[10] das erste Fulldome-Festival Deutschlands statt. Alle Teilnehmer/innen hatten ihre Datenberge plus separatem Ton herangeschafft, die Einzelbildsequenzen wurden vor Ort »ge-sliced« und »ge-stiched«, also von meterhohen Rechnern in einzelne ›Tortenstücke‹ zerteilt, um anschließend von den sechs lichtstarken Projektoren nahtlos zusammengesetzt per Laser in die Kuppel geschrieben werden zu können. Im weltweit betriebsältesten Planetarium[11] feierte man mit allen Beteiligten, Unterstützern, Mentoren und einem kundigen Publikum die unterschiedlichen Ansätze der entstandenen künstlerischen Resultate im neuen Medium. Welch ein atemberaubendes Erlebnis! Welch großartige, lichtstarke Projektion! Welch fetter Sound! Die Offenbacher hatten ein Semester lang den eigenen Film imaginiert, hatten versucht, sich vorzustellen, wie er dramaturgisch

5
Navegar Foundation, Centro Multimeios Espinho, www.multimeios.pt

6
Micky Remann/Wolfgang Kissel.

7
Ralph Heinsohn/Tom Duscher.

8
Eduard Thomas/Jürgen Rienow.

9
Rotraut Pape/Birgit Lehmann.

10
Jürgen Hellwig/Volkmar Schorcht.

11
Das Zeiss-Planetarium in Jena wurde am 18. Juli 1926 eröffnet. Ab Ende Juli 1924 besuchten bereits rund 80.000 Menschen die ersten Versuchsvorführungen des künstlichen Sternhimmels in einer provisorischen Kuppel auf dem Dach der Jenaer Zeiss-Werke, in der Presse als das »Wunder von Jena« gefeiert.

funktionieren, wie er aussehen, wie er sich anhören würde. Das Ergebnis übertraf alle Erwartungen: Zehn HfG-Studierende hatten narrative Kurzfilme entwickelt, die dieser ganz besonderen räumlichen Situation immersiv erlebbaren Films Rechnung tragen. *Expanded cinema = expanded consciousness.* Endlich geht es wie im echten Leben zu: Die Zuschauer/innen sind ringsum von Bildern umgeben und müssen sich bewegen, um die Geschichten zu verfolgen. Jeder sieht genaugenommen einen anderen Film, aus einer anderen Perspektive. Erlöst vom Standpunkt des externen Beobachters sitzen wir nicht mehr *vor* der Bühne oder der Leinwand, sondern mitten drin und rücken als nunmehr teilnehmende Betrachter/innen ins Zentrum der Welt.

Viele Welten existieren nebeneinander. Owi Mahn[12] verwandelt die Kuppel in ein überdimensionales Fahrzeug, in dem alle Zuschauer Platz finden, auf rasanter Fahrt durch die urbane Nacht. Jedes der sechs Fenster, sämtliche Rück- und Seitenspiegel wurden einzeln in größtmöglicher Auflösung gefilmt und anschließend zusammengesetzt. Wir hören den Fahrer, der sich lautstark über Free Jazz in Rage redet und legen uns als ohnmächtige Beifahrer tapfer mit in die Kurven. Anna Pietocha[13] lässt die Kuppel per Zeichentrick zum Innern einer sich um sich selbst drehenden, verrosteten Maschine werden, deren letzter Arbeitstag angebrochen ist. In einem sentimentalen Duett verabschiedet sich der alte Maschinist von seinem eisernen Pendant und schaltet es ab. Daniel Frerix[14] erhebt die Kuppel zum Inneren seines Kopfes. Die Zuschauer – diesmal auf die Größe von Blutkörperchen zusammengeschrumpft – sehen dort, wo die Augen liegen, TV-Bilder aus dem WM-Finale 1990, als Deutschland Fußballweltmeister wurde. Je nach Spielgeschehen knistern die Nervenzellen, und funkensprühende Gehirnströme verweisen auf den Ursprung von Gefühlen. Im Stil der Situationisten protestiert Jos Diegel[15] in analog zerkratztem 16mm/35mm-Filmmaterial gegen *Größere Leinwände, Längere Hälse*, denn alles könne dem virtuellen Film, der sich im Kopf hinter den Augenlidern abspiele, als Leinwand dienen. Aus allen sechs verfügbaren Tonquellen sprudeln Sätze, überlagern und durchdringen sowohl einander als auch die Bilder, die sich flach unter die Kuppel werfen und alle Anstrengungen immersiver Natur in einer großen Geste hinter-

12
Autodrive, Owi Mahn, 4:20 Min., 2007.

13
Der Letzte Arbeitstag, Anna Pietocha, 5:00 Min., 2007.

14
Gefühle im Gehirn, Daniel Frerix, 1:46 Min., 2007.

15
Größere Leinwände, Längere Hälse, Jos Diegel, 7:00 Min., 2008.

fragen. Diese hier begonnene und bis heute kontrovers geführte Diskussion befeuerte Christian Janecke[16] mit jährlichen Vorträgen zur »Immersion in der Kunst« speziell für die studentischen Fulldome-Forscher/innen: »Rundum einzutauchen in eine Illusion ist ein altes Ziel der Kunst – und doch vielleicht auch letztlich gegen die Kunst. Denn die Konzentration auf einen hervorgehobenen Punkt, Bereich oder Gegenstand der Betrachtung entfällt. An die Stelle der Ereignisverdichtung des Bildes tritt die mit dem Raum der Präsentation nahezu deckungsgleiche Repräsentation, in der es sich sehend, suchend und teils überfordert einzurichten gilt.«

So aufregend die ersten Begegnungen der immersiven Art mit den eigenen Rundum-Filmen auch verlaufen waren, so ernüchternd stand anschließend die Befürchtung im Raum, ob man nicht eigentlich für die Schublade – genauer gesagt: für die Festplatte – gearbeitet hatte. Denn noch spärlich waren die Orte gesät, an denen man 360°-Kuppelfilme überhaupt präsentieren oder studieren konnte, und sperrig die Medien, mit denen diese Datenmengen durch Raum und Zeit transportiert werden konnten. Zögerlich begannen Planetarien weltweit, ihre Sternenprojektoren mit der neuen Technik verschiedener Hersteller zu kombinieren oder zu ersetzen, aber erwarteten für ihre Spielorte, bis heute, Inhalte aus der Astronomie oder Astrophysik. Um diese neuen Kurzfilme in unserer bislang mediendomefreien Region überhaupt zeigen zu können, präsentierten wir sie bisweilen in einer mobilen, aufblasbaren Kuppel[17] oder lediglich als runde Bodenprojektion, um die herum man sich bewegen konnte – besonders eindrucksvoll brachte eine Präsentation im Filmmuseum Frankfurt[18] in direkter Nachbarschaft zu den historischen Lebensradscheiben von Stampfer (1833) und dem Zoetrop von Marey (1887) medienarchäologische Schichten zum Vorschein, die bis heute nachwirken –, während sich einige Studierende daran machten, ihre Dome-Filme zurückzurechnen für Projektionen auf die konventionelle, rechteckige Leinwand, um sie überhaupt zeigen zu können. Dementsprechend lief die »Flachfilm«-Version von *The Death of Love*[19] auf zahlreichen Festivals und wurde im Fernsehen ausgestrahlt; *How to Disappear*[20] gewann mit beiden Versionen internationale Preise und Anerkennung, auch

---

16
Christian Janecke lehrt Kunstgeschichte in den Grund-, Haupt- und Promotionsstudiengängen der HfG Offenbach.

17
Matthias Rode, www.fulldomedia.com.

18
Lost Media: Found. Galerieausstellung der HfG Filmklasse im Deutschen Filmmuseum, Frankfurt am Main, 2009.

19
Von Yehonatan Richter-Levin, 2:30 Min., 2007.

20
Vom Verschwinden, Merlin Flügel, 4:00 Min., 2011, VisuaLiszt-Award, FullDome Festival Jena 2011, Students-Nightlife-Award Platin, FH Kiel, Mediendom 2011, Best Narrative Award, Fulldome UK, Leicester 2012.

21
This is Cinerama,
Merian C. Cooper, 1952.

22
Arrivée d´un train à la Ciotat,
Auguste und Louis Lumière, 1896.

23
Fegefeuer, Verfilmung der Erzählung *Miss Thompson* von William Somerset Maugham mit Rita Hayworth, USA 1953.

24
Bei Anruf Mord, Alfred Hitchcock, 1954.

im Internet. Irgendwie fühlt man sich an das letzte Jahrhundert erinnert, als die großen US-Studios den konzertierten *Cinerama*-Angriff gegen rapide sinkende Besucherzahlen in den Kinos starteten, ausgelöst durch die existenzbedrohende Verbreitung des Fernsehens zu Beginn der 1950er Jahre. Der beeindruckende Halbkreis der gekrümmten 146°-Leinwand füllte das Blickfeld schon fast aus, und der Film (drei von Hand synchronisierte 35 mm-Projektionen) wurde quasi physisch erlebbar. Der damalige Blockbuster bot eine Achterbahnfahrt[21], die das Kinopublikum zum Kreischen brachte – so wie die Ankunft eines Dampfzuges auf einem Bahnhof in Frankreich[22] mehr als 50 Jahre zuvor die Zeitgenossen der Brüder Lumière hatte – nämlich infolge der nachgerade topischen Verwechslung von Kunst und Leben – aus dem Häuschen geraten lassen. Als würdiger Nachfolger dieses gruppendynamischen Ansatzes bleibt Owi Mahns Kuppelfilm *Autodrive* im Gedächtnis präsent. Zur Rückgewinnung der Kinogänger brachte man es damals schon auf mehrkanaligen Stereoton und holte auch den »3D-Film« kurzfristig wieder aus dem Keller – der jedoch gleich darauf durch *Cinemascope* an seiner empfindlichsten Stelle getroffen wurde, denn dieses neue Breitwandverfahren funktionierte ohne Brille. Der Markt war – wie heute im Dome-Filmkosmos wieder zu erleben – durch etliche Patente zersplittert, und so stellte man »Flachfilm«-Versionen her, die überall aufgeführt werden konnten. (*Miss Sadie Thompson*[23] kam in 2D, 3D-Standard, 2D-Breitwand und 3D-Breitwand heraus, Alfred Hitchcock drehte *Dial M for Murder*[24] in 3D, der dann allerdings nur im klassischen Format vertrieben wurde.)

Da unsere ersten Dome-Filme die Kuppel vorrangig als geschlossenen Umgebungsraum thematisierten, wurde auch nicht geschnitten. Denn wie nehmen wir die Umwelt wahr? Hoffentlich ungeschnitten – andernfalls wären wir vermutlich krank, eingeschlafen oder auf Drogen! Mit uns im Zentrum bewegt *sie* sich treu um uns herum oder mit uns, wenn *wir* uns bewegen. Rundum-Filme in der mächtigen Kuppel liefern ein bezeichnendes Exempel: »Erlauben sie es doch, jene Illusionen im Bewegtbild zu bedienen und zugleich zu markieren, denen sich in der Zeit *vor* der Erfindung des Films die großen Panoramen letztlich nur mit starren Bildern ohne Anfang und Ende widmeten.«[25] Und könnte man die maschinell rotierenden Besucherplattformen an Tagen regen Zuspruchs nicht auch bereits als Kamerabewegung avant la lettre lesen? Erinnert sei hier auch an das weiterkurbelbare *Moving Panorama* des Montblanc, das Anfang der 1860er Jahre ein Albert Smith in Windsor Castle vor Königin Victoria präsentiert hatte, oder an den Umstand, dass die eigentliche Panoramenrotunde oftmals unterbaut war mit Räumen zur Vorbereitung bzw. Einstimmung des Publikums durch sequentiell angeordnete Stationen eines Erzählzusammenhangs in vielen einzelnen Bildern. Doch erst mithilfe filmisch bewegter Bilder um und ab 1900 (teils auch in raffinierter Vortäuschung eines vermeintlich vom Boden abhebenden Besucherstandorts) sollte es dann gelingen, dem Publikum selbst ein Bewegtwerden zu suggerieren.

Dementsprechend bescheren die kontinuierlichen Kamerabewegungen dem heutigen Kuppel-Publikum die fulldomespezifische Art scheinbar schwereloser Fortbewegung und helfen den klassischen bzw. konventionellen Planetarien-Filmen, ohne Schnitte von einem Ort zum anderen zu gelangen (Fliegen und Tauchen). In David Sarnos[26] Film beginnt sich die Kuppel aufzulösen. Sie wirkt gläsern und gibt den Blick rundum frei auf eine fremde Welt in ungesunden Farben. In einiger Entfernung sehen wir andere gläserne Kuppeln, die gerade von Menschen in Schutzanzügen und Atemmasken gesprengt werden. Wir ahnen Schlimmes, wenn die Truppe auf die Glaskuppel, unter der *wir* sitzen, zusteuert: »Da leben noch welche!« Gonzalo Arilla[27] wandelt die Kuppel zum rechteckigen Zimmer eines Jungen, der lieber grüne Marsmännchen ins Pixelnirwana schießt, als Hausaufgaben zu erledigen. Sein Lieblingsspiel ist ein Kult-Game-Klassiker mit höchstem immersiven Suchtpotential. Wir befinden uns räumlich zwischen ihm und seinem Computer, müssen je nach Standpunkt wie der Schiedsrichter bei einem Tennisspiel den Kopf schnell bewegen und haben die ungewohnte Freiheit auszuwählen – uns entweder für Ursache oder Wirkung zu entscheiden. Aus unterschiedlichen Perspektiven, als Jäger oder Gejagte, erleben wir hautnah, wie dieser moderne Zauberlehrling[28] immer tiefer ins Geschehen eintaucht und die Geister, die er rief, nicht mehr kontrollieren kann, wenn sich sein gesamtes

25
Aus: In The Thick of it – Immersion from an art historian's view. Vortrag von Christian Janecke, FullDome Festival Jena 2012.

26
Aufräumarbeiten, David Sarno, 3:50 Min., 2007, HfG.

27
Space Defender, Version 3.2 Gonzalo Arilla, 2:21 Min., 2007/08, HfG.

28
»Hat der alte Hexenmeister sich doch einmal wegbegeben! Und nun sollen seine Geister auch nach meinem Willen leben!«, J. W. Goethe, 1797.

29
50 Prozent Illusion,
Thorsten Greiner, 5:05 Min., 2008,
Publikumspreis, 2. FullDome
Festival Jena, Best Artistic
Production Award, Domefest,
Chicago 2008.

30
Mit Haut und Haaren,
Anna Pietocha, 1:26 Min., 2008.

31
Die Hessische Film- und Medienakademie ist das Netzwerk der 13 hessischen Hochschulen. Gründung 2007.

32
Micky Remann, Volkmar Schorcht, Jürgen Hellwig mit Tobias Wiethoff, André Wünscher, Hannes Wagner u.v.m.

Zimmer ins Spielfeld auflöst. Basierend auf Textfragmenten aus *Endstation Sehnsucht* von Tennessee Williams lässt Thorsten Greiner[29] die Hauptfigur Blanche tanzend Veränderungen in ihre kleinquaderförmige Eigenwelt halluzinieren. Dabei berührt es den Gleichgewichtssinn des Publikums empfindlich, wenn die mit pulsierenden Quadern gefüllte Kuppel synchron zur Musik aus der Form gerät, aufbricht, wächst oder in sich zusammenfällt. Anna Pietocha[30] bringt die Situation des aktiv einbezogenen Publikums und auch die neuen performativen Möglichkeiten genauer auf den Punkt: Ihr Film beginnt im Dunkeln, wir hören näher kommende Schritte, eine Art Deckel öffnet sich geräuschvoll hoch über unseren Köpfen, eine Hand greift herein und fischt einen zappelnden Menschen aus unserer Mitte. Ein echter Schrei aus dem Publikum im richtigen Moment hebt die Distanz zwischen Publikum und Film vollends auf und macht aus den neunzig Sekunden Film ein Erlebnis der besonderen, bleibenden Art. Mit beginnender Unterstützung der hFMA[31] konnten ab 2009 weitere interessierte Studierende aus dem hessischen Hochschulnetzwerk das Innovationspotential des neuen Mediums kennenlernen, erforschen und anwenden. Gemeinsame Exkursionen nach Jena zu *Carl Zeiss* in die firmeneigene Forschungskuppel zum jährlichen Initiationsworkshop[32] mit anschließenden Mitternachtssitzungen im großen Downtown-Planetarium vertieften den Austausch mit erfahrenen Macher/innen aus Weimar und darüber hinaus. Kriterien und technische Formatvorgaben für die nächste Staffel wurden erarbeitet und beschlossen. Zu divers waren die Formate und Komprimierungen, in denen die ersten Filme hergestellt wurden. Eduard Thomas vom *Mediendom* der FH Kiel lud ein zu vertiefenden Coachings und Screenings und ermöglichte intensive Fachsimpeleien z. B. mit Ralph Heinsohn, visionärem Dome-Filmpionier, der 2004 mit seinem Abschlussfilm *Alien Action* an der Kunsthochschule Kiel, schon quasi stellvertretend für uns alle, die nach wie vor virulenten Fulldome-Fragen thematisiert hatte. Die experimentelle Suche nach Erkenntnissen in Bezug auf Technik, Perspektive, Dramaturgie, Inhalt, Erzählstruktur, Interaktion usw. wurde von einer wachsenden, oft wechselnden, jedoch stets aufs Neue motivierten Gruppe studentischer Pionier/innen an immer mehr Orten vorangetrieben, deren erfrischende Resultate jährlich im Frühling zum *FullDome Festival* in Jena vor kompetentem Publikum uraufgeführt wurden. Bald wurden auch professionelle Fulldome-Shows zum Festival präsentiert, die jedoch fast ausschließlich dem Sternenkosmos huldigen und mithin strikt dem Planetarium verpflichtet sind – oder in der entgegengesetzten schwerelosen Richtung bis in die Tiefen der Meere vordringen. Meist sind diese Wissenschaftsshows als Hochglanz-Computeranimationen unidirektional für angenehme um 30° angekippte Kuppeln mit festgeschraubten Sesseln realisiert und dauern maximal 50 Minuten.

Ginge es nach uns, müsste man sofort die Stühle aus allen Kuppelkinos herausreißen, um sich in diesen neuen begehbaren Projektionen frei bewegen oder je nach Film auch bequem einrichten zu können! Wir fühlen uns der multidirektionalen Fulldome Experience verpflichtet! Wir sind gegen die digitale Rundum-Tapeten-Beschallung und den bereits gefühlte Lichtjahre andauernden Flug durch die Sternenmacht! Wir erwarten Konzepte, Bilder und Töne, die neue, zwangsläufig polylineare, durch die unvorhersehbare multiperspektivische Blickrichtung der bewegten Betrachter entscheidungsabhängige Narrations- und Gestaltungsformen einbinden, *Real Film* miteinbeziehen! Das stellte sich allerdings als besonders schwierig heraus, da »Flachbild«-Kameras bislang nur einen Bruchteil der erforderlichen Kantenlänge hergaben. Wir experimentierten mit adaptierten Inhalten und DIY-Möglichkeiten, um hoch auflösende Real-Film-Dome-Master herzustellen. Darmstädter Studierende[33] lösten das Problem mit einer Geschichte, in der mit Taschenlampen bewaffnete Jugendliche ein Haus durchsuchen. In ihren Lichtkegeln erscheinen Ausschnitte der Räumlichkeiten, die hier und da mit unscharfem Rund im dialogreichen Dunkel aufblitzen und so jeweils die beste Auflösung bieten. Matthias Winckelmann[34] schaffte einen Quantensprung in Sachen Bildqualität mit einem experimentellen Stopptrick-Film, dessen reale Einzelbilder er mittels eines A3-Scanners großzügig »fotografieren« und zur komplexen Weiterverarbeitung digitalisieren konnte. *Chaos, Kosmos, Mu!* gewann den Preis *Best experimental* auf dem renommierten *DomeFest USA* und machte wieder einmal international auf die

33
Awaken, Theresa Maué, Moritz Heimsch, 4:40 Min., 2009, Creative Award, 3. FullDome Festival Jena 2009.

34
Chaos, Kosmos, Mu!, Matthias Winckelmann, 1:30 Min., 2009, Best Experimental Award, DomeFest, Chicago, USA 2010.

35
Polycycle, Thorsten Greiner,
4:30 Min., 2007.

36
Mit Unterstützung von
Alex Oppermann, HfG Friederichs-
Stiftungsprofessur.

37
Niemals dein Leben, Andreas
Thürck, 5:26 Min., 2011.

38
Haie und die, die sie liebt,
Aleksandar Radan, 5:00 Min., 2012.

39
Habitat, Sönke Hahn, Bauhaus
Universität Weimar, 2013.

lebendige Fulldome-Avantgarde in Deutschland aufmerksam. Thorsten Greiner[35] nahm mit zwei digitalen Fotoapparaten nebeneinander im anaglyphischen Verfahren stereoskopische Bildsequenzen auf. Durch rot/cyan-getönte Brillen betrachtet erscheint der Film dreidimensional und löst sich fast völlig von der Projektionsfläche in den Raum hinein. Experimente mit HD-Fotokameras und Fisheye-Linsen wurden aufgenommen[36], hatten jedoch den Nachteil, dass bei bewegten Bildern entweder die Perspektive nicht stimmt oder der Kameramann zwangsläufig mit im Bild ist, wenn er nicht, wie von Andreas Thürck[37] eindrucksvoll gezeigt, die Kamera z. B. auf dem Rücken liegend auf ein Skateboard schnallt und – sich selbst hinter einem Busch versteckt – sie mittels eines unsichtbaren Plastikfadens vorwärtszieht. Aleksandar Radan[38] arbeitete mit einer RedOne-Kamera, die Bilder im 4K-Format liefert, und filmte in einer halsbrecherischen Aktion vertikal von oben in eine auf dem Boden eines gefüllten Swimmingpools liegende Spiegelhalbkugel hinein, die wie eine umgedrehte Fisheye-Linse funktioniert und seine Inszenierung im Wasser in einem durchgehenden Take aufnehmen kann. In Weimar baute Sönke Hahn[39] ein Kamera-GoPro-Rig und filmte rundum mit sechs Kameras gleichzeitig. An der Fachhochschule Potsdam entwickelten Dimitar Ruszev und Christopher Warnow die Softwaretools *DomeMod* und *Dometester* zur Visualisierung von Kuppelfilmen. So wird der langwierige Arbeitsprozess immens erleichtert, da wir Bildkompositionen und Filme nun in einer simulierten Kuppel auf dem Monitor abspielen können – also ohne Zugriff auf eine physische Kuppel den Bildinhalt aus den wechselnden Perspektiven des Publikums überprüfen können. Seit 2010 betreibt das *Interaction Design Lab* der FH Potsdam unter der Leitung von Klaus Dufke und Boris Müller eine 360°-Fulldome-Projektionsanlage, die zudem speziell für die Echtzeit-Visualisierung erweitert wurde, sodass neben hochkarätigen Kuppelfilmen dort nun auch interaktive Anwendungen wie Spiele und wissenschaftliche Visualisierungen entwickelt werden. Neben weiteren spannenden Experimenten im Umgang mit gefilmten Bildern entstanden allerorts reine Computeranimationen neben analogem Trickfilm und hybride Kombinationen verschiedenster

40
Laser Head Explosion,
Denis Carbone, 1:50 Min., 2012,
1. Preis Kategorie FullDome,
Koordinaten Festival der Räumlichen Medien, Kiel 2012.

41
Schwimmende Einhörner,
Stephanie Kayß, 5:00 Min., 2011,
Publikumspreis, 5. FullDome
Festival Jena 2011, Students-
Nighlife-Award Silber, FH Kiel,
Mediendom 2011.

42
Die *All-Dome-Laser-Image-Projektion* von Carl Zeiss und Jenoptik war 2006 die erste laserbasierte Fulldome-Projektion Europas.

Techniken. Denis Carbone[40] spiegelt den Prozess der Bilderzeugung in der Kuppel durch handgemachte Licht-Bilder, die – als Stop Motion-Langzeit-Belichtungen mit farbigen Lasern gezeichnet – immer rasanter in Bewegung geraten, um in einer einzigartigen Welt aus sichtbaren Gedankenblitzen zu explodieren. Stephanie Kayß[41] filmt ihre Schauspieler hochkant in HD und kann sie dann frei in ihre computergenerierten Hintergründe einpassen. Eine weitere vorgeschaltete Ebene (Regen) macht die Illusion einer uns umgebenden nächtlichen Straßenecke perfekt und lindert so auch die Schnitte, mit denen sie ihren Kurzfilm waghalsig strukturiert, denn die klassische Montage funktioniert nicht mehr so recht. Wir haben uns lange daran gewöhnt, Schnitte im klassischen rechteckigen Filmformat zu akzeptieren, als blätterten wir einen Stapel Fotos durch, die wir mal länger, mal kürzer betrachten. Jetzt müssen andere Zeichensysteme und Erzählstrukturen, ein anderes Timing her, um den neuen Anforderungen und Gegebenheiten Rechnung zu tragen.

Besonders der räumlich gesetzte Ton spielt eine noch völlig unterschätzte Rolle – denn der Blick folgt instinktiv dem auditiven Reiz, sobald das Gehirn diesen gemeldet hat. Ende 2011 ist es dann soweit: Beim Austausch des etwas müde gewordenen ADLIP[42]-Projektionssystems im Jenaer Planetarium gegen das lichtstärkere und brilliantere Powerdome®VELVET-System wird auch der Sound erneuert. Das Problem der Reflexion des Lichts in einer Kuppel und damit die Schwierigkeit, *Schwarz* darzustellen, tritt auch im Bereich des Tons auf. Arbeitet man mit Sprache aus verschiedenen Richtungen, war bislang die perfekte Mischung genau genommen nur in der Mitte der Kuppel zu erleben. Befindet man sich am Rand, hört man manches gar nicht mehr und anderes viel zu laut. Das Fraunhofer-Institut für Digitale Medientechnologie (IDMT) hat die räumliche Klangdarstellung in Angriff genommen und als weltweit erste Festinstallation 64 einzeln ansteuerbare Tonquellen hinter die 360°-Leinwand in Jena plaziert. Das auf der Wellenfeldsynthese basierende 3D-Sound-System *SpatialSoundWave* ist ein weiteres innovatives Medium und wird den Umgang mit Ton-*Spuren* revolutionieren, die als separierte Klang-*Objekte* nun bewegt und punktgenau in den Raum hineingesetzt werden können – in Echtzeit oder programmiert. René Rodigast und Kollegen vom Fraunhofer-Institut luden ein zum *Spatial-Sound-Workshop* nach Ilmenau. Mit Unterstützung der hFMA und in Kooperation mit Sabine Breitsameter, Professorin für Sound und Medienkultur am Fachbereich Media der Hochschule Darmstadt, wurde die Forschung auf beiden Gebieten (Bild und Ton) weiter vorangetrieben. Studierende der *h_da* erarbeiteten das wahrscheinlich erste (gänzlich ohne Bilder funktionierende) Soundscape-Hörstück[43] für dieses spezielle 3D-Environment und unterstützten die Kommiliton/innen der HfG bei der Vertonung ihrer raumgreifenden Filme. Kyung-Min Kos Film[44] überzeugte in dieser Kombination die internationale Jury des *FullDome Festivals* und gewann einen *Janus*, den erstmalig verliehenen »Oscar des FullDomeFilms« in Form einer doppelgesichtigen platinfarbenen Keramikstatuette, die vorn und hinten Augen hat. Ihr Film thematisiert das traditionelle Ritual »Gut«, das bis heute in der modernen koreanischen Gesellschaft, Lebensweise und Weltanschauung fest verwurzelt ist. »Gut« ist der Leitgedanke von »Himmel-Erde-Mensch«, bei dem der Mensch als Teil der Natur stets in Bezug zu Himmel und Erde steht und über Leben und Tod hinaus mit allen Lebewesen kommunizieren kann. Es macht Sinn, diese unendlich zirkuläre Reise der Energien im Universum in Planetarien zu zeigen.

Im siebenten Jahr hat sich das *FullDome Festival* im Zeiss Planetarium Jena zum Knotenpunkt der internationalen Kuppelfilm-Community von San Francisco über Moskau bis Melbourne entwickelt. An fünf Tagen im Mai 2013 präsentierten Micky Remann, Volkmar Schorcht und Jürgen Hellwig neue Werke meist als Welturaufführungen in verschiedenen Wettbewerbskategorien zwischen Over- und Underground dem internationalen Fach- und Fanpublikum, das sich nun immer zahlreicher in Jena einfindet, um die innovativen Höhepunkte der Saison zu sehen, zu diskutieren, Know-how auszutauschen, Kooperationen zu vereinbaren und den Nachwuchs zu rekrutieren. Heute gibt es weltweit 1.150 Fulldome-Theater, die Hälfte befinden sich in den USA und nur fünf davon sind größer als die

43
I Water, Felix Deufel, Yannick Hofmann, Natasche Rehberg, Klaus Schüller, h_da , 8:00 Min., 2013, Spatial Sound Recognition Award, Fulldome Festival Jena 2013.

44
Bon Voyage, Kyung-Min Ko , HfG, Sounddesign: Felix Deufel, Yannick Hofmann, h_da, 5:00 Min., 2013, Creative Award, Fulldome Festival Jena 2013.

weltweit dienstälteste Kuppel in Jena. Die wenigsten Projektionskuppeln existieren außerhalb des Planetariumkontexts.

Mit der Idee, künstlerische Kuppelfilme im Rahmen der *B3* erstmals in Frankfurt zu zeigen, stellte sich das FullDome-Kuratorenteam Klaus Dufke, Ralph Heinsohn und Rotraut Pape der Herausforderung, einen mobilen Dome[45] nach Frankfurt zu bringen. An fünf Tagen wird in der Weißfrauenkirche ein internationales »Best Of FullDome-Art« präsentiert, flankierende Workshops geben Einblick in die neuen Möglichkeiten, und auch Programme für Kinder und Jugendliche finden Platz. Die Arbeit an der Evolution der Filmsprache und an Filmen, die sich in berauschender Qualität als gemeinsames Erlebnis nur an diesen Orten und nicht allein zu Hause vor dem Flatscreen erleben lassen, hat überall begonnen.

[45] mit Unterstützung von André Wünscher und Domezelt Deutschland, http://www.domezelt.com.

Rotraut Pape
studierte Freie Kunst an der Hochschule für Bildende Künste Hamburg. Ab 1979 Experimentalfilme, Video und Performancekunst, internationale Festival- und Ausstellungsteilnahmen, Realisation experimenteller Dokumentarfilme, Kurzfilme, Themenabende für arte/ZDF/3sat. Seit 2003 Professorin für Film/Video an der HfG Offenbach, seit 2008 Gründungsmitglied/Vorstandsmitglied der hessischen Film- und Medienakademie (hFMA), Netzwerk der 13 Hochschulen Hessens. Gründungsmitglied der *B3 Biennale des bewegten Bildes*. Screenings, Ausstellungen, Publikationen und Vorträge im In- und Ausland. Lebt in Berlin und Offenbach am Main.

Narrativer Grenznutzen. Format und Immersion beim 360°-Dome-Film

Christian Janecke

[1]
So bei Oliver Grau: Virtuelle Kunst in Geschichte und Gegenwart. Visuelle Strategien. (Diss. 1999), Berlin 2001 (Vgl. kritisch und differenziert dazu Armin Bergmeier: Dominanz der Imagination. Die Konstruktion immersiver Räume in der Spätantike. In: Jahrbuch Immersiver Medien [= JBIM] 2012, S. 37–48, bes. S. 39f.). Sodann bei Nadja Franz: Einreihung des Mediendoms in eine Illusionsgeschichte. In: JBIM 2008/09, S. 27–38 (hier weitere Literatur). Tobias Hochscherf; Heidi Kjär; Patrick Rupert-Kruse: Phänomene und Medien der Immersion. In: JBIM 2011, S. 9–19.

[2]
Man kann hier insbesondere an Effekte suggestiver (uns z. B. in eine Achterbahnfahrt ziehender) *movie ride scenes* oder an jene Kinohelden der 1990er Jahre denken, denen die Ununterscheidbarkeit von digitaler und wirklicher Welt zum Immersionserlebnis geriet. Vgl. Jörg Schweinitz: Totale Immersion und die Utopien von der virtuellen Realität. In: B. Neitzel; R. F. Nohr (Hg.): Das Spiel mit dem Medium. Partizipation – Immersion – Interaktion. Zur Teilhabe an den Medien von Kunst bis Computerspiel. (Schriftenreihe der GfM, Bd. 14), Marburg 2006.

[3]
Ernst Michalsky: Die Bedeutung der ästhetischen Grenze für die Methode der Kunstwissenschaft. (Erstm. Berlin 1932), Neuausg. m. e. Nachwort v. B. Kerber. Berlin 1996.

Im Folgenden geht es weder um eine Vor-, Theater- oder Kunstgeschichte der Immersion als solche noch auch darum, sie, letztlich teleologisch[1], als Fundament späterer bewegtbildnerischen Weiterentwicklungen zu unterlegen. Vielmehr sollen entscheidende Parameter heutigen Immersionsfilms, nämlich das veränderte *Format* nebst etwaigen *Eintauchmöglichkeiten*, in ihren Implikationen erhellt werden. Das erscheint angebracht insofern, als es beim *B3*-Vorhaben ja nicht um technisch-mediale Muskelspiele, sondern um *Neues Erzählen* geht – dessen Vereinbarkeit mit den medialen Koordinaten des Dome-Films allerdings nicht von vornherein ausgemachte Sache ist.

Sieht man von herkömmlicher Entfaltung illusionistischen Sogs[2] im alten Bildgeviert einmal ab, so setzt immersiver Film den Ausbruch aus dem uns allen bestens vertrauten Querformat voraus. Dabei ist nicht primär die Rede von einer Überschreitung der »ästhetischen Grenze«[3] dergestalt, dass die Figuren gewissermaßen im 90°-Winkel zur Leinwand aus dieser heraus in den Zuschauersaal klettern (oder in einem Western vielleicht auch schießen) könnten, wie es als pygmalionisches und gleichermaßen barocker Illusionsstaffelung folgendes Prinzip mitunter filmisch thematisiert wurde. Eher ist die Rede von einer buchstäblichen Ausdehnung bzw. Überschreitung des Projektionsfeldes. Dabei reicht es indes nicht, besagtes Querformat einfach nur zu vergrößern, andernfalls man bei riesigen Kinoleinwänden ja den Leidenswilligen unter den Zuschauern attestieren könnte, sie vermöchten durch bloße Platzierung in der ersten Reihe der Überblickbarkeit des Projektionsfeldes sich lustvoll zu entledigen. Entscheidend ist stattdessen die Okkupation eines größeren Anteils am Sehfeld der einzelnen Zuschauer, was zunächst einer Veränderung des Verhältnisses von Höhe zu Breite gleichkommt. Zwar unterliegt diesbezüglich auch schon das uns vertraute maßvolle Querformat historisch, modisch, apparativ oder auch bloß geschmacklich bedingten Schwankungen, lässt sich aber durchwegs als ein dem Zuschauer obzwar nicht punktuelles, aber eben doch gut verortbares *Gegenüber* definieren – prinzipiell nicht anders als bei jenen allermeisten Bildern, die wir heute noch in Museen, übrigens auch in den Sälen für jüngere Kunst, antreffen. Im Unterschied dazu tendiert ein um den Rezipienten leicht oder stärker gekrümmter Bildträger zu einer *Szenerie*, bei der wir sozusagen immerzu eintreffen, die sich uns also einerseits noch *darbietet*, während sie uns doch, würden wir sie betreten können, andererseits auch regelrecht *umfinge*, wofür der Screen-Verlauf eines IMAX-Kinos ein gutes Beispiel gibt. Und unschwer denken wir an Parallelen zu jener Art aufgelockerten Illusionstheaters, bei welchem das Spiel auf Bühne und Proszenium bereichert wird durch Einbeziehung der Seitzugänge, vielleicht auch der seitlichen Logen oder Ränge. Spätestens dort nun, wo unser Sehfeld überschritten wird, wir also den Kopf wenden müssen, um uns sehend wirklich zu orientieren, sollte man eher von einer *Seh-Umgebung* sprechen. Man kann dabei an das mehr als halbrunde, idealerweise 360° umfassende Panorama[4] denken. Dass dieses Panorama faktisch nur den umlaufenden Rand einer zylindrischen Scheibe einnimmt und zumeist jegliches Oben ausblendet durch eine typischerweise dunkle, über den Köpfen des Publikums schwebende Decke, dass es im Gegenzug den ebenfalls runden Boden gerne recht weit auskragen lässt, auf dass niemand vom viel kleineren und meist eingezäunten Publikumsareal aus ein Unten erspähen kann, all dies tut bzw. tat in älterer Zeit der auf die Zeitgenossen verblüffend wirkenden oder sie doch wenigstens beglückenden Illusion gar keinen Abbruch. Denn das allermeiste Bedeutsame, das um die allermeisten von uns herum und zumal in gebührender Entfernung geschieht oder sichtbar wird, ist plausibel innerhalb einer derartigen Horizontalumgebung unterbringbar (wenn es nicht ausgerechnet um Ikarus oder um Fallschirmspringer geht). Die klassisch requisitäre, bühnenbildnerische Herkunft der dabei eingesetzten plastischen, sodann der reliefierten Partien bzw. Verschmiegungen zum nurmehr täuschend gemalten Hintergrund, schließlich der schieren Versatzstücke (z. B. so genannter »Pappkameraden« im Schlachtenpanorama), also des gesamten *Faux terrain*[5], ist uns indessen untrüglicher Hinweis darauf, dass bei der vom Panorama angestrebten ›Seh-Umgebung‹ der Akzent auf dem *ersten* Teil des Kompositums liegt! Der durchweg auf Distanz gehaltene Betrachter soll eigentlich nur schauend, soll allein schweifenden Blickes durch quasi-bildlich prototypisierte Arrangements sich

[4] Stephan Oettermann: Das Panorama. Die Geschichte eines Massenmediums. (Diss. 1979), Frankfurt am Main 1980. Sehsucht. Das Panorama als Massenunterhaltung des 19. Jahrhunderts. Ausstellungskatalog; Kunst- u. Ausstellungshalle der BRD, Bonn 1993.

[5] Die Kunstlosigkeit dieses Bereiches erkennt richtig Peter Geimer (Faux terrain. Ein Zwischenraum des 19. Jahrhunderts. In: S. Haug; H. G. H. v. Gaertringen; C. Philipp; S. M. Schultz; M. Ziegler; T. Zürn [Hg]: Arbeit am Bild. Ein Album für Michael Diers. Köln 2010, S. 78–85), unterschlägt indes die reliefhaft-bühnenbildnerische Herkunft.

bewegen, darin die Ereignisverdichtung konventionell, also überschaubar formatierter Bilder ineins nutzend und passager auflösend. Zwar mag er sich in nicht weiter bestimmter (mitunter aber auch topographisch minutiös definierter) Mitte wähnen zwischen all dem, was ihm fernansichtig suggeriert wird. Doch es ist zweifellos alles so hergerichtet, als bestünde der von ihm per Aufwärtstreppchen erklommene Aussichtspunkt *auch ohne ihn* weiter – worin das installationsindifferente, wenn nicht anti-installative Moment des Panoramas klar wird, selbst dort noch, wo seine Bildpassagen den Betrachter horizontal rundum komplett umschließen. Dass man zur Spätzeit deutscher Schlachtenpanoramen darauf achtete, nicht allzu momentaneistische Sujets – wie z. B. einen von der Kugel getroffenen, just zu Boden stürzenden Soldaten – zu wählen, weil sie einem allmählich das Panorama rundum durchwandernden Blick auf illusionssabotierende und jedenfalls hässlich störende Weise sich irgendwann ein zweites Mal hätten aufdrängen müssen, ist Hinweis darauf, um wie viel mehr es beim Panorama um dauernde, gewissermaßen nie endende Vergegenwärtigung ging, statt, wie immer wieder mal kolportiert wird, um Protofilmisches. (Das gilt übrigens auch für die motorisiert unmerklich rotierenden Besucherplattformen, die ja keineswegs Bewegung ins Panoramatische, sondern vor allem in den Pulk der Besuchermassen bringen sollten, nämlich um den Einzelnen, vom lästigen Abschreiten der Sehattraktion inmitten vieler weiterer drängelnder Besucher entlastet, aus seinem Schauen gerade *nicht* unsanft aufzustören.[6])

In dem Maße aber, wie das panoramatisch bespielte Format auch in die Höhe sich auswächst und zur Halbkugel respektive Kuppel uns umschließt, die Rundum-Illusion also ein Über-uns einschließt, wird ein räumliches und vor allem szenisches bzw. situatives *Totum* veranschlagt. Offerierte also das Panorama ein, wenn auch ubiquitäres, so doch immer noch latent bildlich sublimer Sphäre verpflichtetes *Vor-uns* (nur eben in jeder Richtung), so bietet erst die vollends immersive Darstellung ein emphatisches *Um-uns*. Aus genau diesem Grunde übrigens konnten im Panorama ja auch längst vergangene Szenerien, wie vielleicht aus dem Alten Rom, die Besucher

6
Das erkennt auch Grau (wie Anm. 1; S. 97), vermengt dann aber – interessiert an der Reklamierung des Panoramas als Vorbereiter späterer bewegtbildlicher Immersion – die allmähliche Bewegung des *Publikums* mit der Bewegung wechselnder *Bilder*, etwa in der Dioramenkunst seit dem frühen 19. Jahrhundert.

erfreuen, ohne dass sie sich in ihrem eigenen Habit, dem des ausgehenden 19. Jahrhunderts, deplatziert vorgekommen wären, während dieselben Besucher in einem *wirklich immersiv* ausgestalteten Raum mit der von ihm gemeinten Welt u. U. hätten kollidieren, d. h. störend von seiner Illusionsabsicht hätten abstechen müssen.

Bislang unerörtert blieb, ob es bei Immersion überhaupt um Illusion gehen muss, und falls ja, ob sie eher einer dimensional verringernden Darstellung in perspektivischer Projektion vermeinter Raumtiefe auf Flächenkompartimente verpflichtet bleibt, oder ob sie, eher der Manier des Trompe l'œil folgend, gleichsam reliefhaft die Anwesenheit und plastische Auswölbung von Gegenständen prätendiert. Oder ob es, wie der Begriff »Immersion« per Wortstamm nahelegen könnte, nur um ein Eintauchen geht in eine vielleicht aus Farbnebeln konstituierte Atmosphäre im künstlerischen Feld, um buchstäblich physisches Eintauchen des Körpers, wie es das so genannte Floating als esoterisch verbrämtes Wellness-Erlebnis verspricht, als sehr bewusstes, an ästhetischer Erfahrung interessiertes Sich-Einlassen auf den Raum bzw. die Räume einer Installation oder einer Klangumgebung. Oder ob womöglich das Eindringen der Einzelnen in die – und zugleich Mitproduktion von – Erfahrungs- und Austauschsphären eines in den letzten Jahren immer ›prosumentischer‹ sich ausgestaltenden Internet 2.0 die eigentlich zeitgenössische Immersion wäre.[7] Oder ob man eher eine an Imagination[8] gekoppelte Immersion voraussetzen sollte, wie sie beispielsweise für Bildräume spätantiker Kunst bedeutsam, ja unabdingbar war – bei der man aber auch an jene einfach nur zu schluckende *Architekturpille* eines Hans Hollein von 1967 denken darf, auf deren Concetto ihr anspielungsreicher Untertitel *Non-physical environment*[9] verwies.

Es leuchtet ein, dass damit nicht nur ein unerhört weites Spektrum an Möglichkeiten aufgerufen ist, sondern dass sich hier nachgerade gegensätzliche Optionen ankündigen. Denn die illusionistische Darstellung beispielsweise eines Käfigs könnte (so es angenommenenfalls darum ginge!) zunächst *täuschende* Kraft nur denjenigen gegenüber entfalten, die monokular von fixier-

[7] So die eloquent und beispielreich vorgetragene These von Frank Rose: The Art of Immersion. How the Digital Generation is Remaking Hollywood, Madison Avenue, and the Way We Tell Stories. New York; London 2011.

[8] Vgl. Bergmeier (wie Anm. 1).

[9] Abb. in: Summer of Love. Psychedelische Kunst der 1960er Jahre. Ausstellungskatalog; Tate Liverpool; Schirn Kunsthalle Frankfurt; Kunsthalle Wien 2006, S. 236.

tem Punkte aus um sich blickten. Und noch zur Aufrechterhaltung jener vermutlich eher interessierenden *ästhetischen Illusion*, die sich zwar »aufdecken«, aber nicht »aufheben«[10] lässt, würde es bei vorausgesetzt binokularem Sehen immer noch einer Einschränkung der Bewegungsfreiheit des Sehenden bedürfen; ja es bedürfte im Fall bewegtbildlich immersiver Darstellung sogar einer körpervergessenen Rezeptionsweise der Einzelnen. Dass die Zuschauer beim spektakulär gezeigten Überflug eines UFOs ihre Köpfe wegducken oder bei immersiv dargestellter Autofahrt sogar Fliehkräfte zu erleben meinen, beweist demgegenüber gerade nicht ihre direkte, sondern nur ihre indirekte Körperinvolviertheit in Gestalt machtvoller Rückkopplungen der allein an die Fernsinne des Auges und des Ohres adressierten Illusionistik auf den Körper.

Auf der anderen Seite, wenn es nämlich eher um illusionsindifferente Eintauchung geht, ist der Körper des Einzelnen nicht nur nicht länger etwas tendenziell zu Erübrigendes, er wird Schnittstelle, wird z. B. in dichtem Nebel Grenze, er wird – etwa in der Dauer-Performance der bestallten Mitstreiter von Tino Sehgal auf der letzten *documenta* (2012) – zum physisch bedrängten Kristallisationspunkt tänzerischer oder quasi-ritueller Anrufung; bei so genannten postdramatischen Formen des Theaters oder Tanzes kommt es vor, dass die Zuschauer regelrecht abgeholt und aus ihrer anfangs rezeptiven Haltung befreit werden sollen, um sie zur Partizipation zu verlocken oder auch zu nötigen. Wie auch immer man das bewerten mag – zweifellos sind die Zuschauer alias Mitmacher hier nicht bloß als Sehende oder Hörende gefragt, wie es beim immersiven Film der Fall wäre. Und zumal dort, wo es weniger überwältigungslogisch zur Sache geht und man sich desgleichen den fraternisierenden Schulterschluss mit dem Betrachter verkneift, also in der ganz normalen Installationskunst, wird das Sich-Bewegen, das Erkunden der Installation zum irreduziblen Moment, wenn auch nicht zur ultima ratio eines sich in Gang setzenden Spiels ästhetischer Erfahrung.[11] Der oder die Einzelne mag hier – buchstäblich physisch oder übertragenen Sinnes – tief eindringen in künstlerischerseits gestiftete evokative Konstellationen, ohne dass es doch vorderhand um Illusion ginge, und stets so, dass Involviertwerden und Rezipie-

10
Lambert Wiesing: Von der defekten Illusion zum perfekten Phantom. Über phänomenologische Bildtheorien. In: G. Koch; C. Voss (Hg.): ... kraft der Illusion, München 2006, S. 90–101, S. 89.

11
Vgl. hierzu und zum nachfolgenden Satz Juliane Rebentisch: Ästhetik der Installation. Frankfurt am Main 2003, exemplarisch etwa angelegentlich der Erörterung der Installationskunst Kabakovs bes. S. 172 ff.

render-Fremdkörper-Bleiben ihre Anteile wahren, um wiederum Reflexion auf das sich hier vollziehende Wechselspiel zu initiieren.

Vor dem Hintergrund dieses Spektrums dürfte nun völlig klar sein, dass der Immersionsfilm, oder sagen wir vorsichtiger: der in einer halbkugelförmigen Kuppel projizierte Dome-Film ganz entschieden an *einem* Ende dieses Spektrums operiert, dem der körpervergessenen, allein über Auge und Ohr operierenden Rezeption. Das kann sich mit größter Illusionistik verbinden, wo in Echtzeit und Lebensgröße ein ungesteuert absichtsloses Naturgeschehen gezeigt wird, etwa submarine Welten, deren Akteure dann auf eine Weise das Sehfeld des Besuchers durchlaufen, wie sie es ungefähr auch unter Wasser vor einem Taucher täten, oder wo es Konstellationen am nächtlichen Sternenhimmel sind, die dann nicht abgefilmt und digital zusammengesetzt, sondern in Lage, Position und Wanderung sogleich präzise errechnet als viele einzelne Lichtpunkte in mannigfachen Einzelprojektionen in ihr verblüffendes Zueinander gebracht werden. Wo sich also manches oder vieles um uns herum bewegen soll, wo zugleich aber auf jene wie auch immer schauspielerisch verkörperten Subjekte, deren Aufeinandertreffen überhaupt erst Voraussetzung von Erzählung wäre, getrost verzichtet wird, dort mag eine veritable Illusionsumgebung sich entfalten und fortwähren; und wie man weiß, erscheint ihr wissenschaftsdidaktisches oder träumerisch eskapistisches Potential etlichen Zeitgenossen bedeutsam oder attraktiv.

Anders aber sieht es aus, wo eine Geschichte, ein Plot erzählt werden soll (von künstlerisch experimentellen Nutzungen wird erst weiter unten die Rede sein). Entsprechende Versuche, den technisch apparativen und mithin formatveränderten Neuerungen filmisch bzw. filmerzählerisch nach- oder gleichaufzuziehen, können allerdings als weitgehend misslungen eingeschätzt werden. Sie blieben Kirmesattraktion oder erwiesen sich als naive Zugabe herkömmlicher Filme, oftmals in Verkehrung von Wirkung und Ursache: Nicht der Film, also das filmisch Erzählte, brauchte immersive Erweiterung[12] – die immersiv erweiterten Möglichkeiten verlangten einen filmischen Vorwand. Folglich wurde in dürftige filmische Erzählung eingebettet, was

12
Hier sehe ich ab von jenem immersiven bzw. immersionsähnlichen Potential, welches im Medium Film, statt *per Illusion* zu wirken, entweder eher nur *thematisiert* wird (vgl. Anm. 2), oder welches diesem Medium sozusagen immer schon qua bewegter Lichtbildprojektion *zueigen* ist und das experimentalfilmisch, etwa im Flicker-Film, aber womöglich auch vermittels intensiver und lange vorgeführter Farbigkeit ausschöpfbar ist.

gut ging: die Vorführung von im 3D-Raum möglichst gleichwertig verteilten Bewegtereignissen, als da notorisch wären: Weltraumschlachten, kriegerisch Berstendes, Submarines, Achterbahnfahrten usw. Man könnte daher zu dem sarkastischen Schluss gelangen, ausgerechnet die Computer Game-Industrie hätte die klügeren Konsequenzen gezogen, indem es etwa bei den Ego-Shootern – obzwar meist gerade auf klassisch formatierten Flachbildträgern! – darum geht, weitgehend narrations*verschont* nicht nur ständig in feindlich kodierte Umgebungen einzudringen (sic!), sondern auch die Richtung dieses Eindringens den Spielenden freizustellen sowie fortwährend deren Aktionen herauszufordern.[13]

Fragt man sich, warum das filmisch eigentlich schieflaufen[14] musste, so gibt es darauf zwei Teilantworten:

Erstens führt der formatbedingte Wechsel vom Primat des *Gegenübers* zu dem der *Umgebung* dazu, dass Ereignisse, die sich vor uns abspielen, die unsere Betrachtung fordern, nun zu solchen werden, die uns zwar involvieren, ohne dass wir doch wirklich intervenieren könnten. Hinzu kommt die Einschränkung, dass wir die basalen Zutaten von Erzählung, von Konflikt, von Drama nirgends gleichzeitig im Blick haben, wir ergo zu ihnen kaum reflexiv Position beziehen können. Man zeigt uns, um es mit einem Beispiel zu sagen, keinen Autounfall auf einer Kreuzung, bei dem wir, wenn er gut gefilmt wäre, recht genau erleben und wiedergeben könnten, wer was wem antat, sondern wir finden uns gewissermaßen selbst auf der Kreuzung wieder, auf der es kracht. Das mag funktionieren, solange es nur darum geht, einen Crash erlebbar zu machen. Doch es sind herbe Abstriche hinzunehmen, was unsere Orientierung, unsere Möglichkeit, das Gezeigte nachvollziehend auf Zurückliegendes oder antizipativ auf Kommendes zu beziehen, betrifft. Überdies vermögen uns aus dieser Unfallszene weder filmische Schnitte[15] schnell herauszuholen, weil sie jene Art Illusion, deren Unterpfand im Fulldome ja gerade wir selbst sind, kompromittieren würden. Noch auch können wir uns mit anderen über das Erlebte erfahrungsbegleitend verständigen oder es in fiktionalisierungsresistenter Kopräsenz mit unseren Besucherkörpern relativieren;

13
Den hier relevanten Aspekt des Involvement betont zurecht Anja Kühn: Computerspiel und Immersion. Eckpunkte eines Verständnisrahmens. In: JBIM 2011, S. 50–62. Vgl. auch die Beiträge von S. Wiemer, J. Distelmeyer und F. Furtwängler in: Das Spiel mit dem Medium (wie Anm. 2).

14
Vgl. etwa die Ausführungen zum Cinerama bei Schweinitz (wie Anm. 2), S. 143 f.

15
Das sieht richtig Matthias Bauer: Immersion und Projektion. In: JBIM 2011, S. 20–36, hier S. 21.

nolens volens verharren wir vielmehr abgedunkelt, körperausgeblendet (jedenfalls nicht körpereingeblendeter als im normalen Kino) und konsumtiv in einer für uns ausgeheckten Widerfahrnis (ebenfalls nicht anders als im normalen Kino, im Unterschied dazu aber ständig ›angefixt‹, es *wäre* anders!).

Der denkbare Gegeneinwand nun, gerade die Vorgeschichte der Immersion in der Kunst belege doch entsprechende Möglichkeiten komplexer Bilderzählung, etwa im wandmalerischen Gesamtprogramm eines barocken Kirchenraumes, unterschlägt gleich mehreres, nämlich zunächst den notorisch euphemistischen Gebrauch des Terminus »Erzählung« durch die Kunstgeschichte (da meistens eben nur Stationen einer hinzuzudenkenden oder anderweitig kommunizierten Erzählung illustriert wurden!), sodann, dass die dortigen Bilder in ihrer auf immer verfügten Anlage und Abfolge zwar auch eine Gesamtwirkung entfalten, aber natürlich auch immer wieder neu gelesen, vor allem nacheinander gelesen und oftmals Stück um Stück abgeschritten werden konnten bei religiös kundiger Nutzung. Das Nämliche gilt für die profane Bilderzählung, die bezeichnenderweise relativ komplexer und zugleich präziser im einzelnen, herkömmlich formatierten Tableau der Historienmalerei gelang als im formaterweiterten Panorama, das, wie ich eingangs angedeutet hatte, aus gutem Grunde vergleichbare Aufgaben nicht in Angriff nahm![16]

Zweitens will uns der von der Projektionsfläche des Dome-Films in Kuppelform umschlossene Raum, ungeachtet seiner unentwegten filmischen Transzendierung, zwar immerzu einladen, ihn zu ›entern‹, indem er unser Beisammensein mit den übrigen Anwesenden zur verschworenen Gemeinschaft im Zentrum stärker hervorkehrt als es das klassische Kino mit seiner eher basilikalen Ausrichtung je zuließe. Und doch muss dieser uns physisch adressierende Raum, wie ich bereits ausführte, gerade *um* der Illusionsgewährung und -aufrechterhaltung willen wieder einkassiert werden. Während also ein vergleichbar physisch präsenter, zumal kuppelförmiger Raum andernorts gut ausschöpfbar wäre, indem er bei entsprechend angelegtem Theatergeschehen gerade unleugbare Kopräsenz von Akteuren und Zuschauern inaugurieren, indem er in der Installationskunst

[16] Das gilt sogar noch für das politpropagandistisch überfrachtete und darin durchaus unrepräsentative Sedan-Panorama des Anton von Werner (vgl. Grau, S. 66–100; wie Anm. 1), das zwar nirgends mit Detailschilderung geizte, aber keinen Raum ließ für das Entfaltete, auch das Sukzessive einer storia.

erfahrungseröffnend (s.o.) fungieren und er bei partizipativ ambitionierten Projekten zu einem temporär emphatischen Ort werden könnte, *auf* den und *von* dem aus Reflexion, Entscheidung, Handlung, Darstellung zielen würde, bleibt er, bleibt genauer gesagt seine halbkugelförmige Hülle im Rahmen des Dome-Films, unhintergehbarer Teil einer schieren Illusionsmaschinerie.[17]

Mit Blick nun weniger auf unterhaltungserpichte oder wissenschaftsdidaktische als vielmehr künstlerisch ambitionierte Nutzung dieses Mediums wäre es m. E. zu kurz gegriffen, ja irreführend, sich von den hier Experimentierenden ›Lösungen‹ zu erhoffen, obgleich genau dies – man schaue sich nur einmal die *Jahrbücher für immersive Medien*[18] an – immer wieder verlangt und ggf. bewundert wird. Daran ändern auch nichts die Versuche, womöglich die Stühle aus dem Dome zu räumen oder vielleicht das Publikum zwischen wechselnd aufscheinenden Projektionsorten flanieren zu lassen, womit man letztlich nur eine Installation aus der Sphäre der Bildenden Kunst in das Raum- und Medienkorsett eines Domes verfrachtet hätte. Ebenso fraglich erscheint mir, ob die des Öfteren gewählte Option, ein gewissermaßen der Projektionskuppel schon von Haus aus affines Sujet zu finden, glückt – obwohl diese Option zunächst einleuchten will: Sind es doch, misslicherweise sowohl beim künstlerisch ambitionierten als auch beim kommerziellen Immersionsfilm, immer wieder Szenen etwa des Dialogs, die nach dem Schema herkömmlichen Querformats dem Betrachter gezeigt werden, mit dem einzigen Unterschied, dass sich ein zu diesem Dialog passender Hintergrund um die von besagtem Dialog *nicht* okkupierten restlichen 300° der Rotunde einfach nur herumzieht. Das erinnert dann an friesartig rundum laufende Dekorationen beim Karneval oder an die Ausstattungskunst beim Volkstheater, wo vielleicht dem Streit zwischen Förster und Wilderer die großen Tannen hinterlegt werden, während das Publikum artig mit kleinem Buschwerk umfriedet wird. So gesehen erschiene es nicht völlig abwegig, wenn angenommenenfalls bei der immersionsfilmischen Darstellung einer rechtlichen Auseinandersetzung statt eines Dialogs dicht benachbarter Kontrahenten lieber ein hehres Tribunal gezeigt würde, in dessen Mitte, gar als

---

17
Dass man Planetarien auch als halbkugelförmigen Saal für Tanzperformances hinterlegen bzw. rundum ausstatten kann mit projiziertem Bühnenbild bzw. Lichtspiel (vgl. etwa Tom Duscher: Ich² – Tanz intermedial für Planetarien. In: JBIM 2007, S. 40–45), widerlegt diese Einsicht natürlich nicht – es handelt sich dann einfach um eine andere Raumnutzung, ja ein anderes Medium.

18
Es erschienen bislang vier Jahrbücher (2007, 2008/09, 2011, 2012), die neben medienwissenschaftlichen Texten überwiegend Berichte von den zahlreichen Wettbewerbsfilmen, Erörterungen technischer Neuentwicklungen und Spezialprobleme sowie Praxistipps für die Macher enthalten – was angesichts des komplexen, indes nicht sonderlich verbreiteten Mediums erklärlich ist.

dessen Gegenstand sich der Zuschauer selbst empfinden sollte. Oder man stelle sich vor, dem Zuschauer würden ringsum vorbeilaufende Passanten gezeigt, die auf ihn – der sich offenkundig als am Boden kauernder Bettler vorkommen sollte – doppelten Sinnes von oben herab, mal mitleidig, mal spöttisch oder ignorant, reagieren würden (wobei der Effekt komisch bliebe, dass es den benachbart sitzenden Kinogängern genauso gehen sollte, man sich gewissermaßen als einzelner Bettler doch zugleich in einem Heer von Bettlern wiederfände). Die Frage bleibt bei all dem, ob ›wir‹ ein abendfüllendes Thema abgeben. Der Immersionsfilmer sieht sich stets in dem Konflikt, entweder ereignisverdichtet, aber in sträflicher Vernachlässigung eines Großteils seines Formats, ja mithin der Spezifik seines Mediums zu erzählen (und damit jene medialiter gegebene, also je schon filmimmanente Art von Immersion zu verwirken oder zu schwächen, die sich auch im klassischen Filmformat bereits aus dem protensiv[19] fortlaufenden Moment von Film ergibt), oder aber, um Verteilungsgerechtigkeit bemüht, die Erzählung in Häppchen über sein riesiges Format auszustreuen. Letzteres kommt leider auch bei der künstlerisch versierten Fraktion oft genug vor und erinnert dann an Goethes Diktum: »Getretener Quark wird breit – nicht stark«. Folglich und verständlicherweise bleibt es ein vorrangiges Movens der hier Aktiven, ihrem Medium konvenierende Sujets und Settings zu finden – nicht anders als auch der Tondo in der Malerei oder die Zirkusarena im theatralen Feld geeignete und weniger geeignete Sujets bzw. Performances kennen.

Indessen muss man achtgeben, mit der mediengerecht gedachten Forderung einer Angemessenheit des Sujets ans Format bzw. Medium nicht das tiefer sitzende Problem zu trivialisieren oder zu verdecken: dass nämlich Narration per se schon Format, und natürlich kein willkürliches Format, aus sich gleichsam entlässt, einen »Richtungssinn des mimischen, vokalen und instrumentalen Ausdrucks«[20] verstetigend; dass per Dialog Distanz zwischen zweien allererst konstituiert wird; dass Narration im Bild sich ihre Räume erst ausbildet[21], statt nur in bereits vorhandene Räume gegossen zu werden; dass eine historisch allmählich erreichte Höhe, Elaboriertheit, Finesse der Bilderzählung nicht darauf verzichten konnte, von der *Umgebung* zum *Gegenüber*

[19]
So den Husserl'schen Begriff der Protention veradjektivierend und unter Bezug auf Barthes' Unterscheidung zwischen Fotografie und Film sowie dessen Verwendung der Husserl'schen Terminologie Robin Curtis: Vicarious Pleasures. Fiktion, Immersion und Verortung in der Filmerfahrung. In: ...kraft der Illusion (wie Anm. 10), S. 191–204, bes. S. 199–202.

[20]
Vgl. Friedrich Dieckmann: Ursprünge des Bühnenbilds. In: Ders.: Theaterbilder. Studien und Berichte, Berlin (Ost) 1979, S. 29–38, S. 31.

[21]
Wolfgang Kemp: Die Räume der Maler. Zur Bilderzählung seit Giotto. München 1996.

sich zu läutern, zusehends davon befreit, sich am Gängelband unseres beschwerenden Dabeiseins entfalten zu müssen.

Das denkbare Gegenargument, die Moderne des 20. Jahrhunderts habe doch recht erfolgreich und keineswegs unter Narrationsverzicht, nur eben in veränderter Narration, vielfältige Formen der Erfassung und Umarmung des Publikums ersonnen oder praktiziert – vom Totaltheater über das Happening bis zur Installation u. a. m. –, verfängt indes kaum, eben weil dort betrachterliche Eingriffs-, Aussetzungs- und Reflexionsmöglichkeiten in situ vorgesehen waren[22]; nicht anders in der Literatur und ihren Weiterungen, wo ein riesiger Zettelkasten oder vielleicht ein ganz mit Text ausgekleideter Raum, der prima facie ja Pendant eines Dome-Films sein könnte, im Unterschied zu Letzterem eben Narrationen *der anderen Art* durchaus erlauben würden. Das immerzu Revidier-, Überprüf-, noch einmal anders Machbare von Erfahrung in all diesen Kunstformen, kurzum die ihrerseits der Narration sich machtvoll entgegenstellende oder sie verändernde *Prozessualität* ästhetischer Erfahrung, kann von der eisernen Fasson des Kinos (zumal in den modernen Totalversionen Bazins und Eisensteins) schon qua Medium nicht aufgeboten werden. Sie muss es auch gar nicht. Im Unterschied aber zum normalen Kino, demgegenüber ja nur ein Narr solche Ermächtigung der Betrachter in der Werkerfahrung verlangen könnte, – prätendiert der Dome-Film sie auf fatale, da ihm medialiter uneinholbare Weise.

Narration bleibt daher ein ungeheurer Anspruch im Dome-Film: Wo in ihm, wie auch immer, Erzählung ihre Schwingen ausbreiten, sich von der Gegebenheit zur Begebenheit fort erheben will, hängen ausgerechnet *wir* uns beschwerend an ihre Flügel – dabei die seitens dieses Mediums vollmundig an uns ausgesprochene Einladung annehmend, uns kopräsent einzubringen. Wo wir dann aber als Subjekte mit Körper und ästhetischer Erkundungslust meinen, wirklich gefragt zu sein, so wie wir es doch in einschlägigen anderen Kunstformen derzeit sind, die unsere Begehrlichkeit darauf noch schüren – dort müssen wir einsehen, dass doch nirgends *wir* mitspielen, sondern etwas wie am Schnürchen *vor uns* abgespielt wird. Unabschüttelbar

[22] Vgl. Benjamin Buchloh: Memory Lessons and History Tableaux. James Coleman's Archaeology of Spectacle. In: James Coleman. Ausstellungskatalog; Fundacio Antoni Tàpies, Barcelona 1999, S. 51–75.

also bleibt dem Immersionsfilm die Paradoxie eines emphatischen Vorortseins, ja Mittendrinseins seiner Zuschauer, die dennoch wegschmelzen müssen zum Aug'-und-Ohr-Sein – doch dies vertrackterweise wiederum für eine Illusion, die, je vollendeter und umfassender sie operiert, desto weniger vom Fleck kommt, deren Format gegen Narration sich stemmt.

Wenn daher in Anna Pietochas nur knapp anderthalbminütigem Dome-Film *Mit Haut und Haaren* (2008) ein Zuschauer, von riesiger Hand ergriffen, in das filmische Himmelszelt entführt wird, noch plausibilisiert durch den punktgenauen Aufschrei eines eingeweihten Helfershelfers aus dem Publikum, so könnte man hier zwar eine spielerische Referenz auf gewisse Genre-Konventionen der Science Fiction erkennen, möglicherweise auch ein Exempel für performative Anreicherbarkeiten des Rahmenmediums. Wichtiger erscheint mir indes, dass hier eine, wenn auch teils unbeabsichtigte, so doch ansehnliche Parabel auf den Dome-Film vorliegt: Da wird erstens umgebungsillusionistisch eine simple Tat über unseren Köpfen inszeniert, wobei die performativ plausibilisierte Zuschauerhimmelfahrt eine Unio Mystica von filmisch illusionierter und realer Sphäre vor- bzw. aufführt; da wird zweitens besagte ›Sphärenharmonie‹ auch schon wieder gebrochen oder auch bloß verscherzt, indem es ja notwendig immer ein *anderer* Zuschauer ist, also nie wir selbst derjenige sein können, der hier vermeintlich geschnappt wird (was sogar noch für den einen per Aufschrei Mitspielenden gälte, der sich ja selbst beim Geraubtwerden zusähe!); da wird drittens in unfreiwillig sinnbildlicher Überhöhung – es ist der göttliche Adler, der sich den Ganymed schnappt, nicht umgekehrt! – nochmals deutlich, *wem* allein die Initiative obliegt beim Immersionsfilm.

Christian Janecke
ist Professor für Kunstgeschichte an der HfG Offenbach. Promotion 1993, Habilitation 2004. Bücher: *Zufall und Kunst* (1995); *Johan Lorbeer* (1999); *Tragbare Stürme. Von spurtenden Haaren und Windstoßfrisuren* (2003); Hg: *Haar tragen – eine kulturwissenschaftliche Annäherung* (2004); *Performance und Bild/Performance als Bild.* FUNDUS 160 (2004); Hg: *Gesichter auftragen. Argumente zum Schminken* (2006); *Christiane Feser. Arbeiten/Works* (2008); *Maschen der Kunst* (2011).

Illusion und ihre Umkehrung. Über die künstlerische Erforschung des stereoskopischen 3D

Erkki Huhtamo

*Der Erinnerung an Ray Zone (1947–2012), einem echten
3D-Enthusiasten und Freund, gewidmet*

Das stereoskopische 3D hat in den letzten Jahren ein Comeback erlebt. Aber seine kulturelle Identität bleibt weiterhin unklar. Es wurde von Hollywood als das Neueste vom Neuen vermarktet, als eine Geheimwaffe, um die Kinobesucher, die sich heute selbst beim Spazierengehen oder Autofahren lieber mit ihren Smartphones beschäftigen, wieder in die Kinos zu locken. Die Werbeteams Hollywoods beanspruchen für sich, die Zukunft der dritten Dimension gesehen zu haben (obwohl ich eher der Meinung bin, dass die Welle mit den 3D-Filmen wieder abebben wird). Tatsächlich aber greift die 3D-Technik auf die Vergangenheit zurück – auf die unzählbaren »tollen« und »phantastischen« 3D-Formate in Kinofilmen, Comicbüchern, Filmrollen, auf den linsenförmigen Postkarten und den Random-Dot-Stereogrammen »Magic Eye«, die in den frühen 1990ern aufgrund der Neugier auf die seinerzeit aufkommenden Computergrafiken zu einer kurzen Modeerscheinung wurden. Man kommt nicht umhin, an Nostalgie zu denken.[1] 3D-Bilder haben in dieser und in vielen anderen Formen eine besondere Rolle in der postmodernen Kultur eingenommen. Sie sind flüchtig und dennoch irgendwie essentiell. Die räumliche Illusion, die sie erzeugen, ist künstlich. Und daher sind sie in der Lage, dass der Zuschauer vor Erstaunen nach Luft schnappt. Sie haben, auf die Leinwand im Kino projiziert, die Kraft, dass die Besucher ihre Zweifel über Bord werfen, anfangen zu schreien und überall versuchen, Phantome, die durch die Luft schweben, zu fangen.[2]

Die Welt des 3D ist eine technische Spielerei – ein Großteil ihrer Faszination entstammt den Geräten. Für den echten 3D-Enthusiasten scheint der Blick durch die Anaglyphen-3D-Brille mit ihren roten und blauen Filtern ebenso wichtig zu sein wie die Illusionen, die sie erzeugen und einem ins Auge hämmern. Man kann sich fragen, wie die Tricks hinter den 3D-Effekten funktionieren, ob das was mit dem Prinzip des Stereoskops oder mit den versteckten Schichten eines computergenerierten Random-Dot-Stereogramms zu tun hat. Aber diese Betrachtungsweise bezüglich der Stereoskopie ist einseitig (oder sollten wir

[1] David Hutchinson (Hg.): Fantastic 3-D. A STARLOG Photo Guidebook. New York 1982. Hal Morgan; Dan Symmes: Amazing 3-D. Boston; Toronto 1982. Peter A. Hagemann: 3-D-Film. München 1980.

[2] Dieser Essay beinhaltet Material, das ich bereits früher veröffentlicht habe; vgl.: Media Art in the Third Dimension. Stereoscopic Imaging and Contemporary Art. In: Jeffrey Shaw; Peter Weibel (Hg.): Future Cinema. Cambridge, Mass. 2003, S. 466–473. Vgl. auch die Version auf Italienisch: Insidiare l'illusione. L'arte e il 3D. In: Moviemento. Speciale 3D. Manduria 2012, S. 62–71.

»einäugig« sagen?). Die stereoskopische Vision ist, seit sie wissenschaftlich untersucht wird, mit Problemen der 3D-Welt, die berühmte Illusionen zurückzuweisen versuchen, verbunden: Analyse, Grund, Kraft, Kontrolle.³ Charles Wheatstones ursprüngliches Spiegelstereoskop (1838) war ein wissenschaftliches Instrument, um den Unterschied zwischen dem externen Reiz, den die Augen wahrnehmen, und seiner Auslegung im menschlichen Gehirn zu untersuchen.⁴ Die antiillusionistische Natur wurde in die offene Struktur des Geräts eingetragen. Der Beobachter konnte die Bilder für das rechte und das linke Auge, die an den Seiten angebracht waren, frei sehen und die 3D-Darstellung in angewinkelten Spiegeln in der Mitte erfassen. Die Analyse und die Illusion verstehen sich in Coexistenz und unterstützen einander.

So wurde aus der Stereoskopie eine Allerweltsware. Sie wurde in Form des kastenförmigen linsenartigen Brewster-Stereoskops (erstmalig bei der Chrystal Palace-Ausstellung in London, 1851, vorgestellt) intensiver vermarktet. Das war eine Art Guckkasten, der den Stereoblick eingrenzte und somit ›geheimnisvoller‹ war. Die analytische Verwendung hält sich bis heute hartnäckig in der Wissenschaft und Medizin. Es wurden spezielle Karten zur »Schulung der Augen« entwickelt, um das als »Wettstreit der Netzhaut« bekannte Phänomen zu untersuchen. Diese Karten fördern ein aktives Sehen (Augengymnastik) und wurden im 20. Jahrhundert von den Optikern verwendet, um die Augen ihrer Patienten zu trainieren. Darüber hinaus fand, wie die meisten optischen Technologien, das Stereoskop als ein professionelles Werkzeug für die Luftraumaufklärung Einzug in die militärische Nutzung. Doch selbst die ›unschuldigen‹ Filmrollen – eine schöne Erinnerung an Kindertage, die über Generationen hinweg erhalten geblieben ist – wurden für militärische Zwecke verwendet, um beispielsweise die Kriegsschiffe des Feinds zu erkennen und um Kampfflieger während des Zweiten Weltkriegs in der Anvisierung der Ziele zu trainieren.⁵ Die Holographie, der spätere Durchbruch im 3D-Bereich, wurde zu einem Sicherheitsgerät, das für Geldscheine und Kreditkarten verwendet wurde, um die wirtschaftlich-soziale Ordnung zu stabilisieren und aufrechtzuerhalten. Die scheinbar harmlosen »Magic Eyes«

3
Francoise Reynaud; Catherine Tambrun; Kim Timby (Hg.): Paris in 3D. From Stereoscopy to Virtual Reality 1850-2000. Paris; London 2000.

4
Thomas L. Hankins; Robert J. Silverman: Instruments and the Imagination. Princeton, N.J. 1995, S. 148–177.

5
John Dennis: View-Master Then and Now. In: Stereo World, März-April 1984 (Sonderausgabe). Die Filmrolle wurde im Jahr 1939 erfunden.

des Stereoskops wurden zu analytischen und panoptischen Instrumenten.

Aber was bietet 3D den Künstlern? Wie kann, wenn überhaupt, 3D für experimentelle Erzählzwecke genutzt werden? Die Künstler haben in einem Jahrhundert Gemälde, Collagen, Drucke, Fotos, Filme, Videos, kinetische Objekte, Darbietungen und virtuelle reale Installationen in 3D angefertigt. Es gibt mehr Verschiedenartigkeit als Uniformität. Die 3D-Gemälde von Salvator Dalí und René Magritte erweiterten die räumliche Erkundung der Surrealisten, wohingegen die 3D-Duschvorhänge von Andy Warhol einen Ausdruck der Pop Art-Sensibilität vermittelten. [6] Die 3D-Filme von Oskar Fischinger (der darüber hinaus auch Stereo-Malereien anfertigte), Dwinell Grant, Hy Hirsh, Harry Smith und anderen verliehen der abstrakten Dynamik der Farben, Formen und dem bewegten bildlichen Ausdruck Tiefe. [7] Andere versuchten, eine Brücke über die Lücke zwischen der Kunst und der Wissenschaft zu schlagen. Margaret Benyon wechselte von stereoskopischen Bildern hin zur Holographie. Medienkünstler wie Ken Jacobs, Jim Pomeroy und Zoë Beloff hingegen haben mit stereoskopischen Folien, Filmen oder »3D-Schatten« auf Objekten vor roten und grünen Lichtern gearbeitet. [8]

Verstecken spielen und sich zwischen 3D und 4D positionieren

Die Geschichte der 3D-Kunst ist so vielschichtig, dass sie hier nicht komplett abgedeckt werden kann. Daher möchte ich mich auf ein paar wenige Künstler konzentrieren, deren Forschungen die Ontologie und die allgemein übliche Nutzung von 3D herausgefordert haben, die Möglichkeiten eröffnet haben, die zu denen, die die Filmbranche gefördert hat, oder zu der Nostalgie, die die 3D-Enthusiasten schätzen, sehr unterschiedlich sind. Die Hauptfigur hierbei ist Marcel Duchamp (1887–1968), der wohl maßgeblichste Künstler des 20. Jahrhunderts. 3D war etwas, das ihn ein Leben lang beschäftigt hat. Es taucht wieder und wieder bereits in seinem berüchtigten frühen Ready-made *Handmade Stereopticon Slide* (einer handgemachten Stereoskopie, 1918) bis hin zu seiner letzten Arbeit

---

6 Siehe Maurice Tuchman (Hg.): A Report on the Art and Technology Program of the Los Angeles County Museum of Art 1967–1971. Los Angeles 1971, S. 330–337. ›Neo-Pop‹-Künstler wie Mariko Mori haben in ihren Installationen ebenfalls 3D-Projektionen verwendet. Warhol gab seinen Namen, um einen 3D-Film von Paul Morrissey zu veröffentlichen. Dieser ist als *Andy Warhol's Frankenstein 3D* (1974) bekannt.

7 William Moritz: La romance du l'animation abstraite en relief. In: Thierry Lefebvre; Philippe-Alain Michaud (Hg.): Le relief au cinéma (1895). Paris 1997 (Sonderausgabe), S. 134–140.

8 Margaret Benyon: Holography as an Art Medium. In: Frank Malina (Hg.): Kinetic Art. Theory and Practice. Selections from the Journal Leonardo. New York 1974, S. 185–192.

The Anaglyphic Chimney (1968) auf. [9] Die zuerst genannte Arbeit, die in Buenos Aires gefunden wurde, fand ihren Ursprung in einem unscheinbaren Stereoblick der Darstellung eines Meeres. Sonst nichts. Duchamp brachte auf diese eher langweilige Darstellung mit einem Bleistift scharf konturierte geometrische Rhombenformen auf. Die Zeichnungen verschmolzen beim Blick mit einem Stereoskop und bildeten dreidimensionale Formen, die in das visuelle Feld ›flossen‹, wohingegen die ursprüngliche langweilige Stereoansicht flach und unscharf blieb (dieser Kontrast muss Duchamp sehr amüsiert haben, denn kurz darauf begannen seine Dada-Jahre).

Obwohl die *Handmade Stereopticon Slide* oftmals nur als eine Studie für Duchamps erstes Meisterwerk, *The Large Glass* (1915–1923), betrachtet wird, kann es doch als eine Art Zusammenfassung eines Meta-Kommentars zur Geschichte der Stereoskopie gesehen werden, mit dem Duchamp mit Sicherheit vertraut war. Er kehrte die Bahn der geschichtlichen Evolution, die sich – zumindest oberflächlich betrachtet – von einem wissenschaftlichen Vorführungsinstrument hin zu einer beliebten Allerweltsware, die für magische Illusionen sorgte, entwickelte, in einer gewissen Art und Weise um. Duchamps von Hand gezeichnete Rhomben brachten die Originalzeichnungen an die Oberfläche, mit denen Charles Wheatstone den stereoskopischen Effekt im Jahr 1838 (die Fotografie stand noch nicht zur Verfügung, die Stereoskopie war also *nicht* ihr Abfallprodukt) aufzeigte, wohingegen der (in diesem Fall fehlgeschlagene) Illusionismus der industriell hergestellten und massenvermarkteten Stereokarte in den Hintergrund rückte. Das Wiedererscheinen von Wheatstones rhombenförmigem Geist glich die Arbeit hinsichtlich der kritischen Abhandlungen der Darstellung der Vertreter der Moderne an: Die zwei Schichten verstehen sich in Koexistenz und sind dennoch bewusst nicht kompatibel. Dies hebt die konstruierte Art des Gegenstands hervor.

Duchamps Faszination an versteckten Zeichen und Bedeutungen einschließlich jener in Bezug auf die Stereoskopie zeigt sich in *Wanted, $2,000 Reward* (1923), einem überarbeiteten Ready-made, das auf einem Probeanzug für ein Fahndungsposter, das Duchamp in einem Restaurant gefunden haben soll, beruht.[10]

9
Der *Anaglyphic Chimney* war von dem Buch *Les anaglyphes geometriques* von H. Vuibert inspiriert. Vgl. Linda Dalrymple Henderson: Duchamp in Context. Science and Technology in the Large Glass and Related Works. Princeton, N.J. 1998.

10
Arturo Schwartz: The Complete Works of Marcel Duchamp. New York 2000, S. 699.

Duchamp gab nicht nur den Namen seines weiblichen Alter Ego, Rrose Sélavy, als das Pseudonym für die gesuchte Verbrecherin an. Er fügte sogar sein eigenes Profilfoto (sowohl im Profil als auch in der Frontalansicht) hinzu. Ein Wissenschaftler hat kürzlich entdeckt, dass man, wenn man sich die Fahndungsfotos anschaut und dabei ein Auge schließt (beim sogenannten freien Sehen), die beiden Fotos wie bei den »Wettstreit der Netzhaut«-Stereokarten verschmelzen und dabei ein verblüffendes plastisches Kompositum von Duchamps Gesicht erzeugen. Diese Räumlichkeit wird durch den doppelten Rahmen betont. [11] Durch diese Entdeckung bekommt die Arbeit eine weitere Bedeutung. Wenn Verbrechen eine »Kunst« verborgener Handlungen ist, ist 3D eine Kunst verborgener visueller Räume. Verbrecher verwenden ebenso wie Künstler gerne Pseudonyme. Es gibt jedoch einen Unterschied: Perfekte Verbrechen sind etwas, das unentdeckt bleibt. Ein perfektes 3D hingegen zeigt, was zuvor unsichtbar war.

Duchamp war neben der Darstellung der Rrose Sélavy in seinen Kunstwerken über Jahre hinweg gleichzeitig damit beschäftigt, eine Rolle als »Präzisionsaugenarzt« zu spielen, eine Art »Künstler-mit-Optiker-mit-Optikwissenschaftler«, der eine Reihe sich drehender optischer Illusionsscheiben (wie die berühmten, sich in einer Kiste befindlichen *Rotoreliefs*, 1935) entwarf. [12] Die Experimente des Präzisionsaugenarztes kombinierten 3D mit 4D. Hinzu kam eine zyklische Bewegung, um den Eindruck der Tiefe und des Reliefs zu erzeugen. [13] Duchamp entwickelte in seiner letzten Hauptarbeit, *Etant donnés* (*Given*, 1946–66) noch eine andere Strategie bezüglich des 3D-Ansatzes. Er konstruierte bewusst eine anstößige Szene, indem er ein nacktes weibliches Model, das sich zurücklehnte, und andere physische Theaterrequisiten nahm und diese Kombination hinter einer alten Holztür verbarg. Der Betrachter konnte die Szene nur durch die beiden Löcher, die in die Tür gebohrt waren, sehen. Die Betrachtungssituation brachte – obwohl man die Installation als den Kommentar eines Künstlers zu illusionistischen Durchscheingemälden in Museen, durch die realistische Objekte realisiert werden (die man in Museen der Naturgeschichte und anderenorts finden kann), auslegen kann – das

---

11 Rhonda Roland Shearer u.a.: Why the Hatrack is and/or is not Readymade. Mit interaktiver Software, Animationen und Videos, die die Leser entdecken können, Teil III: Duchamp's Revolutionary Alternative in the context of competing optical experiments. The Marcel Duchamp Studies Online Journal, Band 1, Ausgabe 3 (Dez. 2000), S. 10; http://www.toutfait.com/issues/issue_3/Multimedia/Shearer/Shearer10.html. Das *Wanted*-Poster wurde erstmals in Duchamps *Boite-en-valise* (1941) herausgegeben. Duchamp gab hinsichtlich dieser Interpretation einen Hinweis auf dem Cover, das er für seinen Werkkatalog (1953) entwarf und ein Kompositum seines Gesichts zeigte.

12 Vgl. Erkki Huhtamo: Mr. Duchamp's Playtoy, or Reflections on Marcel Duchamp's Relationship to Optical Science. In: Tanja Sihvonen; Pasi Väliaho (Hg.): Experiencing the Media. Assemblages and Crossovers. (School of Art, Literature and Music, Media Studies, Series A, Nr. 53), Turku 2003, S. 54–72.

13 Francis M. Naumann: Marcel Duchamp. The Art of Making Art in the Age of Mechanical Reproduction. Ghent 1999.

Stereoskop zum Vorschein. Und das erreichte das bewusst perspektivische Arrangement der Szene hinter den Gucklöchern. Ihre Zusammenstellung hat Ähnlichkeiten mit pornographischen Stereoansichten.[14]

Wie sollen wir Duchamps Engagement hinsichtlich des 3D interpretieren? Es bezieht sich mit Sicherheit auf seinen subtilen, aber bestimmten Ein-Mann-Kreuzzug gegen »retinale Malerei« oder Kunstwerke, hinsichtlich derer er der Meinung war, der Inhalt mit reproduzierenden Oberflächen bringen lediglich die Realität zustande (wie beim Impressionismus). Duchamp befürwortete eine intellektuelle Haltung – Kunst, die das Offensichtliche durchdringt und den Intellekt fördert, die Signifikanz durch die Umkehrung in eine Art bewusst mehrdeutige Zeichen generiert. Die Stereoskopie und andere Arten an optischen Illusionen faszinierten ihn, weil deren Effekte nicht vorher »irgendwo da draußen« existieren, sondern durch ein aktives Sehen im Gehirn des Betrachters verschmelzen. Im 3D flossen viele von Duchamps Interessen wie beispielsweise die Wissenschaft, Technologie, seine streberhafte Faszination in Bezug auf Maschinen und seine eher spöttische Wertschätzung der Handelsware Popkultur.

Der in der Schweiz geborene Alfons Schilling (1934–2013) ist eine weitere Hauptfigur. Auch er erkundete die 3D-Bildgestaltung in all ihrer Vielfalt.[15] Er war wie Duchamp eine Art Künstler-Erfinder, der seine Karriere ebenfalls als Maler begann und, wiederum wie Duchamp, mit vielen verschiedenen Medien und Formen einschließlich rotierender Bildscheiben experimentierte. Der junge Schilling begann unter dem Einfluss des abstrakten Expressionismus damit, Farbe auf große runde Leinwände zu werfen, die sich, von Motoren angetrieben, drehten (die Arbeiten konnten entweder im Stillstand oder in Bewegung betrachtet werden). Die Stereoskopie wurde zu einem ganzheitlichen Aspekt von Schillings Erforschung seiner Vision in den frühen 1970ern. Seine Arbeiten deckten sowohl stereoskopische Zeichnungen und Malereien (sowohl für Betrachtungsgeräte als auch zum »freien Sehen«), ein 3D-Video-Headset und tragbare »Sehmaschinen« als auch stereoskopische Folienprojektionen ab, die mittels rotierender Blendenverschlussscheiben ungewöhnliche optische

14
So, wie ich es sehe, hat bisher niemand die Gucklöcher mit einem Stereoskop in Verbindung gebracht. Haladyn nannte lediglich das »Interieur-Durchscheinbild«, das man durch die »Gucklöcher« sehen kann. Vgl. Julian Jason Haladyn: Marcel Duchamp. Étant donnés. London 2010), S. 84. Duchamp verwendete in seinem Cardboard-Modell für *Étant donnés* den Ausdruck »Trous de Voyeur«. Vgl. Marcel Duchamp: Manual of Instructions for Étant donnés. Philadelphia 1987, separate Beilage.

15
Zu Schilling vgl. vor allem Ich/Auge/Welt. The Art of Vision. Wien 1997.

16
Der experimentelle Filmemacher Ken Jacobs war von dem Schilling-Effekt inspiriert und wendete diesen in seinen eigenen stereoskopischen Projektionen an, die als *The Nervous System* und *The Nervous Magic Lantern* bekannt sind. Jacobs verwendete zwei 16mm-Filmprojektoren und ein maßgefertigtes »Blendverschlussrad«, das sich vorne vor den Linsen drehte. Jacobs projizierte oft zwei Drucke aus dem gleichen Film und ließ sie ein wenig unsynchron laufen. Er manipulierte den filmischen Raum mittels eines rotierenden Blendverschlusses in überraschender Art und Weise. Dies beinhaltete die Erzeugung eines künstlerischen Eindrucks von Tiefe. Vgl. Ken Jacobs: Le Nervous System Film Performance. In: Le relief au cinéma (1897; wie Anm. 7), S. 141–146. Jacobs stellte den 3D-Arbeiten von Schilling seine Tiefe zur Verfügung, scheint sie aber inzwischen ›vergessen‹ zu haben. Vgl. Schilling (1997; wie Anm. 15), S. 185.

17
Der ›Random-Dot-Stereogramm-Wahn‹ war insbesondere in Japan sehr groß. Es kam geradezu eine Lawine an Veröffentlichungen auf den Markt. Hierzu gehörte auch eine Buchreihe mit dem Titel *CG Stereogram*. Vgl. Itsuo Sakane: New Developments in 3-D Perceptual Art. In: 3D – Beyond the Stereography. Images and Technology Gallery Exhibition, Theme III. Tokyo 1996, S. 28–31.

18
Ysabel de Roquette (Hg.): Art/ Photographie Numérique. L'image réinventée. Aix-en-Provence 1995, Farbtf. III. Die Arbeit befindet sich in der Sammlung des Los Angeles County Museum of Art.

Effekte erzeugten (das Prinzip wurde als »Schilling-Effekt« bekannt).¹⁶ Darüber hinaus erfand Schilling (inspiriert von ihrem Erfinder, dem Optikwissenschaftler Béla Julesz) sowohl neue Wege der Erzeugung von Random-Dot-Stereogrammen als auch »auto-binäre« Stereofotos. ¹⁷

Die Ontologie entkleiden: Die 3D-Illusion herausfordern

Duchamps und Schillings Interventionen waren nur implizit politisch. Beide vermieden die offene Konfrontation mit den kulturellen und ideologischen Verzweigungen der Stereoskopie. Künstler wie Esther Parada, Manual (Ed Hill und Suzanne Bloom) und Jim Pomeroy engagierten sich genau für das, was Erstere vermieden. Ihre Erforschungen von 3D entsprangen Debatten über Postmoderne und digitale Fotografie. Manual lagerte in der Fotomontage *Malevich in America* (1991) ein Kreuz (das wie bandagiert aussieht) aus blauen und roten Balken über eine unscharfe monochrome Stereoansicht eines nichtssagenden Waldes.¹⁸ Das Kreuz bezieht sich auf die abstrakten Malereien des russischen Vertreters der Moderne Kasimir Malevich. Hier koexistieren zwei einzelne visuelle sowohl flache als auch dreidimensionale Anordnungen, die an Duchamps *Handmade Stereopticon Slide* erinnern. Es kann sein, dass diese visuellen Anordnungen gemäß dem Hinweis im Titel kulturell bestimmt sind. Wenn der Wald für Amerika steht, was bedeutet dann das russische Kreuz – Dominanz, Fortschritt oder einfach nur abstrakte Flächigkeit? Die Antwort bleibt bewusst mehrdeutig.

Esther Paradas (1938–2005) Arbeiten dekonstruieren ideologische Darstellungen durch subtile digitale Collagen, die sehr mehrdeutige erzählerische Sequenzen erzeugen. Sie wählte für eine Serie mit dem Namen *2-3-4-D: Digital Revisions in Time and Space* (1991–92) die in Masse produzierten alten Stereokarten mit der Keystone-Ansicht eines Unternehmens im kolonialen Lateinamerika aus und kombinierte sie mit anderen visuellen Quellen. Der Startpunkt für die Reihe aus vier Tafeln mit dem Namen *At the Margin* ist eine Stereokarte mit dem Titel *Statue of Columbus, Ciudad Trujillo, The Dominican Republic* aus dem Jahr 1939. ¹⁹ Für Parada steht dies für Imperialismus und Rassismus, ergänzt um die Tatsache, dass Stereoansichten wie diese meist für europäische und nordamerikanische Betrachter gemacht wurden. Parada unterwandert die darin eingebundene Ideologie, indem sie sich auf scheinbar marginale Figuren konzentriert (eine schwarze und eine indische Frau), diese zwei Frauen in die Mitte bewegt und gleichzeitig den 3D-Effekt verzerrt. Auf die dritte Tafel kam eine monoskopische Fotografie mit zwei jungen kubanischen Pionierinnen, die den ursprünglichen Referenten überschatten und die 3D-Illusion weiter ausgleichen. [20]

Paradas Art, mit der Stereoansicht der Kolumbusstatue umzugehen, stellt »eine militante autonome Haltung in Bezug auf die europäische oder nordamerikanische Dominanz in dieser Hemisphäre« dar.[21] Die stereoskopische Illusion zu unterbrechen, hat für sie eine zentrale Wichtigkeit: »Ich hoffe, dass meine Strategie des Nebeneinanderstellens, meine Überlagerung verschiedener Perspektiven durch die digitale Technologie, ähnlich wie die zwei verschiedenen Winkel eines stereographischen Bilds optisch die Illusion einer Dimension erzeugen, konzeptuell eine komplexere oder dimensionalere Sichtweise erzeugt.«[22] Die Keystone-Stereoansichten wurden oftmals mit der Unterstützung von Wissenschaftlern und anderen autoritären Personen vermarktet, die in ihren Bezugnahmen die ontologische Wahrheit der Ansichten, ihre absolute Genauigkeit hinsichtlich der Darstellung der Realität so, wie sie ist, hervorheben wollten. Für Parada stellte der homogene visuelle 3D-Raum eine höchst ideologische Position dar, die andere Ansichten und Stimmen an den Rand drängte. Er musste aufgegliedert werden, damit diese eine Chance hätten, hinter den Kulissen hervorzukommen.

Jim Pomeroy überarbeitete in einer Reihe stereoskopischer Bilder mit dem Namen *Reading Lessons* (1988) alte Keystone-Stereoansichten, indem er digital textliche Fragmente Wortspielähnlich, einfügte.[23] Der Blick des Betrachters wandert in diesen räumlichen Montagen von Ebene zu Ebene und erstellt Verbindungen zwischen den Wörtern und den Dingen. Die offene Ansicht dieser Reihe trägt den Titel *Reading Lessons and Eye Exercises*. Die Ansichten sind auf verschiedenen Ebenen rund um die Figur eines Mannes verteilt, der in einer Position liest, die

---

[19] Timothy Druckrey: Iterations. The New Image. New York; Cambridge, Mass. 1993, S. 108–111. Paradas Projekt war von einem Wohnsitz am California Museum of Photography, UC Riverside, inspiriert.

[20] Diese letzte Tafel, die in den *Iterationen* fehlt, wurde in den *Metamorphosen* veröffentlicht. Vgl. Photography in the Electronic Age. New York 1994, S. 31. Siehe auch Esther Paradas Essay: Taking Liberties. Digital Revision as Cultural Dialogue. In: Leonardo, Band 26, Nr. 5 (2003), S. 445–450.

[21] Esther Parada, Artist Statement auf http://www.uic.edu/depts/lib/projects/parada/html/art/atm.html (15.04.2012).

[22] Esther Parada: ...To Make All Mankind Acquaintance. In: Iterations (1993; wie Anm. 19), S. 110.

[23] Jim Pomeroy fertigte seine Arbeiten wie Esther Parada im California Museum of Photography (Riverside) an. Hier ist die riesige Keystone-Mast-Sammlung beherbergt.

(möglicherweise unbeabsichtigt) an Andrea Mantegnas *Dead Christ* (ca. 1500) erinnert – er schiebt die Sohlen seiner Schuhe virtuell in Richtung des Gesichts des Betrachters. Darüber hinaus bezieht sich Pomeroy spielerisch auf die Stereoskopie in der medizinischen Augenschulung. Die humoristischen und absurden Text-/Foto-Kombinationen, die er erstellt, sind nicht nur Possen. Sie sind auch durchaus kritisch gemeint. »Wir lassen uns nicht von Possen verleiten, sondern sind eher kritisch«, schrieb Pomeroy.[24] Bezeichnenderweise veröffentlichte er diese 3D-Arbeit in einer Box mit drei Filmrollen und einem Betrachtungsgerät als Hommage an die beliebte Stereoskopie.[25]

Pomeroy projizierte in Vorstellungen auch 3D-Folien. Er verwendete in *Apollo Jest, an American Mythology* (1978) eine Reihe an stereoskopischen Folien und eine Stimme aus dem Off, um zu ›beweisen‹, dass die Mondlandung tatsächlich stattgefunden hatte. Dieses Thema wurde zu dieser Zeit in den beliebten Talkshows oft diskutiert. Es gab die eine oder andere konspirative Theorie. Es wurde sogar behauptet, dass die NASA ihre Errungenschaft heimlich in einem Filmstudio in Hollywood aufgenommen hatte. Pomeroy hatte mit dem *Apollo Jest* einen witzigen Weg gefunden, falsche ontologische Gewissheiten, denen Fotos als Beweis beigefügt wurden, anzupacken.[26] Die weibliche Stimme aus dem Off erzählt in einer recht leidenschaftslosen, aber augenzwinkernden Weise von den Ereignissen der Mondlandung, und eine ganze Reihe an gemischten Stereoansichten liefert dann den »unwiderlegbaren« Beweis (das Empire State Building steht beispielsweise für die Rakete usw.). Diese Nichtübereinstimmung von Wort und Bild deckt auf, in welchem Umfang der Bedeutungsgehalt eines Fotos mit den hinzugefügten Texten verbunden ist. Die Stereoansichten, die den Schwindel in einer entsprechenden Art und Weise beendeten, wurden später in einem Set mit 88 3D-Bubblegum-Karten, die mit einem günstigen Cardboard-Stereobetrachtungsgerät geliefert wurden, herausgegeben.[27]

Die Zukunft der Illusion oder die Illusion der Zukunft?

Künstler finden in ihren eigenwilligen Arbeiten immer wieder verblüffende Wege, 3D zu kommentieren und erzählende

---

[24] Jim Pomeroy: Reading ›Reading Lessons‹. In: Multidimensionales/Stereo Views. Syracuse; New York 1988. Diese Publikation kam zu Pomeroys Ausstellung in der Light Work's Robert B. Menchel Photography Gallery heraus (10.1.-13.2.1988).

[25] Ebd.

[26] Es steht online eine Version auf http://www.jim-pomeroy.org/video/hiq.mov zur Verfügung. Zu Pomeroys 3D-Vorstellungen wie *Composition in Deep/Light at the Opera* (1981) vgl. Paul DeMarinis: The Boy Mechanic – Mechanical Personae in the Works of Jim Pomeroy. In: Timothy Druckrey; Nadine Lemmon (Hg.): For A Burning World Is Come To Dance Inane. Essays by and about Jim Pomeroy. Brooklyn, N.Y. 1993, S. 9–10.

[27] Jim Pomeroy: Apollo Jest. An American Mythology (in depth). San Francisco 1983.

Strategien zu weben. Die Beziehung zwischen der Stereoskopie und der Erzählkunst wurde allgemein als ein Problem betrachtet. Ersteres ist mit Gimmicks und Attraktionen verbunden, die aus einem Erzählstrang herausspringen und diesen eher unterbrechen als unterstützen. Ein ungewöhnliches Beispiel, das diese Dimensionen miteinander verwebt, ist William Kentridges meisterhafte Animation *Stereoscope* (1999). Es stellt in Kentridges üblicher Art und Weise eine dunkle und durchgeknallte Gesellschaft kurz vor dem Zusammenbruch dar. Hierbei handelt es sich nicht um einen 3D-Film, obwohl er sich durchgängig auf die Dreidimensionalität bezieht. Er ist, wie Kentridge selbst angab, »eine Art stereoskopische Umkehrung«.[28] Viele dieser Szenen sind als Paare in traditionellen Stereoansichten, jedoch bewegt, dargestellt. Das erzeugt nie eine schlüssige stereoskopische Illusion. Stattdessen »weichen die zwei Bilder voneinander ab. Sie verweigern nicht nur die Stelle der perfekten Annäherung, sondern stellen stattdessen eine schizoide Welt, in der Doppelgänger sich mit Misstrauen begegnen, dar«, wie Tom Gunning beobachtet hat.[29] Auf eigene, spezifische Weise verfolgt *Stereoscope* das ein Jahrhundert alte künstlerische Bestreben, die 3D-Illusion zu durchdringen und deren Koordinaten zu zerschlagen.

Zoë Beloff ist ein weiteres Beispiel für Künstler, die sich damit beschäftigen, Stereoskopie mit erzählenden Experimenten zu verweben. Beloffs Filme und Vorstellungen involvieren projizierte Bilder mit einer Live-Erzählung. Stereoskopische Bilder zaubern spektrale Szenen und Phantome herbei, die für die medienarchäologischen Untersuchungen der Beziehung zwischen Bild und Technologie essentiell sind.[30] Ihre Arbeiten fördern zeitgenössische Diskurse in Bezug auf eine virtuelle Realität zutage, positionieren sie aber in einen breiter gesteckten Kontext der Projektionen der Laterna Magica, Ghostshows aus dem 19. Jahrhundert, des frühen Kinos, der Telepathie und Telegraphie, freudianischen Traumerzählungen und weitschweifigen Traditionen, die den Einfluss der Medientechnologie in Bezug auf schizophrene Wahnvorstellungen erhöhen. Der Betrachter wird in ihrer Installation *The Influencing Machine of Miss Natalija A.* (2001) mit der 3D-Darstellung einer Maschine konfrontiert, die vermeintlich Wahnvorstellungen in das Gehirn

28
William Kentridge, zitiert in: Lillian Tone: William Kentridge. Stereoscope. URL: http://homepage.mac.com/studioarchives/artarchives/liliantone/tonekentridge.html. Das Interview datiert vom 22.02.1999.

29
Tom Gunning: Double Vision. Peering through Kentridge's »Stereoscope«. In: Parkett, Nr. 63 (2001), S. 69.

30
Beloffs Darbietung mit projizierten 3D-Folien und Filmen beinhaltet *Life Underwater*, *Lost* and *Claire and Don in Slumberland*. Beloff hat auch 16mm-3D-Filme wie *Shadow Land or Light from the Other Side* und *Charming Augustine* gemacht. Vgl. www.zoebeloff.com.

einer fiktionalen Person projiziert. Die Berührung der Teile dieser virtuellen Maschine visualisiert die Wahnvorstellungen, die aus Medien des frühen 20. Jahrhunderts abgeleitet sind. Die Stereoskopie dient hier in ihrer Vorführung als ein entsprechendes Medium, um Beloffs künstlerische Interessen auszudrücken.

3D hat sich, wie ich bereits zu Beginn gesagt habe, in den letzten Jahren in der Welt des kommerziellen Kinos ausgetobt. Selbst Filme wie James Camerons *Titanic*, die ursprünglich im traditionellen Format aufgenommen wurden, wurden digital in 3D-Filme umgewandelt. Es gibt die, die sagen, das 3D-Kino sei endlich erwachsen geworden, wohingegen wieder andere einwenden, dass 3D immer eine Modeerscheinung war und ist, die wie in Wellen aufläuft und dann wieder verschwindet. Der Welle an 3D-Filmen in den frühen 1950ern, aus der Kultklassiker wie *It Came from Outer Space* hervorgingen, ging die »Stereoscopomania« des Viktorianischen Zeitalters hundert Jahre früher voraus. Diese 3D-Wellen teilten sich, obwohl sie zeitlich weit auseinanderlagen, viele Motive, insbesondere dann, wenn es um die weitschweifigen Phantasien, die sie inspirierten, ging. Es kann sein, dass beide über signalisierte Risse in der Evolution der Medienkultur verfügen. Eine weitere 3D-Welle kam 1990 auf. Diese war von dem Hype um die virtuelle Realität inspiriert.[31] Der Riss war jedoch offensichtlicher. Man muss nicht darauf hinweisen, dass die Zeit, in der wir jetzt leben, wiederum eine Transformation erlebt, die einen immensen Einfluss auf die Mediennutzung sowie auf die sozialen, ideologischen und wirtschaftlichen Modelle, die sie unterstützen, hat. Mobile Medien überall. Und andere Medienformen sind noch nicht dahingehend geeignet, herausgebracht zu werden. Zumindest nicht ohne große Mühen.

Es ist angesichts dieses Hintergrunds ungewiss, ob 3D-Filme weiterhin die Besucher in die Kinos locken. Zumindest nicht in der Stärke wie in den letzten Jahren. Der 3D-Boom der frühen 1950er war Hollywoods Antwort auf die steigende Popularität eines neuen Rivalen, des Fernsehens. Der aktuelle 3D-Boom ist gleichermaßen eine kalkulierte Maßnahme, die abnehmende Anzahl an Kinobesuchern, deren Hauptbeschäftigung heute aus *Netflix, YouTube* und den immer größer werdenden Sozialen Medien besteht, zurückzugewinnen.

31
Die virtuelle Realität hat Künstler zu zahlreichen Experimenten inspiriert. Aber viele waren einfach nur kleine Erscheinungsformen von ›Demo-Kunstlehren‹. Wichtige digitale Arbeiten in Bezug auf die virtuelle Realität in 3D sind Perry Hobermans *Barcode Hotel* (1994) und Maurice Benayouns und Jean-Baptiste Barrières *World Skin* (1997). Vgl. Erkki Huhtamo (2003; wie Anm. 2) sowie Mary Anne Moser; Douglas MacLeod (Hg.): Immersed in Technology. Art and Virtual Environments. Cambridge, Mass. 1995.

Man kann natürlich sagen, dass digitale Produktions- und Ausstellungsmethoden 3D lukrativ (aber nicht notwendigerweise günstiger) machen. Aber man weiß nicht, wie lange das Interesse noch anhalten wird. Darüber hinaus fragt man sich, ob Innovationen wie das 3D-Fernsehen überhaupt eine Zukunft haben oder ob sie wie viele Modeerscheinungen wieder in der Versenkung verschwinden. Sei es, wie es ist. Es gibt Künstler, die haben sich der Erkundung des 3D verschrieben. Allerdings werden sie von den Geschäftsunternehmen ignoriert. Aber ihr Input wird, vielleicht jetzt mehr denn je, gebraucht, um neue, wichtige Wege in der Erkundung neuer, sich verändernder Bereiche in Bezug auf Visionen und Visualität zu entdecken. Es sind die experimentellen Künstler, die die Kraft, die Beharrlichkeit und die Vorstellungskraft haben, aufgeblasene und trügerische, in Massen produzierte und von der kulturellen Industrie zwangsernährte Illusionen im Namen des Gegengottes mit dem Namen Geld aufzudecken.

Erkki Huhtamo
ist Medienarchäologe, Autor und Ausstellungskurator. Er ist Doktor der Kulturgeschichte und arbeitet als Professor für Mediengeschichte und Theorie an der University of California, Los Angeles, im Fachbereich Design Media Arts. Er gab kürzlich *Media Archaeology. Approaches, Applications, and Implications* (mit Jussi Parikka, University of California Press, 2011) heraus und schrieb die *Illusions in Motion. Media Archaeology of the Moving Panorama and Related Spectacles* (MIT Press, 2013).

Zeitsuchende Verbindungen.
Zwei Interviews

Bjørn Melhus

Yves Netzhammer

Die beiden mit Film und Video arbeitenden Künstler Bjørn Melhus und Yves Netzhammer sind in die Diskussion über neue erzählerische Formen involviert. Auf eine innovative Weise untersucht Bjørn Melhus in seinen Arbeiten verschiedenste alltägliche, narrative Strukturen aus dem Fernsehen und aus US-amerikanischen Kriegsfilmen. Seine Filme führen zu einer Art Metaerzählungen, die sich mit der Dekonstruktion von medienübermittelten Narrativen beschäftigen. Mit Hilfe einer Strategie aus Differenz und Wiederholung verschiebt Melhus bestehende Formate, um unser Mediengedächtnis zu hinterfragen.

Ebenso reflektiert Yves Netzhammer unsere Vorstellungen und Erwartungen, welche die Grundlagen für unser kommunikatives Handeln bilden. Durch seine emphatische, digitale zeichnerische Sprache schafft Yves Netzhammer eine mediale Distanz, die schnell erklärbare Konzepte ablehnt. Seine »mentale Bühne« bietet optimale Probefelder an, welche unser sozial konditioniertes Handeln abtesten. Während Melhus mit Tonsequenzen arbeitet, geht Netzhammer den Weg der bildnerischen Sprache, um unserer gewohnten Beschreibung der Darstellungsform zu widersprechen.

Bjørn Melhus

Liliana Rodrigues
Bjørn, prinzipiell bezieht sich deine Arbeit auf die Welt des amerikanisch-kommerziellen Filmes, Fernsehen, Popmusik und Werbung. Die *B3 Biennale* stellt *The Oral Thing* aus, eine Ikone aus dem Jahr 2001, in der du dich mit den Phänomenen der amerikanischen Tele-Evangelisierung beschäftigst. Welchen Bezug hat das Neue Erzählen zu deiner Arbeit?

Bjørn Melhus
Zunächst möchte ich den im Raum stehenden Begriff des Neuen Erzählens infrage stellen und meine Arbeit davon losgelöst sehen. Fest steht, dass ich zwar ein Geschichtenerzähler bin, mich aber in meiner künstlerischen Praxis immer für das Experiment mit narrativen Strukturen und deren Innovation interessiert habe. Das Video *The Oral Thing* spielt durch die Erscheinung des Hosts, also des Moderators, auf das Bild eines

Fernsehpredigers an, der eine Beichte abnimmt und im Verlauf das anfangs scheinbare Opfer zum Täter werden lässt. Das Video bezieht sich jedoch vielmehr auf das Format so genannter Daytime Talkshows, die als exhibitionistische Beichten einem pseudoreligiösen Ritual nahekommen. (In Deutschland gab es ja mit Fliege sogar mal einen echten Pfarrer, der gefühlvoll auch den letzten Abgrund aus seinen Gästen locken konnte.) *The Oral Thing* zitiert auf der Sprachebene ausschließlich Material der in New York produzierten Show *Maury* mit Maury Povitch als Moderator. Ich habe mich zur damaligen Zeit intensiv mit diesen Sendungen beschäftigt, die eigentlich nur erfunden wurden, um am Tag (deshalb auch »Daytime« im Gegensatz zur »Primetime«) die Sendezeit zwischen den Werbeblöcken zu füllen. Das Grundverständnis des Privatfernsehens ist es, die Konsumenten, durch welche Inhalte auch immer, möglichst lange der Werbung auszusetzen. Im Gegensatz zum Film folgen daher Erzählungen des Fernsehens immer diesen Bedingungen, z. B. durch Cliffhanger vor den Werbepausen. In *The Oral Thing* habe ich formal sehr direkt die Unterbrechung und das Erzählen in Mini-Episoden aufgegriffen, die ich in späteren Arbeiten wie *Captain, Deadly Storms* oder auch zuletzt in *I'm not the Enemy* vertieft habe. Als Zuschauer entziehen wir uns für einen Moment, um nach kurzer Zeit wieder in das Geschehen einzusteigen. Für mich war diese fragmentierte Form auch hinsichtlich einer Endloserzählung, das heißt des Videoloops, im Ausstellungskontext interessant, bei dem die letzte Episode oder Szene zur Vorgeschichte der ersten wird; somit ist der Zeitpunkt des Einstiegs in die Erzählung relativ offen.

LR

Man würde vermuten, dass du als Videokünstler vor allem an Bildern interessiert bist. An erster Stelle nimmst du aber Ausschnitte von Klängen aus verschiedenen medialen Kontexten heraus, um dann die visuelle Komponente als Nächstes zu bilden. Kannst du uns mehr über diese Strategie erzählen? Warum ist es von zentraler Bedeutung für deine Arbeit?

BM

Zum größten Teil handelt es sich dabei um Dialogfragmente, die ich aus ihrem ursprünglichen Zusammenhang reiße, um sie neu strukturiert in eine Art Metaerzählung zu überführen und zu verdichten. Dazu entstehen dann eigene Bilder, die der Tonebene folgen, diese jedoch zum Teil sehr frei interpretieren und dadurch einen neuen Sinnzusammenhang schaffen. Diese Methode bedeutet aber auch, dass ich nur auf das im medialen Archiv Vorhandene zurückgreifen kann. Das Quellmaterial bildet sozusagen einen Rahmen, der mich jedoch in seiner möglichen, aber auch unmöglichen Dekonstruktion interessiert.

LR
Diese Strategie könnte fast mit DJ-ing verglichen werden. Du baust dein Archiv von Tonauszügen und manipulierst sie choreographisch. Würdest du bitte darauf etwas eingehen?

BM
Ein entscheidender Schritt war die Installation *Still Men Out There* (2003), in der ich erstmals vollständig auf das Bild verzichtet habe. Bei dem auf einer Toncollage aus US-amerikanischen Kriegsfilmen basierenden Farbspektakel auf 18 Monitoren geht es weniger um den Krieg selbst als um die Repräsentation des Krieges im amerikanischen Unterhaltungskino. Seit 2003 entstanden neben den sonstigen Filmen auch weitere Arbeiten, die nur mit Farben operieren, wie zuletzt *Murphy* (2008).

LR
Deine Arbeit zerstört deutlich klassische Strukturen des Erzählens. Denkst du, dass die traditionelle Erzählung nicht mehr nützlich ist?

BM
Ich glaube nicht, dass traditionelle Erzählungen nicht mehr nützlich sind. Mich persönlich interessieren sie einfach weniger, ob als Rezipient oder Künstler. Viele traditionelle Erzählformen folgen einem sehr festgelegten, vorhersehbaren Muster. Sie bieten einen festen, wiederkehrenden Rahmen, in dem sich verschiedene Inhalte verhandeln lassen. Sie gleichen eher einem Ritual mit eindeutig festgelegten Regeln.

LR
Hecho in Mexico (2009) meistert mehrere Prinzipien, welche zentral für deine Arbeit scheinen. Er macht Gebrauch von einer Variation weniger Elemente, er grenzt an Narration, die Spannung steigt bis zu einem unerträglichen Punkt, und doch

passiert nichts. Diesen ›Betrug‹ des Publikums definiere ich als eine politische Absicht. Warum interessiert dich das Irreführen des Publikums?

BM

Hecho in Mexico nimmt Bezug auf die Situation in Mexico im Sommer 2009; bis dahin waren in nur wenigen Jahren mehr als 50.000 Menschen dem Drogenkrieg zum Opfer gefallen. Der öffentliche Raum des Landes war geprägt von bis an die Zähne bewaffneten Milizen beider Seiten – der Normalzustand. Die Arbeit entstand im Rahmen des Bicentenario, der Feierlichkeiten zur 200-jährigen Unabhängigkeit Lateinamerikas. Im ersten Teil des Videos sehen wir einen grotesk überbewaffneten, modernen Soldaten auf einem Pferd im Wald, der zu heroisch treibenden Klängen einer Handlung entgegenreitet, zu der es jedoch nicht kommt. Dabei lehne ich mich an die zur Rekrutierung von Soldaten auf der ganzen Welt produzierten Werbefilme an, die heroisch von der Bereitschaft zum Kampf erzählen, jedoch nie vom Feindkontakt und der Schlacht selbst. Filme, die ihre Betrachter oftmals nicht nur in die Irre, sondern auch in den Tod geführt haben. Ich nehme bestehende Formate auf und verschiebe sie in andere Kontexte, um diese Formate wie auch die neuen Kontexte zu reflektieren. In *Hecho in Mexico* steht der Soldat einer vollkommen entvölkerten, postapokalyptischen Großstadt Mexico City gegenüber. Die Arbeit ist sehr minimal, und nicht jeder versteht sie – obgleich sie im lateinamerikanischen Raum wesentlich häufiger gezeigt wurde als z. B. in Europa.

LR

Die *B3 Biennale* (Parcours-Ausstellung) zeigt *Die umgekehrte Rüstung,* einen Film, der 2002 in Kollaboration mit Yves Netzhammer entstanden ist. Wie kam es zu dieser Zusammenarbeit? Was war der Anreiz zu diesem Werk?

BM

Yves Netzhammer und ich haben uns erst in New York getroffen, obgleich wir beide das Werk des anderen schon kannten. Es gab viele Gespräche, aus denen dann die abenteuerliche Idee einer Kollaboration entstand, die wir sehr genau festgelegt haben. Er produziert die Bilder – Sequenzen von Animationen, die sich in irgendeiner Weise mit Blut beschäftigen –, und ich durchforste die Videotheken nach Filmen, um Dialogfetzen und Klänge zu extrahieren, die sich auch im weitesten Sinn um den roten Saft drehen. Nachdem mir Yves Netzhammer eine Vielzahl von Minierzählungen zur Verfügung gestellt hat, habe ich begonnen, das Bildmaterial mit ausgewählten Tonausschnitten zu verschränken, um daraus eine größere Erzählung zu schaffen, die auch das Knistern eines Films aus den 1950ern zulässt und Zitate, die irgendwo in unserem kollektiven Mediengedächtnis hängen, in eine neue, assoziative Erzählung einbettet. Es war für mich eine interessante Herausforderung, erstmals mit dem Prinzip der doppelten Aneignung zu tun zu haben, also diesmal auch nicht die Bilder zu produzieren. Dadurch wurde für mich die Entwicklung der Erzählung selbst zum Hauptakt.

LR

In *I'm not the Enemy* (2011) werden verschiedene Charaktere eingesetzt. Doch anstatt sich zum Storytelling zurückzubegeben, führst du subtile Variationen in der zweiten Hälfte ein. Ist das eine weitere Strategie, um die Narrative zu zerstören?

BM

Ich sehe es als Teil des Narrativen. Es geht oftmals, wie im richtigen Leben auch, um Wiederholung und Differenz. Die Geschichte selbst ist in ihren Episoden in Zwischenbildern von Ein- und Mehrfamilienhäusern eingebettet. Während die Episoden sich zu wiederholen beginnen, tauschen sich die Häuser weiter aus. Es ist also eine Art Hybrid. Ein früheres Experiment war *The Meadow* (2007), in dem ein 28-minütiger Loop aus vier Episoden besteht, die in einigen Abschnitten identisch sind, in anderen jedoch variieren. Neben den offensichtlich verschiedenen Begegnungen der Hauptfigur gibt es geringe Variationen im Schnitt, die eher im Bereich des Spürbaren liegen. Neben dem bewussten Spiel mit Zuschauererwartungen an eine Loopinstallation, die immer dann, wenn man gehen will, doch noch etwas Neues erzählt, ging es für mich auch um Erinnerungsstrukturen von vier zeitlich aufeinanderliegenden Erzählungsfolien. Die Wiederholung prägt sich ein und wird spätestens beim vierten Mal unerträglich, wobei die Differenz und Entwicklung der Geschichte als wahre Erleichterung empfunden wird.

LR

Lass uns über deine neueste Arbeit reden. In der Retrospektive im Haus am Waldsee (2011) hast du dich auf Fragen zu posttraumatischen Belastungsstörungen bei Kriegsveteranen konzentriert. Warum interessiert dich dieses Thema? Wie würdest du deinen Film innerhalb dieser Kontroverse einordnen?

BM

In *I'm not the Enemy* geht es zunächst um die Repräsentation von Kriegsrückkehrern im US-amerikanischen Mainstreamkino. Wie in vielen meiner anderen Arbeiten interessiert mich auch hier eine Verarbeitung der Verarbeitung und Neuverortung. Spätestens seit dem Vietnamkrieg ist der Kriegsveteran eine der beliebtesten Heldenfiguren des amerikanischen Action- und Mainstreamkinos. Ob Rambo oder Avatar. Was und wie es verhandelt wird, hat mich interessiert. Dass dabei auch die derzeitige politische Debatte um Auslandseinsätze in so genannten asymmetrischen Kriegen tangiert wird, ist natürlich unvermeidbar.

LR

Hast du nicht manchmal die Befürchtung, dass durch dein unkonventionelles Erzählen deine Strategie als Bevormundung missverstanden wird?

BM

Diese Schlussfolgerung kann ich wirklich nicht nachvollziehen. Ich empfinde jede Form des konventionellen Erzählens als eine viel stärkere Bevormundung, wenn z.B. ein Film versucht, mich vollständig einzunehmen, und meine kritische Distanz als Betrachter ignoriert. Ich glaube, dass der Unterschied doch gerade darin liegt, sein Publikum herauszufordern, auch mal bewusst spröder oder nerviger zu sein, damit auch fordernder. Davon abgesehen ist es ein Unterschied, ob ich gutes Entertainment oder Kunst mache und welche Erwartungshaltung das Publikum hat.

LR

In deiner Arbeit benutzt du viele Medienformate, verschiedenste TV-Formate, Nachrichten und Hollywood-Kriegsfilme, welche unsere sozialen und kulturellen Wahrnehmungen prägen. Wir befinden uns in einem Digitalisierungszeitalter. Wie ändern sich die Regeln des Spiels?

BM
Ein großer Teil meiner künstlerischen Praxis lässt sich tatsächlich als mediale Archäologie auffassen. In den vergangenen 100 Jahren war das Bewegtbild mit Sicherheit eines der prägendsten Instrumente unserer Gesellschaft, ob als Propaganda, Gegenwartsreflexion oder Traumaverarbeitung. Neben einer Untersuchung der Erzählstrukturen geht es natürlich auch ganz klar um inhaltliche Stellungnahmen von Sendern zu Empfängern. Die mediale Gegenwart heute ist dialogischer und partizipativer. Ob im Bereich der Sozialen Netzwerke, von *YouTube* oder der Gaming-Industrie. Wir sind aufgefordert, zu allem unseren Senf dazuzugeben und Entwicklungen mitzugestalten, was einer extremen Demokratisierung des Bildes gleichkommt. Gleichzeitig besteht hier natürlich die Gefahr einer Beliebigkeit, in der alles im großen Rauschen versinkt, nach dem alten Sprichwort »Zu viele Köche verderben den Brei«.

LR
Deine Arbeiten im öffentlichen Raum, wie *Screensavers* (2008) oder die erweiterte Realitäts-App *Gate-X* für den noch uneröffneten Berliner Flughafen, sind ein Versuch, die Hand nach neuen, herausfordernden Themen des Social Media-Zeitalters auszustrecken und über dessen Problematik zu reflektieren. Wo wird die Reise hingehen?

BM
Bei *Screensavers* (2008) hat eine Spracherkennungssoftware in nahezu Echtzeit verschiedene Schlagworte aus den Radionachrichten abgegriffen und auf großen LED-Displays neben einer stark befahrenen Straße wiedergegeben. Bei Missverständnissen hat die Software einfach ein ähnliches Wort gewählt, wie es auch bei Gerüchten der Fall ist. Als Radio hörender Autofahrer hatte man beides, den öffentlichen Raum des Radios und das visuelle Ereignis im öffentlichen Außenraum.

Hier ist jede erlebte Situation einzigartig und nicht wiederholbar. Das war auch der Reiz. Eine ortsspezifische Augmented Reality Smartphone App als Kunst am Bau für einen internationalen Flughafen ging dann noch ein Stück weiter: Mit Hilfe von Markern finden wir lebensgroße, in die Architektur des Flughafens eingepasste virtuelle Passagiere in Form einer 3D-animierten Kleinfamilie, die in der Transitzone gestrandet ist und sich dort häuslich niedergelassen hat. Als Betrachter können wir mit ihnen den Bildraum und dieses Erlebnis als Bild mit unseren Freunden teilen. Hier werden wir selbst Teil einer Erzählung, die wir dann selbst erzählen.

Neben dem partizipativen Charakter bietet *Gate-X* auch eine Auseinandersetzung mit dem Nichtort Transitzone an, dessen merkwürdiger Status zuletzt wieder mit dem Fall Edward Snowden in die Schlagzeilen geraten ist. Der Technologiewandel bietet eine Vielzahl von Möglichkeiten und somit auch Herausforderungen für Künstlerinnen und Künstler. Ich denke, dabei sollten wir nie unser Grundanliegen sowie das oftmals tragikomische Verhältnis von Mensch und Maschine vergessen, so wie es uns Stanley Kubrick bereits vor über 40 Jahren in seiner *Space Odyssey* prophezeit hat. Eine der großen Erzählungen des 20. Jahrhunderts, die durch ihre starke Autorenschaft in die Geschichte eingegangen ist.

LR
Vielen Dank!

Bjørn Melhus
studierte Kunst und Film an der HBK Braunschweig und dem California Institute of the Arts in Los Angeles. Für sein Werk, das international ausgestellt wurde und in öffentlichen wie privaten Sammlungen vertreten ist, erhielt er zahlreiche Auszeichnungen. Bjørn Melhus lebt und arbeitet in Berlin und lehrt seit 2003 als Professor an der Kunsthochschule Kassel.

Liliana Rodrigues
graduierte 2002 an der Universität Nova in Lissabon mit einem Abschluss in Kunstgeschichte (M.A). Sie arbeitete international im Kunstmanagement und Kommunikationsbereich. 2011 hat sie als kuratorische Assistentin für die 2011 Dublin Contemporary gearbeitet und publizierte über Positionen zeitgenössischer Kunst. Seit 2008 ist sie für Sales & Exhibitions in der Galerie Anita Beckers in Frankfurt am Main zuständig.

Yves Netzhammer

Liliana Rodrigues

Die *B3 Biennale* (Parcours-Ausstellung) zeigt *Die umgekehrte Rüstung,* einen Film, der in 2002 in Kollaboration mit Bjørn Melhus entstanden ist. Wie kam es zu dieser Zusammenarbeit? Was war der Anreiz zu diesem Werk?

Yves Netzhammer

Wir hatten beide im selben Jahr ein Studienstipendium in NYC. Als sich nach dem 11. September die Stadt, die politische Landschaft und auch das persönliche Lebensgefühl derart verwandelt hatten, suchten wir nach einer gemeinsamen Weise der Reflexion. Federführend war die Vorstellung eines verwandlungsfähigen, gleichermaßen physischen und psychischen »Materials«, welches sich in seiner ruhelosen, viralen Beschaffenheit in Identitäten einnistet, diese interpretiert und mit narrativen Elementen so erweitert, dass sich ihre Eigenschaften verändern und damit auch ihr Gebrauch.

LR

Im Sommer 2007 hat deine Arbeit durch die parallel laufenden Ausstellungen in dem Schweizer Pavillon auf der Venedig-Biennale und in der Karlskirche in Karlsruhe das erste Mal internationale Aufmerksamkeit bekommen. Diese Installationen generieren neue bildnerische Wege für alltägliche Problemstellungen, statt die Realität auf die übliche dokumentarische Weise abzubilden. Kannst du die von dir entwickelte künstlerisch-erzählerische Form beschreiben?

YN

Bei beiden Ausstellungen war es mir wichtig, die modellhafte und imaginäre Qualität meiner Arbeit mit der vorherrschenden politischen Situation (Flüchtlingspolitik in Italien, Länderpavillon, Hugenottenkirche in Kassel) zu konfrontieren und mittels präziser installativer Eingriffe die Erzählebene der Bilder und des Sounds mit der Geschichte des Raumes zu konfrontieren.

Obwohl meine Arbeit eher aus einem intrinsischen Prozess geschaffen wird, kann sie in Venedig und Kassel auch politisch gelesen werden. Es gibt viele Einschreibungen, die in unserem kulturellen »Bilder-Code« gespeichert sind. »Politik« ist da vielleicht das falsche Wort, es geht eher um moralische oder gesellschaftsorientierte Regeln und Rollenspiele. Eine Gefahr der Kunst liegt darin, dass oftmals etwas visualisiert wird, das bereits bekannt ist.

Inhaltlich wollte ich meine Arbeit im Kontext eines Länderpavillons noch intensiver in Richtung gegenweltlicher Problemzonen entwickeln. Als Bildermacher fühle ich mich selber oft einem persönlichen Legitimationsdruck ausgesetzt, weil der Wirkungsradius von offenen, zirkulären Bildergeschichten gesellschaftlich nahezu obsolet ist. Dennoch versuche ich, die Qualität der Empfindlichkeit als Ressource zu verstehen, durch die wir einen Punkt der Identifikation mit dem Leiden anderer entwickeln können. Dieser Ausgangspunkt kann ein neues Verhältnis zum tatenlosen Zusehen herausbilden und uns kritischer beurteilen lassen. Die Erfahrungen mit der Arbeit *Die Subjektivierung der Wiederholung* führten mich zum Anfang der introspektiv angelegten Thematik von *Die Möbel der Proportionen*, welche ich fürs SFMOMA entwickelt habe.

LR

Du hast eine einzigartige, digital-bildliche Darstellung kreiert, welche auf eine Syntax aus bestimmten Figuren und Motiven besteht. Diese menschlichen und unmenschlichen Elemente und die Weisen, wie sie in der digitalen Welt interagieren, scheinen unsere traditionellen Handlungen und Verhaltensmuster zu testen. Würdest du bitte etwas darauf eingehen?

YN

Die Figuren sind zwar stilisiert, dennoch sind sie eine Art ›Probekörper‹, welche mentale und körperliche Zustände vorführen und in Verbindung zu mir stehen. Auf einer fiktiven Ebene reichern sie meinen Erfahrungsschatz an. Denn es ist erstaunlich, wie stark selbst fiktionale Erfahrungen das eigene Denken beeinflussen und ergänzen. In gewissem Sinne gehört es zu meinem persönlichen Selbstversuch, dass ich mich als Person über meine Arbeit in etwas Neues hineinverwandle. Ich pendle zwischen den Phantomschmerzen im Bild und den tatsächlichen.

Es entsteht eine »mentale Bühne«, auf der unsere Vorstellungen und Erwartungen, sprich: die Grundlage des kommunikativen Handelns, befragt, aber auch verunsichert werden können.

LR

Entgegen unserer etablierten Logik scheinen die Figuren in deinen Filmen sich zu engagieren. Durch absurde Situationen, auch wenn Absurdität nur eine von mehreren Strategien in deiner Arbeit ist, wird eine gemeinsame Logik gestört. Es fühlt sich an, als ob du gegen Erzählungen arbeitest. Würdest du dem zustimmen?

YN

Es ist der Versuch, mittels Bilder zu anderen, kognitiven Erkenntnissen zu gelangen. Anders als bei textbasiertem Vorgehen entwickle ich meine Fragestellungen über Einfühlungsprozesse. Prozesse, bei denen sich Wissen und Fühlen gegenseitig weiterentwickeln. In einem offenen System zu arbeiten, heißt, sich überraschen zu lassen. Das, was ich vorerst nicht kenne und verstehe, informiert mich widersprüchlicherweise am genauesten über das Andere. Tatsächlich interessiere ich mich für das Ungesagte, das Nichtzusehende. Die Referenzen des Erzählens scheinen mir jedoch verschieden zu sein von textbasiertem Wissen. Mir dünkt es wichtig, dass bei der künstlerischen Arbeit nicht ›Fremdwissen‹, also schnell erklärbare Konzepte, umgesetzt werden. Das zeichnerische Vorgehen entspricht mir deswegen sehr, zumal unmittelbar am eigentlichen Erzählwiderstand gearbeitet werden kann und man infolge der medialen Distanz, also der Stilistik, nicht in einen ›Illustrationsverdacht‹ des Realen gerät, sondern mit dem Mittel der Einbildungskraft operiert.

LR

Ist es deine Absicht, für anfängliche Irritation in deinen Werken zu sorgen und somit einen Weg zu finden, um mit der Erzählung zu brechen? Warst du jemals am Geschichtenerzählen interessiert?

YN

»Bild« ist für mich der Übergang der Wahrnehmung zur anschaulichen Vorstellung. Ich fasse es als ein medial unspezifisches Gegenüber, das der Ablagerung von Erfahrungen und Werten dient und darüber hinaus die Generierung von offenen und imaginativen Verhältnissen ermöglicht. Meine Bildwelt hat viel mit dem Fühlen von Festigkeiten, mit dem Benennen von Anfangsfragen und mit der Erarbeitung des dazu nötigen Vokabulars zu tun.

Der Austausch von innen und außen ist wechselseitig und immer prozessorientiert. Man verändert sich, wenn man sich mit der Frage nach dem Eigenen auseinandersetzt. Innerhalb der Arbeit neige ich dazu, es mir so umständlich wie möglich zu gestalten, um eine ›vivide Art‹ der Beschreibung zu entwickeln. Ich nähere mich den Themen sowohl mit Hilfe eines nicht-naturalisierenden Mediums als auch des ideenbeladenen Beschreibens.

LR

Aber dann fasst der Betrachter die Aktionen auf dem Bildschirm als Folge und Ursache auf und sucht nach einer organischen Entwicklung. Wie nimmst du die natürliche Veranlagung des Betrachters zur Erzählung auf? Wie wirkt sich diese Persistenz auf deine Arbeit aus?

YN

Ist denn die Gesellschaft nur Text? Ich produziere Unmengen von Zeichnungen und unökonomisch lange Filmarbeiten, die kommunizieren wollen und Nähe aufbauen. Mein Bedürfnis zielt auf die Bildfähigkeit in ihren Differenzierungen, die auch humanistische Fragestellungen erfahrbar machen wollen. Normative und funktionsorientierte Vermittlungskonzepte scheinen mir bei diesen Themen oftmals zu verallgemeinernd.

LR

Es scheint, nachdem die digitale Sequenz ihren Platz findet, folgt das Objekt. Diese Objekte sind weder einfache Ready-mades noch Skulpturen im herkömmlichen Sinne. Sie werden aus der Praxis deiner digitalen Zeichnung geboren und bestehen zunächst in den Animationen. Warum die filmische Form in eine skulpturale Form drehen? Warum die geistige Erfahrung des Betrachters in eine physische Welt umsetzen?

YN

Unsere Wahrnehmungskompetenz wird durch Zeit und Raum herausgefordert. Als Subjekt steckt man in verschiedenen Zeitzonen. Wenn man sich an früher erinnert oder sich Zukünftiges vorstellt, dann begegnet man sich als anderer Person. Die

Vermischung digitaler und konkreter Räume ermöglicht eine zeitgemäße Konsistenz unserer Fragestellungen.

LR

Kathleen Bühler, die deine große Einzelausstellung *Das Reservat der Nachteile* im Kunstmuseum in Bern (2010/2011) kuratierte, hat auf die wachsende Theatralität in deinem letzten Stück hingewiesen. Wie ist dieser Aspekt im Zusammenhang mit deinem kontinuierlichen Interesse an der Erforschung der Beziehung zwischen Subjekt und Objekt zu verstehen? Und wie wirkt es sich auf die Narration aus?

YN

Es geht mir in der Installation um eine Vergegenwärtigung kognitiver Möglichkeiten. Dass man als Betrachter mit allen Sinnen angesprochen und zu vernetztem Denken und Erkennen verleitet wird. Das sind Dinge, die mir in Kunsträumen mit ihrer Kühle und ihrem begrenztem sinnlichen Arsenal fehlen, hingegen im Theater und in installativen Werken möglich werden. Allerdings sollten sie nicht nur der Verführung oder Unterhaltung dienen, sondern müssen Synergien erzeugen und Kanäle zum Eigenen öffnen.

LR

Lass uns über deine letzten Arbeiten reden. Kürzlich hast du eine Filmtrilogie beendet: *Dialogischer Abrieb* (2011), *Vororte der Körper* (2012) und zuletzt *Alte Verstecke in neuen Räumen* (2013). Ein Schlüsselmoment ist die Szene mit einem Autounfall. Warum ist Körperverletzung in den letzten Jahren ein so wichtiges Thema für dich geworden?

YN

Ich möchte solche Fragestellungen verfeinern, jedoch nicht bewerten. Durch Unfälle entsteht eine Oberflächenvergrößerung, sie sind eine Art Okular. Zuerst versuche ich, mir die Funktionsweise des Missstandes zu vergegenwärtigen, die Fragen zu klären, wem etwas passiert und was überhaupt passiert. Wenn ich selber gewisse Reaktionen spüre, frage ich mich: Was hat sie ausgelöst? Weshalb reagiere ich auf diese Weise? Dann folgt die nächste Stufe, die Hierarchisierung des Schmerzes: Wie wird sie angewendet auf unbelebte Dinge, auf Tiere, auf Menschen?

Daran zeigen sich gesellschaftliche Zusammenhänge im intuitiven bildnerischen Denken. Bilder sind tolle Probefelder, um etwas auszutesten, da soziales Handeln konditioniert ist und sich an Bildern ablesen lässt. Oft stolpert man über Stereotype – kulturell eingeschriebene Werte, die eigentlich sehr beschränkt, also vereinfachend, sind. Bildnerische Stereotype kommen häufig in der Werbung vor mit den üblichen Polarisierungen: alt – jung, weiß – schwarz, bekannt – fremd.

LR
Dieser besondere Moment des Autounfalls wird in Zeitlupe und in einem diskontinuierlichen Stil erzählt. Die Figuren erinnern an Crashtest-Dummies, welche eine emotionale Distanz schaffen. Du bist dafür bekannt, auch andere Strategien wie Transformation, Zoom und Fusion-Effekte zu benutzen, um unsere Assoziationskette auszulösen. In eigenen Worten: »was ich nachgehe, ist nicht nur visuell, sondern mehr eine Vision in Begleitung von Erzählungen. Ich reflektiere und befrage Konzepte.«

YN
Die metaphorisch angelegte Handlung eines Dialogs in Form eines Autounfalls, in dem sich zwei Subjekte im Zeitlupentempo annähern, letztendlich ineinanderkrachen, bietet die formale Struktur des Filmes. Gegenseitige Abhängigkeiten und Prägungen werden sinnbildlich veranschaulicht.

Die Wucht des Aufeinanderprallens generiert überraschende Körperstellungen, eine Art körpereigenes Erinnerungsarchiv, das die Auseinandersetzung mit den Traumata provoziert. Mittels Überblendungen werden in den verlangsamten Unfallablauf biographische Rück- oder Vorblenden eingefügt.

LR
Vielen Dank!

Yves Netzhammer
studierte an der Hochschule für Gestaltung in Zürich. Seit 1997 entwickelte er eine eigenständige digitale Bildsprache, für die er mehrfach ausgezeichnet wurde. Sein Werk wurde in bedeutenden internationalen Museen gezeigt und auch erworben. 2007 vertrat er die Schweiz auf der Biennale von Venedig. Yves Netzhammer lebt und arbeitet in Zürich.

Loop Narration und hyper-überlagerte Narrative

Eva Paulitsch

Uta Weyrich

Abb. 1
»Die Dinge existieren in mehreren Versionen, wobei die eine nicht wahrer ist die andere ist.« – Parker Ito
#hybride Realität, Foto: Benjamin Franzki

Abb. 2
Der User des sozialen Netzwerks navigiert seinen Geist und sein Profil als
#duale Einheit durch den #Cyperspace

1. Inzwischen...

In unserer modernen konsumorientierten Gesellschaft ist der Einfluss »#des Digitalen« über das bloße Handling digitaler Geräte hinausgewachsen, es ist langsam in unser Bewusstsein gesickert, ist dort gewachsen und nimmt dort nach und nach Einfluss auf unser Denken und Handeln. Neue Routinen werden in unseren Alltag integriert und erweitern so die Grenzen des digitalen Reichs. #Soziale Netzwerke stehen an der Spitze dieser Entwicklung und binden die breite Masse mit einem Belohnungssystem, bestehend aus Aufmerksamkeit und »#Likes«.

Die #Gewinner dieser Welt sind nicht länger nur diejenigen, die im #Alltag erfolgreich sind, sondern jene, die diesen am erfolgreichsten teilen. Plattformen wie *Instagram* vereinfachen nicht nur das Teilen von festgehaltenen Momenten, sondern bereiten sie mittels anwendbarer Filter zudem auch gleich massentauglich visuell auf. Mit verbesserter emotionaler Qualität und kosmetischem Facelift ist das Bild dann bereit, den Laufsteg der Sozialen Netzwerke zu beschreiten, um um Aufmerksamkeit zu buhlen. Jede dieser »#Shares« erweitert schließlich die Biographie und Charaktereigenschaft des digitalen Ich, das kontinuierlich durch das Hinzufügen, Ändern oder Löschen von Informationen die Möglichkeit bietet, optimiert zu werden. Mit nichts anderem als seinen Fingern navigiert der User des Sozialen Netzwerks seinen Geist und sein Profil als #duale Einheit durch den #Cyberspace.

»Die Dinge existieren in mehreren Versionen, wobei die eine nicht wahrer ist die andere.«[1] sagt #Parker Ito. Des weiteren behauptet er, dass wir heute in einer #hybriden Realität leben, in welcher der Raum zwischen dem Physischen und dem Virtuellen fließend, der Übergang zwischen beiden jedoch nicht nahtlos ist.[2] Es ist eben diese #hybride Realität, in der Menschen hinsichtlich des Agierens vor der Kamera, meist der eines Smartphones, sensibilisiert werden. Während einige Menschen ein angeborenes darstellerisches Talent besitzen, wirken andere wiederum vor der Linse der Kamera unbeholfen und angespannt.

Darüber hinaus gibt es weitere situationsbedingte Parameter wie beispielsweise die Szenerie oder die Beziehung zu der filmenden Person, die das Verhalten des Gefilmten beeinflussen.

---

[1] Sometimes people take really good photos and sometimes people look hotter offline. I heard a rumor that I'm hotter in person. More so now than ever things exist in multiple versions and one is not truer than the other. Parker Ito, URL: http://dismagazine.com/blog/36943/interview-with-parker-ito/

[2] Today we live in a hybrid reality where the space between the physical and the virtual is fluid. Gone is the radical internet of the 90's where logging off was an option. Though integrated into our daily lives, the web of today is fluid but not seamless. Parker Ito, URL: http://www.marktholander.dk/today_we_live_in_a_hybrid_reality.html

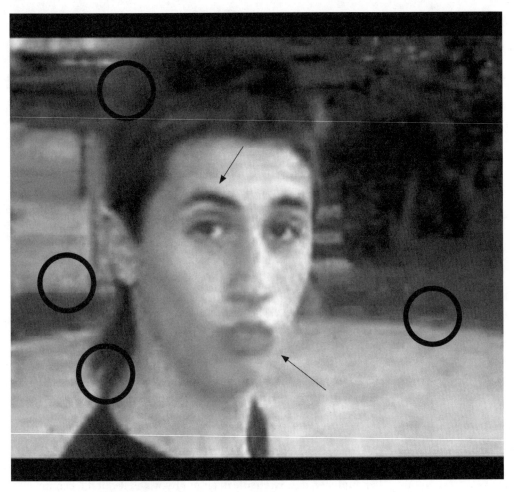

Abb. 3
Einige Menschen haben ein angeborenes darstellerisches Talent,
andere wirken vor der Linse der Smartphones wiederum unbeholfen und
angespannt. #duckface #hochgezogene Augenbraue

Abb. 4
We shape our tools and thereafter our tools shape us. – Marshall McLuhan:
Understanding Media (1964) #gegenseitiger Einfluss #Hybride Realität

Mit der Aktivierung der Aufnahmefunktion wird das Gewöhnliche zum #Spektakel verkehrt und unterbricht so für die Dauer des Aufzeichnens unsere »normale« Realität.[3] Für die fokussierte Person ist der entscheidende Moment nicht notwendigerweise das Auslösen der Funktion, sondern vielmehr, wenn sie diese realisiert. Wenn diese beiden Ereignisse nicht zusammenfallen, wird durch plötzliche charakterliche Veränderungen die wohl persönlichste Seite der Person offenbart.

Jedes Foto und Video gibt Informationen über die Person sowohl vor als auch hinter der Kamera preis. Beide Positionen verschmelzen durch das Phänomen des »#Selfie« zu einer.[4]

All diese Fotos beinhalten Geschichten über Fetische und Aversionen, #Fails, #Wins, Charaktere und soziales Umfeld. Vor diesem Hintergrund werden Bilder oder Videos, die nicht den Sprung in die Sozialen Netzwerke geschafft haben, weil sie zu persönlich sind, zu viel preisgeben oder schlichtweg keinen sichtbaren Wert besitzen, in den privaten Bildergalerie-Festungen der Smartphones und Computer weggeschlossen, leise wartend auf »#Shares«.

Loop Narration und hyper-überlagerte Narrative

Lange #Loops nehmen den Verstand mit auf eine Reise. Eine langer Loop fördert die Generierung vieler Assoziationen, wohingegen ein kurzer Loop durch schnell abfolgende #Wiederholungen eher eine spezifische Idee kultiviert. Jedoch ist auch eine kurze Loop-Sequenz aufgrund ihrer hypnotisierenden Wiederholungen imstande, den Geist des Betrachters auf neue assoziative Handlungswege zu führen.

Laut #Mark Twain verfügt ein Buch idealerweise über keinerlei Reihenfolge, und der Leser sollte diese selbst entdecken. Folgt man dieser Idee, bedeutet dies, dass eine Geschichte idealerweise aus einer Vielzahl eigenständiger Narrative ohne eine vordefinierte Rolle besteht. Ein Loop löst die Wichtigkeit der Positionierung auf, lässt somit jedes Ereignis auf einer unsichtbaren #zirkulären Zeitleiste mehrdeutig werden. Doch selbst mit dem Verlust eines eindeutigen Startpunkts führt der lineare Ablauf (innerhalb eines Videos) den Betrachter immer noch auf der gleichen Strecke entlang. (Deshalb:) »Ist der

---

[3] It may soon be possible, through neurological implants to switch from our »common« reality to another computer-generated reality without all the clumsy machinery of today´s Virtual Reality (the awkward glasses) [...] Slavoj Zizek: NO SEX, PLEASE, WE'RE POST-HUMAN!

[4] Ein »Selfie« ist ein Genre der Selbstportrait-Fotografie. Diese Aufnahmen werden üblicherweise mit einer Digital- oder einer Handykamera gemacht. Selfies sind oftmals mit den Sozialen Netzwerken und Foto-Sharing-Diensten wie *MySpace*, *Facebook* und *Instagram* verbunden, da sie hier üblicherweise gepostet werden. Sie sind oftmals sehr zwanglos, werden üblicherweise mit der Kamera auf Armeslänge entfernt oder in einem Spiegel geschossen und beinhalten normalerweise entweder nur den Fotografen oder den Fotografen und bis zu drei andere Leute. http://en.wikipedia.org/wiki/Selfie

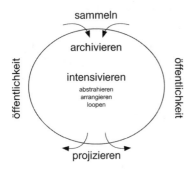

Abb. 5
Künstlerischer Prozess von
Eva Paulitsch und Uta Weyrich
#Öffentlichkeit #sammeln
#archivieren #intensivieren

Abb. 6
Ein Loop lässt die Position jedes
Ereignisses auf einer unsichtbaren
#zirkulären Zeitleiste mehrdeutig
werden

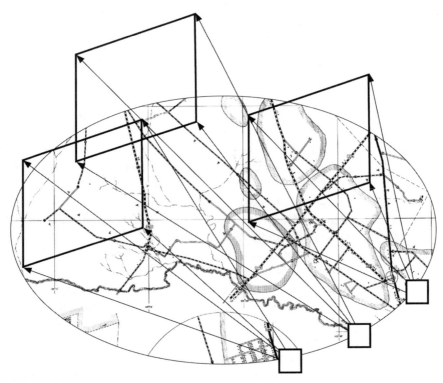

Abb. 7
Durch #räumliches Arrangement des projizierten Materials variiert die Konstruktion einzelner
Narrative nicht nur durch die #mentale, sondern auch durch die #physische Position des Betrachters.

gesamte Loop ein Konstrukt aus mehreren gleichzeitigen und räumlich verteilten Loops, wird der Betrachter zu einem sich frei bewegenden Wanderer inmitten einer Landschaft, bestehend aus assoziierten und vielfach überlagerten Handlungssträngen: #hyper-überlagerten Narrativen.

Durch das Entfernen der Linearität innerhalb des gesamten Erzählkonstrukts bleiben dem Betrachter lediglich interpretierbare Codes als Startpunkte, von denen aus der Verstand des Betrachters im #Hyperraum der Bedeutung von einer semiotischen Basis zur anderen springen kann. Die Einbindung des gesammelten Videomaterials von Alltags- und Amateurkultur dient als #Reiz, um diese Erfahrung zu verstärken. #Videos, die nicht vom Künstler produziert, sondern nur von diesem gesammelt und bearbeitet werden – »werden Elemente als Signifikanten dieses Clips plötzlich zu einer Art digitalem #Objet trouvé?« Eine Unterscheidung zwischen der Relevanz von #Protagonist, #Hintergrundakteur, #Kameramann oder #aufgenommener Person wird überflüssig. Sie werden alle zu interpretierbaren Codes – aussagekräftig oder oberflächlich – abhängig vom individuellen Blickwinkel des Betrachters.

2.1. Der künstlerische Prozess

Ein typischer Arbeitsprozess kann daraus bestehen, zuerst eine Reihe von #Assoziationen zu sammeln, um vorhandene Videos durch den #Künstler zu kategorisieren. Indem Künstler den Dialog innerhalb der Gruppe oder zu einer anderen Partei suchen, ist es möglich, die Limitation eines einzigen Blickwinkels im Bezug auf die Interpretierbarkeit vorhandenen Materials zu überwinden. Dadurch wird der Künstler weniger zu einem #Autor, der versucht eine einzelne These zu etablieren, als vielmehr zu einem Vertreter einer Vielzahl von Positionen.

Die Erzeugung freier #Übereinstimmung sowie das Vermeiden von #Kausalität sind für den Aufbau interpretierbarer Narrative essentiell. Der Betrachter darf nur so viel an Informationen erhalten, um sich seine eigene Bedeutung zu kreieren. Daher müssen jedwede expliziten Features aus der Sequenz entfernt werden. So wird beispielsweise ein Inhalt ohne Sound vage, Stimmen und Umgebungsgeräusche im Kopf des Betrachters

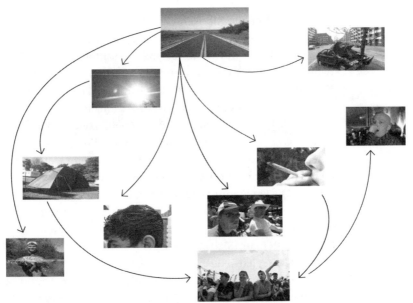

#hiphop #bros #ablenkung #auto #roadtrip #haarschnitt #musik #hell

#Konzept: Timm Häneke,
Eva Paulitsch, Uta Weyrich
#Text #Grafiken: Timm Häneke

werden neu synchronisiert. Personen werden von ihrer #Identität abstrahiert und zu #Vertretern einer sozialen Gruppe, zu #Vertrauten oder #Gegnern. Die ausschnitthafte Verwendung eines Videos kann Raum für Spekulationen über Events vor oder nach der Sequenz schaffen. All diese künstlerischen Eingriffe haben zum Ziel, die Menge an #Assoziationen innerhalb eines Loops zu #maximieren und zu #intensivieren. Durch das #räumliche Arrangement des projizierten Materials variiert die Konstruktion einzelner Narrative schlussendlich nicht nur durch die #mentale, sondern auch durch die #physische Position des Betrachters.

Eva Paulitsch und Uta Weyrich
Studium an der Staatlichen Akademie der Bildenden Künste Stuttgart, seit 2003 künstlerische Zusammenarbeit. Ausstellungen und Projekte (Auswahl): ZKM Medienmuseum, Karlsruhe; Künstlerhaus, Stuttgart; Museum Moderner Kunst Kärnten (Österreich); Künstlerhaus Dortmund; Lothringerstraße 13, München; zeitraumexit, Mannheim; E-WERK, Freiburg; Thurgauische Kunstgesellschaft, Kreuzlingen (Schweiz). Forschung: seit 2011 (Re)präsentationen des Alltags, Handyfilme als jugendkulturelle Ausdrucksform, dreijähriges Forschungsprojekt an der Hochschule der Künste, Zürich.

Der künstlerische Blick von Eva Paulitsch und Uta Weyrich gilt dem Facettenreichtum des Alltäglichen. Bildmaterial dazu suchen sie auf der Straße und finden es auf den Handys von Jugendlichen. Ihr Interesse gilt dabei den *No Story Videos* – selbstgedrehten Filmen, die nebenbei entstehen und die für den Moment gemacht sind. Auf dieses oft schon vergessene Filmmaterial sprechen sie die Jugendlichen an und retten es vor dem »Delete«, indem sie es via *Bluetooth* von den Handys der Jugendlichen auf ihr Handy wandern lassen. Seit 2006 bauen die beiden Künstlerinnen damit weltweit ein einzigartiges digitales Handyfilmarchiv auf, das die Grundlage ihrer künstlerischen Arbeit darstellt.

Timm Häneke
arbeitet als Grafikdesigner in Berlin. Er arbeitet aktuell mit und für Kunden im Bereich Kultur/Kunst und Verlagswesen. Seit 2012 plant er zusammen mit Manuel Bürger die *Transmediale*, ein Festival für Kunst und Designkultur. Er beschäftigt sich mit kultureller Wahrnehmung und der damit verbundenen Sichtweise auf Design, mit politischen und sozialen Effekten in Bezug auf Ästhetik, Darstellung und Schriftstellerei.

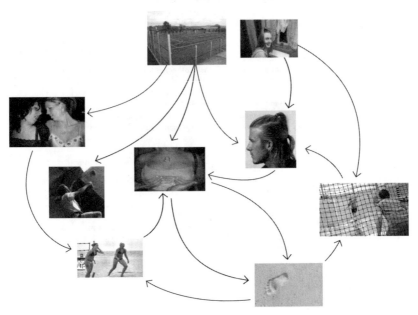

#klettern #brust # hände #zoo #erschöpfung #sport #sand #pferdeschwanz

Eva Paulitsch, Uta Weyrich
Loop Narration und hyper-überlagerte Narrative

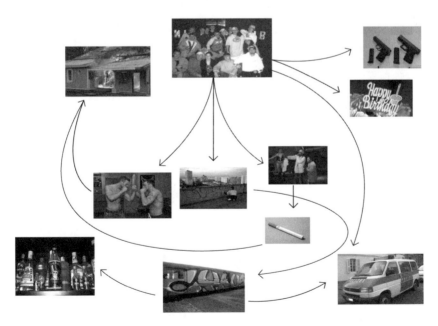

#konzert #gruppe #kampf #houseparty #streit #streetwear #durcheinander #gang

Hören gehen.
Eine kleine Geschichte der Hörspaziergänge

Sabine

Breitsameter

1. Goethes venezianischer Soundwalk

Als sich Johann Wolfgang von Goethe im Oktober 1786 in Venedig aufhielt, beeindruckten ihn beim Durchstreifen der Stadt auch deren Laute. Geprägt waren diese von der Allgegenwart des Wassers und den damit zusammenhängenden Aktivitäten, insbesondere auch den stimmlichen Äußerungen der Einwohner: den Parlandi und Canti der Fischer und Schiffer, deren Nah und Fern an den Stränden, auf den Kanälen, Plätzen und in den Gassen. In einem seiner Briefe an seine Weimarer Freundin Charlotte von Stein beschreibt der Dichter, wie er sich zwischen den einzelnen Schallquellen planvoll im Raum erging, um die Laute, eingebettet in die Stadtlandschaft und ihre Umgebungsgeräusche, adäquat zu hören. Ein Wahrnehmungserlebnis, das ihn tief bewegte: »Warum kann ich dir nicht auch einen Ton hinüber schicken«, so schrieb er an seine ferne Freundin, »den du in der Stunde vernähmest und mir antwortetest. – Gute Nacht, meine Liebe, ich bin müde vom vielen Laufen und Brückensteigen.«[1]

1
Johann Wolfgang von Goethe: Tagebücher Bd. 1, 1770–1810, in: Ders., Gesamtausgabe der Werke und Schriften in zweiundzwanzig Bänden. Zweite Abteilung: Schriften, Elfter Band, hg. v. Gerhart Baumann, Stuttgart 1953, S. 270.

2. Der Hörspaziergang als Bruch kultureller Usancen

Eine gewissen Agilität muss man schon mitbringen: Sich zu Fuß im städtischen Raum zu bewegen, den urbanen Schallquellen von verschiedenen Positionen aus zu lauschen, immer neue Perspektiven zu ihnen einzunehmen und sich die Klanglandschaft über das Ohr zu erschließen: Damit ist bereits umrissen, was seit Ende der 1960er Jahre als »Hörspaziergang« – als *Soundwalk* – hervortrat. Der Terminus »Soundwalk« wurde damals von dem kanadischen Komponisten und Hörforscher Murray Schafer geprägt. Er bringt damit eine Methode auf den Begriff, deren Praxis Ende der 1960er Jahre bereits eine Geschichte aufweist, von der hier im Folgenden die Rede sein wird: Die Geschichte der Hörspaziergänge kann als eine Art Vor- und Frühgeschichte für im 20. Jahrhundert neu aufgekommene, experimentelle und erweiterte Erzählformen gelten, wie sie sich insbesondere in den spartenübergreifenden, audiomedialen Kunstformen Ende der 1960er Jahre herauskristallisiert haben und bis heute – mit vielfältiger Präsenz im Kulturbetrieb – in den ›Grauzonen‹ zwischen Hörspiel, Radiokunst, elektroakustischer Musik, Klanginstallation, Bildender Kunst, Aktionskunstformen und experimentellem Theater siedeln.[2]

Hören und gehen, mobil sein beim Lauschen auf gegebene Laute: Gemäß vorherrschender kultureller Standards und Wahrnehmungsgewohnheiten scheint dies nicht unbedingt eine ideale Verbindung. So weist der Konzertsaal seit gut zweieinhalb Jahrhunderten sein Publikum an, der Bühne und den Interpreten gegenüber die Plätze einzunehmen und still zu sitzen. Analog dazu imaginieren Konzertmitschnitte auf Tonträgern sowie das Kulturradio, v. a. mit seinen künstlerischen Produktionen wie Hörspiel und Feature, den Hörer als jemanden, der idealerweise in seiner Position fixiert ist. Ebenso bauen darauf die vorherrschenden Konzepte der Wissensvermittlung (akademischer Vortrag, schulischer Unterricht). Ohne die Weisung des Still-Seins und Still-Sitzens hätten der so und nicht anders auskomponierte Gesamtklang oder das überlegte Setzen der Worte kaum Chancen, stimmig wahrgenommen zu werden, so die herrschende Ansicht. Hinzu kommt: Man unterstellt dem Herumgehen gegenüber dem Stillsitzen gemeinhin einen ablenkenden Effekt, der angeblich die Intensität der hörenden Aneignung und den damit verbundenen Erkenntnisgewinn schmälert.

Demgegenüber schildert bereits Goethe, dass Gehen und Hören in der beschriebenen Situation ihm besondere Einsichten vermittelten: zum einen durch eine intensivierte Wahrnehmung, zum anderen durch ein vertieftes Verstehen seiner Umgebung. Seine venezianische Erfahrung einer Klanglandschaft, sein Hören auf die akustischen Sensationen beim Durchmessen der Stadt, schlossen ihm deren Kultur und Kunst auf und brachten ihm, nach eigener Aussage, die Einwohner, ihr Empfinden und ihre existentiellen Lebensfragen näher.

3. Von der »Emanzipation der Dissonanz« zur Geräusch-Ästhetik

Goethe muss in diesem Zusammenhang als Vorreiter seiner Zeit betrachtet werden: Dass die Laute im Alltag, also außerhalb ausgewiesener musikalischer Zusammenhänge, Gegenstand ästhetischer Betrachtung sind, war bis zu diesem Zeitpunkt schlichtweg ein Unding. Musik und Geräusch wurden

---

2 Diese elektroakustischen Kunstformen lassen sich kaum auf einen Genrebegriff bringen, der ihrem »Wandern zwischen den Genrewelten« gerecht würde. Die ›Namenlosigkeit‹ hat den Nachteil, dass den audiomedialen Kunstformen das Schicksal aller nichtsichtbaren Kunstformen noch verstärkt zuteil wird, dass nämlich ihre Präsenz und Relevanz marginalisiert oder gar negiert wird. Ihr Vorteil ist, dass sich darin ein genuin Künstlerisches manifestiert, nämlich das Sich-nicht-greifbar-und-verfügbar-Machen, um den Verwertungskategorien des Kulturbetriebs zu entsprechen.

bis zum Ende des 19. Jahrhunderts als unüberbrückbare Antagonisten gesehen. Eine Aufweichung dieses Dogmas begann sich in der zweiten Hälfte des 19. Jahrhunderts abzuzeichnen.

Hermann Helmholtz' 1863 erschienene *Lehre von den Tonempfindungen*[3] erscheint hier als Resultat wie auch Katalysator dieses ästhetischen Wertewandels. Zwar konstatiert Helmholtz zunächst die Unterschiede von Musik und Geräusch, verweist dann aber, naturwissenschaftlich-methodisch begründet, darauf, dass alles Hörbare physikalisch betrachtet nichts anderes sei als in Bewegung versetzte Luft, der Unterschied zwischen einem musikalischen und einem geräuschhaften Schallereignis mithin also eine kulturspezifische und zeitbedingte Erscheinungsform der Ästhetik sei.[4]

Zur selben Zeit leitet der »Tristan-Akkord« Richard Wagners und seine »unstete« Harmonik das ein, was im frühen 20. Jahrhundert als »Emanzipation der Dissonanz«[5] bezeichnet wurde: Diese ist eng verbunden mit Arnold Schönbergs Entwicklung eines dodekaphonischen Systems zu Beginn des 20. Jahrhunderts, in welchem die überkommenen Wertungen von »Harmonie vs. Dissonanz« und damit »Musik vs. Geräusch« keine Rolle mehr spielten.

Damit war die Voraussetzung geschaffen, die nur wenig später dem Alltagsgeräusch zu seinem Einzug in den ästhetischen Materialkanon verhelfen sollte und in der Folge den Hörspaziergang als auditive Aneigungsmethodik hervortreten ließ.

Der italienische Futurismus liefert hierzu ein prototypisches Zeugnis: 1913 publizierte Luigi Russolo sein Manifest *L'Arte dei Rumori* – Die Kunst der Geräusche: »Das Leben der Vergangenheit war Stille. [...] Heute triumphiert und herrscht das Geräusch souverän über die Sensibilität der Menschen.«[6] Die Innovationen des 20. Jahrhunderts, insbesondere ihre expandierenden Städte und die immer machtvolleren Maschinen, so postulierte Russolo, hätten das Hören verändert und dadurch dem Auditiven neue ästhetische Maßstäbe geöffnet: »Wir Futuristen haben die Harmonien der großen Meister alle tief geliebt und ausgekostet. [...] Heute sind wir ihrer überdrüssig und genießen es weitaus mehr, die Geräusche der Tram, der Explosionsmotoren, der Wagen und der schreienden Menschen-

---

3
Hermann Helmholtz: Die Lehre von den Tonempfindungen als physiologische Grundlage für die Theorie der Musik. Braunschweig 1863.

4
Ebd., S. 551ff.

5
Arnold Schönberg: Die formbildenden Tendenzen der Harmonie. Mainz 1957, S. 186. Weiteres dazu in: Arnold Schönberg: Harmonielehre. Leipzig und Wien 1911, S. 19.

6
Luigi Russolo: Futuristisches Manifest (1913). In: Berliner Festspiele (Hg.): Für Augen und Ohren. Von der Spieluhr zum akustischen Environment. Berlin 1980, S. 254.

mengen zu kombinieren als beispielsweise erneut die *Eroica* oder die *Pastorale* zu hören.«[7]

Konsequenterweise ruft er zum Hörspaziergang auf, der die visuellen Eindrücke zugunsten der auditiven suspendierte: »Wenn wir eine moderne Großstadt mit aufmerksameren Ohren als Augen durchqueren, dann werden wir das Glück haben, den Sog des Wassers, der Luft oder des Gases in den Metallröhren, das Brummen der Motoren, die zweifellos wie Tiere atmen und beben, das Klopfen der Ventile, das Auf und Ab der Kolben, das Kreischen der Sägewerke, die Sprünge der Straßenbahn auf den Schienen, das Knallen der Peitschen und das Rauschen von Vorhängen und Fahnen zu unterscheiden. Wir haben Spaß daran, den Krach der Jalousien zu unterscheiden, der Geschäfte, der zugeworfenen Türen, den Lärm und das Scharren der Menge, die verschiedenen Geräusche der Bahnhöfe, der Spinnereien, der Druckereien, der Elektrizitätswerke und der Untergrundbahnen im Geiste zu orchestrieren.«[8] Schon die Futuristen fassten also Hörspaziergänge nicht nur als rezeptive Aktion auf, um die urbanen Hörsensationen, die Laute der maschinellen Moderne, aufzunehmen, sondern auch als Anlässe, sich in gestaltendem Hören zu üben.

4. Das Hervortreten spartenübergreifender Hörkunst-Ansätze in den 1920er Jahren

Ab den 1920er Jahren begann sich das Geräusch als integraler Bestandteil des künstlerischen Materialkanons zu etablieren: Der Komponist Kurt Weill, der Radiomacher Hans Flesch, die Filmkünstler Dziga Vertov und Walter Ruttmann, der Medientheoretiker Rudolf Arnheim – sie alle stehen Mitte, Ende der 1920er Jahre für eine Entwicklung, die dem Geräusch der alltäglichen Umwelt eine herausragende und zentrale Stellung einräumt und es gegenüber dem musikalischen Klang oder dem gesprochenen Wort als gleichwertig postuliert. Daraus, so der Rundfunkpionier Hans Flesch, erwachse eine innovative Hör-Kunstform, welche nicht mehr mit dem traditionellen Begriff »Musik« erfasst werden könne und durch das neue Medium Radio vorangetrieben werde.[9]

---

[7] Ebd.

[8] Ebd.

[9] »Wir können uns heute noch keinen Begriff machen, wie diese noch ungeborene Schöpfung aussehen kann. Vielleicht ist der Ausdruck ›Musik‹ dafür gar nicht richtig. Vielleicht wird einmal aus der Eigenart der elektrischen Schwingungen, aus ihrem Umwandlungsprozeß in akustische Wellen etwas Neues geschaffen, das wohl mit Tönen, aber nichts mit Musik zu tun hat.« Hans Flesch: Rundfunkmusik. In: Rundfunkjahrbuch 1929, S. 150.

Bahnbrechend in vielfacher Hinsicht war hier 1929 Walter Ruttmanns Audio-Produktion *Weekend*, welche die signifikanten Geräusche eines Berliner Wochenendes chronologisch arrangierte, raffiniert aushörte und montierte. Die Laute wurden z.T. als sekundenkurze Elemente mit präzisen Schnitten zusammenfügt. Dies war nur möglich, weil dem Filmemacher Ruttmann die schneidbare Filmtonspur erstmals die Möglichkeit bot, Laute ebenso beliebig zu schneiden und zu montieren wie die Bilder eines Films.

Weekend lässt sich als erstmals reproduzierbare Version eines Soundwalk auffassen, zeigt sie doch, wie neue Produktions- und Reproduktionstechniken im Tonbereich, ebenso wie der Film, die überkommene Einheit von Ort, Zeit und Handlung mühelos überwinden können. Somit kommen sie einem »Gang« durch das heterogene Nebeneinander von Lokalitäten, Aktivitäten und »Augen«-Blicken nahe. Noch viel mehr verdeutlicht das Stück durch seinen Verzicht auf Bilder die Autonomie der akustischen Phänomene, in sowohl ästhetischer als auch semantischer Hinsicht. Die Stärke von *Weekend* liegt nicht im veranschaulichenden Referentiellen und Evozierenden seiner akustischen Materialien. Sie entfaltet sich vor allem in den Passagen, wo dem Auge und seinen Einbildungen kein Zugang möglich ist und prototypische Wesensstrukturen, das quasi »Inwendige«, von Materialien, Geschehnissen und Charakteren v. a. deshalb freigelegt werden können, weil sie nicht von einem visuellen »Schein« überlagert werden. Das Auditive tritt nicht als Surrogat in Ermangelung des Visuellen auf, sondern als Einblick in eine andere Erscheinungsform der Realität. Dieser Grundgedanke Akustischer Kunst beginnt bei Ruttmann zu glimmen. Doch es bedurfte politischer Freiheit ebenso wie weiterer technischer Fortschritte, um derartige Verhältnisse weiter auszuloten und diese Essenz auditiven Gestaltens zu zünden.

5. Die Musique concrète und das akustische Objet trouvé

Erst im befreiten Frankreich der 1940er Jahre, unter der Ägide des französischen Staatsrundfunks wird das ästhetische Explorieren der Alltagslaute und ihres Signifié-Gehalts systematisch vorangebracht: in der Musique concrète, namentlich von ihren Gründern Pierre Schaeffer und Pierre Henry. Geräusche jedweder Art werden in der Musique concrète aufgenommen und durch Manipulation tontechnischer Geräte verändert: anfangs mittels Schallplatten, wenig später dann mittels Magnetophon, wie man das Tonband damals nannte. So wurden Originalgeräusche etwa – um die wichtigsten Verfahrensweisen zu nennen – verlangsamt oder beschleunigt abgespielt, sodass sich ihre Tonhöhe dabei änderte, sie wurden geschnitten, sodass lediglich Bruchteile eines Lauts – etwa nur der Einschwingvorgang – verwendet wurden, oder sie wurden nach dem Prinzip der »geschlossenen Rille« – das noch auf die Herkunft aus Schallplatten-Zeiten erinnert und heute, als Reminiszenz der Tonband-Ära, als »Schleife« bezeichnet wird – repetiert. Die so prozessierten Schallereignisse, sollten – gemäß der Programmatik Pierre Schaeffers – bis zur Unkenntlichkeit verändert werden, sodass möglichst nichts mehr auf ihren ursprünglichen Laut verweist. Dieses Verändern von Lauten hin zur Abstraktion gelang nicht immer und nicht umfassend, wie eine der berühmtesten Kompositionen, Schaeffers *Etude aux Chemins de Fer* (1948), zeigt. Diese besteht aus Geräuschen, die auf Bahnhöfen und von Eisenbahnen und Lokomotiven aufgenommen wurden. Entgegen der postulierten Programmatik ließ sich die Herkunft des Materials nicht vollständig abschütteln. Selbst nach sorgfältig vorgenommener Manipulation der Aufnahmen erzählen die prozessierten Laute immer noch von Maschinenrhythmen, getakteten Bewegungsvorgängen, metallischen Materialien, machtvoller Mechanik und grellen Signallauten. Sie evozieren den Geräuschkosmos von Bahnhöfen zu Zeiten der Dampflok und verdichten ihn.

Gestalterischer Ausgangspunkt für die Musique concrète ist das Objet trouvé, das real vorgefundene, zuallermeist im Alltag auffindbare Lautobjekt: Eisenbahnen, Straßenverkehr, Schritte, Türenquietschen, Brummkreisel, Materiallaute, Radiorauschen usw. usf. Wo sich der klangliche Ursprung nicht völlig ins Abstrakte überführen ließ, öffnet sich das narrative Potential dieser akustischen Kunstform. Vor allem in der Gegenüberstellung vom Status Nascendi eines Geräuschs zu seinen akustisch prozessierten Abstraktionen vermag dieses sein Potential zu entfalten. Wo das Originalgeräusch anklingt, wird dessen Bedeutungskontext »verbildlicht«, und seine unterschiedlichen Grade vom Original zum gestalterisch-technisch manipulierten Laut bis zu ›surrealen‹ Hörphänomenen teilen sich in bilderlosen Erscheinungsformen mit etwa in Raum-, Bewegungs- und Materiallauten. Bildliche Konkretion und auditive Abstraktion treten damit in ein Spannungsverhältnis, dessen narratives Potential in den folgenden Jahrzehnten in der Audiokunst auch jenseits der Musique concrète entwickelt und ausgelotet wurde.

6. Die Musique anecdotique des Luc Ferrari

Mit den Gestaltungsgrundsätzen der Musique concrète brach ausgerechnet einer ihrer Schüler: Luc Ferrari machte »Spaziergang« (promenade) und »Landschaft« (paysage) zur Essenz seines kompositorischen Konzepts[10] und thematisierte den Gedanken der Landschaft und des mobilen und agilen Sich-darin-Befindens. Dem Verändern der Laute wird eine Absage erteilt, auch einer Suche, die ausschließlich auf spektakulären Wohlklang aus ist und ihn dadurch konstruiert. Sein Hörstück *Lever du Jour au Bord de la Mer* (1969)[11] besteht aus vermeintlich unmanipulierten Alltagsgeräuschen. Es führt einen frühmorgendlichen akustischen Spaziergang am Meer vor, sodass der Hörer Ohrenzeuge des Tagesanbruchs wird. Das Rattern der Bootsmotoren, das Schreien der Möwen, das Rauschen der Gezeiten, die beginnenden Aktivitäten der Menschen, das Zwitschern der Zikaden, dies alles nimmt Ferrari über mehrere Stunden auf, führt es durch raffinierte Schnitte zu sich selbst und kondensiert damit über einen Zeitraum von 21 Minuten zu dokumentarischer wie ästhetischer Authentizität. »Musique anecdotique« nennt Ferrari sein kompositorisches Konzept und unterstreicht damit ihr narratives Potential.[12]

7. Der Spaziergang als Happening und Intervention

Nicht nur in der zeitgenössischen Musik, auch in Fluxus, Happening, Performance Art und dem Neuen Hörspiel nehmen Umweltlaute ab Mitte, Ende der 1960er Jahre eine herausragende Stellung ein. Besonders bemerkenswert ist hierbei, dass sich

---

10 Mit Werken wie *Musique promenade* (1964–69) oder *Petite symphonie intuitive pour un paysage de printemps* (1973–74).

11 Teil seines vierteiligen Werkzyklus *Presque rien*.

12 Nach ähnlichen inhaltlichen und auditiven Prinzipien, wenngleich mit einer plakativeren Schnitttechnik, verfährt Ennio Morricone 1969 zu Anfang mit dem Soundtrack des Films *Spiel mir das Lied vom Tod*: ein akustischer Streifzug über einen scheinbar ausgestorbenen Wildwest-Bahnhof. Die Umweltgeräusche stehen dabei weniger für Gegenstände oder Personen als vielmehr für Zustand und Atmosphäre, in diesem Fall für Ereignislosigkeit, Dösigkeit und die Abwesenheit von Aktion.

daraus spartenübergreifende Kunstformen ergeben, die nicht in die Felder des üblichen Kunstkanons einsortiert werden können.[13] Das in den 1920er Jahren u. a. von Hans Flesch formulierte Konzept auditiver Kunstformen jenseits der Musik entwickelte sich seit Ende der 1960er Jahre zu einer wirkungsmächtigen künstlerischen Realität.

Inspiriert von Fluxus, Dadaismus und dem aufkommenden Happening fiel auch die Grenze zwischen Akustischer und Bildender Kunst, etwa mit Künstlern wie Nam June Paik und Joseph Beuys. Die Idee des Umherstreifens von Ort zu Ort, um besonders intensive Wahrnehmungen zu machen, kristallisierte sich in einer Reihe spektakulärer Aktionen, so etwa in einer *24-Hours-Tour* durch Paris von Ben Patterson und Robert Filiou im Sommer 1962 oder in Wolf Vostells *Guided Tour Happenings* durch urbane Räume zahlreicher Städte: In seinem legendären *In Ulm, um Ulm und um Ulm herum* wurden die Teilnehmer an 24 Stationen geführt, u. a. auch auf einen Militärflughafen, wo sie den laufenden Triebwerken von Jets ausgesetzt wurden, sowie auf einen Acker bei Dunkelheit, wo sie der Lebensgeschichte eines Menschen lauschen sollten.[14]

Ein Katalysator dieser Entwicklung hin zu einer Geräuschkunst war – neben einer Reihe bedeutender Fluxuskünstler – auch der US-amerikanische Komponist John Cage, u. a. mit seinem bereits 1952 aufgeführten, programmatischen Werk *4'33*, das die Erwartungshaltung des Publikums anlässlich eines Klavierkonzerts nutzte, dabei aber die Aufmerksamkeit auf die vorhandenen Geräusche der unmittelbaren Umgebung richtete. Cage griff Edgar Varèses Diktum, Musik sei die »organization of sound«[15], auf und machte es populär.[16]

Auch eine allgemeine Politisierung und das antiautoritäre Infragestellen von Verbürgtem im Zuge der 1968er-Bewegung legitimierten und popularisierten den Bruch mit Wahrnehmungsgewohnheiten sowie den überkommenen Vorstellungen von Material, Form und Rezeption. Das Bedürfnis nach Provokation und systemkritischen »Anti-Kunst«-Haltungen motivierte zahlreiche mobile Aktionen der frühen 1960er Jahre, die in diesem Sinne als Interventionen gedacht waren, welche die Gleichförmigkeit und die »Normalität« des Alltags durchbrechen sollten.

---

13 Zentral für diese Entwicklung war dabei das so genannte *Neue Hörspiel*, in welchem sich sowohl Elemente aus Literatur, Musik und Performance Art vermischten. Es versammelt Protagonisten wie u. a. Mauricio Kagel, John Cage, Dieter Schnebel und Luc Ferrari (Komponisten), Franz Mon, Ernst Jandl, Friederike Mayröcker, Peter Handke, Wolf Wondratschek (Autoren), Barry Bermange, Ferdinand Kriwet, Paul Pörtner als Audiokünstler jenseits tradierter Sparten.

14 Vgl. hierzu auch: Lisa Bosbach: Wolf Vostells Guided-Tour-Happenings. Interventionsstrategien im öffentlichen Raum. In: kunsttexte.de, Nr. 4, 2012, 6 Seiten. http://edoc.hu-berlin.de/kunsttexte/2012-4/bosbach-lisa-7/PDF/bosbach.pdf (Stand: 19.08.2013).

15 Edgard Varèse; Chou Wen-chung: Perspectives of New Music, Bd. 5, Nr. 1, Herbst–Winter, 1966, S. 18.

16 John Cage: Die Zukunft der Musik – Credo (1937). In: Für Augen und Ohren. Berlin 1980, S. 112f.

8. Max Neuhaus' LISTEN-Spaziergänge

Alltagswahrnehmung als Herrschaftskritik nahm im politisierten Klima der späten 1960er und der 1970er Jahre eine zentrale Rolle ein.[17] In diesem Milieu konnte der US-amerikanische Musiker Max Neuhaus ab 1966 Hörspaziergänge entwickeln, wenngleich jenseits politisierender Rhetorik: Mit seinen LISTEN-Aktionen, die er zunächst in New York City, dann an den verschiedensten Orten in die USA unternimmt, will er die Aufwertung des Hörens generell befördern und als schöpferisches kulturelles Handeln verdeutlichen: »As a percussionist I had been directly involved in the gradual insertion of everyday sound into the concert hall, from Russolo through Varese and finally to Cage who brought live street sounds directly into the hall. I saw these activities as a way of giving aesthetic credence to these sounds [...].«[18] Neuhaus beschreibt, wie er mit seinen Hörspaziergängen die Erwartungen seines Publikums zunächst konterkariert, da sie am vereinbarten Treffpunkt eine Vorlesung oder ein Konzert erwarten. »I asked (the audience) to meet me on the corner of Avenue D and West 14th Street in Manhattan. I rubber-stamped LISTEN on each person's hand and began walking with them down 14th Street towards the East River. At that point the street bisects a power plant and [...] one hears some spectacularly massive rumbling. We continued, crossing the highway and walking along the sound [...] passing through the Puerto Rican street life of the lower east side to my studio, where I performed some percussion pieces for them.«[19]

Die LISTEN-Spaziergänge sah Neuhaus als eine neue, vorbereitende Strategie um die Aufnahmebereitschaft gegenüber zeitgenössischer Musik zu steigern: »The group would proceed silently, and by the time we returned to the hall many had found a new way to listen for themselves.«[20]

9. Urban Sounds als künstlerische Bewegung

Dieses damals verstärkt aufkommende, vielfältige Suchen und Auffinden von »unerhörten« Lauten der Stadt,[21] ihre Ästhetisierung als gestalterisches und »musikalisches« Material führten zu einer breiten, anhaltenden künstlerischen Bewegung, welche sich wohl am besten mit dem Schlagwort *Urban Sounds*

---

17 Zahlreiche Kulturtheoretiker setzten damals politische und soziale Realität mit den herrschenden ästhetischen Gestaltungsprinzipien in enge Beziehung und legitimierten daraus die künstlerische Avantgarde, vgl. hierzu prototypisch: Herbert Marcuse. Versuch über die Befreiung. Frankfurt am Main 1969, S. 43f.

18 Max Neuhaus über seine LISTEN-Aktionen auf: http://www.maxneuhaus.info/soundworks/vectors/walks/LISTEN/ (Stand: 19.08.2013).

19 Ebd.

20 Ebd.

21 Max Neuhaus verweist etwa auf die faszinierenden Laute, die unter der Brooklyn Bridge gehört werden konnten: »[A] long fascination of mine with sounds of traffic moving across that bridge – the rich sound texture formed from hundreds of tires rolling over the open grating of the roadbed, each with a different speed and tread.« vgl. ebd.

umschreiben lässt[22]. Die gestaltende Arbeit mit Geräuschen, die entweder semantisch oder atmosphärisch das Wesen einer Metropole fasslich machen, zielt auf die Erweiterung deskriptiver und narrativer Prinzipien gegenüber sprachlich oder visuell-filmischen Verfahrensweisen. Das Aushören des städtischen Raums im mikro- als auch makroskopischen Sinn – dies bezogen auf Material-, Raum- und Bewegungsklänge – löst sich von der sinnlichen Verbürgtheit des Sehens und führt hinein in die alltäglichen, dabei aber überraschenden Laute der Stadt, und nicht zuletzt in deren Gegensätze und Widersprüche: Der Hörspaziergang ist Voraussetzung für das Suchen und Finden von einzelnen Lauten sowie Soundscapes mit dem Mikrophon.

10. Hörspaziergang und Akustische Ökologie

Statt Sehenswürdigkeiten nun also Hörenswürdigkeiten: Das realitätskonstituierende wie imaginationsfördernde Potential von Hörspaziergängen hat – ebenfalls Ende der 1960er Jahre – der kanadische Klangforscher, Hörpädagoge und Komponist Murray Schafer herausgearbeitet als integrale Methode der von ihm entwickelten Akustischen Ökologie. Diese thematisiert, getragen von einer Kritik am hörbaren Erscheinungsbild der Umwelt, das akustische Wechselverhältnis zwischen den Lebewesen und ihrer Umwelt und arbeitet kulturgeschichtlich den Zusammenhang zwischen den akustischen Erscheinungen einer Epoche und dem darin jeweiligen Stellenwert des Hörens heraus.[23]

Die beim Hörspaziergang gebotene »Aufmerksamkeit des Hörers auf ungewöhnliche Laute und Umgebungsgeräusche«[24] zu lenken und dies gleichzeitig mit einer umfassenden Hörhaltung auf die Soundscapes zu verbinden, soll dazu dienen, nicht nur zum differenzierten Gebrauch der Ohren zu befähigen und den Reichtum der Umwelt in die sinnliche Wahrnehmung zu integrieren. Sie hat auch zum Ziel, die physische und mentale Zuträglichkeit der akustischen Umwelt zu hinterfragen und ihre ästhetische Qualität zu bewerten.[25]

Schafers ehemalige Forschungsmitarbeiterin, die deutsch-kanadische Komponistin und Hörpädagogin Hildegard Westerkamp, hat diese Methode weiter ausgelotet und verfeinert[26]: »A soundwalk is any excursion whose main purpose

---

[22]
Es würde den Raum des vorliegenden Artikels sprengen, hier alle darunter zu subsumierenden Phänomene darzustellen. Besonders hingewiesen sei auf die – ebenfalls von Max Neuhaus geprägte – innovative Form der Klanginstallation im öffentlichen Raum einer Stadt (vgl. hierzu seine Arbeit *Times Square* a.d.J. 1976) und das Hervortreten einer Radiokunst aus dem experimentellen Hörspiel, für die – bezogen auf unsere Thematik – seit den 1970er Jahren prototypisch die Sendereihe *Metropolis* des Studios für Akustische Kunst des WDR steht. Audiokünstler wie Klarenz Barlow (Kalkutta), Charles Armirkhanian (San Francisco) oder Pierre Henry (Paris) (einer der Gründer der Musique concrète) komponierten aus Alltagsgeräuschen poetisch-erzählerische Porträts von Großstädten.

[23]
Aufgrund der gebotenen Kürze kann an dieser Stelle nicht auf Schafers Unterscheidung zwischen »Listening Walk« und »Soundwalk« eingangen werden. Vgl. dazu: R. Murray Schafer: Die Ordnung der Klänge. Eine Kulturgeschichte des Hörens, übersetzt und neu herausgegeben von Sabine Breitsameter. Mainz 2010, S. 347f. Der Geograph Justin Winkler erhellt diesen Unterschied prägnant in: Justin Winkler: Landschaft hören. http://www.musik-for.uni-oldenburg.de/soundscape/blatt6.htm (Stand: 19.08.2013).

[24]
Winkler, S. 347 (wie Anm. 23).

[25]
Mittels Hörspaziergängen, Tonaufnahmen und Kartographierungen untersuchten Schafer und sein Forschungsteam im Rahmen des *World Soundscape*-Projekts während der 1970er Jahre an der Simon-Fraser-Universität in Burnaby bei Vancouver zahlreiche akustische Umgebungen, mit dem

is listening to the environment. It is exposing our ears to every sound around us no matter where we are. [...] Wherever we go we will give our ears priority. They have been neglected by us for a long time and, as a result, we have done little to develop an acoustic environment of good quality.«[27]

Im Mittelpunkt der Aktion selbst steht – neben der kritischen Sensibilisierung für die Vielzahl ignorierter Laute – das gestaltende Hören als Ausgangspunkt für das eigene künstlerische Schaffen: Die Bezeichnung »Soundscape Composition« wurde zu einer Genrebezeichnung für akusmatisch-elektroakustische Kompositionsweisen, deren Materialgrundlage die Gesamtheit aller Laute aus Alltag und Natur sind. Sie umfasst das gesamte Spektrum geräuschbasierter Kompositionsanlässe über den anspruchsvollen Filmsound und die Klanginstallation bis hin zur Radiokunst und der ihr verwandten Ars Acustica. Das flexible, sich immer wieder neu formierende gestaltende Hören, das sich »unbewaffneten Ohrs« – d. h. unmedialisiert – auf einem Hörspaziergang gezielt probieren lässt, sieht Westerkamp als zentrale Grundvoraussetzung audiomedialer Kreativität: »In the same way in which architects acquaint themselves with the landscape into which they want to integrate the shape of a house, so we must get to know the main characteristics of the soundscape into which we want to immerse our own sounds. [...] [L]ift the environmental sounds out of their context into the context of your composition, and in turn make your sounds a natural part of the music around you.«[28]

An diese Idee des Dialogs zwischen Hörspaziergänger und Umwelt knüpft die kanadische Komponistin und Sound-Wissenschaftlerin Andra McCartney an: Hörspaziergänge als Eingriffe in den Alltag, wobei nicht nur die wahrgenommenen Laute Aussagen über die Umgebung treffen, sondern auch die wechselseitigen Reaktionen zwischen Umgebung und Hörspaziergänger aufschlussreich sind.[29] Was hier hervortritt, ist ein dynamisches Wechselverhältnis, in welchem die Umweltlaute nicht Produkt oder Objekt, sondern Prozess sind. Das erzählerische Potential der so gefundenen Laute expandiert daher hin zum Involvement des Hörers als Beteiligtem, sodass die rezepti-

---

Ziel, ihre physiologische, mentale und ästhetische Zuträglichkeit zu analysieren und die Faktoren, die zur Veränderung der Soundscapes beitragen, zu identifizieren. Die Innenstadt von Vancouver war genauso Gegenstand der Untersuchungen wie der autofreie Ort Cembra in Italien oder das Dorf Bissingen in Baden-Württemberg. Im Zentrum stand dabei die Frage nach der Lebensqualität und Humanität der Städte.

26
Westerkamp produzierte Ende der 1970er Jahre im Vancouver Cooperative Radio eine wöchentliche Sendung namens *Soundwalking*, in welcher sie verschiedene Areale ihrer Heimatstadt Vancouver mit dem Mikrophon dokumentierte und ihre Höreindrücke kommentierte. Vgl. dazu auch: Hildegard Westerkamp: The soundscape on Radio. In: Daina Augaitis/Dan Lander (Hg.): Radio Rethink. Art, sound and transmission. Banff/Canada 1994, S. 87–94. Ihr Hörstück *Kits Beach Soundwalk* (1989) thematisiert das Wechselverhältnis zwischen kritisch-hörendem Erleben der Realität und akustischer Imagination.

27
Hildegard Westerkamp: Soundwalking. In: Autumn Leaves. Sound and the Environment in Artistic Practice. Angus Carlyle (Hg.): Double Entendre. Paris, 2007, S. 49. Überarbeitete Version des gleichnamigen Artikels aus: Sound Heritage. Vol. III, Nr. 4, Victoria B.C., 1974, S. 18.

28
Westerkamp (2007), S. 49 (wie Anm. 26).

ven Voraussetzungen nicht auf ein Wahrnehmen begrenzt bleiben, sondern dieses ohne ein Teilnehmen, ein prozesshaftes In-der-Welt-Sein, nicht denkbar ist.

Sabine Breitsameter
ist seit 2006 Professorin für Sound und Medienkultur an der Hochschule Darmstadt, war 2002–2008 Mitbegründerin des Masterstudiengangs *Soundstudies* an der UdK Berlin. Seit Mitte der 1980er Jahre tätig als Autorin, Regisseurin und Redakteurin insbesondere für Hörspiel-Redaktionen der ARD und Nordamerika. Zahlreiche Workshops, Vorträge, Publikationen und künstlerische Audioproduktionen. Wissenschaftliche und Künstlerische Leitung zahlreicher Symposien und Festivals, u. a. an der Akademie der Künste Berlin, dem ZKM Karlsruhe, der Ars Electronica Linz sowie im Rahmen der Documenta Kassel.

29
Andra McCartney: Performing Soundwalks for Journées Sonores, Canal de Lachine. In: Gabriella Giannachi; Nigel Stewart (Hg.): Performing Nature. Explorations in Ecology and the Arts. Bern 2005, S. 217–234. David Paquette; Andra McCartney: Soundwalking and the bodily exploration of places. In: Canadian Journal of Communication, Bd. 37, Nr. 1, 2012, S. 135–145.